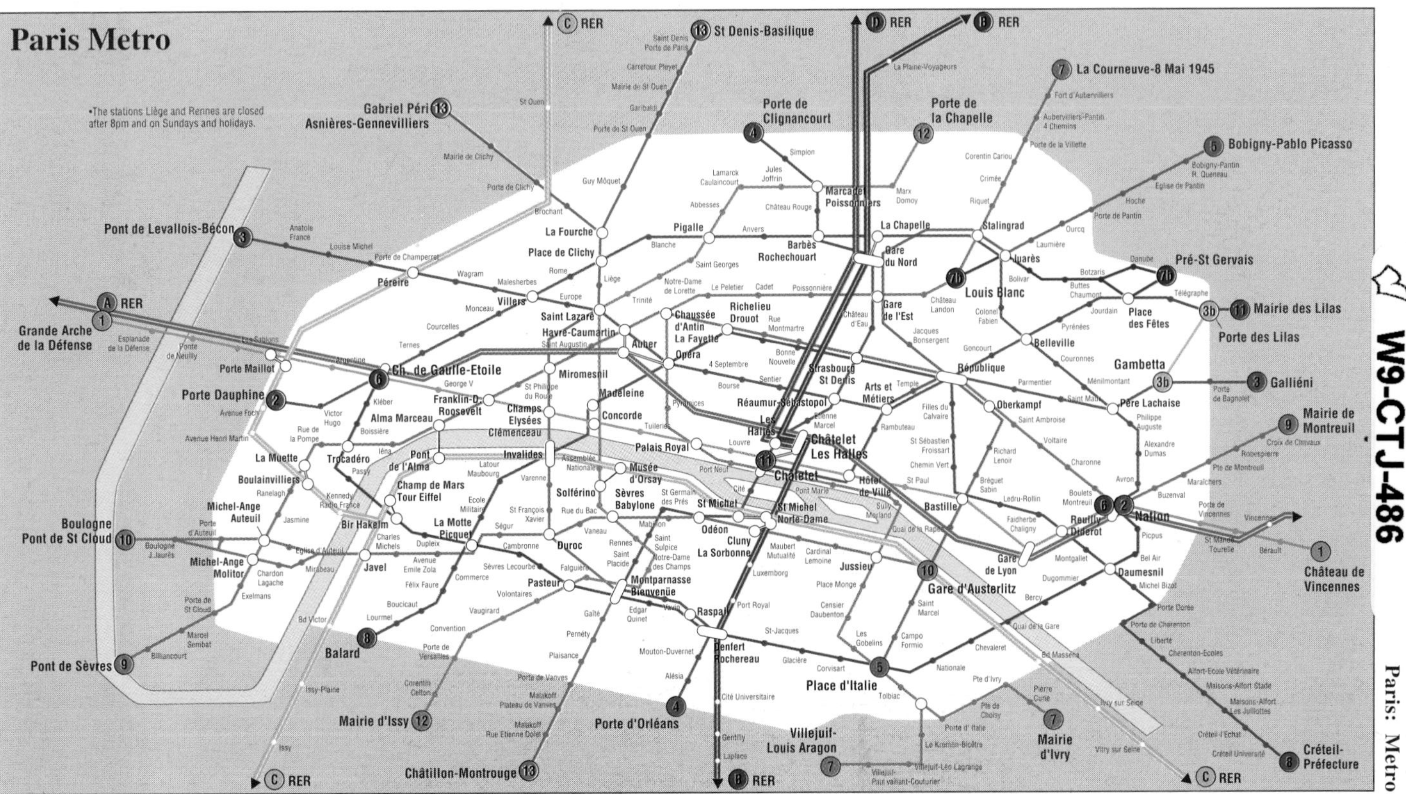
Paris Metro
•The stations Liège and Rennes are closed after 8pm and on Sundays and holidays.
Grande Arche de la Défense
Esplanade de la Défense
Pont de Neuilly
Les Sablons
Porte Maillot
Argentine
Porte Dauphine
Avenue Foch
Avenue Henri Martin
Pont de Levallois-Bécon
Anatole France
Louise Michel
Porte de Champerret
Pereire
Wagram
Malesherbes
Villiers
Gabriel Péri Asnières-Gennevilliers
Mairie de Clichy
Porte de Clichy
Brochant
Guy Môquet
La Fourche
Place de Clichy
St Ouen
St Denis-Basilique
Saint Denis Porte de Paris
Carrefour Pleyel
Mairie de St Ouen
Garibaldi
Porte de St Ouen
Porte de Clignancourt
Simplon
Jules Joffrin
Marcadet Poissonniers
Château Rouge
Lamarck Caulaincourt
Abbesses
Pigalle
Anvers
Barbès Rochechouart
Porte de la Chapelle
Marx Dormoy
La Chapelle
Gare du Nord
Gare de l'Est
La Plaine-Voyageurs
La Courneuve-8 Mai 1945
Fort d'Aubervilliers
Aubervilliers-Pantin 4 Chemins
Porte de la Villette
Corentin Cariou
Crimée
Riquet
Stalingrad
Jaurès
Louis Blanc
Bobigny-Pablo Picasso
Bobigny-Pantin R. Queneau
Église de Pantin
Hoche
Porte de Pantin
Ourcq
Laumière
Pré-St Gervais
Danube
Botzaris
Buttes Chaumont
Bolivar
Colonel Fabien
Château Landon
Télégraphe
Place des Fêtes
Mairie des Lilas
Porte des Lilas
Jourdain
Pyrénées
Belleville
Couronnes
Ménilmontant
Gambetta
Galliéni
Porte de Bagnolet
Père Lachaise
Philippe Auguste
Alexandre Dumas
Mairie de Montreuil
Croix de Chavaux
Robespierre
Pte de Montreuil
Maraîchers
Buzenval
Avron
Nation
Château de Vincennes
Bérault
St Mandé Tourelle
Porte de Vincennes
Vincennes
Picpus
Bel Air
Daumesnil
Michel Bizot
Porte Dorée
Porte de Charenton
Liberté
Charenton-Écoles
Alfort-École Vétérinaire
Maisons-Alfort Stade
Maisons-Alfort Les Juilliottes
Créteil-L'Échat
Créteil Université
Créteil-Préfecture
Ivry sur Seine
Vitry sur Seine
Boulets Montreuil
Reuilly Diderot
Charonne
Voltaire
Saint Ambroise
Parmentier
Oberkampf
Saint Maur
Goncourt
République
Jacques Bonsergent
Château d'Eau
Strasbourg St Denis
Arts et Métiers
Temple
Filles du Calvaire
St Sébastien Froissart
Chemin Vert
Bréguet Sabin
Richard Lenoir
Ledru-Rollin
Faidherbe Chaligny
Montgallet
Dugommier
Bercy
Gare de Lyon
Quai de la Gare
Chevaleret
Bd Masséna
Bastille
Quai de la Rapée
Gare d'Austerlitz
St Paul
Rambuteau
Hôtel de Ville
Sully Morland
Pont Marie
Châtelet Les Halles
Châtelet
Étienne Marcel
Réaumur-Sébastopol
Sentier
Bonne Nouvelle
Poissonnière
Cadet
Le Peletier
Richelieu Drouot
Rue Montmartre
Bourse
4 Septembre
Chaussée d'Antin La Fayette
Opéra
Pyramides
Les Halles
Louvre
Palais Royal
Pont Neuf
Cité
St Michel
St Michel Notre-Dame
Maubert Mutualité
Cardinal Lemoine
Jussieu
Place Monge
Censier Daubenton
Les Gobelins
Campo Formio
Saint Marcel
Nationale
Place d'Italie
Corvisart
Tolbiac
Porte d'Italie
Pte de Choisy
Pte d'Ivry
Pierre Curie
Mairie d'Ivry
Le Kremlin-Bicêtre
Villejuif-Léo Lagrange
Villejuif-Paul Vaillant-Couturier
Villejuif-Louis Aragon
Cité Universitaire
Gentilly
Laplace
Glacière
St-Jacques
Denfert Rochereau
Port Royal
Luxembourg
Odéon
Cluny La Sorbonne
St Germain des Prés
Mabillon
Saint Sulpice
Notre-Dame des Champs
Raspail
Vavin
Edgar Quinet
Montparnasse Bienvenüe
Saint Placide
Rennes
Mouton-Duvernet
Alésia
Porte d'Orléans
Gaîté
Pernety
Plaisance
Porte de Vanves
Malakoff Plateau de Vanves
Malakoff Rue Etienne Dolet
Châtillon-Montrouge
Falguière
Pasteur
Volontaires
Vaugirard
Convention
Porte de Versailles
Corentin Celton
Mairie d'Issy
Sèvres Babylone
Vaneau
Duroc
Rue du Bac
Solférino
Assemblée Nationale
Musée d'Orsay
Invalides
Varenne
St François Xavier
Ségur
Cambronne
Sèvres Lecourbe
La Motte Picquet
Ecole Militaire
Latour Maubourg
Commerce
Félix Faure
Avenue Emile Zola
Dupleix
Charles Michels
Javel
Boucicaut
Lourmel
Balard
Bd Victor
Issy-Plaine
Issy
Champ de Mars Tour Eiffel
Bir Hakeim
Pont de l'Alma
Alma Marceau
Iéna
Passy
Kennedy Radio France
Trocadéro
Boissière
Kléber
Victor Hugo
Rue de la Pompe
La Muette
Ranelagh
Jasmine
Boulainvilliers
Église d'Auteuil
Mirabeau
Michel-Ange Auteuil
Michel-Ange Molitor
Chardon Lagache
Exelmans
Porte d'Auteuil
Porte de St Cloud
Marcel Sembat
Billancourt
Pont de Sèvres
Boulogne J.Jaurès
Boulogne Pont de St Cloud
Ch. de Gaulle-Etoile
George V
Franklin-D. Roosevelt
Champs Elysées Clémenceau
St Philippe du Roule
Miromesnil
Saint Augustin
Havre-Caumartin
Saint Lazare
Europe
Rome
Liège
Trinité
Notre-Dame de Lorette
Saint Georges
Blanche
Auber
Madeleine
Concorde
Tuileries
Ternes
Courcelles
Monceau
RER

Paris: Overview and Arrondissements
1 Cimetière de Montmartre
2 Sacré Coeur Basilica
3 Parc La Villette
4 Parc des Buttes Chaumont
5 Jardins du Trocadero
6 Palais Chaillot
7 Cimetière de Passy
8 American Embassy
9 British Embassy
10 Petit Palais
11 Grand Palais
12 Arc de Triomphe
13 Madeleine
14 Gare St-Lazare
15 Parc Monceau
16 Palais de la Découverte
17 Opéra Garnier
18 Galeries Lafayette
19 Printemps
20 Gare du Nord
21 Gare de l'Est
22 Opéra Bastille
23 Palais Omnisports de Bercy
24 Ministère des Finances
25 Gare de Lyon
26 Parc de Montsouris
27 Cité Universitaire
28 Cimetière Montparnasse
29 Gare Montparnasse
30 Bureau des Objets Trouvés (Lost and Found)
31 Louvre
32 Palais Royale
33 Forum des Halles
34 Musée de l'Orangerie
35 Central Post Office
36 Bourse
37 Bibliothèque Nationale
38 Ecole des Arts et Métiers
39 Archives Nationales
40 Musée Carnavalet
41 Musée Picasso
42 Centre George Pompidou
43 place des Vosges
44 Musée Victor Hugo
45 Notre Dame
46 Mémorial de la Déportation
47 Université de Paris (Sorbonne)
48 Ecole Normal Supérieure
49 Musée de Cluny
50 Museum Nationale d'Histoire Naturelle
51 Panthéon
52 Eglise St-Etienne du Mont
53 La Mosquée
54 Jardin des Plantes
55 Jardins du Luxembourg
56 Eglise St-Sulpice
57 Théatre Nationale de l'Odéon
58 Eiffel Tower
59 Champs de Mars
60 Ecole Militaire
61 UNESCO
62 Hôtel des Invalides
63 Assemblée Nationale
64 Musée d'Orsay
65 Cimetière de l'Est du Pere Lachaise
17e
8e
16e
7e
15e
14e
Bois de Boulogne
rue Victor Hugo
rue du Président Wilson
bd. Victor Hugo
bd. Bineau
bd. Bessières
PORTE DE CLICHY
av. de la Porte de Clichy
rue Pouchet
rue Guy Môquet
rue Legendre
av. de St-Ouen
rue Lamarck
rue Cardinet
bd. Berthier
bd. Reims
bd. Péreire
rue de Jouffroy
r. de Tocqueville
rue de Rome
rue des Dames
bd. des Batignolles
rue de Clichy
PÉREIRE LEVALLOIS
PL. DU MAL JUIN
bd. Gouvrion St-Cyr
av. du Roule
TO LA DÉFENSE
av. Charles de Gaulle
bd. Maillot
NEUILLY/ PORT MAILLOT
av. de la Grande Armée
bd. Pereire
rue Pierre Demours
av. des Ternes
av. Niel
av. de Wagram
av. de Villiers
r. de Prony
bd. de Courcelles
rue de Courcelles
bd. Malesherbes
rue du Rocher
PL. DE L'EUROPE
PL. DES TERNES
av. Hoche
bd. Haussmann
r. St-Lazare
PL. CHARLES DE GAULLE/ ETOILE
av. Friedland
rue La Boétie
PL. ST-AUGUSTIN
rue du Faubourg St-Honoré
AUBER
bd. de la Madeleine
AV FOCH
av. Foch
bd. de l'Amiral Bruix
av. R. Poincaré
av. Victor Hugo
av. Kléber
av. d'Iéna
av. Marceau
av. des Champs Elysées
av. F. D. Roosevelt
r. François 1er
av. George V
av. Montaigne
PL. DE LA CONCORDE
bd. Lannes
r. de la Faisanderie
av. des Belles Feuilles
rue de Longchamp
rue de la Pompe
PL. DU TROCADERO
av. du Prés. Wilson
av. de New York
cours de la Reine
INVALIDES
Jardin des Tuilleries
quai des Tuilleries
Seine
quai Anatole France
av. Henri Martin
AV HENRI MARTIN
av. G. Mandel
av. Paul Doumer
rue de la Tour
Pont d'Iéna
PT DE L'ALMA
quai d'Orsay
rue de l'Université
rue St- Dominique
MUSÉE D'ORSAY
bd. St-Germain
BOULAINVILLIERS LA MUETTE
av. Ingres
r. des Vignes
rue du Ranelagh
rue Reynouard
quai Branly
av. Rapp
av. Bosquet
av. de la Bourdonnais
PL. DES INVALIDES
CHAMP DE MARS/TOUR EIFFEL
Pont de Bir Hakeim
r. de la Fédération
rue Piquet
rue de Varenne
bd. Suchet
bd. Exelmans
av. Mozart
KENNEDY/ MAISON RADIO
av. du Prés. Kennedy
Voie Georges Pompidou
quai de Grenelle
bd. de Grenelle
av. de la Motte Piquet
PL. VAUBAN
bd. des Invalides
rue de Babylone
rue de Sèvres
bd. Raspail
rue de Rennes
rue la Fontaine
PL. JEAN-LORRAIN
rue Chardon Lagache
r. Mirabeau
av. de Versailles
rue Linois
rue St. Charles
rue du Théâtre
av. Emile Zola
rue des Entrepeneurs
rue du Commerce
av. de Lowenthal
av. de Ségur
av. de Saxe
bd. Garibaldi
bd. du Montparnasse
JAVEL
rue Molitor
bd. Exelmans
bd. Murat
quai André Citroën
rue Balard
rue Guttenberg
rue de la Convention
av. Félix Faure
r. de la Croix Nivert
rue de Lourmel
rue Lacourbe
rue Blomet
rue de Vaugirard
r. Dr. Roux
bd. Pasteur
r. Falguière
bd. de Vaugirard
BD VICTOR
Pont du Garigliano
q. St. Exupéry
rue Desnouettes
bd. Victor
GARE PARIS-VAUGIRARD
r. de Vouille
rue des Morillons
rue Vercingétorix
rue Losserand
av. du Maine
av. du Général Leclerc
rue Raymond
rue d'Alésia
rue Branicon
bd. Lefebvre
bd. Brune
RER

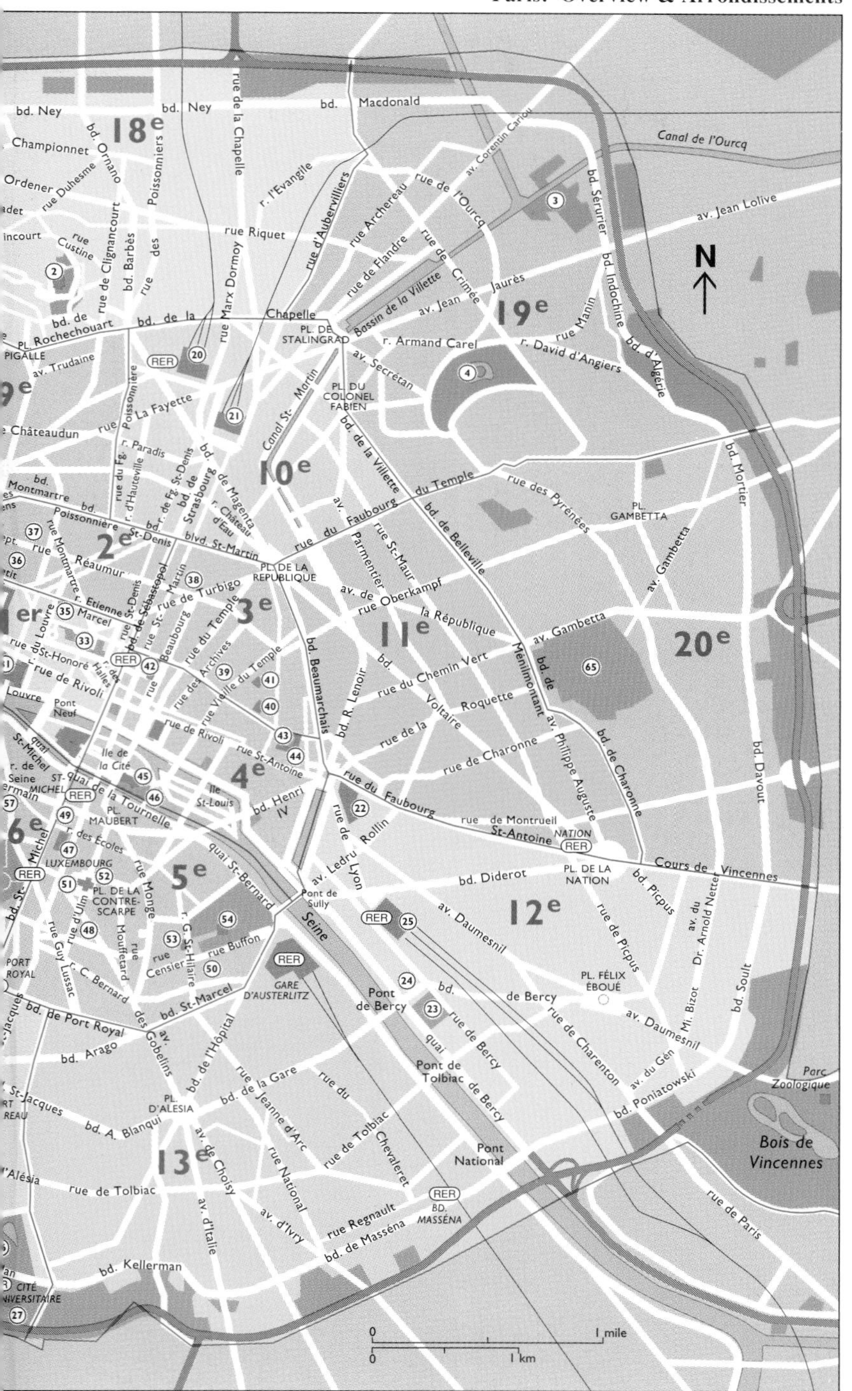
18e
19e
10e
2e
3e
11e
20e
4e
5e
12e
13e
bd. Ney
bd. Macdonald
Canal de l'Ourcq
av. Jean Lolive
rue de la Chapelle
rue d'Aubervilliers
rue Riquet
rue Marx Dormoy
r. l'Evangile
rue Archereau
rue de l'Ourcq
av. Corentin Cariou
bd. Sérurier
bd. Indochine
bd. d'Algérie
rue de Flandre
rue de Crimée
Bassin de la Villette
av. Jean Jaurès
rue Manin
r. David d'Angiers
r. Armand Carel
PL. DE STALINGRAD
av. Secrétan
PL. DU COLONEL FABIEN
Canal St. Martin
bd. de la Villette
bd. de Rochechouart
bd. de la Chapelle
PL. PIGALLE
av. Trudaine
RER
rue La Fayette
rue Poissonnière
rue Châteaudun
r. Paradis
r. de Fg. St-Denis
bd. de Strasbourg
bd. de Magenta
r. Château d'Eau
bd. Montmartre
bd. Poissonnière
bd. St-Denis
blvd. St-Martin
rue du Faubourg du Temple
PL. DE LA REPUBLIQUE
rue des Pyrénées
PL. GAMBETTA
av. Gambetta
bd. Mortier
bd. de Belleville
rue St-Maur
av. Parmentier
rue Oberkampf
av. de la République
rue Réaumur
r. Etienne Marcel
rue de Turbigo
rue St-Martin
bd. de Sébastopol
rue du Temple
rue Beaubourg
rue des Archives
rue Vieille du Temple
rue St-Honoré
rue de Rivoli
Louvre
Pont Neuf
r. des Halles
bd. Beaumarchais
bd. R. Lenoir
bd. Voltaire
rue du Chemin Vert
rue de la Roquette
Ménilmontant
bd. de Charonne
av. Philippe Auguste
rue de Charonne
Ile de la Cité
Ile St-Louis
rue St-Antoine
bd. Henri IV
quai de la Tournelle
quai St-Michel
PL. MAUBERT
r. des Écoles
LUXEMBOURG
bd. St-Michel
PL. DE LA CONTRE-SCARPE
rue Monge
rue Mouffetard
rue d'Ulm
rue Guy Lussac
r. C. Bernard
rue Censier
rue Buffon
r. G. St-Hilaire
quai St-Bernard
Seine
Pont de Sully
rue du Faubourg St-Antoine
rue de Montreuil
NATION
PL. DE LA NATION
Cours de Vincennes
bd. Diderot
av. Ledru Rollin
rue de Lyon
av. Daumesnil
rue de Picpus
bd. Picpus
av. du Dr. Arnold Netter
bd. Davout
bd. Soult
Mi. Bizot
PL. FÉLIX ÉBOUÉ
bd. de Bercy
rue de Charenton
av. du Gén
bd. Poniatowski
Parc Zoologique
Bois de Vincennes
GARE D'AUSTERLITZ
Pont de Bercy
rue de Bercy
quai de Bercy
Pont de Tolbiac
Pont National
bd. de Port Royal
PORT ROYAL
bd. St-Marcel
bd. Arago
av. des Gobelins
bd. de l'Hôpital
bd. de la Gare
rue du Chevaleret
rue Jeanne d'Arc
rue de Tolbiac
rue National
PL. D'ALESIA
bd. A. Blanqui
av. de Choisy
av. d'Italie
av. d'Ivry
rue Regnault
bd. de Masséna
BD. MASSÉNA
bd. Kellerman
CITÉ UNIVERSITAIRE
rue de Paris
0
1 mile
1 km
N

Paris: 1er and 2e

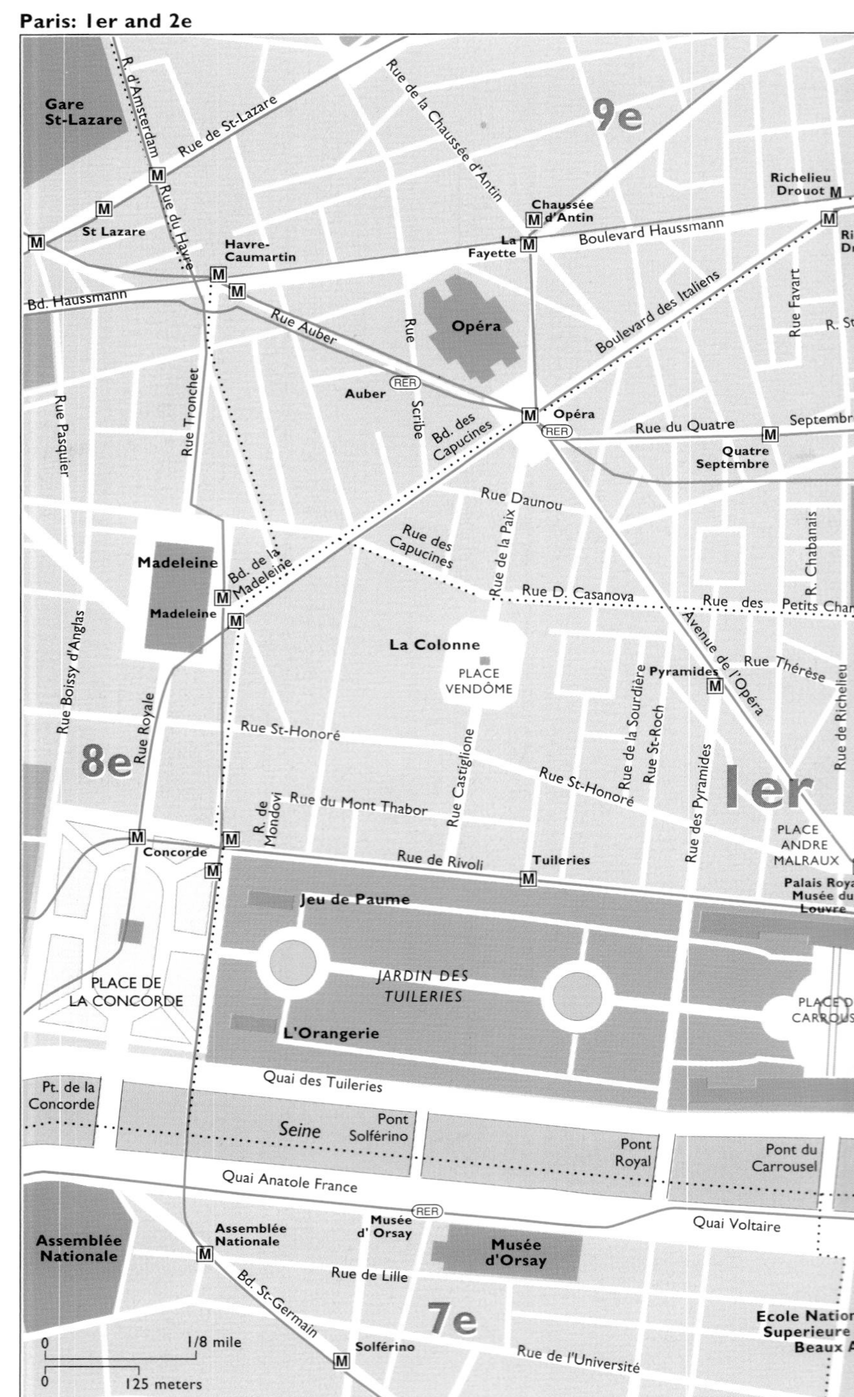

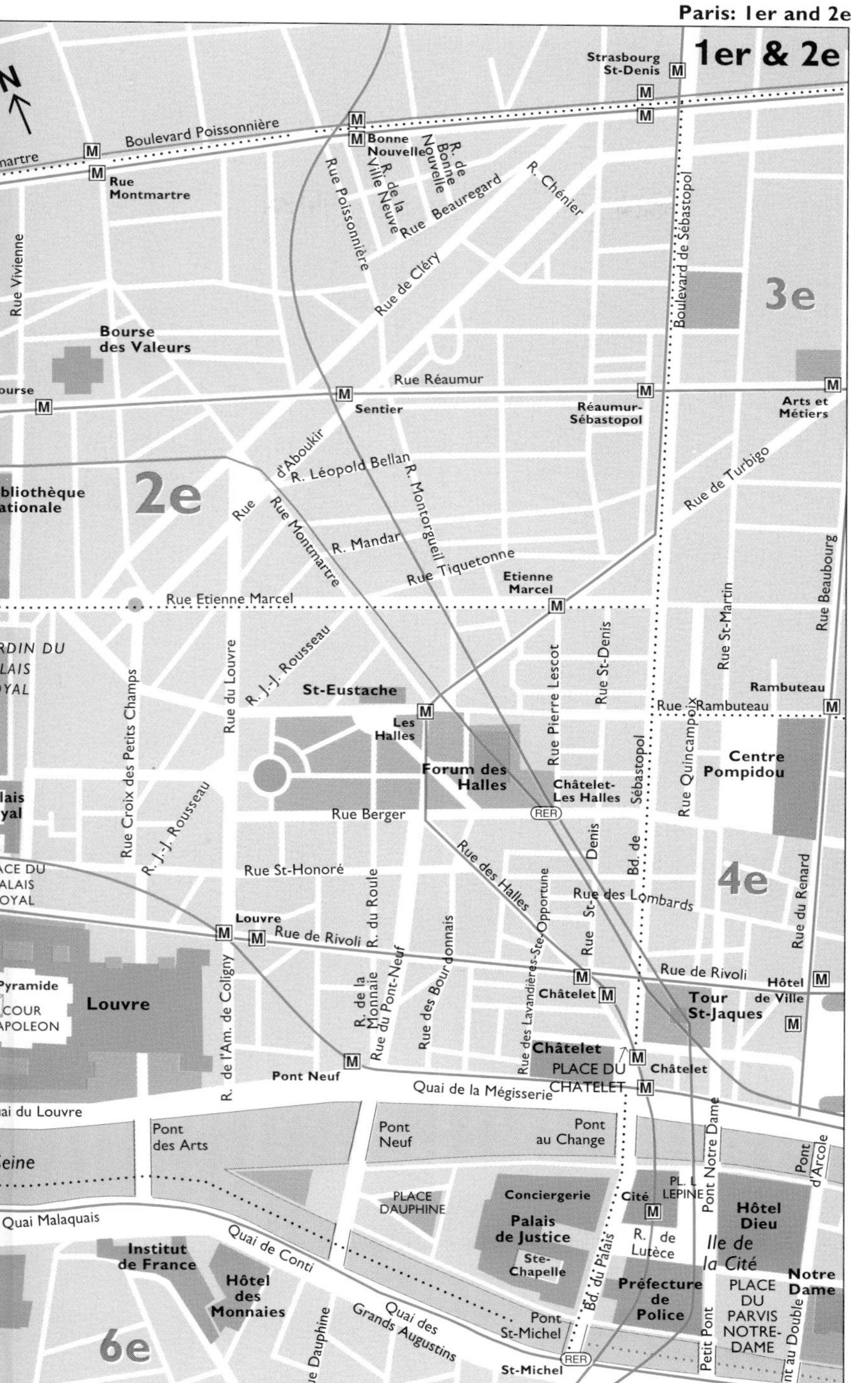

1er & 2e
N
Boulevard Poissonnière
Strasbourg St-Denis
Bonne Nouvelle
Rue Montmartre
Rue Poissonnière
R. de la Ville Neuve
R. de Bonne Nouvelle
Rue Beauregard
R. Chénier
Boulevard de Sébastopol
Rue de Cléry
Rue Vivienne
Bourse des Valeurs
3e
Rue Réaumur
Sentier
Réaumur-Sébastopol
Arts et Métiers
2e
d'Aboukir
R. Léopold Bellan
R. Montorgueil
Rue de Turbigo
Rue Montmartre
R. Mandar
Rue Tiquetonne
Etienne Marcel
Rue Etienne Marcel
Rue Beaubourg
Rue St-Martin
Rue du Louvre
R. J.-J. Rousseau
Rue Pierre Lescot
Rue St-Denis
St-Eustache
Rambuteau
Rue Rambuteau
Les Halles
Forum des Halles
Châtelet-Les Halles
Sébastopol
Rue Quincampoix
Centre Pompidou
Rue Croix des Petits Champs
Rue Berger
RER
Rue St-Honoré
Rue des Halles
4e
Rue des Lombards
Rue du Renard
Louvre
Rue de Rivoli
R. du Roule
Rue des Bourdonnais
Rue des Lavandières-Ste-Opportune
Hôtel de Ville
Pyramide
Louvre
R. de l'Am. de Coligny
R. de la Monnaie
Rue du Pont-Neuf
Châtelet
Tour St-Jaques
PLACE DU CHATELET
Pont Neuf
Quai de la Mégisserie
Pont Notre Dame
Pont au Change
Pont des Arts
Pont d'Arcole
PLACE DAUPHINE
Conciergerie
Cité
PL. L LEPINE
Hôtel Dieu
Quai Malaquais
Palais de Justice
R. de Lutèce
Ile de la Cité
Institut de France
Quai de Conti
Ste-Chapelle
Bd. du Palais
Préfecture de Police
Notre Dame
Hôtel des Monnaies
PLACE DU PARVIS NOTRE-DAME
Rue Dauphine
Quai des Grands Augustins
Pont St-Michel
Petit Pont
Pont au Double
6e
St-Michel

Paris: 5e and 6e

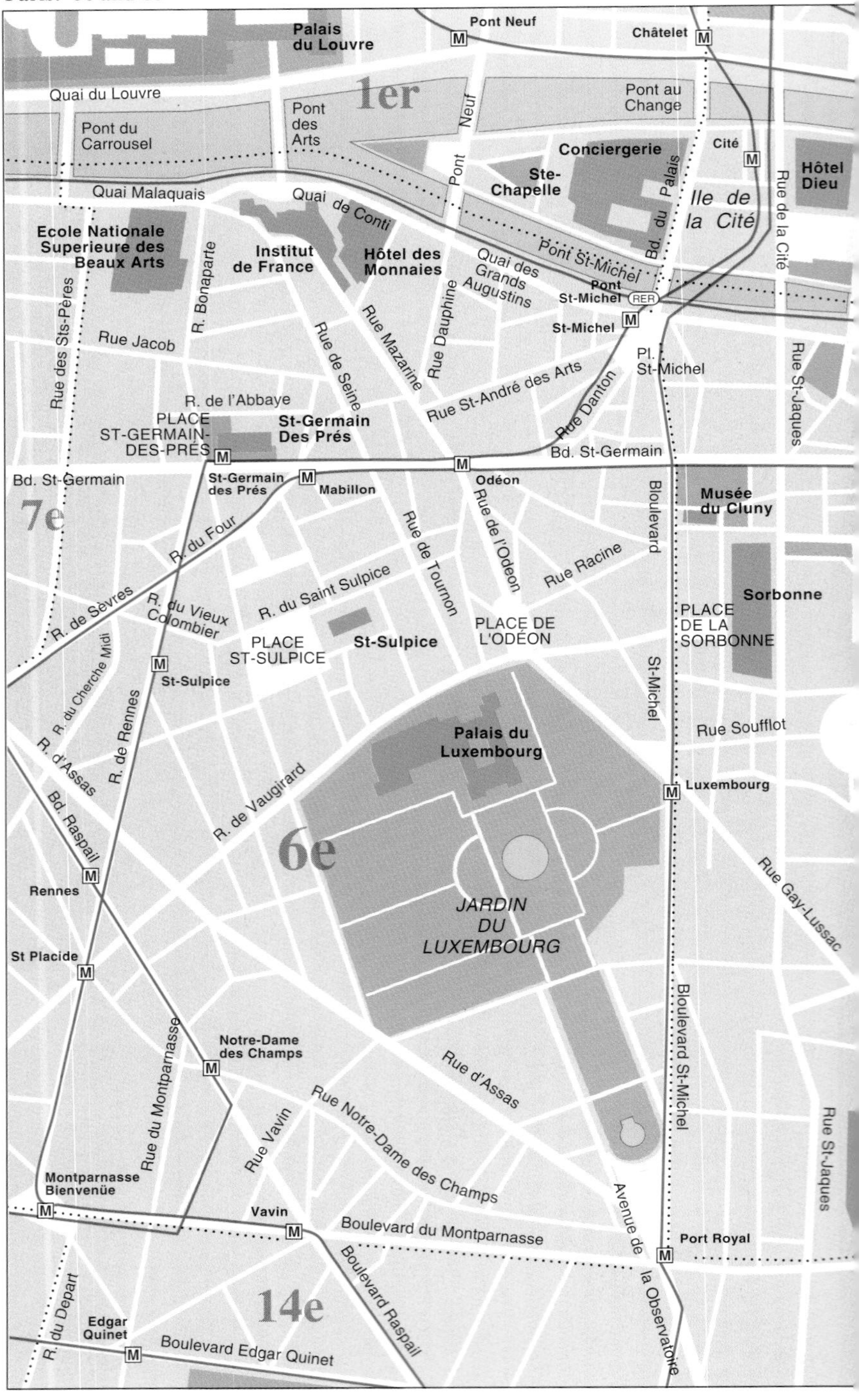

Palais du Louvre
Pont Neuf
Châtelet
1er
Quai du Louvre
Pont au Change
Pont des Arts
Pont du Carrousel
Pont Neuf
Conciergerie
Cité
Hôtel Dieu
Ste-Chapelle
Quai Malaquais
Quai de Conti
Ile de la Cité
Rue de la Cité
Bd. du Palais
Ecole Nationale Superieure des Beaux Arts
Institut de France
Hôtel des Monnaies
Quai des Grands Augustins
Pont St-Michel
R. Bonaparte
Pont St-Michel
RER
St-Michel
Rue des Sts-Pères
Rue Jacob
Rue de Seine
Rue Mazarine
Rue Dauphine
Pl. St-Michel
Rue St-Jaques
Rue St-André des Arts
R. de l'Abbaye
PLACE ST-GERMAIN-DES-PRÉS
St-Germain Des Prés
Rue Danton
Bd. St-Germain
Bd. St-Germain
St-Germain des Prés
Mabillon
Odéon
Musée du Cluny
7e
Rue de l'Odeon
Rue de Tournon
Boulevard St-Michel
R. du Four
Rue Racine
Sorbonne
R. de Sevres
R. du Vieux Colombier
R. du Saint Sulpice
PLACE DE LA SORBONNE
PLACE DE L'ODÉON
PLACE ST-SULPICE
St-Sulpice
St-Sulpice
R. du Cherche Midi
R. de Rennes
Rue Soufflot
Palais du Luxembourg
R. d'Assas
Luxembourg
R. de Vaugirard
Bd. Raspail
6e
Rennes
Rue Gay-Lussac
JARDIN DU LUXEMBOURG
St Placide
Notre-Dame des Champs
Rue du Montparnasse
Rue d'Assas
Rue Notre-Dame des Champs
Rue Vavin
Boulevard St-Michel
Rue St-Jaques
Montparnasse Bienvenüe
Vavin
Avenue de la Observatoire
Boulevard du Montparnasse
Port Royal
Boulevard Raspail
R. du Depart
14e
Edgar Quinet
Boulevard Edgar Quinet

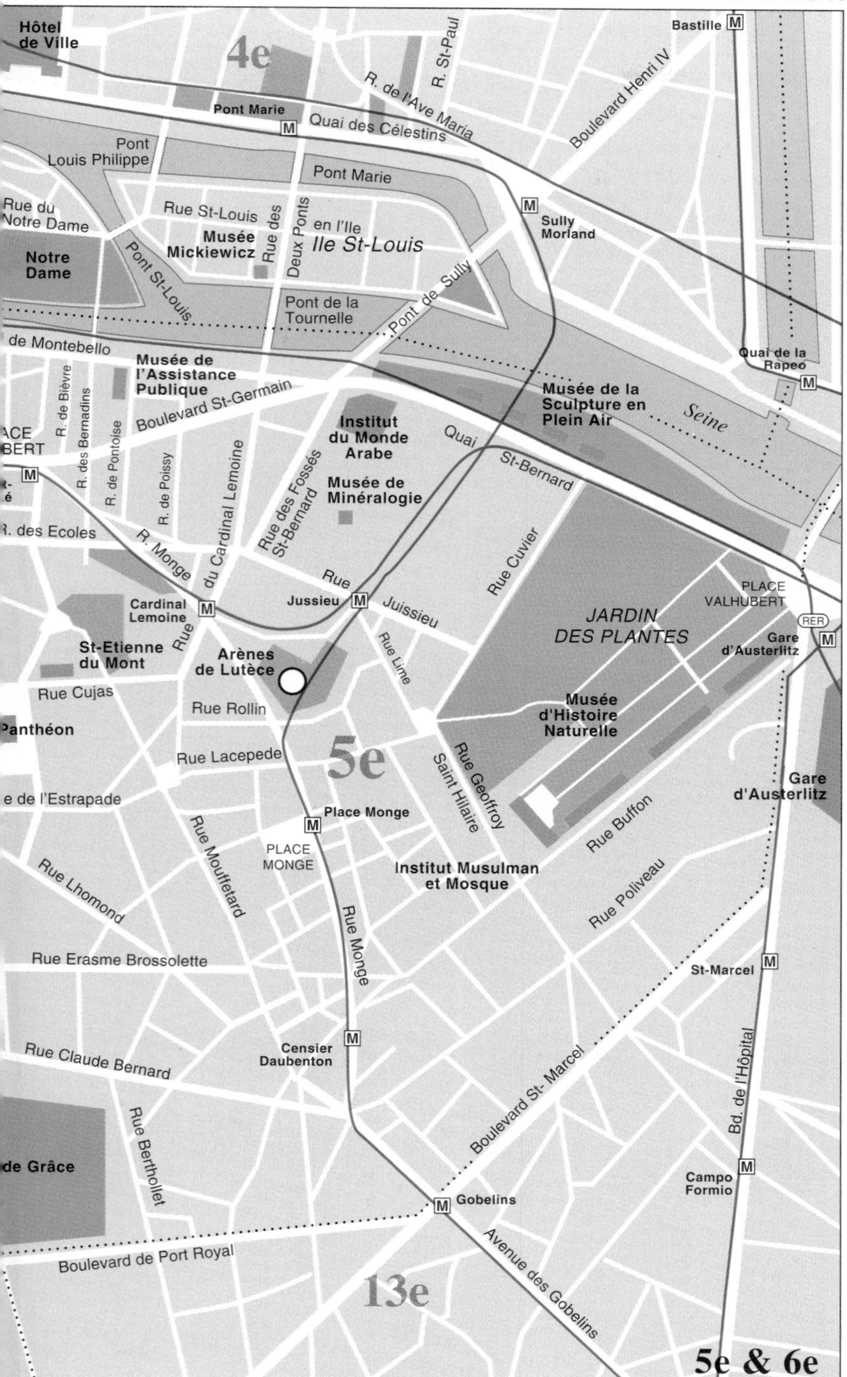
Hôtel de Ville
4e
Pont Marie
Quai des Célestins
R. St-Paul
R. de l'Ave Maria
Boulevard Henri IV
Bastille
Pont Louis Philippe
Pont Marie
Rue du Notre Dame
Rue St-Louis
Musée Mickiewicz
Rue des Deux Ponts
en l'Ile
Ile St-Louis
Sully Morland
Notre Dame
Pont St-Louis
Pont de la Tournelle
Pont de Sully
de Montebello
Musée de l'Assistance Publique
Boulevard St-Germain
R. de Bièvre
R. des Bernadins
R. de Pontoise
R. de Poissy
Rue du Cardinal Lemoine
Rue des Fossés St-Bernard
Institut du Monde Arabe
Musée de Minéralogie
Quai St-Bernard
Musée de la Sculpture en Plein Air
Seine
Quai de la Rapeo
R. des Ecoles
R. Monge
Rue Cuvier
Rue Jussieu
Jussieu
Cardinal Lemoine
PLACE VALHUBERT
JARDIN DES PLANTES
RER
Gare d'Austerlitz
St-Etienne du Mont
Arènes de Lutèce
Rue Lime
Rue Cujas
Rue Rollin
Panthéon
Musée d'Histoire Naturelle
Rue Lacepede
5e
Rue Geoffroy Saint Hilaire
de l'Estrapade
Place Monge
PLACE MONGE
Rue Mouffetard
Rue Buffon
Gare d'Austerlitz
Rue Lhomond
Institut Musulman et Mosque
Rue Poliveau
Rue Monge
Rue Erasme Brossolette
St-Marcel
Censier Daubenton
Rue Claude Bernard
Boulevard St-Marcel
Bd. de l'Hôpital
Rue Berthollet
de Grâce
Campo Formio
Gobelins
Boulevard de Port Royal
Avenue des Gobelins
13e
5e & 6e

Paris RER

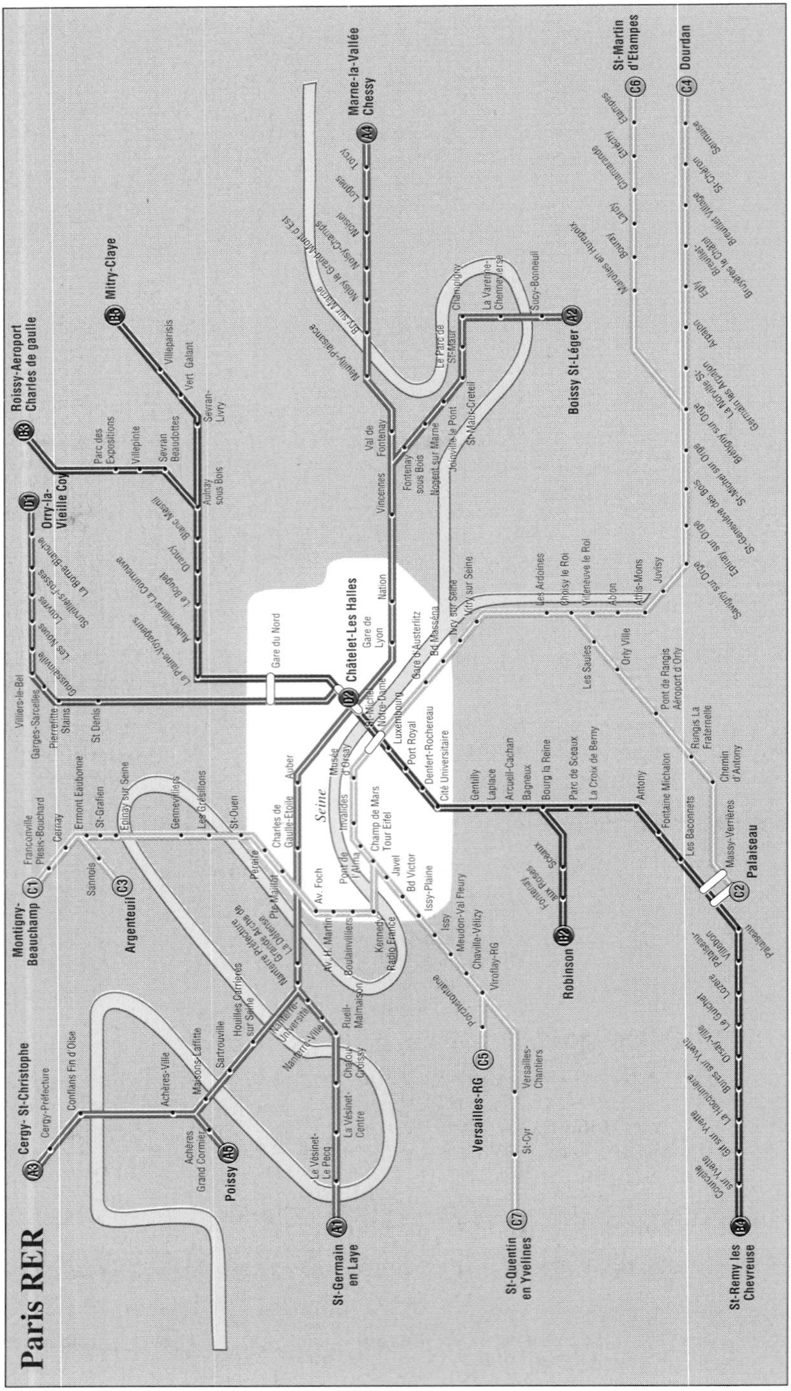

A3 Cergy- St-Christophe
Cergy-Préfecture
Conflans Fin d'Oise
Achères-Ville
Achères Grand Cormier
Poissy A5
Maisons-Laffitte
Sartrouville
Houilles Carrières sur Seine
Nanterre Préfecture
Grande Arche de La Défense
Nanterre-Université
Nanterre-Ville
Rueil-Malmaison
Chatou-Croissy
Le Vésinet-Centre
Le Vésinet-Le Pecq
St-Germain en Laye A1
Montigny-Beauchamp C1
Franconville Plesis-Bouchard
Cernay
Ermont Eaubonne
Sannois
St-Grafien
Argenteuil C3
Epinay sur Seine
Gennevilliers
Les Grésillons
St-Ouen
Pereire
Pte Maillot
Av. Foch
Av. H. Martin
Boulainvilliers
Kennedy Radio France
Pont de l'Alma
Champ de Mars Tour Eifel
Javel
Bd Victor
Issy-Plaine
Issy
Meudon-Val Fleury
Chaville-Vélizy
Viroflay-RG
Porchetontaine
Versailles-RG C5
St-Quentin en Yvelines C7
St-Cyr
Versailles-Chantiers
Charles de Gaulle-Etoile
Auber
Seine
Invalides
Musée d'Orsay
St-Michel Notre-Dame
Luxembourg
Port Royal
Denfert-Rochereau
Cité Universitaire
Gentilly
Laplace
Arcueil-Cachan
Bagneux
Bourg la Reine
Sceaux
Fontenay aux Roses
Robinson B2
Parc de Sceaux
La Croix de Berny
Antony
Fontaine Michalon
Les Baconnets
Massy-Verrières
C2 Palaiseau
Palaiseau
Palaiseau-Villebon
Lozère
Le Guichet
Orsay-Ville
Bures sur Yvette
La Hacquinière
Gif sur Yvette
Courcelle sur Yvette
St-Remy les Chevreuse B4
Chemin d'Antony
Rungis La Fraternelle
Pont de Rangis Aéroport d'Orly
Orly Ville
Les Saules
Villiers-le-Bel
Garges-Sarcelles
Pierrefitte Stains
St Denis
Goussainville
Les Noues
Louvres
Survilliers-Fosses
La Borne-Blanche
Orry-la-Vieille Coy D1
Roissy-Aeroport Charles de gaulle B3
Parc des Expositions
Villepinte
Sevran Beaudottes
Mitry-Claye B5
Villeparisis
Vert Galant
Sevran-Livry
Aulnay sous Bois
Blanc Mesnil
Drancy
Le Bouget
Aubervilliers-La Courneuve
La Plaine-Voyageurs
Gare du Nord
Châtelet-Les Halles D2
Gare de Lyon
Nation
Vincennes
Val de Fontenay
Neuilly-Plaisance
Bry sur Marne
Noisy le Grand-Mont d'Est
Noisy-Champs
Noisiel
Lognes
Torcy
Marne-la-Vallée Chessy A4
Fontenay sous Bois
Nogent sur Marne
Joinville-le Pont
St-Maur-Creteil
Le Parc de St-Maur
Champigny
La Varenne-Chennevierse
Sucy-Bonneuil
Boissy St-Léger A2
Gare d'Austerlitz
Bd Masséna
Ivry sur Seine
Vitry sur Seine
Les Ardoines
Choisy le Roi
Villeneuve le Roi
Ablon
Athis-Mons
Juvisy
Savigny sur Orge
Epinay sur Orge
St-Geneviève des Bois
St-Michel sur Orge
Brétigny sur Orge
La Norville St-Germain les Arpajon
Arpajon
Egly
Breuillet-Bruyères le Châtel
Breuillet Village
St-Chéron
Sermaise
Dourdan C4
Marolles en Hurepoix
Bouray
Lardy
Chamarande
Etréchy
Etampes
St-Martin d'Etampes C6

Let's Go: Paris

"Its yearly revision by a new crop of Harvard students makes it as valuable as ever." **—*The New York Times***

"Value-packed, unbeatable, accurate, and comprehensive." **—*The Los Angeles Times***

"A world-wise traveling companion—always ready with friendly advice and helpful hints, all sprinkled with a bit of wit." **—*The Philadelphia Inquirer***

"Lighthearted and sophisticated, informative and fun to read. [Let's Go] helps the novice traveler navigate like a knowledgeable old hand." **—*Atlanta Journal-Constitution***

"All the essential information you need, from making a phone call to exchanging money to contacting your embassy. [Let's Go] provides maps to help you find your way from every train station to a full range of youth hostels and hotels." **—*Minneapolis Star Tribune***

"Unbeatable: good sight-seeing advice; up-to-date-info on restaurants, hotels, and inns; a commitment to money-saving travel; and a wry style that brightens nearly every page." **—*The Washington Post***

Let's Go researchers have to make it on their own.

"The writers seem to have experienced every rooster-packed bus and lunar-surfaced mattress about which they write." **—*The New York Times***

"Retains the spirit of the student-written publication it is: candid, opinionated, resourceful, amusing info for the traveler of limited means but broad curiosity." **—*Mademoiselle***

No other guidebook is as comprehensive.

"Whether you're touring the United States, Europe, Southeast Asia, or Central America, a Let's Go guide will clue you in to the cheapest, yet safe, hotels and hostels, food and transportation. Going beyond the call of duty, the guides reveal a country's latest news, cultural hints, and off-beat information that any tourist is likely to miss." **—*Tulsa World***

Let's Go is completely revised each year.

"Up-to-date travel tips for touring four continents on skimpy budgets." **—*Time***

"Inimitable.... Let's Go's 24 guides are updated yearly (as opposed to the general guidebook standard of every two to three years), and in a marvelously spunky way." **—*The New York Times***

Let's Go Publications

Let's Go: Alaska & The Pacific Northwest
Let's Go: Britain & Ireland
Let's Go: California
Let's Go: Central America
Let's Go: Eastern Europe
Let's Go: Ecuador & The Galápagos Islands
Let's Go: Europe
Let's Go: France
Let's Go: Germany
Let's Go: Greece & Turkey
Let's Go: India & Nepal
Let's Go: Ireland
Let's Go: Israel & Egypt
Let's Go: Italy
Let's Go: London
Let's Go: Mexico
Let's Go: New York City
Let's Go: Paris
Let's Go: Rome
Let's Go: Southeast Asia
Let's Go: Spain & Portugal
Let's Go: Switzerland & Austria
Let's Go: USA
Let's Go: Washington, D.C.

Let's Go ***Map Guide:*** *Boston*
Let's Go ***Map Guide:*** *London*
Let's Go ***Map Guide:*** *New York City*
Let's Go ***Map Guide:*** *Paris*
Let's Go ***Map Guide:*** *San Francisco*
Let's Go ***Map Guide:*** *Washington, D.C.*

LET'S GO

The Budget Guide to Paris

1997

Lauren J. Feldman
Editor

St. Martin's Press New York

HELPING LET'S GO

If you want to share your discoveries, suggestions, or corrections, please drop us a line. We read every piece of correspondence, whether a postcard, a 10-page e-mail, or a coconut. All suggestions are passed along to our researcher-writers. Please note that mail received after May 1997 may be too late for the 1998 book, but will be retained for the following edition. **Address mail to:**

Let's Go: Paris
67 Mt. Auburn Street
Cambridge, MA 02138
USA

Visit Let's Go at **http://www.letsgo.com,** or send e-mail to:

Fanmail@letsgo.com
Subject: "Paris"

In addition to the invaluable travel advice our readers share with us, many are kind enough to offer their services as researchers or editors. Unfortunately, the charter of Let's Go, Inc. enables us to employ only currently enrolled Harvard-Radcliffe students.

Map revisions pp. 2, 3, 152, 153, 172, 173, 176, 177, 182, 183, 187, 190, 191, 198, 199, 203, 285 by Let's Go, Inc.

Distributed outside the USA and Canada by Macmillan.

ISBN: 0-312-14662-0

First edition
10 9 8 7 6 5 4 3 2 1

Let's Go: Paris is written by Let's Go Publications, 67 Mt. Auburn Street, Cambridge, MA 02138, USA.

Printed in the USA on recycled paper with biodegradable soy ink.

Contents

Maps

Color Maps

Acknowledgements

First of all, thank you Mom, Dad, Jeff, Jay, Melinda, and Nanny for supporting me this summer, I love you all. Mom, Dad, and Jeff—thank you for trekking out to Somerville to see me, and for keeping me well-fed and well-advised. Jay and Melinda, thank you for being the guardians of my sanity. Nanny, thank you for inspiring my interest in Paris and for taking care of me. Thank you Joëlle, Alain, Stéphane, Violaine, et Cecile Gras, my Parisian family. Paris wouldn't have been the same without you. Je vous remercie, Je vous aime. Morgann Mobry—you are one extraordinary woman. Thank you for looking out for me. Jennifer Elizzzzzabeth Frauson, thanks for schlepping all the way up to Boston to visit sorry ol' me—I think you're the coolest dog on the block—I miss you already. Thank you to the Romance room, especially Tom, Julie, and Corey. Tom and Julie—thank you for imparting your wisdom upon me and for helping out whenever possible. Corey—a special thank you to you, you made me smile when absolutely nothing else would. I'll see you in Italy. Liz Squires—you were/are a godsend. You really deserve associate editor credit on this book, thank you for your cheerful dedication. SoRelle- thank you for two years worth of editing/mentoring. Your dedication is astounding and greatly appreciated. Amanda—thanks for all your hard work on the maps. Michelle and the ME posse—thanks for lots of salient advice. Willow, Jenny and Raphie—Thank you for lots of hard work and for making this guide the best it's ever been. And David Joseph—I could fill up the remaining 352 pages of this book just thanking you. This book would never have happened without you. Thank you for infinite support and confidence. Je t'aime mon coeur, beaucoup. —L.J.F.

Willow would like to thank Pop, Mom, Bro-J, Gram, Bev, Ruth, Brenda, Clovis, Gilly and Stanley, Lauren, Tom, Julie and Felix the cat. Jenny gives her thanks to Francois Ecot, and Raphie thanks you, you know who you are.

Researcher-Writers

Willow Crystal *Paris*

Willow did justice (and then some) to the Seine islands and the artistic, quieter arrondissements of the outer-city. Willow wore out her shoes and wrists to churn out prose that was both aesthetic and accurate. Willow's sensitive heart and a poetic pen painted a picture of Auvers and Giverny worthy of their artists, and her never-ending patience and high spirits sent her spinning through Disneyland Paris. Having mastered the R-W job, ferocious Willow returned to Cambridge in time to render Paris proof-perfect.

Raphael Folsom *Paris*

Raphie's writing reflects his captivation with Paris; his copy was always as engaging and astounding as the city itself. A veteran R-W, Raphie abandoned the hills of Turkey for the patisseries of central Paris. Intrepid in his research, Raphie's determination to discover what makes this city tick brought hidden Parisian nightlife to light. Raphie used his tremendous gift for language to evoke the color of the Latin Quarter, and infuse even the most mundane hotel with character.

Jennifer Lefcourt *Paris*

Jenny took the Marais by storm, sending us hip new bars and cafés that only the savviest of Parisiennes would know. Fearlessly defending her home territory, the 19ème and 20ème, Jenny brought the outskirts of Paris closer to the heart of this book. After waging a one woman war against chain-restaurants, Jenny set out on a crusade against kitsch. With her artist's eye and discriminating taste, Mme. Lefcourt added a touch of class to everything that she researched.

Robert Lagueux *Normandy*

Rob's fine sense of humor sent us laughs along with stellar research.

Amy Kristen Brown *Loire Valley*

The most seasoned of R-Ws Amy spiced up the Loire in her own sizzling style.

About Let's Go

THIRTY-SIX YEARS OF WISDOM

Back in 1960, a few students at Harvard University banded together to produce a 20-page pamphlet offering a collection of tips on budget travel in Europe. This modest, mimeographed packet, offered as an extra to passengers on student charter flights to Europe, met with instant popularity. The following year, students traveling to Europe researched the first, full-fledged edition of *Let's Go: Europe*, a pocket-sized book featuring honest, irreverent writing and a decidedly youthful outlook on the world. Throughout the 60s, our guides reflected the times; the 1969 guide to America led off by inviting travelers to "dig the scene" at San Francisco's Haight-Ashbury. During the 70s and 80s, we gradually added regional guides and expanded coverage into the Middle East and Central America. With the addition of our in-depth city guides, handy map guides, and extensive coverage of Asia, the 90s are also proving to be a time of explosive growth for Let's Go, and there's certainly no end in sight. The first editions of *Let's Go: India & Nepal* and *Let's Go: Ecuador & The Galapagos Islands* hit the shelves this year, and work toward next year's series has already begun.

We've seen a lot in 37 years. *Let's Go: Europe* is now the world's bestselling international guide, translated into seven languages. And our new guides bring Let's Go's total number of titles, with their spirit of adventure and their reputation for honesty, accuracy, and editorial integrity, to 30. But some things never change: our guides are still researched, written, and produced entirely by students who know first-hand how to see the world on the cheap.

HOW WE DO IT

Each guide is completely revised and thoroughly updated every year by a well-traveled set of 200 students. Every winter, we recruit over 120 researchers and 60 editors to write the books anew. After several months of training, Researcher-Writers hit the road for seven weeks of exploration, from Anchorage to Ankara, Estonia to El Salvador, Iceland to Indonesia. Hired for their rare combination of budget travel sense, writing ability, stamina, and courage, these adventurous travelers know that train strikes, stolen luggage, food poisoning, and marriage proposals are all part of a day's work. Back at our offices, editors work from spring to fall, massaging copy written on Himalayan bus rides into witty yet informative prose. A student staff of typesetters, cartographers, publicists, and managers keeps our lively team together. In September, the collected efforts of the summer are delivered to our printer, who turns them into books in record time, so that you have the most up-to-date information available for *your* vacation. And even as you read this, work on next year's editions is well underway.

WHY WE DO IT

At Let's Go, our goal is to give you a great vacation. We don't think of budget travel as the last recourse of the destitute; we believe that it's the only way to travel. Living cheaply and simply brings you closer to the people and places you've been saving up to visit. Our books will ease your anxieties and answer your questions about the basics—so you can get off the beaten track and explore. Once you learn the ropes, we encourage you to put Let's Go away now and then to strike out on your own. As any seasoned traveler will tell you, the best discoveries are often those you make yourself. When you find something worth sharing, drop us a line. We're Let's Go Publications, 67 Mt. Auburn St., Cambridge, MA 02138, USA (e-mail: fanmail@letsgo.com).

HAPPY TRAVELS!

How To Use This Book

Paris has been the center of the universe for over a thousand years. Millions have visited, lived in, and fallen in love with (and in) this city. And yet somehow the town stays fresh; each new discovery is as exciting as the first. *Let's Go* will let you dive right into this chic, cultural, and culinary capital.

Paris: An Introduction fills you in on Paris's history, politics, architecture, art, and literary life. The chapter is organized chronologically to give you a sense of the major periods of Paris' past and the various cultural, political, and social developments that marked them. **Essentials** offers practical advice for before you go and after you arrive. **Planning Your Trip,** with its helpful information on necessary documents, useful maps, and currency, will help you think ahead. Students, seniors, families, women, and other travelers with specific needs can find tips and resources to help them get the most out of the trip. **Getting There** gives tips on the cheapest ways to get to Paris. **Once There** provides information on useful organizations within the city, emergency services, and the layout of the city—as well as explaining the difference between the metro and the RER, and why newcomers should stick to the former until they get their bearings.

In the **Accommodations** chapter, hotels, hostels, and foyers are grouped by arrondissement—one of the 20 Parisian neighborhoods—and then listed within the arrondissements in order of value, based on price, location, safety, and comfort, as determined by our researcher-writers. Neighborhood laundromats are listed after the accommodations. **Food and Drink** begins with the budget traveler's staple: groceries and markets. It goes on to give a list of restaurants organized by type, followed by restaurant reviews organized by location and listed in order of value. After that, we list cafés (from the historical sights to the cybercafés), *salons de thé,* and sweets. Also organized by arrondissement, the **Sights** chapter gives a sense of the hidden and not-so-hidden treasures in Paris' different neighborhoods. Organized roughly as a series of walking tours, it features some great strolls, too. **Museums** get a section of their own, with detailed descriptions of the large museums—the Louvre, the Musée d'Orsay, and more—and brief listings of smaller collections that will appeal to every taste. **Entertainment** is chock-full of film, theater, music, and dance; people who aren't interested in our coverage of participatory and spectator sports might take more kindly to what we say about the city's finest bars and dance clubs. **Shopping**—entertainment for some—includes the city's major department stores as well as harder-to-find specialty shops, bookstores, and markets. Travelers hankering for respite from the big-city grind should turn to **Trips from Paris. Daytrips** offers a large selection of nearby châteaux, churches, parks, and, yes, a theme park; **Weekend Trips** has longer get-aways to the châteaux of the Loire and to Normandy, including Mont-St-Michel. Check out our **Appendices** for metric conversions, useful phrases, and a menu reader. Finally, relax, wander about Paris, and remember that the best discoveries are the ones you make on your own.

A NOTE TO OUR READERS

The information for this book is gathered by *Let's Go*'s researchers during the late spring and summer months. Each listing is derived from the assigned researcher's opinion based upon his or her visit at a particular time. The opinions are expressed in a candid and forthright manner. Other travelers might disagree. Those traveling at a different time may have different experiences since prices, dates, hours, and conditions are always subject to change. You are urged to check beforehand to avoid inconvenience and surprises. Travel always involves a certain degree of risk, especially in low-cost areas. When traveling, especially on a budget, always take particular care to ensure your safety.

Paris: An Introduction

A Paris on peut s'amuser, s'ennuyer, rire, pleurer, faire tout ce qui vous plaît; nul ne vous jette un regard car il y a des milliers qui y font la même chose et chacun à sa manière.
(In Paris you can enjoy yourself, bore yourself, laugh, cry, do all that pleases you, and no one casts a glance at you because there are thousands who do the same thing and each one in her own way.)
—Frédéric Chopin, 1831

Ancient Paris

To have been Lutèce and to have become Paris—what could be a more magnificent symbol! To have been mud and to have become spirit!
—Victor Hugo

In the beginning, there was a crossroads and an island, the Ile de la Cité, home to a Gallic tribe called the Parisii. Caesar's Gallic wars inaugurated the grand Paris tradition of invasions and massacres: slaughtering the tribesfolk as they came, the Romans moved into Paris just before the official defeat of Vercingetorix and the Gauls in 52 BC. The Romans imported aspects of their bureaucracy to the city, but considered it little more than a provincial outpost of the Roman empire for the next several centuries, even as the empire itself was crumbling. Ste. Geneviève became patron saint of the grateful city by first turning Attila and his Huns away from Paris in 451 (they attacked Orléans instead). Two decades later, she deflected the wrath of the Franks by becoming wisewoman to Clovis, their chief; partly in deference to her and her counsel, he made Paris the capital of his lands. What the Parisii had called *Loutonheze,* "a dwelling in the midst of the waters," and the Romans referred to as *Lutetia Parisiorum* (the Parisii's Lutèce) finally became *Paris.*

Over the next few centuries, the Vikings raided Paris repeatedly, stopping by every time they headed up the Seine to attack Bourgogne. The city reclaimed its regional power in 987 when Hugh Capet, count of Paris, became King of France—which at the time was little more than Paris and its immediate surroundings. Philippe II (Philippe Auguste) married his way into more land and fought Paris' way into being the capital of Normandy and Anjou, a kingdom that was still only one of many in France. During the Hundred Years War with England (1337-1453), the duke of Burgundy allied with the English against the French, and Paris was stuck in the middle. Were it not for the now mythical Jeanne d'Arc, who allied with the Valois King Charles VII against Henry V of England, Paris might have remained a second-rate city or become an English colony. Instead, Jeanne d'Arc revitalized the Valois troops and led them to a string of victories. Attempting to win Paris back from the Burgundians in 1429, she was wounded in what is now the 1er arrondissement (see "Sights—1er," p. 146). Although she was captured two years later by the English and burned at the stake for heresy in Rouen, her efforts nonetheless bore fruit. In 1437, Charles VII, the king Jeanne crowned, recaptured Paris and France was born.

ARCHITECTURE: THE ROMAN ERA

The Romans transformed Paris from a collection of fishing huts into a place of civilization, a title the city has prided itself on ever since. They rebuilt the city in their own image, with vineyards, baths, an arena, and the north-south rue St-Jacques/St-Martin, a road that led to Rome and that was a prototype for the major Parisian axes of today. The remnants of Roman Paris can be found in the partially reconstructed Arènes de

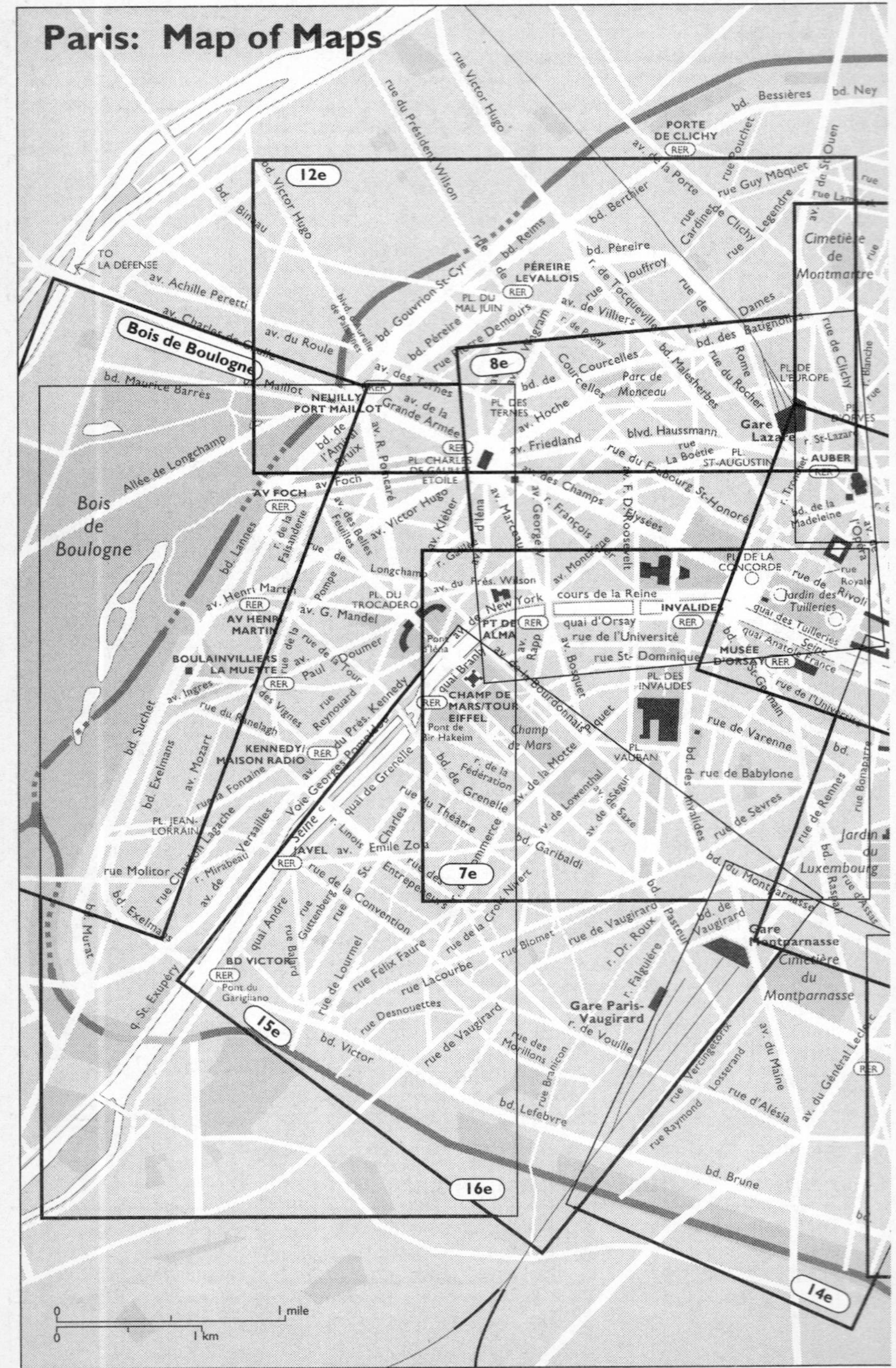
Paris: Map of Maps
12e
8e
7e
15e
16e
14e
Bois de Boulogne
Bois de Boulogne
TO LA DÉFENSE
PORTE DE CLICHY
PÉREIRE LEVALLOIS
PL. DU MAL JUIN
NEUILLY PORT MAILLOT
PL. DES TERNES
PL. CHARLES DE GAULLE ÉTOILE
AV FOCH
AV HENRI MARTIN
BOULAINVILLIERS LA MUETTE
KENNEDY/ MAISON RADIO
PL. JEAN-LORRAIN
JAVEL
BD VICTOR
Pont du Garigliano
PL. DU TROCADERO
Pont d'Iéna
PT DE L'ALMA
CHAMP DE MARS/TOUR EIFFEL
Pont de Bir Hakeim
Champ de Mars
INVALIDES
PL. DES INVALIDES
PL. VAUBAN
MUSÉE D'ORSAY
PL. DE LA CONCORDE
Jardin des Tuileries
Parc de Monceau
PL. ST-AUGUSTIN
Gare Lazare
PL. DE L'EUROPE
AUBER
Cimetière de Montmartre
Jardin du Luxembourg
Gare Montparnasse
Cimetière du Montparnasse
Gare Paris-Vaugirard
Seine
RER
0
1 mile
0
1 km

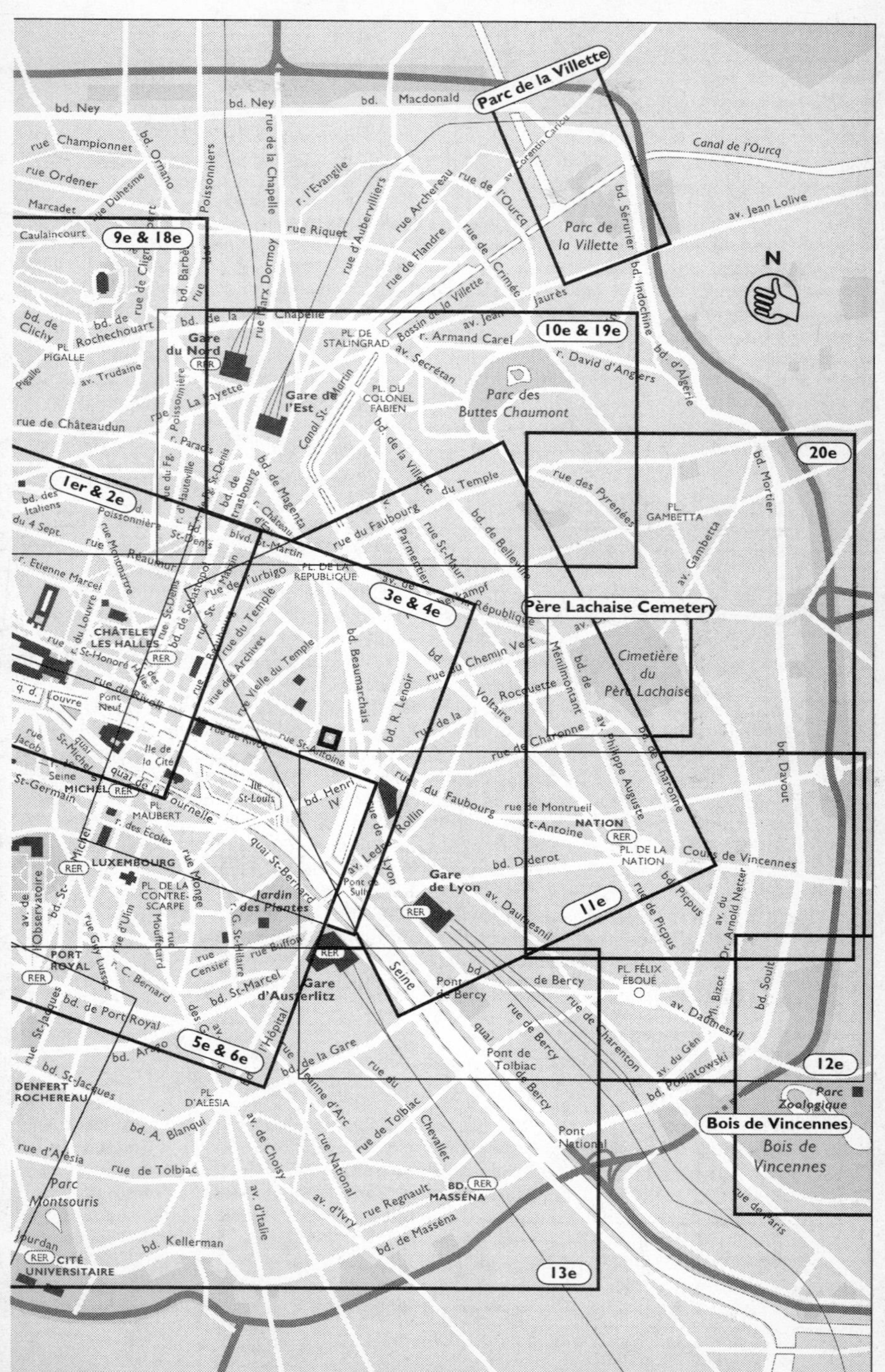

Parc de la Villette
9e & 18e
10e & 19e
1er & 2e
3e & 4e
20e
Père Lachaise Cemetery
11e
5e & 6e
12e
Bois de Vincennes
13e
N
bd. Ney
bd. Macdonald
Canal de l'Ourcq
av. Jean Lolive
av. Corentin Cariou
Parc de la Villette
bd. Sérurier
bd. Indochine
bd. d'Algérie
rue Championnet
bd. Ornano
rue Ordener
Marcadet
rue Duhesme
Caulaincourt
rue Poissonniers
rue de la Chapelle
rue Marx Dormoy
r. l'Evangile
rue d'Aubervilliers
rue Archereau
rue de l'Ourcq
rue Riquet
rue de Flandre
rue de Crimée
Bassin de la Villette
Jaurès
bd. de Clichy
bd. de Rochechouart
PL. PIGALLE
Pigalle
av. Trudaine
Gare du Nord
RER
Gare de l'Est
La Fayette
PL. DE STALINGRAD
r. Armand Carel
av. Secrétan
r. David d'Angers
PL. DU COLONEL FABIEN
Parc des Buttes Chaumont
Canal St-Martin
rue de Châteaudun
r. Paradis
bd. de Magenta
bd. de Strasbourg
bd. de la Villette
du Temple
bd. de Belleville
rue des Pyrenées
PL. GAMBETTA
bd. Mortier
av. Gambetta
bd. des Italiens
du 4 Sept.
Poissonnière
rue Montmartre
Réaumur
St-Denis
bd. St-Martin
rue du Faubourg
rue St-Maur
Parmentier
PL. DE LA RÉPUBLIQUE
av. de la République
r. Etienne Marcel
CHÂTELET LES HALLES
rue de Turbigo
bd. de Sébastopol
rue du Temple
rue des Archives
rue Vielle du Temple
bd. Beaumarchais
rue du Chemin Vert
bd. R. Lenoir
Voltaire
Roquette
Ménilmontant
Cimetière du Père Lachaise
rue St-Honoré
q. d. Louvre
rue de Rivoli
Pont Neuf
Ile de la Cité
rue St-Antoine
rue de Charonne
av. Philippe Auguste
bd. de Charonne
bd. Davout
rue Jacob
quai St-Michel
Seine
St-Germain
MICHEL
quai de la Tournelle
Ile St-Louis
PL. MAUBERT
r. des Ecoles
bd. Henri IV
rue de Lyon
rue du Faubourg St-Antoine
rue de Montreuil
NATION
PL. DE LA NATION
Cours de Vincennes
bd. Diderot
av. Ledru Rollin
Pont de Sully
quai St-Bernard
Gare de Lyon
av. Daumesnil
rue de Picpus
bd. de Picpus
av. du Dr. Arnold Netter
LUXEMBOURG
rue Monge
PL. DE LA CONTRESCARPE
Jardin des Plantes
av. de l'Observatoire
bd. St-Michel
rue d'Ulm
rue Mouffetard
rue Buffon
rue Censier
rue G. St-Hilaire
rue Gay Lussac
PORT ROYAL
r. C. Bernard
bd. St-Marcel
Gare d'Austerlitz
Seine
Pont de Bercy
bd de Bercy
rue de Bercy
quai de Bercy
PL. FÉLIX ÉBOUÉ
rue de Charenton
av. Daumesnil
rue Bizot
bd. Soult
rue St-Jacques
bd. de Port Royal
bd. Arago
bd. de l'Hôpital
bd. de la Gare
Pont de Tolbiac
av. du Gén
bd. Poniatowski
Parc Zoologique
DENFERT ROCHEREAU
bd. St-Jacques
PL. D'ALESIA
rue Jeanne d'Arc
rue du Chevallet
Pont National
Bois de Vincennes
bd. A. Blanqui
av. de Choisy
rue de Tolbiac
rue d'Alésia
rue National
rue de Tolbiac
Parc Montsouris
av. d'Italie
av. d'Ivry
rue Regnault
BD. MASSÉNA
rue de Paris
Jourdan
CITÉ UNIVERSITAIRE
bd. Kellerman
bd. de Masséna

Lutèce, the baths under the Hôtel de Cluny, and the residential excavations in the square in front of Notre-Dame. An early type of architecture modeled after Roman basilicas blossomed into the massive Romanesque cathedrals of the 11th century. The oldest parts of St-Germain-des-Prés show the immense walls and semicircular arches characteristic of this style. Prosperity in the 12th century allowed the invention of a new, far more ornate architectural style—the Gothic. From this period, Paris gained St-Denis, Europe's first Gothic cathedral, as well as the cathedral of Notre-Dame and the jewel-like Ste-Chapelle.

King Philippe Auguste made Paris into a defensive capital, responding to regular raids by beginning work on the fortress of the Louvre and building the first walls around the city. The 12th century also saw the basic segregation of functions that still characterizes the city's geography: Philippe Auguste's construction established political and ecclesiastical institutions on Ile de la Cité, academic ones on the Left Bank, and commercial ones on the Right. By the 14th century, Paris' 80,000 inhabitants made it one of the great cities of Europe; at the same time, the war with the English and Burgundians threatened the city's lifeblood. To cope with the danger, Charles V replaced the earlier wall with a larger wall on the Right Bank, guarded by the new Bastille fortress. Though it was destroyed in the 17th century, its path can be followed down boulevard St-Martin and boulevard Beaumarchais (see "Sights—10ème," p. 188).

FINE ARTS: THE MEDIEVAL PERIOD

Smidgens of Gallo-Roman housewares and artworks, mostly coins, torques, and small statues, survived the centuries and have now come to rest in the Musée Carnavelet. The Middle Ages is the first period from which Paris has a substantial artistic legacy. Much of the surviving medieval art is religious in purpose and public in tone: stunning stained glass and intricate stone façades at Chartres, Ste-Chapelle, and Notre-Dame, among other churches, retell biblical stories for the benefit of the (usually illiterate) medieval churchgoer. Replicas of Parisian and provincial ecclesiastical masonry can be seen at close range in the Musée National des Monuments Français, while panes of glass from many of the greatest windows in the Paris region are displayed in the Musée de Cluny. The latter also has a fabulous collection of medieval domestic arts, including breath-taking tapestries. The rise of monasteries brought the art of illumination to its height, as monks added ornate illustrations to the manuscripts they recopied. Some of the monks became so nearsighted because of their work that their vision was almost microscopic, as apparent in the fantastic detail of some of the illuminations in collections like that of the Musée Marmottan. Another stellar example is the *Très Riches Heures du Duc de Berry,* an illuminated prayer book now in the collection of the Chantilly Museum whose portrayal of the seasonal work of peasants ushered in the naturalism of the Northern Renaissance.

Strong and Absolute Monarchs

L'état c'est moi!
(I am the state!)

—Louis XIV

Religion was at the center of daily life in the Middle Ages and the Renaissance. The Protestant Reformation and its response within the Catholic Church, the Counter-Reformation, tore Europe apart during the 16th century. Though solidly Catholic, Paris hosted many of the key theologians of the time and witnessed some of the most grotesque fighting. One figure stood at the helm of the state during this period: Catherine de Médicis. From 1547, when her husband, Henri II, assumed the throne, until 1589, when her third (and final) son died, Catherine ruled France with subterfuge and guile. A moderate Italian Catholic, she tried without success to control passions by playing the Guise faction (a powerful, rabidly Catholic family bent on gaining power) against the rising Huguenot, or French Protestant, forces. Tensions broke in 1572 at the marriage between her daughter, Marguerite de Valois (Queen Margot), and the Protestant Henri of Navarre. When all of the leading Protestants in France had assembled in Paris for the wedding, Catherine signaled the start of the St-Bartholomew's Day Massacre. A wild Parisian mob slaughtered some 2000 Huguenots; Henri's life was only saved by a temporary, not-exactly-voluntary conversion. When that same Henri became King Henri IV in 1589, he converted to Catholicism for good, waving off the magnitude of his decision with *"Paris vaut bien une Messe"* (Paris is well worth a mass). His heart still lay with the Huguenots, though: in 1598, he issued the Edict of Nantes, which enforced tolerance of Protestants across the land and quelled the religious wars for almost a century.

Marie de Médicis, Henri IV's widow, was left to raise Louis XIII herself, but it was the boy king's first minister, Cardinal Richelieu, who was the era's driving political force. Laying aside his papal loyalty, Richelieu began to fashion the greatest absolutist state Europe has ever seen, a nation where sovereignty rested solely and entirely with the monarch. The power of the king reached its height during the reign of Louis XIV, the *Roi Soleil* (Sun King), who rose to the throne as a five-year-old in 1642 and ruled for 72 years. In 1648, a coalition of dissatisfied and power-hungry nobles stirred up the masses in a revolt known as the Fronde. The people tossed up barricades in the streets and essentially chased the pre-teen king from the city. When the nobles invited Spanish troops (with whom the French were at war at the time) into Paris, however, the shocked bourgeoisie removed their support from the rebellion, and the Fronde was quenched. Louis XIV never again felt quite at home in the city and moved his capital to Versailles as soon as he could. The palace became a showcase for regal opulence and noble privilege as the king surrounded himself with exquisite luxuries and submissive nobles—more to keep an eye on them and an ear open to their rebellious whispers than for the company. The Sun King's great-grandson and immediate successor, Louis XV, continued the tradition of expensive wars and lavish consumption into the late 18th century. Indifferent to actual government, Louis XV left the task to anyone who wanted it. Partly as a result, his mistresses, including Madame de Pompadour and Madame du Barry, wielded considerable social and political power.

ARCHITECTURE: THE RENAISSANCE

The most overwhelming remnant of this era in present day Paris is its color. Fire regulations decreed in the 16th century that wooden exteriors had to be plastered over, creating the gray city that you see today. The strife of the late Middle Ages kept royalty out of Paris and in the suburbs, building and rebuilding their chateaux in the Loire. François I had his nest at Fontainebleau, Catherine de Médicis had hers at Blois and Chenonceau. Though both repeatedly promised to renovate the Louvre and move back into the city, nothing came out of it except Catherine's Tuileries palace—which was destroyed by Revolutionaries in the 19th century anyway. Henri IV had different plans: after fighting for almost four years to get into Paris, he was not about to leave. He changed the face of Paris, building the Pont Neuf, a gallery linking the Louvre to the Tuileries, the Hôpital Saint-Louis, the place Dauphine, and the place des Vosges. At the same time, he widened the roads and banned merchant overflow into the streets, all to accommodate carriages; ironically, it was obstacles blocking the street that slowed his carriage and enabled François Ravaillac to leap in and assassinate him in 1610. Meanwhile, the Paris merchants constructed the first Hôtel de Ville, and the city's population skyrocketed, reaching almost 400,000 by the mid-17th century.

Under Louis XIII's reign, Marie de Médicis built the Palais du Luxembourg to remind herself of home (Italy), and Cardinal Richelieu fixed up the Palais Royal to remind himself of power (his). The 17th century—reign of the Sun King, Versailles, and the Absolute Monarchy—ushered in the Baroque age. Louis XIV banned Gothic architecture; in its place, Italianate domes popped up across the city like toadstools. Le Nôtre, Le Brun, and Le Vau reigned as the triumvirate of French art, designing respectively the gardens, architecture, and all-important interior paintings of châteaux like Versailles and Vaux-le-Vicomte.

One of the last constructive acts of the monarchy was Louis XVI's *mur des fermiers généraux* (farmers-general wall, named after an agricultural organization), built to regulate and tax produce brought into the cities. Generally resented, it was replaced by the "exterior boulevards" in the 19th century and mostly exists now in negative, as the outer borders of the 8ème, 9ème, 10ème, and 11ème arrondissements. A few old tollhouses exist, though, including one in the Parc Monceau (see "Sights—8ème," p. 181).

FINE ARTS: THE ACADÉMIE

When human achievement (and Greek and Roman influence) became the center of attention in the Renaissance, France imported its styles from Italy. François I brought the best Italian artists up north to decorate his palace at Fontainebleau, which is how works such as Leonardo da Vinci's *Mona Lisa* got to the Louvre in the first place. Later, under Louis XIV, indigenous French art flourished, and the center of Western painting and sculpture shifted decisively from Rome to Paris. Nicolas Poussin elaborated the theory of the "grand manner," with its huge canvases and panoramic subjects taken from mythology and history. The French Académie Royale, founded in 1648, came to value this style above all others, and all subsequent French painters had to contend with these weighty "academic" precepts. Claude Lorraine's idyllic landscapes defined the Académie's landscape tradition. In 1725, the Académie inaugurated annual Salons, held in the vacant halls of the Louvre. A sober 18th-century bourgeoisie admired scenes of everyday life by Chardin and Greuze before turning its attention to Jacques-Louis David, whose historical scenes frequently had political or moral "meanings." The more playful French aristocracy hired Rococo artists like Boucher and Fragonard to decorate its gold-embossed salons and bedrooms with flying cherubs and mischievous escapades. Watteau painted the *fêtes* and secret *rendezvous* of the aristocracy as a magnificently theatrical display; and Elisabeth Vigée-Lebrun painted the French nobility with a charm that years later earned her great success with the court of Russia.

LITERARY LIFE: THE EARLY YEARS

During the Middle Ages, the Sorbonne (recognized by the pope in 1209) and other academies attracted such intellectual giants as Pierre Abélard (of the celebrated romance with Héloïse), St. Thomas Aquinas, and Roger Bacon to a city that had become Europe's most prestigious center for theological study. The Humanism of the 15th-century Renaissance, coupled with the invention of the printing press in about 1450, resulted in a widely circulated literature addressing the foundations of human nature. At one time or another, many of the biggest names of the Reformation and the Counter-Reformation called Paris home. That humanist wonder and proto-Reformer, Erasmus, spent time in Paris; Calvin studied here for five years before leaving to reform Geneva. François Xavier and Ignatius Loyola (who later founded the Society of Jesuits) weighed in on the Counter-Reformation side, both attending college in the capital. Similar reform issues were worked through in the secular domain by Rabelais's social satire and Montaigne's personal essays.

Within the walls of the aristocracy's elaborate palaces, a system of patronage tied the age's most respected literati to the whim of their ruler. The rigidly rhythmed and court-subsidized tragedies of Corneille and Racine explored the issues of love, honor, and duty. Molière's brilliant satires were performed in the gardens of Vaux-le-Vicomte and Versailles and sponsored by the king's cousin at the Comédie Française. La Fontaine read his moralistic fables in the salons of the immoral aristocracy, who were in turn serenaded by the operas of Jean-Baptiste Lully. Pascal, in his pessimistic *Pensées*, wrote "the heart has its reasons of which reason knows nothing," while his colleague Descartes summed up the Enlightenment (see below) with a more cerebral "I think, therefore I am." Commentary on the leading intellectuals of the day was provided by *salon* hostess Mme. de Sévigné, who recorded her reflections in hundreds of letters to her daughter. All this was overseen by the newly formed Académie Française (1635), which gathered 40 men to regulate and codify French literature, grammar, spelling, and rhetoric. The rules and standards they set loosely at this time would soon solidify into rigid regulations, launching the "Classical" age of French literature. The Académie has ever since acted as the church of classical French letters, with Racine's *Phèdre* as its Bible and the crystal clear poetry of Malherbe as its *Book of Songs.*

In 1666, Colbert founded the Académie des Sciences to argue over such important issues as whether a dead fish weighs more than a live fish (actually weighing two such fish was *not* considered conclusive evidence). The publication of Newton's *Principia* in 1687 ushered in the era of faith in reason known as the Enlightenment, during which Voltaire declared that "if God did not exist, we would have to invent Him." A generation later, Diderot gathered around him a group of young intellectuals, intent on creating the *Encyclopédie,* a multi-volume work that sought to catalogue, systematize, and rationalize the whole of human knowledge. Rousseau's *Social Contract* and autobiographical *Confessions* rejected rationality, claiming that only a return to nature could save humanity, corrupted by modern society.

Choderlos de Laclos illuminated the increasingly depraved world of the elite with sparkling wit and licentiousness in his controversial *Dangerous Liaisons.* Beaumarchais's *Marriage of Figaro,* produced in 1784, was hugely popular with nobility and working class alike, yet its sharp wit and eloquent dialogues openly condemned the aristocracy. Louis XVI, when he first saw the play, exclaimed prophetically "the Bastille would have to be destroyed if the performance of the play is not to have dangerous consequences;" the playwright was imprisoned, not in the Bastille as protocol dictated, but in the St-Lazare prison for delinquent boys. The sentiment that inspired the play, however, continued to thrive.

From Revolution to Empirical Order

It appears that France must soon be governed by a single despot...a dictator produced by the revolution.

—Gouverneur Morris, American ambassador to France

Discontent with the monarchy, its policies, and its excesses exploded into the French Revolution. By 1787, a financial crisis beset Versailles and Louis XVI called an Assembly of Notables to seek solutions. They suggested that an Estates General, an archaic French parliament including clergy, nobility, and bourgeoisie, be called for the first time since Louis XIII had dismissed it in 1614. Debate ensued over the proper balance of power between the estates. In frustration, the bourgeoisie broke away and declared itself to be a National Assembly. When locked out of their usual chamber, the delegates moved to the Versailles tennis courts (of all places). There they swore the Oath of the Tennis Court on June 20, 1789, promising to draft a new constitution. The Paris mob soon joined in the rebellion, angered by high prices for bread and worried by the disarray of the government.

Marie-Antoinette, Louis XVI's extravagant and much-maligned Austrian queen, lives on in paintings and in popular legend, which credits her (in sentiment, if not speech) with the reply, "Let them eat cake," when told that the people were starving and without bread. The patience of the masses soon snapped under the weight of this cluelessness. On July 14, 1789, an impatient mob stormed the old fortress of the Bastille looking for arms and political prisoners to liberate (they only found a few petty debtors), and the Revolution acquired the violent character that would haunt it until its end. The French now celebrate July 14 *(le quatorze juillet)* as the *Fête Nationale,* Bastille Day.

In September 1792, efforts at revolt bore fruit and the French republic was declared. The Revolution's declared goal was twofold, at once destructive and constructive: to tear down the vestiges of feudalism and to erect in its place a new society built on the tripartite ideal of *liberté, égalité,* and *fraternité.* Major reforms, such as the abolition of guilds and the dismantling of the Church, transformed the nation, but could not bring lasting peace to Paris. In 1793, the radical, Jacobin faction, led by Maximillien Robespierre and his Committee of Public Safety, took over the Convention and began a period of suppression and mass execution known as the Terror. The Jacobins guillotined the king and queen, their enemies, and eventually one another. The place de la Concorde, now a glorified traffic circle, was once the site for more than 1300 beheadings. Thankfully, such a system did not last, and the leading Jacobins were arrested in the revolutionary month of Thermidor (August) 1793.

An exhausted French people yearned for stability and welcomed the rise of a man they felt could achieve it: Napoleon Bonaparte. This famed military commander and megalomaniac took power in a coup in 1799 and by 1804 had declared himself emperor. Napoleon established a strong central bureaucracy and a system of law that still rests at the foundation of legal systems around the world. He was not satisfied with ruling France alone, and soon initiated a series of military campaigns that nearly yielded him control of the entire European continent. The combined power of the Royal Navy, the Russian winter, and the opposing armies proved too much, and on March 30, 1814, the Prussians occupied an undefended Paris. A short period of monarchical government followed. Napoleon brought a temporary end to the short reign of Louis XVIII when he returned to Paris from his exile on the island of Elba in 1815. His ultimate defeat in Belgium at Waterloo came that same year. The Restoration of the monarchy followed, and Louis XVIII resumed his throne.

ARCHITECTURE: UNDER SIEGE

Not too surprisingly, destruction outweighed construction during the French Revolution. Most of its impressive architectural achievements were temporary: an artificial mountain on the Champ de Mars, a cardboard Neoclassical interior for Notre-Dame, and sundry plaster statues of Liberty. More lasting were the various defacements, especially of churches and kings' statues. At the same time, the Jacobins were not too busy beheading people to open up to development parts of the city center previously owned by the Church and the nobility. Napoleon made further improvements in the early 19th century: he planned cemeteries, dug sewers, numbered houses, widened the streets, and carried the artistic riches of a continent to the Louvre. More of a fighter than a builder, though, he left less of a mark on the city than he did on the nation's character.

FINE ARTS: PARTISAN PAINTING

Art during the Revolution, with its emphasis on classical style and public display, was a far cry from the Rococo. Ceremonies, with elaborate Neoclassical props and costumes planned by David, fêted such state occasions as the transfer of Voltaire's body to the Panthéon. David himself joined the Jacobin party, painting such striking works as *The Oath in the Tennis Court* and *The Dead Marat.* In 1793—the year of the Terror—the Louvre opened the royal collection to the public, providing the beginnings of what would become the world's most famous art museum. After being imprisoned (and then released) by the Directory in 1794, David changed allegiance, moving to the camp of the Corsican Emperor-to-be and painting the monumental *Coronation of Napoleon.* Napoleon encouraged painters and carpet-makers alike to use Egyptian and Greek motifs, which expressed his notion of himself as the heir of the Roman emperors; in decorative arts this is now called the Empire style.

Revolt and Repression

Le vieux Paris n'est plus (la forme d'une ville change plus vite, hé las! que le coeur d'un mortel).

(The old Paris is no more (the shape of a city changes more quickly, alas! than the heart of a mortal).)

—Charles Baudelaire, "Le Cygne," Les Fleurs du Mal.

Louis XVIII's repressive successor, Charles X, was France's last Bourbon king, overthrown in 1830 by violent, armed protests that once again cried for liberty and equality. Power passed to Louis-Philippe, the "citizen-king." His July Monarchy—a constitutional monarchy—was seen as a compromise between the Bourbon kings' autocracy and the Republic's excess. He was king not of France, but of the French; and in a symbolic gesture, he kept the Revolutionary tricolor as his flag.

Revolution hit again in 1848 when veterans of the 1830 revolt joined students in a march on the Chambre des Députés, demanding a republic. Louis-Philippe abdicated peacefully, and the Second Republic was declared. Even more than in 1792, the change in regime had been determined solely by events in the capital. Despite Paris' power, in 1851 an anti-Parisian, conservative peasantry elected to the presidency an ambitious man named Louis-Napoleon Bonaparte, nephew to the great Napoleon. Aided by his popular slogan *"l'Empire c'est la paix"* (the Empire means peace), he successfully proclaimed himself Emperor Napoleon III. His downfall came soon after he launched the Franco-Prussian War in July 1870; he was captured by the Prussians and deposed.

Paris responded by declaring the Third Republic. Unfortunately, the Prussians were at war with France, not a particular form of French government, and the Prussian army advanced to Paris to besiege the city for months, leaving its residents so desperate for food that they eventually slaughtered most of the animals in the zoo. At the end of January, 1871, the leaders of the Third Republic capitulated and the conservative regime of Adolphe Thiers began to make heavy restitutions to the Prussians. Parisians rebelled again, this time by establishing the Paris Commune. For four months, a committee of leftist politicians (many based in the workers' suburb of Montmartre) assumed power and thumbed its nose at the Thiers government, which had fled to Versailles. The Commune threw up barricades to defend against the inroads of the Republican government, but the wide boulevards designed by Baron Haussmann (see below) enabled the regulars to outflank the defenders. The crushing of the Commune was quick and bloody: many estimate that over 20,000 Parisians died, slaughtered by their compatriots in about a week. The defeat broke both the power of Paris over the provinces and of the Parisian proletariat over the city. (See "Sights—18*ème*," p. 208, and "Sights—20*ème*," p. 212, for more.)

ARCHITECTURE: GEORGES HAUSSMAN

Despite two bloody revolutions, the early 19th century was a prosperous time for Paris. The government's decision that France's major railroads would all terminate in the capital guaranteed Paris' position at the center of the newly industrialized French economy. Paris thrived as the center of manufacture, a magnet attracting thousands of migrants from the provinces. It continued to be innovative in architecture, adopting the (now ubiquitous) apartment building, imitated throughout the world. Industrialization made many living quarters more pleasant, as glass became cheap and windows proliferated. But unchecked growth continued to swamp improvements, and many of Paris' one million people lived in congested slums.

Though traces of the past abound, parts of pre-19th century Paris would be virtually unrecognizable to a modern visitor. Today's city is the Paris remade under the (somewhat dictatorial) direction of Baron Georges Eugène Haussmann. From 1852 to 1870, Haussmann transformed Paris from an intimate medieval city to a centralized modern metropolis. Commissioned by the government to modernize the city, Haussmann tore long, straight boulevards through the tangled clutter and narrow alleys of old Paris, creating a unified network of *grands boulevards.* These avenues were designed not only to increase circulation of goods and people, but also to make Paris a work of art, a splendid capital worthy of France. Not incidentally, the wide avenues and oblique intersections also impeded insurrection, limiting once and for all the effectiveness of street barricades.

The changes during this period were momentous. The city doubled its area and Haussmann shifted the boundaries of the 20 existing *quartiers*, establishing Paris' present organization into 20 arrondissements. Five of Paris' seven hills were leveled; only Montmartre and the Montagne Ste-Geneviève remain. Twelve thousand structures were destroyed to create 136km of straight avenues. Wide sidewalks (demolished in the next century to make room for automobiles) encouraged strollers, sidewalk cafés, kiosks, and general crowds, giving birth to Paris' famed street culture. But the transformation was not without its costs. Intimate neighborhoods were destroyed by the avenue de l'Opéra and the boulevard St-Michel. Their homes demolished to make room for boulevards and luxury apartments, the workers of Paris were forced eastward to Belleville and beyond.

The transformation of Paris continued along the same lines into the early 20th century. Traffic circles, varied façades, electrical lamps, and (tiny) elevators became important elements in the development of the city's appearance. Paris continued to establish itself as an international center of innovation with the Exhibitions of 1889 and 1900. Both left several quintessential Parisian landmarks in their wake: the Métropolitain, the Grand and Petit Palais, and of course, the Eiffel Tower, a celebration of steel construction.

FINE ARTS: CLASSICISM AND ROMANTICISM

The Restoration and July Monarchy marked the division that would define the rest of the century: the Classical school led by Jean-Auguste Dominique Ingres, a student of David, and the Romantic school led by Eugène Delacroix. Ingres' sinuous lines and sensual surfaces contrasted with Delacroix's emphasis on brilliant colors, dramatic movement, and emotional excess. Meanwhile the invention of photography by Parisians Nièpce and Daguerre provided a new artistic medium, sparking an intense debate over the relative merits of painting and photography.

Paris had also become a capital of classical music. Frederic Chopin, arriving from Poland, brought Romanticism to piano music with his sensitive, highly personal works; Hector Berlioz—who grew up in the mountains without a piano—brought strong feeling and original instrumentation to French orchestral music. The concerts of Hungarian-born pianist and composer Franz Liszt drew swooning crowds any modern rock star might envy.

Napoleon III's declaration of the Second Empire spawned a generation of artists utterly disillusioned with a government that no longer represented their ideals. Like the itinerant gypsies after which they were named, the Bohemians proclaimed for themselves a life free from normal conventions. This "race of obstinate dreamers for whom art has remained a faith and not a career" gathered in the cafés of the *quartier latin* and starved proudly in the garrets of Paris. Charles Baudelaire, Champfleury, Nadar, and Rodolphe Bresdin were but a few of the characters whose way of life was made famous in Henry Murger's bestselling *Scènes de la Vie de Bohème* (later turned into Puccini's opera, *La Bohème*).

While urban Bohemians starved in the attics of Paris, artists like Millet and Rousseau followed the Romantics' urge to escape from nature, retreating to Barbizon to paint the Fontainebleau forest and the French peasantry. Influenced by the social-Utopian theories of Charles Fourier, Gustave Courbet rejected Academic historical painting in favor of a "living art" that would portray what he saw around him. As Europe spread its tentacles across the globe, the East became an inspiration for fashion, painting, and the decorative arts. Academic artists like Jean-Léon Gérôme created lush scenes of Turkish baths and snake-charmers. Japanese *ukiyoe* prints inundated the market from 1853 on, inspiring the nascent Impressionist movement.

Claude Monet, Pierre-Auguste Renoir, and Frédéric Bazille met during the 1860s in Paris and began to develop their now-famous technique. Accustomed to the smooth surfaces and clear-cut lines of Academic painting, critics objected to the "mess"—the rough brushwork and the sketchy quality—the soon-to-be Impressionists produced.

Edouard Manet's *Déjeuner sur l'Herbe* was refused by the Salon of 1863; in defiance he exhibited his painting just outside in a separate *"Salon des Refusés"* (Salon of the Rejected), with a 50-*centimes* entrance fee. As the Commune faded, the Impressionists were beginning to bloom.

LITERARY LIFE: ROMANTICISM TO REALISM

The Romantic movement in literature came to a focus in the essays of Mme. de Staël and the novels of Chateaubriand. Chateaubriand's isolated, melancholy young hero in *René* provided an early example of the *mal du siècle*—a feeling of disillusionment and alienation among 19th-century literati, rooted in the conviction that their century was a dying age. The *petit cénacle,* a group of poets led by Victor Hugo and including Gérard de Nerval and Théophile Gautier, espoused an emotional, lyrical style. Alfred de Vigny's *Chatterton* blamed society for the tragic suicide of a young, idealistic poet. Alfred de Musset eloquently expressed the gloomy outlook of his contemporaries when he declared that "I came too late in a century that is too old."

The prolific Honoré de Balzac rejected the Romanticism of his peers, focusing on the harsh realities of bourgeois society under Louis-Philippe, the "citizen-king." His *Comédie Humaine*—a series of novels that attempted to describe all of Parisian society—covered everyone from the melancholy poet to the bejeweled courtesan and the *nouveau riche* noble. At the same time, George Sand, the preeminent female literary figure of the 19th century, was celebrated for her *romans champêtres* (pastoral novels) and for her scandalous habit of wearing trousers and smoking cigars. She kept equally well-known company, spending nine years as Chopin's on-again-off-again lover. A second affair, between Sand and de Musset, ended unhappily—in the best of romantic traditions, both used the failed romance as a subject for their next books.

In the Second Republic, Hugo himself served in the Assemblée Nationale, eloquently defending the cause of *"liberté."* After Louis-Napoleon Bonaparte's coup d'état, Hugo was exiled and spent the next 19 years on the isle of Guernsey, where he penned *Les Chatîments,* a book of vehemently anti-Bonaparte poems.

Hugo's exile became the clarion-call for a new generation of artists utterly disillusioned with a government that no longer represented their ideals. Their world, together with that of the bourgeois society they rejected, was described by Emile Zola in his *Rougon-Macquart* series. Inspired by Balzac's *Comédie Humaine,* Zola added a newly "scientific" element of detail and called his movement Naturalism. Flaubert's *Madame Bovary,* published in 1857, described a married woman's affair and hinted at a widespread unhappiness with the role of bourgeois women in the 19th century. Charged with "offense to public and religious morality and to good morals," Flaubert was exonerated in a sensational trial.

At the same time, Charles Baudelaire led the way to modernism with his perverse, disturbingly beautiful *Fleurs du Mal* (Flowers of Evil), a collection of poems that focused on the sordid world of modern Paris, seen through the eyes of the elderly, the poor, the prostitutes, and, amid all these, the poet. With this alternative guidebook to Paris, the *flâneur* (wanderer) came into being—the Bohemian ideal of someone who wanders endlessly without direction, roaming among the crowds, yet standing apart from them. In August 1857, half a year after the *Madame Bovary* trial, *Les Fleurs du Mal* was put on trial for the same charge; the same prosecutor this time succeeded. Baudelaire was fined and six poems were censored from his book, not to be reinstated until a second trial in 1949.

Belle Époque and World War I

"La guerre est une chose trap grave pour être confiée à des militaires."
("War is too serious to be left to the military.")

-Georges Clemenceau

The Third Republic introduced modern politics and political parties to France; a nationalist, religious, "blood and soil" Right emerged behind Barrès and Maurras, while the labor-oriented Left crystallized behind Jaurès, as a new political culture took shape around the turn of the century over the Dreyfus Affair. Alfred Dreyfus, a Jewish captain in the French Army, was framed for treason in 1894; when novelist Emile Zola's 1898 article *J'accuse* declared Dreyfus innocent (and the French military establishment venal and corrupt), all of France agonized over, and took sides in, the "Dreyfus affair." Dreyfusards invoked, with Zola, the Rights of Man and the weight of the facts; anti-Dreyfusards (generally anti-Semitic conservatives of the Old and New Right) wanted to preserve the honor of the state and the army by preserving Dreyfus' conviction. Dreyfus spent years on Devil's Island before eventually being declared innocent of all charges in 1906, long after the intelligentsia had finished its debate.

World War I devastated the youth of Europe, but its specific effects on Paris weren't much to see: the German army never made it into the French capital, and by 1916, despite occasional air raids, the theaters, cinemas, and galleries of Paris were humming once again. After the war, delegates from around the world arrived to redraw the map of Europe at the Paris Peace Conference, which eventually produced the flawed Treaty of Versailles.

FINE ARTS: IMPRESSIONISM TO ART NOUVEAU

Many modern viewers are surprised to learn that Impressionism was once considered shocking art. In 1874, a gap of young radicals lead by Monet and Pissarro established an independent exhibition free from juries and establishment taste. Housed in the former photographic studio of Nadar, the exhibit consisted of 165 canvases of which one was Monet's *Impression: Soleil Levant* (Impression: Sunrise). A snide critic made fun of this canvas, labeling its creator an "Impressionist." Monet and his colleagues gleefully adopted this name, and the show became an annual event. The newly dubbed Impressionists set about playing with light and color to capture perceived reality. For the first time, *la foule* (the crowd)—already so aptly described by Hugo and in Baudelaire's *Les Fleurs du Mal*—became a subject worthy of painting. Impressionist paintings, like Manet's *A Bar at the Folies-Bergères* (1882) and Degas' *The Glass of Absinthe* (1876), focused on cafés, balls, cabarets, and ballets. At the same time, a new interest in the countryside created an ideal arena for the Impressionists' credo of *plein air* (open-air) painting.

The next generation—the "Post-Impressionists"—took painting even farther from mere depiction: Paul Cézanne's overlapping planes of color evoked sculpture and geometry and gave viewers the sense of touching, or even of being, apples, bowls, and mountains. Vincent Van Gogh's now-beloved thick brush strokes, odd colors and risky emotions left the viewers of his own time cold. Paul Gauguin, to whom Van Gogh mailed his severed ear, left a family and a highly successful career as a stockbroker to paint the peasants of Brittany and the "natives" of Tahiti. Meanwhile, Pointillists like Seurat explored a highly scientific type of painting, with works made up of tiny dots in primary colors. In sculpture, Rodin and Camille Claudel focused on a highly energetic, muscular shaping of bronze and stone.

During the last decades of the 19th century, Bohemia had moved outside Haussmann's city to the cabarets and cafés of Montmartre—an oasis for artists and bourgeois alike from the sterility of the modern city below. Offenbach composed his celebrated cancan; Toulouse-Lautrec captured the spirit and flashy theatricality of the Belle Époque in the vibrant silkscreen posters that covered Paris, as well as in his starkly linear paintings of brothels, circuses, and cabarets. "Impressionist" composers like Debussy and Ravel in turn evoked the sounds of the ocean, the winds, and the rising sun. The same sort of rejection of decayed traditions formed the basis of a new, decorative style—Art Nouveau. Art Nouveau quickly embraced architecture, furniture, lamps, jewelry, fashion, and book illustration in its search for an all-inclusive aesthetic in which style was more important than function.

ARTS: CUBISM TO DADAISM

The 20th century brought with it a deeply self-conscious, chaotic art world, following the previous generation in its search for a new and modern art. Erik Satie, a wandering Bohemian of Montmartre, composed his pensive, ponderous *Gymnopèdes.* A young group of artists led by Henri Matisse and inspired by Gauguin painted with increasingly brilliant colors and decorative surfaces. Critics labeled them the *fauves* (wild beasts), yet their "wildness" barely hinted at the extreme to which Pablo Picasso and George Braque would carry art with their Cubist experiments of 1907 to 1914. Together with Braque and a poet friend—Guillaume Apollinaire—Picasso formulated rigid precepts for the movement: Cubist painting sought to represent the idea of an object, rather than the object itself. In order to represent a three-dimensional "idea" on a flat canvas, Picasso presented his subjects from several angles at once. Marcel Duchamp added an element of dynamic movement to Cubism with his *Nude Descending a Staircase.* Utrillo and Man Ray formed part of the same set, while Eugène Atget, a photographer who documented the streets and shop fronts of Paris, provided Picasso and his friends with photographic "sketches" to use as a basis for their art. Marc Chagall and Giorgio de Chirico immigrated to Paris from Russia and Italy respectively and brought with them their own visions: Chagall created his Cubist fairy-tale pictures of Russian villages and Jewish legends, while de Chirico's dark-green skies and spilt statuary anticipated Surrealism.

On the eve of World War I, Paris argued over ballets: Debussy's *L'Après-midi d'un faune* (1912), for example, danced and choreographed by the famous Nijinsky. Debussy's symphonic setting of Mallarmé's poem, in which the flute takes the role of Pan, provided perhaps the era's most perfect expression of the union between musical sound and words, while Nijinsky's highly erotic choreography caused a truly magnificent scandal. Yet no one was prepared for the 1913 opening of Stravinsky's *Rites of Spring:* the plot (a maiden dances herself to death in a tribal ritual in order to hasten spring) was disturbing enough, but the music was fraught with violent passages and scandalous atonalities. The opening show on May 29, 1913 at the Théâtre des Champs-Elysées erupted almost immediately into an uproar; to Stravinsky's amazement, the conductor kept going and was able (amid catcalls, fights, whistles, and applause) to finish the show.

In 1917 came the *ballet russes*'s final great triumph—*Parade,* written by the poet Jean Cocteau, inspired by the audience "participation" at the opening of *Rites of Spring,* with music by Satie, Cubist costumes and set by Picasso, and choreography by Nijinsky. As the war continued, however, the Cubists and their circle dispersed, and Apollinaire died at the front. Horrified by the slaughter of the war, Duchamp switched from painting his futurist machine-worshiping images to leading the Dadaists, a group of artists who focused on nonsense and non-art—drawing a mustache on a picture of the Mona Lisa and exhibiting a urinal titled *La Fontaine.*

LITERARY LIFE: SYMBOLISTS

As the century closed, a circle of Symbolist poets—Verlaine, Rimbaud, and, later, Mallarmé—followed Baudelaire to create a "musical" poetry, founded in sounds and images *(vers libérés)* rather than in meaning, reaching its epitome in Mallarmé's *l'Après-midi d'un faune.* Rimbaud's career as a poet was precocious and short; he began writing at fifteen only to abandon it later for life as a gunrunner and explorer in the depths of Abysinnia. Rimbaud's involvement with the Parisian poetry scene included a stormy relationship with fellow poet Verlaine; which ended violently when Verlaine wounded Rimbaud in a drunken quarrel. Rimbaud's work (and his life) had a strong and lasting influence on modern French poetry.

Politics and the arts overlapped as Paris erupted into the controversy of the Dreyfus Affair in 1898. Artists and writers took sides in a public dialogue that swept Paris. Manet, Pissaro, Signac, and Mary Cassatt joined Zola in the *dreyfusard* camp; Cézanne, Renoir, Rodin, and the anti-Semitic Degas joined the *anti-dreyfusards.*

In 1909, André Gide, whose own novels and journals reflected a pure, classical detachment, founded the *Nouvelle Revue Française,* a journal which would become the springboard for up-and-coming writers in the inter-war period.

Through World War II

"La France a perdu une bataille, mais la France n'a pas perdu la guerre."
("France has lost one battle, but France has not lost the war.")
- Charles de Gaulle

The Great Depression inaugurated a decade of disorder in French politics, as government after government rose and fell. For a brief period (1936-37), power was held by the Popular Front, a leftist coalition formed in response to the rise of the Nazis in Germany. French generals were ill-prepared for the German attack when it came, and Paris was occupied easily on June 14, 1940. The French government, pushed south to the resort town of Vichy, signed a treaty that ceded the northern third of the country to the Nazis. This put Paris at the heart of occupied France; for four years it swarmed with German officials, diplomats, and the occasional Resistance spy. Well-attended exhibits purported to show the evils of Freemasonry, Bolshevism, and Jewry, and a detention center was set up just outside Paris in Compiègne. The future leader of the Resistance, General Charles de Gaulle, was in England when France surrendered to the Germans; from London he delivered his now famed appeal for French patriots to resist, and declared his Comité National Français to be the legitimate government-in-exile. While the Nazi presence in Paris made it unsuitable as a Resistance center for most of the war, some heroes did emerge: Albert Camus, for example, directed the underground newspaper *Combat.*

Paris narrowly avoided destruction in the waning months of World War II. With Allied troops approaching from Normandy in the summer of 1944, Hitler ordered the occupying troops to lay waste to the city. Fortunately, his garrison commander disobeyed the order. By August, Allied armies had swept east to liberate Paris. Even if the physical results of the occupation were not catastrophic, this period certainly left its mark on Paris and the Parisians. Recently, the French government has acknowledged some national degree of responsibility for the deportations, but Vichy collaboration with the Nazis left scars that are still tender. Today's government has attempted half-heartedly to bring to trial high-ranking officials of the Vichy government, including Vichy police chief Réné Bousquet, who was murdered in June 1993 before he could be tried. 1993 saw the much-publicized case of Paul Touvier, who allegedly collaborated in Lyon with the Gestapo, and then was harbored by laymen and priests within France's Catholic church for nearly forty years.

ARTS: SURREALISM TO ABSTRACTION

World War I shocked the artists and sensitive souls of Europe. In 1924, André Breton published his *Surrealist Manifesto,* the birth of the Surrealist movement. The Surrealists claimed to create an art of the subconscious, seeking out the dream world that was more real than the rational world around them—or what passed as rational, in the wake of the wholesale slaughter of the Great War. René Magritte, Salvador Dalí, Yves Tanguy, and Max Ernst painted and etched their playful images of top hats, castles, angels, misplaced nude bodies, and melting clocks. Many constructed Surrealist "objects"—modifications of ready-made things. Meret Oppenheim's *Furred Teacup* and Man Ray's nail-studded iron, *The Gift,* were both silly and menacing in their disruption of the natural order of things. Cocteau, now a full-fledged Surrealist, wrote *Les Enfants Terribles* and produced such dreamily evocative films as *La Belle et la Bête.*

During the 30s, photographers like Brassaï and Kertész, both emigrants from Hungary, recorded the streets and *quartiers* of Paris, especially Montmartre, in black and white. Jean Renoir (son of the painter) made his poetic, witty films which investigated the state of culture in the 20th century; *Boudu is Saved from Drowning* tells the story of a beggar saved from the Seine and taken in by a book-seller. On a more serious level, *La Grande Illusion* presents the interactions of three French prisoners of war, each from a radically different social background, with the aristocratic German head of their World War I camp. In 1937, Picasso exhibited the huge and violent mural, *Guernica*, at the Paris International Exposition, in the pavilion of the Spanish Republic. Based on the bombing of a Basque town during the Spanish Civil War, *Guernica* provided the century's most conclusive condemnation of the horrors of the war—three years before the Germans invaded Paris—bringing on the brutality of World War II.

As the Germans advanced on Paris, the masterpieces of the Louvre (except for the *Nike*, which was too heavy) were evacuated to basements and gardens in Paris and the provinces. Within days of the German entry into Paris, the invaders filled the Opéra and the theaters, which staged uncontroversial farces to avoid offense. Braque and Picasso just kept painting, and musicians pulled out their Wagner and Beethoven scores. Jacques Prévert and Marcel Carné teamed up to create two films, *The Devil's Envoy* (1942) and the epic *Children of Paradise* (1945). Edith Piaf and Maurice Chevalier sang in the music halls. On May 27, 1943, hundreds of "degenerate" paintings by Miró, Picasso, Ernst, Klee, and Léger were destroyed in a bonfire in the garden of the Jeu de Paume. Tens of thousands more "respectable" masterpieces belonging to Jewish collectors were appropriated and shipped to Germany, but were mostly returned after the war.

LITERARY LIFE: THE INTERWAR YEARS

French literature of the inter-war lull was dominated by Colette's multi-layered descriptions of the sensual world of Paris in the 20s; her work was unique in its focus on issues of love and sexuality, especially between women. In the years between 1913 and 1927, Marcel Proust wrote his monumental *A la recherche du temps perdu (Remembrance of Things Past)* a semi-autobiographical summation of the Belle Époque and its complex social undercurrents. Proust sent his first chapter to the *Nouvelle Revue;* in one of history's great miscalculations, Gide refused the piece without even unwrapping the package, claiming that the aristocratic Proust—"a snob, a dilettante, and a man-about-town"—was incapable of producing good literature. The journal's history was not always illustrious: under a collaborationist editor during World War II, the journal promoted fascism as an alternative to communism. The 1920s and 30s were also the decades of the expatriates. Even before the war, much of the cutting edge had belonged to foreigners, such as Stravinsky and Picasso. After the Armistice, a "lost generation" of literati streamed in from America and western Europe—James Joyce, Ernest Hemingway, Ford Madox Ford, Ezra Pound, Gertrude Stein, and F. Scott Fitzgerald among them. The Americans, above all, sought a freedom in Paris they could not find at home—and enjoyed the power of the American dollar against the highly devalued French franc. Gertrude Stein expressed the feelings of her fellow expatriates: "America is my country, but Paris is my hometown." Soon they were joined by a different kind of migrant: refugees from the tyrannical states that were sprouting up around Europe. Walter Benjamin, for example, fled to Paris from Nazi Germany, only to flee again (unsuccessfully) after the fall of France. Robert Capa, a Hungarian Jew who grew up in Germany, escaped to Paris before beginning his two decades as a war photographer.

Postwar Paris

Soon after the war, the Fourth Republic was declared, with de Gaulle as its first president (although he resigned out of frustration within months). Its twelve years (1946-58) saw the reconstruction of French transport and industry, the formation of the European Economic Community (EEC) in 1957, and the faltering of French colonial rule in Indochina, Tunisia, and Morocco. But problems with the colonies continued to plague the Fourth Republic, and a 1958 revolution in Algeria triggered its final collapse. De Gaulle returned in triumph to inaugurate the Fifth (and current) Republic in 1958. He allowed Algeria to become independent by referendum in 1962, and focused on building a strong, independent France.

The Fifth Republic came close to collapse in May 1968. Frustrated by racism and sexism, by capitalism's failure to collapse, by an outdated curriculum, and by the threat of a reduction in the number of students allowed to matriculate, university students seized the Sorbonne. Barricades were erected in the *quartier latin,* and an all-out student revolt had begun. The situation escalated for several weeks; police used tear gas and clubs to storm the barricades, while students fought back by throwing Molotov cocktails and lighting cars on fire. Though no one was killed, hundreds of students and police officers were wounded in the fighting. Workers in state industries went on strike in support of the students, paralyzing the country. The government, planning for the worst, arranged for tanks and commando units to be brought into the city in the event of a Communist insurrection. But a march of hundreds of thousands of de Gaulle's supporters down the Champs-Elysées confirmed public support of the government, and helped to extinguish the crisis. By then, de Gaulle had resigned for the last time after losing a referendum in 1969. Ironically, the Paris revolt—settled, in part, by concessions over university textbooks and curriculum committees—became a model for radical "student uprisings" in Mexico and many other nations in the next few years. Less surprising, the Parisian university system was almost immediately decentralized, with various campuses being scattered throughout the city and the nation so that student power could never again come together as explosively as it had (see "Sights—5ème," p. 161).

ARCHITECTURE: ON THE EDGE

Paris' cityscape and its architectural styles survived two World Wars fundamentally unchanged. In the interwar period, a few radical architects began to focus on new building materials. Le Corbusier, a Swiss citizen who lived and built in Paris, was a pioneer in the new material of reinforced concrete. During the postwar years, architects began to make buildings that would stand out, rather than blend in. Most of the changes were made in the outer arrondissements, like the 13ème and the 17ème, leaving the historic core intact. The old marketplace of Les Halles, now a subterranean shopping mall, was torn down, and the *quais* of the Left Bank, like those of the Right, were almost converted into expressways—acts that inspired popular calls for conservation. In response, Paris' growth was relegated mostly to its periphery.

The city's history of expansion into the surrounding territory dates back to the emergence of working-class districts *(faubourgs)* in the late 18th century. In the 19th century, rail lines and trolleys made the suburbs more inviting by enabling workers to commute from the outer districts and suburbs. During the 1950s and 60s, the government sponsored housing developments and a plan for a ring of "new towns" surrounding Paris. Five of these towns have been built, including Marne-la-Vallée, where the movie *Brazil* was filmed and where Disneyland Paris is located. Parisian suburbs, often the only source of affordable housing, are home mainly to the working class and immigrants. As high rents have pushed the working class out to the suburbs, Paris' middle class has gentrified the old workers' quarters, making them tidy but, some would say, dull.

ARTS: FILM AND JAZZ

Post-war Paris responded to American dominance by remaking the USA's newer art forms in its own image: the *Nouvelle Vague (New Wave)* of French cinema, inspired by gangster films and Alfred Hitchcock, burst into 50s cinema, using black and white to capture the fragmented, hurried quality of life on the edge. François Truffaut's *Les 400 Coups,* Alain Resnais's *Hiroshima mon amour,* and Jean-Luc Godard's *A bout de souffle,* all made in 1959, are prime examples. More recently, Eric Rohmer's skillful movies—*A Tale of Winter,* for example—focus on character and not technique.

The late Krzysztof Kieslowski, a transplant (like Chopin) from Poland, made an international splash with his trilogy *Blue, White,* and *Red.*

After World War II, the city's clubs began to fill with first-rank American players, and Paris' proverbial rain-slick streets took on their saxophonic gloss. When Duke Ellington dropped by to play the new Club St-Germain in 1948, he was greeted at the train station by a plaid-clad mob of trendy young jazz fans nicknamed *cavistes,* or *rats du cave,* after the Left Bank's jazz hotspot. The Caveau de la Huchette (see "Jazz," p. 258). Miles Davis' "April in Paris" supposedly "describes" his two-week stay here (at the age of 22) and infatuation with Parisian actress Juliette Greco; legend has it that Sartre tried to convince Davis to marry her, and that interest in jazz among the intellectuals of St-Germain-des-Prés grew out of Davis' visit. Other American players stayed in Paris, drawn by factors as varied as the low cost of living in postwar France, the city's reputation as a haven for arts, the relative lack of racism in continental Europe, the romance of drinking in Paris, heroin, and simply the French love for this American music. But drawn they were: between 1948 and 1963, the roster of transplanted jazz greats included Bud Powell, Kenny Clark, and Dexter Gordon (about whose stay in the capital the movie *Round Midnight* was made).

LITERARY LIFE: EXISTENTIALISM AND FEMINISM

The years before World War II were marked by the beginnings of Existentialism, led by Jean-Paul Sartre. Sartre's *Being and Nothingness,* written at Café de Flore in the midst of the Occupation, became the veritable encyclopedia of Existentialism. Albert Camus published *The Stranger* in 1942, telling the story of the young Meursault, who is fundamentally incapable of relating to his fellow human beings. After the war, the Existentialists met at the cafés of Montparnasse to discuss the absurdity and meaninglessness of the world around them. Sartre published *Huis Clos* in 1945, with its telling assertion that *"L'Enfer, c'est les autres"* (Hell is other people). Simone de Beauvoir, his lifetime companion, wrote the revolutionary feminist work *The Second Sex,* as well as existentialist novels like *The Mandarins.* Camus' *The Plague* (1947) provided the spiritual summation of the movement, with its description of a town quarantined by a renewed epidemic of the bubonic plague. Paris moved into the 1950s with the absurdist plays of Eugène Ionesco and expatriate Samuel Beckett. Ionesco's plays *The Bald Soprano* and *The Lesson* have been running for 34 years in the *quartier latin's* Théâtre de la Huchette (see "Private Theaters," p. 254).

Despite philosophies which de-emphasized the meaning of political events, politics and the arts and letters mixed as the Fourth Republic (1947-58) witnessed the collapse of the French Empire in Indochina, Tunisia, and Morocco. By 1958, France, reluctant to give up control, was embroiled in a war in Algeria. Writers of the political left in Paris, such as Sartre, made an outcry, torn between loyalty to the French government and their desire to condemn imperialism.

Parisian Politics

The French political system under the Fifth Republic blends the European parliamentary system with the American concept of an independent executive. Parliament—the 317-member *sénat* and the 491-member Assemblée Nationale, both elected by universal suffrage—holds legislative power. The Assemblée is housed in the Palais Bourbon in the 7ème; the *sénat* meets in the Palais du Luxembourg in the 6ème. The prime minister is elected by popular vote for a seven-year term and holds executive power. He (or perhaps she, someday) appoints a Council of Ministers, headed by the Prime Minister, which manages the country and is responsible to Parliament. When the majority in the Assemblée is not of the President's party, the President must appoint a Prime Minister from a rival party and share power.

Three parties and their leaders have dominated the French political scene since de Gaulle's exit. Two are parties of the center-right which formed when de Gaulle's old allies split in 1974: the Union pour la Démocracie Française (UDF), led by Valery Giscard d'Estaing; and the Rassemblement pour la République (RPR), led by Jacques Chirac, now France's President. On the left is the Socialist Party, in power throughout the 1980s under former President François Mitterrand. Although the Communists retain some support in the so-called "red belt" that crosses the 12*ème* and the 20*ème* arrondissements, they are minor players today.

The neo-Gaullists on the center-right reigned during the 1970s. De Gaulle's former Prime Minister Georges Pompidou won the presidency in 1969, followed after his death in 1974 by the UDF's Giscard d'Estaing. The elections of 1981 swept the Socialists into a majority in the Assemblée and Mitterrand into the presidency; within weeks they had raised the minimum wage and added a fifth week to the French worker's annual vacation. The Socialists' popularity began to wane, however, as the 1983 recession hit, and the party met with serious losses in the 1986 parliamentary elections. Mitterrand was forced to appoint Chirac as Prime Minister, ushering in two years of uncomfortable cohabitation with a conservative cabinet.

The Socialists made a timely recovery in the 1988 elections, giving Mitterrand another term. He proceeded to run through a series of Socialist governments, including one briefly led by Edith Cresson, who became France's first woman Prime Minister in 1992, but never gained popularity. One problem was the issue of European integration, spearheaded by France since World War II. In the wake of 1991's Maastricht treaty, which pulled the 12-nation European Community into an even tighter-knit European Union, the French have manifested profound unease about further integration. Mitterrand led the campaign for a "oui" vote in France's September 1992 referendum on the treaty, which won by the slimmest of margins.

The French people's isolationist tendencies showed themselves even more clearly in the 1986 parliamentary elections. These saw the emergence of an ugly new force in French politics—the ultra-right, ultra-nationalist Front National, led by Jean-Marie Le Pen, which picked up 10% of the vote by blaming France's woes (unemployment in particular) on immigrants and foreigners. Since World War II, much of France's immigration has come from its former colonies in Asia and Africa; today, almost half of the immigrants in France live in or around Paris—particularly in the 13*ème*, 19*ème*, and 20*ème* arrondissements, as well as in the suburbs—making up 13% of the city's population. Only the second generation born in France can gain French citizenship, but non-citizens are eligible for many state-provided benefits. With economic hardship increasingly widespread, Le Pen's slogan of *"La France pour les français"* ("France for the French"—with a very narrow definition of French identity) has struck a chord with some. Le Pen's popularity has grown only slightly since his debut on the national stage. However, his Front National won its first major mayorship in Toulon in 1995, and his mere presence has pulled the entire political spectrum a bit to the right.

This Just In

In May, 1995, Jacques Chirac was elected to the French Presidency; Mitterrand, the favorite, chose not to run because of his failing health. The primary issue of the election was France's high unemployment rate—12.2% at the time of the election—long a problem for the Socialist regime. Chirac proposed a solution based on encouraging private companies to invest and employ new workers. France also continued to press for tangible action in Bosnia. Feeling the sting of the deaths of dozens of French soldiers participating in the UN peacekeeping mission, Chirac led the movement to increase the UN presence in Bosnia and retaliate against Serbia. The year ended in national paralysis, with a prolonged strike *(grève)* by government workers—and anyone who wanted to join in—against budget and benefit cuts proposed by Chirac and his prime minister, Alain Juppé. French train workers, among others, protested measures that interfered with their pension and benefit plans.

France moved slowly into 1996, recovering from the strike and mourning former president François Mitterrand, who died in early January. Mitterrand succumbed to prostate cancer after a year of fending off party financial scandals and controversial

Strike a Pose

The strikers of 1995 hoped to paralyze France; as its nerve center, Paris was perhaps most effected. It started in late October with students and civil servants protesting budget cuts. They took to the streets, banners held high, screaming and singing about injustice and proudly shouting *"en grève"* (on strike). Train workers joined in, and electricians, postmen, bus drivers, and subway operators were quick to follow. Paris crawled without its Métro, bus, train, or postal service; occasional blackouts added to the fun. People couldn't get to work, stores kept reduced hours, and traffic ensnarled the narrow streets. The French have a word for "whatever works," *système D*—for several months, this became the Parisian modus operandi. As in the siege of 1870, when Parisians dined on zoo animals to keep going, the city endured the strikes with spirit and ingenuity. Executives lined the Champs-Elysées sporting appropriate hitchhiking wear: designer trench coats, high heels, attaché cases, and tiny signs hand-lettered with destinations in ritzy suburbs. The *bateaux mouches* shuttled passengers along the Seine for free. People walked, waited, and smiled. There was only a muted call to end the strike—most held the strikers in high regard, and wished them well. Smaller strikes are as much a part of Parisian life as high fashion and croissants. All one can do is shrug and say *"C'est la vie parisienne."*

media coverage of his collaboration with the Vichy government. Shortly after his death, President Chirac was denounced around the globe for conducting underground nuclear weapons tests in the South Pacific. Greenpeace and foreign governments responded to the indignation of South Pacific island countries opposing these tests by collectively condemning the French government. Despite rioting in Tahiti and demonstrations worldwide, Chirac insisted that the tests were necessary to assure that France would have at its disposal "a viable and modern defense." After a series of tests beneath Pacific atolls—the last test six times more powerful than the atomic bomb dropped on Hiroshima—Chirac announced an end to nuclear testing.

Following France's termination of nuclear underground testing and subsequent rescinding of nuclear warhead production, Chirac introduced yet another cost-cutting measure: downsizing the French military. His plan to abolish conscription and to cut the military from 500,000 to 350,000 in a volunteer-only force by 2002 has met with mixed reactions. Chirac's proposal may reflect his goal of cutting the $59.3 billion budget deficit by 1997, in order to conform with requirements to join the common European currency by the end of the century.

Chirac acknowledges: "You can't change France without the French." Still, he and Prime Minister Juppé have been criticized for sweeping changes in the national health care system that are intended to cut spending and trim the deficit. The new French system resembles the changes proposed in American health care, including centralized tracking of individual doctors and identity cards for all health care users.

ARCHITECTURE: LARGER THAN LIFE

The last two decades may go down in history as one of the greatest periods of building in Paris. Presidents Giscard d'Estaing and Mitterrand were enthusiasts of dramatic architectural endeavors. Mitterrand initiated the famous (some say infamous) 15-billion-franc Grands Projets program to provide a series of modern monuments symbolic of what he perceived as France's role at the center of art, politics, and the world economy. From La Défense to La Villette, these government offices, museums, and public buildings constitute some of the boldest and most controversial additions to the city. I.M. Pei's 1989 modernist glass pyramid was planted smack in the middle of the courtyard of the Louvre. One of the most recent Mitterrand-sponsored projects was construction of the Bibliothèque Nationale, designed by architect Dominique Perrault. Whether Paris should be preserved as a city of another era (or eras) or be host to jarringly innovative projects, and who should make these aesthetic and economic decisions, remain the subjects of public debate.

LITERARY LIFE: THE NOUVEAU ROMAN

Sartre and Camus may have rejected God and country, but they preserved traditional literary styles. Not until the 50s and 60s did experimental writing produce the *nouveau roman* (the new novel), which abandoned conventional narrative techniques, embracing subject matter previously considered trivial and mundane. Among its best known exponents are Alain Robbe-Grillet, Nathalie Sarraute, and Marguerite Duras. Sarraute presents character dialogue with an emphasis on *sous conversation* (what people think as they converse) as opposed to spoken dialogue. Marguerite Duras' novels and her script for the haunting film *Hiroshima mon amour* claim to present the abstract painting of literature. France is also home to many of the great names in modern philosophy—Lacan, Foucault, Saussure, Barthes, Baudrillard, and Derrida—who have been at the center of such movements as Cultural Criticism, Semiology, Structuralism, and Deconstructionism. For more on the latest in French writing (in French), check the list of best sellers in the weekly magazine *Livre,* or look for reviews in the literary section of a French newspaper.

LANGUAGE: ABSOLUTE FRENCH

In 1461, François Villon wrote, "Il n'est bon bec que dans Paris" (There is no good speech except in Paris). For centuries, France has been a country obsessed with language. Spelling standardizations proposed by the state in the 1980s brought purists to the brink of riot. All such changes occur under the watchful eye of the Académie Française, which compiles the French dictionary and oversees the language. In the summer of 1992, the Assemblée Nationale amended the constitution: French is now the official language of France. Parisian French, although full of anglicisms, remains the "official" dialect. Like the city itself, the language of Paris was instrumental in forging the nation's political unity and in creating its culture. The Jules Ferry laws of the Third Republic sent state instructors to spread Parisian lingo and culture to the provinces. While a regional twang lingers, the upper-class Parisian pronunciation, like the BBC accent among the British, endures as the standard of sophistication.

■ La Politesse and Other Necessities

MANNERS: VISITING PARIS

Many visitors from abroad have returned with stories of the Parisians' xenophobia and snobbery. This reputation of Parisian discourtesy may reveal itself if you address people in English without the prefatory *"Parlez-vous anglais, Madame/Monsieur?"* Although some Parisians have the vexing habit of answering all queries in English, even the simplest of efforts to speak French will be appreciated. Be lavish with your *Monsieurs, Madames,* and *Mademoiselles*—unlike English, French demands use of titles when addressing strangers—and greet everyone with a friendly *bonjour* or *bonsoir*. When you do encounter rude locals, consider their point of view. Every summer, tourists more than double the city's population. Many do not speak French and are unwilling to accept the challenge of dealing with people who do not understand them. Parisians have a soft spot for those who wish to share their language and culture, but Paris is not about to pamper you.

Hugs and Kisses

It will not take the foreign visitor to Paris long to realize that hugs are not a traditional form of greeting for the French. The French are, of course, always kissing. The French greeting kiss, or *bisou,* is exchanged by friends, or in introduction to new friends, but not by random strangers. Much more confusing than who to kiss is how to kiss. Parisians tend to give one quick kiss to each cheek. However, in the provinces where people are warmer and the pace of life is slower, friends may deliver as many as three kisses to each cheek.

Let's Go Picks

These are the *crème-de-la-crème,* those special little spots that give Paris that certain *je ne sais quoi,* that infuse Paris with its distinctive and superlative character. Of course, there are many more "bests" of Paris out there yet to be discovered, so treat these as sure stepping-stones to your own adventures.

Best Views of Paris: The Jardin des Tuileries, 1er, offers a fantastic view of the Louvre, the Musée d'Orsay, and the Eiffel tower. Climb the elevated terrace or ride on the giant ferris wheel for the fabulous panoramas or Paris. **Samaritaine,** 1er, one of the oldest departement stores in Paris, offers a fabulous view from its roof. The top of the **Arc de Triomphe**, 8ème, reveals a unique view of the sprawling avenue Foch. The top of the **Tour Montparnasse,** in the 14ème, provides an unobstructed view of the Paris skyline. The narrow climb up the 112-m bell tower at **Sacre Coeur,** 18ème, offers the highest vantage point in Paris and a view that stretches as far as 50km on clear days.

Best Views Underground: Les Catacombs, a series of subterranean tunnels 20m below ground level that compose an underground city (note the "street" names on the walls) with bones for bricks and marrow for mortar. Navigate your way through femur-lined tunnels, complete with fibulas, and anchored by craniums. **Musée des Egouts de Paris** (Museum of the Sewers of Paris), actually inside the sewers, is fascinating if you can stand the stench. **Caveau de la Huchette,** a swing, and blues club in housed in a thrilling *cave* once used as tribunal, prison, and execution rooms.

Best Nightlife: Taste the fiercest funk in town where drag queens, superstars, models, moguls, and Herculean go-go demigods get down to the rhythms of a 10,000 gigawatt sound system at **Le Queen,** 8ème. Relax to the best of French Jazz at the **Au Duc des Lombards,** 1er, in a dark, smoky room always packed with regulars. **Le Piano Zinc,** 4ème is *the* seasoned gay hangout in the Marais, but fun for everyone. Xeroxed lyric sheets allow all to join in bar theme song: *"Moi je suis dingue dingue dingue du Piano Zinc."*

Best Fêtes: Bastille Day, *Vive la République* and pass the champagne. French Independence Day. The day starts with the army parading down the Champs-Elysées and ends with fireworks. The fireworks can be seen from any bridge on the Seine or from the Champs de Mars. July 14. **Course des Serveuses et Garçons de Café,** If you thought service was slow by necessity, let this race change your mind. Tuxedoed waiters sprint through the streets carrying a full bottle and glass on a tray. One day in mid-June; look for posters. **Fête de la Musique,** when everyone in the city makes as much of a racket as possible; noise laws don't apply on this day. Closet musicians fill the streets, strumming everything from banjos, to ukuleles, to Russian balalaikas. June 21.

Best Taste Sensations: Berthillon, 4ème on Ile-St-Louis. M. Cité or Pont Marie. The best ice cream and sorbet in Paris. Choose from dozens of *parfums* (flavors), ranging from chocolate to *tiramisu* to *cassis* (black currant). **Poilâne**, 6ème is the bakery responsible for Paris' most famous bread. Fragrant, crusty, sourdough loaves are baked throughout the day in wood-fired ovens. **Les Deux Magots,** 6ème Simone de Beauvoir's favorite café, serves the world's best hot chocolate, *chocolat des Deux Magots.*

Essentials

Addresses: In address listings, "M." indicates the nearest metro stop. Arrondissement names are abbreviated with the French contraction for ordinal numbers. Thus, the eighth arrondissement contracts to 8ème, an abbreviation for *huitième*. The postal code of Paris addresses is formed by affixing the two-digit arrondissement number to 750. Thus, the code of an address in the 8ème is 75008.
Calling Paris: France converted to 10-digit phone numbers in October, 1996. Even if you are familiar with French phones, you may want to turn to page 67 for an explanation of the new system. Any international call to France requires dialing 33 (France code) plus the 10-digit number.

PLANNING YOUR TRIP

When To Visit

There is no bad time to go to Paris, but if you do have a choice, there are a few factors to keep in mind. In August, tourists move in and Parisians move out—on vacation. Smaller hotels, shops, and services may be closed in observance of this unofficial national vacation month, while tourists flood those that remain open. If you evade the Champs-Elysées, Versailles, and the Eiffel Tower, though, August can be pleasingly calm. In fact, on August 15, a national holiday, Paris (except for its tourist hotspots) is eerily deserted. Early and late summer are often quite cool. Evenings can be windy and cold throughout the summer, and hot days don't hit Paris until mid-July. Keep the weather in mind when renting rooms in your hotel. Top floors become unbearable in real heat.

Traveling during the off-season is a great way to minimize damage to your bank account. Airfares and hotel rates drop and travel becomes less congested. Paris is a city best appreciated outdoors, while wandering through its narrow streets and along the banks of the Seine. In spite of the rain, spring is the time to visit. In fall and winter, however, the city is just as beautiful, if somewhat wet. Off-season visitors with strong constitutions will reap their share of rewards—pop corks with Parisians on New Year's Eve, avoid long museum lines, and take in a dynamic city that rises above gray weather. For temperature and rainfall info, see page 323.

Useful Information

FRENCH GOVERNMENT INFORMATION OFFICES

Tourism is France's largest industry. The French government will gladly provide prospective visitors with sundry brochures (see also "French Consulates," p. 24).

French Government Tourist Office: Write for info on French regions, festival dates, tips for travelers with disabilities, and a youth travel guide. They also provide a travel planner called *The France Discovery Guide* and the paper *France Insider's News.* **U.S.,** (tel. (900) 990-0040, costs 50¢ per minute); 444 Madison Ave., 16th floor, New York, NY 10022; 9454 Wilshire Bd. #715, Beverly Hills, CA 90212. **Canada,** 30 St-Patrick St., Suite #700, Toronto, Ontario M5T 3A3 (tel. (416) 593-4723; fax (416) 979-7587). **U.K.,** 178 Piccadilly, London W1V OAL (tel. (0171) 629 1272). **Ireland,** 35 Lower Abbey St., Dublin 1 (tel. (01) 703 4046). **Australia,** BNP building, 12th fl., 12 Castlereagh St., Sydney, NSW 2000 (tel. (02) 231 52 44). **New Zealanders,** contact this branch or the Consular Section of the French Embassy for info at 1 Willeston St., Wellington (tel. (64) 4 4720 200).

Cultural Services of the French Embassy: U.S., 972 Fifth Ave., New York, NY 10021 (tel. (212) 439-1400). **U.K.,** 23 Cromwell Rd., London SW7 2EL (tel. (0171) 838 20 55). General information about France including culture, student employment, *au pair* jobs, and educational possibilities.

USEFUL PUBLICATIONS AND ORGANIZATIONS

Council on International Educational Exchange (Council), 205 East 42nd St., New York, NY 10017-5706 (tel. (888) COUNCIL (268-6245); fax (212) 822-2699; e-mail info@ciee.org; http://www.ciee.org). A private, nonprofit organization, Council administers work, volunteer, and academic programs around the world. They also offer identity cards (including the ISIC and the GO25) and a range of publications, among them the magazine *Student Travels* (free), *The High School Student's Guide to Study, Travel and Adventure Abroad* (US$14, postage US$1.50), *Work, Study, Travel Abroad: The Whole World Handbook* (US$14, postage US$1.50), and *Volunteer! The Comprehensive Guide to Voluntary Service in the U.S. and Abroad.* Available at Council offices (see "Student and Budget Travel Agencies," p. 51), campus study abroad offices, or by mail. Write to: Marketing Services Dep't., 205 E. 42nd St., New York, NY 10017-5706.

Federation of International Youth Travel Organizations (FIYTO), Bredgade 25H, DK-1260 Copenhagen K, Denmark (tel. (45) 33 33 96 00; fax (45) 33 93 96 76; e-mail mailbox@fiyto.org), is an organization promoting educational, cultural, and social travel for young people. Member groups include language schools, educational travel companies, national tourist boards, accommodations centers and suppliers of travel services to youth and students. FIYTO sponsors the GO25 Card (see "Youth, Student, & Teacher Identification," p. 29).

Michelin Travel Publications, in the U.S.: Michelin Tire Corporation, P.O. Box 19001, Greenville, SC 29602-9001 (tel. (800) 423-0485; fax (800) 378-7471; in France: Michelin Services de Tourisme, 46, av. de Breteuil 75324 Paris, Cedex 07 (tel. 01 45 66 12 39). Publishes three major lines of travel-related material: excellent road maps and atlases; Green Guides, for sight-seeing and driving routes; and Red Guides, for hotels and restaurants. All available at bookstores.

Press and Information Division of the French Embassy, 4101 Reservoir Rd. NW, Washington, D.C. 20007 (tel. (202) 944-6060; fax (202) 944-6040; e-mail info@amb-wash.fr; http://www.info-france-usa.org). Write for info about political, social, and economic aspects of France. Publishes a bi-weekly newsletter, *News from France,* as well as *France Magazine,* a quarterly.

INTERNET AND WORLD WIDE WEB RESOURCES

Along with everything else, budget travel is moving rapidly into the information age. With the growing user-friendliness of computers and Internet resources, reams of info can be yours with the click of a mouse. Commercial Internet providers, such as **America Online** (tel. (800) 827-6394) and **Compuserve** (tel. (800) 433-0389) charge for access, while many companies and schools offer gateways free of charge.

The Internet's **World Wide Web** provides users with graphics and sound, as well as textual information. This and the huge proliferation of "web pages" (individual sites within the web) have made the web the most active and exciting of the Internet destinations. They have also made it the newest path from corporate advertisers to the minds of the masses; be sure to distinguish between useful info and marketing. Another difficulty with the web is its lack of hierarchy (it is a web, after all). **Search engines** (services that search for web pages under specific subjects) have made resources easier to find. **Lycos** (http://a2z.lycos.com) and **Infoseek** (http://guide.infoseek.com) are among the most popular. **Yahoo!** is a slightly more organized search engine, with travel links at http://www.yahoo.com/recreation/travel.

It is often better to know a specific site, and start "surfing" by links from one web page to another from there. France-specific resources include **Webfoot's Guide to France** (http://www.webfoot.com/travel/guides/france/france.html), a directory to guide the on-line traveler in the initial stages of planning his or her trip, and **Le Coin des Francophones et autres Grenouilles** (http://www.cnam.fr/fr/welcome.html), useful information on French culture, history, education, and politics. Here are a few more general starting points for finding budget travel information on the Web.

Dr. Memory's Favorite World Wide Web Travel Pages (http://www.access.digex.net/~drmemory/cybertravel.html) has links to endless web pages of interest to travelers of all kinds.

City.Net (http://www.city.net) is a very impressive collection of country-, region- and city-specific web pages. You select a geographic area, and it provides you with all available links related to that area.

The CIA World Factbook (http://www.odci.gov/cia/publications/95fact) has tons of vital statistics on countries' economies and systems of government.

The Student and Budget Travel Guide (http://asa.ugl.lib.umich.edu/chdocs/travel/travel-guide.html) is just what it sounds like.

Documents & Formalities

Be sure to file all applications several weeks or months in advance of your planned departure date. Remember, you are relying on government agencies to complete these transactions. A backlog in processing can spoil your plans.

When you travel, always carry on your person two or more forms of identification, including at least one photo ID. A passport combined with a driver's license or birth certificate usually serves as adequate proof of your identity and citizenship. Many establishments, especially banks, require several IDs before cashing traveler's checks. Keep photocopies of your documents in a separate place, and never carry all your forms of ID together, since you risk being stranded without ID or funds in the event of theft or loss. Also, carry a few passport-size photos to attach to the sundry IDs or railpasses you will eventually acquire. If you plan an extended stay, register your passport with the nearest embassy or consulate.

U.S. citizens seeking information about documents, formalities and travel abroad should request the booklet *Your Trip Abroad* (US$1.25) from the **Superintendent of Documents,** U.S. Government Printing Office, P.O. Box 371954, Pittsburgh, PA 15250-7954 (tel. (202) 512-1800; fax 512-2250).

FRENCH CONSULATES

The French consulate in your home country can provide info for your trip, arrange for visas, and direct you to info about tourism, education, and working in France.

U.S.: Consulate General, 31 St. James Ave., Park Square Building, Suite 750, Boston, MA 02116 (tel. (617) 542-7374; fax 542-8054); **Visa Section,** (tel. (617) 542-7374; open 8am-noon). There are 12 branch offices across the U.S.; contact the Consulate General to locate the branch nearest you.

Canada: 1, pl. Ville Mairie, 02601 Montréal, Québec 83B4S3 (tel. (514) 878-4385); other consulates in Moncton, Québec City, Toronto, Edmonton, and Vancouver. The French Embassy is in Ottawa.

U.K.: 21 Cromwell Rd., London SW7 2DQ (tel. (0171) 838 2000). **Visa Section,** 6A Cromwell Pl., London SW7 2EW (tel. (0891) 887 733).

Ireland: Contact the Consular Section within the French Embassy at 36 Ailesbury Road, Ballsbridge, Dublin 4 (tel. (01) 260 1666; fax (01) 283 0178).

Australia: 31 Market St., 26th fl., Sydney, NSW 2000 (tel. (02) 261-5931 or 261-5779). **New Zealanders** should contact this consulate or the Consular Section within the French Embassy (see "Embassies and Consulates," page 62).

ENTRANCE REQUIREMENTS

Citizens of the U.S., Canada, the U.K., Ireland, Australia, New Zealand, and South Africa all need valid **passports** to enter France and to re-enter their own country. Some countries do not allow entrance if the holder's passport expires in under six months, and returning to the U.S. with an expired passport may result in a fine.

When you enter France, dress neatly and carry **proof of your financial independence,** such as a visa to the next country on your itinerary, an airplane ticket to depart, enough money to cover the cost of your living expenses, etc. Admission as a visitor does not include the right to work, which is authorized only by a work permit. Entering France to study requires a special visa, and immigration officers may also ask to see proof of acceptance from a school, proof that the course of study will take up most of your time in the country, and proof that you can support yourself. (For specific visa information, see p. 27; customs allowance info begins on p. 27.)

PASSPORTS

Before you leave, photocopy the page of your passport that contains your photograph and identifying information, especially your passport number. Carry this photocopy in a safe place apart from your passport, and leave another copy at home. These measures will help prove your citizenship and facilitate the issuing of a new passport if you lose the original. Consulates also recommend that you carry an expired passport or an official copy of your birth certificate in a part of your baggage separate from other documents. You can request a duplicate birth certificate from the Bureau of Vital Records and Statistics in your state or province of birth.

If you lose your passport, immediately notify the local police and the nearest embassy or consulate of your home government. To expedite replacement, you will need to know all information previously recorded and show identification and proof of citizenship. Some consulates can issue new passports within two days with proof of citizenship. In an emergency, ask for immediate temporary traveling papers that will permit you to reenter your home country. It may take weeks to process a replacement passport, and your new one may be valid only for a limited time. In addition, any visas stamped in your old passport will be irretrievably lost.

Your passport is a public document belonging to your nation's government. You may have to surrender it to a foreign government official; but, if you don't get it back in a reasonable amount of time, inform the embassy of your home country.

United States US citizens may apply for a passport, valid for 10 years (five years if under 18), at any federal or state **courthouse** or **post office** authorized to accept passport applications, or at a **U.S. Passport Agency,** located in Boston, Chicago, Honolulu, Houston, Los Angeles, Miami, New Orleans, New York, Philadelphia, San Francisco, Seattle, Stamford, or Washington, D.C. Refer to the "U.S. Government, State Department" section of the telephone directory, or call your local post office for addresses. Parents must apply in person for children under 13. You must apply in person if this is your first passport, if you're under 18, or if your current passport is more than 12 years old or was issued before your 18th birthday. You must submit the following: 1) proof of U.S. citizenship (a certified birth certificate, certification of naturalization or of citizenship, or a previous passport); 2) identification bearing your signature and either your photograph or physical description (e.g. an unexpired driver's license or passport, student ID card, or government ID card); and 3) two identical, passport-size (2in. by 2in.) photos with a white or off-white background taken within the last six months. It will cost US$65 (under 18 US$40). You can **renew** your passport by mail or in person for US$55. Processing takes two to four weeks. Passport agencies offer **rush service** for a surcharge of US$30 if you have proof that you're departing within ten working days (e.g., an airplane ticket or itinerary). A U.S. embassy or consulate can usually issue a new passport, given proof of citizenship abroad. In the U.S., report lost or stolen passports in writing to Passport Services, U.S. Department of State, 111 19th St., NW, Washington D.C. 20522-1705, or to the nearest passport agency. For more info, contact the U.S. Passport Information's **24-hour recorded hotline** (tel. (202) 647-0518).

Canada Application forms in English and French are available at all **passport offices, post offices,** and most **travel agencies.** Citizens may apply in person at any one of 28 regional Passport Offices across Canada. Travel agents can direct the applicant to the nearest location. Canadian citizens residing abroad should contact the nearest Canadian embassy or consulate. Along with the application form, a citizen must provide: 1) citizenship documentation (an original Canadian birth certificate, or a certificate of Canadian citizenship); 2) two identical passport photos taken within the last year; 3) any previous Canadian passport; and 4) a CDN$60 fee (paid in cash, money order, or certified check) to Passport Office, Ottawa, Ont. K1A OG3. The application and one of the photographs must be signed by an eligible guarantor (someone who has known the applicant for two years and whose profession falls into one of the categories listed on the application). Complete information is outlined in both English and French on the application form. Processing takes approximately five business days for in-person applications and three weeks for mailed ones. Children under 16 may be included on a parent's passport, though some countries you may visit require children to carry their own passports. A passport is valid for five years and is not renewable. If a passport is lost abroad, Canadians must be able to prove citizenship with another document. For additional info, call (800) 567-6868 (24hr.; from Canada only), or the Passport Office at (819) 994-3500. In metro Toronto, call (416) 973-3251. Montréalers should dial (514) 283-2152. Refer to the booklet *Bon Voyage, But...* for further help and a list of Canadian embassies and consulates abroad. It is available free of charge from any passport office.

Britain British citizens, British Dependent Territories citizens, British Nationals (overseas), and British Overseas citizens may apply for a **full passport.** Residents of the U.K., the Channel Islands, and the Isle of Man may apply for a more restricted **British Visitor's Passport.** For a full passport, valid for 10 years (five years if under 16), apply in person or by mail to a passport office in London, Liverpool, Newport, Peterborough, Glasgow, or Belfast. The fee is UK£18. Children under 16 may be included on a parent's passport. Processing by mail usually takes four to six weeks. The London office offers same-day, walk-in rush service; arrive early. A Visitor's Passport, valid for one year in some western European countries and Bermuda only, is available at main post offices in England, Scotland and Wales, and passport offices in Northern Ireland, the Channel Islands, and the Isle of Man. The fee is UK£12.

Ireland Citizens can apply for a passport by mail to either the Department of Foreign Affairs, Passport Office, Setanta Centre, Molesworth St., Dublin 2 (tel. (01) 671 16 33), or the Passport Office, 1A South Mall, Cork (tel. (021) 627 25 25). Obtain an application at a local Garda station or request one from a passport office. The Passport Express Service offers a two-week turn-around and is available through post offices for an extra IR£3. Passports cost IR£45 and are valid for 10 years. Citizens under 18 or over 65 can request a three-year passport that costs IR£10.

Australia Citizens must apply for a passport in person at a post office, a passport office, or an Australian diplomatic mission overseas. An appointment may be necessary. Passport offices are located in Adelaide, Brisbane, Canberra City, Darwin, Hobart, Melbourne, Newcastle, Perth, and Sydney. A parent may file an application for a child who is under 18 and unmarried. Application fees are adjusted frequently. For more info, call toll-free (in Australia) 13 12 32.

New Zealand Application forms for passports are available in New Zealand from travel agents and Department of Internal Affairs Link Centres, and overseas from New Zealand embassies, high commissions, and consulates. Completed applications may be lodged at Link Centres and at overseas posts, or forwarded to the Passport Office, PO Box 10-526, Wellington, New Zealand. Processing time is 10 working days from receipt of a correctly completed application. An urgent passport service is also available. The application fee for an adult passport is NZ$80 in New Zealand, and NZ$130 overseas for applications lodged under the standard service.

South Africa Citizens can apply for a passport at any Home Affairs Office. Two photos, either a birth certificate or an identity book, and a $12 fee must accompany a completed application. South African passports remain valid for 10 years. For further information, contact the nearest Department of Home Affairs Office.

VISAS

A visa is an endorsement that a foreign government stamps into a passport; it allows the bearer to stay in that country for a specified purpose and period of time. Most visas cost US$10-70 and allow you to spend about a month in a country, within six months to a year from the date of issue. Visas are currently *not* required of visitors to France from EU member countries, the U.S., Canada, New Zealand, Andorra, Austria, the Czech Republic, Cyprus, Finland, Hungary, Iceland, Japan, the Republic of Korea, Liechtenstein, Malta, Monaco, Norway, Poland, San Marino, Sweden, and Switzerland. Note that Australia is absent from this list. A visa is required for *anyone* planning to stay more than three months (see below). It must be obtained from the French consulate *in your home country*. In the U.S., for more information send for *Foreign Visa Requirements* (50¢) from **Consumer Information Center,** Pueblo, CO 81009 (tel. (719) 948-3334), or contact **Center for International Business and Travel (CIBT),** 25 West 43rd St. #1420, New York, NY 10036 (tel. (800) 925-2428 or (212) 575-2811). CIBT secures visas for travel to and from all countries. The service charge varies; the average cost for a U.S. citizen is US$50 per visa.

Requirements for a long-stay visa vary with the nature of the stay: work, study, or *au pair*. Apply to the nearest French consulate at least three months in advance. For a **student visa,** you must present a passport valid until at least 60 days after the date you plan to leave France, an application with references, a passport photo, a letter of admission from a French university or a study abroad program, a notarized guarantee of financial support for at least $600 per month, and a fee which fluctuates according to the exchange rate (about US$60).

To obtain a **work visa,** you must first obtain a work permit. After you have secured a job and a work contract, your French employer will obtain this permit for you and will forward it with a copy of your work contract to the consulate nearest you. After a medical checkup and completion of the application, the visa will be issued on your valid passport. Note, however, that it is illegal for foreign students to work during the school year, although they can receive permission from a *Direction départementale du travail et de la main-d'oeuvre étrangère* to work in summer. (For more info on working in France, see "Work," p. 40.)

For an *au pair* stay of more than three months, an **au pair's visa** is required and can be obtained by submission of a valid passport, two completed application forms, two passport photos, a fee (between US$15-25), a medical certificate completed by a consulate-approved doctor, two copies of the *au pair's* work contract signed by the *au pair,* and proof of admission to a language school or university.

In addition to securing a visa, if you are staying longer than 90 days in France for any reason, you must obtain a **carte de séjour** (residency permit) once in France. Report to the local *préfecture* of the *département* in which you are residing. You must present a valid passport stamped with a long-stay visa, a medical certificate, six (yes, six) application forms completed in French, six passport photos, a letter of financial guarantee, and, if you're under 18, proof of parental authorization. Be prepared to jump through hoops, bark like a dog, and stand in line, perhaps repeatedly. Bring your Proust.

CUSTOMS: ARRIVING IN FRANCE

Unless you plan to import a BMW or a barnyard beast, you will probably pass right over the customs barrier with minimal ado. Visitors have an allowance of what they can bring into France. Anything exceeding the allowance is charged a duty. All travelers must declare articles acquired abroad, but only the truly profligate budget traveler will have to pay duties. Before leaving you should record the serial numbers of expensive (especially foreign-made) items that will accompany you abroad. Have this list stamped by a customs office before you leave; this will prevent your being taxed on items you already own. To avoid problems transporting prescription drugs, carry them in the original containers and bring a copy of the doctor's prescription to show the customs officer.

CUSTOMS: GOING HOME

Upon returning home, you must declare all articles you acquired abroad and must pay a duty on the value of those articles that exceed the allowance established by your country's customs service. Holding onto receipts for purchases made abroad will help establish values when you return. Keep in mind that goods and gifts purchased at duty-free shops abroad are not exempt from duty or sales tax at your point of return. You must declare these items; "duty-free" merely means that you need not pay a tax in the country of purchase.

United States Citizens returning home may bring US$400 worth of accompanying goods duty-free and must pay a 10% tax on the next US$1000. You must declare all purchases, so have sales slips ready. Goods are considered duty-free if they are for personal or household use (this includes gifts) and cannot include more than 100 cigars, 200 cigarettes (1 carton), and 1L of wine or liquor. You must be over 21 to bring liquor into the U.S. If you mail home personal goods of U.S. origin, you can avoid duty charges by marking the package "American goods returned." For more information, consult the brochure *Know Before You Go,* available from the U.S. Customs Service, Box 7407, Washington, D.C. 20044 (tel. (202) 927-6724).

Canada Citizens who remain abroad for at least one week may bring back up to CDN$500 worth of goods duty-free once per calendar year. Canadian citizens or residents who travel for a period between 48 hours and six days can bring back up to CDN$200 with the exception of tobacco and alcohol. You are permitted to ship goods except tobacco and alcohol home under this exemption as long as you declare them when you arrive. Citizens of legal age (which varies by province) may import in-person up to 200 cigarettes, 50 cigars, 400g loose tobacco, 400 tobacco sticks, 1.14L wine or alcohol, and 24 355mL cans/bottles of beer; the value of these products is included in the CDN$500. For more information, write to Canadian Customs, 2265 St. Laurent Blvd., Ottawa, Ontario K1G 4K3 (tel. (613) 993-0534).

Britain Citizens or visitors arriving in the U.K. from outside the EU must declare any goods in excess of the following allowances: 200 cigarettes, 100 cigarillos, 50 cigars, or 250g tobacco; still table wine (2L); strong liqueurs over 22% volume (1L), or fortified or sparkling wine; other liqueurs (2L); perfume (60 cc/mL); toilet water (250 cc/mL); and UK£136 worth of all other goods including gifts and souvenirs. You must be over 17 to import liquor or tobacco. These allowances also apply to duty-free purchases within the EU, except for the last category (other goods), which has an allowance of UK£71. Goods obtained duty- and tax-paid for personal use (regulated according to set guide levels) within the EU do not require any further customs duty. For more info about U.K. customs, contact Her Majesty's Customs and Excise, Custom House, Nettleton Road, Heathrow Airport, Hounslow, Middlesex TW6 2LA (tel. (0181) 910-3744; fax (0181) 910-3765).

Ireland Citizens must declare everything in excess of IR£34 (IR£17 per traveler under 15 years of age) obtained outside the EU or duty- and tax-free in the EU, above the following allowances: 200 cigarettes; 100 cigarillos; 50 cigars; or 250g tobacco; 1L liquor or 2L wine; 2L still wine; 50g perfume; and 250mL toilet water. Goods obtained duty- and tax-paid in another EU country up to a value of IR£460 (IR£115 per traveler under 15) will not be subject to additional customs duties. Travelers under 17 are not entitled to any allowance for tobacco or alcoholic products. For more information, contact The Revenue Commissioners, Dublin Castle (tel. (01) 679

27 77; fax (01) 671 20 21; e-mail taxes@ior.ie; http:\\www.revenue.ie), or The Collector of Customs and Excise, The Custom House, Dublin 1.

Australia Citizens may import AUS$400 (under 18 AUS$200) of goods duty-free, in addition to the allowance of 1.125L alcohol and 250 cigarettes or 250g tobacco. You must be over 18 to import either of these. There is no limit to the amount of Australian and/or foreign cash that may be brought into or taken out of the country. However, amounts of AUS$5000 or more, or the equivalent in foreign currency, must be reported. All foodstuffs and animal products must be declared on arrival. For information, contact the Regional Director, Australian Customs Service, GPO Box 8, Sydney NSW 2001 (tel. (02) 213 20 00; fax (02) 213 40 00).

New Zealand Citizens may bring home up to NZ$700 worth of goods duty-free if they are intended for personal use or are unsolicited gifts. The concession is 200 cigarettes (1 carton) or 250g tobacco or 50 cigars or a combination of all three not to exceed 250g. You may also bring in 4.5L of beer or wine and 1.125L of liquor. Only travelers over 17 may bring tobacco or alcoholic beverages into the country. For more information, consult the *New Zealand Customs Guide for Travelers,* available from customs offices, or contact New Zealand Customs, 50 Anzac Ave., Box 29, Auckland (tel. (09) 377 35 20; fax (09) 309 29 78).

South Africa Citizens may import duty-free: 400 cigarettes; 50 cigars; 250g tobacco; 2L wine; 1L of spirits; 250mL toilet water; and 50mL perfume; and other items up to a value of SAR500. Amounts exceeding this limit, but not SAR10,000, are dutiable at 20%. Certain items such as golf clubs and firearms require a duty higher than the standard 20%. Goods acquired abroad and sent to the Republic as unaccompanied baggage do not qualify for any allowances. You may not export or import South African bank notes in excess of SAR500. Persons who require specific information or advice concerning customs and excise duties should contact the Commissioner for Customs and Excise, Private Bag X47, Pretoria 0001. This agency distributes the pamphlet *South African Customs Information,* for visitors and residents who travel abroad. South Africans residing in the U.S. should contact the Embassy of South Africa, 3051 Massachusetts Ave., NW, Washington, D.C. 20008 (tel. (202) 232-4400; fax (202) 244-9417) or the South African Home Annex, 3201 New Mexico Ave. #380, NW, Washington, D.C. 20016 (tel. (202) 966-1650).

YOUTH, STUDENT, & TEACHER IDENTIFICATION

The **International Student Identity Card (ISIC)** is the most widely accepted form of student identification. Flashing this card can procure you discounts for sights, theaters, museums, accommodations, train, ferry, and airplane travel, and other services. It also provides accident insurance of up to US$3000 with no daily limit. In addition, cardholders have access to a toll-free Traveler's Assistance hotline whose multilingual staff can help in medical, legal, and financial emergencies abroad.

Many student travel offices issue ISICs (see "Student and Budget Travel Agencies," p. 51). The card is valid from September to December of the following year. The fee is US$18. Applicants must be at least 12 years old and degree-seeking students of a secondary or post-secondary school. Many airlines and some other services require other proof of student identity: a signed letter from the registrar attesting to your student status and stamped with the school seal and/or your school ID card. The US$19 **International Teacher Identity Card (ITIC)** offers similar but limited discounts, as well as medical insurance coverage. For more info on these handy cards, consult the organization's web site (http:\\www.istc.org).

The Federation of International Youth Travel Organizations (FIYTO; see p. 23) issues a discount card to travelers who are under 26 but not students. Known as the **GO25 Card,** this one-year card offers many of the same benefits as the ISIC, and most organizations that sell the ISIC also sell the GO25 Card. To apply, you will need a passport, valid driver's license, or copy of a birth certificate; and a passport-sized photo with your name printed on the back. The fee is US$16, CDN$15, or UK£5. (For agencies that sell the GO25, see "Student and Budget Travel Agencies," p. 51.)

DRIVING PERMITS AND INSURANCE

If you plan to drive a car while abroad, you must have an **International Driving Permit (IDP),** though France and other countries allow travelers to drive with a valid American or Canadian license for a limited number of months. Most rental agencies don't require the permit. A valid driver's license from your home country must accompany the IDP. The IDP must be issued in your own country before you leave. U.S. license holders can get info or obtain an IDP (US$10), valid for one year, at any **American Automobile Association (AAA)** office or by writing to the main office, AAA Florida, Travel Agency Services Department, 1000 AAA Drive (mail stop 28), Heathrow, FL 32746-5080 (tel. (407) 444-4245; fax (407) 444-4247). Canadian license holders can obtain an IDP (CDN$10) through any **Canadian Automobile Association (CAA)** branch office in Canada, or by writing to CAA Central Ontario, 60 Commerce Valley Drive East, Thornhill, Ontario L3T 7P9 (tel. (416) 221-4300).

Most credit cards cover standard insurance. If you rent, lease, or borrow a car, you will need a **green card,** or **International Insurance Certificate,** to prove that you have liability insurance. Obtain it through the rental agency; most include coverage in their prices. If you lease a car, you can obtain a green card from the dealer. Verify that your auto insurance applies abroad; if it does, you will still need a green card to certify this to foreign officials. If you have a collision abroad, the accident will appear on your domestic records if you report it to your insurance company.

Money

The old adage warns us that a love of money is at the root of all evil. For travelers, money—and its plastic and paper permutations—is at the root of most woes. If you stay in hostels and prepare your own food, expect to spend from 175-250F per person per day in Paris, depending on your needs. Research thoroughly how your own cash and credit cards will work in French ATMs before your departure.

CURRENCY AND EXCHANGE

US$1 = 5.008F	**1F = US$0.200**
CDN$1 = 3.646F	**1F = CDN$0.274**
UK£1 = 7.776F	**1F = UK£0.129**
IR£1 = 8.076F	**1F = IR£.124**
AUS$1 = 3.729F	**1F = AUS$0.258**
NZ$1 = 3.317F	**1F = NZ$0.292**
SAR1 = 1.383F	**1F = SAR0.723**

A Note on Prices and Exchange Rates

The information in this book was researched in the summer of 1996. Since then, inflation will have raised most prices at least 10%. The exchange rates listed were compiled on August 2, 1996. Since rates fluctuate, confirm current rates before you go. The rate listed in the finance section of major newspapers is the bulk trading rate for currency. This is better than the rate you will find at banks and exchange offices, but is the rate you usually receive from ATM withdrawals.

The basic unit of currency in France is the franc, divided into 100 centimes and issued in both coins and paper notes. It is more expensive to buy francs at home than in France, but converting some money before you go will allow you to zip through the airport while others languish in exchange lines. It's a good idea to bring enough French currency to last for the first 24-72 hours of a trip, depending on the day of the week you will be arriving (and allowing for unexpected French holidays).

When looking to change money in Paris, try to approach the event with a spirit of competition. Not every *bureau de change* offers the same rates and most do not charge commission. Don't be fooled by what seem like fantastic rates. Make sure that no strings (like having to exchange at least 15,000F worth of currency) apply. A good rule of thumb is to go to banks or *bureaux de change* that have only a 5% margin between their buy and sell prices. Anything more, and they are making too much profit. Be sure that both prices are listed.

Avoid exchanging money at airports, train stations, hotels, or restaurants; their convenient hours and locations allow them to offer unfavorable rates. To minimize losses on commission, exchange large sums at one time, though never more than is safe to carry around. Carry some traveler's checks or bills in small denominations (US$50 or less), especially for times when you are forced to exchange money at less-than-stellar rates. Many banks will not exchange large bills (US$100 or equivalent) due to the proliferation of counterfeits. Most Parisian banks are open 9am-noon and 2-4:30pm, but not all exchange money. Check before you get in line.

American Express: 11, rue Scribe, 9ème (tel. 01 47 77 77 07). M. Opéra or Auber. Across from the back of the Opéra. Tolerable exchange rates and long lines in summer, especially Mon. and Fri.-Sat. No commission. Cardholders can cash US$1000 in personal checks from a U.S. bank account every 21 days; bring your passport. The office receives moneygrams and will hold mail for cardholders or for those with AmEx Traveler's Cheques; otherwise, 5F per inquiry. English spoken. Open Mon.-Fri. 9am-6:30pm, Sat. 9am-5:30pm.

At Train Stations: These offices offer less-than-attractive rates intended for impatient travelers. **Gare d'Austerlitz,** 13ème (tel. 01 45 84 91 40). Open daily 7am-9pm. **Gare de Lyon,** 12ème (tel. 01 43 41 52 70). Open daily 6:30am-11pm. **Gare de l'Est,** 10ème (tel. 01 46 07 66 84). Open Mon.-Fri. 9am-6:30pm, Sat. 9:30am-5:00pm. **Gare du Nord,** 10ème (tel. 01 42 80 11 50). Open daily 6:15am-10:30pm. **Gare St-Lazare,** 8ème (tel. 01 43 87 72 51). Open daily 8am-6:45pm.

At Airports: Also not the best place to change your currency. Exchange just enough to get to Paris and change the rest within the city. **Orly-Sud:** located at Gate H (tel. 01 49 75 78 41). Open daily 6:30am-11pm. **Roissy-Charles de Gaulle:** (tel. 01 48 62 87 62); open daily 6:30am-11:30pm.

TRAVELER'S CHECKS

Traveler's checks are one of the safest and least troublesome means of carrying funds. They are essentially vouchers for a certain amount you purchase from the company that guarantees them—much like a cashier's check. With most, you sign them when you purchase them, and again when you cash them. Several agencies and many banks sell traveler's checks, usually at face value plus a 1% commission. American Express and Visa are the most widely recognized, though other major checks are sold, exchanged, cashed, and refunded with almost equal ease.

Each agency provides refunds if your checks are lost or stolen, and many provide additional services. (Note that you may need a police report verifying the loss or theft.) You should expect a fair amount of red tape and delay in the event of theft or loss of traveler's checks. To expedite the refund process, keep your check receipts separate from your checks and store them in a safe place or with a traveling companion. Record check numbers when you cash them and leave a list of check numbers with someone at home; ask for a list of refund centers when you buy your checks. Never countersign your checks until you're prepared to cash them. And always be sure to bring your passport with you when you plan to use the checks.

While British and U.S. citizens can easily exchange their respective currencies for francs in France, New Zealanders and Australians may have difficulty exchanging theirs. Buying **French franc traveler's checks** eliminates the need for expensive multiple transactions (such as Canadian to U.S. dollars and then U.S. dollars to francs). Most banks will cash French franc traveler's checks commission-free (but be sure to ask *before* you give them your money). Depending on the changing value of the franc, you may gain or lose money by buying checks in francs in advance.

American Express: Call (800) 221-7282 in the U.S. and Canada; in the U.K. (0800) 52 13 13; in New Zealand (0800) 44 10 68; in Australia (008) 25 19 02). Elsewhere, call U.S. collect (801) 964-6665. American Express Traveler's Cheques are available in 11 currencies, including French francs. **Purchase checks** for a small fee at American Express Travel Service Offices, banks, and American Automobile Association offices (AAA members can buy the checks commission-free). Cardmembers can also purchase checks at American Express Dispensers at Travel Service Offices at airports and by phone (tel. (800) ORDER-TC (673-3782)). You can also buy Cheques for Two which can be signed by either of two people traveling together. Request American Express's booklet *Traveler's Companion,* listing travel office addresses and stolen check hotlines for each European country. Traveler's checks are also available over America OnLine. American Express offices all over the world **cash their checks** commission-free, although they generally offer worse rates than banks. In France, for refund of **stolen checks,** call toll-free 0 800 90 86 00 (24hr.).

Citicorp: Call 24hr. (800) 645-6556 in the U.S. and Canada; in the U.K. (0181) 297 4781; from elsewhere call U.S. collect (813) 623-1709. Sells both Citicorp and Citicorp Visa traveler's checks (not in francs, though). Citicorp's World Courier Service guarantees hand-delivery of traveler's checks when a refund location is not convenient.

Thomas Cook Mastercard: Call (800) 223-9920 in the U.S. and Canada; elsewhere call U.S. collect (609) 987-7300. From the U.K. call toll-free (0800) 62 21 01; collect (1733) 50 29 95 or (1733) 31 89 50. Offers checks in U.S. dollars, British pounds, and French francs—among others. Commission 1-2% for purchases. Try buying the checks at a Thomas Cook office for potentially lower commissions; cash them at Cook offices commission-free.

Visa: Call (800) 227-6811 in the U.S.; in the U.K. (0800) 89 54 92; from anywhere else, call (01733) 31 89 49—a toll call, but Visa can reverse the charges. At any of the above numbers, if you give them your zip code, they will tell you where the closest office to you is to purchase Visa traveler's checks. Report **lost checks** to these numbers, too.

CREDIT CARDS

Credit cards in Europe do everything they do in America. Some offer services for travelers, from rental collision insurance to emergency legal aid—these depend completely, however, on the issuer. The easiest way to reserve a hotel room before you leave is to send a confirming fax with your card number after requesting a room by phone. Cards also extract cash advances in francs from associated banks and teller machines. This can be a bargain since credit card companies get the wholesale exchange rate, which is about 5% better than the retail rate used by banks.

MasterCard (tel. (800) 999-0454) and **Visa** (tel. (800) 336-8472) are the most welcomed in shops and hotels; heavy surcharges keep small businesses and hotels out of the **American Express** (tel. (800) 528-4800) loop. American Express cards do work in ATMs at Crédit Lyonnais banks, at AmEx offices, and at airports. Visa and Mastercard can access most ATMs in Paris; look for stickers saying CB/VISA or EC. Keep in mind that MasterCard and Visa have aliases here, **Eurocard** and **Carte Bleue.** Cashiers are more familiar with the French equivalents.

American Express cardholders can sign up through AmEx's Express Cash service to access cash from their home account at any ATM with the AmEx trademark. Cardholders may withdraw up to US$1000 every seven days. There is a 2% fee for each cash withdrawal (minimum fee $2.50). For a list of AmEx ATMs, call (800) CASH-NOW (227-4669). Make sure to set up your Express Cash account a few weeks before you plan to travel. In the Paris office, American Express cardholders can cash up to US$1000 in personal checks (US$5000 for gold card holders) every three weeks. Global Assist, a 24-hr. hotline offering information and legal assistance in emergencies, is also available to cardholders (tel. (800) 554-2639 in the U.S. and Canada; from abroad call U.S. collect (301) 214-8228). Call American Express Travel Service (tel. (800) 221-7282) for more info on services.

All automatic teller machines require a 4-digit **Personal Identification Number (PIN),** which credit cards in the United States do not always carry. You must ask your credit card company to assign you one before you leave; without this PIN, you will be unable to withdraw cash with your credit card abroad.

If you **lose your card** in Paris, call the following numbers for help. **Mastercard:** tel. 01 45 67 84 84; customer service tel. 01 43 23 41 52. **Visa:** tel. 01 42 77 11 90. **American Express:** tel. 01 47 77 72 00.

CASH CARDS

Automatic Teller Machines—popularly called ATMs—are everywhere in Paris. Depending on the system that your bank at home uses, you will probably be able to access your own personal account when you're in need of funds. Keep in mind that the ATM machines get the wholesale exchange rate, which is generally 5% better than the retail rate most banks use (which is in turn better than the rate most *bureaux de change* use). Don't rely too heavily on automation. There is often a limit on the amount you can withdraw per day, and computer network failures are not uncommon. Finally, there are no letters on the keypads of most European bank machines, but the correspondence is the same as on telephones: ABC correspond to 2; DEF to 3; GHI to 4; JKL to 5; MNO to 6; PRS to 7; TUV to 8; and WXY to 9.

In the U.S., you can call the **Cirrus** network (tel. (800) 4-CIRRUS (424-7787)) for a list of their international ATMs. In Paris, **Crédit Mutuel's Minibanque/24** and **Crédit Agricole** teller machines are on Cirrus. See "ATMs," p. 71, for a short list of ATMs on this network and consult Crédit Agricole's brochure *Rencontrez un specialiste* for an extensive list of that bank's ATM locations.

The **PLUS** system (U.S. tel. (800) 843-7587) works in most Visa ATMs. Institutions supporting PLUS are: **Crédit Commercial de France, Banque Populaire, Union de Banque à Paris, Point Argent, Banque Nationale de Paris, Crédit du Nord, Gie Osiris,** and ATMs in many **post offices.**

Visa TravelMoney is new a system by which you pay a bank a sum of money and receive in return a cash card with that amount pre-coded onto it. You choose a PIN code when you buy the card and can call a 24-hr. assistance line if it is lost or stolen, making TravelMoney more secure and easily replaced than traveler's checks. You'll pay roughly 2% in commission, but your card will work in any Visa ATM, you'll get the wholesale exchange rate, and there's no transaction fee. In the U.S. call (800) 847-2399 for more information; elsewhere call U.S. collect (410) 581-9091.

GETTING MONEY FROM HOME

One of the easiest ways to get money from home is to bring an **American Express** card. AmEx allows card holders to draw cash from their checking accounts at any of its major offices and many of its representatives' offices, up to US$1000 every 21 days (no service charge, no interest). AmEx also offers Express Cash, with over 100,000 ATMs around the world. Express Cash withdrawals are automatically debited from the Cardmember's specified bank account or line of credit. Green card holders may withdraw up to $1000 in a seven day period. There is a 2% transaction fee for each cash withdrawal ($2.50 minimum fee). To enroll in Express Cash, Cardmembers may call 1-800-CASH NOW. Outside the U.S. call collect (904) 565-7875. Unless using the AmEx service, avoid cashing checks in foreign currencies; they usually take weeks and a US$30 fee to clear.

Money can also be wired abroad through international money transfer services operated by **Western Union** (tel. (800) 325-6000). Charging money to be wired to your credit card, an option in the U.S., does not work overseas, you must pay in cash. Money is usually available abroad within an hour, although it may take longer.

In emergencies, U.S. citizens can have money sent via the State Department's **Overseas Citizens Service, American Citizens Services,** Consular Affairs, Public Affairs Staff, Room 4831, U.S. Department of States, Washington, D.C. 20520 (tel. (202) 647-5225, at night and Sun. and holidays (202) 647-4000; fax (202) 647-3000;

http://travel.state.gov). For US$15, the State Department will forward money within hours to the nearest consular office, which will disburse it according to instructions.

OPENING A BANK ACCOUNT

If you are planning a long-term stay in Paris, consider opening a bank account. Once you have a Paris address, you can open an account at any convenient financial institution. You will be eligible for an ATM card drawn on your French account, and have yet another method for getting money from home. Most foreign banks can instantly wire money to French accounts. Required minimum balances vary, but are usually not steep for residents. Foreigners can open non-resident bank accounts, but banks expect that these will be long-term (a few years). They often require a hefty opening deposit, and the maintenance of a high minimum balance (30,000F). Banks' main offices (often located near the Opéra) have foreign affairs departments that deal with such issues.

VALUE-ADDED TAX

The Value-Added Tax (abbreviated TVA, in France) is a varying sales tax levied in the European Union. The French rate is 18.6% on all goods except books, food, and medicine. Luxury items such as video cassettes, watches, jewelry, and cameras are taxed at 33%. If you spend more than 2000F (4200F for EU members) in a particular store, you can participate in a complex, over-the-counter export program for foreign shoppers that exempts you from paying TVA. Ask the store for an official *formulaire de détaxe pour l'exportation* (detax invoice) and a stamped envelope. At the border, show the invoices and your purchases to the French customs officials, who will stamp the invoices. If you're at an airport, look for the window labeled *douane de détaxe,* and be sure to budget at least an hour for your encounter with the French bureaucracy. On a train, find an official (they won't find you) or get off at a station close to the border. Then send a copy back to the vendor. With this official TVA-exempt proof, they will refund the agreed amount. The refunds are sent to your bank account, a process which may take as long as six months. Whew.

TIPPING AND BARGAINING

Service is almost always included at meals in restaurant and cafés; look for the phrase *service compris* on the menu. If service is not included, tip 15-20%. Even when service is included, it is polite to leave extra *monnaie* (change) at a café, bistro, restaurant, or bar—one franc for a glass of wine, several francs for a meal. Similarly, you should tip hairdressers, cabbies, and others 15%. Theater ushers are not shy about letting you know how much to tip; signs are often posted instructing patrons to tip 2F. Museum and tour guides may expect 5-10F after a tour. If you stay in a (swank) hotel for some time, you should tip the chambermaid and bellhop.

Safety and Security

Personal safety should be every traveler's first priority. Self-preservation, as Frenchman Jean-Jacques Rousseau once argued, is essential to life. Protection of your belongings, of course, always comes second. Savvy travelers take a few precautions, however, and enjoy themselves, rather than cowering in constant fear.

PERSONAL SAFETY

While France is a relatively safe and stable country, tourists are particularly vulnerable to crime for two reasons: they often carry large amounts of cash and they are not as street smart as locals. To avoid such unwanted attention, try to blend in as much as possible. Walking directly into a cafe or shop to check your map beats checking it on a street corner. Know where you are going, or look like you do, at all times.

Paris has far less violent crime than American big-city equivalents, but incidence of crime is rising disturbingly. Certain areas of Paris can be rough at night, including Les Halles and the Bastille area; others are outright dangerous. Travelers should not walk around Pigalle, Barbès-Rochechouart, or Belleville alone at night, and should venture into Montmartre with caution. In general, the northern and eastern arrondissements are less safe than the southern and western ones. Both men and women may want to carry a small whistle to scare off attackers and attract attention.

At night, daytime precautions become essential mandates. Steer clear of empty train compartments, and avoid large metro stations. Stick to busy, well-lit streets. Do not attempt to cross through parks, parking lots or any other large, deserted areas. Whenever possible, *Let's Go* warns of unsafe neighborhoods and areas, but only your eyes can tell you for sure if you've wandered into one; be wary of buildings in disrepair, vacant lots, and general desertedness. A district can change drastically in the course of a single block. Many notoriously dangerous areas have safe sections; look for children playing, women walking in the open, and other signs of an active community. If you feel uncomfortable, leave as quickly and calmly as you can.

There is no sure-fire set of precautions that will protect you from all of the situations you might encounter when you travel. A good self-defense course will give you more concrete ways to react to different types of aggression, but it might cost you more money than your trip. **Model Mugging,** with offices in several major cities, teaches a fairly comprehensive course on self-defense. Contact Lynn S. Auerbach on the East Coast (617) 232-7900); Alice Tibits in the Midwest (612) 645-6189); and Cori Couture on the West Coast (415) 592-7300). Courses for men and women cost US$400-500. Women's and men's courses offered. Community colleges and YWCA centers frequently offer self-defense courses at more affordable prices.

For official **United States Department of State** travel advisories, including crime and security, call their 24-hour hotline at (202) 647-5225. To order publications, including a pamphlet entitled *A Safe Trip Abroad,* write them at Superintendent of Documents, U.S. Government Printing Office, Washington, D.C. 20402, or call (202) 783-3238.

FINANCIAL SECURITY

Among the more colorful aspects of Paris are **con artists.** They often work in groups, and children, unfortunately, are among the most effective at the game. Be watchful for groups of children who might distract you while others seize your belongings. A firm "no," or *"laissez-moi tranquille"* (LAY-say mwah trahn-KEEL) should communicate that you are no dupe. Be especially alert. Do not respond or make eye contact, walk quickly away, and keep a tight grip on your belongings.

Like so much else, **pickpocketing** has been honed to a fine art in Paris. Pros can unzip (or slash) a bag in just a few seconds. Thieves in metro stations may try to grab your bag as you walk through the turnstile or as you board the subway, just before the doors close. **Don't put money in a wallet in your back pocket.** Never count your money in public and carry as little as possible. If you carry a purse, buy a sturdy one with a secure clasp and carry it crosswise on the side away from the street, with the clasp against you. For backpacks, buy some small combination padlocks which slip through the two zippers. A **money belt** is the best way to carry cash; you can buy one at most camping supply stores. The best combination of convenience and invulnerability is the nylon, zippered pouch with a belt that should sit inside the waist of your pants or skirt. A **neck pouch** is equally safe, although less accessible. Refrain from pulling out your neck pouch in public; if you must, be discreet. Avoid keeping anything precious in a waist- or fanny-pack; your valuables will be highly visible and easy to steal.

Keep some money separate from the rest of your cash to use in an emergency or in case of theft. Don't trust anyone to "watch your bag for a second." Never leave your belongings unattended; even the most demure-looking hostel may be a den of thieves. Keep valuables on your person if you're staying in low-budget hotels where someone else may have a key. If you feel unsafe, look for places with either a curfew or a night attendant. Try to leave expensive jewelry, valuables, and anything you couldn't bear to part with at home. More complete information on travel safety may be found in *Americans Traveling Abroad: What You Should Know Before You Go,* by Gladson Nwanna (World Travel Institute, US$40).

DRUGS AND ALCOHOL

Possession of drugs in France can end your vacation abruptly; convicted offenders can expect a jail sentence and fines. Never bring any illegal drugs across a border. Prescription drugs, particularly insulin, syringes, or narcotics, should be accompanied by a statement from a doctor and left in original labeled containers. Bring a copy of your prescription with you. In France, police may stop and search anyone on the street—no reason is required. It is not unknown for a pusher to increase profits by selling drugs to a tourist and then turning that person in for a reward. If you are arrested, your country's consulate can visit you, provide a list of attorneys, and inform family and friends, but it cannot get you out of jail. If you become involved in illegal drug trafficking, you're on your own. Write the Bureau of Consular Affairs, Public Affairs #5807, Department of State, Washington, D.C. 20520 (tel. (202) 647-1488) for more information and the pamphlet *Travel Warning on Drugs Abroad.*

Health

For emergency health information, see "Emergency Health and Help," p. 69.

All food, including seafood, dairy products, and fresh produce, is normally safe in Paris. The water is chlorinated and also quite safe; to avoid the infamous traveler's diarrhea, you might drink mineral water while your body adjusts to new bacteria.

Although no immunizations are necessary for travel to France, be sure that your **inoculations** are up-to-date. Typhoid shots are good for three years, tetanus for 10.

Always travel with any **medication** you may need on the road. Allergy sufferers in particular may suffer unexpected flare-ups in new surroundings, and should obtain a supply of their medications before a trip. Carry up-to-date prescriptions and/or a statement (with a translated version) from your doctor, especially if you use insulin, syringes, or narcotic drugs. Keep important medicines in your carry-on luggage.

If you wear **glasses** or **contact lenses,** take an extra prescription with you. Try to use chemical disinfection for contacts while you're traveling; remember that you may not be able to find equivalents abroad when you run out of chemicals. For heat disinfection you'll need outlet and low-watt voltage adapters, and a back-up plan. North American heat units often act up, even with adapters, on European current.

Those with medical conditions (e.g. diabetes, allergies to antibiotics, epilepsy, heart conditions) may want to obtain a **Medic Alert** identification tag (US$35 the first year, and $15 annually thereafter), which identifies the disease and gives a 24-hour collect-call information number. Contact Medic Alert at (800) 825-3785, or write to Medic Alert Foundation, 2323 Colorado Avenue, Turlock, CA 95382. **Global Emergency Medical Services (GEMS)** provides 24-hr. international medical assistance and support coordinated through registered nurses who have on-line access to your medical information, your primary physician, and a worldwide network of screened, credentialed English-speaking doctors and hospitals. Subscribers also receive a pocket-sized, personal medical record that contains vital information. For info call (800) 860-1111; fax (770) 475-0058; or write: 2001 Westside Drive, Suite 120, Alpharetta, GA 30201.

AIDS, HIV, STDS

Acquired Immune Deficiency Syndrome (AIDS, *SIDA* in French) is a growing problem around the world. The World Health Organization estimates that there are around 13 million people infected with the HIV virus. Well over 90% of adults newly infected with HIV acquired their infection through heterosexual sex; women now represent 50% of all new HIV infections.

The easiest mode of HIV transmission is through direct blood-to-blood contact with an HIV+ person; *never* share intravenous drug, tattooing, or other needles. The most common mode of transmission is sexual intercourse. Health professionals recommend the use of latex condoms; follow the instructions on the packet. For more information on AIDS, call the **U.S. Center for Disease Control's** 24-hr. hotline at (800) 342-2437 (Mon.-Fri. 10am-10pm; Spanish 800-344-7332, daily 8am-2am). In Europe, write to the **World Health Organization,** attn.: Global Program on AIDS, 20 Avenue Appia, 1211 Geneva 27, Switzerland (tel. (22) 791-2111), for statistical material on AIDS internationally. Or write to the **Bureau of Consular Affairs,** CA/P/PA, Department of State, Washington, D.C. 20520. Council's brochure, *Travel Safe: AIDS and International Travel,* is available at all Council Travel offices (see "Student and Budget Travel Agencies," p. 51).

Sexually transmitted diseases (STDs) such as gonorrhea, chlamydia, genital warts, syphilis, and herpes are a lot easier to catch and are far more common than HIV. Though hardly foolproof, it's a wise idea to actually *look* at your partner's genitals before you have sex. If things look bad, that may be a warning sign. Condoms may protect you from certain STDs, but oral or even tactile contact can lead to transmission.

BIRTH CONTROL AND ABORTION

Contraception is readily available in most pharmacies. To obtain **condoms** in France, visit a pharmacy and tell the clerk, "*Je voudrais une boîte de préservatifs*" (zhuh-voo-DRAY oon BWAHT duh pray-ZEHR-va-TEEF). The French branch of the International Planned Parenthood Federation, the **Mouvement Français pour le Planning Familiale (MFPF)** (tel. 01 42 60 93 20), can provide more information.

Abortion is legal in France, where the abortion or "morning after" pill, RU-486, was pioneered. The American **National Abortion Federation's** hotline (tel. (800) 772-9100; Mon.-Fri. 9:30am-12:30pm and 1:30-5:30pm), 1436 U St. NW, Washington, D.C. 20009, can direct you to organizations which provide information on the availability of and techniques for abortion in France and other countries.

Insurance

Beware of unnecessary insurance—your current policies may cover travel-related incidents. **Medical insurance** often covers costs incurred abroad. **Medicare** does not cover travel to Paris. Canadians are protected by their home province's health insurance plan for up to 90 days after leaving the country; check with the provincial Ministry of Health or Health Plan Headquarters for details. Australians should requests info about their country's Reciprocal Health Care Agreements (RHCAs) from the Commonwealth Department of Human Services and Health.

Homeowners' insurance may cover theft during travel, and loss of documents up to about US$500. **ISIC, Council, STA** (see p. 51), and **American Express** provide varying levels of insurance. As a supplement to ISIC insurance, **Council** offers the inexpensive Trip-Safe plan with options covering medical treatment and hospitalization, accidents, baggage loss, and charter flights missed due to illness (see p. 51), in addition to their more comprehensive policies. Remember that insurance companies require a copy of the police report for thefts, or evidence of having paid medical expenses before they will honor a claim, and may have time limits on filing for reimbursement. Always carry policy numbers and proof of insurance.

Globalcare Travel Insurance, 220 Broadway Lynnfield, MA 01940 (tel. (800) 821-2488; fax (617) 592-7720; e-mail global@nebc.mv.com; http://www.nebc.mv.com/globalcare). Complete medical, legal, emergency, and travel-related services. On-the-spot payments and special student programs, including benefits for trip cancellation and interruption. GTI waives pre-existing medical conditions with their Globalcare Economy Plan for cruise and travel, and provides coverage for the bankruptcy or default of cruise lines, airlines, or tour operators.

Travel Assistance International, by Worldwide Assistance Services, Inc., 1133 15th St. NW, Suite 400, Washington, D.C. 20005-2710 (tel. (800) 821-2828 or (202) 828-5894; fax (202) 828-5896); e-mail wassist@aol.com). TAI provides members with a free 24-hr. hotline for travel emergencies and referrals. Their Per-Trip (starting at US$52) and Frequent Traveler (starting at US$226) plans include medical, travel, and financial insurance, translation, and lost document/item aid.

Alternatives To Tourism

If the often madcap pace of tourism loses its appeal, consider a longer stay in Paris. Study, work, or volunteering will help you get a better sense of parts of the city that are often hidden to the short-term visitor.

STUDY

If you choose your program well, study in Paris could be one of the most exciting experiences you'll ever have. Research your options carefully, as programs vary in expense, academic quality, living conditions, and exposure to French culture and language. French educational terminology and equivalencies are radically different from almost anywhere else. For pamphlets on various fields of study in France, contact the **Cultural Services of the French Embassy** (see p. 23). Many American undergraduates enroll in programs sponsored by U.S. universities, and most colleges give advice and info on study abroad. **Council** sponsors over 40 programs around the world, and publishes *The High School Student's Guide to Study, Travel and Adventure Abroad* and *Work, Study, Travel Abroad: The Whole World Handbook* (see "Student and Budget Travel Agencies," p. 51). See "French Universities," p. 39, for information on enrolling yourself in the Université de Paris.

American Field Service (AFS), 220 E. 42nd St., 3rd floor, New York, NY 10017 (tel. (800) AFS-INFO or 237-4636, 876-2376; fax (212) 949-9379; http://www.afs.org/usa). AFS offers summer, semester, and year homestay programs for high school students and graduating high school seniors, and short-term service projects for adults. Financial aid available. Often a long waiting list for France.

American Institute for Foreign Study, College Division, 102 Greenwich Ave., Greenwich, CT 06830 (tel. (800) 727-2437) for high school students, (800) 888-2247; http://www.aifs.org. Organizes year, semester, quarter, and summer programs for study in French and other foreign universities. Open to adults. Minority and AIFS International scholarships available. Also offers Au Pair in Europe for those aged 18-26 to provide childcare in exchange for room and board for families in Paris and the French Riviera.

Central College Abroad, Office of International Education, 812 University, Pella, IA 50219 (tel. (800) 831-3629; fax (515) 628-5316; e-mail admissions@central.edu). Offers semester- and year-long study abroad programs in Paris. US$20 application fee. Scholarships available. Applicants must be at least 18 years old, have completed their freshman year of college, and have a minimum 2.5 GPA.

College Semester Abroad, School for International Training, Admissions, Kipling Rd., P.O. Box 676, Brattleboro, VT 05302 (tel. (800) 336-1616 or (800) 258-3279; fax (800) 258-3500). Runs semester and year programs featuring cultural orientation, intensive language study, homestay, and field and independent study. Programs cost US$8200-10,300, all expenses included. Financial aid available and U.S. university financial aid is transferable. Most U.S. colleges will transfer credit for semester work done abroad in France at accredited institutions.

Institute of International Education (IIE), 809 United Nations Plaza, New York, NY 10017-3580 (tel. (212) 984-5413 for recorded information; fax (212) 984-5358). A nonprofit, international and cultural exchange agency. IIE's library of study abroad resources is open to the public Tues.-Thurs. 11am-3:45pm. Publishes *Academic Year Abroad* (US$43 plus US$4 shipping) detailing over 2300 semester- and year-long programs worldwide and *Vacation Study Abroad* (US$37 plus US$4 shipping) which lists over 1800 short-term, summer, and language school programs. Write for a list of publications. For book orders: IIE Books, Institute of International Education, PO Box 371, Annapolis Junction, MD 20701 (tel. (800) 445-0443; fax (301) 953-2838; e-mail iiebooks@iie.org.).

World Learning, Inc., Summer Abroad, P.O. Box 676, Brattleboro, VT 05302 (tel. (800) 345-2929 or (802) 257-7751; http://www.worldlearning.org). Founded in 1932 as The Experiment in International Living, it offers high school programs in France as well as language-training programs with elective homestays. Programs are 3-5 weeks long. Positions as group leaders are available world-wide if you are over 24, have previous in-country experience, are fluent in the language, and have experience with high school students.

Language Schools

Language instruction is a booming business in France; programs are run by foreign universities, independent international or local organizations, and divisions of French universities. The **tourist office** in Paris has a list of language schools. Make sure the program you choose matches your age and commitment to study; some cater to businesspeople, others to preteens. Ask to speak with former participants.

Alliance Française, École Internationale de Langue et de Civilisation Françaises, 101, bd. Raspail, 6ème, Paris or 75270 Paris Cedex 06 (tel. 01 45 44 38 28; fax 01 45 44 89 42; e-mail: info@paris.alliancefrancaise.fr; http://www.paris.alliancefrancaise.fr). M. Notre-Dame-des-Champs, St-Placide, or Rennes. French language courses at all levels and for all needs starting at US$250.

Cours de Civilisation Française de la Sorbonne, 47, rue des Ecoles, 75005 Paris (tel. 01 40 46 22 11; fax 01 40 46 32 29). The Sorbonne has been giving its French civilization course since 1919. Academic-year course can be taken by the semester; 4-, 6- 8- and 11-week summer programs with culture lectures and language classes at all levels. Also offers a special course in commercial French during the academic year, and a 3-week session for high-level students during the summer. You can also take the Cours de Civilisation through **AIFS,** which also arranges accommodations and meals for its students (see "AIFS", p. 38).

Eurocentres, 101 N. Union St. #300, Alexandria, VA 22314 (tel. (800) 648-4809; fax (703) 684-1495; http://www.clark.net/pub/eurocent/home.html), or Eurocentres, Head Office, Seestrasse 247, CH-8038 Zurich, Switzerland (tel. (01) 485 50 40; fax (01) 481 61 24). Long and short intensive courses, holiday courses, and teacher refresher courses. Coordinates language programs and homestays. Programs US$500-5000 for 2 weeks to 3 months. Some financial aid available. Center in **Paris** at 13, passage Dauphine, F-75006 (tel. 01 40 46 72 00; fax 01 40 46 72 06). Open Mon.-Fri. 8:30am-6pm.

Institut Catholique de Paris, 21, rue d'Assas, 6ème Paris, (tel. 01 44 39 52 00). M. St-Placide. Semester-long and summer classes at all levels, taught during the school year by the institute's full-time professors.

French Universities

If your French is already extremely competent, direct enrollment in a French university can be more rewarding than a language or civilization class filled with Americans and Australians. It can also be up to three or four times cheaper than an American university program, though it's harder to receive academic credit at your home university. After 1968, the **Université de Paris** split into ten isolated universities, each occupying a different site and offering a different range of fields. The centuries-old Sorbonne, now the Université de Paris IV, devotes itself to the humanities. For a more experimental approach, try one of the more modern universities. Each of them requires at least a *baccalauréat* degree or its equivalent (British A-levels or two years of college in the United States) for admission. For details contact the cultural services office at the nearest French consulate or embassy.

As a student at a French university, you will receive a student card *(carte d'étudiant)* from your school upon presentation of your residency permit and a receipt for your university fees. In addition to standard student benefits, many additional benefits available to students in France are administered by the **Centre Régional des Oeuvres Universitaires et Scolaires (CROUS).** Founded in 1955 to improve the living and working conditions of students of each academy, this division of the Oeuvres Universitaires welcomes foreign students and can be of great help in answering your (doubtless many) questions. The regional center for Paris is at 39, av. Georges-Bernanos, 5ème Paris or 75231 Paris Cedex 05 (tel. 01 40 51 36 00; open Mon.-Fri. 9am-5pm; RER Port-Royal). CROUS also publishes the brochure *Le CROUS et Moi,* which lists addresses and information on student life in Paris. Pick up their helpful guidebook *Je vais en France* (free), in French or English, from any French embassy.

WORK

There's no better way to submerge yourself in a foreign culture than to become part of its economy. To work in France, you need both a **work permit** and a **work visa.** With the exception of *au pair* jobs, it is illegal for foreign students to hold full-time jobs during the school year. Students registered at a French university may get work permits for the summer with a valid visa, a student card from a French university, and proof of a job. After spending one academic year in France, Americans with a valid student *carte de séjour* can find part-time work if they will be enrolled at a French university again in the fall. Check the fact sheet *Employment in France for Students,* put out by **Cultural Services of the French Embassy.**

If you are a full-time student at a U.S. university, one easy way to get a job abroad is through work permit programs run by **Council** and its member organizations (see "Student and Budget Travel Agencies," p. 51). For a US$225 application fee, Council can procure three- to six-month work permits (and a handbook to help you find work and housing) for France, and has a French office to help with finding accommodations, openings, and connections. Positions require evidence of language skill.

There are many books purporting to list opportunities for working abroad; the following are some of the better resources:

Council publishes *Work, Study, Travel Abroad: The Whole World Handbook,* which covers specific programs on all continents. Includes both summer and long-term work abroad. Published by St. Martin's Press (US$14). (See "Useful Publications and Organizations," p. 23.)

Transitions Abroad Publishing, Inc., 18 Hulst Rd., P.O. Box 1300, Amherst, MA 01004-1300 (tel. (800) 293-0373; fax (413) 256-0373; e-mail trabroad@aol.com). Publishes a bimonthly magazine listing all kinds of opportunities and printed resources for those seeking to study, work, or travel abroad. They also publish *The Alternative Travel Directory,* a truly exhaustive listing of info for the "active international traveler." For subscriptions (USA US$20 for 6 issues, Canada US$26, other countries US$38), contact Dep't. TRA, Box 3000, Denville, NJ 07834.

Perpetual Press, P.O. Box 45628, Seattle, WA 98145-0628 (tel. (206) 633-0561; fax (206) 633-3815). Publishes ever-expanding *Now Hiring!* series with resources on finding (and creating) jobs abroad (US$10-20). Call or write for a catalog.

Vacation Work Publications, 9 Park End St., Oxford OX1 1HJ (tel. (01865) 24 19 78; fax (01865) 79 08 85). Publishes a wide variety of guides with job listings and information for the working traveler. Opportunities for summer or full-time work in countries all over the world. Write for a catalog of their publications.

Finding a Job

Once in Paris, start your job search at the **American Church in Paris,** 65, quai d'Orsay, 7ème (tel. 47 05 07 99; M. Pont de l'Alma), which posts a bulletin board full of job and housing opportunities targeting Americans abroad. Those with ambition and an up-to-date resume, in both French and English, should stop by the **American Chamber of Commerce in France,** 21, av. George V, 1st floor, 8ème (tel. 01 40 73 89 90; fax 01 47 20 18 62; M. George V or Alma Marceau; open Mon.-Fri. 9am-5pm), an association of American businesses in France. Your resume will be kept on file for two months and placed at the disposal of French and American companies. Chamber of Commerce membership directories may be purchased at the Paris office for 500F (members 300F; 50F for older editions), or browse through the office's copy (library open Tues. and Thurs. 10am-12:30pm; admission 50F). The chamber also publishes a brochure (50F) describing paid and unpaid internships. Filled with practical information on working as an American abroad, it is most useful to have it sent to you before your arrival in France. The **Agence Nationale Pour l'Emploi (ANPE),** 4, impasse d'Antin, 8ème (tel. 01 43 59 62 63; M. Franklin D. Roosevelt; open Mon. 8:45am-12:30pm and 1:30-5pm, Tues. 10am-noon and 1:30-5pm, Wed-Thurs. 8:45am-noon and 1:30-5pm, Fri. 8:45am-noon and 1:30-5pm), has specific info on employment. Remember to bring your work permit and, if you have one, your *carte de séjour.* There are branches with the same hours at 5, rue Emile Allez, 17ème (tel. 01 45 74 90 01) and 4, rue Galilée, 16ème (tel. 01 49 31 74 00).

You should also visit the **Centre d'Information et de Documentation Jeunesse (CIDJ),** 101, quai Branly, 15ème (tel. 01 4 49 12 33; RER Champ de Mars/Tour Eiffel; open Mon.-Sat. 10am-6pm), a government-run information clearinghouse on every imaginable practical concern for young people, including education, resumes, employment, careers, long-term accommodations, camping, touring, and sports. Part-time jobs are posted at 9am on the bulletin boards outside. Of particular interest are pamphlets on university enrollment for foreign students (reference 1.63212 and 1.633), French language courses (ref. 5.576), *au pair* positions for foreigners (ref. 5.573), concerns and associations related to handicapped visitors (ref. 5.584-5.5888), and general tourism in France (ref. 7.51-7.53), all including extensive contact lists. English-speaking representatives are available. You can consult these pamphlets for free in the reading room or buy a copy of the pertinent ones for 10-19F each (20-25F by mail). First pick up a free brochure entitled *Les publications du CIDJ,* which lists the holdings and their reference numbers. To buy pamphlets, list their reference numbers on a ticket from the front desk and take it to the cashier.

Also check help-wanted columns in newspapers, especially *Le Monde, Le Figaro,* and the English-language *International Herald Tribune,* as well as *France-USA Contacts,* a free weekly circular filled with classifieds, which can be picked up in Yankee hang-outs: the American Church, Häagen-Dazs, and other stores. Many of these jobs are "unofficial" and therefore illegal, but many people find them convenient because they don't require work permits.

Teaching English

Post a sign in markets, high schools, or learning centers stating that you are a native speaker, and scan the classifieds of local newspapers, where residents sometimes advertise for language instruction. Securing a position will require patience and legwork; teaching English abroad has become enormously popular of late. Professional English-teaching positions are harder to get; most European schools require at least a bachelor's degree and training in teaching English as a foreign language. Because so many foreigners in Paris offer English lessons, visitors shouldn't expect to support themselves on this alone.

Office of Overseas Schools, A/OS Room 245, SA-29, Department of State, Washington, D.C. 20522-2902 (tel. (703) 875-7800). Keeps a list of schools abroad and agencies that arrange placement for Americans to teach abroad.

International Schools Services, P.O. Box 5910, Princeton, NJ 08543 (tel. (609) 452-0990) publishes a free newsletter, *NewsLinks;* call or write to get a copy. Its Educational Staffing Department coordinates placement of teachers and publishes the free brochure *Your Passport to Teaching and Administrative Opportunities Abroad.* The *ISS Directory of Overseas Schools* (US$34.95) is also helpful.

Au Pair Positions

Au pair positions are reserved primarily for single women aged 18 to 30 with some knowledge of French; a few men are also employed. The *au pair* cares for children and does light housework five or six hours each day for a French family while taking courses at a French university or at a school for foreign students. Talking with children can be a great way to improve your French, but looking after them may be extremely strenuous. Make sure you know in advance what the family expects of you. *Au pair* positions usually last six to 18 months; during the summer the contract can be as short as one to three months, but you may not be able to take courses. Expect to receive room, board, and a small monthly stipend. *Au pair* jobs can also be arranged through individual connections, but make sure you have a contract detailing hours per week, salary, and living accommodations. (See also "Cultural Services of the French Embassy," p. 23 and "AIFS," p. 38.)

L'Accueil Familial des Jeunes Étrangers, 23, rue du Cherche-Midi, 6ème Paris (tel. 01 42 22 50 34; fax 01 45 44 60 48; M. Sèvres-Babylone). Arranges summer *au pair* jobs of one to three months, 6-month *au pair* jobs Jan.-June, and 10-month *au pair* jobs beginning in Sept. They have a placement fee of 650F for summer stays and 700F for longer stays, and will help you switch families if you are not happy at your initial location. They also have a service to help you find a room in exchange for two hours of work a day (you must have a student visa).

InterExchange, 161 Sixth Avenue, New York, NY 10013 (tel. (212) 924-0446; fax (212) 924-0575). Provides information in pamphlet form on international work programs and *au pair* positions.

Childcare International, Limited, Trafalgar House, Grenville Place, London NW7 3SA (tel. (01819) 59 36 11 or (01819) 06 31 16; fax (01819) 06 34 61; e-mail: office@childint.demon.co.uk; http://www.ipi.co.uk/childint). Offers *au pair* jobs in France, western Europe, and North America. UK£60 application fee. The organization prefers a 1-year placement, but does arrange summer work.

VOLUNTEERING

Volunteer work can provide a wonderful opportunity to meet people and, in some cases, to receive free room and board in exchange for your work. International firms, museums, art galleries, and non-profit organizations like UNESCO may have unpaid internships available. The **American Center** (tel. 01 44 73 77 77), has a service on Wednesday afternoons providing cultural info on the Paris area and referrals to Franco-American organizations in Paris. Contact the center at 51, rue de Bercy, 12ème Paris or 75592 Paris Cedex 12 (open Wed.-Sat. noon-8pm, Sun. noon-6pm).

Council offers 2- to 4-week environmental or community service projects in over 30 countries around the globe through its Voluntary Services Department (US$250-750 placement fee). Participants must be at least 18 years old. Council also publishes *Volunteer! The Comprehensive Guide to Volunteer Services in the U.S. and Abroad* (see "Useful Publications and Organizations," p. 23). Participants must be at least 18 years of age.

Global Volunteers, 375 E. Little Canada Rd., St. Paul, MN 55117-1628 (tel. (800) 487-1074 or (612) 482-1074; fax (612) 482-0915). Facilitates approximately 90 teams of North Americans on short-term social and economic development in 13 countries in Europe and Central America.

REMPART, 1, rue des Guillemites, 4ème Paris (tel. 01 42 71 96 55; fax 01 42 71 73 00). Works to protect the environment and restore churches, castles, and historical monuments. Offers summer- and year-long programs. Anyone 15 or over is eligible. Programs cost about 40F per day (plus a 220F insurance fee).

Club du Vieux Manoir, 10, rue de la Cossonnerie, 75001 Paris (tel. 01 45 08 80 40). Works to protect the environment and restore churches, castles, fortresses, and other French monuments. The club offers summer and year programs. Anyone 15 or over is eligible; the application fee is 80F.

Service Civil International Voluntary Service, 5474 Walnut Level Rd., Crozet, VA 22932 (tel. (804) 823-1826; fax (804) 823-5027; e-mail sciivsusa@igc.apc.org). Arranges placement in workcamps in Europe (ages 18 and over) and North America (ages 16 and over). Local organizations sponsor groups for physical or social work. Registration fees US$50-250, depending on camp location.

Volunteers for Peace, 43 Tiffany Rd., Belmont, VT 05730 (tel. (802) 259-2759; fax (802) 259-2922; e-mail vfp@vermontel.com; http://www.vermontel.com/~vfp/home.htm). A non-profit organization that arranges for speedy placement in over

800 workcamps in more than 60 countries in Europe, Africa, Asia, and the Americas. Many camps last for 2-3 weeks and are comprised of 10-15 people. Complete and up-to-date listings provided in the annual *International Workcamp Directory* (US$12). Registration fee US$175. Some workcamps are open to 16 and 17 year olds for US$200. Free newsletter.

Specific Concerns

WOMEN TRAVELERS

While traipsing happily through Paris à la Audrey Hepburn, exercise reasonable caution. Foreign women in Paris are sometimes beset by unwanted and tenacious followers. To escape unwanted attention, walk with assurance, look straight ahead, and try not to look anyone directly in the eye. Remember that Americans are often approached because they have a reputation for openness and availability. Stick to centrally located accommodations and avoid late-night treks or metro rides; see "Personal Safety," p. 34, for specific danger spots. The best answer to verbal harassment may be no answer at all. Seek out a police officer or a female passerby before a crisis erupts, and don't hesitate to scream for help (*"Au secours:"* oh suh-KOOR). Ask women or couples for directions if you're lost or if you feel uncomfortable. Always carry a *télécarte,* change for the phone, and enough extra money for a bus or taxi. Carry a whistle on your keychain, and don't hesitate to use it in an emergency.

SOS Viol, the national **rape hotline,** answers calls (in French) Monday through Friday, 10am to 6pm (tel. 0 800 05 95 95). A self-defense course will not only prepare you for a potential mugging, but will raise your level of awareness of your surroundings (see "Safety and Security," p. 34). These warnings should not discourage women from traveling alone. Keep your spirit of adventure, but don't tempt fate.

For general info, contact the **National Organization for Women (NOW),** which boasts branches across America that can refer women travelers to rape crisis centers and counseling services and provide lists of feminist events. Main offices include 22 W. 21st St., 7th Fl., **New York,** NY 10010 (tel. (212) 260-4422); 1000 16th St. NW, 7th Fl., **Washington, DC** 20004 (tel. (202) 331-0066); and 3543 18th St., **San Francisco,** CA 94110 (tel. (415) 861-8960). The following books may be useful:

Handbook For Women Travelers by Maggie and Gemma Moss (UK£9). Encyclopedic and well-written. From Piaktus Books, 5 Windmill St., London W1P 1HF (tel. (0171) 631 07 10).

A Journey of One's Own, by Thalia Zepatos, (Eighth Mountain Press US$17). The latest thing on the market, interesting and full of good advice, plus a specific and manageable bibliography of books and resources.

Women Travel: Adventures, Advice & Experience by Miranda Davies and Natania Jansz (Penguin, US$13). Info on specific foreign countries plus a decent bibliography and resource index. The sequel, *More Women Travel,* is US$15.

Women Going Places, a women's travel and resource guide emphasizing women-owned enterprises. Geared towards lesbians, but offers advice appropriate for all women. US$14 from Inland Book Company, 1436 W. Randolph St. Chicago, IL 60607 (tel. (800) 243-0138), or order from a local bookstore.

OLDER TRAVELERS

Cut-rate tours and transportation discounts have made travel abroad convenient and affordable for those over 65. Proof of age is required for most discounts. Write the Superintendent of Documents (see "Useful Publications and Organizations," p. 23) for a copy of *Travel Tips for Older Americans* (US$1). Although the Parisian Tourist Office has no specific publications concerning seniors, most museums, concerts, and sights in Paris offer reduced prices for visitors over 60. For additional discounts on sights, special events, and transportation, you may want to invest in the **Carte Vermeille** (see "From the Train Stations," p. 59). For travel in Paris, the RATP publishes a free brochure which outlines metro and city bus service for senior travelers called *Circuler sans fatigue dans le metro et le RER;* pick one up at the main RATP office or order one by phone (in French only; RATP, 53ter, quai des Grands Augustins, 6ème or 75271 Paris Cédex 06; tel. 01 43 46 14 14; open Mon.-Tues. 9am-4pm and Wed.-Fri. 9am-5pm). The Ministère des Anciens Combattants (Ministry of Veteran Affairs), 37, rue de Bellechasse, 7ème (tel. 01 45 56 50 00) can offer information for **veterans** in Paris.

The following foundations provide info, assistance, and discounts to seniors.

AARP (American Association of Retired Persons), 601 E St., NW, Washington, D.C. 20049 (tel. (202) 434-2277). Members 50 and over receive benefits and services including the AARP Motoring Plan from AMOCO (tel. (800) 334-3300), and discounts on lodging, car rental, and sight-seeing. Annual fee US$8 per couple; lifetime membership US$75.

Elderhostel, 75 Federal St., 3rd Fl., Boston, MA 02110-1941 (tel. (617) 426-7788; fax 426-8351; http://www.elderhostel.org). For those 55 or over (spouse of any age). Programs at colleges, universities, and other learning centers in over 50 countries on varied subjects lasting 1-4 weeks.

Gateway Books, 2023 Clemens Road, Oakland, CA 94602 (tel. (510) 530-0299; credit card orders (800) 669-0773; fax (510) 530-0497; e-mail donmerwin@aol.com; http://www.hway.com/gateway). Publishes *Europe the European Way: A Traveler's Guide to Living Affordably in the World's Great Cities* (US$14) and *Adventures Abroad* (US$13), which offer general hints for the budget-conscious senior considering a long stay or retiring abroad.

Pilot Books, 103 Cooper St., Babylon, NY 11702 (tel. (516) 422-2225). Publishes a large number of helpful guides including *The International Health Guide for Senior Citizens* (US$5, postage US$2) and *The Senior Citizens' Guide to Budget Travel in Europe* (US$6, postage US$2). Call or write for a complete list of titles.

Unbelievably Good Deals and Great Adventures That You Absolutely Can't Get Unless You're Over 50, by Joan Rattner Heilman. After you finish ogling the title page, check inside for some great tips on senior discounts and the like. Contemporary Books, US$10.

BISEXUAL, GAY, AND LESBIAN TRAVELERS

Next to London, Amsterdam, and Berlin, Paris has one of the largest gay populations in Europe: an estimated 100,000 gay and lesbian people. The recent national increase in right-wing intolerance, combined with the enormous toll taken by *le SIDA* (AIDS—in 1993, the second largest killer of Parisian men 24-44 years old), has helped rally political consciousness and activism within Paris' gay community. The following books also provide general information that may help plan your trip (see also **Women Going Places,** p. 43).

Are You Two...Together? A Gay and Lesbian Travel Guide to Europe. Includes anecdotes and tips and overviews of regional laws relating to gays and lesbians, lists of gay/lesbian organizations, and establishments catering to, friendly to, or indifferent to gays and lesbians. Random House, US$18.

Ferrari Guides, PO Box 37887, Phoenix, AZ 85069 (tel. (602) 863-2408; fax 439-3952; e-mail ferrari@q-net.com). Gay and lesbian travel guides: *Ferrari Guides' Paris for Gays & Lesbians, Ferrari Guides' Gay Travel A to Z* (US$16), *Ferrari Guides' Men's Travel in Your Pocket* (US$14), *Ferrari Guides' Women's Travel in Your Pocket* (US$14), and *Ferrari Guides' Inn Places* (US$16). Available in bookstores or by mail order (postage/handling US$4.50 for the first item, US$1 for each additional item mailed within the US).

Spartacus International Gay Guides (US$32.95), published by Bruno Gmunder, Postfach 110729, D-10837 Berlin, Germany (tel. 615 00 30; fax 615 91 34). Lists bars, restaurants, hotels, and bookstores around the world catering to gays. Lists hotlines for gays in various countries and homosexuality laws for each country.

Once you reach Paris, you may wish to visit the gay and lesbian bookstore **Les Mots à la Bouche,** an excellent resource for travelers just arriving in the city (see "Books and Magazines," p. 274). Consult the encyclopedic **Guide Gai** (69F, at Paris newsstands and in most American gay bookstores), with almost 400 pages of information in French and English about gay hotels, restaurants, nightlife, organizations, and services throughout France. For information on HIV, AIDS, and safer sex, call the 24-hour free and anonymous AIDS information hotline, **SIDA Info Service** (tel. 0 800 36 66 36). Other Parisian organizations that may be useful include:

ACT-UP PARIS, BP231 Paris Cedex 17 (tel. 01 48 06 13 89). The Paris chapter of ACT-UP (the AIDS Coalition to Unleash Power) meets Tues. 7:30pm at Amphitheater 1, 106, bd. de l'Hôpital, 13ème, to discuss issues related to HIV, AIDS, and homophobia. Foreign members are welcome, but are not expected to take part in actions and protests that could lead to arrest.

Association des Médecins Gais (tel. 01 48 05 81 71). Doctors answer all your questions about health and sexuality. Takes calls Wed. 6-8pm and Sat. 2-4pm.

Centre du Christ Libérateur (Metropolitan Community Church), 5, rue Crussol, 11ème (tel. 01 48 05 24 48 or 01 48 06 35 15). M. Oberkampf. Founded by Pasteur Doucé, this center provides cultural, medical, legal, and personal advice and counseling for bisexual, gay, and lesbian people.

Centre Gai et Lesbien, 3 rue Keller, 11ème (tel. 01 43 57 21 47 or 01 43 57 75 95; fax 01 43 57 27 93). M. Ledru Rollin or Bastille. A variety of documentation, fellowship, services and associations concerned with homosexuality, including AIDS information. Café and library of gay info. English spoken. Open Mon.-Sat. 2-8pm, Sun. 2-7pm.

Ecoute Gaie (tel. 01 44 93 01 02). A gay hotline. Mon.-Fri. 6-10pm.

Fréquence Gaie/Radio Orient, 94.3FM (tel. 01 45 02 12 12), 24-hr. gay and lesbian radio station providing news, music, and information in French and English.

Maison des Femmes, 8, Cité Prost, 11ème (tel. 01 43 48 24 91). Info and cultural center for lesbians and bisexual women. Open Wed. 4-7pm, Fri. from 7pm.

Le Projet Ornicar, 8, rue Auguste Blanqui, 93200 St-Denis (tel. 01 44 79 07 82). Political action group which organizes protests, lobbying, and the dissemination of information regarding homophobia, discrimination, and public policy on gay, bisexual, and lesbian issues. Some English spoken.

S.O.S. Homophobie, (tel. 01 48 06 42 41). A hotline for gay, lesbian, and bisexual concerns, especially around issues of homophobia, discrimination, and gay-bashing. Takes calls Sept.-June Mon.-Fri. 8-10pm; July-Aug. Tues.-Fri. 8-10pm.

TRAVELERS WITH DISABILITIES

Many museums and sights are fully accessible to wheelchairs and some provide guided tours in sign-language. Unfortunately, budget hotels and restaurants are generally ill-equipped to handle the needs of handicapped visitors. The index of this book contains a partial list of **wheelchair-accessible** places in Paris, under the heading "wheelchair accessibility." Handicapped-accessible bathrooms are virtually non-existent among hotels in the one-to-two star range. Many hotel elevators could double as shoe-boxes; even travelers with narrow wheelchairs will find it a tight squeeze. As a result, the hotels described in this book as wheelchair-accessible are those with reasonably wide (but not regulation size) elevators or with ground-floor rooms wide enough for wheelchair entry. Travelers are encouraged to ask restaurants, hotels, railways, and airlines about their facilities: *"Etes-vous accessibles aux fauteuils roulants?"* In general, modern buildings in Paris are wheelchair-accessible, as are the more expensive hotels. If transporting a **seeing-eye dog** to France, you will need a rabies vaccination certificate issued in your home country, or a certificate showing that there have been no cases of rabies in your country for over three years. The following provide general info that can be useful in planning your trip.

Graphic Language Press, P.O. Box 270, Cardiff by the Sea, CA 92007 (tel. (619) 944-9594). Publishers of *Wheelchair Through Europe* (US$13). Comprehensive advice for the wheelchair-bound traveler. Specifics on wheelchair-related resources and accessible sites in various cities throughout Europe.

Mobility International, USA (MIUSA), P.O. Box 10767, Eugene, OR 97440 (tel. (514) 343-1284 voice and TDD; fax 343-6812). Headquarters in Brussels, rue de Manchester 25, Brussels, Belgium, B-1070 (tel. (322) 410 6297; fax 410 6874). Information on travel programs, work camps, accommodations, access guides, and organized tours for those with physical disabilities. Membership US$25 per year, newsletter US$15. Sells the periodically updated and expanded *A World of Options: A Guide to International Educational Exchange, Community Service, and Travel for Persons with Disabilities* (US$16, members US$14). Also offers courses that teach strategies for travelers with disabilities.

Access Project (PHSP), 39 Bradley Gardens, West Ealing, London W13 8HE, England. Distributes access guides to Paris and London for a donation of UK£5. Researched by persons with disabilities. They cover traveling, accommodations, and access to sights and entertainment.

Moss Rehab Hospital Travel Information Service, (tel. (215) 456-9600, TDD 456-9602). A telephone information resource center on international travel accessibility and other travel-related concerns for those with disabilities.

Society for the Advancement of Travel for the Handicapped (SATH), 347 Fifth Ave., #610, New York, NY 10016 (tel. (212) 447-7284; fax 725-8253). Publishes quarterly travel newsletter *SATH News* and information booklets (free for members, US$13 each for nonmembers) with advice on trip planning for people with disabilities. Annual membership US$45, students and seniors US$25.

The following organizations arrange tours or trips for disabled travelers:

Directions Unlimited, 720 N. Bedford Rd., Bedford Hills, NY 10507 (tel. (800) 533-5343, in NY (914) 241-1700; fax (914) 241-0243). Specializes in arranging individual and group vacations, tours, and cruises for the physically disabled.

The Guided Tour Inc., Elkins Park House, Suite 114B, 7900 Old York Road, Elkins Park, PA 19027-2339 (tel. (800) 783-5841 or (215) 782-1370; fax (215) 635-2637). Organizes travel programs for persons with developmental and physical challenges and those requiring renal dialysis. Call, fax, or write for a free brochure.

Few metro stations are wheelchair-accessible, but most RER stations are. For a guide to metro accessibility, pick up a free copy of the RATP's brochure, *Circuler sans fatigue dans le metro et le RER* (in French), which provides a list of stations equipped with escalators, elevators, and moving walkways (for the RATP address, see "Older Travelers," p. 43). To speak with an RATP rep, call 01 36 68 77 14 (French), tel. 01 36 68 41 41 (English), cost 2F23 per minute. The main office also distributes *Handicaps et déplacements en région Ile-de-France,* which provides transit info on the Ile-de-France region (open daily 6am-9pm). Check with the following Parisian groups for more info on accessibility and traveling with disabilities.

Association Valentin-Hauy, 5, rue Duroc, 7ème (tel. 01 44 49 27 27). Houses a cassette and Braille library for vision-impaired tourists and residents of Paris (free admission). Also provides a free metro map in Braille. Open Mon.-Thurs. 9am-noon, Fri 9am-noon and 2-5pm.

Audio-Vision guides, at Parisian theaters such as the Théâtre National de Chaillot, 1, pl. Trocadéro, 11 Novembre, 16ème (tel. 01 47 27 26 27), the Comédie Française, 2 rue de Richelieu, 1er (tel. 01 40 15 00 15), and the Théâtre National de la Colline, 15, rue Malte-Brun, 20ème (tel. 01 44 62 52 00). Service for the blind or vision-impaired, which describes the costumes, sets, and theater design 4 performances per each show currently running.

Neut Orthopedio: Orthopédie, Prothèse, Chaussures, 9, rue Léopold Bellan, 2ème (tel. 01 42 33 83 46). M. Sentier. This store sells wheelchairs, canes, and other important accessories. Open Mon.-Fri. 9am-7:30pm.

L'Association des Paralysées de France, Délégation de Paris, 22, rue de Père Guérion, 13ème (tel. 01 44 16 83 87). Publishes *Où ferons-nous étape?* (85F), which lists French hotels and motels accessible to persons with disabilities. Open Mon.-Thurs. 9am-12:30pm and 2-5:30pm, Fri. 9am-12:30pm and 2-5pm.

Comité National Français de Liaison pour la Réadaption des Handicapés (CNFLRH), 236bis, rue de Tolbiac, 13ème (tel. 01 53 80 66 66). Publishes several guides to hotels and tourist attractions which are wheelchair accessible.

VEGETARIAN AND KOSHER TRAVELERS

Vegetarians may have trouble eating cheaply in restaurants, since *menus à prix fixe* usually feature meat or fish. Most restaurants do have vegetarian selections, and some cater specifically to vegetarians. If you don't eat eggs or dairy products, you should clearly state this to the server. Try eating at Tunisian, Moroccan, Indian, Vietnamese, and Chinese restaurants; such establishments often offer couscous or rice and hearty vegetable platters. Health food stores, called *diététiques* or *maisons de régime,* are expensive. Health food products are referred to as *produits diététiques* and can be found more cheaply in large supermarkets. For more, contact the **North American Vegetarian Society,** P.O. Box 72, Dolgeville, NY 13329 (518-568-7970), publisher of travel-related publications, such *Transformative Adventures,* a guide to vacations and retreats (US$14.95). Membership to the Society is US$20; family membership is $26 and members receive a 10% discount on all publications.

In Paris, **kosher** delis and restaurants abound in the 3ème and 4ème *arrondissements,* particularly on rue des Rosiers and rue des Ecouffes. If you are strict in your observance, consider preparing your own food on the road.

The European Vegetarian Guide to Restaurants and Hotels US$13.95, plus US$1.75 shipping) at Vegetarian Times Bookshelf (tel. (800) 435-9610, orders only).

The International Vegetarian Travel Guide (UK£2) was last published in 1991. Order back copies from the Vegetarian Society of the U.K. (VSUK), Parkdale, Dunham Rd., Altringham, Cheshire WA14 4QG (tel. (161) 928 07 93). VSUK also publishes other titles, including *The European Vegetarian Guide to Hotels and Restaurants.* US$12. Call or write for info.

The Jewish Travel Guide (US$12, postage US$1.75) lists synagogues, kosher restaurants, and Jewish institutions in over 80 countries. Available from Ballantine-Mitchell Publishers, Newbury House 890-900, Eastern Ave., Newbury Park, Ilford, Essex, U.K. IG2 7HH (tel. (0181) 599 88 66; fax 599 09 84). It is available in the U.S. from Sepher-Hermon Press, 1265 46th St., Brooklyn, NY 11219 (tel. (718) 972-9010; US$13.95 plus US$2.50 shipping).

MINORITY TRAVELERS

In France, as in much of the world, xenophobia and hate-crimes seem to be on the rise. The blood and soil National Front party, led by Jean-Marie Le Pen, emerged in the 1986 legislative elections and has since remained a major force in French electoral politics. In France, anti-immigrant sentiments toward North Africans and others were taken to a higher register in 1993, when Interior Minister Charles Pasqua proposed there be "zero immigration" (later amended to "zero illegal immigration"). The situation has been further exacerbated by the 1995 rash of Algerian terrorist attacks, provoking a wave of fear and anger among Parisians.

Those of Arab or North African descent may still face suspicious or derogatory glances from passersby. People of color might also find it difficult to gain entry to Paris's nightclubs, where unofficially discriminatory door policies can exclude non-whites, particularly those of Arab descent. Should you confront race-based exclusion or violence, you will be advised to make a formal complaint to the police. We encourage you to work through either SOS Racisme or MRAP in order to facilitate your progress through a confusing foreign bureaucracy.

S.O.S. Racisme, 1, rue Cail, 10ème (tel. 01 42 05 44 44 or 01 42 05 69 69). Occupied primarily with helping illegal immigrants and people whose documentation is irregular. They provide legal services and are used to negotiating with police.

MRAP (Mouvement contre le racisme et pour l'amitié entre les peuples), 89, rue Oberkampf, 11ème (tel. 01 43 14 83 53). Handles immigration issues and monitors racist publications and propaganda.

TRAVELING WITH CHILDREN

Since Disney annexed Hugo's classic *Nôtre-Dame de Paris,* the rug rats may be hankering for a hunk of brie. Paris is a wonderful place to travel with children, as long as you don't drag them to every possible museum, historic monument, church, and nearby château. Try following them for a change; you'll see the city in a new and very different light. Parks, most of which have playgrounds, fountains, and lots of interesting people-watching opportunities, provide excellent spots for a relaxed, fun, and very Parisian afternoon. Despite their miniature Izod shirts and fussy Benetton pullovers, French kids like to get just as messy as their American counterparts.

A climb up the tower of **Notre-Dame,** with its steep, winding stairs, its view of Paris at the top, and—most of all—its leering gargoyles, will liven up any child's tour of the cathedral. The **Jardin du Luxembourg** has a *guignol* (puppet show), pony rides, go-carts, a carousel, boats to rent and sail on the ponds, and swings with attendants who, for a tip, will push the swings while you catch up on Sartre. In the summer, the carnival at the **Tuileries** has rides suitable for all ages. Parents will enjoy the ferris wheel—with its outstanding view of central Paris—as much as their kids. **La Villette,** a huge science museum, aquarium, and Omnimax theater complex, offers an entire day's worth of innovative entertainment. The **Jardin d'Acclimatation** (tel. 01 45 01 88 91 or 01 40 67 97 66) in the **Bois de Boulogne** offers a children's zoo, a hall of mirrors, and a playground, for only 10F. Donkey rides and remote-control speed boats cost extra (7-10F). The **Jardin des Plantes** (with its museum La Grande Galérie de l'Evolution) and the Paris **Zoo** are also fun. Even the most clichéd sights, such as the Eiffel Tower and the *bateaux mouches* (tour boats on the Seine), rejuvenate jaded travelers when seen with children. Remember that not all museums in Paris are devoted to traditional art; flip through our Museum section for some more unusual selections. For a surrender to international capitalist homogeneity and children's occasionally unrefined tastes, take the RER out to **Disneyland Paris.** You may not like the idea of shaking hands with Mickey on "Main Street USA" while you're in France, but remember that your child put up with you in the Louvre.

In the culinary domain, don't fight the siren song of *le hot dog, le croque monsieur* (a grilled ham-and-cheese sandwich), *les frites* (french fries), or even the dreaded "McDonald's!" If your kids don't take to the subtleties of *haute cuisine,* they aren't any different from French kids. Not all restaurants have high chairs; you may want to ask first *("Est-ce que vous avez une chaise haute?").*

For bedtime stories before or during your trip, follow the 12 little girls around the sights of Paris in Hugo Bemelmans's *Madeleine* picture books. *Crin blanc* and *Le ballon rouge,* both by Albert La Morisse, are two stories that exemplify a peculiarly French sentimentality regarding early childhood. Kids will enjoy seeing scenes from them come to life on the streets of Paris. Goscinny and Sempé's *Le Petit Nicolas* and *Nicolas en Vacances* recount the antics of the mischievous little Nicolas and friends in rural France. The well-known Tintin and Astérix comics appeal to a wide range of ages, and the hardbound copies are both travel- and child-proof (well, almost).

The Paris magazine *L'Officiel des Spectacles* (2F) has a section entitled *Pour Les Jeunes* that lists current exhibits, programs, and movies appropriate for children (see "Publications About Paris," p. 71). For more general hints on traveling with children (and on parent-survival) see the following publications:

Take Your Kids to Europe by Cynthia W. Harriman (US$14). A budget travel guide geared towards families. Published by Mason-Grant Publications, P.O. Box 6547, Portsmouth, NH 03802 (tel. (603) 436-1608; fax (603) 427-0015; e-mail charriman@masongrant.com).

Travel with Children by Maureen Wheeler (US$11.95, postage US$1.50). Published by Lonely Planet Publications, Embarcadero West, 155 Filbert St., #251, Oakland,

CA 94607 (tel. (800) 275-8555 or (510) 893-8555; fax (510) 893-8563; e-mail info@lonelyplanet.com; http://www.lonelyplanet.com). Also P.O. Box 617, Hawthorn, Victoria 3122, Australia.

TRAVELING ALONE

There are many benefits to traveling alone, among them greater independence. Without distraction, you can write a travel log in the grand tradition of Mark Twain and John Steinbeck, and meet and interact with natives more easily. On the other hand, you may also be a more visible target for robbery and harassment. Solo travelers need to be well-organized and look confident at all times—no wandering around back alleys looking confused. If questioned, even casually, never admit that you are traveling alone. Try to maintain regular contact with someone who knows your itinerary. **A Foxy Old Woman's Guide to Traveling Alone** by Jay Ben-Lesser touches on practically every concern, offering anecdotes and tips for anyone interested in solitary adventure. It is available in bookstores and from Crossing Press in Freedom, CA (tel. (800) 777-1048; US$11).

Packing

Pack light: lay out everything you think you'll need, and pack only half of it. Remember that you can buy almost anything you'll need in Paris, and the more luggage you carry, the more alien you'll feel. The following are a few overlooked items to bring:

Daypack, rucksack, or courier bag: Bringing a smaller bag in addition to your pack or suitcase allows you to leave your big bag in the hotel while you go sight-seeing. More importantly, it can be used as an airplane carry-on; keep the absolute bare essentials with you to avoid the lost-luggage blues.

Walking shoes: Not a place to cut corners. Well-cushioned **sneakers** are good for walking. Bring a pair of **flip-flops** for protection against the foliage and fungi that inhabit some hostel showers. Talcum powder in your shoes and on your feet can prevent sores, and moleskin is great for blisters. Break shoes in before you leave.

Rain gear: Essential. A waterproof jacket will take care of you at a moment's notice. Gore-Tex® is a miracle fabric that's both waterproof and breathable, if expensive. Avoid cotton as outer-wear, it is useless when wet.

Sleepsacks: If planning to stay in youth hostels, make the requisite sleepsack yourself (instead of paying the linen charge). Fold a full size sheet in half the long way, then sew it closed along the open long side and one of the short sides.

The following items are perhaps more trouble than they are worth.

Electrical appliances: If you must take them, remember that electricity in France is 220 volts AC, enough to fry appliances made for North America's weak 110 volts. In France, sockets accommodate two-pin round plugs; get an **adapter.** If the appliance is not dual voltage, you'll also need a **converter** (US$15-18). Both can be purchased in most hardware stores, or wait until you arrive. For more information, contact **Franzus,** Murtha Industrial Park, P.O. Box 142, Railroad Ave., Beacon Falls, CT 06403 (tel. (203) 723-6664; fax (203) 723-6666), for their free pamphlet, *Foreign Electricity is No Deep Dark Secret.*

Camera equipment: If you take expensive equipment abroad, it's best to register everything with customs at the airport before departure. Buy a supply of film before you leave; it's more expensive in France. Unless you're shooting with 1000 ASA or more, airport X-rays should not harm your pictures. It never hurts, however, to buy a lead pouch, available at any camera store. Either way, pack film in your carry-on, since the X-rays employed on checked baggage are much stronger.

Computers: If you're bringing a laptop computer, be sure to have both computer and discs hand-inspected, lest stray X-rays wipe out your as-yet-unpublished *chef-d'oeuvre.* Officials will ask you to turn it on, so be sure the batteries are loaded. Think twice about shipping a desktop computer; most arrive in pieces, if at all.

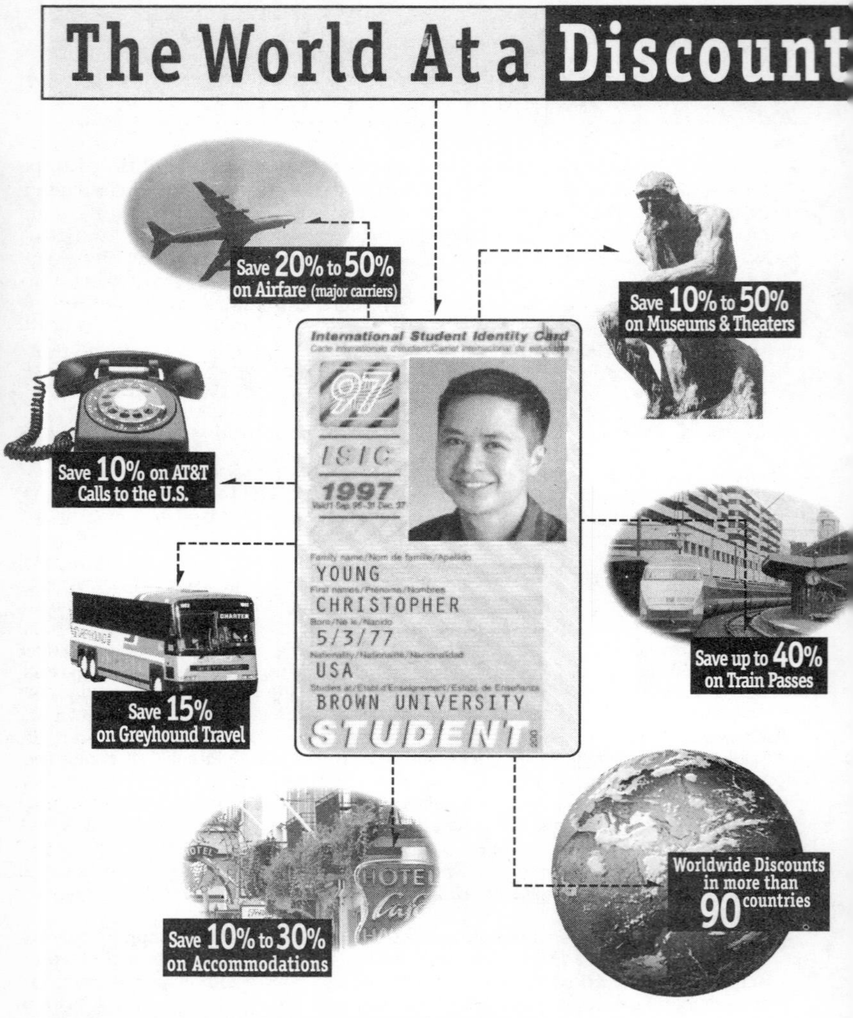

ESSENTIALS

GETTING THERE

Student and Budget Travel Agencies

The following budget travel organizations typically offer discounted flights for students and youths, railpasses, ISICs and other identification cards, hostel memberships, travel gear, travel guides, and general expertise in budget travel.

Council Travel (http://www.ciee.org/cts/ctshome.htm), the travel division of Council, is a full-service travel agency specializing in youth and budget travel. They offer discount airfares, railpasses, hosteling cards, low-cost accommodations, guidebooks, budget tours, travel gear, and international student (ISIC), youth (GO25), and teacher (ITIC) identity cards. U.S. offices include: Emory Village, 1561 N. Decatur Rd., **Atlanta,** GA 30307 (tel. (404) 377-9997); 2000 Guadalupe, **Austin,** TX 78705 (tel. (512) 472-4931); 273 Newbury St., **Boston,** MA 02116 (tel. (617) 266-1926); 1138 13th St., **Boulder,** CO 80302 (tel. (303) 447-8101); 1153 N. Dearborn, **Chicago,** IL 60610 (tel. (312) 951-0585); 10904 Lindbrook Dr., **Los Angeles,** CA 90024 (tel. (310) 208-3551); 1501 University Ave. SE, **Minneapolis,** MN 55414 (tel. (612) 379-2323); 205 E. 42nd St., **New York,** NY 10017 (tel. (212) 822-2700); 953 Garnet Ave., **San Diego,** CA 92109 (tel. (619) 270-6401); 530 Bush St., **San Francisco,** CA 94108 (tel. (415) 421-3473); 4311½ University Way, **Seattle,** WA 98105 (tel. (206) 632-2448); 3300 M St. NW, **Washington, D.C.** 20007 (tel. (202) 337-6464). **For U.S. cities not listed,** call 888-COUNCIL (268-6245). Also 28A Poland St. (Oxford Circus), **London,** W1V 3DB (tel. (0171) 437 7767); 22 Rue des Pyramides 75001; **Paris** (01 44 55 55 65).

STA Travel, 6560 Scottsdale Rd. #F100, Scottsdale, AZ 85253 (tel. (800) 777-0112 nationwide; fax (602) 922-0793). A student and youth travel organization with over 100 offices worldwide offering discount airfares for young travelers, railpasses, accommodations, tours, insurance, and ISICs. 16 offices in the U.S. including: 297 Newbury Street, **Boston,** MA 02115 (tel. (617) 266-6014); 429 S. Dearborn St., **Chicago,** IL 60605 (tel. (312) 786-9050); 7202 Melrose Ave., **Los Angeles,** CA 90046 (tel. (213) 934-8722); 10 Downing St., Ste. G, **New York,** NY 10003 (tel. (212) 627-3111); 4341 University Way NE, **Seattle,** WA 98105 (tel. (206) 633-5000); 2401 Pennsylvania Ave., **Washington, D.C.** 20037 (tel. (202) 887-0912); 51 Grant Ave., **San Francisco,** CA 94108 (tel. (415) 391-8407); **Miami,** FL 33133 (tel. (305) 461-3444). In the U.K., 6 Wrights Ln., **London** W8 6TA (tel. (0171) 938 47 11 for North American travel). In New Zealand, 10 High St., **Auckland** (tel. (09) 309 97 23). In Australia, 222 Faraday St., **Melbourne** VIC 3050 (tel. (03) 349 69 11).

Let's Go Travel, Harvard Student Agencies, 67 Mount Auburn St., Cambridge, MA 02138 (800-5-LETS GO/553-8746) or (617) 495-9649). Railpasses, HI-AYH memberships, ISICs, ITICs, FIYTO cards, *Let's Go* guidebooks, maps, bargain flights, and budget travel gear. All items available by mail; call or write for a catalog.

Campus Travel, 52 Grosvenor Gardens, London, England SW1W 0AG; http://www.campustravel.co.uk. Telephone booking service: in Europe call (0171) 730 3402; in North America call (0171) 730 2101; worldwide call (0171) 730 8111; in Manchester call (0161) 273 1721; in Scotland (0131) 668 3303). 41 branches in the U.K. Student and youth fares on plane, train, boat, and bus travel. Flexible airline tickets. Discount and ID cards for youths, travel insurance for students and those under 35, and maps and guides. Puts out travel suggestion booklets.

Travel CUTS (Canadian Universities Travel Services Limited): 187 College St., **Toronto,** Ontario M5T 1P7 (tel. (416) 979-2406; fax (416) 979-8167; e-mail mail@travelcuts). Canada's national student travel bureau and equivalent of Council, with 40 offices across Canada. Also in the U.K., 295-A Regent St., **London** W1R 7YA (tel. (0171) 637 3161). Discounted domestic and international airfares open to all; special student fares to all destinations with ISIC. Issues ISIC, FIYTO, GO25, and HI hostel cards, as well as railpasses. Offers free *Student Traveller* magazine, as well as information on the Student Work Abroad Program (SWAP).

Usit Youth and Student Travel, 19-21 Aston Quay, O'Connell Bridge, **Dublin** 2 (tel. (01) 677 8117; fax (01) 679 8833). In the USA: New York Student Center, 895 Amsterdam Ave., **New York,** NY, 10025 (tel. (212) 663 5435). Additional offices throughout Ireland. Specializes in youth and student travel. Offers low cost tickets and flexible travel arrangements. Supplies ISIC and GO25 cards.

By Plane

Finding a cheap airfare amid the confusion that the airlines deliberately create will be easier if you understand the system better than the airlines think you do. Call every toll-free number and ask about discounts. Have a knowledgeable travel agent (or two) guide you through the options. Students and people under 26 should never pay full price for a ticket (see "Student and Budget Travel Agencies," p. 51). Many airlines offer senior traveler deals or airline passes and discounts for seniors' companions as well. Outfox airline reps with the phonebook-sized *Official Airline Guide* (at large libraries); this monthly guide lists every scheduled flight in the world (including prices). **TravelHUB** (http://www.travelhub.com) finds travel agencies on the web; the **Air Traveler's Handbook** (http://www.cis.ohio-state.edu/hypertext/faq/usenet/travel/air/handbook/top.html) is a clearinghouse for air travel info.

Most airlines maintain a fare structure that peaks between mid-June and early September. Midweek (Mon.-Thurs.) flights run about US$30-40 cheaper each way than on weekends. Leaving from a travel hub such as New York, Atlanta, Dallas, Chicago, Los Angeles, San Francisco, Vancouver, Toronto, Melbourne, or Sydney will win you a better fare than you'd get leaving from smaller cities; the gains are not as great when departing from travel hubs monopolized by one airline, so call around. Flying to London is usually the cheapest way across the Atlantic, though special fares to other cities—such as Amsterdam, Luxembourg, or Brussels—can cost even less. A New York-Paris round-trip summer student fare should cost $800 at absolute most.

Traveling with an "open return" ticket can be pricier than fixing a return date and paying to change it. Avoid one-way tickets, too: the return fares can be outrageous; it may be cheaper to throw away the return portion of a roundtrip ticket. When flying internationally, pick up your ticket in advance of the departure date and arrive at the airport several hours before your flight with plenty of identification.

COMMERCIAL AIRLINES

The commercial airlines' lowest offer is the **APEX** (Advance Purchase Excursion Fare); specials advertised in newspapers may be cheaper, but have more restrictions and fewer available seats. APEX fares provide confirmed reservations and allow "open-jaw" tickets (landing in and returning from different cities). Reservations must usually be made at least 21 days in advance, with 7- to 14-day minimum and 60- to 90-day maximum stay limitations, and hefty cancellation and change-of-reservation penalties. For summer travel, book APEX fares early. Call **Air France** (tel. (800) 237-2747) and ask for student discounts; be sure to inquire about restrictions.

Most airlines no longer offer standby fares; standby has given way to the **three-day-advance-purchase youth fare.** It's available only to those under 25 (sometimes 24) and only within three days of departure—a gamble that could backfire if the airline's booked (watch out in summer). Return dates are open, but you must come back within a year, and you can book your return seat no more than three days ahead. Youth fares in summer aren't really cheaper than APEX, but off-season prices drop precipitously. Call **Icelandair** (tel. (800) 223-5500) or **Virgin Atlantic Airways** (tel. (800) 862-8621) for info on their last-minute offers. Icelandair also offers a Supergrouper plan that takes travelers to Luxembourg and back.

TICKET CONSOLIDATORS

Ticket consolidators resell unsold tickets on commercial and charter airlines that might otherwise have gone begging. There is rarely a maximum age; tickets are also heavily discounted, and may offer extra flexibility or bypass advance purchase requirements. Unlike tickets bought through an airline, however, you won't be able to use your tickets on another flight if you miss yours, and you will have to go back to the consolidator—not the airline—to get a refund. Consolidators come in three varieties: wholesale, who sell only to travel agencies; specialty agencies (both wholesale and retail); and **"bucket shops"** or discount retail agencies. Look for bucket shops' tiny ads in weekend papers (in the U.S., the *Sunday New York Times* is best). In London, the bucket shop center, the Air Travel Advisory Bureau (tel. (0171) 636-5000) provides a list of consolidators.

Be a smart shopper. Among the many reputable and trustworthy companies are, unfortunately, some wheeler-dealers. Ask to receive your tickets as quickly as possible so you have time to fix any problems. Keep a record of your conversations with the company, including dates and times of calls and the full name of the salesperson helping you. Get the company's policy in writing: insist on a **receipt** that gives full details about tickets, refunds, and restrictions. It may be worth paying with a credit card (despite the 2-5% fee) so you can stop payment if you don't receive your tickets. Beware of the "bait and switch" gag: shady firms will advertise a super-low fare and then tell a caller that it is sold-out. This is a viable excuse, but if they can't offer you a price near the advertised fare on *any* date, it may be a sign of trouble ahead.

CHARTER FLIGHTS

The theory behind a charter is that a tour operator contracts with an airline (usually a fairly obscure one that specializes in charters) to use its planes to fly extra loads of passengers to peak-season destinations. Charter flights thus fly less frequently than major airlines and have correspondingly more restrictions. They are also almost always fully booked. Schedules and itineraries may change at the last moment and flights may be cancelled suddenly; pay with a credit card. You'll probably be better off with a scheduled airline. You might also consider travelers insurance against trip interruption. Find charters through **Interworld** (tel. (305) 443-4929); **Travac** (tel. (800) 872-8800) or **Rebel** in Valencia, CA (tel. (800) 227-3235) and Orlando, FL (tel. (800) 732-3588). Don't be afraid to call every number and hunt for the best deal.

STAND-BY SERVICES

Two stand-by travel companies offer a mile-high version of hitchhiking. **Airhitch,** 2641 Broadway, Third Floor, New York, NY 10025 (tel. (800) 326-2009 or (212) 864-2000) and Los Angeles, CA (tel. (310) 726-5000), adds a certain thrill to the prospects of when you will leave and where exactly you will end up. Complete flexibility on both sides of the Atlantic is necessary; flights cost US$169 each way when departing from the Northeast, US$269 from the West Coast or Northwest, and US$229 from the Southeast and Midwest. The snag is that you buy not a ticket, but the promise that you will get to a destination near where you're intending to go within a window of time (usually 5 days) from a location in a region you've specified. You call in before your date-range to hear all of your flight options for the next seven days and your probability of boarding. You then decide which flights you want to try to make and present a voucher at the airport which grants you the right to board a flight on a space-available basis. This procedure must be followed for the return trip. Be aware that you may only receive a refund if all available flights which departed within your date and destination-range were full. Their Paris office (tel. 01 47 00 16 30) is the main European office where you can register for your return.

Air-Tech, Ltd., 584 Broadway #1007, New York, NY 10012 (tel. (212) 219-7000, fax (212) 219-0066) offers a very similar service. Their travel window is one to four days; rates to and from Europe (continually updated; call and verify) are: Northeast US$169; West Coast US$249; Midwest/Southeast US$199. Upon registration and payment, Air-Tech sends you a FlightPass with a contact date falling soon before your travel window, when you are to call them for flight instructions. Note that the service is one-way—you must go through the same procedure to return—and that *no* *refunds* are granted unless the company fails to get you a seat before your travel window expires. Air-Tech also arranges courier and regular flights at discount rates.

Be sure to read all the fine print in your agreements with either company. It is difficult to receive refunds, and the companies' vouchers will not be honored if an airline fails to receive timely payment from them. Note also that your "savings" in ticket prices may turn quickly into bills for lodgings and food while you wait for a flight, or travel to and from the cities that have available tickets.

Eleventh-hour **discount clubs** and **fare brokers** offer members savings on European travel, including charter flights and tour packages. Research your options carefully. **Last Minute Travel Club,** 1249 Boylston St., Boston, MA 02215 (tel. (800) 527-8646 or (617) 267-9800), and **Discount Travel International** New York, NY (tel. (212) 362-3636; fax 362-3236) are among the few travel clubs that don't charge a membership fee. Others include **Moment's Notice** New York, NY (tel. (718) 234-6295; fax (718) 234 6450) for air tickets, tours, and hotels (US$25 annual fee); **Travelers Advantage**, Stanford, CT, (tel. (800) 835-8747; US$49 annual fee); and **Travel Avenue** (tel. (800) 333-3335). Study these organizations' contracts closely; you don't want to end up with an unwanted overnight layover.

COURIER COMPANIES

Those who travel light should consider flying to Europe as a courier. As a courier, you register with a courier company and trade your baggage allowance for a steep discount on a roundtrip ticket. The company hiring you will use your checked luggage space for freight; you're only allowed to bring carry-ons. You are responsible for the safe delivery of the baggage claim slips (given to you by a courier company representative) to the representative waiting for you when you arrive. You will probably never see the cargo you are transporting—the company handles it all—and airport officials know that couriers are not responsible for the baggage checked for them.

Restrictions to watch for: you must be over 18, have a valid passport, and procure your own visa (if necessary); most flights are roundtrip only with short fixed-length stays (usually one week); only solo tickets are issued (but a companion may be able to get a next-day flight); and most flights are from New York. The service isn't always a money-saver; roundtrip fares to Western Europe from the U.S. range from US$250-400 (in the off-season) to US$400-700 (in summer). **NOW Voyager,** 74 Varick St. #307, New York, NY 10013 (tel. (212) 431-1616), acts as an agent for many courier flights. They offer last-minute deals to such cities as London, Paris, and Rome for as little as US$200 roundtrip plus a US$50 annual registration fee. Other agents to try are **Halbart Express,** 147-05 176th St., Jamaica, NY 11434 (tel. (718) 656-5000), and **Discount Travel International**, (tel. (212) 362-3636).

Check your bookstore or library for handbooks such as *The Courier Air Travel Handbook* (US$10 plus US$3.50 shipping) which explains how to travel as an air courier and contains names, phone numbers, and contact points of courier companies. It can be ordered directly from Bookmasters, Inc., P.O. Box 2039, Mansfield, OH 44905 (tel. (800) 507-2665).

By Ferry

Ferries link France with England and Ireland. From the French ferry ports, you will be able to catch a train to Paris. Le Havre has the fastest road connections to Paris.

Brittany Ferries (tel. (01752) 22 13 21 or (01705) 82 77 01) run from Portsmouth to Caen (3 per day, 6-7hr.; Jan.-March and Nov.-Dec. 140F, students 120F; April-June and Sept.-Oct. 180F, students 160F; July-Aug. 225F, students 210F), from Poole to Cherbourg (1-2 per day, 2½hr., overnight 5hr.; one-way or 5-day return Nov.-March 270-330F, students 220-290F; April-Oct. 390-430F, students 350-380F.), from Plymouth to Roscoff (5hr.; June-Sept. 1 per day, 240F, students 220F; April-May and Oct. 1 per day, 200F, students 180F; Nov.-March 2-5 per week, 155F, students 135F), from Portsmouth to St-Malo (1 per day March 12-Nov. 15, irregular service Nov. 16-March 11; April-Oct. 19, 210F, students 180F. Oct. 20-March 31 180F, students 150F; 7hr., same prices for 5-day return), and from Poole to St-Malo (May-Sept. only; 4 per week; 8½hr.; May-June and Sept. 200-240F, students 180-210F; July-Aug. 240-250F, students 210-230F; same prices for 5-day return).

Irish Ferries (tel. (01) 661 05 11) offer year-round service from Rosslare in Ireland to Le Havre (8-13 per month, 20hr. overnight, May-June and Sept. 530F, students 450F; July 1-5 and Aug. 11-31 580F, students 500F; July 6-Aug. 10 635F, students 555F; Oct.-April 415F, students 335F), and from Rosslare to Cherbourg (June-Aug. 2 per week; Sept.-May 1 per week; 16hr. overnight; July 1-5 and Aug. 11-31 580F, students 500F; July 6-Aug. 10 635F, students 555F; May-June and Sept. 530F, students 450F; Oct.-April 415F, students 335F). During the summer, they also run ferries from Cork to Le Havre (June-Aug. 1 per week, 20½hr. overnight, same prices as Rosslare-Le Havre). Eurailpass holders travel free after paying a 30F tax.

P&O European Ferries (tel. (0181) 575 85 55) cross from Dover to Calais (every 45min., 1¼hr., oneway or 5-day return 220F, open return 440F) and from Portsmouth to Cherbourg (4 per day, 5hr., 9hr. overnight; Jan.-March 24 and Nov.-Dec. 170F; March 25-July 22 and Sept. 5-Oct. 190F; July 23-Sept. 4 280F).

Sealink Stena Lines (tel. (01233) 64 70 47 or (01233) 24 02 80) chug from Southampton to Cherbourg (2-3 per day, 6hr., oneway or 5-day return April-Dec. 24 180F, students 170F; Jan.-March 31 110F, students 90F), and from Newhaven to Dieppe (4 per day, Jan.-Feb. 3 per day, 3hr., 220F, students 200F, bikes free).

Traveling by **hovercraft** is quicker (50min.), but you should book in advance. **Hoverspeed** (tel. 1304 240 241) departs for Calais or Boulogne from Dover, with extra craft operating to Dunkerque from Ramsgate during the summer (oneway or 5-day return 240F). Service is suspended in rough weather.

ESSENTIALS

GETTING IN AND OUT OF PARIS

Please consult "Public Transportation," p. 73, for details on transport and taxis.

From the Airports

ROISSY-CHARLES DE GAULLE

Most transatlantic flights land at **Aéroport Roissy-Charles de Gaulle,** 23km northeast of Paris. As a general rule, Terminal 2 serves Air France and its affiliates (recorded arrivals and departures tel. 08 36 68 10 48, live operator tel. 01 44 08 24 24; 9am-9pm). Most other carriers operate from Terminal 1; for info call the 24-hr. English-speaking passenger information center at 01 48 62 22 80.

The two cheapest and fastest ways to get into the city from Roissy-Charles de Gaulle and vice versa make use of the RATP local transit system (tel. 08 36 68 77 14). The **Roissy Rail** bus-train combination begins with a free shuttle bus from Aérogare 1 arrival level gate 28, Aérogare 2A gate 5, Aérogare 2B gate 6, or Aérogare 2D gate 6 to the Roissy train station. From there, the **RER B3** (one of the Parisian commuter rail lines) will transport you to central Paris. To transfer to the metro, get off at **Gare du Nord, Châtelet-Les Halles,** or **St-Michel,** which are both RER and metro stops. To go to Roissy-Charles de Gaulle from Paris, take the RER B3, any train with a name starting with the letter "E", to "Roissy," which is the end of the line. Then change to the free shuttle bus (RER daily 5am-12:30am, every 15min., train 30–35min., bus 10min., 45F). For more direct service to the airport, the **Roissybus** (tel. 01 48 04 18 24) runs from in front of the American Express office on rue Scribe, near M. Opéra, to gate 10 of Terminal 2A (which also serves terminal 2C), to gate 12 of Terminal 2D (which also serves Terminal 2B), and to gate 30 of Terminal 1, arrivals level (every 15min., to airport 5:45am-11pm, from airport 6am-11pm, 45min., 40F).

Alternatively, daily **Air France Buses** (tel. 01 44 08 24 24) run to and from the **Arc de Triomphe** (M. Charles de Gaulle-Etoile) at 1, av. Carnot (every 12min. 5:40am-11pm, 35min., 55F); to and from the **pl. de la Porte de Maillot/Palais des Congrès** (M. Porte de Maillot), near the Air France booking agency (same schedule and prices); and to and from 13, bd du Vaugirard near the **Gare Montparnasse** (M. Montparnasse-Bienvenue; to the airport hourly 7am-9am and 2pm-9pm, every ½hr. 9am-2pm; from the airport hourly 6:30am-7:30pm, 45min., 65F). At Roissy, the shuttle stops between terminals 2A and 2C; between 2B and 2D; and at terminal 1 on the arrivals level, outside exit 34. Call 01 41 56 89 00 for recorded information, available in English, on all Air France airport shuttles.

Taxis take at least 50 minutes to the center of Paris and cost about 250F during the day, 280F at night.

ORLY

Aéroport d'Orly (tel. 01 49 75 15 15 for info, in English 6am-midnight), 12km south of the city, is used by charters and many continental flights. From Orly Sud gate H or gate I, platform 1, or Orly Ouest arrival level gate F, take the shuttle bus known as Orly-Rail (every 15min. 5:40am-11:15pm) to the **Pont de Rungis/Aéroport d'Orly** train stop where you can board the **RER C2** for a number of destinations in Paris (daily 5:50am-11pm, every 15min., 25min., 30F; call RATP at 08 36 68 77 14 (French) or 08 36 68 41 14 (English) for info). The **Jetbus** (every 12min. 5:45am-11:30pm, 22F), provides a quick connection between Orly Sud- gate H- platform 2, or Orly Ouest arrival level gate C and M. Villejuif-Louis Aragon on line 7of the metro.

Another option is the **RATP Orlyval** (tel. 01 43 46 14 14) combination of metro, RER, and VAL rail shuttle. To get to Orly, buy a combined Orlyval ticket (52F), take the metro to Gare du Nord, Châtelet-les-Halles, St-Michel, or Denfert-Rochereau, and change to the RER B. Make sure that the station Antony-Orly is lit up on the changing

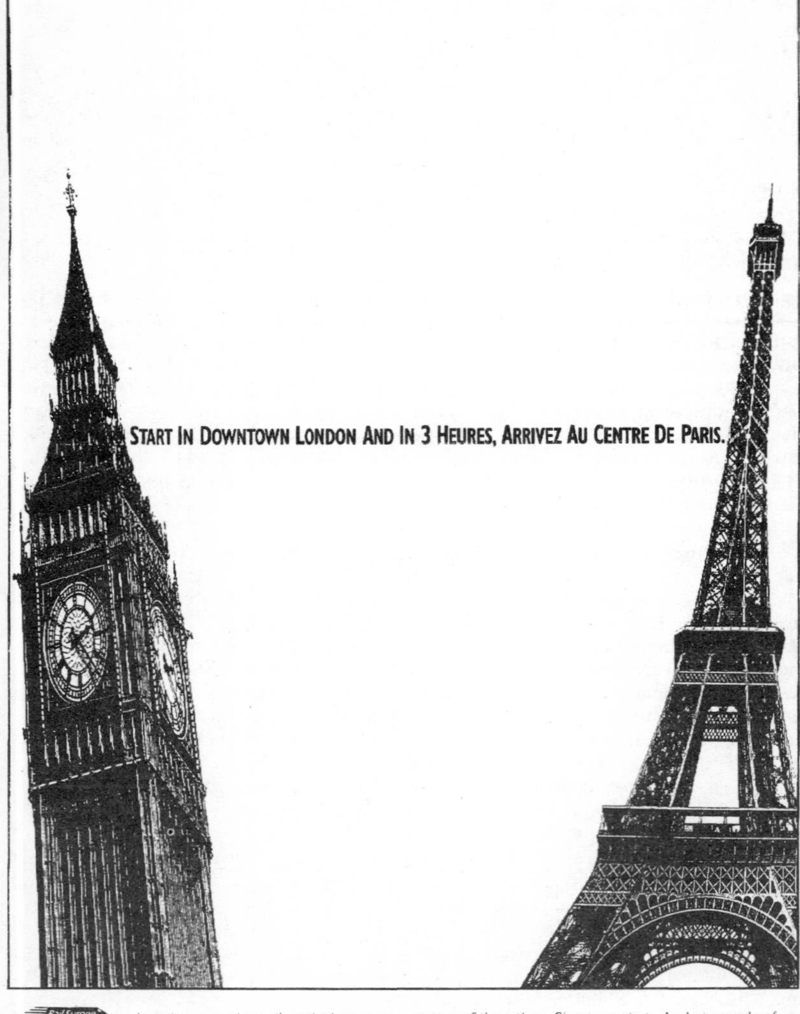
START IN DOWNTOWN LONDON AND IN 3 HEURES, ARRIVEZ AU CENTRE DE PARIS.

schedule panel next to the track (see "RER," p. 74). Get off at Antony-Orly and transfer to the VAL train. Reverse these instructions to enter the city from Orly, and remember that with the combined ticket, your subsequent transfers in the Paris metro are included. From the airport, buy a ticket at an RATP office (Ouest gate W level 1 or gate J level O; sud gate E or gate F, baggage area). Note that weekly or monthly yellow or orange cards are not valid for Orlyval. (VAL trains run from Antony to Orly Mon.-Sat. 6am-10:30pm and Sun. 7am-10:55pm; trains arrive at Orly Ouest 2min. after reaching Orly Sud. They run from Orly to Antony Mon.-Sat. 6am-10:30pm and Sun. 7am-10:57pm, every 7min., 30min. from Châtelet.)

Air France Buses run between Orly Montparnasse, 36, rue de Maine, 6ème (M. Montparnasse-Bienvenue), and the Invalides Air France agency, 2, rue Robert Esnault Pelterie (every 12min., 30 min., 40F). Air France shuttles stop at Orly Sud, gate F and Orly Ouest, gate E, arrivals level. In addition, the RATP runs **Orlybus** to and from metro and RER stop Denfert-Rochereau, 14ème. Board at Orly Sud gate H, platform 4 or Orly Ouest level O, gate J (Mon.-Fri. every 13min., Sat.-Sun. every 16-20min., 6am-11pm, 30min., 30F).

Taxis from Orly to town cost at least 120F during the day, 160F at night and on weekends. Allow at least 45 minutes for the trip.

ESSENTIALS

LE BOURGET

Paris's third airport, **Le Bourget** (tel. 01 48 62 12 12), is most remembered as Charles Lindbergh's landing site after his historic transatlantic flight. In odd-numbered years, it now hosts an internationally renowned air show, the **Salon International de l'Aéronautique et de l'Espace.** For the most part, however, Le Bourget is used for charter flights, generally within France. Should you land at Le Bourget, take **Bus #350** (every 15min. 6:10am-11:50pm, 2 metro tickets) to Gare du Nord or Gare de l'Est. **Bus #152** also makes these stops and, for the same price, will take you to Porte de la Villette, where you can catch the metro or another bus.

From the Train Stations

Each of Paris's six train stations is a veritable community of its own, with resident street people and police, cafés, *tabacs,* and banks, plus stores selling perfume and Flashdance fashions. Locate the ticket counters *(guichets),* the platforms *(quais),* and the tracks *(voies),* and you will be ready to roll. Each terminal has two divisions: the *banlieue* and the *grandes lignes.* **Grandes lignes** depart for and arrive from distant cities in France and other countries—each of the six stations serves destinations in a particular region of France or Europe. Trains to the **banlieue** serve the suburbs of Paris and make frequent stops. Within a given station, each of these divisions has its own ticket counters, information booths, and timetables; distinguishing between them before you get in line will save you hours of frustration. Don't forget to **"composter" your ticket** (time-stamp it) at the orange machines on the platform before you board the train, or you may be slapped with a heavy fine. All train stations are reached by at least two metro lines; the metro stop bears the same name as the train station. For **train information** or to make reservations, call the SNCF at 08 36 35 35 35 (2F23 Per min.), or use Minitel 3615 SNCF (see "Minitel," p. 68; reservations open daily 7am-9:30pm). The SNCF line may seem perpetually busy—visiting a local travel agency will let you buy your tickets or make your reservations with more personal attention and little or no fee. There is a free telephone with direct access to the stations on the right-hand side of the Champs-Elysées tourist office. In addition, there are yellow automatic guichets known as **Billetterie** at every train station; if you know your PIN, you can use a Mastercard, Visa or American Express to buy your own tickets. Mastercard and Visa are also accepted at the ticket booths. Some cities can be accessed by both regular and **très grande vitesse (TGV;** very fast speed) trains. TGVs are faster (hence the name) but more expensive; they also require reservations that cost a small fee. Regular trains require no reservations; this means that tickets for regular trains can be used as far after purchase date as you wish, although they must be used within 24hrs. of being stamped.

A word on safety: though full of atmosphere, each terminal also shelters its share of thieves and other undesirables. Gare du Nord becomes rough at night, when drugs and prostitution take over; Gare d'Austerlitz can also be unfriendly. Be cautious in and around stations. In many stations and metro stops, you will encounter friendly-looking people who will try to sell you a train or metro ticket at exorbitant prices. It is not advisable to buy anything in the stations except at official counters.

A number of special discounts can be applied to point-to-point tickets purchased in France. The **Carrissimo,** available for travelers under 25 years old, offers discounts of 20-50%; the **Carte Vermeil** entitles travelers over 60 to similar discounts. Another reduction, **Prix Joker,** is for tickets reserved 30-60 days in advance. All of these discounts may be shared with your friends if they fit into the same age categories. These discounts are sold only in Europe; inquire at major train stations for other discounts, including ones for couples and families.

Note: The following prices are for one-way, second class tickets unless otherwise noted. In general, prices vary according to the day of the week, season, and other criteria. Call ahead.

Gare du Nord: Trains to northern France, Britain, Belgium, the Netherlands, Scandinavia, the Commonwealth of Independent States, and northern Germany (Cologne, Hamburg). To: Brussels (19 per day, 2hr., 220F); Amsterdam (6 per day., 5hr., 366F); Cologne (6 per day, 5-6hr., 332F); Boulogne (18 per day, 2½hr., 163F); Copenhagen (1 direct, 2 indirect per day, 16hr., 1343F); London (by the Eurostar chunnel, 7-9 per day, 2hr., 410-645F one way).

Gare de l'Est: To eastern France (Champagne, Alsace, Lorraine), Luxembourg, parts of Switzerland (Basel, Zürich, Lucerne), southern Germany (Frankfurt, Munich), Austria, and Hungary. To: Zürich (7 per day, 6hr., 412F); Munich (4 per day, 13hr., 613F); and Vienna (2 per day, 13hr., 923F).

Gare de Lyon: To southern and southeastern France (Lyon, Provence, Riviera), parts of Switzerland (Geneva, Lausanne, Berne), Italy, and Greece. To: Geneva (6 per day, 3½hr., 498F); Florence (1 per day, 12hr., 650F); Rome (3-4 per day, 14-16hr., 630F); Lyon (20 per day, 2hr., 286-381F); Nice (12 per day, 7hr., 300-432F); Marseille (10 per day, 4-5hr., 180-357F).

Gare d'Austerlitz: To the Loire Valley, southwestern France (Bordeaux, Pyrénées), Spain, and Portugal. TGV service to southwestern France leaves from Gare Montparnasse. To: Barcelona (3 per day, 12-14hr., 600F) and Madrid (4 per day, 12-16hr., 600F).

Gare St-Lazare: To Normandy. To: Caen (10-15 per day, 2½hr., 153F); Rouen (20 per day, 1½hr., 102F).

Gare Montparnasse: To Brittany, and the TGV to southwestern France. To: Rennes (15 per day, 2-2½hr., 258F plus 32-80F TGV reservation).

From the Bus Stations

Most international buses to Paris arrive at **Gare Routière Internationale du Paris-Gallieni,** 28, av. du Général de Gaulle, Bagnolet 93170 **Eurolines** (tel. 01 49 72 51 51; Minitel 3615 Eurolines; M. Gallieni). Call ahead, check Minitel, or go by to pick up schedules for departures to other European countries. For reservations on buses to England, contact **Hoverspeed Voyages** (tel. (16) 21 46 14 14; Minitel 3615 Hoverspeed). The Paris office of **Hoverspeed Voyages** is at 75, av, des Champs-Elysées, 8ème. The company's Paris terminal is located at 165, av. de Clichy, 17ème (tel. 01 40 25 22 00; M. Porte du Clichy), where passengers are deposited and picked up.

Hitchhiking and Ridesharing

While *auto-stop* (hitchhiking) is more common in Europe than in the States, don't feel pressured to save money by putting yourself at risk. Women should never hitch-hike alone or in pairs. And anyone who values their own safety will take a train or bus out of Paris. *Let's Go* does not recommend hitchhiking, and no information in this book is intended to encourage this often dangerous practice.

For a registered and probably safer "hitch," **Allostop-Provoya,** 8, rue Rochambeau, 9ème (in Paris tel. 01 53 20 42 42; Minitel 3615 Provoya; M. Strasbourg-St-Denis), will try to match you with a driver going your way. All fees included, the following approximate prices cover one-way trips out of Paris: to Brussels about 111F; to Frankfurt 186F; to Cologne 153F; to Geneva 173F. An economical way to travel—and a way to meet people. Open Mon.-Fri. 9am-7:30pm, Sat. 9am-1pm and 2-6pm.

ONCE THERE

Embassies and Consulates

If anything serious goes wrong, make your first inquiry to your country's consulate in Paris. The distinction between an embassy and a consulate is significant: an embassy houses the offices of the ambassador and his or her staff; you won't gain access unless you know someone inside. All facilities for dealing with nationals are in the consulate. If your passport gets lost or stolen, your status in France is immediately rendered illegal—go to the consulate as soon as possible to get a replacement. A consulate is also able to lend (not give) up to 100F per day (interest free), but you will be forced to prove you are truly desperate, and with no other source of money. The consulate can give you lists of local lawyers and doctors, notify family members of accidents, and give information on how to proceed with legal problems, but its functions end there. Don't ask the consulate to pay your hotel or medical bills, investigate crimes, obtain work permits, post bail, or interfere with standard French legal proceedings. If you are arrested during your stay in France, there is little, if anything, that your own government can do to help you.

U.S.: 2, av. Gabriel, 8ème (tel. 01 43 12 22 22; fax 01 42 66 97 83), off pl. de la Concorde. M. Concorde. Open Mon.-Fri. 9am-6pm. **Consulate** at 2, rue St-Florentin (tel. 01 43 12 48 45 or 01 40 39 82 91 for automated information), 3 blocks away. Passports replaced for $55 (under 18 $30). Open Mon.-Fri. 9am-3pm. Closed for both American and French holidays.

Canada: 35, av. Montaigne, 8ème (tel. 01 44 43 29 00). M. Franklin-Roosevelt or Alma-Marceau. Open Mon.-Fri. 9am-noon and 2-5pm. **Consulate** at same tel. and address. Ask for "consular services;" you will need to make an appointment. New passport 380F. Open Mon.-Fri. 9:30-10:30am and 2-3pm.

U.K.: 35, rue du Faubourg-St-Honoré, 8ème (tel. 01 42 66 91 42). M. Concorde or Madeleine. **Consulate** at 16, rue d'Anjou (same phone). M. Concorde. New passport 144F, cash only. Open Mon.-Fri. 9:30am-noon and 2:30-5pm. Visa bureau open Mon.-Fri. 9:30am-noon.

Australia: Embassy at 4, rue Jean-Rey, 15ème (tel. 01 40 59 33 00; fax 01 40 59 33 10). M. Bir-Hakeim. **Consular services:** new passport 450F. Open Mon.-Fri. 9:30am-noon and 2-4pm.

New Zealand: Embassy at 7ter, rue Léonard de Vinci, 16ème (tel. 01 45 00 24 11; fax 01 45 01 26 39). M. Victor-Hugo. New passport 880F, children 660F. Open Mon.-Thurs. 9am-1pm and 2-5:30pm, Fri. 9am-2pm.

Ireland: Embassy at 12, av. Foch, 16ème (tel. 01 45 00 20 87; passport services fax 01 45 00 81 50). M. Argentine. Open 9:30am-noon. **Consular Services** at same phone and address. New passport 380F, children 85F. Open 9:30am-noon.

South Africa: Embassy at 59, quai d'Orsay, 7ème (tel. 01 45 55 92 37; fax 01 47 53 99 70). M. Invalides. New passport 100F. Passports are processed only in South Africa and take 6-8 weeks to arrive. Open Mon.-Fri. 9am-noon.

ESSENTIALS

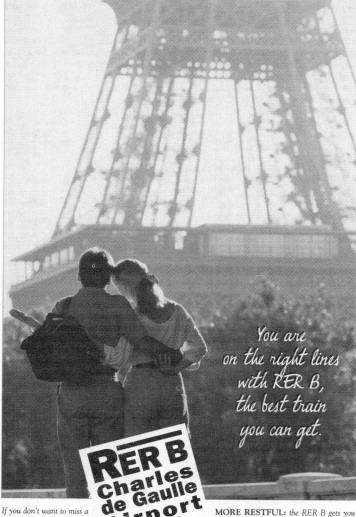

Tourist Offices

Though packed in the summer, the following offices are usually able to keep the wait down to an hour at most. Lines are worst in the afternoon. They all stock the requisite reams of brochures, maps, and pamphlets, as well as information on special seasonal events. Tourist offices will help you find a room in a one-star hotel for 20F, two-star for 25F, three-star for 40F, and hostels for 8F, but they can only arrange for a room the day of your arrival. The central branch also exchanges currency at decent rates with no commission, and always has English-speaking representatives.

Bureau d'Accueil Central: 127, av. des Champs-Elysées, 8ème (tel. 01 49 52 53 54). M. Charles-de-Gaulle-Etoile. English-speaking staff. Mobbed in summer. Open daily April-Oct. 9am-8pm; Nov.-March Mon.-Sat. 9am-8pm, Sun 11am-6pm. Also call **Tourist Information** (tel. 01 49 52 53 56), where a recorded message in English (updated weekly) gives the major events in Paris—call 01 49 52 53 55 for recording in French. There are 6 smaller Bureaux d'Accueil, also operated by the *office de tourisme,* located in the following train stations and at the Eiffel Tower:

Bureau Gare du Nord, 10ème (tel. 01 45 26 94 82). M. Gare du Nord. Open May-Oct. Mon.-Sat. 8am-9pm; Nov.-April Mon.-Sat. 8am-8pm.

Bureau Gare de L'Est, 10ème (tel. 01 46 07 17 73). M. Gare de l'Est. Open May-Oct. Mon.-Sat. 8am-9pm; Nov.-April Mon.-Sat. 8am-8pm.

Bureau Gare de Lyon, 12ème (tel. 01 43 43 33 24). M. Gare de Lyon. Open May-Oct. Mon.-Sat. 8am-9pm; Nov.-April Mon.-Sat. 8am-8pm.

Bureau Gare d'Austerlitz, 13ème (tel. 01 45 84 91 70). M. Gare d'Austerlitz. Open Mon.-Fri. 8am-3pm, Sat. 8am-1pm.

Bureau Tour Eiffel, Champs de Mars, 7ème (tel. 01 45 51 22 15). M. Champs de Mars. Open May-Sept. daily 11am-6pm.

Bureau Gare Montparnasse, 15ème (tel. 01 43 22 19 19). M. Montparnasse-Bienvenue. Open May-Oct. Mon.-Sat. 8am-9pm; Nov.-April Mon.-Sat. 8am-8pm.

Both international airports run tourist offices where you can make same-day hotel reservations (with deposit equal to 12% of room rate) and receive info about Paris.

Orly, Sud: Near gate H (tel. 01 49 75 00 90). **Orly, Ouest:** Near gate F (tel. 01 49 75 01 39). Both open daily 6am-midnight.

Roissy-Charles de Gaulle: Near gate 36 arrival level (tel. 01 48 62 27 29). Open daily 7:30am-10pm.

Budget Travel Offices

Accueil des Jeunes en France (AJF): 119, rue St-Martin, 4ème (tel. 01 42 77 87 80). M. Rambuteau. Across from the pedestrian mall in front of the Pompidou Center. Open Mon.-Sat. 10am-6:45pm. Also 139, bd. St-Michel, 5ème (tel. 01 43 54 95 86), in the *quartier latin.* M. Port-Royal. Open Mon.-Thurs. 10am-12:30pm and 1:45-6pm, Fri. 10:30am-12:30pm and 1:45-6pm. Another in Gare du Nord arrival hall next to Agence de Voyages SNCF (tel. 01 42 85 86 19). Open Mon.-Fri. 8am-5pm. The small Gare du Nord office only books accommodations. The other offices will give you free maps, sell ISICs (60F, cash only), and make reservations in Paris hotels and hostels (10F reservation fee for rooms approximately 115F per night). Discounted student plane, train, and bus tickets, budget weekend holidays, and meal vouchers for Paris youth hostels are also available. Branches are friendly, centrally located, English-speaking, and often absurdly crowded. MC, V.

Centre Régional des Oeuvres Universitaires (CROUS): 39, av. Georges Bernanos, 5ème (general tel. 01 40 51 37 10 or 01 40 51 37 14, lodging tel. 01 40 51 37 17, or 01 40 51 37 19). M. Port-Royal. This helpful university organization has information on student dormitory housing in Paris (min. stay 2 days, max. stay 1 month) and on the many university restaurants scattered throughout the city that offer simple but filling meals for rock bottom prices. For more information, see "University Restaurants," p. 110.

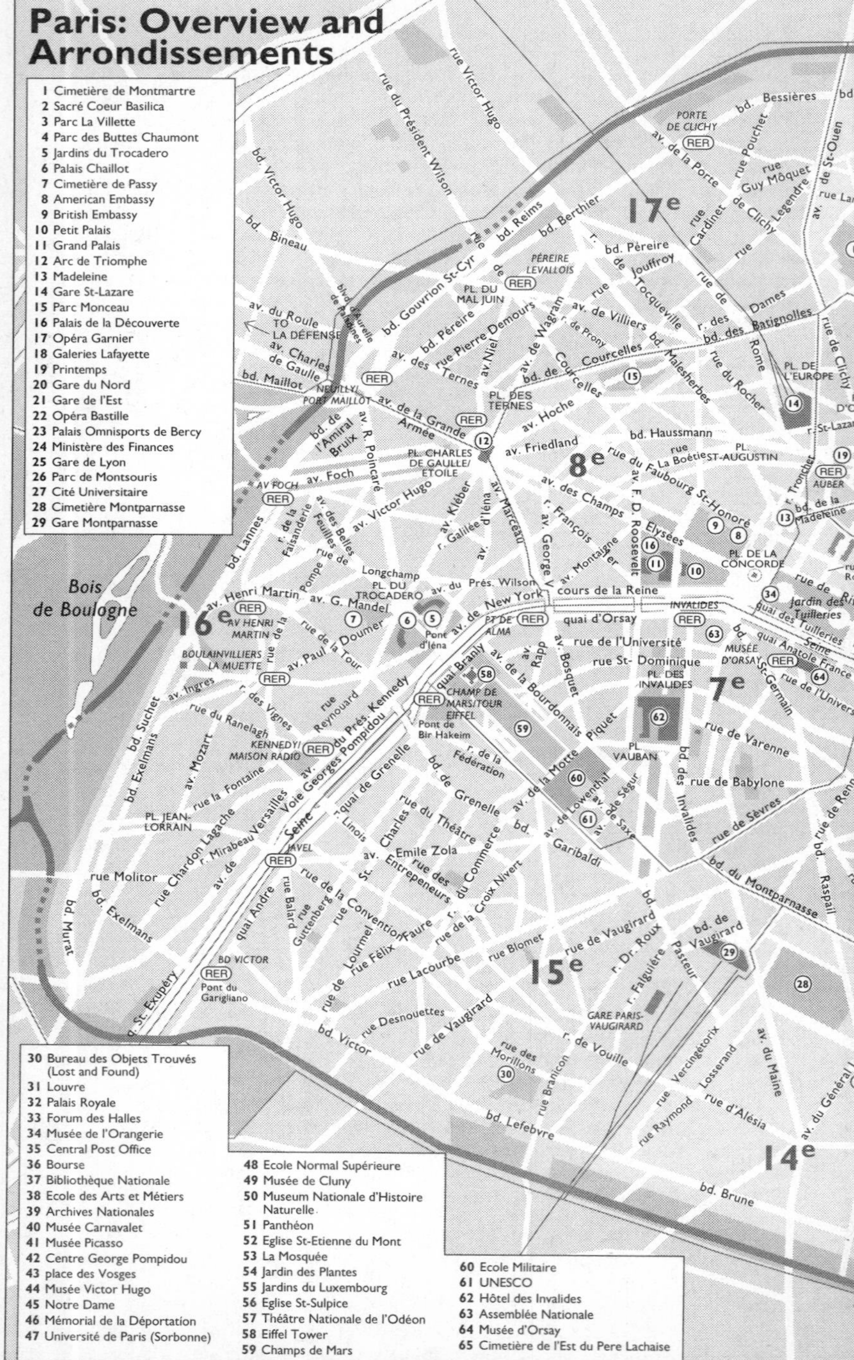
Paris: Overview and Arrondissements
1 Cimetière de Montmartre
2 Sacré Coeur Basilica
3 Parc La Villette
4 Parc des Buttes Chaumont
5 Jardins du Trocadero
6 Palais Chaillot
7 Cimetière de Passy
8 American Embassy
9 British Embassy
10 Petit Palais
11 Grand Palais
12 Arc de Triomphe
13 Madeleine
14 Gare St-Lazare
15 Parc Monceau
16 Palais de la Découverte
17 Opéra Garnier
18 Galeries Lafayette
19 Printemps
20 Gare du Nord
21 Gare de l'Est
22 Opéra Bastille
23 Palais Omnisports de Bercy
24 Ministère des Finances
25 Gare de Lyon
26 Parc de Montsouris
27 Cité Universitaire
28 Cimetière Montparnasse
29 Gare Montparnasse
30 Bureau des Objets Trouvés (Lost and Found)
31 Louvre
32 Palais Royale
33 Forum des Halles
34 Musée de l'Orangerie
35 Central Post Office
36 Bourse
37 Bibliothèque Nationale
38 Ecole des Arts et Métiers
39 Archives Nationales
40 Musée Carnavalet
41 Musée Picasso
42 Centre George Pompidou
43 place des Vosges
44 Musée Victor Hugo
45 Notre Dame
46 Mémorial de la Déportation
47 Université de Paris (Sorbonne)
48 Ecole Normal Supérieure
49 Musée de Cluny
50 Museum Nationale d'Histoire Naturelle
51 Panthéon
52 Eglise St-Etienne du Mont
53 La Mosquée
54 Jardin des Plantes
55 Jardins du Luxembourg
56 Eglise St-Sulpice
57 Théâtre Nationale de l'Odéon
58 Eiffel Tower
59 Champs de Mars
60 Ecole Militaire
61 UNESCO
62 Hôtel des Invalides
63 Assemblée Nationale
64 Musée d'Orsay
65 Cimetière de l'Est du Pere Lachaise
16e
17e
8e
7e
15e
14e
Bois de Boulogne
TO LA DÉFENSE
PORTE DE CLICHY
PÉREIRE LEVALLOIS
PL. DU MAL JUIN
NEUILLY/ PORT MAILLOT
PL. DES TERNES
PL. CHARLES DE GAULLE/ ETOILE
PL. DU TROCADERO
PL. DE LA CONCORDE
PL. DE L'EUROPE
PL. ST-AUGUSTIN
PL. DES INVALIDES
PL. VAUBAN
PL. JEAN-LORRAIN
BOULAINVILLIERS LA MUETTE
AV HENRI MARTIN
KENNEDY/ MAISON RADIO
CHAMP DE MARS/TOUR EIFFEL
PT DE ALMA
INVALIDES
MUSÉE D'ORSAY
AUBER
JAVEL
BD VICTOR
GARE PARIS-VAUGIRARD
Pont d'Iéna
Pont de Bir Hakeim
Pont du Garigliano
Seine
av. des Champs Elysées
av. de la Grande Armée
av. Foch
av. Victor Hugo
av. Kléber
av. Marceau
av. Friedland
av. Hoche
av. de Wagram
bd. Haussmann
rue du Faubourg St-Honoré
bd. Malesherbes
bd. de Courcelles
bd. des Batignolles
bd. Berthier
bd. Pereire
cours de la Reine
quai d'Orsay
rue de l'Université
rue St- Dominique
rue de Varenne
rue de Babylone
rue de Sèvres
bd. du Montparnasse
bd. Raspail
bd. de Grenelle
bd. Garibaldi
av. de la Bourdonnais
av. de la Motte Piquet
av. de Suffren
rue de Vaugirard
rue de la Convention
rue Lecourbe
av. Emile Zola
av. de Versailles
rue Molitor
bd. Murat
bd. Exelmans
bd. Suchet
bd. Lannes
av. Henri Martin
av. Paul Doumer
av. du Prés. Kennedy
av. de New York
Voie Georges Pompidou
quai de Grenelle
bd. Lefebvre
bd. Brune
rue d'Alésia
av. du Maine
bd. Victor

18e
19e
10e
2e
3e
11e
20e
4e
5e
6e
9e
12e
13e
N
bd. Ney
bd. Ney
bd. Macdonald
Canal de l'Ourcq
rue Championnet
bd. Ornano
rue Ordener
rue Duhesme
rue de la Chapelle
rue des Poissonniers
r. l'Evangile
rue d'Aubervilliers
rue Archereau
rue de l'Ourcq
av. Corentin Cariou
bd. Sérurier
av. Jean Lolive
rue Riquet
rue Custine
rue de Clignancourt
bd. Barbès
rue Marx Dormoy
rue de Flandre
rue de Crimée
Bassin de la Villette
av. Jean Jaurès
bd. Indochine
rue Manin
bd. d'Algérie
bd. de Rochechouart
bd. de la Chapelle
PL. DE STALINGRAD
r. Armand Carel
r. David d'Angiers
PL. PIGALLE
av. Trudaine
av. Secrétan
Canal St-Martin
PL. DU COLONEL FABIEN
rue La Fayette
rue Poissonnière
rue de Châteaudun
r. Paradis
bd. de Magenta
bd. de la Villette
bd. Mortier
bd. de Strasbourg
r. Château d'Eau
rue du Faubourg du Temple
rue des Pyrénées
PL. GAMBETTA
bd. Montmartre
bd. des Italiens
bd. Poissonnière
bd. St-Denis
blvd. St-Martin
av. Parmentier
rue St-Maur
bd. de Belleville
av. Gambetta
rue Réaumur
PL. DE LA REPUBLIQUE
rue de Turbigo
rue Montmartre
r. Etienne Marcel
av. de la République
rue Oberkampf
rue du Louvre
rue St-Honoré
r. des Halles
bd. de Sébastopol
rue St-Martin
rue Beaubourg
rue du Temple
rue des Archives
rue Vieille du Temple
bd. Beaumarchais
bd. R. Lenoir
bd. Voltaire
rue du Chemin Vert
av. Gambetta
bd. de Ménilmontant
rue de Rivoli
rue de Rivoli
rue de la Roquette
rue de Charonne
av. Philippe Auguste
bd. de Charonne
bd. Davout
Pont Neuf
quai St-Michel
Ile de la Cité
rue St-Antoine
ST-MICHEL
quai de la Tournelle
Ile St-Louis
bd. Henri IV
rue du Faubourg St-Antoine
rue de Montreuil
NATION
rue de Lyon
r. de Seine
bd. St-Germain
PL. MAUBERT
r. des Écoles
av. Ledru Rollin
Cours de Vincennes
bd. Diderot
PL. DE LA NATION
bd. Picpus
bd. St-Michel
LUXEMBOURG
rue Monge
quai St-Bernard
Pont de Sully
Seine
av. Daumesnil
rue de Picpus
av. du Dr. Arnold Netter
PL. DE LA CONTRE-SCARPE
rue d'Ulm
rue Mouffetard
r. G. St-Hilaire
rue Buffon
rue Censier
av. de l'Observatoire
rue Guy Lussac
PORT ROYAL
r. C. Bernard
GARE D'AUSTERLITZ
Pont de Bercy
bd. de Bercy
PL. FÉLIX ÉBOUÉ
bd. Soult
Mi. Bizot
bd. de Port Royal
bd. St-Marcel
av. des Gobelins
bd. de l'Hôpital
rue de Bercy
quai de Bercy
rue de Charenton
av. Daumesnil
av. du Gén Michel Bizot
rue St-Jacques
bd. Arago
Pont de Tolbiac
Parc Zoologique
bd. St-Jacques
DENFERT ROCHEREAU
PL. D'ALESIA
bd. de la Gare
rue Jeanne d'Arc
rue du Chevaleret
bd. Poniatowski
bd. A. Blanqui
rue de Tolbiac
rue National
av. de Choisy
Pont National
Bois de Vincennes
rue d'Alésia
rue de Tolbiac
av. d'Ivry
av. d'Italie
BD. MASSÉNA
rue Regnault
bd. de Masséna
rue de Paris
bd. Kellerman
CITÉ UNIVERSITAIRE
RER
0
1 mile
0
1 km
2
3
4
20
21
22
23
24
25
26
27
31
33
35
36
37
38
39
40
41
42
43
44
45
46
47
48
49
50
51
52
53
54
57
65

Council on International Educational Exchange: 1, pl. de l'Odéon, 6ème (tel. 01 44 41 74 74; fax 01 43 26 97 45). M. Odéon. Answers questions about work abroad, and offers mail service, phone service, and computers for use in the office. The branch at pl. de l'Odéon has a comprehensive library with useful information about jobs, travel, and housing opportunities, but the library is only available to students and recent graduates who are registered Council participants. American and Canadian students may register in Paris (1020F), although it may be easier to do so before arriving in France. Students from other countries must contact their local CIEE branch for application materials (library open 3-6:30pm). Open Mon.-Fri. 9am-6pm.

Council Travel, 16, rue de Vaugirard, 6ème (tel. 01 44 41 89 89; fax 01 40 51 89 12). M. Odéon. 22, rue des Pyramides, 1er (tel. 01 44 55 55 65). M. Pyramides. English-speaking travel service for young people. Books international flights. Sells student train tickets, guidebooks, and ISICs (60F). BIJ/Eurotrain tickets. If you lose your Council Travel flight ticket, one of the offices will telex the U.S. for a substitute; penalty fee for lost ticket varies by flight. Vaugirard branch open Mon.-Fri. 9:30am-6:30pm, Sat. 10am-5pm. Pyramides branch open Mon.-Fri. 9am-7pm, Sat. 10am-6:30pm. MC, V.

Office de Tourisme Universitaire (OTU): 39, av. Georges Bernanos, 5ème (tel. 01 43 36 80 27). M. Port-Royal, also 119 rue St. Martin, 4ème (tel. 01 42 77 87 80). A French student-travel agency. English spoken. The same reduced train and plane tickets for students under 26 that are sold at any travel agent in Paris, but more crowded. Bring an official form of ID. Also sells ISIC (60F) and BIJ tickets. Open Mon. 11am-12:45pm and 2-6:45pm, Tues.-Fri. 10am-6:45pm, Sat. 11am-12:45pm and 2-5:45pm.

Keeping in Touch

MAIL

Post offices are marked on most Paris maps by their abstract flying-letter insignia; on the streets, look for the yellow and blue PTT signs. Blocks with post offices are usually marked by a cheerful sign at the corner. In general, post offices in Paris are open weekdays 8am-7pm (they stop changing money at 6pm) and on Saturday 8am-noon, though the **Poste du Louvre,** 52, rue du Louvre, 1er (tel. 01 40 28 20 00; M. Louvre; open 24 hrs. daily) and the **Poste des Champs-Elysées,** 71, av. des Champs-Elysées (tel. 01 44 13 66 00; M. Franklin D. Roosevelt or George V; open Mon.-Sat. 8am-10pm, Sun. 10am-noon and 2-8pm) have longer hours. Avoid long lines by purchasing stamps at local *tabacs* or from the yellow coin-operated vending machines inside major post offices.

Air mail between Paris and North America takes five to ten days and is fairly dependable. Send mail from the largest post office in the area. Surface (*par eau* or *par terre*) mail is by far the cheapest way to send mail, but takes one to three months to cross the Atlantic. It's adequate for getting rid of books or clothing you no longer need; a special book rate makes this option more economical. It is vital to distinguish your airmail from surface mail by labelling it clearly **par avion.** To airmail a 20g (about 1 oz.) letter or postcard from France to the U.S. or Canada costs 4F40, to Australia or New Zealand 5F20. The **aerogramme,** a sheet of fold-up, pre-paid airmail paper, requires no envelope and costs more (5F to the U.S. or Canada, no enclosures allowed). To airmail a package, you must complete a green customs slip. Registered mail is called **avec recommandation** and costs 28F40. To be notified of a registered letter's receipt, ask for an **avis de récéption** and pay an additional 7F70. In France there are two grades of express mail: letters mailed **exprès** cost 32F40 and arrive within 5 days to North America; letters mailed **chronopost** arrive in 2-3 days at a soaring cost of 230F for a letter, plus 56F for pickup. Chronopost is only available until 6pm in most post-offices, but until 7pm at major branches; call toll-free 0 800 05 24 00. Finally, for mail to the U.S., **Federal Express** (toll-free tel. 0 800 33 33 55) charges

254F to send a 500g package overnight. Call Monday-Friday for pick up. If they get it in the morning, the parcel will arrive in the U.S. the next business day.

If you're writing from home to France and expect a reply (e.g., when making hotel reservations), enclose an **International Reply Coupon** (available at post offices for US$1) for a response by surface mail; send two for airmail.

Postcards and letters sent from the U.S. cost 50¢ and 60¢. The post office also sells aerograms for 50¢. Many U.S. post offices offer Express Mail service, which sends packages under 8 oz. to major overseas cities in 40 to 72 hours (US$11.50-14). Private mail services provide the fastest, most reliable overseas delivery. **DHL** (US$30), **Federal Express** (US$32), and **Airborne Express** (US$34, max. 8 oz.) can get mail from North America to Paris in 2 days. You must complete a customs form to send any package over 1kg (2kg for letter-post rate) via air mail.

If you do not have a specific address in Paris, you can receive mail through the **Poste Restante** system, handled by the 24-hr. post office at 52, rue du Louvre, 1er (tel. 01 42 80 67 89 for postal info, tel. 01 40 28 20 00 for urgent telegrams and calls; M. Châtelet-les-Halles). To ensure the safe arrival of your letters, they should be addressed with your last/family name in capital letters, followed by a comma and your first name, followed by *Poste Restante,* the address of the specific post office, and Paris, FRANCE. You will have to show your passport as identification and pay 3F for every letter received.

American Express, 11, rue Scribe, 75009, Paris (tel. 01 47 77 79 59) also receives and holds mail for up to 30 days, after which they return it to the sender. If you want to have it held longer, just write "Hold for x days" on the envelope. The envelope should be addressed with your name in capital letters, with "c/o American Express: Client Mail" printed below your name. In Paris, this service is free with presentation of your American Express traveler's checks or card.

TELEPHONES

Almost all French pay phones accept only **télécartes;** in outlying districts and in many cafés and bars, some phones are still coin-operated. You may purchase the card in two denominations: 40F60 for 50 unités, and 97F50 for 120 unités, each worth anywhere from six to 18 minutes of conversation, depending on the rate schedule. Local calls cost one *unité* each. The *télécarte* is available at post offices and most metro stations and tabacs. The best places to make calls are phone booths and post offices. If you phone from a café, hotel, or restaurant, you risk paying up to 30% more. Emergency or collect calls do not require coins or a *télécarte.*

A small digital screen on the phone issues a series of simple commands. A call is *un coup de téléphone* or *un appel;* to dial is *composer;* a collect call is made *en PCV* (pay-say-vay); a person-to-person call is *avec préavis. Décrochez* means pick up, *racrochez* hang up. On some *télécarte* phones, you need to *fermer le volet,* pull down the lever directly above the card slot, and wait for a dial tone.

On October 18, 1996 all the phone numbers in France changed from eight digits to 10. It will take the country awhile to catch on; most people still provide their number in the old eight-digit format. Any eight-digit number you see listed anywhere, though, is wrong. Phone numbers in Paris and the Ile-de-France acquired **01** in front of them, in the northwest of France **02,** in the northeast **03,** in the southeast and Corsica **04,** and in the southwest **05.** Emergency calls and numbers beginning with **0 800** (formerly 05) are free. Numbers beginning with **08** (formerly 36) are much more expensive than others (the equivalent of 900 numbers in the USA; from about 2F per minute).

You can make **intercontinental calls** from any phone booth, or have the other person call you back. Most European pay phones receive incoming calls. The number is posted on a sticker inside the booth, prefaced by *ici le.*

To call France, dial the **international access code** (011 from the U.S. and Canada, 00 from the U.K., 0011 from Australia, 00 from New Zealand, 09 from South Africa), 33 (France's country code), and the ten-digit local number. Calling overseas can cost as little as 5F, and it's much cheaper this way (the French tax calls by as much as

30%). This technique is cheaper than calling collect or via credit card. Country codes are posted inside most telephone booths. If your credit isn't good at home, the 96 *unités télécarte* will serve you well (call to the U.K. 20min. for 120 units; call to the U.S. or Canada 12min. for 120 units).

Another alternative is AT&T's **USA Direct** service, which allows you to be connected instantly to an operator in the U.S. USA-France rates vary according to the day and time of calls, but average US$1-2 per minute. One more AT&T service is **World Connect,** which is for calling between two countries other than the United States. Calls must be made either collect (US$2.75 surcharge) or billed to an AT&T calling card (US$2.50); the people you are calling need not subscribe to AT&T service. For more information call AT&T at (800) 331-1140 or (800) 545-3117. To call **Canada Direct** from France, dial 19, wait for the tone, then dial 0016 and the number. It will be billed as a person-to-person call. **Australia Direct** and **New Zealand Direct** are similar, though not as extensive. For information in Canada, call (800) 561-8868; in Australia, dial 0102; and in New Zealand, dial 018. **MCI** provides a service called **World Phone.** The service lets you call the U.S. using your MCI calling card and an access code, which you'll receive before you leave for France. For more information, call MCI at (800) 444-3333.

Telephone rates are reduced Monday through Friday 9:30pm-8am, Saturday 2pm-8am, and Sunday all day for calls to the European Community and Switzerland; Monday through Friday noon-2pm and 8pm-2am, and Sunday afternoon to the U.S. and Canada; Monday through Saturday 9:30pm-8am and Sunday all day to Israel. Remember **time differences** when you call—Paris is one hour ahead of Greenwich Mean Time and six hours ahead of New York (Eastern Standard Time).

A brief **directory:**

AT&T operator: tel. 00 00 11.
MCI operator: tel. 00 00 19
Direct international calls: tel. 00+ country code (listed in most phone booths) + area/city code + the number.
Direct calls within France: To call to or from anywhere in France, dial the ten digit number. Paris numbers always begin with 01.
Directory information (Renseignements téléphoniques): tel. 12.
International information: tel. 00 33 12 + country code (Australia 61; Ireland 353; New Zealand 64; U.K. 44; U.S. and Canada 1).
International Operator: tel. 00 33 11.
Operator (Téléphoniste): tel. 10.

TELEGRAMS, FAXES, AND MORE

To send a **telegram** to France from the U.S., Western Union (tel. (800) 325-6000) charges $14.32 for the first seven words and then 76 cents per each additional word. Delivery is same-day. To send a telegram to the U.S. from France, the Parisian post offices charge 133F for the first 15 words, and 27F per five words after that.

Most Parisian post offices have public **fax** machines, called *les télécopieurs* by the members of the Académie, but *les faxes* by many (if not most) other people. Rates to the U.S. are approximately 70F for the first page, 40F per page after that. For post office hours and specific post offices with fax machines, see "Mail," p. 66.

MINITEL

Minitel is what the French invented while the rest of the world was working on the Internet: a computer system with the awesome power of an average Commodore 64 which provides telephone numbers, addresses, and professions of French telephone subscribers, as well as on-screen newspapers (including the *International Herald Tribune*), the weather, train schedules, and lots of other information. If you have a listed telephone number, you can lease your own from the phone company. But at 2F a minute, Minitel could break your budget before you're even aware of it. Minitel has a free cousin found in post offices. Use the little yellow machines as phone books to find numbers and services. They can be used with the most rudimentary knowledge of French. Several post offices have public, full-service Minitels, including the Poste du Louvre and Poste des Champs-Elysées (see "Mail," p. 66); bring your *télécarte* and get ready to rack up a bill.

Emergency Health and Help

Fire: tel. 18.

Emergency Medical Assistance: Ambulance (SAMU): tel. 15. Outside of Paris, call 01 45 67 50 50.

Poison Control: tel. 01 40 37 04 04, or 01 42 05 63 29.

Police Emergency: tel. 17.

Police: Each arrondissement of Paris has its own *gendarmerie* (police force) to which you should take all your non-emergency concerns. Call the operator (tel. 12) and ask where your local branch is.

Rape Crisis: SOS Viol, tel. 0 800 05 95 95. Call from anywhere in France for counseling, medical and legal advice, and referrals. Open Mon.-Fri. 10am-6pm.

Hospitals: Hospitals in Paris are numerous and efficient. They will generally treat you whether or not you can pay in advance. Settle with them afterward and don't let financial concerns interfere with your health care. Unless your French is exceptionally good, you'll have the best luck at one of the anglophone hospitals. **Hôpital Franco-Britannique de Paris:** 3, rue Barbès, in the Parisian suburb of Levallois-Perret (tel. 01 46 39 22 22). M. Anatole-France. Considered a French hospital and bills as one. Has some English-speakers and a good reputation. **Hôpital Américain de Paris:** 63, bd. Victor Hugo, Neuilly (tel. 01 46 41 25 25). M. Port Maillot, then bus #82 to the end of the line. In a suburb of Paris. Employs English-speaking personnel, but much more expensive than French hospitals. You can pay in U.S. dollars. If you have Blue Cross, your hospitalization is covered as long as you fill out the appropriate forms first. They can also direct you to the nearest English-speaking doctor and provide dental services.

Late Night Pharmacies: Pharmacie Dhéry, in the Galerie des Champs, 84, av. des Champs-Elysées, 8ème (tel. 01 45 62 02 41). M. George V. Open 24hr. **Grande Pharmacie Daumesnil,** 6, pl. Félix-Eboué, 12ème (tel. 01 43 43 19 03). M. Daumesnil. Visible as you exit the metro. Open 24hrs. **Pharmacie Européenne de la Place Clichy,** 6, pl. de Clichy 9ème (tel. 01 48 74 65 18). M. Place de Clichy. Open 24hr. **Drugstore St-Germain,** 149, bd. St-Germain, 6ème (tel. 01 42 22 80 00). M. St-Germain-des-Prés or Mabillon. Open Mon.-Sat. 8:30am-2am, Sun. 10am-1am. **Pharmacie Opéra Capucines,** 6, bd. des Capucines, 9ème (tel. 01 42 65 88 29). M. Opéra. Open Mon.-Sat. 8am-12:30am, Sun. 5pm-12:30am. MC, V, AmEx. In addition, every arrondissement should have a **pharmacie de garde** (pharmacy on call), which will open in case of emergencies. The locations change, but your local pharmacy can give the name of the nearest one; after hours, the information for the area will be posted on each pharmacy's door.

AIDS information: AIDES, Fédération Nationale, 247, rue de Belleville, 19ème (tel. 01 44 52 00 00). AIDES is one of the oldest and most prolific AIDS public service organizations in France. Roughly equivalent to the AIDS Action Committees found in most major American cities. AIDES runs a hotline that provides information in French and English (tel. 0 800 36 66 36; open 24hrs.; Minitel 3615 Aides).

Alcoholics Anonymous: 3, rue Frédéric Sauton, 5ème (tel. 01 46 34 59 65). M. Maubert-Mutualité. A recorded message in English will refer you to several numbers you can call to talk to telephone counselors. Daily meetings. Open 24 hrs.

Birth Control: Mouvement Français pour le Planning Familial, 10, rue Vivienne, 2ème (tel. 01 42 60 93 20). M. Bourse. Open Mon.-Fri. 9:30am-5:30pm. Resources for information on birth control, pregnancy, and STD prevention.

Drug Problems: Hôpital Marmottan, 17-19, rue d'Armaillé, 17ème (tel. 01 45 74 00 04). M. Charles de Gaulle-Etoile. You're not always guaranteed an English speaker. For consultations or treatments, open Sept.-July Mon.-Wed. and Fri. 11am-7pm, Thurs. and Sat. noon-7pm; Aug. Mon.-Fri. only.

Emotional Health: Services and aid are provided by a number of organizations. Try calling **SOS Crisis Help Line: Friendship** (tel. 01 47 23 80 80). English-speaking.

Support and information for the depressed and lonely. Open daily 3-11pm. For personalized crisis-control and counseling (for anything from pregnancy to homesickness), the **American Church,** 65, quai d'Orsay, 7ème (M. Invalides or Alma-Marceau) offers the **International Counseling Service (ICS),** and the adjunct **American Student and Family Service (ASFS)** provides access to psychologists, psychiatrists, social workers, and a clerical counselor. Payment is nominal and negotiable. Open Mon.-Sat. 9:30am-1pm. The office is staffed irregularly July-Aug., but will respond if you leave a message on its answering machine. Call for an appointment (tel. 01 45 50 26 49 for both) at the American Church. The American Church also offers **Free Anglo-American Counseling Treatment and Support** (FAACTS) for people affected by HIV.

HIV Testing: 218, rue de Belleville, 20ème (tel. 01 47 97 40 49). M. Télégraphe. Also at 3-5, rue de Ridder, 14ème (tel. 01 45 43 83 78; M. Plaisance; open Mon.-Fri. noon-6:30pm, Sat. 9:30am-noon). Mandatory counseling, some English spoken. Results in 1 week. Free and anonymous. Open Mon.-Fri.1-6pm, Sat. 9:30am-noon.

STD Clinic: 43, rue de Valois, 1er (tel. 01 42 61 30 04). M. Palais-Royal. Testing and treatment for sexually transmitted diseases. Free consultations, blood tests, and injection treatments. Syphilis tests are free. Plasma and chlamydia tests usually around 300F each, but free if you are in dire straits. Tests for HIV are free, anonymous, and include mandatory counseling. Open Mon.-Fri. 9am-7pm. Call for an appointment English-speaking doctors available). HIV testing at lunchtime and late afternoon.

English-Language Religious Services

American Church in Paris: 65, quai d'Orsay, 7ème (tel. 01 47 05 07 99). M. Invalides or Alma-Marceau. As much a community center as a church. Bulletin boards with notices about jobs, rides, apartments, personals, etc., both in the lobby and downstairs. *Free Voice,* a free English-language monthly specializing in cultural events and classifieds, is published here; submit your ad by the 22nd of the month before it runs (60F for 30 words). Inter-denominational services Sun. at 11am, followed by a coffee break at noon. Counseling service (tel. 01 45 50 26 49), call to make an appointment. Church open Mon.-Sat. 9am-10:30pm, Sun. 9am-7:30pm. Free student concerts Oct.-June Sun. at 6pm. Hosts meetings for AA, AL-ANON, ACOA, and FAACTS (workshops for people affected by AIDS, ARC, or with HIV+ status). In Oct., the church sponsors an orientation program for newcomers to Paris. There is a minimal fee (150F, call for more info). The church also holds a flea market on the 1st and 3rd Sat. of each month (2-5pm).

Anglican and Episcopalian: St. Michael's Church, 5, rue d'Aguesseau, 8ème (tel. 01 47 42 70 88). M. Concorde. Services in English Sun. at 10:30am. On the 1st floor, outside the offices, bulletin boards list jobs offered and wanted, accommodations available and sought, as well as info on activities of interest. Office open Mon.-Tues. and Thurs.-Fri. 9:30am-12:30pm and 2-5:30pm. Even if the office is closed, boards and pamphlets should be accessible. **Eglise Anglicane St-Georges,** 7, rue Auguste-Vacquerie, 16ème (tel. 01 47 20 22 51). M. Kléber. Communion services in English on Sun. at 8:30 and 10:30am. Other services Tues. 6:30pm, Wed. noon, Thurs. 6:30pm, Fri.-Sat. noon, Sun. 8:30am. Office open Mon.-Fri. 3-6pm. Also **American Cathedral,** 23, av. George-V, 8ème (tel. 01 47 20 17 92). M. George-V. English services daily at 9am; Communion services Sun. 9am and 11am, Wed. 12:30pm. Office open Mon.-Fri. 9am-5pm.

Catholic: St. Joseph's Church, 50, av. Hoche, 8ème (tel. 01 42 27 28 56). M. Charles de Gaulle-Etoile. Services in English on Sun. at 9:45, 11am, 12:15, and 6:30pm. Office open Mon.-Sat. 10am-6pm. **Catholic Information Center,** street address 8, rue Massillon, 1er; mailing address 6, pl. du Parvis Notre-Dame, 4ème (tel. 01 46 33 01 01). M. Cité. Info about religious activities, prayer, and pilgrimages. English speaker usually present. Open Mon.-Fri. 9am-noon and 2-6pm.

Society of Friends (Quaker), 114bis, rue de Vaugirard, 6ème (tel. 01 45 48 74 23). M. St-Placide or Montparnasse-Bienvenue. Enter through the garage door and walk down the courtyard stairs. Small, intimate, and friendly meeting, with many seniors and a fair number of students during the school year. Messages are delivered in

French, but nearly everyone is fluent in English. 10am discussion hour and Bible reading, 11am meeting, followed by communal lunch at noon.

Synagogue: Union Libéral Israélite de France, 24, rue Copernic, 16ème (tel. 01 47 04 37 27). M. Victor-Hugo. 1-hr. services Fri. at 6pm and 1½-hr. service Sat. at 10:30am, mostly in Hebrew with a little French. English-speaking rabbi stays after the service to chat. Services also on the evenings and mornings of the High Holy Days; call for specifics, as well as info about religious groups. Secretariat open Mon.-Thurs. 9am-noon and 2-6pm, Fri. 9am-noon.

Other Services

ATMs: A selected list of ATM machines on the **Cirrus** network: 5, rue de la Feuillade, 1er (M. Bastille); 8, rue St-Antoine, 4ème (M. Bastille); corner of rue Monge and rue des Bernardins, 5ème (M. Maubert-Mutualité); 22, rue de Sèvres at Le Bon Marché, 7ème (M. Sèvres-Babylone, open during store hours); 7, bd. Malesherbes, 8ème (M. Madeleine); 26, rue de Naples, 8ème (M. Europe); 35bis, rue de Provence, 9ème (M. Le Peletier); 94-96 bd. Magenta, 10ème (M. Gare du Nord); 82, bd. Soult, 12ème (M. Porte Dorée); 53, av. des Gobelins, 13ème (M. Gobelins); 58, rue St-Charles, 15ème (M. Dupleix); 2, rue de l'Arrivée, 15ème (M. Montparnasse-Bienvenue); 28, rue d'Auteuil, 16ème (M. Eglise d'Auteuil); 30, av. Niel, 17ème (M. Pereire-Levallois); 13, rue des Abbesses, 18ème (M. Abbesses); 7, pl. des Fêtes, 19ème (M. pl. des Fêtes); 167-171, av. Gambetta, 20ème (M. Porte des Lilas).

Lost Property: Bureau des Objets Trouvés, 36, rue des Morillons, 15ème (tel. 01 55 76 20 20). M. Convention. When you visit or write, describe the object and when and where it was lost. No info given by phone. Open Mon.-Thurs. 8:30am-5pm; Sept.-June Mon. and Wed. 8:30am-5pm, Tues. and Thurs. 8:30am-8pm.

Public Baths: 8, rue des Deux Ponts, 4ème (tel. 01 43 54 47 40). M. Pont-Marie. Shower 7F, with soap and towel roughly 15F. For the same price you can also rub-a-dub-dub at 42, rue du Rocher, 8ème (tel. 01 45 22 15 19; M. St-Lazare), and at 40, rue Oberkampf, 11ème (tel. 01 47 00 57 35; M. Oberkampf). These are clean, respectable, and quite popular in summer. All open Thurs. noon-7pm, Fri. and Sat. 7am-7pm, Sun. 8am-noon.

Public Libraries: Bibliothèque Publique Information, in the Centre Pompidou, 4ème (tel. 01 44 78 12 33). M. Rambuteau. Many books in English. Record and video listening room, free Internet classes. Novels are arranged alphabetically by century on the 1st floor. Guidebooks and books about France and Paris abound. Books cannot be checked out. Open Mon. and Wed.-Fri. noon-10pm, Sat.-Sun. 10am-10pm. There are many other public libraries in Paris that circulate books; this one should be able to direct you to the one nearest you. Anybody can visit the library and read there; in order to take books out, you need a passport ID and two proofs of French residency (phone and electricity bills, *carte de séjour,* etc.).

Weather: Allo Météo, 5-day recorded forecasts. Call from touch-tone phones. **Paris,** tel. 08 36 68 02 75; **Ile de France,** tel. 08 36 68 00 00; **France,** tel. 08 36 68 01 01; **mountain regions** (choice of northern Alps, southern Alps, Pyrénées, and Massifs), tel. 08 36 68 04 04; **marine conditions,** tel. 08 36 68 08 08. All in French. You can also check out a map of the day's predicted weather at the corner of Rapp and Université in the 7ème, posted by **Météorologie Nationale.**

Publications About Paris

On those heartbreaking and rare occasions when *Let's Go* falls just short, consult the following guides. *Le Petit Futé* (65F), *Paris Pas Cher* (98F), and *Paris Combines* (98F) can guide you to the best and cheapest stores, services, restaurants, and options especially useful for the long-term traveler. *Connaissance de Vieux Paris* (120F) is a street-by-street guide to the history of Paris. Popular among the French is *Guide du Routard* (79F); basically a French *Let's Go,* complete with smart-alec comments, it provides useful info on how to live on a budget in Paris. *Gault Millau* (155F) is a respected guide to Parisian eateries. Patricia Wells' *The Food Lover's Guide to Paris* (US$15, about 120F in France) lists most of the city's greatest and most famous restaurants, cafés, bakeries, cheese shops, *charcuteries,* wine shops, etc. Gourmets may not share all of Wells' opinions (and budget travelers may not be able to verify them), but the guide is generally reliable. Both of the above are available at Gibert Jeune and other bookstores (see "Books and Magazines," p. 274).

Your most important printed resource will invariably be a map (see "Maps," p. 73). The tourist office distributes a free monthly booklet entitled *Paris Sélection* that highlights exhibitions, concerts, suggested walking tours, and other useful information. Similarly, the Mairie de Paris publishes the monthly *Paris le Journal* (free) with articles and listings about what's on, touristically and culturally, around the city. It is available at the Mairie's Salon d'Accueil, 29, rue de Rivoli, 4ème (tel. 01 42 76 42 42; M. Hôtel-de-Ville), at most *mairies,* and some tourist offices.

The weeklies *Pariscope* (3F) and *Officiel des Spectacles* (2F; both published every Wed.) list current movies, plays, exhibits, festivals, clubs, and bars. *Pariscope* is the most comprehensive—buy one as soon as you arrive to get the rundown on Parisian life. *Pariscope* includes an English-language section called *Time Out Paris*, a joint venture with the British entertainment magazine *Time Out.* The Wednesday edition of *Le Figaro* includes *Figaroscope,* a supplement about what's happening in Paris. *Free Voice,* a free monthly English-language newspaper published by the Cooperative for Better Living at the American Church, is available there and at many student centers. *France-USA Contacts (FUSAC),* printed twice monthly and available free from English-speaking establishments (bookstores, restaurants, travel agencies) throughout Paris, lists job, housing, and service information for English speakers.

Although the newspapers in France do have political leanings, this does not necessarily determine who reads them. *Libération* (7F), a socialist newspaper, is carried everywhere by students in search of amusingly written but comprehensive news coverage of world events. Heavy on culture, including theater and concert listings, *"Libé"* (as it is known in France) has excellent, controversial interviews and thought-provoking full-page editorials. Readers with a penchant for politics will disappear behind a copy of *Le Monde* (7F), decidedly centrist with a tendency to wax socialist. The equally respectable, solid *Le Figaro* (7F) leans to the right, with an entire section of financial news. *Le Parisien* (4F80), *France-Soir* (5F), and *Quotidien* (7F) also write from the right, though their efforts tend toward the more-style-than-substance end of the journalistic spectrum. *La Tribune* (7F) is France's Wall Street Journal. The Communist Party puts out *L'Humanité* (7F) for the good of the people. Militants and revolutionaries will want to buy *Lutte Ouvrière,* carried at few newsstands; look for it in the streets and metro. Those homesick for the *Washington Post* and the *New York Times* will find solace in their wire studies in the *International Herald Tribune* (10F). *L'Equipe* (4F90), the sports and auto daily, offers stats on most sports you can think of and some that you cannot. Hippofanatics will gallop to get *Paris-Turf* (7F), the horse-racing daily.

Getting Around

Orientation

LAYOUT

Coursing languidly from east to west, the Seine River forms the heart of modern Paris. Perhaps single-handedly the basis of the city's legendary romantic aura, the river played midwife to Paris' birth on an island some 2300 years ago. Today, the Ile de la Cité and neighboring Ile St-Louis remain the geographical center of the city, while the Seine splits Paris into two large expanses—the renowned *rive gauche* (Left Bank) to its south and the *rive droite* (Right Bank) to its north. By the time of Louis XIV, the city had grown to 20 *quartiers;* Haussmann's 19th-century reconstructions shifted their boundaries but kept the number, dividing Paris into 20 *arrondissements* (districts), which spiral clockwise around the Louvre. The arrondissement system provides the organizational framework for this guide. See the Sights chapter for a detailed description of what each arrondissement has to offer.

MAPS

A map of Paris is essential if you plan to do any serious strolling. Convenient for a long day of touring, *Let's Go Map Guide: Paris* provides highlights from Let's Go's Paris coverage along with detailed fold-out maps and a street index, all in a pocket-sized format (US$7.95). The most exhaustive guide to Paris, **Plan de Paris par Arrondissement** includes a detailed map of each arrondissement, all the bus lines, a wealth of miscellany, and an essential index of streets and their nearest metro stops. You can pick up a copy of the red- or black-covered *plan* at almost any newsstand, bookstore, *papeterie* (stationery store), or *tabac* for 56F. When you buy any map, check that you've got one of the more expansive versions, with maps of the *banlieue* (city outskirts). Unfortunately, the metro maps in guides are often out of date. Pick up a free, updated one that also includes bus lines and the RER suburban system in any metro station. If you get lost, each metro station has a map of its neighborhood, with a street index. **L'Astrolabe,** 46, rue de Provence, 9ème (tel. 01 42 85 42 95; M. Chaussée d'Antin), or 14, rue Serpente, 6ème (tel. 01 46 33 80 06; M. Odéon or St-Michel), stocks an extremely comprehensive collection. Both locations sell guidebooks, magazines, and travel literature in almost every language. At the 9ème location, an entire floor is dedicated just to France (both open Mon.-Sat. 9:30am-7pm).

■ Public Transportation

The **RATP (Régie Autonome des Transports Parisiens)** coordinates an efficient network of subways, buses, and commuter trains in and around Paris. For information on the services of RATP, contact their office at the **Bureau de Tourisme RATP,** pl. de la Madeleine, 8ème (tel. 01 40 06 71 44; M. Madeleine; open Mon.-Sat. 8:30am-6:45pm, Sun. 6:30am-1pm). RATP can also be reached by telephone at the helpful information number (tel. 01 36 68 77 14; open daily 6am-9pm). An English-speaking representative is usually available. For information about metro services for people in wheelchairs or with impaired vision, see "Travelers with Disabilities," p. 45.

If you're only staying in Paris for one day but expect to do a lot of traveling, consider buying a **metro pass.** At 70F for two days, 105F for three days, and 165F for five, the **Paris Visite** tourist tickets are valid for unlimited travel on bus, metro, and RER, and discounts on sightseeing trips, bicycle rentals, and more. A more practical saver-pass is the **Formule 1;** for 30F per day, you get unlimited travel on buses, metro, and RER within Paris. If you're staying in Paris for more than a few days, get a weekly *(hebdomadaire)* **Coupon Vert** or a monthly *(mensuel)* **Coupon Orange,** which allow unlimited travel (starting on the first day of the week or month) on the metro and buses in Paris. Both of these must be accompanied by the ID-style **Carte Orange.** To get your *carte orange,* bring an ID photo (taken by machines in most major stations) to the ticket counter, ask for a *carte orange* with its plastic case, and then purchase your handsome *coupon vert* (63F) or equally swanky *coupon orange* (219F). No matter which *coupon* you have, write the number of your *carte* on your *coupon* before you use it. Also remember that these cards have specific start and end dates and may not be worthwhile if bought in the middle or at the end of the month or the week. All prices quoted here are for passes in zones 1 and 2 (the metro and RER in Paris and the immediate suburbs). If you intend to travel to the distant 'burbs, you'll need to buy RER passes for more zones (up to 5). Ask at the ticket windows for details. Finally, if you read some French and can use a Minitel, dial 3615 RATP to learn the fastest way to travel between any two Parisian streets or metro stops.

METRO

Inaugurated in 1898, the *Paris Métropolitain* (metro) is one of the world's oldest and most efficient subway systems, able to whisk you within walking distance of nearly any spot in the city. Stations are marked with an "M" or with the *"Métropolitain"* lettering designed by Art Nouveau pioneer Hector Guimard. Trains run frequently, and connections are easy. The first trains start running around 5:30am; the last ones leave the end-of-the-line stations (the *"portes de Paris"*) for the center of the city at about 12:15am. For the exact departure times of the last trains from the *portes,* check the poster in the center of each station marked *Principes de Tarification* (fare guidelines). Most stations can also provide free, pocket-sized metro maps. Transport maps are posted on train platforms and near turnstiles; all have a *plan du quartier* (map of the neighborhood). Connections to other lines are indicated by orange *"correspondance"* signs, exits by blue *"sortie"* signs. Lines are numbered (1 is the oldest), but referred to by their final destinations. Transfers to other lines are free if made within a station, but it is not always possible to reverse direction on the same line without exiting the station and using another ticket.

Each trip on the metro requires one ticket. Tickets can be bought individually (8F), but a *carnet* of 10 (46F) is more practical. Don't buy tickets from anyone except the people in the ticket booths. To pass through the turnstiles, insert the ticket into the small slit in the metal divider just to your right as you approach the turnstile. It disappears for a moment, then pops out about a foot farther along, and a little green or white circle lights, reminding you to retrieve the ticket. If a small electric whine sounds and a little red circle lights up, your ticket is not valid; take it back and try another. **Hold onto your ticket** until you exit the metro, past the point marked **Limite de Validité des Billets;** a uniformed RATP *contrôleur* (inspector) may request to see it on any train. If caught without one, you must pay a hefty fine. Also, any *correspondances* (transfers) to the RER require you to put your validated (and uncrumpled) ticket into a turnstile. Otherwise you might need to buy a new ticket in order to exit—or may not be able to exit. Keep in mind that a metro ticket is valid only within Paris. There is no longer first-class metro service; any cars still marked "1" are waiting to be repainted. A word on being helpful to people who have "lost" their ticket and need to get through an entrance or exit: while it may seem a small matter to allow someone to follow you through the gate, be warned that **thieves** often use this strategy to insinuate their way into your bag or pocket.

Do not count on buying a metro ticket home late at night. Some ticket windows close as early as 10pm, and many close before the last train is due to arrive. Always have one ticket more than you need. Stay away from the most dangerous stations (Barbès-Rochechouart, Pigalle, Anvers, Châtelet-Les-Halles, Gare du Nord, Gare de l'Est). Despite the good neighborhoods in which some of these stops are located, they are frequented by troublemakers looking to prey on tourists or the wealthy. When in doubt, take a taxi. If you choose to walk home, stay on well-lit streets.

RER

The RER *(Réseau Express Régional)* is the RATP's local suburban train system, which passes through central Paris. Introduced in 1969, the RER runs through deeper tunnels at higher speeds. Within the city, the RER travels much faster than the metro, and for all intents can be regarded as a faster, though more confusing, set of metro lines. There are four RER lines, marked A-D, with different branches designated by a number, such as the C5 line to Versailles-Rive-Gauche. The principal stops within the city, which link the RER to the metro system, are Gare du Nord, Nation, Charles de Gaulle-Etoile and Châtelet-les-Halles on the Right Bank and St-Michel and Denfert-Rochereau on the Left Bank. To check for the right train, watch the electric signboards next to each track. These signs list all the possible stops for trains running on that track. Be sure that the little square next to your destination is lit up. There are two transit classes on RER trains. Unless you indicate otherwise, you'll be sold a second-class ticket. Every RER car is marked "1" or "2"; second-class ticket holders are excluded from first-class cars under penalty of fine. First class caters to commuters, with nicer seats and more leg-room. Second-class tickets cost 8F within the city and are the same ones used for the metro or bus. First-class tickets cost 12F. To get to the suburbs, you'll need to buy special tickets, prorated to your destination's distance from the center city (10-38F one-way). Classier and more confusing, the RER differs from the metro on yet another count; you'll need your ticket to *exit* RER stations. Insert your ticket just as you did to enter, and pass through.

BUS

Because the metro is so efficient and convenient, the Parisian bus system is often neglected by both locals and visitors. Though slower and more costly than the metro (one ticket takes you as far as you want on one line, but connections between bus lines require a new ticket), bus rides can be cheap sight-seeing tours and helpful introductions to the city's layout. The free bus map *Autobus Paris-Plan du Réseau* is available at the tourist office and at some metro information booths. The routes of each line are also posted at each stop. Bus tickets are the same as those used in the metro, and can be purchased either in metro stations or on the bus. Enter the bus through the front door and punch your ticket by pushing it into the machine by the driver's seat. If you have a *coupon orange,* flash it at the driver. Inspectors may ask to see your ticket, so hold onto it until the end of the ride.

Most buses run 7am-8:30pm, although those marked **Autobus du Soir** continue until 12:30am. Still others, called **Noctambus,** run all night. Night buses (3 tickets needed, 4 if you use 2 buses) start their runs to the *portes* of the city from the "Châtelet" stop and leave every hour on the half hour from 1:30 to 5:30am. Buses departing from the suburbs to Châtelet run every hour on the hour 1 to 6am. Buses with three-digit numbers come from or are bound for the suburbs, while buses with two-digit numbers travel exclusively within Paris. Buses with numbers in the 20s come from or are bound for Gare St-Lazare, in the 30s Gare de l'Est, in the 40s Gare du Nord, in the 70s Châtelet/Hôtel de Ville (with exceptions), in the 80s Luxembourg (with exceptions), and in the 90s Gare Montparnasse.

For more detailed diagrams of all bus routes, consult the *Plan de Paris par Arrondissement* (see "Maps," p. 73). The RATP prints a number of useful brochures. Ask for their *Grand Plan de Paris* which includes legible maps of all Parisian bus routes and numbers. Some routes pass by enough sights to make them mini-tours in themselves. Worthwhile bus rides include the following; they can be taken from any stop in either direction; all stops are not listed here.

Bus #20: From Opéra to Montmartre-Poissonière, République, Bastille. A trip down the grands boulevards. Open platform in back.
Bus #21: From Opéra to Palais Royal, the Louvre, Pont Neuf, Châtelet, St-Michel.
Bus #29: From Opéra to the Bibliothèque Nationale, the Centre Pompidou, Bastille. Intrepid ride through narrow streets of the Marais. Open platform in back.
Bus #82: From Gare du Luxembourg to Montparnasse, École-Militaire, Champs-de-Mars, Tour Eiffel.
Bus #83: From pl. d'Italie, along bd. Raspail, Gare des Invalides, pl. des Ternes (34-45min.). Paris's finest real estate and views of the quais. Open platform in back.
Bus #95: From Tour Montparnasse past St-Germain-des-Prés, the Louvre, Palais Royal, the Opéra, and to Montmartre, near Sacré-Coeur (50min.).

In addition, a special tourist bus, **Balabus,** stops at virtually every major sight in Paris (from Gare de Lyon to Bastille, St-Michel, Louvre, Musée d'Orsay, Concorde, Champs-Elysées, Charles-de-Gaulle-Etoile, Porte Maillot, Pont de Neuilly, Grande Arche de La Défense, about 75min.). *Balabus* costs 1-3 tickets, depending on how far you ride it, and runs only April 2-Sept. 24 on Sundays and holidays. The first bus leaves Grande Arche at 1pm and Gare de Lyon at 1:30pm; the last bus leaves Grande Arche at 8:10pm and Gare de Lyon at 8:50pm. Buses run about every 20 minutes.

■ Taxi

Taxi trips within Paris represent the height of decadence for the budget traveler. Rates vary according to time of day and geographical area, but they're never cheap.

Tarif A, the basic rate, is in effect in Paris proper 7am-7pm (3F23 per km). **Tarif B** is in effect in Paris proper Mon.-Sat. 7pm-7am, all day Sunday, and during the day from the airports (5F10 per km). **Tarif C,** the highest, is in effect from the airports 7pm-7am (6F88 per km). In addition, there is a *prix en charge* (base fee) of about 11F. All taxis have lights on their roofs indicating the rate being charged, so you can check to see that the driver is playing it straight. Should you call a taxi, rather than getting one at a taxi stand, the base fee will increase according to how far way you are and how long it takes the driver to get there. For all cabs, stationary time (at traffic lights and in traffic jams) costs 120F per hour. Additional charges (5-10F) are added for luggage weighing over 5kg, a pet in the backseat, a fourth adult in the cab, or for taxis leaving from train stations and marked taxi stops. Taxis can refuse to take more than three people. Illegal overcrowding of cabs can bring heavy fines upon the driver. A 15% tip is customary (round up to the nearest 5F).

If you must take a taxi, try to pick one up at a train station or taxi stand, called *arrêt taxis,* usually found near bus stops. Calling a radio-cab (**Alpha Taxis,** tel. 01 45 85 85 85, **Taxis Radio Etoile,** tel. 01 41 27 27 27, **Taxis G7,** tel. 01 47 39 47 39, **Taxis Bleus,** tel. 01 49 36 10 10, or **Taxis 7000,** tel. 01 42 70 00 42) is more expensive; you must pay for the distance the cab drives to pick you up. If you have a complaint, write to **Service des Taxis de la Préfecture de Police,** 36, rue des Morillons, 75015 (tel. 01 55 70 20 00 M. Convention). Ask the driver for a receipt; if you file a complaint, record and include in your complaint the driver's cab license number.

■ Car

"Somewhere you have heard a dark apocryphal statistic—that one driver out of every twelve in Paris has killed his man. On foot, the Parisian is as courteous as the citizen of any other city. But mounted, he is merciless." So wrote Irwin Shaw, and he liked

Parisians. The infamous rotary at the Arc de Triomphe has trapped many an unwary tourist; at rush hour, cars move in any direction they want. **Priorité à droite** gives the right of way to the car approaching from the right, regardless of the size of the streets, and Parisian drivers make it an affair of honor to take this right even in the face of grave danger. Drivers are not allowed to honk their horns within city limits unless they are about to hit a pedestrian, but this rule is often broken. The legal way to show discontent is to flash the headlights; keep an eye peeled in case a law-abiding driver refrains from honking until just before impact. If you don't have a map of Paris marked with one-way streets, the city will be impossible to navigate. Parking is hard to locate (although Parisians park on sidewalks, corners, etc.) and garages are expensive. Foreigners need a passport, a valid license that is at least one year old, and a credit card to rent in Paris; an international license is not required. None of the agencies in Paris will rent to drivers under 21. The following prices represent quotes for the agency's smallest economy car available. Note that only one of these agencies offers cars with automatic transmissions.

Rent-a-Car, 79, rue de Bercy, 12ème (tel. 01 43 45 15 15; fax 01 43 45 65 00). For a Fiat Panda with unlimited miles: 199F per day, 298F with insurance; 499F per weekend (Fri. noon to Mon. 10am), 698F with insurance; 999F per week, 1398F with insurance. Must be 23 years old with a 2-yr.-old license. Open Mon.-Fri. 8am-6:30pm, Sat. 9am-5:30pm. Call for locations of 10 other offices in town. MC, V.

Inter Touring Service, 117, bd. Auguste Blanqui, 13ème (tel. 01 45 88 52 37; fax 01 45 80 89 30). M. Glacière. Fiat Panda 267F per day with 200km and insurance, 1407F per week. Also provides vehicles equipped for **drivers with disabilities.** Open Mon.-Sat. 8:30am-8:30pm. MC, V.

Autorent, 98, rue de la Convention, 15ème (tel. 01 45 54 22 45; fax 01 45 54 39 69). M. Boucicaut. Also at 35, rue Fabert, 7ème (tel. 01 45 55 12 54). M. Invalides. Rents Fiat Pandas for 280F per day, 250km included. 1500F for a week with 1000km; 1800F with unlimited mileage. Some cars with **automatic transmission.** Open Mon.-Fri. 8:30am-7pm, Sat. 8:30am-noon. Renters must have had a license for at least one year. MC, V, AmEx.

■ Two Wheelers

During the metro strike of December 1995, bike stores sold out to car-less Parisians, and the community of cyclists dreaming of an autoless Paris became more vocal. The government has promised that 1997 will bring 50km of Parisian streets reserved for motorless wheels. Nonetheless, if you have never ridden a bike in heavy traffic, don't use central Paris as a testing ground. The Bois de Boulogne and the Bois de Vincennes should be more your speed (see "Participatory Sports—Cycling," p. 269). The metro cannot accommodate bikes, but local trains list specific times when they allow bicycles on board for free. When renting from the following agencies, ask for a helmet.

Paris Bike, 83, rue Daguerre, 14ème (tel. 01 45 38 58 58). M. Denfert-Rochereau. Leads 3hr. tours that focus on the west side of Paris; commentary in French, but the guide is bilingual (tours start 10am and 2pm on Sun.; 195F per person).

La Maison du Vélo, 11, rue Fénelon, 10ème (tel. 01 42 81 24 72). M. Poissonière. Follow rue Lafayette in the direction of traffic. Rue Fénelon is the street running along the left side of the St. Vincent de Paul church. "The English speaking bike store in Paris" since 1979. Sells new and used bikes, repairs all models. Rent mountain or hybrid bikes 150F per day, 260F two days, 300F three days, 575F per week. Deposit 200F per bike.

Paris-Vélo, 2, rue de Fer-à-Moulin, 5ème (tel. 01 43 37 59 22). M. Censier Daubenton. Bikes 80F for 5hrs., 100F per day, 495F per week. Bike rental with deposit, includes accident insurance. Open Mon.-Sat. 10am-12:30pm and 2-7pm.

For **motorcycles** or **scooters,** stop by **Agence Contact Location,** 24, rue Arc de Triomphe, 17ème (tel. 01 47 66 19 19; M. Etoile). Scooters 235F per day, 870F per week. 7000F credit card deposit required. Motorcycles 660-815F per day, 2850-3350F per week. 20,000-30,000F credit card deposit required.

Accommodations

Three basic types of Parisian accommodations are suitable for the budget traveler: hotels, hostels, and *foyers.* While hotels are comfortable and give you complete privacy and independence, hostels and *foyers* are the least expensive options, especially for people traveling alone. According to the Office du Tourisme, high season in Paris falls around Easter, May-June, and September-October (when trade shows—*salons*—take over the city). The peak of high season however, is July and August. Unless otherwise noted, we list hostel prices per person; prices elsewhere are per room. Be aware that the city of Paris has a *Taxe de Séjour* of 1-5F per person per day within the city. Most hostels and *foyers* include this *Taxe* in their listed prices, but hotels may or may not consider it part of the room's cost. It is advisable to check for this as well as other add-on expenses such as direct telephone service (some hotels will even charge you for collect calls), before making a reservation.

Try to make a reservation in advance, but if you do arrive in Paris without one, don't panic. The **Office du Tourisme** on the Champs-Elysées or one of its other bureaus should be able to find you a room, although the lines may be long and the selections not necessarily among the cheapest in Paris (see "Tourist Offices," p. 63). The following booking offices, located near major metro lines, are also frequently crowded, but their English speaking staff can arrange for stays in hostels and budget hotels throughout the city:

La Centrale de Réservations (FUAJ-HI), 4, bd. Jules Ferry, 11ème (tel. 01 43 57 02 60; fax 01 40 21 79 92). M. République. Follow the rue du Faubourg du Temple away from pl. de la République until you reach the park-like entity which divides Blvd. Jules Ferry in two. Cross to far side and turn right—"La Centrale" is half a block up on your left. One of the best ways to secure a bed in a hostel or to book any other budget accommodation (90-125F per night per person) in Paris. Provides same-day reservations in one of their affiliated youth hostels or budget hotels—a total of 10,000 beds in and around the city. The earlier you show up the better, but they can usually help anyone anytime. Books beds for groups throughout France and Europe, arranges excursions, and procures plane and bus tickets. Open Mon.-Sat. 9am-6pm. If "La Centrale" is closed, the 24-hr. reception at the Jules Ferry Hostel, two doors down, has access to the same network of affiliates and may be able to find you a bed.

Accueil des Jeunes en France (AJF), 119, rue St-Martin, 4ème (tel. 01 42 77 87 80). M. Rambuteau. Across the pedestrian mall from the Pompidou. Even in the busiest months, AJF guarantees "decent and low-cost lodging" in hostels and hotels for same-day reservation and immediate use. You must pay the full price of the *foyer* room when making your reservation, even before seeing the room. Employees speak English and one other foreign language. 10F service charge. Open Mon.-Sat. 10am-6:45pm. See "Budget Travel Offices," p. 63, for more info.

■ Hostels and Foyers

Paris' big-city hostels don't bother with many of the restrictions—sleepsheets, curfews, and the like—that characterize most hostels in the world, but they do have maximum stays, though even these are flexible. Accommodations usually consist of single sex rooms containing two to eight beds, but you may be asked whether you're willing to be in a co-ed room. You will almost certainly be required to share a room with strangers.

To stay in a **Hostelling International (HI)** hostel, you must be a member. If you show up at an HI hostel without a membership card, the hostel should issue you a blank card with space for six validation stamps. Each night you'll pay a nonmember supplement (19F) and earn one Guest Stamp; get six stamps and you're a member. Membership purchased this way costs 114F, so it's cost-efficient for prospective hostelers to become members before leaving home. Most student travel agencies issue

HI cards on the spot, or you can contact a national hostel organization (see "Student and Budget Travel Agencies," p. 51). Another benefit of an HI membership is HI's recently instituted **International Booking Network,** whereby you can reserve a room in advance. Information on French hostels can also be obtained through the world wide web at http://www.fuaj.fr.

Despite the hype, there are only two official HI hostels in the city proper. Most of the hostels and *foyers* in the city are privately run organizations, usually with services comparable to those at HI and often preferable to the HI hostels because of their more central locations. Normally intended for university students during the academic year, *foyers* offer the security and privacy of a hotel, while providing the lower prices and camaraderie of a youth hostel.

■ Hotels

Of the three classes of Parisian budget accommodations, hotels may be the most practical for the majority of travelers. There is total privacy, no curfew, and (usually) concerned managers. Most important, hotels routinely accept reservations. Budget hotels in Paris are not significantly more expensive than their hostel and *foyer* counterparts. Groups of two, three, and four may find it more economical to stay in a hotel since, unlike *foyers,* hotels rent doubles by the room and not by the body.

The French government publishes a comprehensive guide that classifies hotels with a star system: 4L (luxury), 4, 3, 2, and 1, depending on the services offered, the percentage of rooms with bath, and other such indicators. Most hotels in *Let's Go* are one-star or unclassified establishments, though two-star hotels offering inexpensive rooms are sometimes included. Most rooms come with full-size beds. In our listings, double refers to rooms with one full-size bed; two-bed double refers to the rare room with two separate (usually twin) beds. Expect to pay at least 150F for singles. If your room has no shower, you'll usually have to pay extra (15-25F) to get the key to the hall shower. Showers in your room are included in the room charge.

Paris has a number of very nice hotels in the 150-200F range. These hotels are often small, simple, and do not offer the amenities of the Sheraton or the Hilton. But the hotels listed here are clean, have well-furnished rooms, and have adequate toilet and shower facilities. Most newly renovated hotels have double-paned glass windows which provide insulation against cold and street noise.

A few tips about Parisian hotels: Keep in mind that the French call the ground floor the *rez-de-chaussée,* and start numbering with the first floor *above* the ground floor *(premier étage).* Many hotels serve breakfast for 20-30F. Since local cafés often serve croissants and coffee for less, you may want to eat breakfast out. Remember that there are usually rules against bringing food into your rooms. Parisian law forbids hanging laundry from windows or over balconies to dry. Most hotels in Paris are not wheelchair accessible; in the index of this book, we list the few hotels we cover that are. It is advisable to call for more information as accessibility is almost always limited to a few rooms and may require advance reservations or preparation.

RESERVATIONS

Confirm your dates before making a reservation. If you decide to leave Paris before you intended, or if you want to switch hotels, don't expect to get back all your money. Make reservations at least two weeks in advance; a number of hotels claim that they are fully booked two months in advance for the summer. To help guarantee that you have a room waiting when you arrive, the following process is advised:

1) Call, write, or fax the hotel asking for a reservation for a specific date and specifying the type of room (single, double, with bathroom, shower, etc.).

2) If you write, enclose an International Reply Coupon (sold at post offices), so that the hotel need not bother with postage expenses.

3) When you receive positive confirmation, send *la caution* (a deposit) for one night. Most hotels will confirm reservations only upon receipt of a check for the first

night, although some will accept a credit card number instead. The easiest way to send this deposit is to mail a traveler's check in French francs, double signed.

4) Call one or two days in advance to confirm (or cancel) and inform the manager of your intended arrival time.

■ Alternative Accommodations

STUDENT ACCOMMODATIONS

For travelers planning a summer visit to Paris, student housing is available in the dormitories of most French universities. Contact the **Centre Régional des Oeuvres Universitaires (CROUS)** for more information. Additional lodging is available on a month-to-month basis at the **Cité Universitaire** (15, bd. Jourdan, 14ème; tel. 01 53 80 68 88; M. Cité Universitaire). Over 30 different nations maintain dormitories at the Cité Universitaire, where they board their citizens studying in Paris. In summer, dorms lodge anyone on a first-come, first-served basis. Reserve a bed months in advance—at least by April for June and July. To stay in the American House write to Fondation des Etats-Unis, 15, bd. Jourdan, 75690 Paris Cedex 14 (tel. 01 53 80 68 88). Room rates vary according to demand in summer: 2900F per month. Office open Monday-Friday 10-11:30am and 4-6pm. For info about other dorms, write to M. le Délégué Général de Cité Universitaire de Paris, 19, bd. Jourdan, 75690 Paris Cedex 14. Kitchen facilities available. The restaurant in the Maison Internationale offers decent institutional fare at rock-bottom prices (open Mon.-Sun. 11:45am-2:30pm and 5:30-9pm; meal ticket 12F).

LONG-TERM ACCOMMODATIONS

If you plan to stay in Paris for a longer period of time, consider renting an apartment. Though rent is high and utilities are expensive, apartments offer convenience, privacy, and a kitchen. Call, fax, write, or visit **Allô Logement Temporaraire,** 64, rue du Temple, 3ème (tel. 01 42 72 00 06; fax 01 42 72 03 11; M. Chapelle; open Mon.-Fri. noon-8pm). This helpful, English-speaking association charges a membership fee of 300F if they succeed in finding an apartment for you, which is followed by an additional charge of 200F per month beginning in the second month of your stay. The company suggests writing or calling before you leave for France. Be sure to leave a phone or fax number where you can be reached easily; vacancies come and go very quickly. Consult the French Department at your local university; it may be able to connect you with students abroad who want to sublet. Remember that short-term rentals, usually more expensive per month than longer rentals, can be difficult to procure, especially in winter months.

If possible, stay in a hotel your first week in Paris and find an apartment while you're there. This will allow you to see what you're getting. Among the best places to look are the bulletin boards in the **American Church.** Those upstairs tend to advertize for long-term lessors, while those downstairs list short-term, often cheaper arrangements. A smaller list of apartments to rent or share can be found at the bookstore **Shakespeare and Co.** (see "Books and Magazines," p. 274). Check listings in any of the English-French newsletters like **Free Voice** or **France-USA Contacts (FUSAC).** FUSAC is a free publication found in English bookstores and restaurants throughout Paris. It is also distributed in the U.S. (write or fax to FUSAC, 104 W. 14th St., New York, NY 10011-7314, USA; tel. (212) 989-8989; fax (212) 255-5555). It includes an extensive classifieds section, in which anglophones offer apartments for rent or sublet. An earlier generation often found cheap rooms on the top floor of regular hotels, where the cramped space under the eaves rents for less; if they haven't added elevators or renovated, some hotels still have cut rates for these simple singles and rent them for longer stays.

HOTELS, HOSTELS, AND FOYERS

■ First Arrondissement

In the shadow of the Louvre, much of the 1er remains true to its regal past. Cartier, Chanel, and the Banque de France set an intimidating mood for the budget traveler. Yet while financiers and ladies-who-lunch may whisk past you haughtily, don't let them scare you away: a few budget finds are still scattered around the area here. Single travelers who stay near Châtelet-les-Halles will revel in their central location, but should use a safer metro station at night.

Henri IV, 25, pl. Dauphine (tel. 01 43 54 44 53). M. Cité. Walk toward the Conciergerie, turn right on bd. du Palais, and left on quai de l'Horloge; turn left at the front of the Conciergerie onto pl. Dauphine. The last outpost of cheap accommodations on Ile de la Cité; one of the best-located hotels in the city. Overlooking a quiet park. Somewhat run-down, average-sized rooms with squishy beds. To reach the quirky first floor toilet, follow the staircase that curls around the building. All other toilets located (inside) on each floor. Collection of guidebooks for guests' use. Singles 115-140F. Doubles 145-200F, with shower 225-255F. Triples 200-225F. Quads 260F. Reserve 2 months in advance; send a check for 1 night.

Hôtel Montpensier, 12, rue de Richelieu (tel. 01 42 96 28 50; fax 01 42 86 02 70). M. Palais-Royal. Walk left around the Palais Royal to rue de Richelieu. Clean rooms, fresh scents, lofty ceilings, and friendly staff welcome the Montpensier's clientele. Its spaciousness, good taste, and elevator distinguish it from most hotels in this region and price range. Brightly lit lounge with stained glass ceiling. 43 rooms, 36 with private baths. TVs in rooms with shower or bath. Singles 250F, doubles 260F. Singles or doubles with toilet 295F, with shower, toilet, and sink 385F, with bath, toilet, and sink 450F. Extra bed 70F. Shower 25F. Breakfast 35F in lounge or bedroom. Reserve 2 weeks in advance. MC,V, AmEx.

Hôtel du Palais, 2, quai de la Mégisserie (tel. 01 42 36 98 25; fax 01 42 21 41 67). M. Châtelet. Location by the Seine, at the corner of pl. du Châtelet and quai de la Mégisserie, gives all rooms (except those on top floor) splendid views—though the sounds of street traffic waft through open windows. 18 rooms have sound dampening double-pained windows. High ceilings on first floor; crazy, funky eaves and tiny rooms on top floor. Singles with shower 280F, with shower and toilet 320F, with bath and toilet 350F. Doubles with shower 320F, with shower and toilet 350F, with bath and toilet 380F. Triples 420F. Large quad (480F) and quint (550F) with 2-sink bathroom and huge windows. On garret-like top floor: singles 180F, doubles 230F. Extra bed 70F. Hall shower included for top-floor, no-frill rooms. Breakfast 30F. Reserve 3 weeks in advance. MC, V.

Hôtel Lion d'Or, 5, rue de la Sourdière (tel. 01 42 60 79 04; fax 01 42 60 09 14). M. Tuileries or Pyramides. From M. Tuileries walk down rue du 29 Juillet away from the park, turn right on rue St-Honoré; turn left on rue de la Sourdière. Carpeted, sparsely decorated rooms with colorful bedspreads and double-paned glass; you'll hear the bells toll from nearby Eglise St-Roch, but little else. English-speaking staff. Prices "change with the season." In general, singles 195F, with shower 260F. Doubles 270F, with shower 320F-340F, with bath and toilet 390-395F. Extra bed 60F. Showers 20F. Breakfast 35F. 5% discount for stays of more than three nights. MC, V, AmEx.

Hôtel de Lille, 8, rue du Pélican (tel. 01 42 33 33 42). M. Palais-Royal. From the Metro walk toward the Palais-Royal and turn right onto rue St-Honoré, left on rue Croix des Petits Champs, and take your first right on rue du Pélican. Located on a quiet street close to the Louvre. What it lacks in extras it makes up in calm and price. Big, clean, red-carpeted rooms. Coin-operated phone on 1st floor. Outside door locked at 9pm; arrive before 7pm to pick up your personal and outside door keys. Singles 180F. Doubles 220F, with shower 270F. Showers 30F. No breakfast. Reserve 1-2 months in advance with check for one night's payment.

Hôtel Saint-Honoré, 85, rue St-Honoré (tel. 01 42 36 20 38 or 01 42 21 46 96; fax 01 42 21 44 08). M. Louvre, Châtelet, or Les Halles. From M. Louvre, cross rue de Rivoli onto rue du Louvre and turn right on rue St-Honoré. Recently renovated, comfortable, bright, good-sized rooms with firm beds and simple decor. Some renovations may be ongoing. Friendly, English-speaking staff, and young clientele. Guests have access to fridge. No singles. All rooms have shower and toilet. Doubles 280-320F. Triples 380F. Quads 450F. Breakfast 24F. Reserve one month in advance and confirm the night before or upon arrival. MC, V.

Hôtel Richelieu-Mazarin, 51, rue de Richelieu (tel. 01 42 97 46 20). M. Palais-Royal. Walk left around the Palais Royal to rue de Richelieu. Industrial carpeting, plastic flowers, and faux Monet prints. Doubles in converted attic are an oasis of taste—muted flowered wallpaper, pine furniture, and skylight (but no view). Otherwise, smallish rooms have radios, phones, and a view of the bustling thoroughfare. Little English spoken. Singles 190-210F, with shower or bath and toilet 280-310F. Doubles 230F, with shower or bath and toilet 300-330F. Triple with shower and toilet 390F. Extra bed 60F. Showers 10F. Breakfast 25F in the *salle,* 30F in your room. Reserve 3 weeks ahead in summer. MC, V, traveler's checks.

Hôtel de Rouen, 42, rue Croix des Petits Champs (tel. and fax 01 42 61 38 21). M. Palais-Royal. Walk toward the Palais-Royal, turn right on rue St-Honoré and left on rue Croix des Petits Champs. Steep, narrow staircase leads to small rooms with smaller bathrooms. Rooms on higher floors are quieter and hotter. One triple on the courtyard priced as a double. Singles or doubles 180F, with shower 240F, with shower, toilet, and TV 290F. Triple with shower and toilet 290F. Quads with shower, toilet, and TV 350F. Free hall shower. Breakfast 20F. MC, V.

Hôtel du Centre, 20, rue du Roule (tel. 01 42 33 05 18; fax 01 42 33 74 02). M. Pont Neuf, Louvre, Châtelet, or Les Halles. Take rue de la Monnaie toward Les Halles straight onto rue du Roule. If inexpensive accommodations and location at the center of the cultural/touristic mosh-pit of inner Paris are your overriding concerns, the Hôtel du Centre is the place for you. Quiet helps compensate for the hotel's stuffy air and cramped stairwell. Rooms with mushy beds, red carpeting on the floor, and pink fur on the walls. Singles or doubles with shower and toilet, most with TV 340F. Extra double bed (only available for some rooms) 30% extra. Breakfast 29F. Reserve 2 weeks in advance with 1 night's deposit. Basic English spoken. No elevator. MC, V, AmEx.

Hostels and Foyers

Centre International de Paris (BVJ)/Paris Louvre, 20, rue J.-J. Rousseau, (tel. 01 42 36 88 18; fax 01 42 33 40 53). M. Palais-Royal. 200 beds. High-ceilinged, bright, dorm-style rooms. Courtyard hung with brass lanterns and strewn with *brasserie* chairs. 2-10 beds per room. Lunch or dinner 55F. Groups must pay for 1 meal per day, lunch or dinner. Open 6am-2am. No families. Rooms available at 2:30pm. 120F per person, breakfast and showers included. No singles. Meals usually 55F. Weekend reservations up to 1 week in advance; reserve 1 day ahead for weekday bookings. Rooms held 1 hr. after your expected check-in time; call if you'll be late.

Maisons des Jeunes Rufz de l'Avison, 18, rue J.-J. Rousseau (tel. 01 45 08 02 10). M. Louvre or Palais-Royal. From M. Louvre take rue du Louvre away from river, turn left on rue St.-Honoré and right on rue J.-J. Rousseau. During the academic year, it's a private residence for male college students. In summer it's a coed *foyer*. Quiet, spacious and sunny rooms. Flower-filled open-air courtyard—hay fever sufferers, beware. Reception open 9am-7pm. No curfew. Singles 200F, 3 day minimum stay, 160F per night if you stay more than 5 days. Doubles 140F per person, 5-day minimum stay. Shower and breakfast included.

■ Second Arrondissement

Although there's little to see in the 2*ème* itself, it's within easy walking distance of the Marais, the Centre Pompidou, and the Louvre. The 2*ème*'s safe, animated southern half sports the cobbled market street rue Montorgueil and the pedestrian rues Tiquetonne and Léopold Bellan, while the streets radiating away from pl. de l'Opéra are littered with designer boutiques and theatres. In general, try not to stray too far into the northeastern quarter, especially near the seedy rue St-Denis; below rue Réamur, it glows with flashing sex shop signs, while further north and especially near Porte St-Denis it supports a large number of prostitutes.

Hôtel Bonne Nouvelle, 17, rue Beauregard (tel. 01 45 08 42 42; fax 01 40 26 05 81). M. Strasbourg-St-Denis or Bonne Nouvelle. From M. Bonne Nouvelle follow traffic down rue Poissonnière and turn left on rue Beauregard. A bright, calico-trimmed lobby and somber men's club hallways lead toward sizeable rooms with TVs and antique-style furnishings. Spotless, modern bathrooms come equipped with hairdryers. Singles 250F, with shower and toilet 310F. Doubles with toilet and shower or bath 310-370F. Triples with toilet and bath 450-580F. One quad with toilet and bath 540-580F. Breakfast 30F, in room 35F. Reserve with 1 night's deposit. MC, V.

Hôtel Vivienne, 40, rue Vivienne (tel. 01 42 33 13 26; fax 01 40 41 98 19). M. rue Montmartre. Walk down bd. Montmartre past the Théâtre des Variétés and turn left on rue Vivienne. From its ungainly, tiled hallway to spacious rooms outfitted with armoires, TVs, and full-length mirrors, this hotel successfully reconciles gracious living with budget accommodations. Some rooms have balconies, and from the top floor you can see across the surrounding rooftops. Singles and doubles with shower 350F, with shower and toilet 420F, with bath and toilet 440F. 2-bed doubles with bath and toilet 460F. 3rd person under 10 yrs. free, over 10 yrs. 30% extra. Breakfast 40F. Elevator. MC, V.

Hôtel La Marmotte, 6, rue Léopold Bellan (tel. 01 40 26 26 51). M. Sentier. Follow traffic on rue Réaumur, turn right onto rue Montorgueil, and then turn right again at rue Léopold Bellan. Reception located in ground-floor bar. Unlike many French budget hotels, the building itself is relatively modern. Clean, quiet rooms come with fairly good mattresses, classy patterned bedspreads, and TVs. Some English spoken. Singles and doubles with shower and toilet 270-300F. 2-bed doubles with shower and toilet 320F. Extra bed 80F. Breakfast 25F. Shower 15F. Reserve 2-3 weeks in advance. MC, V, AmEx.

Hôtel Ste-Marie, 6, rue de la Ville Neuve (tel. 01 42 33 21 61; fax 01 42 33 29 24). M. Bonne Nouvelle. From the rue Poissionnière metro exit, turn right on rue Poissonnière, then left on rue de la Lune and right onto rue de la Ville Neuve. This route allows you to avoid the X-rated movie theater on rue de la Ville Neuve, the one blemish in an otherwise good area. This bright little hotel has recently been renovated and refurbished with candy-striped walls, new mattresses, and clean, tiled bathrooms. Some English spoken. Singles 173F, with shower and toilet 243F. Doubles 206F, with shower and toilet 281F. Triples with shower and toilet 392F. Shower 10F. Breakfast 20F.

Hôtel Tiquetonne, 6, rue Tiquetonne (tel. 01 42 36 94 58; fax 01 42 36 02 94). M. Etienne-Marcel. Walk against traffic on rue de Turbigo and turn left on rue Tiquetonne. Near Marché Montorgueil, but uncomfortably close to the sex shops on rue St-Denis, this affordable hotel has fake-marble corridors and large rooms shouting in various shades of red and pink. Singles 136F, with shower and toilet 203-233F. Doubles with shower and toilet 236F. Showers 25F. Breakfast 22F served in your room. Elevator. Closed Aug. MC, V.

■ Third Arrondissement

Once the address of Paris' noblest families, the southern portion of the 3ème hides many restored 17th-century mansions, some of which now house museums, boutiques and galleries. Meanwhile, budget hotels cluster in the 3ème's noisy, commercial northwest—particularly around rue Turbigo, where budget hotels sidle up to Paris' garment district.

Hôtel du Séjour, 36, rue du Grenier St.-Lazare (tel. 01 48 87 40 36). M. Etienne Marcel or Rambuteau. From M. Rambuteau, walk opposite traffic on rue Beaubourg and turn left on rue du Grenier St.-Lazare. One block from Les Halles and the Centre Pompidou. This inexpensive hotel is in the process of being re-done one room at a time. Ask for a renovated room. The hotel isn't oozing with charm, but the Portuguese couple who run it love to chat and will gladly watch your bags the day you check out. Reception 7am-9:30pm, call ahead if you're going to arrive later. Singles 130F. Doubles 180F, with shower 250F, with shower and toilet 270-280F. Shower 20F. No elevator or breakfast.

Hôtel de Roubaix, 6, rue Greneta (tel. 01 42 72 89 91; fax 01 42 72 58 79). M. Réaumur-Sébastopol or Arts-et-Métiers. From M. Réaumur-Sébastopol, walk opposite traffic on bd. de Sébastopol and turn left on rue Greneta. This hotel (which is upscale for the price) is run by a wonderful older couple who enjoy giving advice to travelers. They will keep your bags in a safe place the day you leave. Very clean rooms with flowered wallpaper and brand new bathrooms. Breakfast room, 2 other lounges. All rooms have shower, toilet, and cable TV. Rooms on the street are noisy if the windows are open, rooms on the courtyard are quiet. Singles 300-330F. 2-bed doubles 390-410F. Triples 415-435F; 3-bed triple 480F. Quad 500F, 5 people 525F. Breakfast included. Elevator. MC, V.

Hôtel Picard, 26, rue de Picardie (tel. 01 48 87 53 82; fax 01 48 87 02 56). M. République or Filles-du-Calvaire. From M. République walk down rue du Temple, make your first left on rue Béranger, turn right on rue de Franche-Comté, then turn left on rue de Picardie. Quiet, clean hotel which feels like it hasn't been renovated in years. 5-min. walk to the Centre Pompidou or the Musée Picasso. Twin doubles are bunk-bed style. Mention *Let's Go* for a 10% discount. English spoken. Elevator. Singles 200F, with shower and toilet 250F, with bath and toilet 320F. Doubles 240-260F, with shower and toilet 320F, with bath and toilet 390F. Extra bed 120F. Showers 20F. Breakfast 30F. MC, V.

Hôtel Bellevue et du Chariot d'Or, 39, rue de Turbigo (tel. 01 48 87 45 60; fax 01 48 87 95 04). M. Arts-et-Métiers. Clean, modern rooms with new bathrooms. Some look onto a quiet courtyard. Elegant breakfast room, bar, and lobby. All rooms have telephones, toilets and bathtub or shower. Singles 305F, Doubles 330F. Triples 415F. Quads 475F. Breakfast 30F.

Hôtel Bretagne, 87, rue des Archives (tel. 01 48 87 83 14). M. Temple. From the metro, walk opposite traffic on rue du Temple, turn left on rue de Bretagne and right onto rue des Archives. The hotel is next to a small park which makes a good spot for picnics. Variable room quality and size: cheaper rooms are simple, while more expensive ones have TVs and snazzy new bathroom fixtures. Many rooms are on the noisy street, others are on a nondescript courtyard. No real breakfast room. Singles 155F, with bath, toilet, and TV 300F. Doubles 195-220F, with bath, toilet, and TV 350F. 2-bed double 220F. Triples 330F, with bath, toilet, and TV 500F. Quad 440F, with bath, toilet and TV 600. Breakfast 30F. No credit cards.

Hôtel Paris France, 72, rue de Turbigo (tel. 01 42 78 00 04, reservations 01 42 78 64 92; fax 01 42 71 99 43). M. République or Temple. From M. République take rue de Turbigo, the hotel is on the left. The lobby has pleasant lounges where breakfast is served. Rooms and lobby are feebly lit at night. Noisy rooms with tiny showers but spacious, tiled baths. English spoken. Singles with shower 255F, doubles with shower 290F, with bath, toilet, and TV 320F. Extra bed 100F. Breakfast 25F. Elevator. MC, V, AmEx.

Laundromats

Laverie, 40, rue de Montmorency; M. Rambateau. Walk against traffic on rue Beaubourg and turn left. Wash 6kg (20F). Dry 5F per cycle. One dose of detergent 2F. Open 7am-9pm.

■ Fourth Arrondissement

On either side of the rue de Rivoli, a web of narrow streets and alleyways harbors galleries, boutiques, historic sites, small museums, quiet squares, and funky bars (homo and hetero). The Marais is famed for its old Jewish quarter, its **pl. des Vosges** (the oldest square in Paris), and its many hidden courtyards—in all, making the 4*ème* a great place to get lost, and an ideal base for tourists.

Hôtel Practic, 9, rue d'Ormesson (tel. 01 48 87 80 47; fax 01 48 87 40 04). M. St-Paul. From the metro, walk opposite traffic on rue de Rivoli, turn left on rue de

Sévigné and right on rue d'Ormesson. No elevator or fresh flowers, but nevertheless, this is the kind of low-budget hotel one always hopes for: clean, quiet, and right on a cobblestone square in the heart of the Marais (ask for a room with a view of the square). Reserve 2 weeks in advance (longer for singles). TV in all rooms. English spoken. Singles 150F. Doubles 230F, with shower 275F, with toilet and shower 340F. Hall shower free. Breakfast 25F. No credit cards.

Castex Hôtel, 5, rue Castex (tel. 01 42 72 31 52; fax 01 42 72 57 91). M. Bastille or Sully-Morland. Exit M. Bastille on bd. Henri IV and take the third right on rue Castex. Rooms in this family-run hotel are spotless and quiet (they look onto either a side street or a courtyard with a slanting metal roof and plants). TV room on main floor. English spoken. Check-in 1pm. Reception open 7am-12pm. All rooms with telephone, sink, and shower or bath. Singles 220F, with toilet 240-270F. Doubles 300F, with toilet 320-340F. 2-bed doubles with toilet 320F, with bath and toilet 340F. Triple with bath and toilet 440F. Extra bed 70F, for baby 30F. Breakfast 25F. Reserve with 1 night's deposit 7-8 weeks in advance. MC, V.

Hôtel Sansonnet, 48, rue de la Verrerie (tel. 01 48 87 96 14; fax 01 48 87 30 46). M. Hôtel-de-Ville. Walk down rue du Temple with your back to the Hôtel de Ville and turn left on rue de la Verrerie. A long white staircase with a Persian rug leads up to the reception area. Clean, tasteful rooms look out on a rather quiet street or courtyard. All rooms have cable TV, and most have hair dryers. English spoken. Singles 245-255F, with shower 285F, with shower and toilet 340F, with bath and toilet 365F. Doubles with shower and toilet 355F, with bath and toilet 380F. Showers 20F. Breakfast 32F. Reserve 3 weeks in advance. MC, V.

Hôtel Andréa, 3, rue St-Bon (tel. 01 42 78 43 93). M. Hôtel-de-Ville. Follow traffic on rue de Rivoli and turn right on rue St-Bon. Located on a quiet side street 5min. from Châtelet. Clean rooms with varying color schemes. Some have non-functioning fireplaces. To avoid noise, reserve a room on a high floor if possible. Travelers in cheaper rooms must descend to use the 1st-floor shower. Rooms with shower or bath also have TV. Singles 210F, with toilet and shower or bath 300F. Doubles 210F, with toilet and shower or bath 330-350F. Extra bed 60F. Showers 15F. Breakfast 30F. Reserve 2 weeks in advance with 1 night's deposit. Elevator. MC, V, AmEx.

Hôtel de la Herse d'Or, 20, rue St-Antoine (tel. 01 48 87 84 09). M. Bastille. Exit metro on rue St-Antoine and continue two blocks. Rooms look onto a tiny, box-like cement courtyard, a wall, or the noisy street. (There is also an old church across the street that makes for a "picturesque" view if you're up high enough that the noise isn't intrusive). Fairly clean. Singles 160F, with toilet and shower 260F, with toilet and bath 280F. Doubles 200F, with toilet and shower 260F, with toilet and bath 280F. Triples with toilet and shower 380F. Shower 10F. Breakfast 25F. Tax 3F per person, per night. Reserve 2-10 days in advance.

Hôtel de la Place des Vosges, 12, rue de Birague (tel. 01 42 72 60 46; fax 01 42 72 02 64). M. Bastille. From the metro take the third right off rue St-Antoine. Go for it, if you can afford it! Elegant hotel on a quiet street, steps away from pl. des Vosges. Plush red carpets and dark wood. Rooms are tiny, except on the top floor, and some look onto a wall (but are quiet and get a little sun anyway). TV in all rooms. English spoken. During summer months rooms on higher floors are also useful as steam baths. Singles with toilet and shower 305F, with toilet and bath 415F. Doubles with toilet and bath 420F. 2-bed doubles with toilet and bath 440F. One quad on top floor 670F. Extra beds for children under 12 110F. Breakfast 40F. Reserve 1-2½ months ahead. Elevator starting on 2nd floor. MC, V, AmEx.

Grand Hôtel Jeanne d'Arc, 3, rue de Jarente (tel. 01 48 87 62 11; fax 01 48 87 37 31). M. St-Paul or Bastille. From M. St-Paul walk opposite traffic on rue de Rivoli, turn left on rue de Sévigné, then right on rue de Jarente. Elegant hotel on a quiet street in the Marais. Rooms have peach-colored wallpaper, Renoir prints, and views ranging from "Ah, Paris!" (slanting roofs, courtyard, chimneys) to the airshaft, "I thought it was sunny out." Queen-sized beds, remote control cable TV, table cloths in the breakfast room, and a large selection of guide books on the wooden bookshelves. English spoken. 2 rooms on ground floor wheelchair-accessible. Singles or doubles with toilet and shower, small room 295F. Larger singles or doubles with toilet and shower or bath 380F. Doubles with two big beds, toilet, and bath or shower 450F. Triples with toilet and bath or shower 500F. Quads with toilet and bath or shower 550F. Extra bed 75F. Breakfast 35F. 5F tax per person, per night. Reserve 1 month in advance. Elevator. MC, V.

Hôtel de Nice, 42bis, rue de Rivoli (tel. 01 42 78 55 29; fax 01 42 78 36 07). M. Hôtel-de-Ville. From the metro, walk opposite traffic on rue de Rivoli for about four blocks; the hotel is on the left. A place with character! The owners wanted to respect this 19th-century building by using 19th-century decorations. Lots of rugs, colors, and (slightly faded) patterns. Many rooms have balconies, and rooms high up have great views. A bit hot in the summer (there are fans in the rooms) and noisy if the window is open. Sparkling bathrooms and lots of light. English spoken. Singles and doubles with toilet 380F, with shower or bath 400-420F, depending upon the size. Triples with toilet and bath 520F. Breakfast 30F. Check-in 2pm, check-out 11am. Extra bed 100F. Reserve with 1 night's deposit a month in advance for summer. Elevator from 2nd floor. MC, V.

Hostels

Hôtel des Jeunes (MIJE) (tel. 01 42 74 23 45; fax 01 42 74 08 93 or 01 42 71 61 02) books stays in "Le Fourcy," "Le Fauconnier," and "Maubuisson." Three small, charming hostels located on quiet streets in former Marais aristocratic residences. No smoking. English spoken. Public phones and free lockers (with a 2F deposit) For groups, no age specifications or limits on length of stay. Individuals must be 18-30 and have a 7-day maximum. Reception open 7am-10pm. Check out by noon. Lockout noon-4pm. Silence after 10pm. No entry to hostels after 1am. Singles 168F. Doubles 148F per person. Larger rooms (3-8 beds) 120F per person. Shower in room, toilet down the hall, breakfast served 7:30-10am—all included. No towels, but there are sheets and blankets. Individuals may reserve rooms only in person and by paying in full in advance. Rebooking must be requested before 10pm the day before. Groups may reserve 1 year in advance. The budget **Restaurant la Table d'Hôtes,** entered through le Fourcy, offers an entrée with drink and coffee (32F) and 3-course "hosteler special" (52F). Open Mon.-Fri. 11:30am-1:30pm and 6:30-8:30pm.

Le Fourcy, 6, rue de Fourcy. M. St-Paul or Pont Marie. From M. St-Paul, walk opposite traffic for a few meters down rue François-Miron and turn left on rue de Fourcy. Hostel surrounds a large courtyard ideal for meeting travelers or for open-air picnicking at one of the tables. In summer, school groups raise Cain under evening skies; light sleepers should shun rooms on the courtyard. Elevator. Call ahead for wheelchair accessibility.

Le Fauconnier, 11, rue du Fauconnier. M. St-Paul or Pont Marie. From M. St-Paul take rue du Prevôt, turn left on rue Charlemagne and take the first right on rue du Fauconnier. Spacious rooms, most of which have 6 beds, some doubles, some singles.

Maubuisson, 12, rue des Barres. M. Hôtel-de-Ville or Pont Marie. From M. Pont Marie, walk opposite traffic on rue de l'Hôtel de Ville and turn right on rue des Barres. A former girls' convent that looks out onto a carless cobblestone street and faces the St. Gervais monastery. Lively Maubuisson offers smaller rooms of 2-7 beds (mostly 4 beds). Two of the doubles look at the Seine; many rooms have nice views. Elevator. Call ahead for wheelchairs.

■ Fifth Arrondissement

With the Sorbonne as its focal point, the 5ème is a bookish neighborhood with the feel of a bustling village. Wander its café-filled squares and outdoor markets, take in a movie, and then launch yourself on its action-packed nightlife. Most hotels fill up for August far in advance; try to reserve rooms at least a month ahead.

Hôtel d'Esmeralda, 4, rue St-Julien-le-Pauvre (tel. 01 43 54 19 20; fax 01 40 51 00 68). M. St-Michel. Walk along the Seine on quai St-Michel toward Notre-Dame and turn right at the park. Friendly staff, perfect location, and homey rooms make the Esmeralda a diamond in the rough of this bustling neighborhood. Beautiful views of the parc Vivani, the Seine, and Notre Dame. Nit-pickers might notice that the halls are a little tight, the ceilings a little low, and the staircase a bit steep. English spoken. Singles 160F, with shower and toilet 320F. Doubles with shower and toilet 420-490F. Triples with shower and toilet 550F. Quads with shower and toilet 600F. Breakfast 40F. Shower 10F.

Hôtel des Argonauts, 12, rue de la Huchette (tel. 01 43 54 09 82; fax 01 44 07 18 84). M. St-Michel. Rue de la Huchette is off of bd. St-Michel, near the Seine. Located above a Greek restaurant of the same name; a pleasant surprise that may have vacancies when other hotels in the 5*ème* do not. Beautiful lobby decorated entirely in flower patterns. The clean, spacious rooms are surprisingly quiet given the bustling (and sometimes noisy) street. Singles 200F, doubles with shower 250-350F, with toilet and shower 300-350F. Breakfast 25F. MC, V, AmEx.

Hôtel des Grandes Ecoles, 75, rue Cardinal Lemoine (tel. 01 43 26 79 23; fax 01 43 25 28 15). M. Cardinal Lemoine. From the metro take a left on rue Cardinal Lemoine in the direction of the Panthéon. The place to go all-out on a hotel in Paris. Built around a flower garden where guests breakfast in warm weather, this ivy-covered establishment maintains impeccably clean, tasteful rooms to the great pleasure of its faithful guests. Singles and doubles 510F and up. Triples 610F. Several smaller, less well-equipped rooms available as singles or doubles 320-350F. Extra bed 100F. Breakfast 40F. Reserve well ahead. MC, V.

Hôtel St-Jacques, 35, rue des Ecoles (tel. 01 43 26 82 53; fax 01 43 25 65 50). M. Maubert-Mutualité. Walk up rue des Carmes and turn right on rue des Ecoles. Clean, quiet hotel, with relatively big rooms that are well-maintained. Impressive lobby with a glass chandelier and red carpet. English spoken. Singles 190F, with shower or bath and toilet 420F. Doubles with shower 320F, with shower and toilet 480F. Triples with shower and toilet 560F. Shower 25F. Breakfast 30F. Elevator. MC, V, AmEx.

Hôtel des Alliés, 20, rue Berthollet (tel. 01 43 31 47 52; fax 01 45 35 13 92). M. Censier-Daubenton. Walk down rue Monge in the direction of bd. Port-Royal, turn right on rue Claude Bernard and left on rue Berthollet. Less scenic than other hotels in the 5*ème*, but offers very cheap, clean, comfortable rooms and is close to the markets of rue Mouffetard. Singles 145-160F. Doubles 200-300F, with shower and toilet 295F. Showers 15F. Breakfast 28F. MC, V.

Hôtel Marignan, 13, rue du Sommerard (tel. 01 43 54 63 81). M. Maubert-Mutualité. Turn left on rue des Carmes and right on rue du Sommerard. Quiet, spacious rooms, many redone with new handmade cabinets and paint jobs. Has a boarding-house feel, with clientele ranging from backpacking students to suitcase-lugging families. Laundry room and a breakfast room (with microwave) where residents can fix daytime meals. Singles with shower and toilet 190F. Doubles 290-310F. Triples 380-420F, with shower 440-490. Quads 440-480F, with shower 550-650F. Free hall shower and washing machine for clients use. Breakfast included. Reserve far in advance. Rates fall in winter.

Hôtel Gay Lussac, 29, rue Gay-Lussac (tel. 01 43 54 23 96). M. Luxembourg. From the metro walk down rue Gay-Lussac to rue St-Jacques; hotel is at the intersection. An old but well-preserved hotel on a noisy street: the floors are slightly warped and creaky, but the rooms are clean, sunny, and in good repair. Some even have balconies. Lots of tour groups. Doubles and singles 185F, with shower 350-360F. Triples with shower 425F. Quads 550F. Hall shower free. Breakfast 25F. Reserve by phone at least 2 weeks in advance; no deposit required. Elevator.

Grand Hôtel du Progrès, 50, rue Gay-Lussac (tel. 01 43 54 53 18). M. Luxembourg. Multilingual proprietors welcome you to clean, bright rooms with big windows and simple decor; expect balconies, as well as linoleum floors, frayed rugs, and some peeling paint. Tiny, yet cute, annexes on the top floor overlook the Panthéon. Plant-filled breakfast room has a piano and a small library (for your travel literature needs). Singles 150-172F, with shower and toilet 310F. Doubles 240F, with shower and toilet 330F. 2-bed double 285F, the same room with a third bed 330F. Showers free. Breakfast included.

Hôtel le Central, 6, rue Descartes (tel. 01 46 33 57 93). M. Maubert-Mutualité. Walk uphill on rue de la Montaigne Ste. Geneviève from the metro. Great location near the rue Mouffetard with abundant cafés and bars nearby. Narrow stairs, odd wallpaper, sparkling clean rooms, bathrooms and sheets. Rooms facing the street get brilliant sunlight. Singles 153-173F. Doubles with shower 216-246F. Triples with folding bed for same price as doubles.

Hôtel Gerson, 14, rue de la Sorbonne (tel. 01 43 54 28 49; fax 01 44 07 13 90). M. Cluny-Sorbonne. Left on bd. St-Michel, then left on rue des Ecoles and right on rue de la Sorbonne. Site facing the Sorbonne and bright, clean rooms compensate for mismatched furnishings. Singles 210F, with shower and toilet 283F. Double with toilet 250F, with toilet and shower 310F. Large two or three person rooms with shower and toilet 360-400F. Shower 20F. Breakfast 25F. MC, V.

Hôtel des Médicis, 214, rue St-Jacques (tel. 01 43 54 14 66). M. Luxembourg. From the metro turn right onto rue Gay Lussac, and then left onto rue St-Jacques. Kerouak, Burroughs, and a hardy breed of backpacker would find this hotel to be a fine nesting place. Travellers with more delicate sensibilities probably will not. A lack of upkeep comes with bottom of the barrel prices. English spoken, lots of American youths. Check your room before accepting. Reception open 9am-11pm. Some 85F singles, usually occupied. Singles and doubles 150F, with toilet 160F. Showers 10F. No reservations in summer; arrive early in the morning and hope for a vacancy.

Hostels and Foyers

Young and Happy (Y&H) Hostel, 80, rue Mouffetard (tel. 01 45 35 09 53; fax 01 47 07 22 24). M. Monge. Cross rue Gracieuse and take rue Ortolan to rue Mouffetard. Clean, cramped rooms. Lively hostel in the heart of the raucous student quarter on rue Mouffetard. Claustrophobes beware the serpentine staircase and tight hallways. Telephones in some rooms, which have 2-4 beds (mostly bunks). Lockout 11am-5pm. Curfew 2am. 107F per person per night for doubles, 97F per person per night for quads, 670F per week. Shower included. Sheets 15F. Towels 5F. Reserve with 1 night's deposit by mail (by telephone only on the day you arrive); otherwise show up at 8am.

Centre International de Paris (BVJ): Paris Quartier Latin, 44, rue des Bernardins (tel. 01 43 29 34 80; fax 01 42 33 40 53). M. Maubert-Mutualité. Walk down bd. St-Germain to rue Monge and turn right on rue des Bernardins. 138 beds. Spacious, spotless ultra-modern hostel with tile and chrome décor. Filled with a friendly, boisterous crowd that congregates in the sprawling common areas on the ground floor and basement. Photocopier, typewriter, kitchen, TV, message service, work space, airport shuttle service (de Gaulle 79F; Orly 59F) all available to guests. Showers in rooms. Reception open 24hrs. Check-in before 2:30pm. Check-out 9am. Singles 130F. Doubles, quads, and 10-bed rooms 120F per person. Breakfast included. Lockers 10F. Come by around 9am to check for available rooms. Discounts for longer stays and groups. Students may stay from one month to a year; call for info and prices.

Laundromats

Lavabo, 214bis, rue St-Jacques. M. Luxembourg. Detergent 2F; wash 20F per 6kg; dry 60F. **Laverie,** 36, rue des Bernardins. M. Maubert-Mutualité. Detergent 2F; wash 20F per 6kg; dry 2F per 5 min. Open daily 7am-10pm. **Laverie,** 8, rue Larrey. M. Monge. Detergent 2F; wash 20F per 6kg; dry 2F per 5 min. Open daily 8am-9pm. **Laverie,** 2, rue Jean de Beauvais. M. Maubert-Mutualité. Wash 24F per 7kg, 40F per 10kg; dry 2F per 5min. Open daily 7:30am-9:30pm.

■ Sixth Arrondissement

The 6*éme* combines the most attractive characteristics of the Left and Right Bank: the bohemian caché, the intellectual panache, and the historical richness of the Quartier Latin; the august noblesse of the Palais Royale region, and a thriving artistic culture centered around the École des Beaux Arts. Budget hotels are sparse in this chic neighborhood, but the following exceptions provide surprising bargains.

Hôtel Nesle, 7, rue du Nesle (tel. 01 43 54 62 41). M. Odéon. From the metro walk up rue de l'Ancienne Comédie and onto rue Dauphine; take a left on rue du Nesle.

The Egyptianesque frescoes, ducks in the rose garden, typically warm management, and outrageously low prices make for a whimsical departure from the monotony of Paris' like-seeming budget hotels. Many of the quiet, clean rooms display murals depicting the history of Paris. One of the best hotels on the Left Bank. Laundry. Singles with breakfast and shower 220F. Doubles with breakfast and shower 270-400F. No reservations; arrive between 10am and noon.

Hôtel Stella, 41, rue Monsieur-le-Prince (tel. 01 43 26 43 49; fax 01 43 54 97 28). M. Odéon or Luxembourg. From M. Odéon walk down rue Dupuytren and take a left on rue Monsieur-le-Prince. The hotel may be older than the hills, the hallways may seem under construction, and the office may be a steam bath in summer, but the wood-trimmed rooms are modern, comfortable, pleasant, breezy—basically superlative. Singles with toilet and shower 218F. Doubles with toilet and shower 298F. Triples 447F. Quads 516F. Reserve by fax or telephone.

Hôtel St-André des Arts, 66, rue St-André-des-Arts (tel. 01 43 26 96 16; fax 01 43 29 73 34). M. Odéon. From the metro take rue de l'Ancienne Comédie, walk one block, and take the first right on rue St-André-des-Arts. Unique fabric covers walls, curtains, and bedding. Central location near restaurants and bars. All rooms have toilets. Singles 235F, with shower 310-350F. Doubles with shower 450F, with 2 beds and shower 480F. Triples with double bed, single bed, and shower 550F, rooms with 2 double beds and shower 600F. Breakfast included. MC, V.

Hôtel St-Michel, 17, rue Git-le-Coeur (tel. 01 43 26 98 70). M. St-Michel. From pl. St-Michel walk one block on rue St-André-des-Arts and turn right on rue Git-le-Coeur. Comfortable (if bland) rooms on a quiet street close to the Seine. Friendly staff. Singles 215F, with shower 310F, with shower and toilet 350F. Doubles 240F, with shower 335F, with shower and toilet 375F. 2-bed doubles with shower 390F, with shower and toilet 420F. Shower 12F. Breakfast 25F. Reserve with 1 night's deposit at least 2 weeks in advance.

Hôtel Petit Trianon, 2, rue de l'Ancienne Comédie (tel. 01 43 54 94 64). M. Odéon. *Petit,* sparkling, whitewashed rooms in a loud but central location. Negotiable prices, youthful atmosphere, friendly staff, and discount deals at local attractions keep the Trianon popular. 3 rooms have balconies. Singles 180F. Much larger doubles with shower 320-350F, with shower and toilet 350-390F. Breakfast 30F. Reserve at least 1 week in advance with 1 night's deposit.

Dhely's Hotel, 22, rue de l'Hirlondelle (tel. 01 43 26 58 25). M. St-Michel. On the west side of pl. St-Michel, through the archway and down the stairs, just steps from the Seine. Wood paneling, flower boxes, modern facilities (TVs!), and a quiet location make for a pleasant stay. Singles 230F. Doubles 350F, with shower 430F. Triples 470F, with shower 580F. Extra bed 100F. Showers 25F. Breakfast 30F. Reserve with deposit. MC, V, AmEx.

Hôtel de la Faculté, 1, rue Racine (tel. 01 43 26 87 13; fax 01 46 34 73 88). M. Cluny-Sorbonne. Walk down bd. St-Michel away from the Seine until you find rue Racine on your right. Small, clean rooms, each with private shower and toilet. Singles or doubles 345-385F. Extra bed 85F. Breakfast 29F. Elevator. MC, V.

Hôtel du Dragon, 36, rue Dragon (tel. 01 45 48 51 05; fax 01 42 22 51 62). M. St-Germain-des-Prés. Walk against traffic on bd. St-Germain and turn left on rue Dragon. The justifiably proud owner of this hotel in the chic-er part of the 6*ème* has flocked all rooms with Victorian bird-and-flower wallpaper and with presumably antique furniture. Singles with shower 276F. Doubles with shower and toilet 392F. 2-bed doubles with shower and toilet 452F. Breakfast 30F. Closed Aug. MC, V, AmEx (2000F minimum).

Hostels

Foyer International des Etudiantes, 93, bd. St-Michel (tel. 01 43 54 49 63). M. Luxembourg. Across from Jardin du Luxembourg. Marbled reception area library, TV lounge, kitchenettes, and laundry facilities are all fitted with elegant wood paneling. Spacious and comfortable. Some rooms have balconies. Breakfast and shower included. Oct.-June women only: singles 133F, 2950F per month; doubles 82F per person, 2000F per person monthly; *foyer* open Sun.-Fri. 6am-1:30am, Sat. all night. July-Sept.: men and women; singles 165F, doubles 115F per person, breakfast and shower included; *foyer* open 24hr. Reserve in writing 2 months in advance, 200F deposit if confirmed. Call ahead or arrive around 9:30am to check for no-shows.

Laundromats

Julice Laverie, 24, rue Monsieur le Prince. M. Cluny-Sorbonne or Odéon. Wash 20F per 6kg, 40F per 12kg; dry 5F per 5min. Open daily 7:30am-9:30pm. **Lav'Club,** 126, rue de Vaugirard (tel. 01 47 37 52 21). M. St-Placide. Open daily 8am-9pm. Token dispenser closes at 8pm.

■ Seventh Arrondissement

Budget hotels cluster around the western edge of the 7*ème* arrondissement, all advertising (though not necessarily providing) rooms with views of the Eiffel Tower. Frequented by business travelers and older couples, hotels in this quarter are quieter and more expensive than those which cater to the scraggly backpacker. Pay a little more and enjoy telephones and TVs in most rooms, breakfast in bed, bathtubs, a subdued atmosphere, and a short walk to the tallest thing in Paris.

Hôtel de la Paix, 19, rue du Gros Caillou (tel. 01 45 51 86 17). M. Ecole Militaire. Walk up av. de la Bourdonnais, turn right on rue de Grenelle, then left on rue du Gros Caillou. The only true budget hotel in the 7*ème*, and it shows. Worn carpets, soft mattresses, peeling paint, but fairly quiet. English spoken. Reception open 9am-9pm. Get key if returning after 9pm. Check-out at noon. Singles 160F, with shower 230F. Doubles with shower 295F, with shower and toilet 295-370F. Shower 15F. Breakfast 32F. Reservations recommended. Deposit required if you plan to arrive after 3pm, payable by traveler's checks. Call ahead.

Hôtel Malar, 29, rue Malar (tel. 01 45 51 38 46; fax 01 45 55 20 19) M. Latour Maubourg. Turn left on rue St. Dominique off of Blvd. de la Tour Maubourg, then right on rue Malar. Provincial hotel with inner courtyard, on a quiet side street, near the restaurants and shops of the rue St. Dominique. All rooms have TV and direct telephone service. Singles with shower 280F, with shower and toilet 340-350F, with bath and toilet 350F. Doubles with shower 320F, with shower and toilet 380-400F, with bath and toilet 400F. Triples with shower 380F, with shower and toilet 440-460F, with bath and toilet 460F. Breakfast 28F. MC, V.

Royal Phare Hôtel, 40, av. de la Motte-Picquet (tel. 01 47 05 57 30; fax 01 45 51 64 41). M. Ecole Militaire. Next to metro on a bustling street. Small, tidy, colorful rooms come equipped with TV and hair dryer. Friendly reception. English spoken. Singles with shower and toilet 315-375F, with bath and toilet 405F. Doubles with shower and toilet 350-380F, with bath and toilet 410F. Breakfast 30F, 7-10am in room or in lobby. Reserve with 1 night's deposit. Elevator. MC, V, AmEx.

Hôtel Eiffel Rive Gauche 6, rue du Gros Caillou (tel. 01 45 51 24 5; fax 01 45 51 11 77). M. Ecole Militaire. Walk up av. de la Bourdonnais, turn right on rue de la Grenelle, then left on Gros Caillou. Located on a quiet street this busy, family run hotel is a favorite spot for anglophone visitors to Paris. (The owner speaks five languages.) Inner courtyard is decorated like a Spanish garden. All rooms have cable, TV, radio, and direct phone service. Prices vary according to whether you have a toilet, shower, and/or bath: Singles 220-450F, doubles 250-460F, triples 440-550F. Breakfast is served 8-11am in the large peach dining area (35F), or in your room (45F). Showers 19F. MC, V, AmEx.

Grand Hôtel Lévêque, 29, rue Cler (tel. 01 47 05 49 15; fax 01 45 50 49 36). M. Ecole Militaire. Walk northeast on av. de la Motte-Picquet and make a left onto rue Cler, a cobblestone street right out of a picturebook. Sleep in small rooms with tiled bathrooms overlooking a dimly-lit inner courtyard or the daily bustle of the rue Cler market. Reception open 24hr. Singles 195F, with shower 290F, with shower and toilet 315F, with shower, toilet, and a view onto rue Cler 345F. Doubles 225F, with shower and toilet 360F. Triples 425F. Extra bed 80F. Showers included. Breakfast 25F, served 7-11am. MC, V.

Hôtel du Champ de Mars, 7, rue du Champ de Mars (tel. 01 45 51 52 30; fax 01 45 51 64 36). M. Ecole Militaire, off av. Bosquet. Cheerful blue-and-yellow theme suggests elegant country living. All rooms have satellite TV. Singles with toilet and shower 355F, with toilet, shower, and bath 380F. Doubles with toilet and shower 360F, with toilet and bath, 390-420F. Triples with toilet and bath 505F. Breakfast 35F, in rooms or salon 7-10am. Reserve by phone and confirm in writing with 1 night's deposit. Elevator. Wheelchair-accessible after the first step. MC, V, AmEx.

Hôtel Kensington, 79, av. de la Bourdonnais (tel. 01 47 05 74 00; fax 01 47 05 25 81). M. Ecole Militaire. Compact rooms all have TV, shower or bath, toilet, and pastel paisley wallpaper. Singles 300F. Doubles with shower 380F, with bath 410-480F. Extra bed 80F. Breakfast 28F, served 7:30-11am in dining room or bedroom. Reservations recommended, 1 night's deposit is required. Elevator. MC, V, AmEx.

Laundromats

2, rue de la Comète, M. Latour Maubourg. Wash 22F per 6kg, 24F per 7kg, 36F per 10kg; dry 5F per 10min. Open daily 7am-10pm. 27, rue Angereau, M. Ecole Militaire. Wash 24F per 6kg, 45F per 12kg; dry 5F.

■ Eighth Arrondissement

The 8*ème* is more for jet-setters than for budget travelers. While you might spot a movie star dining at Fouquet's or hopping into a car outside Christian Dior, you'll be hard-pressed to find comfortable, affordable lodging nearby. The places we list are within budget, if without the extras found in less exclusive neighborhoods.

Hôtel d'Artois, 94, rue La Boétie (tel. 01 43 59 84 12 or 01 42 25 76 65; fax 01 43 59 50 70), a stone's throw from the Champs-Elysées. M. St-Philippe de Roule. From the metro take a left on rue la Boétie. Worn rug, has-been mattresses, but impeccable, spacious bathrooms and large bedrooms. Plant-filled lobby and incense-scented breakfast room. English spoken. Singles 240F, with shower 345F, with bath 390F, with bath and toilet 390F. Doubles 270F, with shower 375F, with bath 420F, with bath and toilet 420F. 2-bed doubles with bath and toilet 440F. Extra bed 100-125F. Showers 20F. Breakfast 25F. Elevator. MC, V, AmEx.

Hôtel Wilson, 10, rue de Stockholm (tel. 01 45 22 10 85). M. St-Lazare. Walk up rue de Rome; turn left on rue de Stockholm. No-frills hotel near Gare St-Lazare. Soft mattresses, aged carpet—but at this price, what did you expect? Bathrooms within rooms are newer than those off the halls. The occasional velvet chair offsets drabness. Clean, relatively spacious rooms. Singles 165-200F, with shower and toilet 220-240F. Doubles 225-230F, with toilet 245-260F. Triples 340F, with shower 360F. Quads 365F, with shower 395F. Shower 10F. Breakfast included.

Hostels and Foyers

UCJF (Union Chrétienne de Jeunes Filles) or **YWCA,** 22, rue Naples (tel. 01 45 22 23 49; fax 01 42 94 81 24). M. Europe. From metro take rue de Constantinople and turn left onto rue de Naples. Extremely organized, well-kept, homey environment for women only. Spacious, airy rooms, hardwood floors, large beds. Large oak-paneled common room with fireplace, TV, VCR, books, theater performance space, and family-style dining room with varied daily *menu*. Congenial staff. June-Aug. 3-day min. stay; Sept.-May longer stays for women ages 18-24. All guests must pay 30F YWCA membership fee, as well as 50F (for week stays) or 100F (for stays of 1 month or more) processing fee to stay in YWCA hostels worldwide. Reception open Mon.-Fri. 8am-12:30am, Sat.-Sun. 8am-12:30pm and 1:30pm-12:30am. Visitors until 10pm; men not allowed in bedrooms. No curfew. 200F key deposit returned when you leave. June-Aug. singles 120F per day; doubles or triples 100F per person per day; breakfast included. Weekly: singles 800F, doubles 650F. Monthly: doubles or triples 2195-2700F; breakfast and dinner included. Reserve if you can (200F deposit for stays less than 2 weeks, otherwise 500F). Other locations: 65, rue Orfila, 20*ème* (tel. 01 46 36 82 80; fax 01 46 36 32 61; M. Gambetta), and 168, rue Blomet, 15*ème* (tel. 01 45 33 48 21; fax 01 45 33 70 32; M. Convention). Men should contact the YMCA *foyer* **Union Chrétienne de Jeunes Gens,** 14, rue de Trévise, 9*ème* (tel. 01 47 70 90 94).

■ Ninth Arrondissement

The 9ème bridges some of Paris' wealthiest and most heavily touristed quarters—the 2ème and the 8ème—to the less tantalizing and less affluent 10ème and 18ème. There are plenty of hotels here, but many in the northern half of the area are used by prostitutes and their customers. Avoid M. Pigalle and M. Barbès-Rochechouart; use the Abbesses stop instead. Just a few streets south of bd. de Clichy and rue Pigalle, the neighborhood shifts from red-light district to a quiet, diverse residential quarter. Pricier hotels line side streets near bd. des Italiens and bd. Montmartre.

Hôtel des Trois Poussins, 15, rue Clauzel (tel. 01 48 74 38 20). M. St-Georges. Uphill on rue Notre-Dame-de-Lorette, right on rue H. Monnier, and right on rue Clauzel. Renovations of this quiet, family-owned hotel with cozy courtyard and clean, comfortable rooms will be finished in Jan. 1997. Singles 150F. Doubles 190F, with shower 220-240F, with shower, toilet, and stove 260F. Breakfast 30F. Reserve one month ahead.

Hôtel Beauharnais, 51, rue de la Victoire (tel. 01 48 74 71 13). M. le Peletier. Follow traffic on rue de la Victoire. Elegant array of beds, armoires, and mirrors span the centuries and showcase the owner's passion for antiques; no two rooms are alike. Lots of calm, sun, and fresh flowers. Singles and doubles with shower 300F, with shower and toilet 350F. Triples with shower and toilet 465F. Breakfast 25F.

Hôtel des Arts, 7, Cité Bergère (tel. 01 42 46 73 30; fax 01 48 00 94 42). M. Montmartre. Walk uphill on rue du Faubourg Montmartre; turn right at no. 6 onto Cité Bergère. Two rooms on ground floor decorated with owner's antiques. A very family-oriented place; if you hear someone whistle at you, probably the parrot. All rooms have showers, cable TV, and hair dryer. Singles with shower 355F, with bath 375F. Doubles with shower 375F, with bath 390F. Triple 515F (475F in July and August). Two slightly smaller rooms on the top floor cost a few francs less (singles 335F, doubles 360F). Breakfast 30F. Elevator. MC, V, AmEx.

Hôtel Modial Européen, 21, rue Notre-Dame-de-Lorette (tel. 01 48 78 60 47; fax 01 42 81 95 50.) M. Notre-Dame-de-Lorette. Identical pastel rooms, all renovated. Spotless bathrooms; TVs in rooms. Intimate automated wake-up calls. Rooms on the street are a little noisy. Lovely breakfast salon, a faithful variation on the peach-pink theme. Some English spoken. Doubles with shower and toilet 350-360F. Triples 460-500F. Quads 500F. Breakfast 30F. Elevator. Reserve 1-2 weeks in advance. MC, V.

Hôtel d'Espagne, 9-11, Cité Bergère (tel. 01 42 46 73 30; fax 01 48 00 95 69). M. Rue Montmartre. See directions for Hôtel des Arts, above. Not elegant but clean, with high ceilings and decent beds. Some English spoken by welcoming staff. TVs and/or telephones in some rooms. Singles with toilet 180-260F; with shower 260F. Doubles with shower 260-300F, with shower or bath and toilet 320F. Triples with shower or bath and toilet 320-420F. Quads 100-120F per person. Extra bed 100F. Prices negotiable. Free hall shower. Breakfast 30F. Reserve 2 weeks in advance. Accepts foreign traveler's checks. MC, V, AmEx.

■ Tenth Arrondissement

In response to the ceaseless traffic that pours through the Gare de l'Est and the Gare du Nord, quite a few inexpensive hotels have set up shop in the 10ème—so many that the supply often exceeds demand, making this a good place to look if you've struck out elsewhere. Some portions of this multi-ethnic residential quarter have been hard hit by France's current recession. The most gloomy and depressed areas are found north of the Gare du Nord, particularly along rue du Faubourg St-Denis and bd. de Magenta (especially near M. Barbès). These hotels are far from sights and nightlife, so you'll have to use taxis or your feet once the metro stops running.

Hôtel Palace, 9, rue Bouchardon (tel. 01 40 40 09 46 or 01 42 06 59 32; fax 01 42 06 16 90). M. Strasbourg St-Denis. Walk opposite traffic on bd. St-Denis until the small arch; turn left on rue René Boulanger and left on rue Bouchardon. The privacy of a hotel with the atmosphere of a hostel: friendly, young, and cheap. A dark hallway leads to small, cheerful, sunny doubles and triples, many of which face a plant-filled courtyard. Close to a laundromat and a supermarket. English spoken. Singles 103F. Doubles 136-146F, with shower and toilet 236F, with bath and toilet 256F. Triples with shower and toilet 289F. Quad with shower and toilet 362F. Shower 20F. Breakfast 20F. Reserve 2 weeks ahead in summer. MC, V.

Cambrai Hôtel, 129bis, bd. de Magenta (tel. 01 48 78 32 13; fax 01 48 78 43 55). M. Gare du Nord. Follow traffic on rue de Dunkerque to pl. de Roubaix and turn right on bd. de Magenta. The hotel is almost directly on your left. A homey, family-owned hotel close to the *gare* but without its safety concerns. Clean, airy rooms with high ceilings and lots of natural light, plus an intimate breakfast room. Singles 125-150F, with shower 202F. Doubles 200F, with shower 250F, with shower and toilet 274F. 2-bed double with shower and toilet 313F. Triples with shower 376F. 2-room suite for 4 with shower 400F. Showers 20F. Breakfast included.

Hôtel Lafayette, 198, rue Lafayette (tel. 01 40 35 76 07). M. Louis Blanc. From the metro, walk opposite traffic on rue Lafayette. Nothing fancy: just a good, clean, bright, comfy place to stay. The small, airy bedrooms have high ceilings, great lighting, and hardwood floors with rugs. Singles 128F. Doubles 191F, with toilet 231F, with shower 266F. Showers 20F. Breakfast included. MC, V, AmEx.

Hôtel Sibour, 4, rue Sibour (tel. 01 46 07 20 74; fax 01 46 07 37 17). M. Gare de l'Est. Walk straight from the *gare* on bd. de Strasbourg and turn left on rue de Sibour before church. The halls are nice, bright, and festooned with old-fashioned stained glass. In the rooms creaky floors, droopy ceilings, and a questionable brown-and-yellow color scheme impress less. Otherwise, it's comfortable. TVs in rooms with toilet and shower or bath. Singles and doubles 190F, with toilet 210F, with shower and toilet 280F, with bath and toilet 295F. Extra bed 50-75F. Showers 15F. Breakfast 25F. MC, V, AmEx.

Hôtel Métropole Lafayette, 204, rue Lafayette (tel. 01 46 07 72 69; fax 01 42 09 07 09). M. Louis Blanc. On the far side of the island near metro. Loud unless you get one of the few rooms with double glazing. Labyrinthine staircase. Rooms may be dark and musty, but are otherwise clean. Friendly staff. Make sure to see your room before taking it. Singles 140F, with shower 190F, with toilet and bath 210F. Doubles with shower 240F, with shower and toilet 260F. Triples 260F. Showers 20F. Breakfast 20F. MC, V.

Laundromats

Lav'Club, 43, rue des Vinaigriers. M. Château d'Eau. Detergent 3F; wash 18F per 6kg, 35F per 12kg; dry 5F per cycle. Open daily 7am-10pm. **Laverie,** 195, rue du Faubourg St-Denis. M. Gare de l'Est. Open daily 7am-9pm.

■ Eleventh Arrondissement

The 11*ème* is a crazy quilt of alterno-chic, urban decay, family businesses, and final sales. Inexpensive hotels cluster around the Opéra Bastille, providing travelers with easy access to nightclubs, bars, and record stores. Other budget hotels rim the pl. de la République, a touristed transportation hub; watch your wallet. The 11*ème*'s hotels tend to have vacancies in July and August, though its large-sized youth hostels are popular year-round. The area north of av. de la République near M. St-Maur, M. Couronnes, and M. Belleville can be dangerous at night.

Hôtel de Nevers, 53, rue de Malte (tel. 01 47 00 56 18; fax 01 43 57 77 39). M. Oberkampf or République. From M. République, walk down av. de la République and take a right on rue de Malte. Spacious, bright, clean rooms, with matching wallpaper and curtains. Ask for one on a high floor, away from the noise of the street. The owners generally enjoy Americans and speak some English. Guests have access to a refrigerator. Singles and doubles 170F, with shower 220F, with shower and toilet 245F. 2-bed doubles with shower and toilet 260F. Triples 310F. Quads 380F. Showers 20F. Breakfast 25F, served in the rooms. Reserve 2 weeks in advance with 1 night's deposit by check or credit card. 24-hr. reception. Elevator. MC, V.

Hôtel de Belfort, 37, rue Servan (tel. 01 47 00 67 33; fax 01 43 57 97 98). M. Père-Lachaise, St-Maur, or Voltaire. From M. Père-Lachaise, take the rue du Chemin Vert and turn left on rue Servan. 15-min. walk from pl. de la Bastille (just keep walking on rue de la Roquette, past metro Voltaire and turn left on rue Servan when you hit a grassy square). Ideal if you want to stay out late doing the bar scene at Bastille. Leather couches for lounging in the lobby. Not particularly memorable or attractive rooms except for the *Let's Go* backpacker special: just 100F per person per night in doubles, triples, and quads. All rooms with shower, toilet, phone, and TV. English spoken. Breakfast served in downstairs salon. Breakfast 15F with *Let's Go* special, served 7:30-9:30am. MC, V.

Hôtel Rhetia, 3, rue du Général Blaise (tel. 01 47 00 47 18; fax 01 42 61 23 17). M. St-Ambroise, St-Maur, or Voltaire. From M. Voltaire, take av. Parmentier, turn right on rue Rochebrune and take the next left onto rue du Général Blaise. Some rooms overlook a peaceful park. The hotel is calm and the neighborhood quiet, despite proximity to the Opéra Bastille. No elevator, dimly lit stairwell, and single beds are a bit narrow. Reception open Mon.-Fri. 7:30am-10pm, Sat.-Sun. and holidays 8am-10pm. Singles 170F, with shower or bath and toilet 210F. Doubles 190F, with shower or bath and toilet 230F. Triples 240F, with shower or bath and toilet 280F. Showers 10F. Breakfast 10F. TV 10F.

Plessis Hôtel, 25, rue du Grand Prieuré (tel. 01 47 00 13 38; fax 01 43 57 97 87). M. Oberkampf. From M. Oberkampf, walk north on rue du Grand Prieuré. Five floors of clean, pastel-hued rooms, with hairdryers and fans if you request. The cheaper rooms are not as fully-equipped. Piano, TV, vending machines, and oversized leather chairs in lounge. 10% discount for stays of over 3 nights. Singles 195F, with shower, toilet, and TV 270F. Doubles 215F, with shower, toilet, and TV 295-315F. Triples with shower, toilet, and TV 360F. Shower 10F. Continental breakfast 32F, students 20F. Heartier, "American-style" breakfast 36F. In July singles 150F, doubles 170F; free shower. Ask about the 300F triple. Open Sept.-July. Elevator. MC, V, AmEx.

Hôtel de Vienne, 43, rue de Malte (tel. 01 48 05 44 42). M. Oberkampf or République. From M. Oberkampf, exit at Crussol and turn left on rue de Malte; from M. République, walk down av. de la République and turn right on rue de Malte. Peaceful, pastel rooms with flowered curtains. Some saggy-looking beds. Plastic doors on the bathrooms and sink-areas don't add to the charm of this hotel, however the warm welcome does. Singles 105F, bigger bed 130F. Doubles 155F, with shower 215F. Breakfast 30F. Open Sept.-July.

Hôtel Notre-Dame, 51, rue de Malte (tel. 01 47 00 78 76; fax 01 43 55 32 31). M. République. Walk down av. de la République and take a right on rue de Malte. Clean, sunny rooms with squishy beds; some look onto an airshaft, others onto the street. TV in pricier rooms. Singles 190F, with shower 230-280F, with shower or bath and toilet 330F. Doubles 190F, with shower 280F, with shower or bath and toilet 330F. 2-bed doubles 360F. Extra bed 70F. Showers 20F. Breakfast 32F, served in your room or in the salon. Reserve 1 week ahead. Elevator. MC, V.

Hôtel de l'Europe, 74, rue Sedaine (tel. 01 47 00 54 38; fax 01 47 00 75 31). M. Voltaire. Walk up bd. Voltaire past the rather imposing government building, the Mairie du XI*ème* Arrondissement (a city hall), and take a left on rue Sedaine. Clean, large rooms have suffered some wear. Hotel seems to be popular with German tourists. Doubles 185F, with shower or bath 210F, with shower and toilet 230F, with bath and toilet 250F. Breakfast 20F. Shower 10F. Open Sept.-July.

Pax Hotel, 12, rue de Charonne (tel. 01 47 00 40 98; fax 01 43 38 57 81). M. Bastille. Walk east on rue du Faubourg St-Antoine and turn left on rue de Charonne. Centrally located in the hip Bastille neighborhood. Long hallways and generic rooms with TVs and hair dryers. All but three rooms have bathrooms. Dark hallway, no elevator, some mattresses seem older than others. Singles 200F, with shower 230F, with shower and toilet 250F. Doubles with shower and toilet 280F. Triples 300-360F. Quads 400F. Breakfast 30F in the breakfast room, 40F in bedrooms. Reserve by credit card or check a few days in advance. MC, V, AmEx.

Hôtel Beaumarchais, 3, rue Oberkampf (tel. 01 43 38 16 16; fax 01 43 38 32 86). M. Oberkampf. From M. Oberkampf, exit on rue de Malte and turn right on rue Oberkampf. Charming hotel with salmon walls, blue couches in the lounge, and a cute courtyard with lots of plants. Working-class residential neighborhood worth exploring. Newly refurbished interior with TV, shower or bath, and toilet in each room. Small elevator. 24-hr. reception. English spoken. Call ahead for wheelchair access. *Let's Go* special (you must mention *Let's Go* to get these rates): singles 200F, doubles 300F. Breakfast 30F. Reserve 3 or 4 days in advance. MC, V, AmEx.

Hostels

Auberge de Jeunesse "Jules Ferry" (HI), 8, bd. Jules Ferry (tel. 01 43 57 55 60). M. République. Walk east on rue du Faubourg du Temple and turn right on the far side of bd. Jules Ferry. About 100 beds. Wonderfully located. Clean, large rooms with bunk beds and sinks. Slightly crowded, friendly party atmosphere. Jovial, multilingual staff. The dining room is always open if you want to bring your own food and eat in. Reception open 24hr. Lockout noon-2pm but reception staff always present to answer questions or accept membership cards for reservations. No curfew. Single-sex lodging, but can accommodate couples; all residents of a room are consulted before it becomes co-ed. 4-to 6-bed rooms 110F per person. Doubles 118F per person. Showers and breakfast (self-serve 7-9:30am) included. No reservations, so come by 9am if you can. If there are no rooms left, the **Centrale de Réservations,** next door, will help you get a room in another hostel (see p. 78). Flexible 4-night max. stay. Lockers for bags 5F, lockers for valuables free. Sheets 5F. Wash 20F, dry 10F. Basement bike storage.

Auberge Internationale des Jeunes, 10, rue Trousseau (tel. 01 47 00 62 00; fax 01 47 00 33 16). M. Ledru-Rollin. Walk east on rue du Faubourg St-Antoine and turn left on rue Trousseau. Lively atmosphere with lots of backpackers in the sunny breakfast room. Most of the cramped rooms have 4 beds, though a few have 2 or 6. Rooms on ground floor are off of a quiet, outdoor passage in the back. Rooms on high floors look out over the roofs of Paris, or onto the street. Safebox for valuables. Luggage storage closes at 10pm. Lockout 10am-3pm. Common rooms downstairs. 91F per person; Nov.-Feb. 81F per person. Breakfast and shower included. Sheets 5F. Show up at 8am to get a room. MC, V.

Résidence Bastille (AJF), 151, av. Ledru-Rollin (tel. 01 43 79 53 86). M. Voltaire. Walk across the pl. Léon Blum and head south onto av. Ledru-Rollin. Modern building undergoing slow renovations. 2-4 wooden bunks per room. About 170 beds. Some of the recently redone triples and quads have bathrooms in the room. Other rooms use hall bathrooms; all rooms have sinks. Less crowded and more subdued than most hostels. Friendly, multilingual staff. Ages 18-35 (flexible). Couples can be accommodated in doubles. Reception open 7am-1am. Curfew 1am. Lockout 12:30-2pm. Nov.-Feb. 110F in shared room, 160F in single. March-Oct. 120F in shared room, 171F in singles. 10% reduction for ISIC- and GO25-holders. Showers, breakfast, and sheets included. No reservations, so arrive early in the morning. A welcoming station at the Gare du Nord, inside the suburban station (tel. 01 42 85 86 19) can make same-day reservations.

Maison Internationale des Jeunes, 4, rue Titon (tel. 01 43 71 99 21; fax 01 43 71 78 58). M. Faidherbe-Chaligny. Walk on rue Faidherbe, turn right on rue de Montreuil, and then take your second left onto rue Titon. Well-located and tranquil. An enclosed glass courtyard off the breakfast room hides a pair of pet bunnies. Except for 1st floor, not a bunkbed in sight, but expect a cot. Rooms with 2-8 beds, some new doubles with sinks and hairdryers, some really cramped rooms. Ages 18-30 (flexible). Single-sex rooms, but exceptions made for traveling buddies, couples, and consenting groups over age 18. Co-ed bathrooms without toilet seats. Family housing. Handicapped access. 3- or 4-day max. stay is fairly flexible. If full, they'll find you another place. Reception open 8am-2am. Lockout 10am-5pm (flexible). Check-out 10am. Curfew 2am. Quiet hours 10pm-8am. 110F. Showers and breakfast included. Sheets 15F for entire stay, or bring your own.

■ Twelfth Arrondissement

As in most cities, the area around the train station (Gare de Lyon) is a good bet for budget hotels. This neighborhood is within walking distance of Bastille night life, or even the Marais. In the arrondissement's southeast corner, hotels are far enough from central Paris to be both cheap and quite comfortable. They also provide easy access to the Bois de Vincennes, a lovely park with jogging paths and an artificial lake (see Bois de Vincennes, p. 218).

Hôtel de Reims, 26, rue Hector Malot (tel. 01 43 07 46 18). M. Gare de Lyon. Take bd. Diderot away from the river and make a left onto rue Hector Malot. Charming proprietress tends to this immaculate hotel which, despite its aging wallpaper and dim lighting, deserves its faithful guests. There are always fresh flowers at the reception desk, and breakfast is served in a room that feels like a French grandmother's. Singles 170F. Doubles 220F, with shower 250F, with shower and toilet 270F. Triples with shower 350F. Showers 25F. Breakfast 30F. Reserve by phone and confirm in writing. A good bet if you arrive in the city without reservations.

Mistral Hôtel, 3, rue Chaligny (tel. 01 46 28 10 20; fax 01 46 28 69 66). M. Reuilly-Diderot. Walk west on bd. Diderot and take a left onto rue Chaligny. A spectacularly clean, mostly renovated hotel. The owner's mother pays attention to detail—new cups in each room everyday, maps of Paris, etc. All rooms have TV. Singles and doubles 200F, with shower 250F, with shower and toilet 250F. 2-bed doubles with shower 280F. Triples 300F. Quads 325F. Free hall shower. Breakfast 35F, served in rooms or downstairs. Call 7am-11pm to reserve (1 week in advance) and confirm in writing. English spoken. MC, V.

Nièvre-Hôtel, 18, rue d'Austerlitz (tel. 01 43 43 81 51). M. Gare de Lyon or Quai de la Rapée. Walk away from the train station (and tracks) on rue de Bercy and take a right on rue d'Austerlitz. Slowly progressing renovations promise pleasant, cheerful rooms. Resident cat presides at the entrance. High-ceilinged, often downright big rooms. Rugs are new, mattresses seem less so. Singles 160F. Doubles 200F, with shower 260F, with shower and toilet 300F. Showers free for *Let's Go* readers. Breakfast 20F. Call for reservations and confirm in writing, but most of the time there is room in the morning. MC, V.

Hôtel Printania, 91, av. du Dr. Netter (tel. 01 43 07 65 13; fax 01 43 43 56 54). M. Porte de Vincennes. Walk west on the cours de Vincennes and turn left on av. du Dr. Netter. 25 spotless rooms with brown, office-like carpets and formica headboards. Dark hallways. Climb one flight to elevator. Doubles 160F, with shower and toilet 220F, with shower, toilet, and TV 260F. Extra bed 40F. Showers 15F. Breakfast 25F, served in rooms. Reserve by phone. MC, V.

Hôtel de l'Aveyron, 5, rue d'Austerlitz (tel. 01 43 07 86 86; fax 01 43 07 85 20). M. Gare de Lyon. Walk away from the train station on rue de Bercy and take a right on rue d'Austerlitz. Small, clean, and unpretentious rooms, with aged wallpaper and beds. Capacious bathrooms come stocked with towels. Lounge downstairs in leather and chrome with a huge TV. Clients can use the fridge. English spoken. Singles and doubles 170F, with shower and toilet 245F. Triples 210F, with shower and toilet 290F. Quads with shower 260F, with shower and toilet 320F. Hall showers included. Breakfast 15F. Reservations suggested. MC, V.

Grand Hôtel Chaligny, 5, rue Chaligny (tel. 01 43 43 87 04; fax 01 43 43 18 47). M. Reuilly-Diderot. Walk west on bd. Diderot and take a left onto rue Chaligny. Screams low-budget, but some rooms have been recently redone. Purple-and-blue bedspreads and TVs in all 43 rooms; hair driers in most. While some rooms are dingy and most bedspreads patched, the whole is a decent deal. Singles and doubles 200F, with shower and toilet 250F, with bath and toilet 270F. 2-bed doubles with shower or bath and toilet 300F. Quads 400F. Extra bed 50F. 2 showers 25F. Breakfast 20F. Elevator. MC, V.

Hostels and Foyers

Centre International du Séjour de Paris: CISP "Ravel," 6, av. Maurice Ravel (tel. 01 44 75 60 00; fax 01 43 44 45 30). M. Porte de Vincennes. Walk east on cours de Vincennes, take the first right on bd. Soult, left on rue Jules Lemaître, and right on av. Maurice Ravel. Large, institutional-looking hostel, catering mostly to groups. Large rooms (most with 4 or fewer beds), restaurant, art exhibits, auditorium, and access to outdoor municipal pool next door (50% discount for guests). Flexible 3-day max. stay. Reception open daily 6:30am-1:30am. Singles with shower, toilet, and phone 165F. Doubles with shower, toilet, and phone, 135F per person. Rooms with 2-4 beds and shower (with shared toilet in the hall) 118F per person. Breakfast, sheets, and towels included. Reserve a few days early. Self-serve restaurant open daily 7:30-9:30am, noon-1:30pm, and 7-8:30pm.

■ Thirteenth Arrondissement

Hostels and Foyers

Association des Foyers de Jeunes: Foyer des Jeunes Filles, 234, rue de Tolbiac (tel. 01 44 16 22 22; fax 01 45 65 46 20). M. Glacière. From the metro walk 100m east on bd. Auguste Blanqui, turn right on rue de Glacière, then left on rue de Tolbiac. Large, modern foyer for young women (ages 18-30) with excellent facilities—kitchens on all floors, cable TV, washers, dryers, piano, exercise room, library, cafeteria, and garden. Run by extraordinarily friendly, helpful staff. Elevator. Sunny singles with a sink, desk, chairs, and closet space. Excellent security. Reception open 24hr. 120F per night. Showers and breakfast (served Mon.-Sat., 6:30-8:30am) included. Dinner 47F. 3135F per month, breakfast and dinner included. Mostly workers, not students; call 3-4 months ahead. 30F registration fee (good for one year) required of all first-time visitors. There are usually vacancies in summer. Reserve by fax or call a few days ahead when in Paris. MC, V.

CISP "Kellerman," 17, bd. Kellerman (tel. 01 44 16 37 38; fax 01 44 16 37 39) M. Porte d'Italie. From the metro turn right on bd. Kellerman. Institutional-looking hostel complex, affiliated with CISP Ravel in the 12ème. Rooms in the new wing have snazzy decor. 380 beds. Singles with shower 135F, with shower and toilet 165F. Doubles with shower and toilet 135F per person. 2-4 beds with shower 118F per person, 8 beds 93F per person (shared toilets in hallway). Breakfast included, served 7-9:30am. Restaurant open daily 6:30-9:30pm. Reserve a week in advance. Call ahead for wheelchair access.

Maison des Clubs UNESCO, 43, rue de Glacière (tel. 01 43 36 00 63; fax 01 45 35 05 96). M. Glacière. From the metro walk 100m east on bd. Auguste Blanqui and take a left on rue de la Glacière. Enter through the garden on right. Small, clean rooms, some newly renovated, others in need of paint. Run by helpful, multilingual management. Caters to tour groups; ask about special rates for groups of 10 or more. Reception open 7am-1:30am. Curfew 2am. Singles 160F. Doubles 140F per person. Triples 120F per person. Showers and breakfast included. Breakfast served 7:45-9am. No individual reservations, but call a week ahead for availability.

■ Fourteenth Arrondissement

This commercial district just south of the *quartier latin* was once a haven for political radicals which lured Picasso and his artistic circle from Montmartre. Today, the cafés along the bd. du Montparnasse where Einstein, Sartre, and Hemingway passed their time are lively and popular, while the neighborhoods near rue d'Alésia and rue Raymond Losserand have become residential and sedate.

Hôtel de Blois, 5, rue des Plantes (tel. 01 45 40 99 48; fax 01 45 40 45 62). M. Mouton-Duvernet. From metro, take a left onto rue Mouton Duvernet; at the end, go left onto rue des Plantes. Unquestionably one of the best deals in Paris, with rooms decked-out with cable TV, telephones, and pseudo-Laura Ashley decor. Laundromat across the street. Singles or doubles with toilet 220-260F, with shower 250F, with shower and toilet 270F, with bath and toilet 320-350F. Triples with bath and toilet 360F. Shower 15F. Breakfast 25F. MC, V, AmEx.

Central Hôtel, 1bis, rue du Maine (tel. 01 43 20 69 15; fax 01 43 20 50 09). M. Edgar-Quinet. Facing the Tour Montparnasse, turn left on rue de la Gaîté, then right on rue du Maine. The exterior might not catch your eye, but the interior flashes with its bronze-mirrored lobby ceiling. Simple decor is predominantly peach, and all rooms have toilets, hairdryers, and showers or baths. Singles 345F. Doubles 375F. 2-bed doubles 415F. Triples 445F. Breakfast 35F. MC, V, AmEx.

Hôtel du Midi, 4, av. René-Coty (tel. 01 43 27 23 25; fax 01 43 21 24 58). M. Denfert-Rochereau. From metro, turn off av. Général Leclerc and into the sq. de l'Abbé Migne, then turn right onto av. René-Coty. Catering mostly to business travelers, this large, professionally run hotel's stylish decoration extends to—yes—marbled bathrooms. Every room has hairdryer and satellite TV; some have A/C. Singles with shower 288F, with shower and toilet 298-398F, with bath and toilet 368-488F. Suite with all the extras 490F. Breakfast 38F. MC, V.

Hôtel du Parc, 6, rue Jolivet (tel. 01 43 20 95 54; fax 01 42 79 82 62). M. Edgar-Quinet. Facing the Tour Montparnasse, turn left onto rue de la Gaîté, then right onto rue du Maine, and right instantly onto rue Jolivet. Climb up to the sunny lobby. The level of elegance and spaciousness of the rooms rises and falls with the price, but a mismatching color scheme is constant throughout. Windows open onto either a tranquil courtyard or a park. Each room has TV. Singles 250F. Singles and doubles with shower 335F, with toilet and bath 360F. Twin beds with toilet and shower 410F. Triples 430-450F. Shower 20F. Breakfast 30F. MC, V, AmEx.

Ouest Hôtel, 27, rue de Gergovie (tel. 01 45 42 64 99; fax 01 45 42 46 65). M. Pernety. Walk against traffic on rue Raymond Losserand and turn right onto rue de Gergovie. The jovial welcome gives way to a plain but clean hotel with small rooms and a laundromat down the street. Singles with small bed 120F. Singles and doubles with larger bed 160F, with shower 220F. 2-bed doubles beds 200F, with shower 230F. Showers 20F. Breakfast 20F. MC, V, AmEx.

Hôtel Plaisance, 53, rue de Gergovie (tel. 01 45 42 11 39 or 01 45 42 20 33; fax 01 41 13 74 42). M. Pernety. Walk against traffic on rue Raymond Losserand and turn left on rue de Gergovie. On a quiet street in a dull neighborhood, the cheapest hotel in the 14ème has linoleum stairs, dimly-lit hallways, and stained wallpaper. Some beds have permanent dips. Singles 135F, with shower 190F, with shower and toilet 210F. Doubles 170F, with shower 210F, with shower and toilet 260F. Showers 20F. Breakfast 20F. MC, V, AmEx.

Hostels and Foyers

FIAP Jean-Monnet, 30, rue Cabanis (tel. 01 45 89 89 15; fax 01 45 81 63 91). M. Glacière. From metro, turn left off of bd. Auguste-Blanqui onto rue de la Santé, then right onto rue Cabanis. This international student center has 500 beds, mostly full of tour groups in summer. Comfortable, well-furnished rooms are impeccably maintained and equipped with toilet and shower. The complex contains a game room, TV rooms, a laundry room, conference rooms, an in-house language institute offering French courses, a sunlit piano bar and café, a restaurant, a spacious outdoor terrace, and a *discothèque.* In case you actually choose to leave this city-unto-itself, the lobby has kiosks posting upcoming Parisian events and offering stacks of tourist info. Some rooms wheelchair accessible. Curfew 2am. Singles 260F. 2-bed doubles 170F per person. Triples or quads 150F per person. 8-bed rooms 125F per person. Breakfast included. Tour groups given preference; individual reservations accepted as space permits (2 weeks in advance in summer, more in winter). MC, V.

■ Fifteenth Arrondissement

Because of the nearby Parc des Expositions and other massive commercial centers clustered along *le front*—or, "forehead"—of the Seine, hotels of the 15ème fill with businesspeople who arrive in the tourist off-season for conventions and trade shows. The neighborhood is relatively safe and quiet, though there are several vibrant commercial areas. Many of these hotels consider the summer months, with their lull in business travelers, to be off-season; subsequently, most have vacancies, and offer a quality of service found in few budget hotels of the central arrondissements.

Hôtel Printemps, 31, rue du Commerce (tel. 01 45 79 83 36; fax 01 45 79 84 88). M. La Motte-Picquet. Smack in the middle of a lively section of the 15ème, surrounded by stores (including a Monoprix), this hotel offers a warm welcome and clean, bright, and quiet rooms, all for hostel prices. Singles or doubles 140F, with shower 170F, with shower and toilet 200F. 2-bed doubles with shower and toilet 220F. Extra bed 30F. Shower 15F. Breakfast 20F. Reserve 3 weeks ahead. MC, V.

Mondial Hôtel, 136, bd. de Grenelle (tel. 01 45 79 73 57 or 01 45 79 08 09; fax 01 45 79 58 65). M. La Motte-Picquet. Near cafés, shops, and the metro. The moustached owner will welcome you to bright, clean, flowery rooms with saggy beds, modern showers, and a view of bd. de Grenelle. Singles 183F, with shower 223F, with shower and toilet 293F. Doubles 206F, with shower 246F, with shower and toilet 316F. Extra bed 73F. Shower 10F. Breakfast 20F. TV 20F per day. MC, V.

Hôtel Camélia, 24, bd. Pasteur (tel. 01 47 83 76 35 or 01 47 83 69 91; fax 01 40 65 94 98). M. Pasteur. Close to the metro and shops, this hotel offers clean, simple rooms with fairly good beds and oval-shaped furniture. Majority of rooms have shower and TV. Sept.-Nov. and Feb.-May: singles or doubles 200F, with shower and TV 280-300F, with shower, TV, and toilet 330F, with bath, TV, and toilet 370F. June-Aug. and Dec.-Jan.: singles and doubles 200F, with shower and TV 250F, with shower, TV, and toilet 300F, with bath, TV, and toilet 330F. Extra bed 50F. Shower 20F. Breakfast 28F. MC, V.

Practic Hôtel, 20, rue de l'Ingénieur Keller (tel. 01 45 77 70 58; fax 01 40 59 43 75). M. Charles Michels. From pl. Charles Michels walk up rue Linois, turn left on rue des 4-Frères Peignot, and then turn right on rue de l'Ingénieur Keller. This might be the single most elegant budget hotel in the 15*ème*. Modern, clean, bright rooms with bedspreads worthy of a Sheraton, comfortable mattresses, and TVs, all located on a very quiet street. Singles or doubles 250-290F, with shower and toilet 325F. 2-bed doubles with shower and toilet 370F. Triples with shower and toilet 440F. Free showers. Breakfast 36F. Elevator. MC, V, AmEx.

Hôtel de la Paix, 166, bd. de Grenelle (tel. 01 44 49 63 63; fax 01 45 66 45 27). M. Cambronne. This large, slightly industrial hotel is frequented by British traveling groups and sits on one of the busiest streets in the 15*ème*. The marble entryway gives way to rooms decorated in blues and browns reminiscent of the 1970s. TV room on ground level. Breakfast served in next-door North African restaurant. Singles 185F, with shower and toilet 275F. Doubles 200F, with shower and toilet 290F. Twin beds with shower and toilet 310F, with shower, toilet, and TV 340F. Suites with 3-4 beds, bath, toilet, and television 530-550F. Free shower. Breakfast 35F. English spoken. MC, V.

Hôtel de l'Ain, 60, rue Olivier de Serres (tel. 01 45 32 44 33 or 01 45 32 49 36; fax 01 45 32 58 95). M. Convention. Walk down rue de la Convention and take the first right onto rue Oliver de Serres. On a quiet residential street, but close to the parade of shops along rue de la Convention, this hotel has smallish rooms whose clean, whitewashed walls don't hide the wear and tear of the years. Singles 170F. Doubles 230F, with shower and TV 270F, with shower, toilet, and TV 280F. 2-bed doubles with bath, toilet, and TV 350F. Triples with bath, toilet, and TV 390F. Free showers. Breakfast 25F. MC, V.

Hostels and Foyers

Aloha Hostel, 1, rue Borromée (tel. 01 42 73 03 03; fax 01 42 73 14 14). M. Volontaires. Walk against traffic on rue de Vangirard, then turn right on rue Borromée. Centrally located, but over-run by English-speaking backpackers. Spartan rooms with bunk beds and cots have space for 3-6 guests, with a few doubles and one 8-bed room. Top floor rooms have slanted roofs and are very hot (no A/C). Kitchen facilities, communal refrigerator, and stereo in the café-style common room. Lockout 11am-5pm. Reception open 7:30am-2am. April-Oct. 97F per person, 107F per person in a double; Nov.-March 75F per person, 85F per person in a double. 630F per person per week. Sheets 15F, towels 5F. Curfew 2am. Arrive between 7:30 and 11am or reserve with 1 night's deposit a week in advance.

Three Ducks Hostel, 6, pl. Etienne Pernet (tel. 01 48 42 04 05; fax 01 48 42 99 99). M. Félix Faure. Walk against traffic on the left side of the church, the hostel will be on your left. Without a doubt one of the most rowdy hangouts in the city for young vacationing backpackers during the summer months. Has all the amenities (brand new kitchen, lockers for valuables, sink in each room) and fairly clean dorm-style rooms with bunkbeds for 2-6 people. Yellow, ivy-covered central courtyard becomes a loud café hangout on summer nights when a young, mostly American crowd drinks cheap beer from the hostel's watering hole, **Richie's Bar.** Lockout 11am-5pm. Curfew 1am. April-Oct. 97F per person; Nov.-March 75F per person. April-Oct. 700F per person per week; Nov.-March 490F per person per week. Sheets 15F, towels 5F. Reservations accepted with 1 night's deposit.

■ Sixteenth Arrondissement

Wealthy and residential, the 16ème may inconvenience budget tourists on several counts; though a short walk from the Eiffel Tower, accommodations require a 20-minute metro ride to the more renowned museums and traditional axes of Parisian nightlife. The area also has few of the grocery stores, cheap restaurants, and American tourists abundant elsewhere. Nonetheless, hotels here are comparatively luxurious and apt to have vacancies in the high season.

Villa d'Auteuil, 28, rue Poussin (tel. 01 42 88 30 37; fax 01 45 20 74 70). M. Michel-Ange-Auteuil. Walk up rue Girodet and take a left on rue Poussin. On a street laced with antique shops, this hotel offers spacious, high-ceilinged rooms with graceful wooden beds, good mattresses and baby blue and pink motifs. All rooms have a shower or small bath, toilet, telephone, and TV, and face either the street or a garden. Singles 285-290F. Doubles 320-330F. Triples 405F. MC, V.

Hôtel Ribera, 66, rue La Fontaine (tel. 01 42 88 29 50; fax 01 42 24 91 33). M. Jasmin. Walk down rue Ribera to its intersection with rue La Fontaine. Shades of pink complement shades of brown in spacious rooms, some decked out with marble fireplaces and floor-to-ceiling windows. Rooms with shower have TV. Singles with running water 200F, with shower 230F, with shower and toilet 270F. Doubles with running water 230-280F, with shower 260-280F, with shower and toilet 310-330F. Free showers. Breakfast 28F. MC, V, AmEx.

Hôtel Résidence Chalgrin, 10, rue Chalgrin (tel. 01 45 00 19 91; fax 01 45 00 95 41). M. Argentine or Charles-de-Gaulle-Etoile. From M. Argentine walk down av. de la Grande Armée toward the Arc de Triomphe, take a right on rue Argentine and another right onto rue Chalgrin. Overwhelmed by red and green tapestries, a profusion of antique decorations and somewhat ornate furniture, most rooms in this well-located hotel are dim, small, and very quiet. Rooms with shower or bath have TVs. Dogs receive a warm welcome. Rooms with running water 150-250F, with toilet 230F, with toilet and shower 270-340F, with toilet and bath 380F. Suite 450F. No hall showers. Extra bed 5F. Breakfast 27F. MC, V, AmEx.

■ Seventeenth Arrondissement

The 17ème combines the elegance of its western neighbor Neuilly with the sordidness of its eastern neighbor pl. Pigalle; some of its hotels cater to prostitutes, others to visiting businesspeople and tourists. Safety is a concern where the 17ème bounds the 18ème, especially on bd. des Batignolles and near pl. de Clichy. Most of the hotels listed are found in safer enclaves of this district, near its southern border with the 16ème. Though far from the center, they can be wonderful bargains.

Hôtel Riviera, 55, rue des Acacias (tel. 01 43 80 45 31; fax 01 40 54 84 08). M. Charles-de-Gaulle-Etoile. Walk north on av. MacMahon; turn left on rue des Acacias. Close to the Arc de Triomphe and Champs-Elysées. Don't be alarmed by the sparseness of the lobby. Modern, blue-and-pink rooms face patios and courtyards and have large, comfortable beds, TVs, and hairdryers. One of the best-located, most agreeable hotels in Paris. English spoken. Singles 240F, with shower 275F, with shower or bath and toilet 325-375F. Doubles with shower or bath and toilet 350-400F. Triples with shower and toilet 455F. Breakfast 25F. Free showers. Reservations encouraged, by phone or fax. Elevator. MC, V, AmEx.

Hôtel Belidor, 5, rue Belidor (tel. 01 45 74 49 91; fax 01 45 72 54 22). M. Porte Maillot. Go north on bd. Gouvion St-Cyr and turn right on rue Belidor. Dim halls give way to quiet rooms dressed in floral wallpaper circa the 1970s, most facing a peaceful, tiled courtyard. Singles 220-240F, with shower 280F, with shower and toilet 330F. Doubles 250F, with shower and toilet 360F. 2-bed doubles 360F, with shower 400F, with shower and toilet 440F. Triples 390F. Shower 30F. Breakfast included. Open Sept.-July. MC, V.

Hôtel Jouffrey, 28, passage Cardinet (tel. 01 47 54 06 00; fax 01 47 63 83 12). M. Malesherbes. Follow rue Cardinet across bd. Malesherbes and rue de Tocqueville and turn left into passage Cardinet. Simple, clean rooms with a slightly modern feel. Extremely quiet, mainly residential neighborhood. TVs in every room, and your pet poodle can stay for free. One room is fully handicapped-accessible—once you clear the first two steps into the hotel. Singles with shower and toilets 255-285F. Doubles with shower and toilet 330-350F. 2-bed doubles with shower and toilet 360F. Breakfast 30F, 35F in room. MC, V.

Hôtel des Deux Avenues, 38, rue Poncelet (tel. 01 42 27 44 35; fax 01 47 63 95 48). M. Ternes. Walk 1 block west on av. des Ternes and turn right on rue Poncelet. A bargain for its location only 10min. from the Champs-Elysées and Arc de Triomphe, this hotel offers tidy, no-frills rooms and nearly as much information about Paris as the main tourist office. English spoken. Singles 225F, with shower 285F, with bath, toilet, and TV 345F. Doubles 260F, with shower 310F, with bath, toilet, and TV 390F. One triple with bath, toilet, and TV 510F. Extra bed 70F. Showers 20F. Breakfast 27F. Animals 20F. Elevator. MC, V.

■ Eighteenth Arrondissement

The area known as Montmartre owes its reputation to the fame of artists who lived there, and who were rarely reputable folk. By day, the 18*ème* crawls with tourists; by night, it can be dangerous, especially for those newcomers easily lost in its winding streets. Hotel rates follow the northern, uphill approach to Sacré-Coeur: the higher you go, the higher the prices. Downhill and south at seedy pl. Pigalle, hotels tend to rent by the hour. Avoid M. Pigalle and M. Barbès-Rochechouart at night by using the Abbesses metro stop instead. Do not walk alone through the 18*ème* at night.

Hôtel André Gill, 4, rue André Gill (tel. 01 42 62 48 48; fax 01 42 62 77 92). M. Abbesses. From the metro walk downhill on rue des Abbesses, turn right on rue des Martyrs and left on rue André Gill. Situated on a quiet, dead-end street, this family-run hotel has faux marble and chandeliers at the reception area and sateen bedspreads and glittery, pastel walls upstairs. Liberace couldn't have asked for more—except maybe a pink baby grand. English spoken. Singles 160F. Singles or doubles with toilet and breakfast 240F, with toilet, shower, and breakfast 360F, with toilet, bath, and breakfast 390F. Triples with toilet, bath, and breakfast 530F. Extra bed 140F. Showers 25F. Breakfast 25F. Elevator. MC, V, AmEx.

Hôtel Sofia, 21, rue de Sofia (tel. 01 42 64 55 37; fax 01 46 06 33 30). M. Anvers. Walk up rue de Steinkerque, turn right at pl. St-Pierre onto rue Pierre Picard; cross rue de Clignancourt, and take your first left on rue de Sofia. The oak-timbered lobby leads to bright, colorful rooms with modern bathrooms, new beds, and Impressionist prints. Some rooms have been recently renovated. All of them come equipped with shower and toilet, and look onto the street or into the small, sunlit courtyard. Singles 195F. Doubles 245F. 2-bed doubles 260F. Triples 330F. Quads 400F. Breakfast 20F. Group rates available. Reception open 24hr. Call ahead or fax for reservations. Traveler's checks accepted in francs. MC, V.

Hôtel Pax, 5, rue des Poissoniers (tel. 01 46 06 33 26; fax 01 46 06 89 41). M. Château-Rouge. With rue Custine behind you, leave M. Château-Rouge down bd. Barbès, then take a sharp left onto rue des Poissoniers. On the edge of a lively African market quarter, this recently-renovated hotel has impersonal but neat rooms with new beds, peach walls, and dark, wooden furniture reminiscent of a Sheraton. All rooms have toilets and TVs. Singles 165F, with shower 235F. Doubles 190F, with shower 270F. 2-bed doubles 210F, with shower 290F. Extra bed 80F. Shower 20F. Breakfast 25F. Elevator. MC, V, AmEx.

Ideal Hotel, 3, rue des Trois Frères (tel. 01 46 06 63 63; fax 01 42 64 97 01). M. Abbesses. Walk down rue Yvonne le Tac and turn right on rue des Trois Frères. Respectable, optimistically named hotel on a lively, fairly safe street lined with shops and restaurants. If the breathtaking lobby reminds you of a 19th-century mansion, the small, tidy rooms upstairs say "servants' quarters." Singles 125-140F, with shower 250F. Doubles 190-230F, with shower 290F. Free showers.

Hôtel du Commerce, 34, rue des Trois Frères (tel. 01 42 64 81 69). M. Abbesses. Walk down rue Yvonne le Tac and turn left onto rue des Trois Frères. If you don't mind doors that don't close completely or bare lightbulbs, this hotel's location on a quiet street in the heart of Montmartre is ideal. All rooms have a view of the street or a courtyard, most have faux-wood floors and simple, worn furnishings. Singles and doubles 80-100F, with shower 110-120F. Shower 15F. Call to reserve.

Hôtel Bearnais 42, rue d'Orsel (tel. 01 46 06 38 30). M. Anvers or Abbesses. From M. Abbesses, turn left on rue Abbesses, left on rue des Martyrs, and then right on rue d'Orsel. From the lobby with its tiled floor you climb up linoleum-covered stairs to sparse rooms with more tiled floors and an institutional feel. A real find: cheap, clean, fairly safe, and right around the corner from Sacré Cœur. Singles 100F. Doubles 140F, with shower 180F, with toilet and shower 220F. Shower 20F. Breakfast 20F. Reserve several weeks in advance by telephone.

Laundromats

Laverie Libre Service, 4, rue de Burq. Wash 19F per 6kg, 21F per 7kg, 34F per 10kg; dry 4F per 10min. Open daily 7:30am-10pm. **Laverie Libre Service,** 61, rue Caulaincourt. Wash 31F per 7kg, 35F per 10kg. Dry 2F per cycle. Open daily 7:30am-9:30pm. **Laverie Libre Service,** 122, rue Caulaincourt. Wash 24F per 7kg, 40F per 10kg. Dry 2F per 10min. Open daily 7:30am-9:30pm. **Salon Lavoir Sidec,** 28, rue des Trois Frères. Wash 20F per 7kg, 30F per 10kg. Dry 2F per cycle. Open daily 7am-9pm. **Laverie Libre Service Mièle,** 47bis, rue de Clignancourt. Wash 20F per 7kg, 30F per 10kg. Dry 2F per cycle. Open daily 7am-10pm.

■ Nineteenth Arrondissement

The 19*ème* is far from central; apart from a visit to Parc de la Villette, you'll have to commute to do your sight-seeing. However, the metro line Marie des Lilas-Châtelet will zip you to the center in no time. Less hectic than more central neighborhoods, this quartier can provide needed respite from the tourist hordes along the Seine. The hilly Parc des Buttes-Chaumont is a romantic spot for a picnic lunch, and a worthy place to jog it off.

Hôtel du Parc, 1, pl. Armand Carrel (tel. 01 42 08 08 37 or 01 42 08 86 89; fax 01 42 45 66 91). M. Laumière. Turn up rue Laumière from the metro and follow it to its end at pl. Armand Carrel (or take bus 65 or 70). The owners have done wonders with what was obviously a very old building. Good location next to the Parc des Buttes-Chaumont. Spacious, clean rooms, many with oh-so-delicate pastel tiling in the bathrooms. Most rooms look out onto the park, top floor rooms have a great view over the tree-tops. Singles with shower 235F. Doubles with shower 270F. 2-bed doubles with shower 320F. Triples with shower 380F. Breakfast 40F, served in your room for an extra 5F. Reserve 2 weeks ahead. Parking available at 45F per night, 75F per 24hrs. Elevator. MC, V, AmEx.

La Perdrix Rouge, 5, rue Lassus (tel. 01 42 06 09 53; fax 01 42 06 88 70). M. Jourdain. Hotel is to your left if you are facing the church at the metro exit. Hotel has a long awning leading to an airy lobby, which makes it feel fancier than others in its price range. Modern, small rooms, all of which have TV and toilet. Some rooms overlook the church, other quieter rooms survey a less picturesque patch of green. Pink formica headboards and office carpeting give rooms an impersonal feel. Singles with shower 265F. Doubles with shower 300F, with bath 320F. Triples with bath 355F. No extra beds. Breakfast 26F. Reserve by fax 2-3 weeks ahead in summer. Elevator. MC, V, AmEx.

Crimée Hôtel, 188, rue de Crimée (tel. 01 40 35 19 57 or 01 40 36 75 29; fax 01 40 36 29 57). M. Crimée. Right outside the metro, at the corner of the rue de Flandre, near lots of restaurants. The lobby has tables and chairs where you can order a drink. Modern, clean, box-like rooms with soundproofing, hairdryer, TV, radio, alarm clock, toilet, and shower or bath. Singles with shower 280F, with bath 300-310F. Doubles with shower 310F, with bath 320-340F. Triples with shower 350F. Quads with shower 420F. Breakfast 30F. MC, V, AmEx.

Rhin et Danube, 3, pl. Rhin et Danube (tel. 01 42 45 10 13; fax 01 42 06 88 82). M. Danube. Steps from metro. Located in a square (or rather, a circle) with a fountain and two hip cafés, this hotel is in an out of the way neighborhood worth exploring for its provincial feel. Cobblestone streets are lined with little houses and flower gardens. Most rooms have fully equipped kitchens with coffee-makers, hairdryers,

TV and uncomfortable looking beds. Singles with bath and toilet 300F. Doubles with bath and toilet 350F. Triples with bath and toilet 400F. Quads with bath and shower 450F. Extra bed 50F. MC, V, AmEx.

Hôtel Polonia, 3, rue de Chaumont (tel. 01 42 49 87 15; fax 01 42 06 32 91). M. Jaurès or Bolivar. From Jaurès, walk up avenue Secretan and turn right on rue de Chaumont. From Bolivar, walk down Secretan and turn left on Chaumont. Friendly Polish immigrants run this modest hotel, filling it with Eastern European guests. Old mattresses. TV room. Singles 108F. Doubles 161F, with shower 241F. 2-bed doubles 176F. Extra bed 75F. Showers 25F. Breakfast 27F. No elevator. Reserve 1 month ahead.

Laundromats

Lav'club, 183, rue de Crimée. M. Crimée. Wash 19F per 7kg, 38F per 10kg; dry 5F per 10min. Open daily 7am-10pm. **Laverie Libre Service,** 19, rue Clavel. M. Pyrénées (from metro, go up rue de Belleville and make your first left). Wash 20F per 7kg, 30F per 15kg; dry 2F per 6min. Open daily 7:30am-9:30pm.

■ Twentieth Arrondissement

The 20*ème* often gets a bad rap from Parisians—generally those who have never been there. However, it has recently become a prime destination for funky, young bar-hoppers. While cheap high-rises dot the hillsides and seem to grow at breakneck speed (for Paris), charming streets and inexpensive open-air markets are no strangers to this quartier. In summer, the slowdown in commercial activity leaves the two-star hotels of this arrondissement half empty, which makes them a good bet if you're having trouble finding a place to stay.

Hôtel Printana, 355, rue des Pyrénées (tel. 01 46 36 76 62). M. Jourdain. From rue du Jourdain take a left on rue des Pyrénées. Devoted proprietors, refurbished rooms, and a clientele that always returns. The owner says he prefers to keep prices low and not accept credit cards (since customers end up paying the 3% surcharge at many hotels). Clean, cozy rooms overlooking street vendors and pastry shops. Singles with toilet 145F. Doubles with toilet 210F, with shower and toilet 245F. Triples with shower and toilet 300F. Showers 10F. Breakfast 25F. Elevator.

Hôtel Dauphine, 236, rue des Pyrénées (tel. 01 43 49 47 66; fax 01 46 36 05 79). M. Gambetta. Walk north on rue des Pyrénées. Homey, inoffensively pastel rooms, though not luxurious on the 2-star hotel spectrum. Sparsely furnished with TV and the occasional small refrigerator. Some noise from bustling street vendors. Singles with shower 200F. Doubles with shower 240-260F, with bath 300F. Extra bed 70F. Breakfast (7am-10am) 25F. MC, V, AmEx.

Hôtel Eden, 7, rue Jean-Baptiste Dumay (tel. 01 46 36 64 22). M. Pyrénées or Jourdain. Off rue de Belleville between the two stations. (Turn right if you're coming from Pyrénées, left if you're coming from Jourdain). Good value on clean, no-frills rooms with TVs. Some doubles fairly small, though—pay the extra 20F if you're looking for elbow room. Plant-filled breakfast room downstairs. Singles 185F. Doubles 230F, with shower and toilet 265-285F. Extra bed 60F. Bath 25F, or use shower next to lobby. Breakfast 27F. Elevator. MC, V.

Hostels and Foyers

Auberge de Jeunesse "Le D'Artagnan" (HI), 80, rue Vitruve (tel. 01 40 32 34 56; fax 01 40 32 34 55). M. Porte de Bagnolet or Porte de Montreuil. From Porte de Bagnolet, walk south on bd. Davout and make a right on rue Vitruve. The hostel is on the outskirts of Paris, surrounded by high-rises. A big modern complex with a festive, busy feel to it. 411 beds. 7-floor compound with restaurant, bar (featuring a happy hour and live music about once a week), and even a small movie theater. Vending machines and free microwaves downstairs. Mostly triples; a few doubles; some 8-bed rooms. English spoken. Flexible 3-day max. stay. Open 24hr., but rooms are closed noon-3pm. 110F per person, doubles 129F per person. Breakfast and sheets included. Lockers 10F. Laundry 15F per wash, 5F per dry; soap 3F. Reservations a must; hostel is packed Feb.-Oct.

Food and Drink

At daybreak he woke us again to drink the early morning soups; and after that we ate only one meal, which lasted all day. We did not know whether it was dinner or supper, luncheon or bed-time snacks.

—Rabelais, Gargantua and Pantagruel

Most Parisians and budget travelers have neither the time nor the appetite for the Rabelaisian stupor that six-course meals induce. Fortunately, the breads, cheeses, and pastries that appear as standard fare throughout the capital are both affordable and eminently French. With a bakery on every corner and dozens of open-air markets, food is a high-profile, high-quality affair. The soup and salad the Parisian makes at home for dinner may not be fancy, but they are made from fresh ingredients carefully selected from markets or specialized food stores and prepared with love, respect, and creativity.

FRENCH CUISINE

For a list of French food terms and descriptions of some classic sauces and dishes, please consult the Menu Reader at the back of the book.

The aristocratic tradition of extreme richness and elaborate presentation known as **haute cuisine** is actually not French at all; Catherine de Médicis brought it from Italy along with her cooks, who taught the French to appreciate the finer aspects of sauces and seasonings. In their work and writings, great 19th-century chefs made fine food an essential art of civilized life. To learn about the skills involved—such as preparing base sauces, which are in turn combined with other ingredients to make the classic sauces—leaf through the *Larousse Gastronomique,* a standard reference for chefs, first compiled in the 19th century.

The style made famous in the U.S. by Julia Child is **cuisine bourgeoise,** quality French home-cooking. Both *haute cuisine* and *cuisine bourgeoise* rely heavily on the **cuisine de province** (provincial cooking, also called *cuisine campagnarde,* or country cooking), by creating sophisticated versions of traditional French regional cuisine. Trendy **nouvelle cuisine,** consisting of tiny portions of delicately cooked, artfully arranged ingredients with light sauces, became popular in the 1970s and is now little more than a source of international amusement. Simple, inexpensive meals such as *steak-frites* (steak and fries) or *poulet rôti* (roasted chicken) can be found on just about every corner in Paris.

French **meat** is not all frogs and snails, though those tasty morsels both make great appetizers (frog really does taste like chicken, and snails taste like shellfish; however, most of what they taste like is the garlic butter sauce in which they are usually cooked). It is true that the French tend to eat a wider variety of creatures and creature-parts than do most Anglo-Saxons. *Tripes* (stomach lining of a cow) cooked in herbs is well-loved by many, but doesn't go over as well with foreigners; the sausage version is called *andouille* or *andouillette.* Rabbit is fairly common; pigeon shows up in casseroles and pastry shells. Though not all steaks are *tartare* (raw), most red meat is served quite rare unless you request otherwise. **Fish**-lovers should celebrate seafood specialties of the French southwest and be adept with a blade. Unless clearly marked *filet,* the fish will arrive eyes, tail, and all. Be aware, too, that *fruits de mer* is French for seafood (usually shellfish, shrimp, and the like), and has nothing to do with fruit. **Vegetables** may be overcooked by some standards, but usually so their full flavor can be appreciated. French asparagus (often served in vinaigrette) is a white, stumpy version of the matchstick you've come to love, and *haricots verts* (green beans) are a svelte and tastier cousin of the ones your mother made you eat. Americans may be taken aback by the cost of produce. Don't buy vegetables in the small groceries which stay open late if you can help it, as the prices are exorbitant. Produce markets and stores which sell only fruits and vegetables are your best bet, but some supermarkets are reasonable as well. Restaurants often serve *pommes frites* (french fries) or potato *gratins,* potatoes sliced, doused with cream, butter, and cheese, and baked in an oven.

Bread is served with every meal. It is perfectly polite to use a piece of bread to wipe your plate. The *baguette* is the long, crisp, archetypal French loaf which, at about 4F, has kept many a budgeteer afloat on treks through Paris. The *bâtard* has a softer crust, the smaller *ficelle* a thicker, harder crust. *Pain de campagne,* made with whole wheat flour, is heavier inside than the baguette. The *pain complet* is a whole grain loaf, and the *pain à six céréales* is made with six grains. The cheap, government-subsidized bread you buy from a nameless bakery in Paris may well be the best you have ever eaten; make it your staple.

Tremendously bountiful and various, French **cheeses** fall into three main categories. Cooked cheeses include *beaufort* and *gruyère.* Veined cheeses, such as *bleu* and *roquefort,* gain their sharp taste from the molds that are encouraged to grow on them. Soft cheeses, like brie (the official king of cheeses) and camembert (the unofficial marquis of cheeses), round out a basic cheese tray. Tangy *fromages de chèvre* (goat cheeses) come in two forms: the soft, moist *frais* and crumbly, sharp *sec* (dry). Among **charcuterie** (cold meat products), the most renowned is *pâté,* a spread of finely minced liver and meat. Often a house specialty, it comes in hundreds of varieties, some highly seasoned with herbs. *Pâté de campagne* (from pork) is chunky, while *pâté de foie* (liver) is soft and silky. (Technically, a *pâté* is baked in a pastry crust, and the variety without a crust is a *terrine.* In practice, *pâtés* with crusts are rare, and the terms are used interchangeably.)

French **pastry** is one of the major arguments in favor of civilization. Breakfast pastries include the delectable *pain au chocolat* (croissant or brioche with chocolate) and *croissant aux amandes* (almond croissant). More elaborate choices are *flans* (egg-based, custardy cakes) and fruit tarts, including the *chausson aux pommes,* a light pastry with apple filling. Many *gâteaux* (cakes) were invented in the 19th century, such as the chocolate-and-espresso *opéra* and the cream-filled, many-layered *mille-feuilles*. The Paris-Brest cake, another filo dough and cream delight, is the only dessert named for a round-trip on the SNCF. All of these can be eaten in the afternoon with tea or after dinner as a dessert—eat pastry whenever you want to. Also good with tea are crumbly cookies like macaroons and *madeleines.*

And of course, **wine.** In France, wine is not a luxury, it's a necessity. During World War I, French infantry pinned down by heavy shell fire had only iron rations brought to them: bread and wine. And when France sent its first citizen into orbit on a Soviet space craft, he took the fruit of the vine with him. Wines are distinguished first by color—white wines are produced by the fermentation of grapes carefully crushed to keep the skins from coloring the wine. The fermentation of rosés allows a brief period during which the skins are in contact with the juice; this period is much longer with red wines. In general, white wine is served with fish and red wine with everything else, but it is the color of the sauce, not the color of the meat, that really matters. Red wine is preferred with cheese. The wines of Bordeaux break down into three broad categories: *rouge* (red), *blanc sec* (dry white), and *moelleux,* a sweeter white very easy to drink. Different regions, due to soil, climate, types of grapes, and aging processes, produce widely different wines. Connoisseurs know that French wine is best one to three years after an armistice; the years 1921, 1945, and 1947 are celebrated vintages. When buying wine look for the words *Appellation Controlée* (the government stamp of approval) surrounding the name of a region. Don't get too self-conscious about not knowing anything about wine. Waiters can give recommendations and let you sample expensive wines by the glass. See "Wine Bars" on page 261. Or fall back on the *vin de maison* (house wine) of the restaurant—it's usually pretty good. Among the major *apéritifs* are *kir,* made from white wine and *cassis,* a black currant liqueur *(kir royale* substitutes champagne for the wine). *Pastis,* otherwise known as "51" *(cinquante-et-un),* a licorice liqueur diluted with water, is popular with *tabac* owners, gamblers, and the Bastille crowd. Popular *digestifs* (after-dinner drinks) are cognac and various brandies, such as Normandy's apple-based *Calvados.*

GROCERIES

When cooking or assembling a picnic, buy supplies at the specialty shops found in most neighborhoods. Be careful to buy before lunch, though: *crémeries* (dairy products), *fromageries* (cheese shops), *charcuteries* (meats, sausages, *pâtés,* and *plats cuisinés*—prepared meals by the kilo), and *épiceries* (groceries, with cold salads by the kilo) usually take a two-hour break from noon-2pm. *Epiceries* also carry culinary staples: wine, produce, and a bit of everything else. *Boulangeries* sell several varieties of bread; buying in the morning, when the goods are still hot, is a memorable Parisian pleasure. *Pâtisseries* sell pastries, and a *confiserie* stocks candy and ice cream (though the difference between these two kinds of stores is often unclear). You can buy your produce at a *primeur. Boucheries* sell all kinds of meat and poultry, as well as roast chicken. Your hotel manager or any local can point you to the neighborhood *fromagerie, charcuterie, boucherie,* and *boulangerie.* Note that French store owners are fantastically touchy about people touching their fruits and vegetables; unless there's a sign outside your corner store that says *"libre service,"* ask inside before you start handling the goods displayed.

Supermarkets *(supermarchés)* are found in every neighborhood. Take note that in many *supermarchés* it is up to you to weigh your produce, bag it, and label it. If you're in the mood for a five-and-dime complete with a supermarket, go to any of the **Monoprix, Prisunics, Franprix,** or **Uniprix** that litter the city. Also look for the small chains such as **Casino** and **Félix Potin.** Starving students and travelers-in-the-know swear by the ubiquitous **Ed l'Epicier.** Buy in bulk and watch the pile of francs you save grow; it's possible to end up paying 30-50% less than you would elsewhere. Two of Ed's drawbacks: you can't find non-Ed brands (alas, no Nutella) and some stores do not carry produce. **Picard Surgelés,** with 50 locations throughout the city, stocks every food ever frozen—from crêpes to calamari. Most branches offer free delivery. No luck finding that special ingredient? Try the following:

Alléosse, 13, rue Poncelet, 17ème (tel. 01 46 22 50 45). M. Ternes. An immense and exquisite selection of cheeses, perfect for classy evenings and extravagant sandwiches. Open Tues.-Sat. 9am-1pm and 4-7:15pm, Sun. 9am-1pm. MC, V.

Ecouffes Alimentation, 16, rue des Ecouffes, 4ème (tel. 01 48 87 75 32). M. St-Paul. From the metro, walk in the direction of traffic down rue de Rivoli and take a right on rue des Ecouffes. A kosher grocery store, selling packaged goods, frozen meats, dairy products (including camembert and Philadelphia cream cheeses), and wine, much of it imported. Not too expensive. Also sells *Shabbat* candles. Open Sun.-Thurs. 8am-8pm, Fri. 8am-sundown. MC, V.

Fauchon, 26, pl. de la Madeleine, 8ème (tel. 01 47 42 60 11). M. Madeleine. The Rolls Royce is to the Chevy El Camino as Fauchon is to the ordinary supermarket. Tuxedoed attendants waft about the store helping clients find their favorite pâté of salmon. The Parisian elite shops at this supermarket, which only sells its own brands. The *pâtisserie* and *gastronomie* stores (set in two adjoining buildings) will turn your francs into pastries, rare fruits and vegetables, deli goods, cheese, and all kinds of wine. Indulge. Open Mon.-Sat. 9:40am-7pm. MC, V, AmEx.

Finkelsztajn's, 27, rue des Rosiers, 4ème (tel. 01 42 72 78 91), and 24, rue des Ecouffes, 4ème (tel. 01 48 87 92 85). M. St-Paul. Grab a bagel or *piroghi* on your gambol through the Marais. Serving homemade Eastern European Jewish delicacies since 1946, this is the place to go for everything to-go, from strudel to latkés (13F). *Vatrouchka* (cheesecake) and sweets about 13F. Gargantuan meat sandwiches 30-45F. Rue des Rosiers store open Wed.-Fri. 10am-2pm and 3-7pm, Sat.-Sun. 10am-7pm; rue des Ecouffes store open Thurs.-Mon. 10am-2pm and 3-7pm.

Goldenberg, 69, av. de Wagram, 17ème (tel. 01 42 27 34 79). M. Ternes. This distinguished gourmet delicatessen sells East European and Middle Eastern food, including pastrami, olives, and sausages. Some products are kosher, some are not; be sure to ask. Pastries (e.g., cheesecake, strudel, baklava) 8-15F each. Open daily 8:30am-midnight. MC, V.

La Grande Epicerie, 38 rue de Sèvres (tel. 01 44 39 81 00). M. Sèvres-Babylone. This food annex to Bon Marché, one of Paris' most illustrious department stores, sells high-priced French ingredients. Also a lot of "gourmet" American fare. English aisle stocks ever-elusive Lee and Perkins Worcestershire sauce and a selection of Twinings tea (11-18F). Well-wrapped chocolates and *bonbons* make great souvenirs—if they make it home. Open Mon.-Sat. 8:30am-9pm. MC, V, AmEx.

Jardin de Vie, 13, rue Brézin, 14ème (tel. 01 45 43 54 98). M. Mouton Devernet. This clean, spacious grocery store and pharmacy stocks the healthy versions of your favorite French delicacies, from wine to boxed croque tofu (16F). Soy drink (14F), bio-tortilla chips (13F). Small selection of organically-grown vegetables and natural beauty products. Advice on health and nutrition is always available. Open Mon. 10am-1pm and 2-7pm, Tues.-Fri. 9:30am-7:30pm, Sat. 10am-7pm.

Paul, 4, rue Poncelet, 17ème (tel. 01 42 27 80 25). M. Ternes. Folks from all over come to purchase this bakery's mystically aromatic crusty loaves, baked in wood-fired ovens. Bite-sized samples 2-3F. Pastries 4-12F. 25F *menu* includes a sandwich, dessert, and drink. Open Tues.-Sat. 7:30am-7:30pm, Sun. 7:30am-1pm.

Poilâne, 8, rue Cherche-Midi, 6ème (tel. 01 45 48 42 59), off bd. Raspail. M. Sèvres-Babylone. This tiny, rather sparse shop services the huge bakery responsible for Paris' most famous bread. Fragrant, crusty, sourdough loaves are baked throughout the day in wood-fired ovens. Menus in the city's finest restaurants declare that they serve only *pain Poilâne.* Unlike the *baguette,* these circular loaves don't come cheap; priced according to weight, a whole loaf usually costs 38-40F. For just a taste, ask for a *quart* (a quarter-loaf), about 10F. It's probably enough since they're extraordinarily filling. Bread can also be bought by the slice. Open Mon.-Sat. 7:15am-8:15pm.

Aux Quatre Saisons, 5, rue Tardieu, 18 (tel. 42 54 61 20). M. Anvers or Abbesses. From M. Anvers walk up rue Steinkerque and turn left onto pl. St-Pierre which becomes rue Tardieu. This small health food shop is filled with organic vegetables and a variety of snack foods and refreshments to give you energy before your climb up the *butte* Montmartre. 1L containers of soy drink 10-13F, crackers 10-25F, vegetable pasta 11F. Recipe booklets with a host of tofu concoctions, *tartes,* soups, and desserts 10F. Open Tues.-Sat. 9:30am-1pm and 3:30-7:30pm. MC,V.

Tang Frères, 48, av. d'Ivry, 13ème (tel. 01 45 70 80 00). M. Porte d'Ivry. Look for no. 48 and go down a few steps to this huge grocery in the heart of Chinatown. Come to buy rice (50kg 115-228F), spices, soups, and noodles in bulk. Stocks canned goods and high-quality, hard-to-find Eastern and Western produce. There's also a butcher. Signs in French and Chinese. Open Tues.-Fri. 9am-7:30pm, Sat.-Sun. 8:30am-7:30pm.

Thanksgiving, 20, rue St-Paul, 4ème (tel. 01 42 77 68 29). M. St-Paul or Pont Marie. Grocery store filled with purely "American" products. Find that pancake—not crêpe—mix for your French friends, tortilla chips (16F), "happy birthday" plates and candles, or the Sunday *New York Times* you can't live without (it takes the Concorde and arrives in the store by Sunday afternoon; 65F, 31F for a weekday paper). Upstairs, the restaurant serves up homemade American delicacies like cheesecake (30F), bagels with cream cheese (28F), chili (65F), and jambalaya (65F). Store open Mon.-Sat. 11am-8pm, Sun. 11am-6pm. Restaurant open Tues.-Fri. noon-3pm, Sat.-Sun. 11am-4pm.

Veggie, 38, rue de Verneuil, 7ème (tel. 01 42 61 28 61). M. Rue du Bac. Follow rue de Bac toward the Seine and turn right onto rue de Verneuil. Small health-food store has been specializing in organic grains and vegetables for twenty-five years. Rice cakes (10F), and carob bars (7F). Take-out options include fresh carrot juice (13F), sandwiches (15F), and vegetable pies sold by weight. Open Mon.-Fri. 10:30am-2:30pm and 4:30-7:30pm.

FOOD MARKETS AND NOTEWORTHY STREETS

In the 5th century, ancient Lutèce held the first market on what is now Ile de la Cité. More than a millennium and a half later, markets are not a novelty but an integral part of daily life. Both open-air and covered markets can be found around almost every corner, in every arrondissement. For more information about markets in Paris, ask at the tourist office or your local *mairie*. The freshest produce and best products are often sold by noon, when many stalls start to close up. Quality and price can vary significantly from one stall to the next; you might want to stroll through the market before selecting your purchases. Keep in mind that fruits and vegetables are cheapest and tastiest when in season. Unless there is a sign saying *"libre service,"* you should point to what you want and ask for it; stall owners might become enraged if you touch the produce yourself, even if you do intend to purchase it.

Marché Montorgeuil, 2ème. M. Etienne Marcel. Market extending from rue Réaumur to rue Etienne Marcel, along rue des Petits-Carreaux and rue Montorgeuil. Superabundance of fishmongers, butcher stores, bakeries, and fruit stands in this mall of food which dates back to the 13th century.

Rue Mouffetard, towards the intersection of bd. du Port-Royal, 5ème. M. Censier-Daubenton. Colorful, fun, busy, and—yes—quaint. Find your favorite fresh produce, meat, fish, and cheese here; other tables are loaded with shoes, cheap chic, and housewares. Open Mon.-Sat. 9am-1pm and 4-7pm, Sun. 9am-1pm.

Marché Biologique, on bd. Raspail between rue Cherche-Midi and rue de Rennes, 6ème. M. Rennes. French hippies peddle everything from organic produce to 7-grain bread and tofu patties. A great place to buy natural beauty supplies, to stock up on homeopathic drugs, or just to people-watch. Prices are higher than at other markets, but reflect the quality of the products. Open Sun. 7am-1:30pm.

Marché Raspail, on bd. Raspail between rue Cherche-Midi and rue de Rennes, 6ème. M. Rennes. A small open-air market with fresh fruits and vegetables, meats and cheeses, nuts and dried fruits, and a few household appliances (lampshades and the like). Open Tues. and Fri. 7am-1:30pm.

Marché St-Germain, at 3ter, rue Mabillon, 6ème. M. Mabillon. Walk down rue du Four to rue Mabillon. In a rather upscale building that is currently being renovated to include sports facilities and a parking lot, the market is home to a wide variety of equally chi-chi foods. A variety of foods ranging from the banal to the imported, and perhaps the only *marché* in Paris to sell Corona beer. Open Tues.-Sat. 8am-1pm and 4-8pm, Sun. 8am-1:30pm.

Rue Cler, between rue de Grenelle and av. de la Motte-Picquet, 7ème. M. Ecole Militaire. A bustling market filled with produce, meat, cheese, and bread, on one of the most picturesque streets in Paris. Open Tues.-Sun. 8am-1pm and 4-7:30pm.

Marché Europe, 1, rue Corvetto, 8ème. Covered food-market. Open Mon.-Sat. 8am-1:30pm and 4-7pm, Sun. 8am-1pm.

Marché St-Quentin, 85bis, bd. de Magenta, 10ème. M. Gare de l'Est. Outside, this is a massive construction of iron and glass, built in 1866 and covered by a glorious glass ceiling. Inside you'll find stalls of fresh fruits and vegetables, meats, cheese, seafood, and wines. Open Tues.-Sat. 8am-1pm and 3:30-7:30pm, Sun. 8am-1pm.

Marché Bastille, on bd. Richard-Lenoir from pl. de la Bastille north to rue St-Sabin, 11ème. M. Bastille. Fruit, cheese, veggies, exotic mushroom stalls, bread, meat, and cheap housewares stretch from M. Richard Lenoir to M. Bastille. Expect to spend at least an hour here. Popular as a Sunday morning family outing for area residents. Thurs. and Sun. 7am-1:30pm.

Marché Popincourt, on bd. Richard-Lenoir between rue Oberkampf and rue de Crussol, 11ème. M. Oberkampf. An open-air market close to hotels in the 11ème. The street fills with fresh, well-priced perishables (fruit, cheese, groceries, bread). Less expensive than the Bastille market. Open Tues. and Fri. 7am-1:30pm.

Marché Beauvau St-Antoine, on rue d'Aligre between rue de Charenton and rue Crozatier, 12ème. M. Ledru-Rollin. One of the largest Parisian markets, with the cheapest produce in the city. Browse before buying—the fruit and vegetable qual-

FOOD AND DRINK

ity is wildly variable. Also visit the market's large tag sale, with scattered old clothing, fabrics, and household remnants. Produce market open Tues.-Sat. 8am-1pm and 3:30-7:30pm, Sun. 8am-1pm. Tag sale open daily 8am-12:30pm.

Marché de Grenelle, on bd. de Grenelle starting at rue de Lourmel, 15*ème*. M. Dupleix. A never-ending open-air market with the regular market fare (meat, fish, fruits, veggies, and—oh—cheese), as well as cookies, candies, flowers, housewares, and clothing. Open Wed. and Sun. 8am-1:30pm.

Rue de la Convention, from the intersection of rue de Vaugirard to pl. Charles Vallin, 15*ème*. M. Convention. A bewildering array of fruits, vegetables, meat, fish, cheese, and pastries (not to mention some clothing and housewares), all at reasonable prices. Open Tues., Thurs., and Sun. 7:30am-1pm.

Marché Président-Wilson, on av. Président-Wilson between rue Freycinet and pl. d'Iéna, 16*ème*. M. Iéna or Alma-Marceau. An excellent alternative to the 16*ème*'s exorbitant restaurants. Competitively-priced agricultural and dairy products, as well as meat and fish. Spectacular flower stalls. Clothing, table linens, and other household goods available. Open Wed. and Sat. 8:30am-1pm.

Marché St-Didier, at the corner of rue Mesnil and rue St-Didier, 16*ème*. M. Victor-Hugo. Walk all the way down rue Mesnil. This small market (half covered, half open-air) offers a fair selection of somewhat pricey vegetables, fish, cheese, and flowers. Gourmet salads start at 98F per kg. Open Tues. and Thurs.-Sat. 8am-1pm.

Rue Gros and Rue la Fontaine, 16*ème*. M. Ranelagh. Follow rue de l'Assomption toward the Maison de Radio France, then turn right on rue la Fontaine. A large collection of fish, flowers, cheese, and fresh vegetables at competitive prices. Nuts and dried fruit cost 24-60F per kg. Tues. and Fri. 8am-1pm.

Rue de Lévis, between bd. des Batignolles and rue Legendre, 17*ème*. M. Villiers. A busy pedestrian marketplace with everything from bread and bananas to boots and Benetton. Friendly competition among the meat, fish, and produce markets keeps prices relatively low. Open Tues.-Sat. 10am-7:30pm, Sun. 10am-1pm.

Marché des Batignolles, 96, rue Lemercier, 17*ème*. M. Brochant. Turn left off rue Brochant onto rue Lemercier. An indoor market with all the usual food groups at fair, though not fantastic, prices. The complex also contains a small supermarket for the items on your shopping list which aren't animal or vegetable. Open Tues.-Fri. 8am-12:30pm and 4-7:30pm, Sat. 8am-1pm and 3-7:30pm, Sun. 8am-1pm.

Marché de Ternes, 8bis, rue Lebon, 17*ème*. M. Ternes. Walk west on av. des Ternes. Take a right on rue Pierre Demours and a left on rue Lebon. Closed market hawking a variety of meat, cheese, and produce of decent quality but not-so-rock-bottom prices. Open Tues.-Sat. 8am-1pm and 4-7:30pm, Sun. 8am-1:30pm.

Marché Poncelet-Bayen, on the corner of rue Bayen and rue Poncelet, 17*ème*. M. Ternes. With bd. Courcelles behind you, follow av. des Ternes and turn right on rue Poncelet. Although many of the outdoor vendors take their cue from the surrounding specialty shops and set their prices rather high, the quality and quantity of vegetables, fish, meat, and cheese almost make up for it. Open Tues.-Sat. 8am-1pm and 4-7pm, Sun. 8am-1pm.

Marché Reims, on bd. de Reims between rue de Courcelles and rue du Marquis d'Arlandes, 17*ème*. M. Porte de Champerret. Turn left off bd. Berthier onto rue de Courcelles, then right on bd. de Reims. Hard-selling meat and vegetable vendors needn't try so hard—this market probably has the cheapest produce in Paris. Keep an eye out for North African and Middle Eastern specialties like Turkish bread and *baklava.* Open Wed. and Sat. 8am-1pm.

Marché Dejean, rue Dejean, 18*ème*. M. Château-Rouge. Follow the rising numbers on rue Poulet and turn right on rue Dejean. A small selection of vegetables, fruit, meat, and fish catering to the mostly African neighborhood with specialties like yams and ginger roots. Surrounding streets are filled with shops selling music, fabric, and sculpture. Market open Tues.-Sat. 7:30am-7pm, Sun. 7:30am-1pm.

UNIVERSITY RESTAURANTS

For travelers or long-term visitors strapped for cash, university restaurants provide cheap and dependable meals. Students can purchase meal tickets at each restaurant location while food is being served (tickets 12F70). The following university restaurants are most convenient, but the list is not nearly exhaustive. The university restaurants are open on a rotating schedule during the summer; it is extremely important to get a schedule before showing up. For more information—summer and weekend schedules, a list of other restaurant locations—visit **CROUS (Centre Regional des Oeuvres Universitaires et Scolaires),** 30, av. Georges Bernanos, 5*ème* (tel. 01 40 51 36 00; M. Port-Royal; open Tues.-Sat. 11:30am-1:30pm and 6-8pm). All of the following, except Citeaux, Grand Palais, and C.H.U. Necker, are open between lunch and dinner for sandwiches and drinks: **Bullier,** 39, av. Georges Bernanos, 5*ème* (M. Port-Royal); **Cuvier-Jussieu,** 8bis, rue Cuvier, 5*ème* (M. Cuvier-Jussieu); **Censier,** 31, rue Geoffroy St-Hilaire, 5*ème* (M. Censier-Daubenton; closed for dinner); **Châtelet,** 10, rue Jean Calvin, 5*ème* (M. Censier-Daubenton); **Mazet,** 5, rue Mazet, 6*ème* (M. Odéon); **Assas,** 92, rue d'Assas, 6*ème* (M. Port-Royal or Notre-Dame-des-Champs); **Mabillon,** 3, rue Mabillon, 6*ème* (M. Mabillon); **Grand Palais,** cours la Reine, 8*ème* (M. Champs-Elysées Clemenceau); **Citeaux,** 45, bd. Diderot, 12*ème* (M. Gare de Lyon); **C.H.U. Pitie-Salpetrière,** 105, bd. de l'Hôpital, 13*ème* (M. St-Marcel); **Dareau,** 13-17, rue Dareau, 14*ème* (M. St-Jacques); **C.H.U. Necker,** 156, rue de Vaugirard, 15*ème* (M. Pasteur); **Dauphine,** av. de Pologne, 16*ème* (M. Porte Dauphine).

RESTAURANTS

Do not approach French dining with the assumption that chic equals *cher.* Recent economic hard times have led to the return of the bistro, a more informal, less expensive, often family-run restaurant. Even more casual are *brasseries.* Often crowded and action-packed, *brasseries* are best for large groups and high spirits. The least expensive option is usually a *crêperie,* a restaurant specializing in the thin Breton pancakes filled with various meats, cheeses, chocolates, fruits, and condiments; surprisingly, you can often eat at a crêperie for the price of McDonald's.

Note that the French sit longer at dinner than Americans do. The check *(l'addition)* may be a long time in coming—spending two hours in a restaurant is not unusual. If you are particularly pleased with the service, feel free to leave a small cash tip as a sign of your gratitude (anywhere from a few francs to 5% of the check) but don't feel obligated. The initials BC mean *boisson compris*, drink included; BNC, or *boisson non-compris,* means the opposite.

Also, consider ordering the fixed *menu* or *formule,* a *prix fixe* lunch or dinner usually composed of two or three courses and a choice of several appetizers, main courses, and desserts. Ordering à la carte can be much more expensive, especially at dinner. A note about the organization of the following section: the restaurants we suggest are arranged both by type and by location. "Restaurants By Type" provides a list of restaurants followed by an arrondissement label; turn to "Restaurants By Location" for the full write-up. "Restaurants By Location" groups eateries by arrondisse-

Quel Ironie!

As one story has it, the world's first restaurant was born in Paris over 200 years ago. Ironically, its purpose was not to indulge its clientele with delicious foods and wines, but rather to restore (from the French verb *restaurer*) over-fed party-goers to physical health. Restaurants were a social respite from the high-calorie world of soirées, balls, and private dinner parties. Here one was meant to be in society and eat nothing.

ment, then lists them in order of *value:* the top entry may not be the cheapest, but it will be the best in its price range and area.

Restaurants by Type

All-You-Can-Eat: Country Life, 2ème; Le P'tit Comic, 4ème; Restaurant L'Escapade, 5ème

American: Elliott Restaurant, 8ème; Hard Rock Café, 9ème; Hayne's Bar, 9ème; Texas Blues, 10ème; Slice, 11ème

Bistro: Aux Lyonnais, 2ème; Le Divin, 4ème; Le Temps des Cérises, 4ème; L'Estrapade, 5ème; Restaurant Perraudin, 5ème; Les Bacchantes, 9ème; Au Petit Keller, 11ème; Le Bistro St-Ambroise, 11ème; Chez Paul, 11ème; Le Passage, 11ème; La Route du Château, 14ème; Bistro Bourdelle, 15ème

Cambodian, Thai, and Vietnamese: Le Palais de l'Est, 10ème; Lao Thai, 13ème; Thiên Co, 13ème; Thuy Hong, 13ème; Phetburi, 15ème

Caribbean: Babylone, 2ème; Le Rocher du Diamant, 12ème; La Papaye, 20ème

Chinese: Aux Délices de Széchuen, 7ème; Le Palais de l'Est, 10ème

Crêperie: Crêperie Saint Germain, 6ème; Le P'tit Comic, 4ème; Ty Breiz, 15ème

Deli: Chez Jo Goldenberg, 4ème

Eastern European: Chez Marianne, 4ème; Restaurant Le Beautrellis, 4ème

Greek: Le Colvert, 14ème

Hispanic: Vue du Parc, 3ème; Casa Tina, 16ème; Grill Churrasco, 17ème

Indian: Anarkali, 9ème; La Rose du Kashmir, 10ème

Italian: Restaurant Montecristo, Ile St-Louis; Le Carpaccio, 1er; Saint Joseph, 3ème; Fiorentino Angelo, 5ème; Le Jardin des Pâtes, 5ème; Pizzéria King Salomon, 9ème; Slice, 11ème; La Matta, 16ème

Japanese: Japanese Barbecue, 2ème; Kiotori, 6ème

Kosher: L'as du Fallafel, 4ème; Café des Psaumes, 4ème; Pizzeria King Salomon, 9ème

Mexican and Tex-Mex: Texas Blues, 10ème; Ay, Caramba!, 19ème

Middle Eastern: Chez Marianne, 4ème; L'as du Fallafel, 4ème; Café des Psaumes, 4ème; Café le Volcan, 5ème; Simbad, 5ème; Sannine, 9ème; Samaya, 15ème; Byblos Café, 16ème

North African: Au Clair de Lune, 2ème; L'Ebouillanté, 4ème; Café le Volcan, 5ème; Paris-Dakar, 10ème; Au Berbere Jessica, 14ème

Nouvelle Cuisine: Au Petit Prince, 6ème

Open Late: Pom' Cannelle, Ile St-Louis; L'Emile, 1er; L'Epi d'Or, 1er; Aux Lyonnais, 2ème; Babylone, 2ème; Le Hangar, 3ème; L'as du Fallafel, 4ème; Café des Psaumes, 4ème; Chez Marianne, 4ème; L'Apostrophe, 5ème; Il Fiorentino Angelo, 5ème; Restaurant L'Escapade, 5ème; Le Petit Vatel, 6ème; Kiotori, 6ème; Così, 6ème; Horse's Tavern, 6ème; Le Club des Poètes, 7ème; Anarkali, 9ème; Hayne's Bar, 9ème; Les Bacchantes, 9ème; Hard Rock Café, 9ème; Brasserie Flo, 10ème; Le Palais de l'Est, 10ème; Chez Paul, 11ème; Le Samson, 13ème; N'Zadette-M'foua, 14ème; Restaurant Aux Artistes, 15ème; Casa Tina, 16ème; Suzon-Grisou, 18ème

Organic: Aquarius, 4ème; Le Jardin des Pâtes, 5ème; Le Grenier de Notre Dame, 5ème; Crêperie Saint Germain, 6ème; Aquarius Café, 14ème; L'Epicerie Verte, 17ème

Outdoor Dining: Lescure, 1er; Le Hangar, 3ème; Saint Joseph, 3ème; La Dame Tartine, 4ème; L'Ebouillanté, 4ème; Simbad, 5ème; Horse's Tavern, 6ème; Aux Délices de Széchuen, 7ème; Fontaine de Mars, 7ème; Anarkali, 9ème; La Rose du Kashmir, 10ème; A la Courtille, 20ème

Provençale: Le Divin, 4ème; Fontaine de Mars, 7ème; Au Boeuf Bourgignon, 9ème

Regional Cuisines: Aquarius, 4ème; Auberge de Jarente, 4ème; Le Divin, 4ème; Occitanie, 11ème; Chez Gladines 13ème

Sandwich Shops: Le Dame Tartine, 4ème; Così, 6ème; Antoine's: Les Sandwichs des 5 Continents, 8ème

Seafood: Restaurant le Beautreillis, 4ème; Brasserie Flo, 10ème; Chez Clément, 17ème

Swiss: Chez les Fondues, 18ème

Vegetarian: Country Life, 2ème; Aquarius, 4ème; Piccolo Teatro, 4ème; Le Grenier de Notre Dame, 5ème; Aquarius Café, 14ème; Au Grain de Folie, 18ème; L'Epicerie Verte, 17ème; Joy in Food, 17ème

West African: À la Banane Ivoirienne, 11ème

Restaurants By Location

Ile St-Louis

The restaurants on Ile St-Louis are everything you'd expect: expensive, romantic, and charming to a fault. In summer, rue St-Louis en l'Ile, which traverses the island, becomes a pedestrian mall of just-showered Americans looking for the little restaurant they remember from last year and sticky-fingered adults and children polishing off the last of their Berthillon treats. For the most part, budget travelers in search of bargain *menus* had better look elsewhere. The following establishments are, however, good bets for a dinner date:

Les Fous de l'Isle, 33, rue des Deux-Ponts (tel. 01 43 25 76 67). M. Pont Marie. A cantina for the young neighborhood crowd, this comfortable restaurant displays the work of local artists and has evening concerts every two weeks. An ideal place to read. Appetizers 20-50F. Salads 45-50F. Hot main courses 60-98F, featuring pastas and steak. Our compliments to whomever baked the brownies, cheesecake, and carrot cake (28-38F). Check the blackboard for daily specials. Open Tues.-Fri. noon-3pm and 6-11pm, Sat. 6-11pm, Sun. noon-3pm for brunch; *salon de thé* open Sat.-Sun. 3-7pm. MC, V.

Restaurant Montecristo, 81, rue St-Louis-en-l'Ile (tel. 01 46 33 35 46). M. Pont Marie. An elegant Italian restaurant festooned with plants and Art Nouveau lamps. The specialties are pasta, veal, and pizzas. 2-course lunch *formule* at 69F includes wine or coffee. Desserts (40-45F) and *glaces* (32-50F). Reservations are key. Open daily noon-2:30pm and 7-11:30pm. MC, V, AmEx.

Au Gourmet de l'Isle, 42, rue St-Louis-en-l'Ile (tel. 01 43 26 79 27). M. Pont Marie. Lattice-covered walls and decorative wine bottles create the snug setting for traditional French food. House specialties include fresh artichoke hearts St-Louis and *la charbonné de l'isle au Marcillac* (pork stewed in red wine). 130F menu proffers an appetizer, main dish, salad or cheese, and dessert; 85F *menu* includes appetizer and main dish or main dish and dessert. Open Wed.-Sun. noon-2pm and 7-10pm. Dinner reservations recommended. MC, V.

Pom' Cannelle, 27, rue des Deux Ponts (tel. 01 46 34 68 59). M. Pont Marie. A straightforward place serving up a slice of one of their *tartes salées* (such as *quiche Lorraine*) and a salad for 55F—probably the cheapest, lightest lunch you'll find on the island. Also serves a range of salads, including the *Salade Exotica* with palm hearts, corn stalks, and pineapple on a bed of lettuce for 59F. Like every other place on the island, they have Berthillon ice cream; have a scoop (10F) or a sundae concoction (42-49F). Open daily noon-midnight.

First Arrondissement

The small streets around the Palais-Royal teem with teeny, traditional restaurants, each worth a special visit. Cheaper, louder eateries constellate Les Halles, offering everything from fast food to four-course Italian feasts. The disreputable delights of rue St-Denis may put off first-time visitors. Sex shops and thoroughly respectable restaurants coexist *face à face* down the portion of this street near Les Halles. During daylight hours, travelers should consider these eateries welcome bargains, though we advise steering clear of the area after dark.

Pizza Sicilia, 26, rue de Beaujolais (tel. 01 42 96 93 55). M. Palais-Royal. On the corner of Montpensier and Beaujolais north of the Palais. Budget travel guides exist to publicize gastronomic gems like Pizza Sicilia. Friendly service, low prices and absurdly good food. Try the phenomenal *tortellini aux champignons* (tortellini with mushrooms), at 42F, their most expensive pasta. 56F *menu* includes a salad, main course, and dessert or cheese. Open Mon.-Sat. noon-2:15pm and 5-11pm.

L'Epi d'Or, 25, rue J.-J. Rousseau (tel. 01 42 36 38 12). M. Les Halles. A small restaurant open to the street in the summer, with high ceilings and tasteful antiques, copper pots, majolica, and fresh flowers. Frequented by journalists from the nearby

Figaro offices. The staff is charming and the food ranges from excellent to rapturous. Two course *menu* served until 9pm (105F). Main courses 90F and up. Try the *entrecôte bordelaise* (105F). Open Mon.-Fri. noon-2:15pm and 7:30-2am; Sat. 7:30pm-2am. Last orders at midnight. Closed Aug. and 1 week in Feb. Reserve a few hours in advance. MC, V.

L'Incroyable, 26, rue de Richelieu or 23, rue de Montpensier (tel. 01 42 96 24 64). M. Palais-Royal. Walk along the right side of the Palais Royal and turn right on rue de Montpensier; look for passage Potier on your left. Although it's tiny and hidden in an alleyway, many tourists and locals seem to know it lives up to its name. Scrumptious 3-course *menus* are set at 70F lunch, 80F and 100F in the evening. The kitchen does amazing things with basics like steak and chicken. Friendly, English-speaking staff. Open Tues.-Fri. noon-2:15pm and 6:30-9pm, Sat. and Mon. noon-2:15pm. Closed for the last 3 weeks of Jan.

Lescure, 7, rue de Mondovi (tel. 01 42 60 18 91). M. Concorde. Flowing out onto the street corner, Lescure serves good food and hospitality in generous portions. Ivy, windowboxes, and white umbrellas outside, wooden beams inside. 3-course *menu* (100F) includes wine. Open Mon.-Fri. noon-2:15pm and 7-10:15pm, Sat. noon-2:15pm. Closed Aug. MC, V.

La Mangerie, 17, rue des Petits Champs, not to be confused with rue Croix des Petits Champs (tel. 01 42 97 51 01). M. Bourse. Offers casual, understated refinement and, in the back room only, a view of the Palais Royal and its gardens. It's worth reserving a table in the room with a view. Daily special 60F. A second cheaper one (40F) is offered June-July. *Entrecôte* 65F. Save room for home-baked pastries: fruit tart 22F, *crème caramel* 18F. Open Mon.-Fri. noon-2pm. MC, V.

L'Emile, 76, rue J.-J. Rousseau (tel. 01 42 36 58 58). M. Les Halles. Walk toward the church St-Eustache and bend right onto rue Coquillère; turn right on rue J.-J. Rousseau. Green velvet, mirrors, and marble flagstones create a laid-back ambience, while richness and subtlety define the cuisine. 3-course lunch *menu* including wine changes daily (71F). Evening *menu* changes seasonally (95F). Sumptuous saffron filet of salmon (82F). Open Mon.-Fri. noon-2:30pm and 8pm-midnight, Sat. 8pm-midnight. MC, V.

Le Vieil Ecu, 166, rue St-Honoré (tel. 01 42 60 20 14). M. Palais-Royal. Walk toward the Palais Royal and turn right on rue St-Honoré; the restaurant is on your left. Everything you might expect from a Parisian restaurant: checkered tablecloths, lace-draped lamps, and the exposed beams of a 300-year-old building. 65F lunch *menu* of traditional French food, drink included. Dinner *menu* 69F or 99F. Main courses 79-83F. Feast upon dishes like *confit de canard* and *onglet à l'échalottes* (flank steak with shallots) along with a glass of Beaujolais (20F). Finish with a *tarte tatin* (38F). Vegetarian entrees available. Live piano and folk guitar upstairs Mon.-Sat. 8:30-10pm. Open Mon.-Sat. 11:30am-3pm and 6:30-11pm. MC, V.

Le Carpaccio, 6, rue Pierre Lescot (tel. 01 45 08 44 80). M. Les Halles. Near the Pompidou. Waiters maneuver 4-ft. pepper grinders over this restaurant's Italian food. Cordon Bleu it's not, but Carpaccio's location, prices, and solid cuisine attract Parisians and tourists alike. Large terrace on a pedestrian street in Les Halles. Pizza 41-71F. A variety of 2-course *menus* (59F), coffee included. Try the namesake beef (54F), or salmon carpaccio (67F). Memorable pastries (30-37F). Open daily noon-11pm. MC, V, AmEx.

Au Petit Ramoneur, 74, rue St-Denis (tel. 01 42 36 39 24). M. Les Halles. Walk down Rambuteau toward the Pompidou and turn on rue St-Denis. Crammed with your average (French and Anglo) joes during lunch hour, this is a place to eat—and eat well—but not to relax. 68F *menu* includes appetizer, main course, ½L of wine and either a *salade, fromage,* or *dessert*. Open Mon.-Fri. 11:30am-2:30pm and 6:30-9:30pm.

■ Second Arrondissement

Wedged between the wide, touristed boulevards of the 9ème, and the affluence of the 1er near the Louvre, the 2ème provides inexpensive meals to tourists exploring this and neighboring *quartiers.* Graze along rue Montorgueil, a market street lined with excellent bakeries, fruit stands, and specialty stores, or explore sidestreets like rue

Tiquetonne, rue Marie Stuart, and rue Mandar. The passage des Panoramas and the passage des Italiens are populated with fast, cheap food options.

Aux Lyonnais, 32, rue St-Marc (tel. 01 42 96 65 04). M. Bourse. Walk against traffic on rue Vivienne and turn left on rue St-Marc. Copious, traditional French food set with floral tile and Victorian lamps. The ideal semi-fancy French restaurant for a romantic dinner. Dine upstairs or downstairs on *caille rôtie* 75F (roast quail) or *lapin aux échalotes* (rabbit with shallots, 75F). 2-course *menu* 87F. Glass of wine 25F. Open Mon.-Fri. noon-2:30pm and 7pm-midnight, Sat. 7pm-midnight. Reserve a table for dinner. MC, V, AmEx.

Au Clair de Lune, 27, rue Tiquetonne (tel. 01 42 33 59 10). M. Etienne-Marcel. Walk against traffic on rue de Turbigo and turn left on rue Tiquetonne. Faithful regulars flock to this simple neighborhood restaurant for its huge plates of North African and French food. Couscous (54-70F) for ravenous (though discriminating) eaters. *Entrecôte* 62-65F. Sample Algerian wines like *Gris de Medea* or *Sidi Brahim* (53F per bottle). Open daily noon-2:30pm and 7:30-11pm. MC, V.

Babylone, 34, rue Tiquetonne (tel. 01 42 33 48 35). M. Etienne-Marcel. Walk against traffic on rue de Turbigo and turn left onto rue Tiquetonne. Late-night revelers stream in for Antillean specialties. Zebra skins and African carvings on the walls, banana leaves on the ceiling, zouk and reggae on the stereo, and dancing guests on the tables. Celebrities who've eaten here include Stevie Wonder and Jesse Jackson. Tantalizing side dishes include *aloko* (bananas flambéed in liqueur, 35F). 2-course dinner *menu* at 85F served 9pm-midnight. Main courses 70-120F. Open Mon.-Fri. 9pm-7am, Sat.-Sun. 9pm-9am. MC, V.

La Perdrix, 6, rue Mandar (tel. 01 42 36 83 21). M. Sentier. Follow rue Réaumur, then turn right on rue des Petits-Carreaux, which becomes rue Montorgueil, then take another right on rue Mandar. Catering to a business crowd, this affordable restaurant's long paneled interior and hunting trophies make it resemble a medieval banquet hall. 60F *menu* includes 3 courses and a drink. 82F *menu* spotlights *canard à l'orange* (duck in orange sauce). Even more sumptuous 100F *menu* includes shrimp cocktail and escargot as appetizers. A la carte: *entrecôte* 58F, *cassoulet au confit de canard* (kidney bean and duck stew, 79F). Excellent homemade desserts. Open Mon.-Sat. 11:30am-3pm and 6:30-10pm. MC, V, AmEx.

Country Life, 6, rue Daunou (tel. 01 42 97 48 51). M. Opéra. Treat yourself to fresh vegetarian cuisine in the spacious, light-filled dining area of this smoke-free health-food store. 62F all-you-can-eat buffet includes soups and salads as well as hot main courses and a wide selection of *crudités*. Carrot juice 10F, *infusions* (herbal tea 5F). Take-out available. Open Mon.-Thurs. 11:30am-3pm and 6:30-10pm, Fri. 11:30am-3pm. Store open Mon.-Thurs. 10am-10pm, Fri. 10am-3pm.

Japanese Barbecue, 60, rue Montorgueil (tel. 01 42 33 49 61). M. Sentier. Follow rue Réaumur and turn right on rue des Petits-Carreaux, which becomes rue Montorgueil. A Western clientele gathers in the modest dining room for delicious fish and meat. Sit at the bar and watch the Japanese chef tend the charcoal grill. All *menus* come with broth and rice, some with salad. Grill *menus* 73F, sushi/sashimi *menus* 80-120F, yakitori menus 66-112F. Lunchtime *menus* around 47-56F. Open Mon.-Sat. noon-2:30pm and 7-9:45pm. MC, V.

■ Third Arrondissement

Close to the 3ème's museums, located in elegant *hôtels particuliers,* and next to the clamor of its second-rate wholesale stores, the restaurants listed here are as varied in personality as the arrondissement in which they reside. For the most part, expect sit-down meals of classic Parisian fare. Dinner à la carte can be pricey, but lunchtime *menus* make even the glamorous affordable.

Vue du Parc, 4, rue du Parc Royal (tel. 01 48 04 90 50). M. Chemin-Vert. Take rue St-Gilles, which becomes rue du Parc Royal. Salads, tarts, and Brazilian cuisine in a sunny restaurant overlooking square Léopold Achille. Tasty salads like the *exotique* (with avocado and *roquefort)* are well-priced (40-50F, or 20-25F as appetizer). Brazilian fare includes *boulettes* (rolled and grilled balls of cheese, corn, or ground meat, around 40F). Appetizers 25-27F. Entrees 55-80F (most 55-60F). Desserts 23-28F. Open Mon.-Sat. 11:30am-3:30pm and 7:30-11pm. MC, V.

Le Hangar, 12, impasse Berthaud (tel. 01 42 74 55 44). M. Rambuteau. Take the impasse Berthaud exit from the metro. Tucked in an alley near the Centre Pompidou, Le Hangar is a quiet restaurant removed from the tourist-madness of the neighborhood. Tablecloths, fresh flowers, and a newspaper rack for those who come for tea on Sat. (3:30-7pm). Appetizers 28-58F and many French specialties, like *ravioles de Romans* (cheese ravioli with an eggplant cream sauce, 48F), *foie gras de canard poêlé* (85F), and to-die-for chocolate cake (44F). Open Mon. 7pm-midnight, Tues.-Sat. noon-4pm and 6pm-midnight.

Saint Joseph, 1, rue Perrée (tel. 01 42 71 23 08). M. Temple. Walk opposite traffic on rue du Temple and take the second left onto rue Perrée. On a quiet tree-lined street next to a park, this restaurant has outdoor tables where diners are sheltered from the exhaust of passing cars. Good pizza for 37-52F. 3-course lunch *menu* 59F. Fancier 3-course lunch or dinner *menu* 80F. Take-out available. Open Mon.-Sat. noon-2:30pm and 7-11pm.

Les Lanternes du Marais, 38, rue Debelleyme (tel. 01 42 72 39 24). Traditional French cuisine in an old-fashioned atmosphere. Tablecloths, fresh flowers, and wooden beams. 70F lunch or dinner *menu* includes appetizer and main dish, or main dish and dessert. A la carte is more expensive: appetizers (31-75F), main dish (80-120F), cheese (28F), dessert (22F). 50cl pitcher of wine 40F, bottles 88-265F. Open Mon.-Tues. and Thurs.-Fri. noon-3pm and 7-9:30pm, Wed. and Sat. noon-3pm. Closed Aug.

Les Enfants Rouges, 9, rue de Beauce (tel. 01 48 87 80 61). M. Filles du Calvaire. From the metro walk down rue Filles du Calvaire, continue along rue de Bretagne and make a left on rue de Beauce. Small, simple neighborhood restaurant. Lunch *menu:* appetizer, main course, cheese or dessert (68F). Otherwise, appetizers (21-30F), main dishes (48-78F), cheese (18-19F), dessert (21-29F), 25cl carafe of wine (18-29F). Open Mon.-Fri. 10am-11pm. Closed Sat. and Sun.

■ Fourth Arrondissement

The 4ème arrondissement has undergone gentrification over the past few years, with old mansions being restored, galleries opening, and New York-style bars and restaurants (i.e., places that serve brunch) taking over its old, crooked buildings. Rue des Rosiers is the main street of the Marais' Jewish quarter—a great place to go on Sundays and Mondays, when many French restaurants are closed. The falafel stands found on this street offer an inexpensive, filling, and healthy lunch or dinner. If you're looking for all male bars and restaurants, this *quartier* is your best bet (around rue Vieille du Temple).

Chez Marianne, 2, rue des Hospitalières-St-Gervais (tel. 01 42 72 18 86). M. St-Paul. Follow rue de Rivoli a few steps and turn right on rue Pavée; turn left on rue des Rosiers and right on rue des Hospitalières-St-Gervais. Sample Middle Eastern and Eastern European specialties in this folksy canteen and specialty store. Wine bottles and bins of pickled delicacies, stacked floor to ceiling, provide a cheerfully cluttered backdrop for locals to converge *en famille* or with friends. Eat outdoors if weather permits. Sample four, five, or six specialties (55F, 65F, or 75F), including *zaziki,* tabouli, falafel, hummus, and *tarama;* check out the *vatrouchka,* a *gâteau de fromage* rather different from American cheesecake (35F). Arrive before 7:45pm to avoid the dinner crowd. Take-out available. Open daily 11am-1am. MC, V.

L'Ebouillanté, 6, rue des Barres (tel. 01 42 71 09 69). M. St-Paul or Pont Marie. From M. St-Paul walk opposite traffic down rue François-Miron and turn left on rue des Barres. A casual restaurant and tearoom offering light snacks and meals in ambient calm, just steps from the bustle of cars and *bouquinistes* along the Seine. See "Salons de Thé," p. 135, for full listing. Open Tues.-Sun. noon-10pm.

La Dame Tartine, 2, rue Brisemiche (tel. 01 42 77 32 22). M. Rambuteau. Walk along the back of the Centre Pompidou on rue du Renard and make your first right. You'll see the fountain on your left. Also at 69, rue de Lyon, 12ème (tel. 01 44 68 96

95). This incredibly popular restaurant is almost as zippy as the Stravinsky fountain, which it faces. The terrace fills with a mostly young, dressed-down crowd. Cheapest coffee in the neighborhood (8F). Various ingredients on a slice of brown bread (not always filling, but very tasty): avocado and tomato (20F), chicken and berries (42F). Large selection of wines by the glass (11-15F). Desserts 20F. Open daily noon-11pm. MC, V.

Piccolo Teatro, 6, rue des Ecouffes (tel. 01 42 72 17 79). M. St-Paul. From the metro, walk with the traffic down rue de Rivoli and take a right on rue des Ecouffes. A romantic hideout for the health-conscious vegetarian—come for a candle-lit tryst over bulgar wheat. Various platters (all about 60F) offer a savory combination of grains and vegetables; or try the astonishingly filling *lait mixé framboises* (un-iced milk mixed with raspberries, 25F). Lunch menu at 53F offers soup or appetizer, a *gratin de légumes,* and dessert of *fromage blanc.* 3-course dinner *menu* 115F. ¼L of wine 22-24F. A *kir* on the house for Let's Go readers! Open Wed.-Sun. noon-3pm and 7-11pm. MC, V, AmEx.

Auberge de Jarente, 7, rue de Jarente (tel. 01 42 77 49 35). M. St-Paul. From the metro walk opposite traffic on rue de Rivoli; turn left on rue de Sévigné and then right on rue de Jarente. Disappear into this dim, cottage-like restaurant to feast on Basque specialties like *cailles* (quail, 68F) and *cuisses de grenouilles* (frogs' legs, 44F). 3-course lunch *menu* with wine 77F; 4-course *menu* 117F, with wine 132F. Open Tues.-Sat. noon-2:30pm and 7:30-10:30pm. Reservations recommended on weekend evenings. MC, V, AmEx.

Le Temps des Cérises, 31, rue de la Cerisaie (tel. 01 42 72 08 63). M. Bastille or Sully-Morland. From M. Bastille exit on bd. Henri IV and turn right onto rue de la Cerisaie. A true, down-to-earth neighborhood bistro, café, and wine bar that has been around for 17 years. Hearty 3-course lunch *menu* (68F) changes daily. Sandwiches 12F; coffee 5F60 at bar, 9F50 at table. Open for lunch Mon.-Fri. 11:30am-2:30pm; bar open 7:45am-8pm.

Restaurant le Beautreillis, 18, rue Beautreillis (tel. 01 42 72 36 04). M. Bastille. Exit the metro on rue St-Antoine and take the fifth left onto rue Beautreillis. Jim Morrison fans will want to stop by this restaurant, located across from the address where he died (no. 17). The dark wood walls are covered with Doors photographs. Vieran, the Croatian owner, has quite a story to tell about his "connection" to Jim (he just published a book). 11 volumes of comment books are a fascinating read over goulash (house specialty, 80F). 63F lunch *menu* (goat cheese salad, lamb, and dessert, for example). 95F dinner *menu* features more Slavic cuisine (blinis, smoked salmon, vodka, etc.). Tapes of *tsigane* music fill the silences between Monday *Doors* nights. Open noon-11pm. MC, V, AmEx.

Le P'tit Comic, 6, rue Castex (tel. 01 42 71 32 62). M. Bastille. Exit on bd. Henri IV and take the third right on rue Castex. A small Breton crêperie with bright table cloths and one breathtaking catch: an all-you-can-eat *menu à gogo* (lunch 65F, dinner 90F). Take a glass of cider and then choose from a list of 8 dinner crepes and 8 dessert crepes. Then choose again, and again....(The record so far is held by a woman who had 9 in a row.) Predictably, service is fast and brusque. Specialties include the *comic* (with ham, egg, cheese, and mushrooms, 35F), the *pleuvreuse* ("the crybaby," with onions, 27F), and, for dessert, the *Mont Blanc* (chestnut cream with whipped cream, 28F). Open Mon. 11:30am-3pm, Tues.-Sat. 11:30am-3pm and 7-10:30pm.

L'Arbre Aux Sabots, 3, rue Simon-le-Franc (tel. 01 42 71 10 24). M. Rambuteau. Walk along rue Beaubourg for half the length of the Centre Pompidou and turn left on rue Simon-le-Franc. This tiny, intimate restaurant hidden on a side street offers a huge variety of *menus* for various budgets. 48F gives you a 3-course lunch (steak, chocolate mousse). The 68F lunch has more choices, including calf's liver. 98F and 125F dinners are still reasonable (snails, poultry and *foie gras, profiteroles*). A la carte lunch can be as simple as an omelette and salad (35F). Open Mon.-Fri. noon-2pm and 7-11:30pm, Sat. 7-11:30pm. MC, V, AmEx.

L'As du Fallafel, 34, rue des Rosiers (tel. 01 48 87 63 60). M. St-Paul. From the metro go with the traffic a few steps down rue de Rivoli, make a right on rue Pavée; turn left on rue des Rosiers. This kosher falafel stand and grocery with a few benches outside (pay first at the cashier and give your ticket to the falafel maker) prominently displays pictures of (surprise!) Lenny Kravitz, who credited this modest little booth with "the best falafel in the world, particularly the special eggplant falafel with hot sauce." Gonna go his way with the falafel (22F) or falafel special (25F)? Wander off into the Marais with hummus (25F) or lamb *schawerma* (32F). Open Sun.-Thurs. 10am-midnight. MC, V.

Café des Psaumes, 14-16, rue des Rosiers (tel. 01 48 04 74 77). M. St-Paul. See directions for l'As du Fallafal. A kosher restaurant in the heart of the Jewish quarter whose second floor sports a spiffy mural representing the renowned rue des Rosiers as it was in 1905. The food is great, if occasionally too rich; try the falafel plate (55F) or the *couscous douceur* (couscous with beef, raisins, chick peas, almonds, and cinnamon, 85F). Open Sun.-Thurs. 11am-midnight, Fri. noon-sundown. MC, V.

Chez Jo Goldenberg, 7, rue des Rosiers. M. St-Paul. See directions for l'As du Fallafal. In the heart of the Marais's Jewish quarter, Goldenberg's has become something of a landmark. In business since 1920, it suffered a 1982 terrorist attack which took the life of the owner's son. A pilgrimage site for tourists and celebrities (from Moshe Dayan to Harry Belafonte), but still a neighborhood, family place. Not quite Old World—and not at all kosher. Soups 20-32F, 2 blinis 18F, *plat du jour* (stuffed cabbage; wheat, barley, and veggie stew) 70F, and pastries galore. Take-out available: you know, borscht (25F per L), pickles (45F per kg), gefilte fish (45F), bagels (6F)... Menu translated into English. Lots of tables outside. Deli open daily 8:30am-11pm; restaurant open daily noon-midnight.

Aquarius, 54, rue Ste-Croix-de-la-Bretonnerie (tel. 01 48 87 48 71). M. Hôtel-de-Ville. Walk away from the Hôtel de Ville on rue du Temple and turn right on rue Ste-Croix-de-la-Bretonnerie. Also at 40, rue de Gergovie 14ème (tel. 01 45 41 36 88). Potted plants, straight-backed wooden chairs, and smoke-free air make your meal feel like a stint in a new-age terrarium—and, as a bonus, you can browse through their small occult library. Fresh, wholesome vegetarian dishes borrow from rural regions of France. Have an omelette (25-45F) or the lunch *menu* which includes homemade yogurt and the veggie daily special (56F). The *assiette paysanne* (54F), a combo platter of *chèvre chaud,* garlic bread, roasted mushrooms, and potatoes, is offered only at dinner. *Plats du jour* 45F (noon-2pm and 7-10pm). Soy milk 6F. Take-out available. Open Mon.-Thurs. noon-10pm.

Le Divin, 41, rue Ste-Croix-de-la-Bretonnerie (tel. 01 42 77 10 20). M. Hôtel-de-Ville or Rambuteau. Walk away from the Hôtel de Ville on rue du Temple and turn right on rue Ste-Croix-de-la-Bretonnerie. A taste of Provence in a countrified stucco-and-beam setting with an 8th century *cave* downstairs. House specialties include *terrine du Divin* (pâté with scallops, 42F) and several *assiettes* with salads and cheeses for around 50F. 30-something couples mingle here, drawn by the sophisticated decor, oldies music, and 89F, 3-course *menu.* Open Tues.-Sat. noon-2pm and 7:30-11pm, Sun. 7:30-11pm. MC, V, AmEx.

■ Fifth Arrondissement

Foraging for food in the 5ème requires no special skills. Rue Mouffetard is the undisputed main culinary artery of this lively arrondissement. French, Greek, and Lebanese restaurants dovetail along the "Mouff," extending down rue Descartes all the way to bd. St-Germain. The highest density of cheap eateries is found along the pedestrian rue de Pot-de-Fer. To assemble your own lunch or dinner, spend a morning at one of the 5ème's open-air markets, on rue Mouffetard or on pl. Maubert. (See "Food Markets and Noteworthy Streets," p. 108)

Le Jardin des Pâtes, 4, rue Lacépède (tel. 01 43 31 50 71). M. Jussieu. From the metro walk up rue Linné and turn right on rue Lacépède. Eight tables unassumingly set with woven placemats are the meeting place for organic, gourmet pasta and a host of farm-fresh sauces—from sesame butter to duck and *crème fraîche.* Locals dig into the *pâtes de seigle,* with ham, white wine, and sharp *comté* cheese (56F). Many vegetarian offerings. Appetizers 19-25F, main courses 38-73F. Reservations recommended at night. Open Tues.-Sun. noon-2:30pm and 7-11pm.

Restaurant Perraudin, 157, rue St-Jacques (tel. 01 46 33 15 75). M. Luxembourg. From the metro take rue Royer Collard to rue St-Jacques. At this family-style bistro, locals gather to relax in the burgundy and dark-wood interior. Gamble on *le plat du jour selon l'humeur du chef* (daily special according to the chef's mood), or try old favorites like *sautée d'agneau aux flageolets* (sautéed lamb with white beans, 58F). Come early to avoid crowds. 3-course lunch *menu* 63F. Appetizers 32F. Main dishes 56F. Desserts 28F. Glass of wine 9F. Open daily noon-2:15pm and 7:30-10:15pm.

Café Le Volcan, 10, rue Thouin (tel. 01 46 33 38 33). M. Cardinal Lemoine. Turn left on rue Cardinal Lemoine and take a right on rue Thouin. Boisterous restaurant heats up at night with a youthful crowd of regulars. Posters of Bogart, Chaplin, and Dexter Gordon punctuate the otherwise plain, brick-floored interior. Specializes in *mousaka* and other Greek dishes, with some North African dishes (like couscous) thrown in for good measure. The 3-course 57F *menu* is served until 9pm; at lunch it includes a glass of wine. Dinner *menus* 80-100F. Open Tues.-Sun. noon-2:15pm and 6:30-11:30pm. MC, V.

Simbad, 7, rue Lagrange (tel. 01 43 26 19 05). M. Maubert-Mutualité. Take your pick of tabouli, hummos, stuffed grape leaves—the works—either in sandwich form or as a *plat* (sandwiches 18-20F, *plats* 20-45F). The small terrace outside is often full, but you can bring your food to the parc de St. Julien le Pauvre across the street and absorb good food and a great view of Notre Dame simultaneously. Delivery available in the 1ème-7ème arrondissements with a 75F minimum order (20F for orders 75-150F, free for orders above 150F). Open daily 11am-11pm.

L' Estrapade, 15, rue de l'Estrapade (tel. 01 43 25 72 58). M. Luxembourg. From pl. du Panthéon turn right on rue Clotaire and left on rue de l'Estrapade. Located near the Panthéon, this tiny bistro specializes in modest, exquisitely prepared French cuisine like *poulet de pot* and *soupe à l'oignon.* Antique caricatures of French celebrities and statesmen dot the walls. 67F lunch *menu* includes a salad and main course. 89F lunch *menu* serves up 3 courses and coffee. Dinner a la carte 62-89F. Open Wed.-Mon. noon-2:30pm and 7-11pm. MC, V.

Le Grenier de Notre Dame, 18, rue de la Bûcherie (tel. 01 43 29 98 29). M. St-Michel. Walk along quai St-Michel to quai de Montebello; turn right on rue Lagrange and immediately left on rue de la Bûcherie. Macrobiotics and soybean-freaks delight. A quiet, secluded restaurant that ladles up vegetarian *cassoulet*—a stew of beans, tofu, and soy sausages—along with an appetizer and dessert, all for 75F. Delicious *polenta* with stir-fried vegetables 70F. Open Mon.-Thurs. noon-2:30pm and 7:30-11pm, Fri.-Sun. noon-2:30pm and 7:30-11:30pm. MC, V, AmEx.

Restaurant L'Escapade, 10, rue de la Montagne Ste-Geneviève (tel. 01 46 33 23 85). M. Maubert-Mutualité. From bd. St-Germain turn right on rue de la Montagne Ste-Geneviève. All-you-can-eat meets Paris chic. 95F *menu* includes an hors d'oeuvre, a buffet of cold salads and pâté, a main course, dessert, and wine (as much as you can drink, served from the cask). Escape the hordes and the heat by eating in the cool, dark *cave* downstairs. Reservations accepted. Open daily 8:30pm-midnight. Later Fri. and Sat. MC, V.

L'Apostrophe, 34, rue de la Montagne Ste-Geneviève (tel. 01 43 54 10 93). M. Maubert-Mutualité. From the metro walk down bd. St-Germain toward the Institut du Monde Arabe and turn right on rue de la Montagne Ste-Geneviève. Somewhat garishly decorated with huge candles, this restaurant offers suitable French food with nary a French guest in sight. Two well-priced *menus* keep the tourists coming: 65F, served until 8pm; 85F, served all night. The first two *menus* include an appetizer and main course (10F supplement for dessert or cheese). The third offers 3 courses, with an all-you-can-eat buffet as an appetizer choice. Open Tues.-Sun. 5pm-12:30am. MC, V.

Il Fiorentino Angelo, 3, rue Mouffetard (tel. 01 46 34 71 61). M. Maubert-Mutualité. From bd. St-Germain take a right on rue de la Montagne Ste-Geneviève. Neat little Italian restaurant with a breadth of pasta offerings (45-65F) and a friendly, relaxed ambiance. 69F *menu* includes appetizer, main course, and coffee. 80F *menu* adds in dessert and wine. Open daily 7pm-midnight. MC, V, AmEx.

■ Sixth Arrondissement

Tiny restaurants with rock-bottom *menus* jostle each other for space and customers in the area bounded by bd. St-Germain, bd. St-Michel, and the Seine, making this an excellent quadrangle to wander in search of a filling meal. The rue de Buci harbors bargain restaurants and a rambling daily street market, while the nearby rue Gregoire de Tours has the highest density of cheap restaurants, making it a great place to browse. Toward the boundaries of the 6*ème* restaurants tend to get more expensive. Nonetheless, bargains can still be found along the streets near M. Odéon.

Le Petit Vatel, 5, rue Lobineau (tel. 01 43 54 28 49). M. Odéon or Mabillon. From M. Mabillon, follow traffic on bd. St-Germain, turn right on rue de Seine, and then take your second right onto rue Lobineau. This tiny restaurant offers little in spaciousness—three tables fill the room completely—but provides delicious, inexpensive meals. At lunch and on weekdays, choose a main dish plus an appetizer or dessert from the 61F *menu* scribbled on the chalkboard, including rotating daily specialties like *poivrons farcis* (stuffed peppers), *gratin de courgettes au jambon* (zucchini casserole with ham), mousaka, and vegetarian stews. A vegetarian plate is always offered. Take-out available. Open Mon.-Sat. noon-3pm and 7pm-midnight, Sun. 7pm-midnight. Closed Dec. 25-Jan. 1. MC, V, AmEx.

Orestias, 4, rue Grégoire-de-Tours (tel. 01 43 54 62 01). M. Odéon. Walk against traffic on bd. St-Germain and turn left onto rue Grégoire-de-Tours. Stuffed heads of mammals and birds line the walls of what remains nonetheless an airy restaurant. The food here is French with a heavy Greek influence—*dolmata, baklava,* and Greek wine are offered alongside French foods. Fries and green beans accompany each meal. Offered at both lunch and dinner, their 44F *menu* is an inspired bargain with copious first and second courses and a choice of cheese or dessert. You can't eat more for the price anywhere in the area. Open Mon.-Sat. noon-2:30pm and 5:30-11:30pm. MC, V.

Kiotori, 61, rue Monsieur-le-Prince (tel. 01 43 54 48 44). M. Odéon. From the metro walk all the way down rue Dupuytren, where it intersects rue Monsieur-le-Prince. A youthful international crowd packs this Japanese restaurant for succulent skewers of grilled beef, chicken, and shrimp, and picture-perfect plates of sushi and maki. A large variety of amazingly cheap *menus* 40-91F. All *menus* include a bowl of soup, *salade de crudités,* a main course and a saki *digestif.* Unbelievably fast service. Open Mon.-Sat. noon-3pm and 7pm-midnight. MC, V.

Crémerie Restaurant Polidor, 41, rue Monsieur-le-Prince (tel. 01 43 26 95 34). M. Cluny-Sorbonne or Luxembourg. From M. Cluny-Sorbonne walk down bd. St-Michel away from the river, take a right on rue Racine and your first left on rue Monsieur-le-Prince. The Polidor gleams with the mirrors, brass, and polished wood of over a century's worth of history. When Rimbaud lived on rue Monsieur-le-Prince, he ate here with Verlaine and it's been a neighborhood joint ever since. The Polidor offers traditional French cuisine cooked perfectly; the *escargots* are an excellent introduction to snails for nervous first-timers and the *bavarois au cassis* (a cake soaked in blackberry liqueur) is famous. 2-course lunch *menu* 55F; 3-course dinner *menu* 100F. 3-course dining a la carte 120-130F. Open Mon.-Sat. noon-2:30pm and 7pm-12:30am, Sun. noon-2:30pm and 7-11pm.

Così, 54, rue de Seine (tel. 01 46 33 35 36). M. Odéon. Walk up rue de l'Ancienne Comédie one block, take a left on rue de Buci and your next right on rue de Seine. Another branch at 53, avenue des Ternes, 17*ème* (tel. 01 43 80 86 70). It would be a sandwich shop were it slightly less self-important; let's call it an *atelier aux sandwiches.* Made to order with a choice of ingredients like curried turkey, goat cheese, and tomato and basil salad, sandwiches are all served between slices of warm *focaccia* fresh from the oven. These gargantuan masterpieces (30-50F) will seem more refined with a glass of wine (14-18F). Open daily noon-midnight.

Crêperie Saint Germain, 33, rue St-André-des-Arts (tel. 01 43 54 24 41). M. St-Michel. From the metro find pl. St-André-des-Arts and proceed down rue St-Andre-des-Arts. The Flintstones go Euro in this club-like *crêperie.* Faux boulders serve as chairs and mosaics as tabletops while mirrored disco balls dangle from the ceiling. House specializes in *crêpes noirs,* made from all-natural wheat flour. Try a *rasta*

FOOD AND DRINK

(cucumbers, red beans, and corn) and as many dessert crêpes as you can eat or afford; fillings like chocolate, whipped cream, berries, and coconut appear in every imaginable combination. Most crêpes (20-55F) are unusually filling. For the uninitiated, *cidre* (13F50) is a mildly alcoholic drink more like beer than its American cousin. A 49F *formule* (served until 6pm) includes a fairly simple dinner crêpe, an equally simple dessert crêpe, and a glass of *cidre* and coke. Open daily noon-12:30am. MC, V, AmEx (110F minimum).

Horse's Tavern, 116, Carrefour de l'Odéon (tel. 01 43 54 96 91). M. Odéon. Exit the metro and turn left to get to this small square. A tavern/restaurant *trés sympa,* where 13 different types of beer on tap keep the party happening. The outside seating gives a great view of the busy bd. St-Germain without subjecting you to its busy sidewalk. 3-course 69F *menu* offered 11am-8pm. Salads and dishes à la carte 35-80F. Open Mon.-Sat. 8am-2am. MC, V.

La Cambeuse, 8, rue Casimir Delavigne (tel. 01 43 26 48 84). M. Odéon. Veer right off pl. de l'Odéon. Specializing in traditional French cuisine, this simple restaurant will satisfy your craving for *soupe à l'oignon, boeuf bourgignon,* or *coq au vin.* Expect hearty servings. 3-course *menu* 90F. Open Mon.-Sat. noon-2:30pm and 7-10:30pm (roughly). Closed July 18-Aug. 19. MC, V.

Au Petit Prince, 3, rue Monsieur-le-Prince (tel. 01 43 29 74 92). M. Odéon. From M. Odéon, walk down rue Dupuytren and take a right on rue Monsieur-le-Prince. St-Exupéry fans will love this sophisticated restaurant, offering delicate but rarely filling *nouvelle cuisine.* Try the grilled sole in orange butter. Subtly decorated with a tiny airplane in the window and watercolors of Le Petit Prince himself. 129F lunch *menu* and 135F dinner *menu* provide main course, wine, and coffee; dishes à la carte run 50-100F. Open Mon.-Sat. noon-2:15pm and 7:30-10:15pm. MC, V, AmEx.

Restaurant des Beaux Arts, 11, rue Bonaparte (tel. 01 43 26 92 64). M. St-Germain-des-Prés. Follow traffic on bd. St-Germain and turn left onto rue Bonaparte. Just across from the Ecole des Beaux Arts, with walls decorated by its students and teachers. Smiling service and the sound of English spoken all around make this feel like home—or Epcot Center. The 75F *menu* includes wine, appetizers like *maquereau aux pommes à l'huile* (mackerel with potatoes in oil) and a daily vegetarian dish. Large salads 25-35F. Open daily noon-2:15pm and 7-10:45pm.

■ Seventh Arrondissement

Restaurants are perhaps the only touristed spots in the militaristic 7ème not consecrated to the memory of Napoleon. The emperor himself never allowed more than 20 minutes to dine. Visitors here, however, must commit a few hours and a good deal of cash for a fancy meal they'll certainly remember but probably can't afford. As for low-budget options, expect dependable, generally unadventurous fare.

La Varangue, 27, rue Angereau (tel. 01 45 05 51 22). M. École Militaire. Turn right on rue de Grenelle from av. de la Bourdonnais, then take a left onto rue Angereau. Two sisters make and serve family style dishes and homemade desserts in this bright, intimate restaurant with a plant on every table. 74F *formule* for lunch and dinner includes an appetizer or dessert, main course, salad, and drink. *Grandes salades* with fresh vegetables (56-64F) and other vegetarian meals are always available. Wine is 8F a glass. Desserts run 10-32F. Open Mon.-Sat. noon-2:30pm, Tues.-Fri. 7-10pm; Aug. Mon-Sat. noon-2:30pm. MC, V.

Fontaine de Mars, 129, rue St-Dominique (tel. 01 47 05 46 44), M. Ecole Militaire. Walk north on av. Bosquet and turn left on rue St-Dominique. One of the best places in the 7ème for a dainty helping of sumptuous French fare. Picture-perfect restaurant with lace curtains, pine interior, and red checkered tablecloths features food from southwestern France. Terrace overlooks the fountain after which the restaurant is named. House specialties include tomatoes and basil with fresh *chèvre* (45F) or duckling filet with mushrooms and sauteed potatoes (100F). Unadventurous but ample 85F lunch *menu* includes *steak tartare, pommes de terre* (potatoes), green salad, and dessert. Open Mon.-Sat. noon-2:30pm and 7:30-11pm. MC, V.

Kamal, 20, rue Rousselot (tel. 01 47 34 66 29). M. Duroc. Delicate woodwork, metal masks, and content buddhas cover all the rooms of this northern Indian restaurant specializing in tandoori. Succulent *beignets d'oignon* are 35F. Indian breads come plain (12F), or stuffed with vegetables and cheese (22F). Vegetable dishes 29-60F. Main dishes 60-100F. Open Sun.-Thurs. noon-2pm and 7:30-11pm, Fri.-Sat. noon-2pm and 7:30-11:30pm. MC, V, AmEx.

Le Club des Poètes, 30, rue de Bourgogne (tel. 01 47 05 06 03). M. Varenne. Take rue de Varenne and turn left onto rue de Bourgogne. Small, timbered dining room hosts lunch, dinner, and nightly poetry readings. 96F *menu* of veal, beef, or lamb, appetizer, and dessert. Come for dinner à la carte at 8pm or drinks after 9:30pm and stay for the nightly poetry readings beginning at 10pm. Open Mon.-Sat. noon-3pm and 8pm-1am. MC, V, AmEx. Proprietor Jean-Pierre Rosnay also directs the 24-hr. poetry hotline called **Allô Poésie** (tel. 01 45 50 32 33).

Aux Délices de Széchuen, 40, av. Duquesne (tel. 01 43 06 22 55). M. St-François-Xavier. On the corner of av. Duquesne and av. Breteuil behind the Eglise St-François-Xavier. An elegant, family-run Chinese restaurant which has been serving Szechuan cuisine for two decades. One house speciality is the *poulet sauté aux champignons noirs* (chicken sautéed with black mushrooms, 42F). 96F 3-course *menu*. Vegetarian options available. Large, shaded outdoor terrace in summer. Open Tues.-Sun. noon-2:30pm and 7-10:30pm. MC, V, AmEx.

Sifaridi, 9, rue Surcouf (tel. 01 45 50 20 69). M. Invalides. Sip from playfully painted glasses below somber black and white photographs at this Constantinian restaurant specializing in couscous. The young staff serves up different *formules* (60-140F) and a 39F *formule* at lunch. Take-out available. Open Mon.-Sat. 11:30am-3pm and 6:45-10:30pm.

Grannie, 27, rue Pierre Leroux (tel. 01 43 34 94 14). M. Vaneau. There may be no grandmother on the premises, but the chefs in this rustic restaurant, decorated in bright blues and yellows, remain faithful to traditional French cuisine. Lunchtime *formules* include a main dish, and either a salad or coffee (50F) or an appetizer and wine (75F). Wine is 18-22F a glass. Open Tues.-Fri. noon-1:30pm and 7:30-10:30pm, Mon. and Sat. 7:30-10:30pm. MC, V.

■ Eighth Arrondissement

The 8*ème* is as glamorous and expensive as one might expect of Paris. In fact, most of the charm of this arrondissement lies in its gratuitous extravagance and the bountiful opportunities to spend money that it frivolously offers. If you are more interested in observing the exuberant wastefulness of others than in indulging in it yourself, there are a number of affordable restaurants, especially on the side streets around the rue La Boétie.

Elliott Restaurant, 166, bd. Haussmann (tel. 01 42 89 30 50). M. Miromesnil. Walk up av. Percier and turn left on bd. Haussmann. A taste of home in the arrondissement that makes you feel like a stranger. Bistro-style restaurant with slick decor and food that's all-American. Buffalo wings (43F), hamburgers (62F), and selected American beers (23F). Huge American brunch Sat.-Sun. includes eggs Benedict (98F). Open Mon.-Sat. noon-3pm and 8pm-midnight, Sun. noon-4pm. V, AmEx.

Antoine's: Les Sandwichs des 5 Continents, 31, rue de Ponthieu (tel. 01 42 89 44 20). M. Franklin D. Roosevelt. Walk towards the Arc de Triomphe on the Champs-Elysées, turn right on av. Franklin D. Roosevelt and left onto rue de Ponthieu. Don't give into temptation and grab fast-food on the Champs-Elysées, hop around the corner to this hip sandwich shop. Specialities include the Buffalo sandwich composed of barbecued chicken and melted cheese on hearty bread (23F). American desserts and ice-cream bars fill out the menu for a cheap, but appetizing, meal (12-18F). Beer 12-18F. Take-out available. Open Mon.-Fri. 8am-6pm.

Barry's, 9, rue de Duras (tel. 01 40 06 02 27). M. Champs Elysées-Clemenceau. From the metro, cross the Champs-Elysées and head straight up av. Marigny to pl. Beauvau, hang a sharp right onto the rue du Faubourg St-Honoré and your first left onto rue de Duras. A clean, quiet, low-budget sandwich emporium with *panini* (24-29F), sandwiches (20-25F), and desserts (15-17F). Surprisingly simple and good in this arrondissement of bright lights, big prices, and rip-off tourist traps. Open Mon.-Fri. 11am-3pm.

Le Singe d'Eau, 28, rue de Moscou (tel. 01 43 87 72 73). M. Europe. Opened in 1992, the year of the water monkey *(singe d'eau),* this restaurant serves authentic Tibetan cuisine in a room outfitted in quiet, understated reds, yellows, and blues. Appetizers 10-40F, main courses 45-55F. A vegetarian menu is available. The "Full Moon Momos" and "Drhe," a kind of chicken curry, both get raves from customers. English spoken. Open Mon.-Sat. noon-3pm and 7-11pm.

Vitamine, 20, rue de Bucarest (tel. 01 45 22 28 02). M. Liège. From the metro walk up rue de Moscou. The restaurant is on the first corner on your right. Simple décor, mirrors, and sunshine go well with the light, low-priced, tasty sandwiches and salads you'll find here. Poilâne bread is a specialty here. Sandwiches (13-20F), salads (22-40F). House couscous with curried chicken and saffron 40F. Open Mon.-Fri. 8am-3pm.

Nirvana, 6, rue de Moscou (tel. 01 45 22 27 12). M. Liège. Warm, classy décor bordering on the overdone. Indian cuisine, very popular among those who work in this commercial quarter. 79F summer *menu* includes chicken or fish Tikka, salad and nan. Other *menus* at 95F and 129F. Open Mon.-Sat. noon-4:30pm and 7-11pm.

FOOD AND DRINK

■ Ninth Arrondissement

Except for a few gems, meals close to the heavily touristed Opéra area can be quite expensive; for truly cheap deals, head farther north. Displaced by the projectile force of the city's skyrocketing prices, much of ethnic Paris has found a home here, providing visitors to the 9*ème* with wondrous, affordable delicacies from former French colonies.

Anarkali, 4, pl. Gustave Toudouze (tel. 01 48 78 39 84). M. St-Georges. Walk uphill on rue Notre-Dame-de-Lorette and branch right onto rue H. Monnier. On a secluded cobblestone square. Serves up a standard assortment of spicy South Indian fare. Relax on the terrace under wide, colorful umbrellas and revel in the lack of traffic. Meat dishes 55-60F, veggie dishes 30-40F. Chutneys cost an extra 6-8F. 3-course lunch *menu* 69F, 2-course *menu* 55F. Open Tues.-Sat. noon-2:30pm and 7pm-12:30am. Open Sun.-Mon. 7pm-12:30am in summer. MC, V, AmEx.

Pizzéria King Salomon, 46, rue Richer (tel. 01 42 46 31 22). M. Cadet or Bonne Nouvelle. From M. Cadet descend rue Saulner and turn left on rue Richer. A popular kosher (no, Virginia, there are no meat toppings) pizzeria in the heart of the 9*ème*'s Jewish community. The *King Salomon* (58F) is topped with tomato, cheese, artichoke hearts, egg, basil, mushrooms, and olives. Delicious individual pizzas 42-58F. Slices 12-15F. Take-out available. Open Sun.-Thurs. 11:30am-3pm and 4:30pm-midnight, Sat. 4:30pm-midnight.

Hayne's Bar, 3, rue Clauzel (tel. 01 48 78 40 63). M. St-Georges. Head uphill on rue Notre-Dame-de-Lorette, branch right on rue H. Monnier, and right again on rue Clauzel. Bedecked with photos of jazz and blues greats, this restaurant/bar specializes in down-home New Orleans cooking with soul. Come here for fried or BBQ chicken, New Orleans-style red beans, and fresh-baked cornbread. Southern hospitality, generous portions, and dinner still comes to less than 100F. On Fri. nights, a pianist plays New Orleans jazz. Hot tamales 40F. Ma Sutton's fried chicken 70F. Sister Lena's BBQ spare ribs 70F. Open Tues.-Sat. 7:30pm-1am.

Le Chartier, 7, rue du Faubourg-Montmartre (tel. 01 47 70 86 29; fax 01 48 24 14 68). M. Rue Montmartre. Walk uphill on rue du Faubourg-Montmartre; enter the restaurant through the small passage to your left. A huge restaurant in grand old French style, with chandeliers and wooden booths. Jovial waiters serve a mainly older, local clientele. Specialties include beef in a house tomato sauce, *pot au feu* (stew), and roast veal. Portions are huge. A full meal will cost 95F with the *menu.* Open daily 11am-3pm and 6-9:30pm. MC, V (100F minimum).

Sannine, 32, rue du Faubourg-Montmartre (tel. 01 48 24 01 32). M. rue Montmartre. Walk uphill on rue du Faubourg-Montmartre to its corner with rue Richer. A small, family affair specializing in Middle Eastern basics: kebabs, marinated beef, falafel, and tabouli. Yellow tablecloths and painted murals of the Lebanon that once was.

Dinner à la carte for around 90F; *menu* for 49F (lunch) and 69F (dinner). Take-out available. Open Mon.-Fri. noon-3pm and 6-11:30pm, Sat.-Sun. 6-11:30pm. MC, V, AmEx.

Les Bacchantes, 21, rue de Caumartin (tel. 01 42 65 25 35). M. Havre-Caumartin. Walk south (away from Au Printemps) on rue de Caumartin. Hearty portions of perennial French favorites and wine amid dark wood and lacy chandeliers. Specials advertised on blackboards. Delicious *pommes de terre au munster et au lard paysan* (potatoes with melted munster cheese and bacon, 60F). For dessert, try the cinnamon-y *pêches au vin à la cannelle* (peaches in red wine, 25F). Wine 13-30F by the glass. Open Mon.-Sat. 11:30am-12:30am, Sun. 11:30am-10pm; Aug. Mon.-Sat. 11:30am-6am. MC, V, AmEx.

Le Palmier de Lorette, 19, rue de Châteaudun (tel. 01 48 78 34 41). M. Notre-Dame-de-Lorette. Across from the church. *Brasserie*-style, plush interior. Owned by a couple who take pride in their food and hospitality. Monsieur does the cooking. Lunch and evening menu (94F50) offers farm-fresh French classics and a *kir.* Open Mon.-Fri. 7am-1am; open for meals noon-3pm and 7-11:30pm. MC, V.

Hard Rock Café, 14, bd. Montmartre (tel. 01 42 46 10 00). M. Richelieu Drouot. Loud music, burgers, and guitars on the wall. Same as it ever was, but this time in *Paris.* Remember, the most important thing is the city under the logo. Happy hour Mon.-Fri. 6-8pm. Open daily 11:30am-2am. MC, V, AmEx (100F minimum).

■ Tenth Arrondissement

While many tourists may see no more of the 10ème than their two-hour layover at the Gare du Nord allows, those who venture out will find enough French, Indian, and African food to make any gourmand smile. Catering to locals rather than tourists, these restaurants offer short- and long-term visitors alike the chance to slurp down some of the culinary fruits of New Paris. Passage Brady, for one, overflows with cheap Indian eateries.

Paris-Dakar, 95, rue du Faubourg St-Martin (tel. 01 42 08 16 64). M. Gare de l'Est. African masks and batiks decorate this popular, family-run restaurant. Try *Yassa* (chicken with lime and onions, 71F), *Maffé* (chicken or beef sauteed in peanut sauce, 69F), and *Tiep Bou Dieone,* the "national dish of Senegal" (fish with rice and veggies, 98F). Feast freely but carefully; the red-chili and oil concoction may be hard on the gentle stomachs. 3-course lunch *menu* with drinks 59F; 3-course dinner *menu* 99F. Open Tues.-Sun. noon-3pm and 7pm-2am. MC, V.

Brasserie Flo, 7, cour des Petites-Ecuries (tel. 01 47 70 13 59). M. Château d'Eau. Walk against traffic on rue du Château d'Eau, turn left on rue du Faubourg St-Denis; the entrance to the *cour* is on the right. Elegant dining room with dark wood paneling and tuxedoed waiters specializing in seafood. Every imaginable type of oyster is on the menu; 6 of the cheapest for 60-84F. Dinner à la carte is exorbitant, but the 2-course *menu* provides a superb meal (119F lunch, 189F dinner). Reservations recommended. Open noon-3pm and 7pm-1:30am. MC, V.

La Rose du Kashmir, 64-66, passage Brady (tel. 01 42 46 23 75). M. Château d'Eau or Strasbourg St-Denis. Walk opposite traffic on bd. de Strasbourg and enter passage Brady at no. 33. Two large golden urns flank the entrance to this razzle-dazzle Indian eatery, which serves large portions of wide-ranging Tandoori specialties. Appetizers run 19-90F; main plates 50-149F; curries (with chicken, beef, lamb, or vegetables) 47-58F; and desserts 18-22F. Terrace seating! Open noon-3pm and 6-11:30pm. MC, V.

Le Palais de l'Est, 186, rue du Faubourg St-Martin (tel. 01 46 07 09 99). M. Château Landon. Walk toward Gare de l'Est on rue du Faubourg St-Martin. The food, the price, the place might not inspire—but, oh, the hours are divine. Stop by in the wee hours for Chinese and Vietnamese specialties and fantabulous karaoke. Dinner à la carte around 170F; try the lunch *menu* at 52F or dinner at 78F. Take-out available; dim sum, too. Open daily noon-3pm and 7pm-5am. AmEx.

Le Dogon, 30, rue René Boulanger (tel. 01 42 41 95 85). M. République. From the metro, rue René Boulanger is on your left. Elegant African (mainly Senegalese) restaurant steps away from pl. de la République. White walls, batiks, and animal pelts serve as the backdrop for sumptuous curries, couscous, and *Maffé,* all made affordable by a 2-course, 55F lunch *menu.* Go easy on the chili sauce here. Open Mon.-Fri. 11:30am-3pm and 7pm-midnight, Sat.-Sun. 11:30am-2:30pm. MC, V.

■ Eleventh Arrondissement

The 11ème's restaurants fill to capacity with young and chic regulars who stay through the night. Low rents have inspired low meal prices near and beyond the new Opéra Bastille. Try to reserve tables ahead of time, or expect to wait (and wait, and wait, and wait on weekends) at the restaurant's bar.

Occitanie, 96, rue Oberkampf (tel. 01 48 06 46 98). M. St-Maur. Go northwest on av. de la République, take your first right onto rue St-Maur, and then turn right on rue Oberkampf. Burlap-covered refectory tables provide a rustic setting for southwestern French cuisine. 3-course midday *formule* at 52F includes a wine or coffee and a wide selection of salads and meats. Dinner *menus* are bargains at 62F (for 3 courses) and 89F (for 4 courses). Appetizers 30-50F, main courses 48-98F. Open Sept.-July Mon.-Fri. noon-2pm and 7-11pm, Sat. 7-11pm. MC, V, AmEx.

Au Petit Keller, 13, rue Keller (tel. 01 47 00 12 97). M. Ledru-Rollin. Walk north on av. Ledru Rollin and turn left on rue Keller. Traditional bistro in the heart of the vibrant Bastille district. The filling, wholesome food has something of a neighborhood fan club. At noon, 70F *menu* includes main dish (such as veal) and an appetizer (endive salad with roquefort cheese) or a dessert *(crème caramel),* and beer, wine, or mineral water. *Gâteau de riz* (rice cake) is a house specialty. Open Mon.-Sat. 8am-2:30pm and 7pm-midnight. MC, V.

A la Banane Ivoirienne, 10, rue de la Forge-Royale (tel. 01 43 70 49 90). M. Faidherbe-Chaligny. Walk west on rue du Faubourg St-Antoine and turn right on rue de la Forge-Royale. Run by a gregarious Ivoirian emigré who wrote his doctoral thesis on his country's banana industry. Come for delicious West African specialties, such as *attieke,* made from cassava, and *aloko,* from bananas. Appetizers, like stuffed crabs *à l'Abgidinaise,* 25-35F. Main courses 50-80F. Every Thursday try the *Foutou National* (a dish with plantains) for 80F. Open Tues.-Sat. 7pm-midnight. MC, V (100F minimum).

Le Bistro St-Ambroise, 5, rue Guillaume Bertrand (tel. 01 47 00 43 50). M. St-Maur. Walk against traffic on rue St-Maur and turn left on rue Guillaume Bertrand. Yellow walls and old ads from French magazines cover the walls of this cute bistro hidden away from tourists. Delicious food, an expert wine *carte,* and an unrivaled repertoire of desserts (20-40F). Try the *travers de porc au miel* (honeyed pork) 54F, or the *confit de canard* (59F). 3-course lunch *menu* 68F. MC, V.

Le Passage, 18, passage de la Bonne-Graine (tel. 01 47 00 73 30). M. Ledru-Rollin. From the metro, walk east on rue du Faubourg St-Antoine and take a near-hidden left on passage de la Bonne-Graine. A sequestered Bastille bistro for thirty-something wine lovers. Famous for their *andouillettes* (sausages) served with potatoes and puréed peas or lentils (75-90F). Dare to try the *pieds Janet* (pigs feet cooked in *foie gras*). Daily specials 60F. 270 kinds of wine, many overpriced; order the week's chosen vintage by the glass. Inquire about wine-tasting events. Open Mon.-Fri. noon-3:30pm and 7:30-11:30pm, Sat. 7:30-11:30pm. MC, V, AmEx.

Le Bistrot du Peintre, 116, av. Ledru-Rollin (tel. 01 47 00 34 39). M. Ledru-Rollin. Walk up av. Ledru-Rollin. A neighborhood haunt and Art Nouveau period piece. The original 1900 interior is preserved as a landmark. Locals and tourists convene under the angels on the ceiling for unassuming, honest food. Omelettes 32-35F. Appetizers 28-46F, main courses 48-70F, desserts 18-33F. The house specialty is *confit de canard* with sautéed potatoes (69F). Sit outside on a nice day. Open Mon.-Sat. 9am-2am, Sun. 10am-9pm. (Food served noon-midnight.) MC, V.

Chez Paul, 13, rue de Charonne (tel. 01 47 00 34 57). M. Ledru-Rollin or Bastille. From M. Bastille, go east on rue du Faubourg St-Antoine and turn left on rue de Charonne. Late-night crowds fill this small restaurant with a 1920s zinc bar and black-and-white-tiled floor. Friendly staff serves bounteous traditional food. Try 6 snails (36F), followed by steak with pears, cognac, and potatoes (60F), or rabbit thigh stuffed with goat cheese and mint leaves (72F). Open Sept.-July Mon.-Sat. noon-2:30pm and 7:15pm-2am, food served until 12:30am. MC, V, AmEx.

Slice, 11, rue de la Roquette (tel. 01 43 57 66 67). M. Bastille. The location of this New York-style pizzeria, near the happening bars and clubs of rue de Lappe, makes it a great place to stop by for a late night snack (15-21F a slice) before that next round of Long Island Iced Teas. Those out to satisfy more than just the munchies have a choice of three inexpensive *menus* which include a slice, dessert, and beverage (25F for lunch only, 32F and 33F *menus* for all hours). Delivery service noon-4pm and 7-11:30pm. Open daily 11am-1:30am.

Au Trou Normand, 9, rue Jean-Pierre Timbaud (tel. 01 48 05 80 23). M. Oberkampf. Walk north on rue de Malte until it intersects rue Jean-Pierre Timbaud. This may be the cheapest bistro in Paris. Don't come here if you're looking to have a gourmet French meal. Attracts a youthful lunch crowd of regulars. The *onglet rocquefort* and *frites,* steak and fries, (30F) is a favorite. Have one of the homemade tarts, too. Appetizers 12-15F, *plats du jour* 30F, tasty desserts 10F-14F. Open Sept.-July Mon.-Fri. noon-2:30pm and 7:30-11pm, Sat. 7:30-11pm.

Le Val de Loire, 149, rue Amelot (tel. 01 47 00 34 11). M. Filles du Calvaire. Walk towards the Cirque d'Hiver and turn left on rue Amelot. Locals share tables with tourists from nearby hotels. Traditional decor—red tablecloths and a small wooden cask by the window—complements standard French fare. 2-course 48F *menu* includes a main course and choice of appetizer or dessert. 58F *menu* includes a buffet of appetizers (melon, salami, salad), a main course, and a dessert. Probably not the best place to spring for the 105F *menu;* nothing gourmet here. Open Sept.-July Mon.-Sat. noon-2:30pm and 6:45-10pm. MC, V, AmEx.

■ Twelfth Arrondissement

With the Gare de Lyon as its gravitational center, the 12*ème* provides a monotony of goods and services for the no-frills tourist on a train layover. Restaurants, however, are in short supply, and not many merit special trips from the center city. Here is a sampling of the area's few finds.

L'Ebauchoir, 45, rue de Citeaux (tel. 01 43 42 49 31). M. Faidherbe-Chaligny. Walk down the Rue de Faubourg St-Antoine. Make a left on rue de Citeaux. Great combination of relaxed, funky atmosphere and sophisticated, subtle French food. 3-course lunch menu with drink 66F, dinner à la carte only. Try the *foie de veau au miel et au coriandre* (veal's liver with honey and coriander, 80F) or the *fondant au chocolat* (30F). Open Mon.-Sat. 11:30am-2:30pm and 7-11pm.

Le Rocher du Diamant, 284, rue de Charenton (tel. 01 40 19 08 78). M. Dugommier or Daumesnil. From M. Dugommier walk against traffic on rue Charenton; from M. Daumesnil, walk down rue Claude Decaen, take your first right on rue de la Brèche-aux-Loups and walk until it intersects rue de Charenton. Stuffed turtles in the windows suggest the tropical, palm-and-sea decor of this Antillean outpost of chic on the Paris outskirts. 3-course lunch *menus* at 69F and 89F. Additional 2-course lunch *menu* with main course and choice of an appetizer or dessert. Dinner *menu* at 89F. Split the 2-person *marmite des Caraïbes* (seafood stew, 240F) with a friend. *Colombos* (Caribbean curry dishes) around 75-80F. A la carte: appetizers 25-45F, main courses 59-80F, seafood 60-135F, desserts 40-45F. Open daily 11am-2:30pm and 7pm-midnight. MC, V.

Le Parrot, 5, rue Parrot (tel. 01 43 43 05 64). M. Gare de Lyon. Walk against traffic on rue de Lyon and take a right on rue Parrot. A cheap, old-fashioned, friendly place to go for a meal. 58F *menu* includes appetizer, main course, and dessert. Try various big salads (e.g. lettuce, potato, mushrooms, radish, apples, carrots) and dessert (48F). Open Mon.-Sat. 11:30am-3pm and 6:30-10:30pm. MC, V, AmEx.

■ Thirteenth Arrondissement

AVENUE DE CHOISY

Scores of Vietnamese, Thai, Cambodian, Laotian, and Chinese restaurants cluster south of pl. d'Italie on av. de Choisy. There, Paris' answer to Chinatown caches some of the city's cheapest eats. Note that rice and tea aren't included in the price of your meal. Save room for dessert; some of Paris' best pastries cluster here. Early eaters should note that many restaurants in this neighborhood are open all day.

Thiên Co, 41, av. de Choisy (tel. 01 45 85 55 00). M. Porte de Choisy. Walk north on av. de Choisy. Sidle through the green-trimmed, glassed-in patio to the long, skinny dining room for homestyle Vietnamese food. Reasonably priced, perfectly sized servings of soup or rice dishes with grilled meat (30-45F). Limited, though adequate, menu selection. *Pho* soup specialties 36-41F, desserts 15-17F. Open Mon. and Wed.-Fri. 11am-4pm and 6:30-11pm, Sat.-Sun. 11am-11pm.

Thuy Hong, 15, av. de Choisy (tel. 01 45 86 87 07). M. Porte de Choisy. In the building labeled "le Kiosque de Choisy"—walk through the outdoor alley in the building and turn left; the restaurant is the last one on the left side. Long, marble-topped tables hold large portions of simple Cambodian and Vietnamese food. Try the *poisson vapeur à la crème de coco* (steamed fish with coconut cream; 55F), soup (35F), or the *crêpe combodgienne* (54F). Most entrees around 43F. Save room for their acclaimed desserts. Open Wed.-Mon. noon-10:30pm.

Lao Thai, 128, rue de Tolbiac (tel. 01 44 24 28 10). M. Tolbiac. Asian and French regulars convene for comparatively expensive Thai food. The 47F lunch *menu,* however, is a steal; it includes an appetizer, main dish, rice, and dessert or coffee. Dinner menus 136F, 156F, or 176F (for 2 people) allow you to try a few dishes, soup, and dessert. A la carte main courses 30-50F. Open Thurs.-Tues. noon-2:30pm and 7-11:15pm. MC, V.

BUTTE AUX CAILLES

The Butte aux Cailles district encompasses a handful of streets stretching south of pl. d'Italie. Havens for artists and intellectuals thrown from the Latin Quarter by soaring prices, area restaurants and bars fill with the young and high-spirited.

Le Temps des Cérises, 18-20, rue de la Butte-aux-Cailles (tel. 01 45 89 69 48). M. pl. d'Italie. Take rue Bobillot and turn right on rue de la Butte-aux-Cailles. A restaurant cooperative and venerated neighborhood institution. Locals meet here to discuss everything from art to (liberal) politics, often with live music in the background. 3-course *menu* (lunch 56F, dinner 60F), is served until 9pm (Mon.-Thurs. only). Choices include *paté de foie* and *coquelet sauce poivre.* Open Mon.-Fri. noon-2:15pm and 7:30-11:30pm, Sat. 7:30-11:30pm. MC, V, AmEx.

Le Samson, 9, rue Jean-Marie Jégo (tel. 01 45 89 09 23). M. pl. d'Italie. Take rue Bobillot, turn right on rue de la Butte-aux-Cailles, and then turn right again on rue Jean-Marie Jégo. Spray-painted tables and red, sponge-painted walls flag artsy hipsters to this small restaurant. Daily menu on chalkboards around the room. Reasonably priced, very French food. 61F *menu* includes appetizer, main course, and dessert (*salade Boston, roti de porcauports,* and *crème brulée,* for example). A la carte, appetizers 20-35F and main courses 45-60F. Open Mon.-Fri. noon-2:30pm and 7:30pm-1am, Sat. 7:30pm-1am.

Chez Gladines, 30, rue des Cinq Diamants. M. pl. d'Italie. Take bd. Auguste Blanqui and turn left onto rue des Cinq Diamants; it's at the corner of rue Jonas. A bar/restaurant and café during non-dinner hours. Sit at long wooden tables for snails and other Basque specialties. Main courses 45-65F, salads 28-50F, various *escargots* 48-55F. Good selection of wines by the glass (12-16F). Despite Gladine's multiple rooms, crowds inevitably gather on the sidewalk, waiting for tables. Don't be discouraged; the turnover is quick. Open Sept.-July daily 9am-2am; dinner served 7:30pm-12:30am. No credit cards.

■ Fourteenth Arrondissement

The budget traveler is forever indebted to the Bretons, the French from the northwest who flooded Paris at the turn of the century and settled in Montparnasse. The crepes and *galettes* (a larger, buckwheat version, topped with meat, cheese, or vegetables instead of sweets) which they brought with them are easy to find, easy to eat, and even easier on the wallet. Bypass the overcooked *biftek* and limp *frites* available at one of the hundreds of utterly forgettable restaurants that cluster around the Tour Montparnasse and try a *crêperie* on the rue de Montparnasse instead.

Aquarius Café, 40, rue de Gergovie (tel. 01 45 41 36 88). M. Pernety. Walk against traffic on rue Raymond Losserand and turn right onto rue de Gergovie. Wooden tables, an exceptionally friendly staff, and serene decorations enhance the mouth-watering meals in this inventive vegetarian restaurant. The famous "mixed grill" includes tofu sausages, cereal sausages, wheat pancakes, wheat germ, brown rice, and vegetables in a mushroom sauce (65F). Or get your vitamins via an Aquarius salad (55F) with goat cheese, avocado, egg, vegetable pâté, potato salad, *crudités,* and vinaigrette. Homemade desserts are well worth 25-30F. Open Mon.-Sat. noon-2:15pm and 7-10:30pm. MC, V, AmEx.

Le Château Poivre, 145, rue du Château (tel. 01 43 22 03 68). M. Pernety. Walk with traffic on rue Raymond Losserand and turn right onto rue du Chateau. The owner takes his food seriously, and the generous portions, enhanced by over 60 varieties of wine, will encourage you to do the same. With à la carte prices a little steep (the exquisite *crème caramel* will melt in your mouth, as it slips 35F out of your wallet), the 89F *menu,* with dishes like *escargots, andouillette au sauvignon*, and *mousse au chocolat*, is a steal. "Not just good, it's great!" says the modest owner. Open Mon.-Sat. noon-2:30pm and 7-10:30pm. MC, V, AmEx.

Phinéas, 99, rue de l'Ouest (tel. 01 45 41 33 50). M. Pernety. Follow the traffic on rue Pernety and turn left on rue de l'Ouest. Specializing in *tartes sucrées et salées* made before your very eyes, this delightful restaurant doubles as a shrine to cartoons. The menu, which includes main dishes for 58-80F and a number of vegetarian options, comes inserted in a comic book. While flipping through the pages, don't miss a peak at the bust of Tintin, or the enormous suspended metal crown which occupies most of the back room. The famous *tarte ancitron* and other choices from the *"Hit-Parade des desserts"* are 10-36F. Cheaper take-out options available. Open Tues.-Sat. noon-11:30pm. MC, V, AmEx.

N'Zadette-M'foua, 152, rue du Château (tel. 01 43 22 00 16). M. Pernety. Walk with the traffic on rue Raymond Losserand; turn right on rue du Château. Take a break from French food at this vibrant Congolese restaurant, where African relics and woven wall hangings whisk you away from the infernal Parisian drizzle. You'll be smiling after a *Sourire Congolais,* a fish, tomato, pineapple, cream, and cucumber concoction (42F); or try the *maboke,* meat or fish cooked in a wrapper of banana leaves (69F). 3-course *menu* 85F; à la carte appetizers 25-42F, main dishes 54-88F, vegetables 12-25F. Open daily noon-3pm and 7pm-1am.

Le Colvert, 129, rue du Château (tel. 01 43 27 95 19). M. Penerty. Follow the traffic on rue Raymond Losserand, then turn right on rue du Château. You can't miss this tiny restaurant's shtick: ducks. They're on the walls, on the plates, sitting (ceramic, of course) on the shelves—there's even a quacking duck telephone. The pricey Mediterranean menu features tsaziki (35F) and *confit de canard aux baies roses* (85F) and cheese or Greek desserts (25-42F); the 65F lunchtime *menu* and 89F and 130F dinner *menus* offer 3 courses of traditional French food. Plan to waddle out. Reservations accepted. Open Mon.-Fri. noon-3pm and 7–11:30pm and 7-11pm, Sat. 7-11:30pm. MC, V.

Le Jeroboam, 72, rue Didot (tel. 01 45 39 39 13). M. Plaisance. Off of rue d'Alésia. Authentic French restaurant serving superb traditional fare at utterly reasonable prices. Relax in the intimate dining room under the pastoral ceiling frescoes. 3-course lunch *menus* at 65F and 82F include delectable dishes such as *tarine de poisson aux olives et citron confit* (a fish stew with preserved lemons and olives). Open Mon. noon-2:30pm, Tues.-Sat. noon-2:30pm and 7-10:30pm. MC, V.

La Route du Château, 123, rue du Château (tel. 01 43 20 09 59). M. Pernety. Walk with traffic on rue Raymond Losserand until it crosses rue du Château. This tiny bistro is an oasis of French charm in an otherwise humdrum neighborhood. The antique light fixtures, frosted glass windows, and faded lace curtains have been here at least as long as the 27-year-old restaurant. Specialties include *langue de boeuf* (78F) and rabbit sautéed in cider and mustard (80F). Three-course *menu* 82F, and definitely worth it. Open Mon. 7pm-midnight, Tues.-Sat. noon-2pm and 7pm-midnight. MC, V, AmEx.

Le Biniou, 3, av. du Général Leclerc (tel. 01 43 27 20 40). M. Denfert-Rochereau. This small *crêperie* is decorated in stark tones of yellow, blue, and white, but its twist on the traditional crêpe is far from minimalist. Unusual combinations of calamari or mussels with curry; sophisticated *galettes* with smoked salmon, fresh cream, and lemon (47F); and traditionals like the *complète* (ham, cheese, and egg, 25F). Main course and dessert crepes 16-47F. Open Mon.-Sat. 11:45am-2:30pm and 6:45-11pm.

Au Berbere Jessica, 50, rue de Gergovie (tel. 01 45 42 10 29). M. Pernety. See Aquarius Café, above, for directions. Standard French and North African fare at hugely low prices: appetizers 17-52F, main courses that range from the *omelette aux herbes* (22F) to the lamb for two (152F). Couscous dishes 48-87F. Satisfying 3-course lunch *menu* is 55F. Open Mon.-Sat. noon-3pm and 6-11pm, Sun. 7-10:30pm. MC, V.

■ Fifteenth Arrondissement

Eateries in this vibrant-yet-safe arrondissement remain treasured local establishments, where owners personally welcome regulars to their usual tables and lovingly detail the specials of the day. Traditional bistros, complete with oak and brass bars and mirrored walls, pepper the area around the rue du Commerce, while the streets radiating away from bd. de Grenelle have more Asian restaurants than you could shake a chopstick at.

Restaurant Les Listines, 24, rue Falguière (tel. 01 45 38 57 40). M. Falguière. A neighborhood favorite, this charming family-run restaurant has a simple, classic decor, but takes delicious risks with its French fare. The 2-course, 79F *formule* includes options like warm goat cheese flan dressed in herbs; and monkfish with leeks and cream. A la carte prices are reasonable: appetizers 35F, main dishes 60F, desserts 28-36F, main dish and desert 89F. A glass of wine is 14-21F. Open Mon.-Sat. noon-2:30pm and 7-10pm. MC, V, AmEx.

Ty Breiz, 52, bd. de Vaugirard (tel. 01 43 20 83 72). M. Pasteur or Montparnasse. Scant steps from the picturesque Tour Montparnasse, this bustling *crêperie* is where Bretons choose to eat. Traditional elements such as exposed wood beams, porcelain plates painted with Bretons in native garb on the walls, and rustic copper cookware make for a full immersion experience. Try one of their succulent dinner crêpes (17-51F), like the *forestière* (fried egg, tomato, and mushroom in a *Provençale* sauce, 44F), or go straight for dessert (16-43F) with, oh, say, a *crêpe tropicale* (crêpe flambée with Malibu, coconut, and pineapple, 40F). 59F *formule* includes 3 crêpes and a bowl of cider. Show them your *Let's Go* and get a free aperitif, the *kir breton.* Open Mon.-Sat. 11:45am-2:45pm and 7-10:45pm. MC, V.

Chez Foong, 32, rue Frémicourt (tel. 45 67 3699). M. Cambronne. Walk through pl. Cambronne and turn left on rue Frémicourt. Get your fill of creamy satay and satisfying, spicy curry at this small Malaysian restaurant, while festive moon kites hover on the walls above your head. Try the *ikan pais bernyiur* (grilled fish wrapped in banana leaves with coconut milk and spices, 59F), but save room for dessert: the *kwih ketayapo* (Malaysian crêpes with coconut), *onde onde* (sweet potato balls covered with caramel), and *kaya pope* (tarts coated in coconut jam) are sensational at 25F each, and even better at 35F for all three. 78F and 85F *menus* include an appetizer, main dish, rice, and dessert. Weekday 56F lunch *menu* has a scaled-down version of the same courses. English spoken. Open Mon.-Sat. noon-2:30pm and 7-11pm. MC, V.

Restaurant Aux Artistes, 63, rue Falguière (tel. 01 43 22 05 39). M. Pasteur. Follow bd. Pasteur toward the omnipresent Tour Montparnasse, and turn right on rue Falguière. A cheap restaurant with a humongous menu, where you can eat with young Americans in the shadow of surfboards, an assortment of U.S. license plates, and posters of young Ronald Reagan. The low prices and late hours attract a crowd of less discriminating palates. Gourmets may want to keep looking. 2-course lunch *menu* 56F, 3-course dinner *menu* 76F. You can't discover what the *rêve de jeune fille* (young girl's dream) dessert is about unless you order it (26F). Open Mon.-Fri. noon-2:30pm and 7pm-12:30am, Sat. 7pm-12:30am. MC, V.

Sampieru Corsu, 12, rue de l'Amiral Roussin. M. Cambronne. Walk into the pl. Cambronne and take a left onto rue de la Croix Nivert, then another left onto rue de l'Amiral Roussin. Infamously run by a Marxist Corsican separatist, political posters, petitions, and articles fill all available wall and table space in this simple, comfortable restaurant where—in the spirit of the cause—you may be invited to share a table with other visitors. Eat your fill and pay according to your means, though the suggested price for the simple but copious 3-course *menu* is 36F (beer or wine included). The management does not speak English, so don't expect translations, and don't even think about pulling out a credit card. Open Mon.-Fri. 11:45am-1:30pm and 6:30-9:30pm.

Café du Commerce, 51, rue du Commerce (tel. 01 45 75 03 27). M. Émile Zola. Turn right on rue du Commerce. This venerable institution has been around since 1921, and takes pride in offering great food for less than 100F. The beautiful 3-level, open-air interior surrounds a central atrium courtyard with overflowing vines and flowers. Bright and surprisingly full, this café-restaurant has an 85F *formule commerce menu* (main dish, appetizer or dessert, and drink) and a 110F *menu* (all 3 courses) which feature *saumon cru mariné à l'aneth* (raw salmon in a dill marinade), *côtes d'agneau aux herbes* (lamb with herbs), and *mousse au chocolat.* Open daily noon-midnight. MC, V, AmEx.

Samaya, 31, bd. de Grenelle (tel. 01 45 77 44 44). M. Dupleix. A small eatery specializing in Lebanese cuisine; the bundles of wheat on the walls are for good luck, which is what you'll have here. 68F and 98F *menus* feature tabouli, *laban concombre* (yogurt with cucumber and mint), hummus, and lamb delicacies. Some vegetarian options, like *foul,* a bean salad with olive oil and lemon juice (30F). Tasty Middle Eastern desserts, such as *baklava* (28F). Takeout available. Open daily noon-midnight. MC, V.

Bistro Bourdelle, 12, rue Antoine Bourdelle (tel. 01 45 48 57 01). M. Montparnasse-Bienvenue. From metro walk up Rue de l'Arrive, take a right onto av. de Maine and then a left onto rue Antoine Bourdelle. A traditional, small, dark bistro where dignified old men come to pass their lunch hour drinking decent house wine and feasting on the impeccably prepared meat and fish. 88F *formule* offers two courses (main dish and appetizer or dessert), including such house specialties as *salade aux foies de volaille* (salad with chicken-liver mousse) and *quenelles de brochet.* Open Mon.-Fri. 9:30am-3pm and 6pm-midnight. MC, V.

Phetburi, 31, bd. de Grenelle (tel. 01 40 58 14 88). M. Dupleix. The place to go for Thai if you're not averse to lemon grass—specialties include lemon grass chicken soup (39F), spicy beef with lemon leaves (49F), shrimp salad flavored with lemon grass (42F). Lunch *menu* (69F) and dinner *menu* (92F, Mon.-Fri.) include three courses and a portion of rice, though dinner offers more choices. Takeout available. Open Mon.-Sat. noon-2:30pm and 7-10:45pm. MC, V, AmEx.

■ Sixteenth Arrondissement

If you are staying in the 16ème, eat elsewhere. If you are visiting the 16ème, bring a picnic. Hard-hitting sight-seers can explore one of the area's markets—the marchés Président Wilson and St-Didier, as well as the market at the intersection of rue Gros and rue La Fontaine—to pick up fresh produce and baked goods while en route to yet another of the area's myriad museums. Here are some of the (few) inexpensive restaurants in this otherwise upscale, residential neighborhood:

Casa Tina, 18, rue Lauriston (tel. 01 40 67 19 24). M. Charles-de-Gaulle-Etoile. Walk up av. Victor Hugo 1 block and take a left on rue Lauriston. This tiny Spanish restaurant provides excellent, light meals and a large dose of native charm. Terra cotta tiles, hanging peppers, and a guitar furnish an ambient setting for *tapas* (light Spanish delicacies 15-69F, or 98F for a meal of seven hot and cold dishes). The Andalusian chef also turns out a range of traditional dishes, like *paella* (98-150F). Appetizers 18-28F, main dishes 68-124F. 100F *menu* includes a plate of *tapas*, the daily special, a glass of wine, and coffee. Open daily 11:30am-3:30pm and 6pm-1am, Sat.-Sun. 7pm-2am. Make reservations on weekends. MC, V, AmEx.

Byblos Café, 6, rue Guichard (tel. 01 42 30 99 99). M. La Muette. Walk down rue Passy one block and take a left on rue Guichard. A simply furnished Lebanese café-restaurant with a soothing, pastel orange color scheme. Order a few hors d'oeuvres (28-64F) from a selection which includes tabouli, *moutabal* (puréed eggplant with sesame paste), and a variety of hummus plates. A meatless meal is easy to get here. 2-person dinner *menu* (230F) is a 7-dish sampler. Grilled meats 58-62F. Takeout available; takeout prices are 10-20% lower. Open 11:30am-11pm. Lunch served noon-3pm, dinner served 6:30-11:30pm. MC, V, AmEx.

La Matta, 23, rue de l'Annonciation (tel. 01 40 50 04 66). M. Passy. From the metro, walk up rue de Passy, and turn left on rue de l'Annonciation when you reach pl. de Passy. La Matta has all the elements of the traditional Italian restaurant (straw-bottomed chairs, drawings of Italian sights and scenery on the walls, and Italian waiters and owners—you know the routine), including relatively inexpensive yet utterly tasty food. Try the calzone (with ham, cheese, tomato, and egg, 54F) or the Neptune pizza (with tomato, tuna, and olives, 55F), or attack some of their pasta and meat dishes. Pizza 47-68F, pasta 46-62F, meat dishes 70-125F, salads 25-60F. Takeout available. Open daily noon-2:30pm and 7-11pm. MC, V.

■ Seventeenth Arrondissement

Formed from a patchwork of isolated neighborhoods, the 17*ème* can't lay claim to any single, unifying quality, much less a characteristic meal. This identity deficit creates a sumptuous smorgasbord of choices for the hungry visitor. Francophiles may want to investigate av. des Ternes and the streets which lead away from l'Arc de Triomphe for traditional French fare, although this region—which borders on the staid, wealthy 16*ème*—is not cheap. More varied menus and small bistros pepper the Village de Batignolles between the rue de Rome and the av. de Clichy, while cheaper, livelier spots cluster around rue Guy Hoquet. Use caution in this fun-though-seedy part of town, especially around pl. de Clichy.

Le Patio Provençal, 116, rue des Dames (tel. 01 42 93 73 73). M. Villiers. Follow rue de Lévis away from the intersection and turn right on rue des Dames. You can sit on the sunny terrace, but don't miss a peak indoors where graceful arbors laced with vines shelter the tables, and bunches of dried lavender accent the walls with memories of Provence and the south. A variety of *grandes assiettes* are available in their ample entirety (49-65F) or as half-portions (30-45F). Dessert (35-37F) includes melt-in-your-mouth dark chocolate draped with raspberry purée, but don't forget to sample some of the regional wines (10-12F a glass) or the staple apératif of the South, *Pastis* (24-26F). Reservations recommended. Open Mon.-Fri. noon-2:30pm and 7-10:30pm, Sat. noon-2:30pm. V, MC.

Restaurant Natacha, 35, rue Guersant (tel. 01 45 74 23 86). M. Porte Maillot. Follow bd. Gouvion St-Cyr past the Palais de Congrès and turn right on rue Guersant. A neighborhood favorite, this restaurant offers an extraordinary lunch *menu* with a buffet of hors d'oeuvres (mostly raw vegetables) or a standard appetizer, a filling second course of fish or a *grillade,* as well as dessert for only 85F. Dinner 100F. Both *menus* include as much wine as you can drink, so belly up to the wooden barrels and help yourself. A *formule* at lunch is composed of either the buffet or a main dish, followed by cheese or dessert, with wine, again (60F). Open Mon.-Fri. noon-2pm and 7:30-11pm, Sat. 7:30-11pm. Call for reservations.

Chez Clément, 99, bd. Gouvion St-Cyr (tel. 01 45 72 93 00). M. Porte Maillot. Across from the Palais des Congrès. Also at 123, av. des Champs-Elysées, 8*ème* (tel. 01 40 73 87 00; M. George V), and at 17, bd. des Capucines, 2*ème* (tel. 01 47 42 00 25; M. Opéra). The copper pots and pans gathered in bunches on the doors, stairwells, and walls, and the silverware, clustered gracefully on lamps and all other available surfaces, serve as not-so-subtle reminders to eat. And eat you shall—all you can with the *grande rôtisserie* (79F) which includes beef, pork, and chicken. Seafood offerings (oysters 69-78F, mussels 48F) are balanced with meatier choices, including a hamburger on Poilâne bread and fries (68F) and a filet of duck in raspberry vinegar accompanied by a pasta trio (85F). For dessert try the all-you-can-eat *profiteroles au chocolat*, a mere 38F. Open daily noon-1am. MC, V.

Joy in Food, 2, rue Truffaut (tel. 01 43 87 96 79), on the corner of rue des Dames. M. Rome. Walk one block up rue Boursault and turn right on rue des Dames. A vegetarian restaurant dedicated to taking care of your body, both with a range of quiches served with salad (43F) and with a non-smoking, relaxed atmosphere. Decorated in simple tones of blue and white, Joy in Food has plants in the windows and a friendly chef named Naema in the open kitchen. Don't forget to wash down your meal with a glass of wine (11-13F) or one of Naema's frothy vegetable shakes (carrot juice 12F). Apple crumble and other desserts are 15-22F. Two-course *menu* 58F. 3-course *menu* 71F. Open Mon.-Sat. 11:45-3pm.

Aux Iles des Princes, 96, rue de Saussure (tel. 01 40 54 01 03). M. Wagram. Turn left off av. de Villiers onto rue Jouffroy, then left again onto rue de Saussure. A popular spot for the young and the young at heart, this Turkish restaurant specializes in charcoal-grilled lamb, beef, and chicken *brochettes* (45-70F). The amiable owner speaks only a little French and no English, but lots of hand gestures, a little patience, and either 70F (lunch) or 90F (dinner) will get you a three-course *menu* with selections like *tarama* (a mousse of smoked cod eggs). A la carte appetizers 22-45F. Bottle of Turkish wine 60-65F. Reservations recommended. Open Mon.-Fri. noon-3:30pm and 6pm-midnight, Sat.-Sun. 6pm-midnight. V, MC.

L'Epicerie Verte, 5, rue Saussier Leroy (tel. 01 47 64 19 68). M. Ternes. Walk north on av. des Ternes, take your first right on rue Poncelet, and turn left on rue Saussier-Leroy. This appropriately green grocery sells organic grains and vegetables and runs an excellent lunch counter. Even unyielding carnivores may want to try their salads (16-33F) and warm vegetable *tartes* (with salad 27F, with *crudités* 37F). Counter seating or take-out. Open Sept.-July Mon.-Sat. 9:45am-8pm; food served Mon.-Sat. noon-7pm. MC, V.

Grill Churrasco, 277, bd. Pereire (tel. 01 40 55 92 00), across from the Palais des Congrès. M. Porte Maillot. A friendly Argentinian restaurant specializing in beef. The 84F *menu* "Idée Churrasco," the 96F "Idée Cavaliero," and the 107F "Idée Gringo" all have two courses and few vegetables. Don't forget to drink: *sangria* 22F, and margaritas 34F. Desserts run the gamut from flan to sweet pies (26-34F). Open Sun.-Thurs. 11am-midnight, Fri.-Sat. 11am-1am. MC, V, AmEx.

■ Eighteenth Arrondissement

During the siege of Paris in 1814 Russian cossacks inhabited Montmartre, an ideal location to keep an eye on wily Napoleon, and came to call the restaurants where they grabbed quick bites between battles *bistro,* meaning "fast" in Russian. While the Russians are gone, the *butte* is now liberally sprinkled with tiny, charming *bistros,* especially along the streets between M. Abbesses and pl. St-Pierre. The heavily touristed cafés and restaurants around pl. du Tertre are perfect for coffee breaks, but pricey for meals. Whether simply satisfied or enraptured by your food, remember that safety is always a concern in the 18ème, especially as you descend the *butte.*

Chez les Fondus, 17, rue des Trois Frères (tel. 01 42 55 22 65). M. Abbesses. From the metro stop, walk down rue Yvonne le Tac and take a left on rue des Trois Frères. A small, finger-food restaurant with only two main dishes: *fondue bourguignonne* (meat fondue) and *fondue savoyarde* (cheese fondue). Wine served in baby bottles; Freudian revulsion/American puritanism drive many to remove the nipples. Fun and crowded. The 87F *menu* includes an *apéritif,* wine, appetizer, fondue, and dessert. Call ahead to reserve or show up early. Open daily 5pm-2am, dinner served after 7pm.

Au Grain de Folie, 24, rue la Vieuville (tel. 01 42 58 15 57). M. Abbesses. This intimate restaurant on a quiet street serves a vast array of vegetarian dishes, from couscous and hummus to salads and cheese, in portions so huge that eating à la carte may be more economical than the 100F *menu* (main dish, dessert, and wine). Appetizers, including avocado in roquefort sauce, cost 18-30F; main dishes 45-65F; desserts such as frozen bananas in hot chocolate, 25-40F. Glass of wine 15-25F. Open Mon.-Fri. noon-2:30pm and 6-10:30pm, Sat.-Sun. noon-10:30pm.

Suzon-Grisou, 96, rue des Martyrs (tel. 01 46 06 10 34). M. Abbesses. Follow rue Yvonne le Tac away from the metro, and turn left on rue des Martyrs. You'll know you're in the right place when you've found the frogs. Frog figurines, plush toys, and even a groggy cuckoo clock with bulging eyes watch over this small, welcoming African restaurant. Enticing main dishes (70-80F) include *N'Dole* beef with African leaves, *Mafe* chicken cooked in ground-nut purée, and *Colombo* lamb cooked in curry with eggplant, zucchini, and green pepper. Appetizers such as spicy fish soup or stuffed crab are 30-70F; aside from sweet potato (18F) and igname root (16F) side dishes, not many vegetarian options. 2-course *menu* available before 9pm (79F); 3-course *menu* available all night (130F). Frequent live African music. Open daily 7pm-2am. MC, V.

Au Pierrot de la Butte, 41, rue Caulaincourt (tel. 01 46 06 06 97). M. Lamarck-Caulaincourt. From the metro turn right on rue Lamarck, right on rue de La Fontaine du But, and right again on rue Caulaincourt. Offering excellent French food in an area far enough from Sacré Cœur to be affordable, yet close enough for a pleasant after-dinner walk, this popular French restaurant overlooks a peaceful garden and displays reproductions of famous Montmartrois paintings. 3-course dinner *menu* for 98F includes favorites like *feuilletée de moules à la Provençale* (mussel pastry) and *magret de canard avec griottes* (duck with cherries). Appetizers 34-50F, main dishes 42-78F, desserts 26-30F. Reservations recommended. Open Mon.-Fri. noon-2:15pm and 7:15-11pm, Sat. 7:15-11pm. MC, V, AmEx.

Chez Claude et Claudine, 94, rue des Martyrs (tel. 01 46 06 50 73). M. Abbesses. From the metro walk down rue Yvonne le Tac and turn right on rue des Martyrs. Lit by a skylight during the day and lace-covered hanging lamps at night, this plant-filled restaurant serves large portions of solid, standard French fare. 3-course 69F *menu* includes choices like onion soup, *boeuf bourgignon,* and *poulet à l'éstragon* (chicken with tarragon). 3-course 100F *menu* offers more options. Expect to stagger out. Open daily noon-2:30pm and 6-11:30pm. MC, V.

Rayons de Santé, 8, pl. Charles Dullin (tel. 42 59 64 81). M. Abbesses or Anvers. Follow rue Yvonne le Tac away from M. Abbesses, turn right on rue des Trois Frères and left into pl. Charles Dullin. A feast of vegetarian meals and snacks are available at this intimate, homey restaurant on the edge of a quiet square. On any given day you might savor artichoke mousse (27F), or wholewheat couscous and soy sausage (35F). All main dishes are served with vegetables and grains. 2-course *formule* (48F) and 3-course *menu* (63F) served at lunch and dinner. Desserts include the house soy yogurt (8F) or *clafoutis* (fruit flan, 16F). Carafe of non-alcoholic wine 15-16F. Open Sun.-Thurs. 9:15am-3pm and 6:30-10pm, Fri. 9am-3pm.

■ Nineteenth Arrondissement

The nineteenth is one of the more ethnically diverse arrondissements of Paris. There aren't tons of restaurants here as there are in the touristic center of the city, but then again there aren't tons of tourists once you find the restaurants. Along av. Jean Jaurès and the northern part of rue de Crimée are a lot of fast-food restaurants and Greek sandwich shops which are nothing special. Instead, head to "Little Chinatown" near M.Belleville, whose Chinese, Vietnamese, Thai, and Malaysian restaurants merit a trip from the center.

Lao-Thai, 34, rue de Belleville (tel. 01 43 58 41 84). M. Belleville. Walk up the rue de Belleville a few blocks. Thai and Laotian specialties. "All-you-can-eat" buffet with twelve different dishes, rice, and dessert. Lunch: Mon.-Fri. 49F, Sat.-Sun. 55F. Dinner Sun.-Thurs. 74F, Fri.-Sat., 88F. Air-conditioned. Open Mon. noon-2:30pm, Tues.-Sun noon-2:30pm, and 7-11:15pm.

Baguettes d'or, 61 rue de Belleville (tel. 01 44 52 02 95). M. Belleville. Two *menus* at 52F, including appetizer, main course, rice, and dessert. *Assiète rapide* at 39F (appetizer, main dish, and rice all served on one plate). Soups 22-30F, entrees à la carte 30-40F. Open Tues.-Sun. 11am-3pm and 6pm-midnight. Mon. 11am- 3pm. MC, V.

Ay, Caramba!, 59, rue de Mouzaïa (tel. 01 42 41 23 80). M. Pré-St-Gervais. Turn right onto rue Mouzaïa from the metro. Good food and fiesta atmosphere in a building which also houses a small Tex-Mex grocery and liquor store (with everything from dried banana leaves and hot peppers to pancake mix and pop-tarts). Chili 59F.

Children's menu 49F. Margaritas 39F. *Nachos caramba* (chips, cheese, *pico de gallo*, guacamole, and choice of beef, chicken, or *chile con carne*) 43F. Fajitas 79F. Restaurant open Mon.-Thurs. 7:30-11pm, Fri.-Sun. noon-2:30pm and 7:30-11pm. Store open Tues.-Sat. 10:30am-2pm and 3-7:30pm. MC, V, AmEx.

■ Twentieth Arrondissement

On the edge of the city, the 20*ème* is another part of Paris dominated by hideous high-rises, though a breath of the city as it once was still wafts through the area. Side streets with built-in staircases, cobblestoned squares, and peaceful parks (including Père Lachaise) cling to a tenuous existence here.

La Papaye, 71, rue des Rigoles (tel. 01 43 66 65 24). M. Jourdain. Turn left on rue des Rigoles from rue du Jourdain. Owner/chef has traveled the world over, serving a mix of Caribbean and South American specialties. Lunch *menu* (61F) and dinner *menus* (100F and 149F) feature *colombos* (Caribbean curry dishes), grilled fish, and a delicious, light coconut cake, which hails from Brazil. Ala carte entrées 50-95F, with most hovering around 50F. Open Mon.-Tues. and Thurs.-Fri. noon-2pm and 7pm until last customer leaves, Sat.-Sun. opens at 7pm. MC, V.

A la Courtille, 1, rue des Envierges (tel. 01 46 36 51 59). M. Pyrénées. Walk down rue de Belleville, make your first left on rue Piat and go to the very end of the street. Traditional French Cuisine presented artfully on large white plates. Sit outside on the terrace in a cobblestone square, or inside on comfortable dark green benches. Steps away from a fantastic view of Paris. Lunch *menus* at 70F and 100F available Mon.-Sat. Dinner menu 150F. A la carte appetizers 35-50F, main courses 75-85F, desserts 35-40F. Large selection of wines (80-250F). Open daily 11am-1pm. Lunch service starts at noon. MC, V.

Le Baratin, 3, rue de Jouye-rouve (tel. 01 43 49 39 70). M. Pyrénées or Belleville. From Pyrénées walk down rue de Belleville and take your second left. From Belleville walk uphill and turn right on rue de Jouye-rouve. This intimate, relaxed neighborhood wine bar and restaurant with wooden tables and chairs serves hearty, home-style meals cooked by the owner. She makes two or three different dishes fresh each day. Appetizers (30-35F), entrées (65-70F), dessert (35F). Wine by the glass (9-16F) or bottle (80-118F). Open Tues.-Fri. noon-4pm, and 6pm-1:30am, Sat. 6pm-1:30am. Dinner served until midnight. V.

CAFÉS

The French café has long been suffused with the glamor of languid leisure time absent from its rough American counterpart, the coffee shop. Service can be impossibly slow; entire novels have been written in the time it takes to pay the bill. Visitors to Paris who don't drink coffee should still think of cafés as worthwhile haunts. Take inspiration from the example of the Surrealists, themselves partially responsible for the café's global prestige: at the Café Deux Magots, where André Breton held court, the Communist poet Pierre de Massot sipped his morning bottle of Coke.

On a more practical note: café prices are often two-tiered; it can be cheaper at the counter (*comptoir* or *zinc*) than in the seating area, whether inside *(salle)* or on the *terrasse* (terrace). Both these prices should be posted. Aside from coffee and wine, other popular drinks include *citron pressé,* freshly squeezed lemon juice (with sugar and water on the side). Cafés can also have affordable light lunches and snacks. A *croque monsieur* (grilled ham-and-cheese sandwich), a *croque madame* (the same with a fried egg), and assorted omelettes cost about 15-20F. A more popular choice is a salad. Try the *salade niçoise,* or a *chèvre chaud,* a salad with warm goat cheese. Check the posted menu before you sit down; some cafés (particularly the ones near the big monuments) will charge you inordinately for a snack.

CLASSIC CAFÉS

Listed here are some of the most historically important cafés. By no means is this a list of budget establishments. Think of these cafés as museums, as the price of coffee or soda here is comparable to the average admission fee.

La Closerie des Lilas, 171, bd. du Montparnasse, 6ème (tel. 01 43 26 70 50). M. Port-Royal. Exit the metro and walk one block up bd. du Montparnasse. This lovely flower-ridden café was the one-time favorite of Hemingway (a scene in *The Sun Also Rises* takes place here), and of the Dadaists and Surrealists before him. Picasso came here weekly to hear Paul Fort recite poetry. If the gorgeous dark interior (see the baby grand?) suggests a culinary opulence that you can't afford. In summer, soak up the sun among the plants on the terrace. Coffee 15F, house wine 26F, *marquise au chocolat* 65F. Open daily 11am-1am. MC, V, AmEx.

La Coupole, 102, bd. du Montparnasse, 14ème (tel. 01 43 20 14 20). M. Vavin. Black-and-white-clad waiters get their aerobic exercise vaulting through this enormous Art Deco café decorated with mirrors, modern sculpture, wooden chairs, and elegantly tiled floor. Part café and part restaurant, La Coupole's tables have hosted the likes of Lenin, Stravinsky, Hemingway, and Einstein. The *menus* are expensive, but you can probably still afford coffee (10F). Beer 7-30F, lunchtime *formule* 89F, desserts 29-49F. Open daily 7:30am-2am. Dancing on the weekends: Fri. 9:30pm-4am, Sat. 3-7pm and 9:30pm-4am. MC, V.

Les Deux Magots, 6, pl. St-Germain-des-Prés, 6ème (tel. 01 45 48 55 25). M. St-Germain-des-Prés. Sartre's second choice café and Simone de Beauvoir's first, it was here that the couple first spotted each other. Home to Parisian literati since it opened in 1875, Les Deux Magots is now a favorite among Left Bank youth and tourists. Named after two Chinese porcelain figures (*magots*), this café has beautiful high ceilings, gilt mirrors, and 1930s Art Deco café decor. *Café des Deux Magots* 22F, *café crème* 25F, *chocolat des Deux Magots* (a house specialty) 30F, beer 28-38F, ham sandwich 34F. Desserts such as *gâteau au chocolat amer* (bitter-sweet chocolate cake) 40F, *tarte tatin chaude* (apple turnover) 40F, assorted pastries 38F. Café open daily 7am-1:30am. MC, V. AmEx (100F minimum).

Le Dôme, 108, bd. du Montparnasse, 14ème (tel. 01 43 35 25 81). M. Vavin. This illustrious café shares all the literati history and fame of its neighbors, but its smaller interior and elegant 1920s décor make it one of the best cafés in town—and one of the most expensive, with menu items as high as 400F. The interior boasts marble tables, gilded mirrors with engravings of flappers, and Victorian stained-glass windows. Coffee 15F, beer 20-30F, sandwich of the day 20F. Open Tues.-Sun. noon-3pm and 7pm-12:30am. Closed Sun. in Aug. MC, V, AmEx.

Le Flore, 172, bd. St-Germain, 6ème, next door to Deux Magots (tel. 01 45 48 55 26). It was here, in his favorite hangout, that Jean-Paul Sartre composed *L'être et le néant* (Being and Nothingness). Apollinaire, Picasso, André Breton, and even James Thurber also sipped their brew in this friendly, relaxed atmosphere. *Café espresso spécial Flore* 23F, *café crème* 28F, beer 28-38F, sandwiches 34-62F. Open daily 7am-2am. AmEx.

Le Fouquet's, 99, av. des Champs-Elysées (tel. 01 47 23 70 60). M. George V. "Created" in 1899, in the shadow of the Arc de Triomphe, this is the premier gathering place for Parisian *vedettes* (stars) of radio, television, and cinema. Tourists, oblivious to the celebrities inside, bask on the terrace. James Joyce dined here with relish. Bank-breaking coffee and a chance to be seen 25F. Entrees from 85F. Open daily 8am-1am; food served noon-3pm and 7pm-midnight. MC, V, AmEx.

Café de la Paix, 12, bd. des Capucines, 9ème (tel. 01 40 07 32 32). M. Opéra. On the left as you face the Opéra. This institution just off rue de la Paix (the most expensive property on French Monopoly) has drawn a classy crowd since it opened in 1862. The café is located on the terrace only. The two restaurants inside are pricey, with *menus* around 300F; the people there spend their time fussing over where to go next (shopping at Armani or at St. Laurent?). Coffee 26F, *café crème* 31F, ice cream desserts 40-59F. Open daily 10am-1am.

Le Procope, 13, rue de l'Ancienne Comédie, 6ème (tel. 01 43 26 99 20). M. Odéon. Founded in 1686, the first café in the world. Le Procope has served as stage to weighty, historic moments: Voltaire came here for the 40 cups of coffee per day he needed to finish *Candide;* the young Marat stopped in regularly to plot the Revolution and dodge the police. Figurines of other famous regulars line the café's back wall. *Bien sûr,* history has its price—a 299F *menu*. Frugal diners should choose the café, whose 72F *menu* includes a main course and a choice of appetizer or dessert. 3-course 99F *menu* offers a choice of entrées such as *coquille de crevettes* (shrimp cocktail) or *steak tartare* (raw steak, more or less), and desserts like sorbets. Coffee 14F, beer 21-28F. Open daily 11am-2am.

Le Séléct, 99, bd. du Montparnasse, 6ème (tel. 01 45 48 38 24). M. Vavin. Across the street from Le Coupole. Trotsky, Satie, Breton, Cocteau, and Picasso all frequented this swank bistro-like café. Today, black turtlenecks gather in the hopes that if they hang out long enough, they'll become serious artists. Coffee 12F (before 3pm), 15F (after 3pm), *café au lait* 22F, teas 22-25F, beer 24-50F, iced coffee 32F. Open 7am-3am weekdays, 24hrs on weekends. MC, V.

CYBER CAFES

Café Orbital, 13, rue du Médicis, 6ème (tel. 01 43 25 76 77; fax 01 43 25 78 00). M. Odéon. Serves up access to telnet, newsgroups, and the Web, as well as a variety of hot cyberwiches with green salads (35F). Internet is 1F per min. or 55F per 60min., but you can create a personal e-mail account for free. Students may get a *Carte Sidérante:* 200F for 5hrs., 300F for 10hrs. Open Mon.-Sat. 10am-10pm.

Riva Multimedia, 4, rue du Quatre Septembre, 2ème (tel. 01 42 60 40 81). M. Bourse. Offers free e-mail accounts, 15min. of Internet connection for 10F, and printing (5F per page). Creating a personal home page costs 150F. Sandwiches (14-32F, salads 25-32F). Open Mon.-Sat. 11am-5:30pm. MC, V.

Hammam Café, 4, rue des Rosiers, 4ème (tel. 01 42 78 04 46). M. St.-Paul. This café replaced an actual *hammam* in 1996. Some of the pillars still have small tiles which give it an elegant, bath-house feel. The café is also a restaurant with salads, crêpes, pizza, and ice-cream. Saunter downstairs to hook-up (Internet connections 100F per hour), or upstairs to "hook-up," music nightly at 10:30pm. Cocktails 65F. Open Sun.-Thurs. noon-2am, Fri. noon-4pm, Sat. 4pm-2am.

Cox, 15, rue des Archives, 4ème (tel. 01 42 72 08 00). M. Hôtel-de-Ville. Rope yourself a robo stud at the world's first "Bar Cybergay" with full Internet uplink (Mon.-Fri., 3-6pm). The succinctly-named Cox is new, very popular, and less forbidding than its name would suggest. The crowd is young, stylish, muscular, and predominantly male. Beer 16F. Open daily 1pm-2am.

Café Cyberia, Centre Georges Pompidou, East Mezzanine. 4ème (tel. 01 44 54 53 49; fax 01 44 54 53 39). M. Rambuteau. Not the place to go just to drink a coffee (it's pretty small and computer dominated), but certainly practical for connecting. Half-hour 30F, students 25F, 1hr. 50F. Coffee 10F, sandwiches 18-20F. Open Mon., Wed.-Fri. noon-10pm, Sat.-Sun. 10am-10pm.

SALONS DE THÉ

It was T'ien Yi Heng who said, "one drinks tea to forget the sound of the world." Paris' *salons de thé* (tea rooms) provide low-key refinement and light meals. Long a preferred afternoon meeting spot for mature women, tea rooms now draw alterno-youth for Sunday brunch. Relax and regroup over an *infusion* (herbal tea); sip an invigorating *menthe* (mint), *verveine* (vervain), or *tilleul-menthe* (lime blossom and mint). Ah, yes—and don't forget the pastries.

Angelina's, 226, rue de Rivoli, 1er (tel. 01 42 60 88 00). M. Concorde or Tuileries. Return to the "Age of Innocence" in the refined calm of this venerable establishment. Broad open spaces, leather upholstery, and a thick atmosphere of propriety dampen all sounds but the click of teacups, as mature ladies and sedate tourists enjoy the pleasures of afternoon tea (32F), pastries (25-35F). Angelina's is also a tasty, but not exactly budget, restaurant. Entrées (85-130F). Open Mon.-Fri. 9:00am-7pm, Sat.-Sun. 9:30am-7:30pm. MC, V.

A Priori Thé, 35-37, Galerie Vivienne, 2ème (tel. 01 42 97 48 75). M. Bourse or Palais-Royal. Enter from 6, rue Vivienne; 4, rue des Petits Champs; or 5, rue de la Banque. Shielded from the city noise in one of Paris's most elegant, pleasant *galeries* (see "Sights—2ème," p. 149), this comfortable, classically furnished haven has uncommonly good salads (82-85F) and weekend brunches (75-146F). Desserts, including strawberry rhubarb sauce and the house brownie, are 30F; a soothing selection from the tea repertoire is 25F. Lunch reservations recommended. Open Mon.-Fri. 9am-6pm, Sat. noon-6:30pm, Sun. 12:30-6:30pm. Breakfast served weekdays 9am-noon, lunch on weekdays noon-3pm, Sat. brunch noon-4pm, Sun. brunch 12:30-4pm. Tea service starts at 3pm weekdays, 4pm weekends. MC, V.

L'Arbre à Canelle, 57, Passage de Panoramas, 2ème (tel. 01 45 08 55 87). M. Rue Montmartre turn left into the passage off bd. Montmartre. On the lovely terrace, sample one of the house's 14 varieties of tea (20F). Fruit tart 26F, 2 scoops of Berthillon ice cream 32F, apple crumble 28F. A range of *assiettes gourmandes* (mixed platters, 58-108F), including the *suprême,* with smoked goose and *mousse de foie gras* (goose liver, 64F). Salads 39-56F. Open Mon.-Sat. 11am-6pm; tea service only after 2:30pm. MC, V.

Dalloyau, 2, pl. Edmond Rostand, 6ème (tel. 01 42 99 90 00). M. Luxembourg. Also at 99-101, Faubourg Saint-Honoré, 8ème, and other locations. This chic *pâtisserie* serves salads and lunch but is best known for its tantalizing array of homemade pastries (18-20F). Purchase one to take away to the Jardin du Luxembourg. Young crowd on the terrace, 30+ upstairs. Open daily 8:30am-9:30pm. MC, V, AmEx.

L'Ebouillanté, 6, rue des Barres, 4ème (tel. 01 42 78 48 62). M. Pont Marie or St-Paul. A tiny restaurant and *salon de thé* located on a cobblestone alleyway facing Eglise St-Gervais-St-Protais. Come here in good weather for a picturesque mid-afternoon on the terrace. Watch arty passersby from local galleries cross paths with monks from the adjacent church. House specialities are *bricks*—filled Tunisian crepes (42-60F); try them with salmon and *fromage blanc* or with cheese, eggs, and tomatoes. Salads (57-62F), crêpes, and blini are a cut above. Tea 23F. Homemade pastry 36F. Open Tues.-Sun. noon-9pm (10:30pm in summer).

Ladurée, 16, rue Royale, 8ème (tel. 01 42 60 21 79). M. Concorde. The perfect spot to show your style: sit suavely under the painted ceiling and order one of its famed macaroons (20F), flavored with chocolate, pistachio, coffee, vanilla, or lemon. Ladurée endures as *the* chic tea room near La Madeleine. Pastries 10-20F. You will pay less if you carry your goodies away with you. Lunch served daily 11:30am-3pm. Open Mon.-Sat. 8:30am-7pm, Sun. 10am-7pm. MC, V, AmEx.

Le Loir Dans la Théière, 3, rue des Rosiers, 4ème (tel. 01 42 72 90 61). M. St-Paul. Named "The doormouse in the teapot" after *Alice in Wonderland,* "Le Loir" offers home-baked *tartes* and crumbles in a laid-back, bohemian atmosphere, with assorted 1930s armchairs, wooden tables, and a pile a magazines to read. Tea 20F, coffee to cappuccino 12-30F, homemade cakes and tarts 35-45F. Sunday breakfast includes fresh-squeezed juice, tea, hot chocolate or coffee, croissants, and toast (60F). Sunday brunch includes all the above plus a savory tart (110F). Open daily noon-6:30pm.

Marriage Frères, 30, rue du Bourg-Tibourg, 4ème (tel. 01 42 72 28 11). M. Hôtel-de-Ville. Also at 13, rue des Grands Augustins, 6ème (tel. 01 40 51 82 50; M. St-Michel). An elegant rattan salon which takes tea oh-so-seriously; non-smoking tea room fragrantly showcases the 400 varieties of teas sold in the boutique. Homemade desserts and lunch plates (82-105F), include meals made with tea as an ingredient. Teatime sandwich plate 55F, cake 40F, tea around 34F, depending on the kind. Scoff at house's undisguised colonialist nostalgia; *musée de thé* upstairs chronicles Marriage Frères' forays into the Orient from then to now. Museum and store open daily 10:30am-7:30pm; lunch served after noon. MC, V, AmEx.

Max Poilâne, 29, rue de l'Ouest, 14ème (tel. 01 43 27 24 91). M. Gaîté. Follow av. du Maine away from the Tour Montparnasse and turn right on rue de l'Ouest. A Parisian establishment since the 1940's. This affordable *salon de thé* is a great spot to get a taste of the famous *pain Poilâne.* Sandwiches are 17-36F and desserts are 13F, but you can always have a slice of their fabulous flan for 10F. Take away one of the hearty loaves (21F per kg) or try a dense roll (3-6F). Open Sept.-June Mon.-Sat. 9am-7:30pm; July-Aug. Mon.-Fri. 10am-7pm and Sat. 10am-noon.

Muscade, 36, rue de Montpensier, 1er (tel. 01 42 97 51 36). M. Palais-Royale. Tucked away in the northwest corner of the Palais Royale, Muscade is a high-priced restaurant at lunch and dinner time. In the afternoon however, Muscade becomes an affordable *salon de thé.* With mirrored walls, Renaissance-style tapestries and a meticulously understated sense of style, Muscade is an ideal location for Sunday afternoon reveries. 26 types of tea (22F).

Toupary, 19, rue de Rivoli, 1er (tel. 01 40 41 29 29). M. Châtelet. On the fifth floor of the Samaritaine. Like Muscade, Toupary is a high-priced restaurant at lunch and dinner time. In the afternoon Toupary is a *salon de thé* worth visiting for the incredible view of the city alone. Spacious green, salmon, and blue décor. Tea served 3:30-6pm.

Thé-Troc, 52, rue Jean-Pierre Timbaud, 11ème (tel. 01 43 55 54 80). M. République. From M. République, walk down av. de la République and hang a left on rue Jean-Pierre Timbaud. It is difficult to discern what this place is by looking in the window filled with teas, spices, t-shirts and southeast Asian crafts (all on sale inside). Venture into the non-smoking tea-room (15-20F for a cup of tea), or take 100g of tea home (18-200F)—if you can make up your mind between the 100 different kinds. Open Mon.-Fri. 9am-noon and 2-8pm, Sat. 10am-1pm and 4-8pm.

SWEETS

Paris' pastries and chocolates, fail-safe cure-alls for the weary traveler, are generally made where you buy them. Recently, American desserts—like *brownies* and *cookies* (pronounced kookeys)—have gained a strong following among Parisians young and old, but more traditional vices such as the *tarte au chocolat* deservedly remain local favorites. Neighborhood *pâtisseries* or *confiseries* will satisfy any sweet-tooth, but for serious sugar lovers, the *crème-de-la crème* in specialty sweets can be found sprinkled throughout the city.

The Baker's Dozen, 3, pl. de la Sorbonne, 5ème (tel. 01 44 07 08 09). M. Luxembourg. Fudge brownies (10F), chocolate chip cookies (5F or 3 for 13F), and muffins (9F) are the specialty of this micro-bakery. Indulge on the miniscule terrace facing pl. de la Sorbonne and watch the waitstaff explain to Parisians what brownies are. Open Mon.-Fri. 8am-6:30pm.

Berthillon, 31, rue St-Louis-en-l'Ile, 4ème (tel. 01 43 54 31 61), on Ile-St-Louis. M. Cité or Pont Marie. The best ice cream and sorbet in Paris. Choose from dozens of *parfums* (flavors), ranging from chocolate to *tiramisu* to *cassis* (black currant). Single (9F), double (16F), triple (20F). Sitting down is more expensive (double, 32F). Since lines are quite long in summer, look for stores nearby that sell Berthillon products; the wait is shorter and they're open in late July and August, when the main Berthillon shuts down. A list of participating stores is posted on the Berthillon window after it closes. Open Sept.-July 14th Wed.-Sun. 10am-8pm.

Debauve et Gallais, 33, rue Vivienne, 2ème (tel. 01 45 48 54 67). M. Bourse. Also at 30, rue des Sts-Pères, 7ème (tel. 01 40 39 05 50; M. St-Germain-des-Prés) and 107, rue Jouffrey. A purported "chocolate pharmacy," founded in 1800 by confectioner and quack Sulpice Debauve. Need something for your nerves? Follow the house prescription of two almond milk chocolates. With 40 different kinds of chocolate sold here, come to buy or browse. Ask for a guide to the historic chocolates or select your own *boucheé* (mouthful) for 16F. Open Mon.-Sat. 9am-6pm.

Jeff de Bruges, 95, rue du Commerce, 15ème (tel. 01 40 43 07 06). M. Commerce. Excellent homemade chocolates and candies will practically jump into your hands at the low price of 17F per 100g. For the same price, you can get *pâtes de fruits* (made from fresh fruit, the best gumdrops you'll ever taste); or, pick up some frogs, dogs, trains, or goggle-eyed escargots made out of marshmallow (28-39F). *Dragées aux amandes* (18-25F per 100g) make a great snack for the road. Be-laced and be-ribboned gift baskets are good presents if you can resist the temptation to indulge yourself in the meantime. Open Tues.-Sat. 10am-2pm and 3-7:30pm. MC, V, AmEx.

Gérard Mulot, 76, rue de Seine, 6ème (tel. 01 43 26 85 77). M. Odéon or St-Sulpice. An outrageous selection of handmade pastries, from *clafoutis* with virtually any kind of fruit, to flan and *mille-feuilles,* to marzipan. Pastries 10-12F. Open Thurs.-Tues. 6:45am-8pm.

Maison du Chocolat, 8, bd. de la Madeleine, 9ème (tel. 01 47 42 86 52). M. Madeleine. Every imaginable kind of chocolate: bonbons, blocks, milk chocolate, dark chocolate. Plus delicious ice cream and sorbets (2 scoops for 21F). Open Mon.-Sat. 9:30am-7pm. MC, V.

Le Nôtre, 48, av. Victor Hugo, 16ème (tel. 01 45 02 21 21). M. Victor Hugo. Also at 15, bd. de Courcelles, 8ème (tel. 01 45 63 87 63); and 121, av. de Wagram, 17ème (tel. 01 47 63 70 30). A small chain that hawks wonderful pastries throughout the city. Join the local children pointing out their chosen treat to *maman* at one of the counters. Assorted chocolates and pastries 17-30F, buttery croissants 5F. Gourmet meat and fish selections available for take-out (30-125F). Most branches open daily 9am-9pm. MC, V, AmEx.

Peltier, 66, rue de Sèvres, 7ème (tel. 01 47 83 66 12 or 01 47 34 06 62). M. Vaneau or Duroc. Also at 6, rue St-Dominique, 7ème (tel. 01 47 05 50 02; M. Solférino). A famous and famously self-congratulatory chocolatier. Nonetheless, great desserts. The house specialty, a *tarte au chocolat,* is more gooey than rich (16F). Melt into a chair in the *salon de thé.* Take-out available. Open Mon.-Fri. 9:30am-8:00pm, Sat. 9:00am-8pm, Sun. 8:30am-7pm. Credit cards require 150F minimum.

Pierre Mauduit, 54, rue du Faubourg St-Denis, 10ème (tel. 01 42 46 43 64). M. Château d'Eau. From the metro, turn right on rue du Château d'Eau and left on rue du Faubourg St-Denis. Mauduit catered a party for Madonna in 1992 and now her photo hangs in the shop; can you guess that the place is expensive? Wolf down an *Opéra* or *mille-feuilles* (19-23F). Liqueur chocolates 4-5F each. Open Mon.-Fri. 10am-6pm. MC, V.

Sights

For all its cosmopolitan pizazz and sight-laden glitz, Paris is a small city. In just a few hours, you can walk from the heart of the Marais in the east to the Eiffel Tower in the west, and pass almost every monument there is. Try to reserve one day entirely for wandering: you don't have a true sense of Paris until you know how close medieval Notre Dame is to the modern Centre Pompidou, and the *quartier latin* of students is to the Louvre of kings. With a map, comfortable shoes, and an adventurous spirit, you are ready to discover what makes Paris tick. After dark, the glamor only increases; spotlights go up over everything from the Panthéon to the Eiffel Tower, Notre Dame, to the Obélisque. From dusk until midnight the city glows like a galaxy of multicolored, glittering chandeliers.

When walking gets to be too much, don't forget that buses can give you almost the same experience. In the "Bus" section, page 75, we list some public bus lines that are essentially tours of Paris' sights, minus the commentary and the high cost. In addition, **Parisbus** (tel. 01 42 30 55 50) runs a more traditional bus tour with an English-language commentary that lasts over two hours. The ticket is good for two consecutive days, so you can visit any of the places it stops (Trocadéro, Eiffel Tower, Louvre Museum, Notre Dame, Musée d'Orsay, Opéra, Champs-Elysées, and Grand Palais museum). Tickets cost 125F, students with ID 100F, children 60F; call for departure times.

For a tour of Paris from the water, take a riverboat down the Seine. **Bateaux-mouches** (tel. 01 42 25 96 10) provide a classic, if goofy, tour of Seine-side Paris. Be prepared for one-and-a-half hours of nonstop sight-commentary in five languages, and dozens of tourists straining their necks to peer around you. The ride is particularly worthwhile if taken at night. (Departures every ½hr. 10am-11pm from the Right Bank pier near Pont d'Alma. M. Alma-Marceau. 40F, under 14 20F.) **Vert Galant** boats (tel. 01 46 33 98 38) are another option, with commentaries in French and English. (Departures every ¾hr. 10am-noon, every ½hr. 1:30-6:30pm and 9-10:30pm from the Pont Neuf landing. M. Pont-Neuf or Louvre. 45F during the day, 50F at night, ages 4-10 20F.) The **Canauxrama** (tel. 01 42 39 15 00) boat tours of Paris get excellent reviews for their 3-hour trip down the Canal St-Martin. The tour leaves at 9:30am and 2:45pm from Bassin de la Villette, 5bis, quai de la Loire, 19*ème* (M. Jaurès) and at 9:45am and 2:30pm from Port de l'Arsenal facing 50, bd. de la Bastille, 12*ème* (M. Bastille). (75F, students 60F, under 12 45F, under 6 free; weekend afternoons and holidays 75F.)

Seine Islands

Ile de la Cité

If any one location could be called the heart of Paris, it is this slip in the river. Ile de la Cité sits in the very center of the city, and indeed at the very center of the Ile de France: all distance points in France are measured from the *kilomètre zéro,* a circular sundial on the ground in front of Notre-Dame. The island was first inhabited by a Gallic tribe of hunters, sailors, and fisherfolk called the Parisii, who immigrated to the island in the 3rd century BC in search of an easily fortified outpost from which to defend themselves against the Romans. The first certifiable record left by this tribe was, sadly, their defeat by Caesar's legions in the year 52 BC. The island became the center of the Lutèce colony, languishing for four centuries under the rule of the crumbling Roman empire. In the early 6th century, Clovis crowned himself king of the Franks and adopted the embattled island as the center of his domain. No kingdom being complete without an adequately glorious church, work was begun on St-Etienne, the island's first Christian church. The basilica, built into the wall which surrounded the island-fortress, was finished in the late 6th century under Clovis's son,

Childebert I, and completely destroyed only two centuries later by Norman invaders. It was rebuilt, but razed again to make room for Notre-Dame.

During the Middle Ages, the island began to acquire the features for which it is best known and loved today. In the 12th century work commenced on Notre-Dame and Ste-Chapelle under the direction of Bishop Maurice Sully. The cathedral, completed in the 14th century, was the product of five generations, 200 years, and millions of hours of work, and is one of the most beautiful, and most famous, examples of medieval architecture.

NOTRE-DAME

In 1163, Pope Alexander III laid the cornerstone for the **Cathédrale de Notre-Dame-de-Paris** (tel. 01 42 34 56 10; M. Cité) over the remains of a Roman temple. The most famous and most trafficked of the Cité's sights, this massive structure was not completed until 1361. During the Revolution, the cathedral was renamed the *Temple du Raison* and dedicated to the Cult of Reason; at the same time, the Gothic arches were hidden behind plaster façades of virtuous, Neoclassical design. Although reconsecrated after the Revolution, the building fell into disrepair and was even used to shelter livestock until Victor Hugo's 1831 novel, *Notre-Dame-de-Paris (The Hunchback of Notre-Dame),* inspired King Louis-Philippe and thousands of citizens to push for its restoration. The modifications by Eugène Viollet-le-Duc (including the addition of the spire, the gargoyles, and a statue of himself admiring his own work) remain highly controversial. Regardless of whether the architectural integrity of the medieval structure was violated, the cathedral became a valued symbol of civic unity after its renovation. In 1870 and 1940 thousands of Parisians attended masses to pray for deliverance from the invading Germans—both times without immediate success. But the faithful do not demand instantaneous results; and on August 26, 1944, Charles de Gaulle braved sniper fire to come here and give thanks for his victory. All of these upheavals seems to have left the cathedral unmarked; as have the hordes of tourists who invade its sacred portals every day. In the words of e.e. cummings, "The Cathedral of Notre-Dame does not budge an inch for all the idiocies of this world."

Today, thousands of visitors flood through the doors of the cathedral, depriving themselves of one the most glorious aspects of the structure: the **façade.** "Few architectural pages," Hugo proclaimed, "are as beautiful as this façade...a vast symphony in stone." Although it was begun in the 12th century, the façade was not completed even in the 17th, when artists were still adding Baroque statues of dubious aesthetic value. Highly symbolic, the carvings were designed to instill a fear of God and desire for righteousness in a population of which less than 10% were literate. Revolutionaries, not exactly your regular churchgoers, wreaked havoc on the façade of the church during the ecstasies of the 1790s; not content to decapitate Louis XVI, they attacked the stone images of what they thought were his ancestors above the doors. The heads were found in the basement of the Banque Française du Commerce in 1977, and were installed in the Musée de Cluny (see "Musée de Cluny," p. 235). Chips of paint on the heads led to a surprising discovery: Notre-Dame was once painted in bright and garish colors, a far cry from the pale-yellow and smog-gray that most people associate with medieval churches. Replicas of the heads (unpainted) now crown the severed bodies.

From the inside, the cathedral seems to be constructed of soaring light and seemingly weightless walls, thanks to the spidery flying buttresses which support the vaults of the ceiling from outside, allowing the walls to be opened up for stained glass. The effect is increased by a series of subtle optical illusions, including the use of smaller pillars to surround the bigger ones, diminishing their apparent size. The most spectacular features of the interior are the enormous stained-glass **rose windows** that dominate the transept's north and south ends. Originally, similarly masterful artistry adorned the windows on the ground level, but "Sun King" Louis XIV tried to live up to his nickname by ordering that the lower-level stained glass be smashed and replaced by clear windows. More recent and unimpressive stained glass panels now take their place.

Free **guided tours** of the cathedral are an excellent way to discover its history and architecture; inquire at the information booth to the right as you enter or contact CASA (Communautés d'Accueil dans les Sites Artistiques), 8, av. César Caire, 8ème (tel. 01 42 93 71 87; tours in English Wed. and Thurs. noon, in French Mon.-Fri. noon, Sat. 2:30pm; free). The cathedral's **treasury,** south of the choir, contains an assortment of glittering robes, sacramental cutlery, and other gilded souvenirs from the cathedral's past (open Mon.-Sat. 9:30am-6pm; last ticket at 5:30pm; admission 15F, students 10F, under 17 5F).

Outside again, don't miss the opportunity to visit the haunt of the cathedral's most famous fictional resident, Quasimodo the Hunchback, with a hair-raising climb into the two **towers.** The perilous and claustrophobic staircase emerges onto a spectacular perch, where a bevy of gargoyles survey a stunning view of the heart of the city. The climb generally deters the bus-load tourists, and you may even have the towers relatively to yourself if you come early. Although this is not the highest point in Paris, it affords you a detailed view of both the *quartier latin* on the Left Bank in the 6ème, and the Marais on the Right Bank in the 4ème. Continue on to the south tower, where a tiny door gives access to the 13-ton bell that even Quasimodo couldn't ring: it requires the force of eight people to move. (Towers open April to mid-Sept. daily 9:30am-6pm; mid-Sept. to Oct. 9:30am-5:30pm; Nov. 10am-5pm; Dec.-Jan. 10am-4pm; Feb.-March 10am-5pm. Admission 28F, students ages 18-25 18F, ages 12-17 15F, under 12 free.) Cathedral open daily 8am-6:45pm. Confession can be heard in English. Roman Catholic masses are celebrated here daily; high mass with Gregorian chant is celebrated on Sunday at 10am, and with music at 11:30am, and at 12:30 and 6pm. For a striking view of the cathedral, cross **Pont St-Louis** (behind the cathedral) to **Ile St-Louis** and turn right on quai d'Orléans. At night, the buttresses are lit up, and the view from here is breathtaking. The **Pont de Sully,** at the far side of Ile St-Louis, allows for a more distant, though equally thrilling, vista.

The **Mémorial de la Déportation** (located behind the cathedral at the very tip of the island, in the Square de l'Ile de France and down a narrow flight of steps), is a haunting memorial erected for the French victims of Nazi concentration camps. Two hundred thousand flickering lights represent the dead, and an eternal flame burns close to the tomb of an unknown deportee. The names of all the concentration camps glow in gold triangles which recall the design of the patch that French prisoners were forced to wear for identification purposes. A series of quotations is engraved into the stone walls—most striking of these is the injunction, *"Pardonne; N'Oublie Pas"* (Forgive; Do Not Forget) engraved over the exit. The old men who frequently visit the museum may act as voluntary guides. You may hear one of these men chanting the chillingly beautiful *kaddish,* the Jewish prayer for the dead (square and monument open Mon.-Fri. 8:30am-9:45pm, Sat.-Sun. and holidays 9am-9:45pm; free).

Far below the cathedral towers, in a cool excavation beneath the pavement of the square in front of the cathedral, the **Crypte Archéologique,** pl. du Parvis du Notre-Dame (tel. 01 43 29 83 51), is everything-they-found-when-building-the-parking-garage-on-the-island. Essentially an archeological dig, the *crypte* offers a self-guided tour through the history of Ile de la Cité, allowing you to wander among architectural fragments from Roman Lutèce up through the 19th-century sewers (open daily April-Sept. 10am-6pm; Oct.-March 10am-5pm; last ticket sold one ½hr before closing; admission 28F, students ages 18-25 18F, ages 12-17 15F, under 12 free).

The nearby **Hôtel Dieu** was a hospital built in the Middle Ages to provide aid to foundlings. It became more a place to confine the sick than to cure them: guards were posted at the doors to keep the patients from getting out and infecting the city. More recently, Pasteur did much of his pioneering research inside. In 1871, the hospital's proximity to Notre-Dame saved the cathedral; *communards* were dissuaded from burning the latter by the fear that the flames would engulf their hospitalized wounded. The restful calm of the hospital's garden belies its continuing use as a medical center. (Hall and inner court open daily 7:30am-10:30pm.) Across the street is the **Préfecture de Police,** where at 7am on August 19, 1944, members of the Paris police force began an insurrection against the Germans that lasted until the Allies liberated the city six days later.

The **Palais de Justice** (tel. 01 44 32 51 51), spanning the western side of the island, harbors the infamous **Conciergerie,** prison of the Revolution, and Ste-Chapelle, St. Louis's private chapel. Since the 13th century, the structures here have contained the district courts for Paris; indeed *Chambre 1* of the *Cour d'Appel* witnessed Pétain's convictions after WWII. All trials are open to the public, but don't expect a *France v. Dreyfus* every day. Even if your French is not up to legalese, the theatrical sobriety of the interior, with lawyers dressed in archaic black robes, makes a quick visit worthwhile (criminal courtrooms open Mon.-Fri. 1:30-4pm; trials usually Mon.-Fri. 9am-noon and 1:30-5pm; free).

At the heart of the palais, **Ste-Chapelle** (tel. 01 43 54 30 09) remains one of the foremost examples of flamboyant Gothic architecture and a triumph of transparency. Crowded into an inner courtyard of the *palais,* the church appears plain and unassuming from the outside, a simple structure topped with a 33-m cedar steeple from the 19th century. The Lower Chapel echoes this architectural modesty with a low vaulted ceiling, blank arcades, and painted walls. Inside however, the Upper Chapel is a sublime fusion of space, color, and light. Construction began on the church in 1241 to house the most precious of King Louis IX's possessions, the crown of thorns from Christ's Passion. Bought from the Emperor of Constantinople in 1239 along with a section of the Cross for the ungodly sum of 135,000 livres, the crown required an equally princely chapel. Although the crown—minus a few thorns which St. Louis gave away as political favors—has been moved to Notre-Dame, Ste-Chapelle still remains a masterpiece—"the pearl among them all," as Marcel Proust called it. In the Upper Chapel, formerly reserved for royalty and their court, the brilliantly colored stained-glass windows have a lace-like delicacy; their blues and reds combine to produce a claret-colored lighting, giving rise to the saying "wine the color of Ste-Chapelle's windows." The windows are the oldest stained glass in Paris, tastefully restored in 1845; the glass you see is for the most part the same under which St. Louis prayed to his own personal holy relic. Check weekly publications for occasional concerts held in the Upper Chapel mid-March through October, or ask at the information booth. (Open daily April-Sept. 9:30am-6:30pm; Oct.-March 10am-5pm. Last admission ½-hr. before closing. Admission 32F, students and seniors 21F, ages 12-17 15F, under 12 free.)

The **Conciergerie** (tel. 01 43 54 30 06), 1, quai de l'Horloge, around the corner of the Palais de Justice from the entrance to Ste-Chapelle, lurks ominously, brooding over the memories of the prisoners who died here during the Revolution. The northern façade is that of a gloomy medieval fortress. At the farthest corner on the right, a stepped parapet marks the oldest tower, the Tour Bonbec ("good beak"), which once housed the prison's torture chambers, where the accused were made to "sing." The modern entrance lies between the Tour d'Argent, stronghold of the royal treasury, and the Tour de César, which housed the revolutionary tribunal.

While the Conciergerie doesn't have much to offer in the way of period pieces besides its beautifully restored stonework, its exhibits on daily life in the prison during the Revolution are worth a visit, especially for those who can read the French explanations. If you choose to tread the same flagstones as Queen Marie-Antionette and the 2700 people sentenced to death between 1793 and 1794 who spent their final days in the Conciergerie, you'll follow the *"rue de Paris,"* the corridor leading from the entrance, named for *"Monsieur de Paris,"* the executioner during the Revolution. Past the hall, stairs lead to facsimiles of prisoners' cells, now inhabited by glum-looking mannequins. (The most desperate mannequins are in the *pailleux* cell, where prisoners who weren't rich enough to bribe their jailers for bedding were forced to sleep on straw.) Farther down the hall is the cell where Maximilien de Robespierre, the mastermind behind the Reign of Terror, awaited his death. The cell has been converted into a display of his letters, and engraved on the wall are Robespierre's famous last words: *"Je vous laisse ma Mémoire. Elle vous sera chère, et vous la défendrez"* (I leave you my memory. It will be dear to you, and you will defend it).

Open daily 9:30am-6:30pm; Oct.-March 10am-5pm. Last ticket ½hr. before closing. Admission includes guided tour in French 28F, students ages 18-25 18F, ages 12-17 15F, under 12 free.

Leave Ile de la Cité from here by the oldest bridge in Paris, ironically named **Pont Neuf** (New Bridge). Completed in 1607, the bridge broke tradition by not having its sides lined by houses. Before the construction of the Champs-Elysées, the bridge was Paris' most popular thoroughfare, attracting peddlers, performers, thieves, and even street physicians. More recently, Christo, the Bulgarian performance artist, wrapped the entire bridge in 44,000 square meters of nylon. Unfortunately, the bridge itself is not of particular architectural interest, though it does have individual gargoyle capitals on its supports which can be viewed by craning your neck over the side, or better yet, from a *bateau-mouche* (see "Sights," p. 139).

■ Ile St-Louis

A short walk across the Pont St-Louis will take you to the elegant neighborhood of **Ile St-Louis.** Originally two small islands—the Ile aux Vâches (Cow Island) and the Ile de Notre-Dame—it was considered suitable for duels, cows, and little else throughout the Middle Ages. In 1267, Louis IX departed for the Tunisian Crusade from the Ile aux Vâches, never to return, and the island was later named in memoriam. It became habitable in the 17th century due to a contractual arrangement between Henri IV and the bridge entrepreneur Christophe Marie, after whom the Pont Marie is named. Virtually all of the construction on the island happened within a few short decades in the mid-17th century, giving Ile St-Louis an architectural unity lacking in most Parisian neighborhoods.

Today, the island looks much as it did 300 years ago, with only two small streets altered in any significant sense. Its *hôtels particuliers* and townhouses have attracted an elite that now includes Guy de Rothschild and Pompidou's widow; Voltaire, Mme. de Châtelet, Daumier, Ingrès, Baudelaire, and Cézanne number among its past residents. Floating somewhere between small village and chic address, the island retains a certain remoteness from the rest of Paris. Older residents say *"Je vais à Paris"* (I'm going to Paris) when leaving by one of the four bridges linking Ile St-Louis and the mainland; and in a rare burst of vigor, inhabitants even declared the island an independent republic in the 1930s. While you may not be able to afford the rent, you can afford the view. Many a literary personage has watched the passage of *bateaux-mouches* down this stretch of the Seine, notably Jake Barnes in *The Sun Also Rises.*

Leave Ile de la Cité by the Pont St-Louis and follow the **quai de Bourbon.** Camille Claudel lived and worked at no. 19 from 1899 until 1913, when her brother, the poet Paul Claudel, had her incarcerated in an asylum. Because she was the protégée and lover of sculptor Auguste Rodin, Claudel's most striking work is displayed in the Musée Rodin (see "Musée Rodin," p. 233). At the intersection of the quai and rue des Deux Ponts sits **Au Franc-Pinot,** whose wrought-iron and grilled façade is almost as old as the island. The grapes that punctuate the ironwork gave the café its name; the *pinot* is a grape from Burgundy. Closed in 1716 after authorities found a basement stash of anti-government tracts, the café reemerged as a treasonous address during the Revolution. Cécile Renault, daughter of the then-cabaret's proprietor, mounted an unsuccessful attempt on Robespierre's life in 1794. A young admirer of Charlotte Corday, she was guillotined the following year.

The island's most beautiful old *hôtels* line the **quai d'Anjou,** between Pont Marie and Pont de Sully. No. 29 once housed Ford Madox Ford's *Transatlantic Review, the* expatriate lit mag, to which Hemingway frequently contributed. At no. 17, the **Hôtel Lauzun,** built in 1657 by Le Vau, presents a simple façade but for the gold filigree on the iron balcony and on the fish-shaped drainpipes. The interior may only be seen by guided tour; check the *"Conférences"* section of *Pariscope* or stop by the Caisse Nationale des Monuments Historiques, 62, rue St-Antoine (tel. 01 44 61 00 00). In the 1840s, the *hôtel* became the clubhouse for the Hachischins, a bohemian literary salon. Charles Baudelaire and Théophile Gautier reclined with hookahs at its evening gatherings. Jeanne Duval, Baudelaire's mulatto mistress—the famous "Black Venus"—lived nearby at 6, rue Legrattier. Nine, quai d'Anjou was the address of Honoré Daumier, realist painter and caricaturist, from 1846 to 1863.

Loop around the end of the quai and walk down **rue St-Louis-en-l'Ile.** This is the "main drag" of Ile St-Louis, and harbors gift shops, art galleries, and traditional French restaurants, as well as the famous Berthillon *glacerie* (see "Sweets," p. 137). The **Hôtel Lambert,** at no. 2, was designed by Le Vau in 1640 for Lambert le Riche, and was home to Voltaire and Mme. de Châtelet, his mathematician mistress. **Eglise St-Louis-en-l'Ile,** 19bis, rue St-Louis en l'Ile (tel. 01 46 34 11 60), is another Le Vau creation built between 1664 and 1726. Get beyond the sooty, humdrum façade and you'll find one of the airiest and lightest of Rococo interiors, decorated with gold leaf, marble, and statuettes, and lit by more windows than seemed to exist on the outside (open to the public Mon.-Sat. 9am-noon and 3-7pm). Legendary for its acoustics, the church hosts concerts throughout the year and every night in July and August (check with FNAC for details or call the church at 01 46 34 11 60). Currently a four-star hotel, no. 54 was frequented by sports-lovers during the 17th and early 18th century when *jeu de paume* was in vogue. The ancestor of modern tennis, the game was originally played in rectangular halls painted black so the white leather ball could be more visible. On either side of rue St-Louis-en-l'Ile, residential streets lead to the quais. Follow rue Budé to the **Musée Adam Mickiewicz,** 6, quai d'Orléans; the former home of the famous Polish poet now displays mementos relating to Mickiewicz and his circle of exiled Polish artists, including Chopin (see "Museums," p. 246). Marie Curie lived on the other side of the rue des Deux Ponts at 36, quai de Béthune, until she died of radiation-induced cancer in 1934. Proust fans should remember that Swann lived nearby on **quai d'Orléans.** And, though Marcel's Aunt Léonie found the island "a neighborhood most degrading," Parisians seem to have skipped that page.

First Arrondissement

The spectre of the Ancien Régime walks proudest through the first arrondissement. Hugging the Seine, the Louvre takes up about one seventh of the quartier's surface area; if you count Marie de Médicis's attached formal garden, the Jardin des Tuileries, the entire royal complex occupies a full third of the 1er. An ancient, ponderous elegance characterizes the western half of the arrondissement. From Cardinal Richelieu's 17th-century Palais Royale, to Louis XVI's pl. Vendôme, to the massive 16th-century Eglise St-Eustache (haunt of nobles and royalty throughout the centuries), the 1er is an open-air temple to imperial France. Yet, on the other side of the rue du Louvre lies a grubby hodge-podge of medieval and post-modern. Lurid neon sex-shops stud the rue St-Denis, while punks and free-spirits gather in the parks to pound out the bongo beat that moves this half of the quartier.

The **Jardin des Tuileries,** at the western foot of the Louvre, celebrates the victory of geometry over nature. The views from the elevated terrace by the river and from the central path of the park are spectacular. From the terrace you can see the Louvre, the gardens, the Eiffel Tower, and the Musée d'Orsay (right across the river). From the central path, gaze upon the obelisk of Luxor (in pl. de la Concorde), the Arc de Triomphe, and (on a clear day) the Grande Arche de la Défense in the distance; turn around to see the Arc de Triomphe du Carrousel and the Cour Napoléon of the Louvre. Sculptures are sprinkled throughout the park, including 18 bronze nudes by Auguste Maillol. Catherine de Médicis, missing the public promenades of her native Italy, had the gardens built in 1564; in 1649 André Le Nôtre (designer of the gardens at Versailles) imposed his preference for straight lines and sculpted trees upon the landscape of the Tuileries. The gardens were made public and have since become one of the most popular open spaces in Paris. Flanking the pathway through the gardens are the Jeu de Paume and the Musée de l'Orangerie (see "Museums," p. 240 and p. 245). The Jeu de Paume was originally constructed under Napoleon III as a court on which to play *jeu de paume,* an ancestor of tennis. In 1909, it was converted into a display area, mostly for art exhibits. When the Nazis took over Paris, they sent plun-

SIGHTS

dered art here, where much of it was labeled "degenerate" and burned. After the war, the building housed an Impressionist collection which has now been transferred to the Musée d'Orsay; at the moment, it's not much of anything (temporary exhibits fly through, as they've been doing since 1991). Along with the gardens, Catherine ordered the building of the **Palais des Tuileries,** which stretched along the west end of the Jardin du Carrousel, forming the western wall of the Louvre. Long after most of the Louvre had been converted into an art museum, the Tuileries remained the royal residence, though many of the royals would have rather been elsewhere. In 1791, Louis XVI and Marie-Antoinette attempted to flee this palace, where they had been kept after a mob of Parisian housewives dragged them out of Versailles. Napoleon lived here before his exile; Louis XVIII was chased out upon Napoleon's return in 1814. Louis-Philippe fled in similar haste during the Revolution of 1848, and in 1870, the Empress Eugénie scrambled out as the mob crashed in the main entrance. She then successfully escaped Paris with the help of her American dentist. Nine months later, as *Versaillais* forces streamed into the city to crush the Commune, a Communard official packed the palace with gunpowder, tar, and oil, and the building erupted into flames. The burnt-out ruins of the Tuileries survived until 1882, when the Republican Municipal Council, unwilling to restore a symbol of the monarchy, had them flattened. Today, only the Pavillion de Flore and the Pavillion de Marsan remain.

In recent years, the government has allowed an **amusement park** to spring up seasonally. If you're with kids or want a little adrenaline rush, come for the rides between the first weekend of December and the first weekend of January, or between the last Sunday of June and the first Sunday after August 15. At night, the huge Ferris wheel offers a magnificent view of nocturnal Paris. There are also some more traditional amusements for children, which operate year-round (except for a few weeks in winter). The park opens at 7am on weekdays, and on weekends and holidays at 7:30am. From the last Sunday of March to the Saturday before the last Sunday of September, closing time is 10pm; for the rest of the year it is 8pm.

The **pl. Vendôme,** three blocks north along the rue de Castiglione from the Tuileries, was begun in 1687 according to plans by Jules Hardouin-Mansart, who convinced Louis XIV and a group of five financiers to invest in the ensemble of private mansions and public institutions. The project ran out of funds almost immediately; for several decades before it was finished in 1720, the theatrical and ostentatious pl. Vendôme remained no more than a series of empty façades. Many of the buildings were gutted in the 1930s, but their uniformly dignified, 17th-century exteriors were protected. Today, the same shells mask stores that make the entire *place* shimmer with opulence. Well-known bankers, perfumers, and jewelers sprinkle the area, which is one of the few in Paris safe for high heels. Savor the moment at night by practicing the box-step under the iron lampposts past Chanel and Cartier. Then waltz over to the **Ritz** (no. 15) where Hemingway drank, and drank, and is duly remembered: they named the bar after him. Immediately after riding into Paris with the U.S. Army, Hemingway gathered some Resistance troops and went off to liberate the Ritz. Greeted by his old chum, the assistant manager, Hemingway proceeded to order 73 dry martinis. Raise a glass in his memory at **Hemingway,** 36, rue Cambon (tel. 01 42 60 38 30), and pay through the nose for a taste of this shrine to Papa (open daily 7pm-1am). Chopin died at no. 12; no. 11 and no. 13 house the **Ministry of Justice.** To the left of the entrance is **The Meter,** the mother of all rulers. Nowadays meters are defined using krypton-86 radiation, but this 1848 unit is still a pretty reliable source.

Napoleon presides over the square from atop the central **column,** looking down on the Ministry of Justice and the Bank of Spain. Originally, the square held a 7-m statue of Louis XIV in Roman costume. The statue was destroyed on August 10, 1792, and the square was renamed pl. des Piques. (*Piques* were long spears—pikes, even—used in the Revolution to carry guillotined heads.) In 1805, Napoleon erected a central column modeled after Trajan's column in Rome. Cast from Austrian and Russian bronze cannons captured in battle, surrounding a core of stone, the bas-reliefs of the column showed a series of military heroes; the emperor at the top was represented in a Roman toga like the one that once covered Louis XIV. Nine years later the statue of Napoleon was deposed—not without difficulty. In order to remove it, the Royalist government had to arrest the maker of the statue and force him, on penalty of execution, to figure out how to get rid of it. For all his pains, the return of Napoleon from Elba soon brought the original statue back to its proud stance. Over the next 60 years it would be replaced by the white flag of the ancient monarchy, a renewed Napoleon in military garb, and a classical Napoleon modeled after the original. During the Commune, a group led by Gustave Courbet toppled the entire column, planning to replace it with a monument to the "Federation of Nations and the Universal Republic." Later, in Napoleon's final victory, the original column was recreated. New bronze reliefs were made from the original molds and the intact Emperor returned to the top, where he still presides over the square.

Nearby, at 328, rue St-Honoré, is the former site of the **Jacobin convent,** a Dominican convent which furnished a meeting-place for Robespierre, who lodged at no. 398-400. The **Feuillants Monastery** arranged for an apartment house to be built nearby between 229 and 235, rue St-Honoré, where the Feuillants club (a group of moderates such as Lavoisier) met in 1791, just down the street from their opposition, the Jacobins. The monastery's gardens extended as far as the Tuileries riding school, known as the **Manège** and located at 230, rue de Rivoli. The National Assembly met at the Manège from 1789 to 1793, and in 1792 the Convention condemned Louis XVI to death here by a majority of only one vote.

The **Palais-Royal** lies farther down rue de Rivoli, across from the Louvre. Constructed in 1632 by Jacques Lemercier as Cardinal Richelieu's Palais Cardinal, it became a Palais Royal when Richelieu gave it to Louis XIII, a few years before both of them died. Louis XIV was the first king to truly inhabit the palace, and it was from here that he fled when the Fronde broke out. Louis-Philippe d'Orléans, the Duc de Chartres whose son became King Louis-Philippe, inherited the palace in 1780. Strapped for cash in 1784, the Duc de Chartres built and rented out the elegant buildings that enclose the palace's formal garden, turning the complex into an 18th-century shopping mall. It had boutiques, restaurants, prostitutes, and (in lieu of a multiplex cinema) theaters, wax museums, and puppet shows. On July 12, 1789, 26-year-old Camille Desmoulins leaped onto a café table here and urged his fellow citizens to arm themselves, shouting, "I would rather die than submit to servitude." The crowd filed out and was soon skirmishing with cavalry in the Tuileries garden. The Revolutions of 1830 and 1848 also began with angry crowds in these gardens. In the second half of the 19th century, the Palais recovered as a center of luxury commerce, preserving a serene aristocracy amid the commercialism of Haussmann's boulevards and the nearby modern department stores.

Today, the galleries of the venerable buildings contain small shops and a few cafés with a splendid view of the palace fountain and flower beds. In the summer, the fountain becomes a mecca for tourists and natives in need of a therapeutic foot bath. The levels above the cafés and shops, as well as the older parts of the palace, are occupied by government offices (including the Ministry of Culture). The *colonnes de Buren*—a set of black and white striped pillars and stumps that completely fill the *cour d'honneur* (the main courtyard)—are popular among couples with a large height disparity. Planted here in 1986, Daniel Buren's columns created a storm of controversy comparable to the one that greeted I.M Pei's Louvre pyramid. Separating this courtyard from the gardens stands a more conventional collonade, built in the early 19th century. On the southwestern corner of the Palais-Royal, facing the Louvre, the **Comédie Française,** formerly the Théâtre Français, is home to France's leading dramatic group. The theater was built in 1790 by architect Victor Louis. The entrance displays a number of busts of famous actors, including Mirabeau by Rodin, Talma by David, and d'Anges and Voltaire by Houdon. Molière, the company's founder, was taken ill here on stage; ironically, he was playing the role of the "Imaginary Invalid." The chair onto which he collapsed can still be seen. A monument to the great playwright rises not far from here at the corner of rue Molière and rue Richelieu, a few steps away from no. 40, where he was declared dead. The Fontaine de

Molière, designed by Visconti, splashes nearby. Several centuries earlier, the square witnessed another dramatic first-aid attempt. In 1429, when the Burgundians and the English held Paris, the city walls were only a few steps to the east down rue St-Honoré. Jeanne d'Arc tried to lead her troops across a moat to penetrate these walls, at what is now 163, rue St-Honoré, but was hit by an arrow while testing the depth of the water. Her troops carried her back to the place André-Malraux, but the wound was serious and the attack was called off. (See "Ancient Paris," p. 1, for more about the Hundred Years War.)

Stretching north from the Comédie into the 2ème and 9ème arrondissements is the glittering **Avenue de l'Opéra.** Haussmann leveled the *butte de Moulins* and many old homes to connect the old symbol of royalty, the Louvre, to the new symbol of imperial grandeur, the Opéra. The grand creation was intended to bear the mightiest name of all—avenue Napoléon—but the Franco-Prussian war interrupted this scheme, and when finished, the avenue was named for its terminus instead.

The **Bourse du Commerce** is the large round building between the rue du Louvre and the Forum des Halles. Not to be confused with the stock exchange (the *"bourse des valeurs"* or the *"bourse"*), the Bourse du Commerce is a commodities exchange where deals on agricultural produce are made; it also has an iron-and-glass cupola surrounded by paintings that you can see if you step inside (open Mon.-Fri. 8:30am-7pm). In the Middle Ages, a convent of repentant sinners occupied the site. Catherine de Médicis threw out the penitent women in 1572, when a horoscope convinced her that she should abandon construction of the Tuileries and build her palace here instead. Catherine's palace was demolished in 1748, leaving only the observation tower of her personal astrologer (a huge stone pillar that stands right next to the wall of the Bourse du Commerce) as a memorial to her superstition. Louis XV replaced the structure with a grain market; it was transformed into a commodities market in 1889, when the current building was built.

St-Eustache (M. Les Halles, Châtelet-Les Halles) is the large Gothic/Renaissance church visible from all over Les Halles, right next to the Turbigo exit of the Les Halles metro. In front of the church is a large cobblestone area with fountains and a distinctive sculpture of a huge human head and hand. Come to this area with a frisbee on a summer evening; and you'll be sure to meet plenty of local youths and foreign backpackers who want to play. Eustatius was a Roman general who is said to have adopted Christianity upon seeing the sign of a cross between the antlers of a deer. As punishment, he and his family were locked into a brass bull which was then placed over a fire until it became white-hot. Construction of the church in his honor began in 1532, and dragged on for over a century. In 1754, the unfinished façade was knocked down and replaced with the Romanesque one that stands today—incongruous with the rest of the building, but appropriate for the saint in question. You can get a good view of the older parts of the church if you go down the stairs of the Porte St-Eustache. To visit the interior you can just look around, or take a guided tour (in French only). See Colvert's tomb and Pigalle's exquisite statue of the Madonna. Perhaps the best way of taking in the architecture and the stained glass is to attend one of the **organ concerts** organized in June and July. The organ is one of the best in Paris; classical music lovers will not want to miss the experience of its thrilling baritone. Berlioz heard his *Te Deum* at St-Eustache for the first time, and Liszt conducted his *Messiah* here in 1886. For information on the organ festival, check *Pariscope,* call 01 45 22 28 74, or read the posters in front of the church. (Organ festival tickets 120F, students 80F. Church open Mon.-Sat. 8:30am-7pm, Sun. 8:15am-12:30pm and 3-7pm. Guided tours 3pm on Sun.; June-July daily 2pm. Mass Mon.-Fri. 10am and 6pm, Sat. 6pm, Sun. 8:30, 9:45, and 11am, and 6pm. On Sun., the 11am mass is with choir and organ; the 6pm mass is with organ only.) The statue in front of the church was created in 1986 by sculptor Henri de Miller. Its apt title is *The Listener.*

Les Halles (M. Les Halles, Châtelet-Les Halles) was called *"le ventre de Paris"* (Paris' belly) by Emile Zola, for the sprawling food market that had thrived there since 1135, when King Louis VI built two wooden buildings in the quartier to house a bazaar. The Les Halles that Zola described received a much-needed facelift in the

1850-60s with the construction of large iron and glass pavilions to shelter the vendors' stalls. Designed by Baltard, the pavilions resembled the one that still stands over the small market at the Carreau du Temple in the 3*ème* arrondissement. In the 1960s, the market had again slipped into disrepair. This time, however, the authorities decided to solve the problem simply by sending the vendors to a suburb near Orly. After moving the old market in 1970, politicians and city planners debated how to fill *le trou des Halles* (the gap at Les Halles), 106 open acres which presented Paris with the largest urban redesign opportunity since Haussmannization. Most of the city adored the elegant pavilions and wanted to see them preserved. But planners insisted that only by destroying the pavilions could they create a needed transfer point between the metro and the new commuter rail, the RER; demolition began in 1971. The city retained architects Claude Vasconi and Georges Penreach to replace the pavilions with a subterranean shopping mall, the **Forum des Halles.** Whatever their original intentions, the forum is now at once chipper and sordid, like a Disney remake of Blade Runner. Two hundred ebulliently colorful boutiques encrust the bowels of this metro-station-like mall (the most fashionable of which have floated to the upper levels). A small vidéothèque de Paris offers screening of videos concerning Paris (tel. 01 44 76 63 33; open Tues.-Sun. 12:30-9pm; 20F).

Getting around the Forum can be quite confusing; computerized maps scattered throughout the complex tell you what's available and how to get there. The computers will communicate with you in English—if you see a French screen, keep pressing the words *sommaire* or *fin* until you get to a display which features a button marked "change language."

Putting the mall underground allowed its designers to landscape the vast Les Halles quadrangle with greenery, statues and fountains. Striking a delicate balance between hypermodernity and verdure, the gardens avoid some of the aesthetic pitfalls of the forum beneath them. Both forum and gardens, however, present the danger of pickpockets; hold onto your wallet and stay above ground at night.

South of the forum along the rue St-Honoré is the **rue de la Ferronnerie.** In 1610, as Henri IV passed no. 11 in his carriage, he was assassinated by François Ravaillac, who leaped into the coach and stabbed the king. Ravaillac was upset that Henri was not persecuting the Protestants. He was later seared with red-hot pincers and scalded with boiling lead in an effort to uncover his accomplices. Finally, the torturers concluded that Ravaillac had acted alone and left him in the hands of the angry mob, which tore him to pieces. (See also "Strong and Absolute Monarchs," p. 4.) The nearby **Fontaine des Innocents,** built in 1548, is the last trace of the church and cemetery that used to stand there: **L'Eglise** and **La Cimetière des Sts-Innocents,** which once bordered and overlapped Les Halles. Until its demolition in the 1780s, the edges of cemetery were crowded by tombstones and the smell of rotting corpses, as well as by merchants trying to sell their wares. The cemetery was closed during the Enlightenment era's hygienic reforms; the corpses were relocated to the city's catacombs. The fountain, once attached to the church, now attracts punks and the overflow lunch-time crowd from McDonald's.

Tucked behind the Louvre near the Pont Neuf is the Gothic church **St-Germain l'Auxerrois.** On August 24, 1572, the church's bell functioned as the signal for the St. Bartholomew's Day Massacre. Huguenots were rounded up by the troops of the Duc de Guise and slaughtered in the streets, while King Charles IX shot at the survivors from the palace window. Pont Neuf itself, the oldest and most famous of the Seine bridges, connects the first arrondissement to the Ile de la Cité (see "Seine Islands," p. 139). At its left, **Samaritaine** is one of the oldest department stores in Paris. Founded in 1869, it ushered in the modern age of consumption. The building you see today began as a delicate iron and steel construction in 1906; and was revamped in the Art Deco style of 1928. The roof has a fabulous view of Paris that you, too, can enjoy for free (see "Department Stores," p. 272, for more information).

SIGHTS

Second Arrondissement

Since the 19th century, the 2ème has centered around barter and trade, whether in the *quartier*'s many indoor, glass-covered shopping arcades called *galeries* or *passages*, at the **Bourse des Valeurs** (national stock exchange), or among the prostitutes on rue St-Denis and rue d'Aboukir. Abundant fabric shops and cheap women's clothing stores hover between rue du Sentier and rue St. Denis, while theatres crowd the streets in the arrondissement's western half.

Galerie Colbert and **Galerie Vivienne,** near the Palais Royal, are the finest remaining examples of Parisian *galeries*—marbled, pedestrian walkways built within city blocks to house quaint, often exclusive boutiques (e.g. antique cork-screw stores, antiquarian print shops). Both arcades, recently restored, date from the early 19th century, and, like others of their kind, are the predecessors of the modern shopping mall. Enter Galerie Vivienne at 4, rue des Petits Champs, and you'll encounter a spectacular showcase of pastel luxury, dainty shops, and *trompe l'oeil* marble columns, actually made of wood. Turn left at the end of the corridor to visit the Galerie Colbert which houses a bronze statue (1822) within the rotunda. Catch your reflection in the *vitrine* of Madonna's preferred designer, **Jean-Paul Gaultier,** 6, rue Vivienne (tel. 01 42 86 05 05). Other *galerie* windows display treasures (or copies thereof) belonging to the Bibliothèque Nationale, which uses portions of this building as a storage annex.

The **Passage des Panoramas,** between bd. Montmartre and rue St-Marc, is less conspicuously posh, but perhaps just as beautiful. It contains a fully intact 19th-century glass-and-tile roof and a more recently installed multicultural food-court. Other *galeries* in the 2ème include the **Passage du Grand-Cerf** (between rue St-Denis and rue Marie Stuart), with several small art galleries and the **Passage des Princes** (between bd. des Italiens and rue de Richelieu), home to a cheap fast-food court.

The **Bibliothèque Nationale,** 58, rue de Richelieu (tel. 01 47 03 81 26), is the largest library in Continental Europe. Its collection of 12 million volumes includes two Gutenberg Bibles and assorted other first editions dating from the 15th century to the present. Since 1642, a year before Richelieu founded the Académie Française, every book published in France has been legally required to enter the national archives. The current library evolved out of the **Bibliothèque du Roi,** the royal book depository, and further expanded with sizeable donations from noted bibliophiles and authors, such as Victor Hugo and Émile Zola. To accommodate the ever-increasing volume of books, annexes have been purchased near the library, notably in the Galerie Vivienne. In the late 1980s, the French government eschewed annexes as a short-term solution and resolved to build the monstrously inadequate **Bibliothèque de France** (see "Sights—13ème," p. 194), where the Bibliothèque Nationale's collection is presently being relocated. When the move is complete in the fall of 1997, the old B.N. will become the Bibliothèque Nationale des Arts.

To enter the **Salle des lecteurs** (main reading room), scholars must pass through an often strict screening process. For the most part, only graduate students and professors qualify. To receive a **carte de lecteur,** bring a letter from your university, publisher, or publication that explains your research project in as much detail as possible; the library has a number of specialized departments to which individuals must be granted specific entry. Stop by the library's main office (tel. 01 47 03 81 26; open Mon.-Sat. 9am-4:30pm). Non-scholars may peek into the main reading room from its semi-circular antechamber. In summer, the library fills to capacity soon after it opens at 9am. Those who arrive late must take a number from the clerk who sits at the entry to the reading room, and wait for a seat to vacate. (Main reading room open Sept.-July, Mon.-Fri. 9am-8pm, Sat. 9am-5:30pm; in Aug, Mon.-Fri. 9am-8pm, Sat. 9am-6pm.) A gallery within the building hosts excellent temporary exhibitions of books, prints and lithographs from the B.N. archives; call 01 47 03 81 10 for information; gallery hours vary with exhibit and season. Upstairs, the **Le Cabinet des Médailles** displays coins and medallions, as well as 18th-century armoires and other treasures (open Mon.-Sat. 1-5pm, Sun. noon-6pm; admission 22F, reduced 15F).

Across from the Bibliothèque Nationale main entrance is the **sq. Louvois.** The sculpted fountain at its center, completed by Visconti in 1839, depicts, among other things, the four great rivers of France, the Seine, the Saône, the Loire, and the Garonne, in womanly form. At the fountain's base, cherubs ride sea creatures that charmingly spout water through their nostrils.

The Neoclassical exterior of the **Bourse des Valeurs** (stock exchange), 4, place de la Bourse (tel. 01 40 41 62 20; M. Bourse), is the architectural version of a poker face. Its massive Corinthian columns might, according to Victor Hugo, be those of "a royal palace, a house of commons, a town hall, a college, a riding school, an academy, a trade market, a tribunal, a museum, a barracks, a sepulchre, a temple, a theater." Founded in 1724, Paris' stock exchange opened well after those of Lyon, Toulouse, and Rouen. Bourbon kings soon began issuing worthless bonds there, which helped finance their expensive taste in palaces and wars. Jacobins closed the exchange during the Revolution in order to fend off war profiteers, but it reopened under Napoleon. Construction of the present building began in 1808, proceeded slowly, and halted between 1814 and 1821 for lack of funds. The wings of the building were added from 1902-1907. Tours of the building (in French, 1hr.; Mon.-Fri. 1:15-4:15pm on the ¼-hour; 30F, students 15F) will appeal either to those already passionate about foreign stock exchanges or to those caught outside in a sudden downpour. The traders' pit is tame compared to those of London or New York.

To the west of the *bourse*, the Salle Favart between rue Favart and rue Marivaux (M. Richelieu Drouot) has resonated with the laughs, sobs, and cries of the Opéra Comique since 1783. Inside and out the building itself is a veritable recipe for opera with its numerous statues signifying music, poetry, and tragedy. It was here that Bizet's Carmen first hitched up her skirts, cast a sweltering side-long glance at the audience, and seduced Don José with the trilled declaration "Si, tu m'aimes pas, je t'aime. Et si je t'aime prends garde à toi." (If you don't love me, I love you. And if I love you watch out.)

SIGHTS

A center of food commerce and gastronomy since the 13th century, rue **Montorgueil** is composed of a number of wine, cheese, meat and produce shops. To the left of rue Montorgueil (literally Mt. Pride) stand the well-preserved remnants of a 15th century tower built next to what was once the city wall and is now rue Étienne Marcel. Soon after ordering the successful assassination of his cousin (Louis d'Orléans, brother to the king) in 1408, Jean Sans Peur erected a tower in the middle of his house, the Hôtel de Bourgogne. To crown this mountain of pride he named it in his own honor, **Tour de Jean Sans Peur**.

Further north, the rue de Cléry and rue d'Aboukir run parallel along the line of another city boundary, the old rampart of Charles V. The buildings between the two streets were constructed shortly after the wall's destruction in the 17th century. Their façades are modified versions of the fanciest Italianate forms, using lintels instead of arches and plaster instead of stone. These buildings are known to serve as scrim to many of the city's prostitutes.

In the mid-1970s Paris' prostitutes demonstrated in churches, monuments, and public squares demanding unionization. They marched down **rue St-Denis,** the central artery of the city's prostitution district, to picket for equal rights and protection under the law. Their campaign was successful—prostitution is now legal in France. In recent years, rue St-Denis has resettled many of the sex workers who once plied their trade in the Bois de Boulogne; routed from the park by French police in 1993, many now work streets, like rue Blondel, just south of M. Strasbourg-St-Denis.

Third Arrondissement: The Marais

The 3*ème* and 4*ème* arrondissements comprise the neighborhood otherwise known as the Marais, or "the swamp." The Marais earned its name as a result of its distinctive dampness before it was drained by monks in the 13th century. With Henri IV's construction of the place des Vosges (see "Sights—4*ème*," p. 156) at the beginning of the 17th century, the area became the city's center of fashionable living. Leading architects and sculptors of the period designed elegant mansions with large front courtyards and rear gardens called *hôtel particuliers.* These "hotels" are not places where tourists can rent rooms—a hôtel was the city residence of a *grand seigneur.* Under Louis XV, the center of Parisian life moved from the Marais to the *faubourgs* St-Honoré and St-Germain, and construction of *hôtels* in the Marais ceased.

The 19th and early 20th centuries were not kind to this old *quartier.* Many *hôtels* fell into ruin or disrepair. In a misguided attempt to widen the narrow, medieval streets, laws specified that any new building had to be constructed several meters back from the curb. No one seemed to realize that given the longevity of city buildings, widening a street in this manner would take several hundred years. By the time the plan was abandoned in 1964, all that had been accomplished was that streets which had seen any recent construction now had jagged, saw-toothed curbs (e.g., rue du Temple). At the same time, a section of the Marais was declared a historic neighborhood and protected from further destruction—the first step in the gentrification that has since proceeded apace, with boutiques, trendy cafés, and museums (such as the **Musée de la Chasse,** the **Musée Picasso,** and the **Musée Cognacq-Jay**—see "Museums", page 223) moving quickly into restored old *hôtels.*

To the modern tourist the district still retains the stamp of a bustling medieval village whose storefronts have, over time, begun to sway with gravity. Many of Paris' oldest buildings are to be found here. Some buildings on the rue de Montmorency and rue Volta date from the 14th century. This is a great neighborhood for a stroll, and a peek into many of the *hôtels* is free.

The **square Emile-Chautemps** leads from **boulevard Sébastopol,** Haussmann's great north-south thoroughfare, to the **Conservatoire National des Arts et Métiers,** 292, rue St-Martin (tel. 01 40 27 20 00; M. Réaumur-Sébastopol or Arts-et-Métiers; information office through the archway to the left of the main courtyard open Mon.-Fri. 10am-noon and 1:30-5:30pm, Sat. 9am-noon), a polytechnical institute housed in a compound about 13 centuries old. In 1060, Henri I built a church here over the ruins of an 8th-century parish church. The prióry St-Martin des Champs, now restored, is a 12th-century addition to the complex. The school itself evolved out of a repository for technical inventions assembled at this site during the Revolution. Walk through the main gate towards the former prióry, where you'll see commanding statues of Coulomb and Chaptal. Coulomb, the better-known of the two scientists, established a law of electrical attraction; Chaptal, a true French hero, was a chemist whose discoveries improved methods used to dye cotton and to preserve wine. Exit left out the main gate, turn left on rue Réaumur, and take a left on rue Volta. At no. 3 sits the oldest residential building in Paris, a four-story structure dating from 1300. It would take some imagination, however, to dream away the modern bustle of this stooping medieval street.

From rue Volta, turn right on rue Notre-Dame de Nazareth and continue up rue du Temple to **place de la République** (M. République), the meeting point of the 3ème, 10ème, and 11ème arrondissements. In the center, a monument to the Republic of France celebrates the 23 years of intermittent republican rule between 1789 and the monument's inauguration in 1880. The statue of *La République* by Morice stands on a base by Dalou, with bronze reliefs representing various revolutions in French history. During the day, *brasseries* and cafés attract folks to this noisy *place*. Avoid the area at night, however, when prostitutes and swindlers abound.

This area is crowded with low-budget stores of all sorts, including the astounding, almost terrifying **Tati,** and a few blocks southeast, the blue steel and glass of the **Carreau du Temple** market. (See "Department Stores," p. 272, and "Markets," p. 277.) After frenetic bargaining, the benches in the **square du Temple** may provide welcome respite. Follow rue du Temple south from pl. de la République to reach this public park, next to the 3ème's impressive *mairie,* and laden with a tumultuous past. Just beyond the playground was the **quartier du Temple,** the 12th-century headquarters for the Knights of the Templar. Under the direction of the Prince de Conti, the Grand Prior, the palace became quite the spot for society gatherings. Home to Jean-Jacques Rousseau in 1765, it became another kind of aristocratic hot spot during the

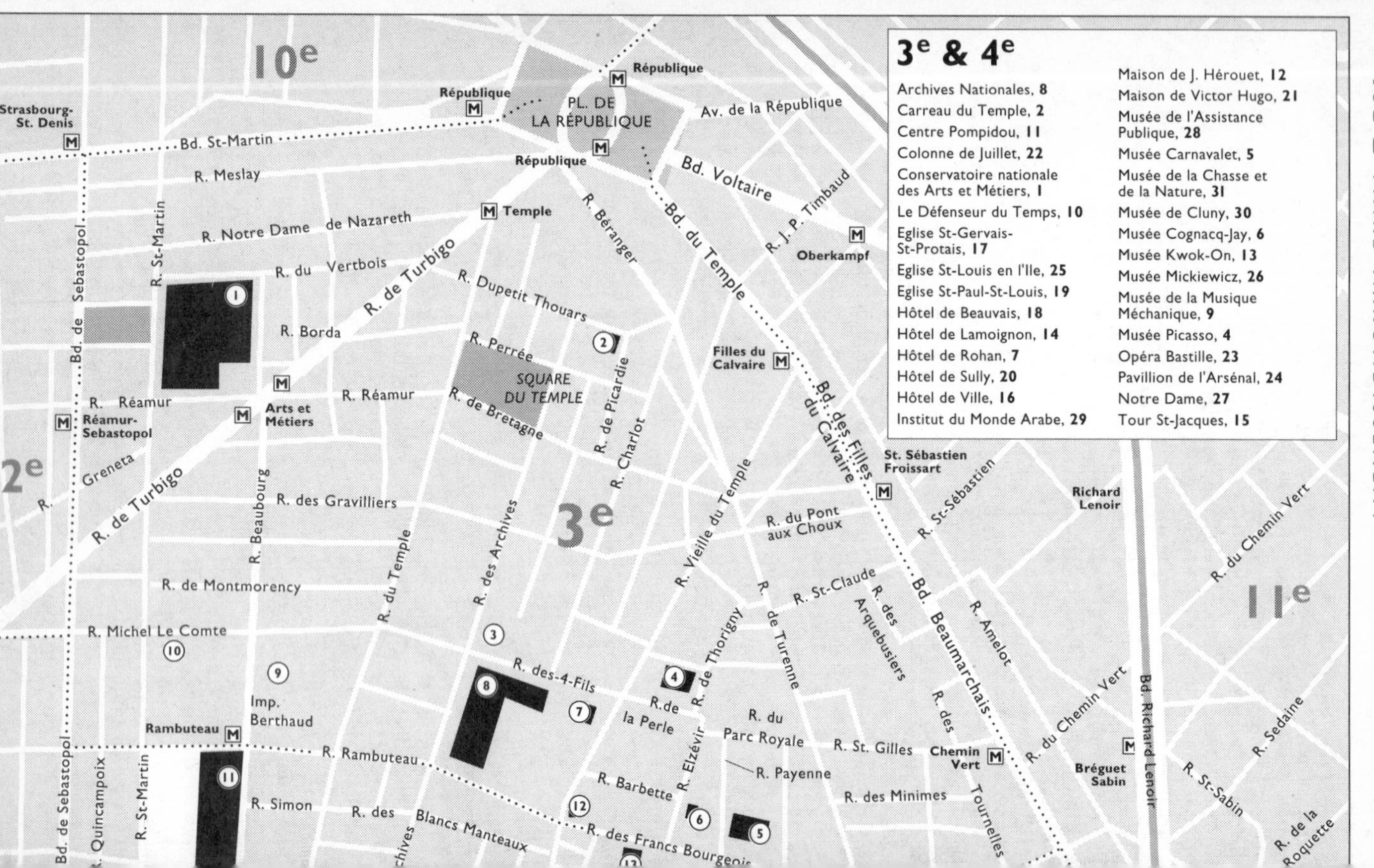
3e & 4e
Archives Nationales, 8
Carreau du Temple, 2
Centre Pompidou, 11
Colonne de Juillet, 22
Conservatoire nationale des Arts et Métiers, 1
Le Défenseur du Temps, 10
Eglise St-Gervais-St-Protais, 17
Eglise St-Louis en l'Ile, 25
Eglise St-Paul-St-Louis, 19
Hôtel de Beauvais, 18
Hôtel de Lamoignon, 14
Hôtel de Rohan, 7
Hôtel de Sully, 20
Hôtel de Ville, 16
Institut du Monde Arabe, 29
Maison de J. Hérouet, 12
Maison de Victor Hugo, 21
Musée de l'Assistance Publique, 28
Musée Carnavalet, 5
Musée de la Chasse et de la Nature, 31
Musée de Cluny, 30
Musée Cognacq-Jay, 6
Musée Kwok-On, 13
Musée Mickiewicz, 26
Musée de la Musique Méchanique, 9
Musée Picasso, 4
Opéra Bastille, 23
Pavillion de l'Arsénal, 24
Notre Dame, 27
Tour St-Jacques, 15
10e
11e
3e
2e
PL. DE LA RÉPUBLIQUE
SQUARE DU TEMPLE
République
Temple
Oberkampf
Filles du Calvaire
St. Sébastien Froissart
Richard Lenoir
Bréguet Sabin
Chemin Vert
Arts et Métiers
Réaumur-Sebastopol
Strasbourg-St. Denis
Rambuteau
Bd. Richard Lenoir
Bd. Beaumarchais
Bd. des Filles du Calvaire
Bd. du Temple
Bd. Voltaire
Av. de la République
Bd. St-Martin
Bd. de Sebastopol
R. du Chemin Vert
R. Sedaine
R. de la Roquette
R. St-Sabin
R. Amelot
R. St-Sébastien
R. des Tournelles
R. des Arquebusiers
R. St-Claude
R. du Pont aux Choux
R. de Turenne
R. St. Gilles
R. des Minimes
R. du Parc Royale
R. Payenne
R. de Thorigny
R. Vieille du Temple
R. Elzévir
R. de la Perle
R. Barbette
R. des Francs Bourgeois
R. des-4-Fils
R. des Archives
R. Charlot
R. de Picardie
R. Béranger
R. J. P. Timbaud
R. Dupetit Thouars
R. Perrée
R. de Bretagne
R. de Turbigo
R. du Temple
R. Rambuteau
R. des Blancs Manteaux
R. Notre Dame de Nazareth
R. du Vertbois
R. Borda
R. Réaumur
R. des Gravilliers
R. Meslay
R. St-Martin
R. Beaubourg
R. de Montmorency
Imp. Berthaud
R. Simon
R. Michel Le Comte
R. Quincampoix
R. Greneta

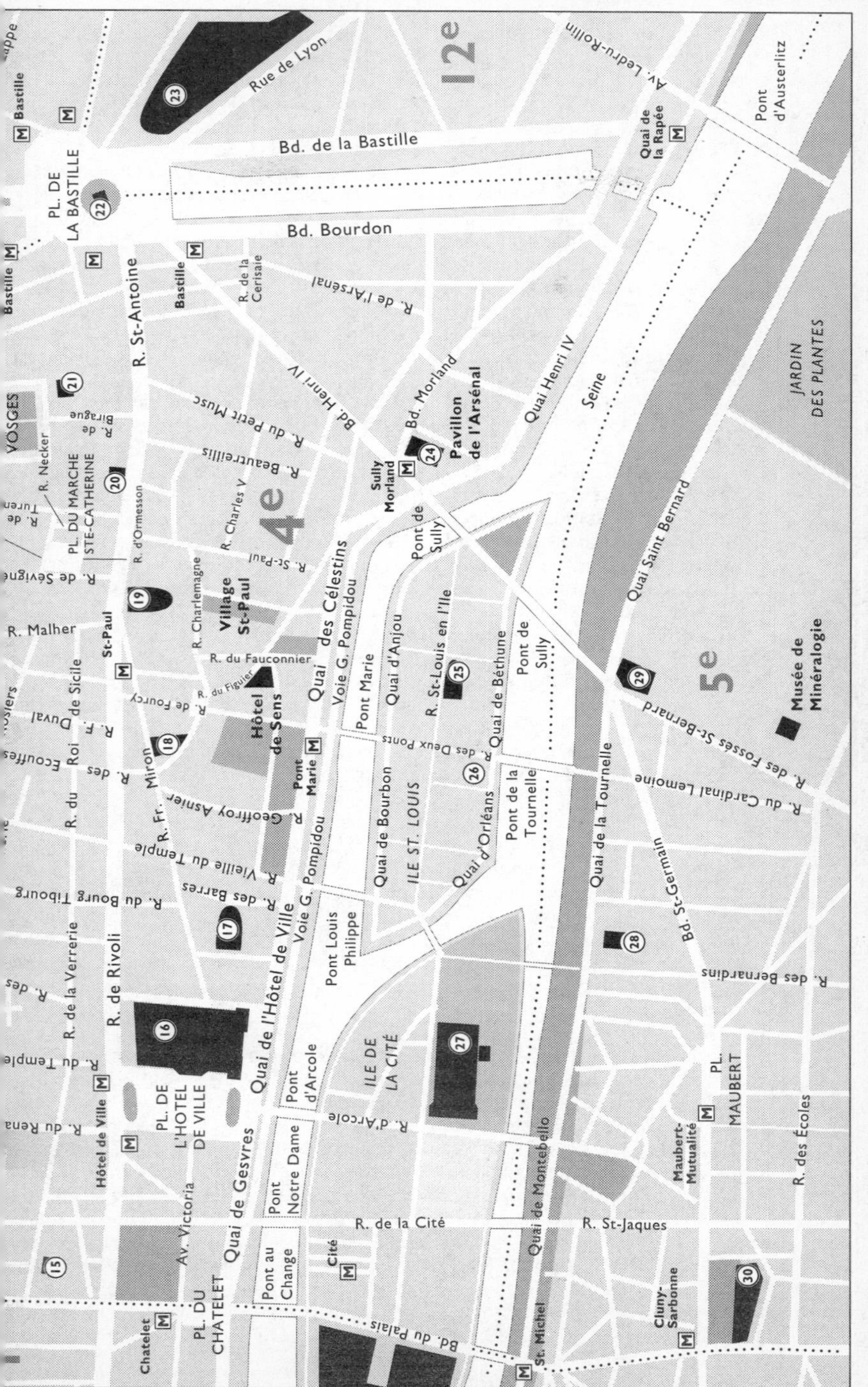
12e
4e
5e
Rue de Lyon
Av. Ledru-Rollin
Pont d'Austerlitz
Quai de la Rapée
Bd. de la Bastille
PL. DE LA BASTILLE
Bastille
Bd. Bourdon
R. de la Cerisaie
R. de l'Arsénal
R. St-Antoine
Bd. Henri IV
Bd. Morland
Pavillon de l'Arsénal
Quai Henri IV
Seine
JARDIN DES PLANTES
VOSGES
R. Necker
R. de Birague
R. de Turenne
PL. DU MARCHE STE-CATHERINE
R. du Petit Musc
R. Beautreillis
R. Charles V
R. d'Ormesson
R. St-Paul
Sully Morland
Pont de Sully
Quai Saint Bernard
R. de Sévigné
R. Malher
St-Paul
R. Charlemagne
Village St-Paul
Quai des Célestins
Voie G. Pompidou
R. du Fauconnier
R. du Figuier
R. de Fourcy
Hôtel de Sens
R. F. Duval
R. du Roi de Sicile
R. des Ecouffes
R. Fr. Miron
Pont Marie
Quai d'Anjou
R. St-Louis en l'Ile
Quai de Béthune
R. des Deux Ponts
Musée de Minéralogie
R. des Fossés St-Bernard
R. du Cardinal Lemoine
Quai de la Tournelle
Pont de la Tournelle
Quai d'Orléans
ILE ST. LOUIS
Quai de Bourbon
R. Geoffroy Asnier
R. Vieille du Temple
R. du Bourg Tibourg
R. des Barres
R. de la Verrerie
R. de Rivoli
Quai de l'Hôtel de Ville
Pont Louis Philippe
Bd. St-Germain
R. des Bernardins
R. du Temple
PL. DE L'HOTEL DE VILLE
Hôtel de Ville
R. du Renard
Pont d'Arcole
R. d'Arcole
ILE DE LA CITÉ
PL. MAUBERT
Maubert-Mutualité
R. des Écoles
Quai de Gesvres
Av. Victoria
Pont Notre Dame
R. de la Cité
R. St-Jaques
Quai de Montebello
Pont au Change
Cité
PL. DU CHATELET
Chatelet
Bd. du Palais
St. Michel
Cluny-Sorbonne

Revolution: it was the state prison where the royal family lived while awaiting exec tion. While everyone agrees that Louis XVI was taken directly from this prison to th guillotine, the fate of the young Louis XVII is still contested. Nonetheless, most thin that he died here in 1795; to find what is presumed to be his grave, see "Sights-$11^{\text{ème}}$," page 188. Napoleon destroyed most of the fortress in 1809; during the Se ond Empire the lot was replaced by the square you see today.

From the far end of the park, if you turn left on rue du Temple, you'll walk throug the garment district on the way to a landmark-packed section of the Marais. You' wade through a slough of junk jewelry, handbag, and button stores. Bargain hunte may be disappointed though; many of these wholesale dealers only sell *en gros*—i bulk. If you see a sign that says *vente aux particuliers* (sale to individuals), you ca try your luck. Take a right on Montmorency and behold the **Auberge Nicolas Flame** built in 1407. The French alchemist Flamel ran a charity house here, providing mec eval indigents with free food and lodging. In its current state, the *auberge* feeds a le needy crowd; the elegant restaurant will probably be above your budget, even you're far from a charity case.

Pick up the trail on rue du Temple and turn left on rue des Haudriettes. One bloc down on the left side is the **Hôtel Guénégaud,** at 60, rue des Archives. The hôtel w built by Mansart in the 17th century and is the current address of the **Musée de Chasse** (see "Museums," p. 242). A glimpse at the sculptures in the courtyard (si bodiless bronze deer heads and two suspiciously fat lions), is both free and fun. At 5 rue des Archives, stands the only surviving portion of the Hôtel de Clisson, built i 1380. The unusual angle between the gate and the road was chosen to facilitate th entrance of litters and carriages. On the opposite side of the street is a beautiful 18t century fountain, the **fontaine des Haudriettes,** whose sculpted lion's head sti spouts water today.

Turning left onto rue des Francs Bourgeois will lead you to the entrance of th **Musée de l'Histoire de France** (see "Museums," p. 244). Housed in the **Hôtel d Soubise,** this is the exhibition space of the **Archives Nationales.** The majestic cour yard of the Hôtel de Soubise, built between 1705 and 1709, is a classic example 18th-century aristocratic architecture. The lavish interior decorations (execute between 1730 and 1745) remain intact. Some of the most important French historic documents are stored in this hôtel and in the other old residences occupying th block. Located here are the Treaty of Westphalia, the Edict of Nantes and its Revoc tion, the first *Declaration of the Rights of Man,* a will from 627, the wills of Louis X and Napoleon, Marie-Antoinette's last letter, and correspondence between Benjami Franklin and George Washington. Also cached here is Louis XVI's famous diary. Onl the word *"rien"* (nothing) is scrawled here to describe the events of July 14, 178 (Bastille Day)—it had been a bad day for hunting. While the public might clamor t see the most intriguing of these documents, access to them is limited to specialist The only documents on view for the general public are those displayed in tempora exhibits at the museum. Scholars should apply to the **Centre d'Accueil et de Recher che des Archives Nationales,** 11, rue des Quatre-Fils (tel. 01 40 27 64 19 or 01 40 2 64 20 for recorded information).

The museum is on the corner where the rue des Francs-Bourgeois and rue Rambu teau meet. Going right on Rambuteau will bring you past the Centre Pompidou (few streets further on your right is the rue Quincampoix—one of the streets mos dense with galleries). Going left on rue des Francs-Bourgeois will lead you throug the spiritual heart of the Marais. This street divides the third and fourth arrondiss ments. Window-shop, stop at a *salon de thé,* or look for corner *brasseries* sellin famed Berthillon ice cream and sorbet (expect to pay about 12F for a small singl scoop and 17F for a double). As you proceed toward the intersection of rue de Francs-Bourgeois and rue Vieille du Temple, you may notice an odd crack betwee nos. 57 and 59. This gap hides a vestige of Philippe-Auguste's city wall, built fro 1180 to 1220; it's the stone base of the red brick building in the background. Th next building (no. 55) is the home of the **Crédit Municipal de Paris,** nicknamed *M Tante* (my aunt—as in, "oh, I have to go see my aunt today"). Impoverished arist crats have been discreetly selling off their family heirlooms since 1777 at this glorified pawnshop. The building still auctions jewelry, paintings, sculptures, and other artworks on a regular basis; it buys, too, though not as publicly. Take a peak at the fountain in the courtyard. (Open Mon.-Thurs. 8:30am-4:30pm, Fri. 8:30am-3:30pm.)

A few meters down, an alleyway at no. 38 gives a sense of what Henri IV's Paris actually felt like: dark and claustrophobic. The oldest houses here date from the 1600s, and most of them have overhanging second floors that jut out over the street. No. 36 houses a 19th-century apothecary that has been preserved, with a dark wood interior and blue glass jars for herbs and medicines. A few steps back, at the intersection of rue des Francs-Bourgeois and rue Vieille-du-Temple, stands the flamboyant Gothic **Hôtel Hérouët,** built in 1528 for Louis XII's treasurer. Hérouët had to get special permission to build the bold angle turret, which he used to observe the action on his street; normally such extravagances were reserved for royalty.

Rue Vieille-du-Temple is lined with stately residences. No. 75 marks the 18th-century **Hôtel de la Tour du Pin,** with an attractive private garden opposite the entrance. The **Hôtel de Rohan,** one of the most famous *hôtels* in the Marais, stands at no. 87, rue Vieille du Temple (tel. 01 40 27 60 00). Built between 1705 and 1708 for Armand-Gaston de Rohan, Bishop of Strasbourg and alleged love child of Louis XIV, the *hôtel* has housed many of his descendants. Cardinal Rohan, Louis XVI's treasurer, was arrested here as a result of the infamous *affaire du collier de la reine.* One can only see the palace's sumptuous interior by visiting one of the frequent temporary exhibits, often held in the *Cabinet des Singes*, the only room with its original decoration (admission 10F). If there's no exhibit when you visit, you can still see the impressive courtyard and rose garden (open Mon.-Fri. 9am-6pm; free).

Farther along rue Vieille du Temple on the right is a pleasant park, the garden of the **Hôtel Salé** (Salted Hôtel), once the Hôtel de Juigné and currently home of the **Musée Picasso** (see "Museums," p. 248). Built for a salt merchant and profiteer of the hated *gabelle* (salt tax), the hôtel has served many different functions in its transition from parvenu residence to Picasso museum. In 1793, it was the Dépôt Nationale Littéraire, a warehouse for books seized by Revolutionary censors; then it was a 19th-century pension for students and artists, including Honoré de Balzac. Today, Picasso's sculptures and paintings thumb jagged noses and raise one, long eyebrow at the cupids on the ceiling and the rest of the high-falutin' decor. Light fixtures by Diego Giacometti, brother of Alberto, share this incongruous setting.

Turn right from the Musée Picasso's courtyard and walk down rue de Thorigny. Straight ahead, at 1, rue de la Perle, is the five-room **Musée de la Serrure** (Lock Museum), located in the **Hôtel Libéral-Bruant** (see "Museums," page 249). The recently restored hôtel was built in the 17th century by Bruant, architect of the Invalides, as his private home.

Follow rue du Parc Royal to **square Léopold Achille.** The twin **square Georges Cain,** several yards down rue Payenne on the left, is quieter and shadier, but without the architectural scenery. All along rue du Parc Royal are impressive *hôtels particuliers;* nos. 4 and 8 have superb façades of stone and pink brick.

Winding around the corner down rue de Sévigné, an imposing gate at no. 52 is all that's left of the Hôtel de Flesselles, built in the 18th century and demolished in 1908. No. 48 houses a workshop of the Ecole des Beaux-Arts; the woman generously doing the breast-feeding is Charity, as sculpted by Fortin in 1806. On the right side of the street (no. 23), in the former home of Mme. de Sévigné, the **Musée Carnavalet** contains paintings and knick-knacks which portray Paris' changing face from prehistoric to present times (see "Museums," p. 241). Even if you don't visit the museum, it's worth looking at the building's gate and courtyard, built in the mid-16th century for Jacques des Ligneris, the ambitious president of the Parlement de Paris. The statue of Louis XIV in the middle of the courtyard was once in front of the Hôtel de Ville (see "Sights—4ème," p. 159). To maintain architectural unity, the walls to your left and right, added in 1655, were given similar bas-reliefs; to the left are the Four Elements, and to the right, the Four Winds. In the 1860s, architects tried to restore the building to its original appearance. Unfortunately, they mistook a 17th-century proposal to

The Affair of the Queen's Necklace

This infamous *affaire* unraveled in 1785 on the eve of the Revolution, when a certain Countess de La Motte convinced Louis XVI's treasurer, Cardinal Rohan, that Marie-Antoinette was deeply in love with him and only needed a small token of his affection. He gave his official authorization for a diamond necklace costing one and a half million francs to be carried to the queen by La Motte herself. As soon as she received the necklace, the countess sprinted to London and began selling the diamonds one by one, all the while counterfeiting letters from Marie-Antoinette acknowledging receipt of the goods and continued affection for the anxious Cardinal. It was only a matter of time before the equally anxious jewelers demanded payment for the sumptuous necklace the Queen had never even glimpsed. The ensuing trial concluded that Rohan was a fool for believing the story, and that La Motte was guilty of forgery and theft. However, a rebellious public found it easy to believe that Marie-Antoinette had in fact stiffed the Parisian artisans and then abandoned her friend.

remodel the building for the original plans, and ended up carrying out the proposed remodeling two centuries late. From the Hôtel Carnavalet, continue your Marais tour by proceeding south to the 4ème.

Fourth Arrondissement: The Marais (Lower Half)

Relatively undisturbed by Haussmann's reconstruction, the 4ème arrondissement encourages visitors to wander past decaying edifices once inhabited by kings and their mistresses, through cobblestone streets lined with *galeries* and falafel stands, and into parks and *places* in which the well-heeled mix with the unshod. From pl. des Vosges on the north and Ile St-Louis on the south, to the Hôtel de Ville on the west and the boulevard Henri IV on the east, the 4ème offers a panoply of elegant historic monuments, market streets, and sudden, fanciful extravagance, bisected by the busy rue de Rivoli and rue St-Antoine. Royals and literary greats as well as a centuries-old and still thriving Jewish community have left their mark here.

The **Hôtel de Lamoignon,** 24, rue Pavée (M. St-Paul), directly south of the Musée Carnavalet (see "Sights—3ème," p. 155*),* is one of the finest *hôtels particuliers* in the Marais, built in 1584 for Diane de France, daughter of Henri II. The noble façade, with its two-story Corinthian pilasters, is the first example in Paris of the "colossal" style of decoration later to appear in the Louvre. In the staid 16th century, these ground-to-roof pilasters were quite daring, but no one was going to tell that to the princess. The left wing, which blends rather clumsily into the original building, was added a generation later by Diane's heir, Charles de Valois. The buildings of the cobblestone courtyard to the right date from 1968. Added to make room for the library that moved here that year, they provide a surprisingly graceful counterpoint to the left wing. The unfortunate modern construction visible behind the library dates from 1992. Through a door in the courtyard, you can enter the **Bibliothèque Historique de la Ville de Paris** (tel. 01 42 74 44 44). This non-circulating library of Parisian history lets anyone read its 800,000 volumes, including foreigners with valid passports; however, it is not a tourist attraction. Visit only for information (open Mon.-Sat. 9:30am-6pm). To peek through the fence and see the gardens of the *hôtel*, which are closed to the public, exit onto rue Pavée (thus named because it was the first street in the city to be paved) and turn right on rue des Francs Bourgeois. Next door once stood the prison de la Force, where more than 60 citizens were massacred in 1792.

At the end of rue des Francs Bourgeois, **pl. des Vosges** (M. Chemin Vert or St-Paul), Paris' oldest remaining public square and one of its most charming, promises a fantastic stroll. The central square, now the site of a park, is surrounded by 17th-century townhouses built at the height of the French Renaissance. Kings built several mansions on this site; the last was the Palais de Tournelles, which Catherine de Médicis ordered destroyed after her husband Henri II died there in a jousting tournament in 1563. The newly vacant space was the site of a horse market until 1605, when Henri IV expelled the market and decreed the construction of a new public square, to be known as the pl. Royale. Wishing to promenade in courtly opulence, he wanted a *place* large and central enough to accommodate leisurely walks. Each of the 36 buildings has arcades on the street level, topped by two stories decorated with pink brick capped by a steep, slate-covered roof. The "brick" on most of the façades is just a layer of mortar; this money-saving measure is most evident on the south side of the square (near the rue St-Antoine and the Seine), where the mortar has wrinkled and cracked. The largest townhouse, forming the square's main entrance on the south side, was the majestic king's pavilion; directly opposite, the pavilion of the queen is smaller but equally gracious.

Henri IV was assassinated in 1610, two years before the place Royale's completion. The marriage of Louis XIII's sister to the crown prince of Spain in 1612 would inaugurate the square as a place of spectacle. The event drew a crowd of 10,000 spectators and 150 buglers. Although Henri intended the *place* as a home and workplace for merchants (hence the arcades), the king's design restrictions made the *place* an address only gentlefolk could afford. Mme. de Sévigné (born at 1bis on February 6, 1626) and Cardinal Richelieu number among the illustrious few. Another character who occupied and then was bounced from the *place* was Marion Delormé, renowned for her beauty and number of lovers. As a friend of Richelieu, Marion would visit his home in the guise of a man. Marion's fortunes took a turn for the worse as her looks faded: her house was repossessed in 1648, and she died in (and of) middle age, a pauper.

Molière, Racine, and Voltaire filled the grand parlors with their *bon mots.* Mozart played a concert here at the age of seven. Even when the majority of the city's nobility moved across the river to the fbg. St-Germain, the pl. Royale remained among the most elegant spots in Paris. During the Revolution, however, the 1639 Louis XIII statue in the center of the park was destroyed (the statue there now is a copy erected by the restored monarchy in 1818) and the park was renamed pl. des Vosges after the first department in France to pay its taxes (1800). After that, successive liberal and right-wing regimes changed the name back and forth from "Vosges" to "Royale" until 1870 and the Third Republic, when "Vosges" finally won out.

Follow the arcades around the edge of pl. des Vosges for an elegant promenade, some delightful window-shopping, and a glimpse of plaques that mark the habitations of famous residents. Théophile Gautier and Alphonse Daudet lived at no. 8; Rachel, the 19th century's most famous classical tragedy actress, lived at no. 9. Victor Hugo lived at no. 6, now an excellent museum with displays on his life, work, and contemporaries (see "Museums," p. 245). During summer weekends, these arcades fill with an array of talented musicians who play and sing mostly classical music, from harp medleys to Mozart arias. On a bench in the park, under the shade of the tall trees and next to the fountains, visitors are entirely isolated from the traffic noises and fumes of central Paris. The most scenic way of leaving the pl. des Vosges is through the little corner door at the right of the south face (near no. 5), which leads into the garden of the Hôtel de Sully.

The **Hôtel de Sully,** 62, rue St-Antoine (M. St-Paul), is a restful enclave best appreciated on summer afternoons. The small inner courtyard offers the fatigued tourist several stone benches and an elegant formal garden. If you're lucky, you'll come upon one of their frequent concerts—either pre-scheduled, often free chamber music, or the impromptu concerts of penniless students. The main building in the courtyard, adorned with allegorical statues of the four elements and the four seasons, was built in 1624 and acquired by the Duc de Sully, minister to Henri IV. Sully, often cuckolded by his young wife, would say when giving her money, *"voici tant pour la maison, tant pour vous, et tant pour vos amants"* (here's some for the house, some for you, and some for your lovers), asking only that she keep her paramours off the staircase.

The **Caisse Nationale des Monuments Historiques** (tel. 01 44 61 20 00), a government agency dedicated to preserving historic monuments, occupies a few rooms in the *hôtel.* At the information office (tel. 01 44 61 21 50), you can pick up free brochures (in French) about monuments and museums all over France, as well as maps of France (open Mon.-Fri. 9am-6pm, Sat. 10am-1:15pm and 2-5pm). The Hôtel de Sully also holds a small gallery that displays temporary photography exhibits. Be sure to look up at the ornate ceiling in the gift shop. (Admission 25F; students, groups of 6 or more, under 25, or over 60 15F. Open Tues.-Sun. 10am-6:30pm.) If you tire of relaxation, culture, and people-watching, cross through the gardens to the **rue St-Antoine,** the major thoroughfare of the 4ème arrondissement. Along this boulevard, you'll find cafés, fruit and vegetable stands, *fromageries,* and boutiques, together with the more prosaic Monoprix supermarket.

On your right, the **Eglise St-Paul-St-Louis,** 99, rue St-Antoine (M. St-Paul), one of the earliest examples of the Jesuit style in Paris, dates from 1627, when Louis XIII placed its first stone. Its large dome—one of the trademarks of Jesuit architecture—is visible from afar, but hidden at close range by ornamentation on the façade. The royal origin of the church is recalled by paintings inside the dome of four great French kings: Clovis, Charlemagne, Robert the Pious, and St. Louis. The regal ties to the church were most hearteningly solidified when the embalmed hearts of Louis XIII and Louis XIV, kept in vermeil boxes carried by silver angels, were hung from the arches on each side of the choir. Small wonder that the Revolutionary Convention sacked the church with particular vehemence, destroying the dynastic relics. The church, where the Jesuit Bossuet preached, retains a rich Baroque interior, complete with three 17th-century paintings representing the life of St. Louis. There used to be four, but one was lost and replaced by Eugène Delacroix's equally dramatic *Christ in the Garden of Olives* (1826). The two large holy water vessels were a gift from Victor Hugo. (Open Mon.-Sat. 7:30am-7:30pm, Sun. 9am-8pm. Free guided visit at 3pm, every 2nd Sun. of the month. Masses Sat. 6pm, Sun. 10, 11:15am, and 7pm; July and Aug. no 7pm mass; Aug. no 10am mass.)

Leaving the church, follow rue St-Antoine on your right, turn right on rue St-Paul, and then right on rue Charlemagne. Facing no. 14, you can still see part of Philippe-Auguste's wall. This is the longest and best-preserved fragment left from the defensive ramparts he built before departing for the Crusades. Farther down, no. 20 is a medieval building on which the area's old street names are inscribed.

Turning right on rue du Figuier, you come to the **Hôtel de Sens,** 1, rue du Figuier (M. Pont Marie), one of the city's three surviving examples of medieval residential architecture. (The others are the Hôtel de Cluny in the *quartier latin* and Jacques Coeur's House at 40, rue des Archives.) Built in 1474 for Tristan de Salazar, the archbishop of Sens, its military features reflect both Salazar's life as a soldier and the violence of the day. The turrets on rue du Figuier and rue de l'Hôtel de Ville were designed to survey the streets outside, while the square tower at the far left corner of the courtyard served as a dungeon. An enormous Gothic arch for the entrance—complete with chutes for pouring boiling water on invaders—and steep chimneys and spires contribute to the mansion's intimidating air.

The former residence of romantic heroine Queen Margot, Henri IV's first wife, Hôtel de Sens has witnessed some of Paris' most daring romantic escapades. One Sunday in 1606, the 55-year-old "Queen Venus" drove up to the door of her home, in front of which her two current lovers were arguing. One of them strode to open the lady's carriage door, and the other shot him dead. Unfazed, the queen demanded the execution of the other, which she watched from a window the next day. The same tempestuous queen had a fig tree that encumbered her carriage immediately removed from the street; this episode gave rue du Figuier its name. The *hôtel* now houses the **Bibliothèque Forney** (tel. 01 42 78 14 60), a library that focuses on fine, decorative, and graphic arts, and artisanship. The collection includes 200,000 books, 15,000 posters, and 1,000,000 postcards. Anyone with an ID can consult works in the library, but to check out books you must live in the Paris area. There are also temporary exhibits (admission 20F, students under 28 and those over 60 10F, under 12 free). (Library and exhibits open Tues.-Sat. 1:30-8:30pm, library also open Sat. 10am-1:30pm; the Caisse Nationale des Monuments Historiques gives irregular tours of the building; call 01 44 61 21 69 for info.)

Until the 13th century, Paris' Jewish community was concentrated in front of Notre Dame; however, when Philippe-Auguste expelled the Jewish population from the city limits, it moved to the Marais, just outside the walls. Since then, this quarter has been the Jewish center of Paris, with the area around rue des Rosiers and rue des Ecouffes still forming the spine of the Jewish community—as one oratory (18, rue des Ecouffes), two synagogues (at 25, rue des Rosiers, and at 10, rue Pavée; the latter was designed by Hector Guimard in 1913), and dozens of kosher restaurants and delis attest. Down towards the river, at 17, rue Geoffroy de l'Asnier, the solemn 1956 **Mémorial du Martyr Juif Inconnu** (Memorial to the Unknown Jewish Martyr; M. St-Paul), commemorates European Jews who died at the hands of the Nazis and their French collaborators. Due to a 1980 terrorist attack, the center now asks that visitors pass through a metal detector. The crypt downstairs contains ashes brought back from concentration camps and from the Warsaw ghetto. Comment books at the base of the stairwell provide a moving record of reflections and reactions by survivors, partisans, and many others who have visited (open Sun.-Thurs. 10am-1pm and 2-6pm, Fri. 10am-1pm and 2-5pm; 15F). Upstairs, the **Centre de Documentation Juive Contemporaine** (Jewish Contemporary Documentation Center; tel. 01 42 72 44 72) has frequent temporary exhibits (admission to the memorial gives access to the exhibits). The center also holds a library with more than 600,000 documents relating to the Nazi era (open Mon.-Thurs. 2-6pm; library admission 30F per day, or join for a longer period and lower daily fee).

Two streets and centuries away at 68, rue François-Miron, stands the **Hôtel de Beauvais,** built in 1655 for Pierre de Beauvais and his wife Catherine Bellier. The fortune used to build the *hôtel* was given to Catherine, Anne d'Autriche's chambermaid, because of Catherine's tryst with Anne's son, 15-year-old Louis XIV. As the story goes, Anne was overjoyed to learn that her son would please his future wife more than Anne's impotent husband Louis XIII had pleased her. From the balcony of the hôtel, Anne d'Autriche and Cardinal Mazarin watched the entry of Louis XIV and his lucky bride, Marie-Thérèse, into Paris. A century later, as a guest of the Bavarian ambassador, Mozart played his first piano recital here. The decline of the hotel began after the Revolution, when its new owner tried to increase his profit from apartment rentals by adding another floor to the building. Now the place appears cheapened and worn down, with crude iron banisters and visible lines of caulking.

At the end of rue François-Miron, on your left, you'll find the **Eglise St-Gervais-St-Protais,** one of the city's most beautiful examples of 16th- and 17th-century ecclesiastical architecture. The exterior is Neoclassical; the soaring interior, with its intricate vaulting and stained glass, is flamboyant Gothic. Look for the Baroque wooden Christ by Préault, the less dramatic 16th-century Flemish Passion painted on wood, the beautiful 16th-century stained glass in the choir, and the strange Boschian misericords in the 16th-century choir stalls of the nave. François Couperin (1688-1733), together with eight other members of his family (spanning two hundred years of the church's history), was the main organist here; the organ on which they played is the same used in services today. St-Gervais-St-Protais is part of a working monastery, and if you come at the right time (check posted services), you will hear the nave filled with Gregorian chant and psalms.

At the other side of the *place* is the back of the **Hôtel de Ville** (M. Hôtel de Ville), Paris' grandiose city hall. Walk around to the front, where the hôtel dominates a large square with refreshing fountains and Victorian-style lampposts. The present edifice is a 19th-century creation little more than a century old. It replaced the medieval structure built originally as a meeting hall for the *hause,* the cartel which controlled traffic on the Seine. In 1533, under King François I, the old building was destroyed; construction of a more spacious version, meant to house Paris' municipal government, began on the same spot. The newer building, designed by Boccadoro, recalled the Renaissance style of the châteaux along the Loire.

On May 24, 1871, *communards* doused the building with petrol and set it afire. Lasting a full eight days, the blaze spared nothing but the frame. The Third Republic built a virtually identical structure on the ruins, with only a few incongruous changes. The republican Gambetta regime integrated statues of its own heroes into the façade. Michelet, rhapsodic historian of the Revolution, flanks the right side of the building; and Eugène Sue, author of *Les Mystères de Paris,* a novel about the city's underbelly, can be seen forever surveying the rue de Rivoli which he made (in)famous. In addition to updating the façade's cast of *Grands Hommes,* the Third Republic added a group of bronze knights to the roof. All dressed up and nowhere to go, the knights share much with the officials who commissioned them.

The Third Republic spared not a *centime* for the finest of crystal chandeliers, and gilded every possible interior surface, even creating a Hall of Mirrors in conscious emulation of the one at Versailles. In choosing painters, the officials in charge were suspicious of the new-fangled Impressionists; when Manet, Monet, Renoir, and Cézanne offered their services, they were all turned down in favor of ponderous, didactic artists. Bare-breasted women act out *Philosophy* (in the Salon des Lettres), *The Triumph of Art* (in the Salon des Arts), and *Light Guiding the Sciences in the Heavens* (in the Salon des Sciences). Some of the paintings aren't too shabby, and the ostentatious decoration can be quite impressive. Rodin's bronze bust of the Republic (in the Salon Laurens) is one work of note.

Foreign heads of state are welcomed with receptions at the **Hôtel de Ville,** but it is closed to the public, except for groups that make appointments for guided visits one to two months in advance. However, the Information Office holds temporary exhibits in its lobby (open Mon.-Sat. 9am-6pm).

In front of the Hôtel de Ville, the **pl. Hôtel de Ville** entered the language under its former name, the pl. de Grève. The old name was derived from the Right Bank's medieval topography. A marshy embankment *(grève)* of the Seine, the *place* served as a meeting ground for angry workers throughout the Middle Ages, giving France the extremely useful phrase *en grève* (on strike). In the late 18th and early 19th centuries, the pl. de Grève became a theater of political conflagration and metamorphosis. The first Paris Commune declared itself into existence there in 1789; later the July Monarchy and Second Republic followed suit. The only hordes demanding bread today are the flocks of plump, swaggering pigeons, but strikes still gather here with some regularity. You'll know if one is expected: busloads of gun-toting riot police will dramatically block off the entire *place.*

Two blocks west of this area, the **Tour St-Jacques** (between 39 and 41, rue de Rivoli) stands alone in the center of its own park. This flamboyant Gothic tower is the only remnant of the 16th-century Eglise St-Jacques-la-Boucherie which stood here until 1802. The 52m tower has a meteorological station at its top, continuing a long scientific tradition that began with Pascal's experiments on the weight of air performed here in 1648; the statue of Pascal at the base of the tower commemorates this event. The tower marks the grand intersection of the rue de Rivoli and the bd. Sébastopol, Haussmann's treasured *grande croisée* (great crossing). Here was the intersection of the builder's new east-west and north-south axes for the city, only meters from where the earliest Roman roads crossed two thousand years ago.

In the northwest corner of the fourth, the **Centre Pompidou** (also referred to as the **Beaubourg**) looms like an oversized engine abandoned next to the Seine. An anti-Hôtel de Ville, the Beaubourg's inside-out architecture has looked down on the surrounding buildings of the *quartier* since 1977: escalators, elevator shafts, and color-coded pipes (blue conducts air; green, water; red, electricity) pop out along the sides of the Centre. The center sits on the former site of a slum whose high rate of tuberculosis earned it the classification of an *îlot insalubre* (unhealthy block) and demolition in the 1930s. The lot remained vacant for many years, and two decades after the building's construction, some Parisians wish it remained so. Nonetheless, more people visit the Centre each year than step inside the Louvre (see "Centre Pompidou," p. 232).

In afternoon and early evening, the vast cobblestone *place* in front of the center gathers a mixture of caricature artists, street musicians, monologuists, mimes, grunge rebels, and curious passersby. Pickpockets also frequent this area. In this chaotic scene, talent does not seem to matter; the police are quite tolerant just as long as you don't make *too* much noise. Consult the big numerical display that counts the seconds until the year 2000; if you want a precise record of your visit, buy a postcard which will tell you the date and time to the millisecond (30F). Late at night when the tourists have left, the square can get dangerous due to the plethora of drunks who hang around and pick fights.

The **Fontaine Stravinsky,** part of the museum complex, complements the Beaubourg's crowd of minstrels and eccentrics with its cartoon-like kinetic sculptures. Its dancing g-clef, spinning bowlers, and multi-colored elephants and birds spit water on passing crowds. A collaborative effort between Jean Tinguely and Niki St-Phalle, the work does justice to the memory of Igor Stravinsky, whose dissonant music shocked and dismayed audiences nearly a century ago (see "Théâtre des Champs-Elysées," p. 257). Tinguely created the iron works, St-Phalle the animals.

Next to the fountain, the **Eglise St-Merri** conceals some impressive Renaissance painted-glass windows behind its flamboyant Gothic exterior. Ravaged during the Revolution, this church was known as the "Temple of Commerce" from 1796-1801, a sly reference to the flesh trade that has dominated this area since the 14th century. Free concerts are held here on weekends (Sat. 9pm, Sun. 4pm, except Aug.). After the concert on the first and third Sunday of each month, there is a guided tour of the church (in French). Another clue to the widespread trade in this arrondissement can be found in the name of the rue du Petit Musc, which originated from *"Pute y muse"* (the prostitute idles here). One street away, on the third floor of 17, rue Beautreillis, pop culture icon Jim Morrison died, allegedly of a heart attack, while in his bathtub. His grave can be found at Père Lachaise (see "Sights—20^éme^," p. 212).

Fifth Arrondissement: The Quartier Latin

Though the Romans built some of the 5ème's ancient streets, the Latin in the *quartier's* name refers to the language of scholarship and daily speech heard here until 1798. Home since the 13th century to the famed **Sorbonne,** the *quartier* has come to evoke bookish bohemians scribbling works-in-progress in attic apartments or corner cafés. Nonetheless, throughout most of the 19th century it was something of a slum, and students themselves spent as much time as possible on the more glamorous Right Bank.

1968 was one of the most exciting years in recent French history, a year when student dissent over outmoded educational and administrative practices within the French university system exploded. During the appropriately named *jours de mai* (May days), violent protests spread from the Nanterre University campus, the anarchist and socialist hotbed of the day, to the Sorbonne (see "Postwar Paris," p. 15, for more). Partly because of his inability to comprehend or subdue the riots, then-President de Gaulle resigned; also in response to the protests, the University of Paris was split into 13 autonomous campuses. With this decentralization, the *quartier latin* lost a good number of its youthful, scholarly, and impetuous inhabitants. In the 28 years since, a tourist invasion has caused many of the small bookstores and cafés that were once the *quartier's* hallmark either to expand or to go out of business. Nonetheless, students still leave their mark on the area: yes, the stores are big and impersonal, but they're big and impersonal *bookstores.* Smaller used book and record shops and repertory cinemas are located for the most part along rue des Écoles, though there are some intensely cheap record stores on bd. St-Michel, too.

Bounded by the Seine to the north, the Jardin des Plantes to the east, bd. St-Michel to the west, and the bd. de Port Royal and bd. St-Marcel to the south, the 5ème arrondissement still swarms with students from the University of Paris at the Sorbonne and from the *grandes écoles* (prestigious exam-entry schools such as the École Normale Supérieure). While artists and hipper intellectuals have migrated towards the Bastille, the *quartier latin* maintains an eternally youthful air, especially around the Panthéon. Intact medieval streets twist their way past cafés, restaurants, and neighborhood *pâtisseries* and *charcuteries.* The many dead-end streets petering out at walls testify to Haussmann's demolition of the hills that used to roll through the neighborhood. A few hills still remain; the tiny rue Rollin (M. Monge) drops down to rue Monge, a major thoroughfare.

The **boulevard St-Michel,** with its fashionable cafés, restaurants, bookstores, and movie theaters, is the pulsing center of tourist and, at certain hours of the day, student life in the *quartier.* **Place St-Michel,** at the northern tip of this *grand avenue,* excludes no one and attracts everyone—tourists, students, and drunken indigents. The majestic fountain dates from 1860, but includes a memorial to the liberation of France after World War II. (The *place* was the scene of student fighting against the Germans in August, 1944.) At the intersection of bd. St-Germain and bd. St-Michel at 6, pl. Paul-Painlevé, the **Hôtel de Cluny** (the city's second-oldest extant residential building) is now home to the **Musée de Cluny,** featuring one of the world's finest collections of medieval art, jewelry, architecture, and tapestry (see "Musée de Cluny," p. 235).

Farther south on bd. St-Michel, the **place de la Sorbonne** (M. Cluny-La Sorbonne, RER Luxembourg), a square lined with cafés, lounging students, and bookstores, is one of the many sites of student life in the *quartier latin.* At the eastern end of the square stands the Sorbonne, 45-7, rue des Écoles, which claims to be Europe's oldest university. (The other contenders are Oxford and Bologna.) Founded in 1253 by Robert de Sorbon as a dormitory for 17 theology students, the Sorbonne soon became the administrative base for the University of Paris. Its scholars were treated as nobility; they wore swords and were not subject to arrest while on campus. In 1469, Louis XI established France's first printing house here. One of the Sorbonne's many famous students was the 15th-century poet and criminal François Villon. Later, Roger Bacon haltingly developed the scientific method, and Pierre Lombard assembled an early encyclopedia here. As it grew in power and size, the Sorbonne often contradicted the authority of the French throne, and even sided with England over France during the Hundred Years War.

All the original buildings have been destroyed and rebuilt, the last time in 1885, with one exception: **Ste-Ursule de la Sorbonne** (the main building), commissioned in 1642 by Cardinal Richelieu. The cardinal, himself a *sorbonnard,* lies buried inside, his hat suspended above him by a few threads hanging from the ceiling. Legend has it that when Richelieu is freed from purgatory, the threads will snap and the hat will tumble down. The public is allowed only in the chapel, which occasionally hosts art exhibits (open Mon.-Fri. 9am-5pm). Behind the Sorbonne is the less exclusive **Collège de France,** an institution created by François I in 1530 to contest the university's supreme authority. The outstanding courses at the Collège, given over the years by such luminaries as Henri Bergson, Paul Valéry, and Milan Kundera, are free and open to all. Check the schedules that appear by the door in September. (Courses run Sept.-May. For more information, call 01 43 29 12 11.) Just south of the collège lies the **Lycée Louis-le-Grand,** where Molière, Robespierre, Victor Hugo, Baudelaire, and Pompidou spent part of their student years. Sartre taught there as well. If you're hooked on academic sight-seeing, the **École Normale Supérieur,** France's leading liberal arts college and longtime home to deconstructionist Jacques Derrida, is located southeast of the Sorbonne on rue d'Ulm.

The **Panthéon,** its proud dome visible from any point in the *quartier latin,* towers as the highest point on the Left Bank (tel. 01 40 51 75 81; M. Cardinal Lemoine). The monument began as a mere church among many on this hill, the Montagne Ste-Geneviève. It all started with the Romans, who used it for a temple to Mercury; later, Clovis built a shrine to the saints Peter and Paul on the same spot. The people of Paris, however, were faithful to their patron saint, Geneviève, whose prayers had deflected Atilla's hordes to Orléans; Parisians soon renamed the church and surrounding hill in her honor. (Oddly enough, the *Orléannais* prefer Jeanne d'Arc, as saints go.) After being destroyed by Norman invasions in the late 9th century, the church was rebuilt and remained basically untouched until 1754, when a new church was requisitioned by Louis XV. As a sign of his gratitude to Ste. Geneviève for helping him recover from a grave illness in 1744, the king commissioned the current enormous Neoclassical structure. Jacques-Germain Soufflot's design challenged the conventions of architecture of the period, launching a Greek revival in France. The church took 40 years to build and was completed on the eve of the Revolution.

The Revolution converted the church into a mausoleum of heroes, designed to rival the royal crypt at St-Denis. On April 4, 1791, the great parliamentarian Mirabeau was interred, only to have his ashes expelled the next year when his correspondence with Louis XVI was revealed. Voltaire's body was moved here, with great ceremony. Dubbed the Panthéon in this epoch, the building underwent minor alterations under the direction of Quatremere du Quincy, a renowned 18th-century design theorist. With nearly all its windows sealed to showcase light emanating from the dome, the building took on its current tomb-like aspect. Quincy also had a statue of Liberty mounted atop the dome to replace the cross. Over the next few centuries, the purpose of the Panthéon bounced between church and mausoleum, reflecting fluctuations in France's religio-political climate. In 1885, it became a national necropolis. Whoever France's next darling may be will enjoy immortality among an illustrious few: in the crypt you'll find Voltaire, Rousseau, Hugo, Zola, Jean Jaurès, Louis Braille, and Jean Moulin. At Hugo's interment here in 1885, two million mourners, and Chopin's *Marche funèbre,* followed the coffin to its resting place. In his *Souvenirs littéraires,* Léon Daudet recalled the scene: "A cold crypt, where glory is represented by an echo which the *gardien* will make you admire. A room full of the leftovers of republican and revolutionary immortality. It's freezing in there, even in the summer, and the symbolic torch held up by a hand from Rousseau's tomb has the air of a cruel joke, as if the author of the *Confessions* could not even light a cigarette for the author of *Les Misérables.*"

From the crypt, a twisting staircase winds upward to the roof and dome, where you can get an up-close view of garish Neoclassical frescoes proclaiming the glory and justice of France. While you can walk around the outside of the roof, the building is not high enough to offer a view of anything but nearby rooftops. The dome's interior is an extreme example of Neoclassical architecture, replete with grand Corinthian columns and expansive heights (admission 32F, students 21F). The dome will be closed until spring 1997, due to repairs.

While at the Panthéon, don't miss the fanciful **Église St-Etienne du Mont** next door. St-Étienne was built between 1492 and 1626; the resulting edifice is a mix of flamboyant Gothic and gingerbread castle. Delicate rose windows are outlined by broken Renaissance pediments, topped off by a clock tower that would better suit a parish church in the Alps. Move inside and feast your eyes on the huge 17th-century rood screen, used in the abbey churches of Western Europe to separate the chancel (occupied by monks) from the nave (where the congregation sat). On the right side of the nave are epitaphs for Pascal and Racine, both of whom are buried farther down at the opening of the choir. Also on your right is the sanctuary of Ste. Geneviève, a chapel and reliquary of gilt copper built in the 19th century. Ste. Geneviève's actual remains were burnt during the Revolution; the reliquary holds a piece of her original tombstone together with a few bones and other scraps. A blank book placed in front allows you to render homage to these fragments, as well as to ask for a few favors. You may want to peer at the 16th- and 17th-century stained glass, particularly that found in the cloister (accessible through the back of the choir).

From St-Etienne du Mont, head south on rue Descartes, past the Lycée Henri IV (one of the most prestigious high schools in the country), to the picturesque **place de la Contrescarpe.** The geographical center of the 5ème, it has the feel of a tiny medieval village. The streets leading to it are even older; many, like rue Mouffetard, served as ancient Roman causeways. The festive atmosphere and cheap rent drew Hemingway here during his first years in Paris. He rented a studio at 39, rue Descartes and

SIGHTS

lived at 74, rue du Cardinal Lemoine with his wife, Hadley. To the left of no. 74's unassuming brown door once resided the Bal du Printemps, a dance hall that Hemingway used as a raucous setting for parts of *A Moveable Feast* and *The Sun Also Rises.* At no. 67, Pascal died in 1662. John Dos Passos and Samuel Beckett were also former residents. The days of budget living are gone now, though; residents watch as the renovated buildings are snapped up by French yuppies.

If you get hungry, head down rue Mouffetard towards **boulevard de Port-Royal.** Here you'll find one of the liveliest street markets in Paris (daily 9am-1pm and 4-7pm). Wade through tables piled high with lingerie, shoes, and random housewares to reach the *charcuteries, fromageries,* and fruits and vegetables that taste even better than they look. Also on rue Mouffetard, notice the old, picturesque houses; in 1938, 3500 gold coins were discovered at no. 53, presumably hidden more than 150 years earlier by the Royal Counselor to Louis XV.

The remains of the **Arènes de Lutèce** are further east from the Panthéon, at the intersection of rue de Navarre and rue des Arènes. A 100 by 130m oval Roman amphitheater, the Arènes was built by the Romans to accommodate 15,000 spectators (far surpassing the needs of the still-tiny colony of Lutetia). The ruins were unearthed during construction of rue Monge and were restored in the 1910s; all the seats are reconstructions. Benches that line the winding paths above the arena provide serene settings for a picnic supper.

However circuitous the streets, lively the outdoor markets, or atmospheric the cafés, much of the 5*ème* is a neighborhood-turned-tourist-attraction. Not so, however, for the **Jardin des Plantes,** where actual Parisians go for trysts or family outings (tel. 01 40 79 30 00 for information concerning the entire complex; M. Jussieu; main entrance at pl. Valhubert, off quai St-Bernard). The park, 45,000 square meters in all, was opened in 1640 by Guy de la Brosse, personal doctor to Louis XIII. Originally intended for the sole purpose of growing medicinal plants to promote His Majesty's health, it became a general garden for botanical research, beloved by that avid naturalist Thomas Jefferson, among others. The garden has since been converted into a group of museums, including a three-part natural history museum, an insect gallery across the street, a hedge maze, an arboretum, greenhouses, and a full-fledged zoo (see below). Check out the size of the bugs at the insect gallery, then head over to admire 5cm-long diamonds and meter-high quartz formations. While attractions such as the arboretum—a series of rare trees labeled with metal nameplates, scattered throughout the park—and the hedge maze, located at the northeastern end of the park, are free, all of the museums have separate tickets and hours (see "Museums," p. 244 and p. 245). Ask at the entrance gate for a free park map. The Jardin des Plantes also has two botanical theme parks, the **Jardin Alpin** and **Serres Tropicales;** the first is full of rare flowers and plants from the Alpine domain and the second full of those from tropical and desert regions (Jardin Alpin open Mon.-Fri. 8-11 am and 1:30-5pm, free. Serres Tropicales temporarily closed for repairs, call for more info. Usually open Wed.-Mon. 1-5:30pm, admission 15F, students 10F). A recent addition to the complex is the **Grande Galerie de l'Evolution,** which houses temporary exhibits, a cultural center, and a conference hall (open weekdays 10am-5pm, weekends 10am-6pm, closed Tues; admission 30F, students 20F).

The **Ménagerie,** also found in the Jardin des Plantes, is a dejected-seeming zoo with an unhappy past. During the siege of Paris in 1871, the zoo was raided for meat; elephant became a great delicacy for starving Parisians, though no one dared to try slaughtering the lions. The cages here are painfully small, the weather damp, and the countenances of the animals downtrodden. The great German poet Rainer Maria Rilke wrote a series of poems describing the animals lodged here. Of the panther he wrote: "His vision, from the constantly passing bars,/ has grown so weary that it cannot hold/ anything else. It seems to him there are/ a thousand bars; and behind the bars, no world." Meanwhile, in the Reptile House, pythons, cobras, rattlesnakes, and boa constrictors sleep peacefully in their tree displays. (Open April-Sept. 9am-12:30pm and 2-6pm; Oct.-March 9am-12:30pm and 2-5pm; admission 30F, students and ages 4-16 20F.)

Behind the Jardin des Plantes stands the **Mosquée de Paris,** a Muslim place of worship constructed in 1922 by French architects to honor the role played by the countries of North Africa in World War I. Admire the graceful ivory and aqua tower; enter the sculpted archways to tour the courtyard with its soothing fountain, carved wooden doors, and ornate detailing. One may even indulge in a steambath in the *hammam* (65F, bring your own towel and swimsuit) and enjoy a cup of mint tea (10F) in the *salon de repos* or the peaceful outdoor courtyard at 39, rue Geoffroy St-Hilaire (tel. 01 43 31 18 14; M. Jussieu; mosque open Sat.-Thurs. 10am-noon and 2-6pm. Guided tour 15F, students 10F. *Hammam* open to men Tues. 2-9pm, Sun. 10am-9pm. Open to women Mon., Wed., Sat. 10am-9pm.)

Walking west along the Seine back toward pl. St-Michel, you can stop to rest in the beautiful **Jardin des Sculptures en Plein Air,** quai St-Bernard, a lovely collection of modern sculpture on a long stretch of green along the Seine, with works by such artists as Zadkine, Brancusi, and Scheffer. Although it can be a great place to read and sunbathe by day, this area should be avoided at night. Across the street and not to be missed is the **Institut du Monde Arabe** (see "Museums," p. 246). Just next door to the institute, **La Tour d'Argent,** 15, quai de la Tournelle (M. Maubert), is one of Paris' most prestigious and most expensive restaurants.

Farther west along the Seine, **square René Viviani** (M. St-Michel) sequesters the oldest tree in Paris (a false acacia dating from 1693), one of the best views of Notre-Dame, and the **Église St-Julien-le-Pauvre.** The church, all spikes and dirty stone, was completed in 1165 and thus predates Notre-Dame, making it officially the oldest church in Paris. (Some parts of St-Germain-des-Prés are older, but were constructed back when St-Germain was a suburb of Paris.) The church now hosts musical concerts (check gates for upcoming events). Two more Paris records are set right around the corner: the shortest and most narrow street in Paris is the rue du Chat-qui-pêche (the fishing cat), just off of rue de la Huchette.

Sixth Arrondissement: St-Germain-des-Prés

Less frenzied and more sophisticated than its neighbors, the sixth arrondissement combines the youthful vibrancy of the *quartier latin* to the east with the fashionable cafés, restaurants, and movie theaters of Montparnasse to the south. This area has long been the focus of literary and artistic Paris and remains less ravaged by tourists than other, more monumental quarters. Watch well-dressed Parisians watch one another at one of the famous cafés on the bd. St-Germain, former haunts of Picasso, Sartre, de Beauvoir, Camus, Prévert, Apollinaire, and Hemingway.

"There is nothing more charming, which invites one more enticingly to idleness, reverie, and young love, than a soft spring morning or a beautiful summer dusk at the **Jardin du Luxembourg,"** wrote Léon Daudet in 1928 (RER: Luxembourg). Parisians are to be seen here sunbathing, writing, romancing, strolling, or just gazing at the beautiful rose gardens and into the central pool. A mammoth task force of gardeners tends to this most beloved of Parisian gardens; each spring they plant or transplant 350,000 flowers and move the 150 palm and orange trees out of winter storage. Thanks to the 19th-century Parisians who defended this park against Haussmann's intentions to carve a street through it, you can still sail a toy boat, ride a pony, attend the *grand guignol* (a puppet show—see "Guignols," p. 255), or play *boules* with a group of elderly men.

The **Palais du Luxembourg,** located within the park, was built in 1615 at Marie de Médicis's behest. Homesick for her native Tuscany, she did her best to recreate it in central Paris; her builders finished the resulting Italianate palace in a mere five years, giving it a symmetry and uniformity of design rare among Parisian buildings. Marie set up housekeeping in the palace in 1625, but her feud with the powerful Cardinal Richelieu made her time there brief. Her son, Louis XIII, promised her that he would dismiss the cardinal, but revoked his promise the following day. Richelieu thought ill of the Queen's slights. In 1630, he took his revenge, banishing Marie to Cologne, where she died penniless. The palace would later house various members of the royal family and of the high nobility, including the Duchesse de Montpensier (known as La Grande Mademoiselle because of her girth). The palace served as a prison during the Terror, then as a prison for its Revolutionary perpetrators. Jacobin artist Jacques-Louis David used his time confined there to paint his haunting self-portrait, now displayed in the Louvre.

Almost everyone important involved with either Empire passed through the palace at some point. Future Empress Joséphine was imprisoned in the palace together with her republican husband, Beauharnais; she returned five years later to take up official residence there with her second husband, the new Consul Bonaparte. Under the Restoration and July Monarchy, the Chamber of Peers met there to judge the trials of traitors, including those of Maréchal Ney and the young Louis-Napoleon Bonaparte. One of Napoleon's marshals, Ney rallied support for the ex-emperor in his unsuccessful attempt to escape Elba and return to power (see below). The young Louis-Napoleon led several abortive rebellions against the July Monarchy, for which he was sentenced to life imprisonment. Engineering his escape, he slipped past jailers disguised as a mason and fled abroad, only to return to France years later and become Napoleon III.

In 1852 the palace first served its current function as the meeting place for the *sénat,* the upper house of the French parliament. Despite (or perhaps because of) its large and increasing membership, the *sénat* is a fairly ineffectual body that may be overruled by the Parliament. The president of the *sénat* lives in **Petit Luxembourg,** originally a conciliatory gift from Marie de Médicis to her nemesis, the Cardinal Richelieu. The **Musée du Luxembourg** (tel. 01 42 34 25 95), next to the palace on rue de Vaugirard, often shows free exhibitions of contemporary art.

The main entrance to the garden is from bd. St-Michel through lovely gold-leaved and wrought-iron gates. Bring a book and relax in one of the folding chairs in front of the palace, or saunter through the park's convolution of paths, past statues of the queens of France and through to one of the garden's secluded glens, each with monuments to poets and heroes of French history. Never expect to be alone, however. The Jardin du Luxembourg is one of Paris' favorite parks, which means that it is constantly packed with people. You may steal a moment's peace at the **Fontaine Médicis,** a tranquil spot in the northeast corner at the end of a long alleyway and reflecting pool. Tall shade trees line the alley, giving the spot the feel of an enchanted bower. A row of chairs along the reflecting pool provides a traditional spot for daydreaming. Unfortunately, the fountain tends to run dry in summer.

South of the park stretch its elegant, linear annexes, the Jardin R. Cavelier-de-la-Salle and the Jardin Marco Polo, both forming the northern half of the **avenue de l'Observatoire.** The elaborate **Fontaine de l'Observatoire** (1875) marks the halfway point between the Observatory and the Jardin du Luxembourg; its rearing horses provide a fittingly sumptuous perspective on the *grand avenue* that stretches at either side. At the extreme southeastern corner of the 6ème proudly stands Rude's statue of Maréchal Ney, whom Napoleon deemed "le plus brave des braves." After a lifetime as a soldier, the courageous marshal gave his last command to the firing squad assembled before him; he asked that they punish his treason: "Comrades, fire on me, and aim well."

At the nearby **Closerie des Lilas** café, such notables as Baudelaire, Verlaine, Breton, Picasso, and Hemingway listened to poetry and discussed their latest works (see "Classic Cafés," p. 134). Hemingway described it as "one of the best cafés in Paris. It was warm inside in the winter and in the spring and fall it was fine outside." Other expatriate watering holes extend farther down the bd. Montparnasse: Le Séléct at no. 99, to which Jake Barnes and Brett Ashley taxied in *The Sun Also Rises,* and La Coupole at no. 102-104. French artists sought refuge in this neighborhood as well. Picasso, along with Matisse, found encouragement and financial support at 27, rue de Fleurus, off bd. Raspail west of the *jardin,* where Gertrude Stein and her brother Leo welcomed the century's greatest artists. Curving down from bd. Raspail towards

SIGHTS

Montparnasse is rue Notre-Dame-des-Champs. American artist James MacNeill Whistler had a studio at no. 86, and Ezra Pound lived in a rear garden apartment at no. 70.

At the end of rue Notre-Dame-des-Champs and running up one edge of the Jardin du Luxembourg, the **boulevard Saint-Michel**—central axis of the *quartier latin*—marks the eastern boundary of the 6ème. For another view of the Panthéon (especially beautiful at night), walk up bd. St-Michel to pl. Edmond-Rostand, where a small fountain marks the end of the rue Soufflot (see "Sights—5ème," p. 161, for more about the Panthéon).

Follow the arcades of rue de Médicis around the edge of the Jardin du Luxembourg to Paris' oldest and largest theater—the **Théâtre Odéon** (M. Odéon). Completed in 1782, the Odéon was built for the **Comédie Française,** which, though it had once been Paris' only officially recognized actors' troupe, did not have a theater of its own. Beaumarchais' *Marriage of Figaro,* nearly banned by Louis XVI for its attacks upon the nobility, premiered here in 1784 before delighted aristocratic audiences. Prior to the Revolution, the Odéon became a frequent stage for republican posturing. In 1789 the actor Talma staged a performance of Voltaire's *Brutus* in which he imitated the pose of the hero in David's painting of the same scene (see "Musée du Louvre," p. 224), an act illustrating his liberal sympathies. As the Revolution approached, the Comédie-Française splintered over the issue of political loyalties. Republican members followed Talma to the Right Bank, settling into the company's current location near the Louvre (see "Sights—1er," p. 146). Those actors who remained behind were jailed under the Terror, causing the theater to close abruptly. The Odéon went on to earn the title of *théâtre maudit* (cursed theater) after a chain of failures left it nearly bankrupt. Destroyed twice by fire, its present Greco-Roman incarnation dates from an 1818 renovation overseen by the painter David. The Odéon's fortunes changed after World War II, when it became a venue for contemporary, experimental theater. Nobody missed the irony when rioting students staged their own real-life, experimental theater there on May 17, 1968, seizing the building and destroying much of its interior before police quelled the rebellion. The Odéon now enjoys middle-aged languor living on its state-supported pension. Around the corner at 12, rue de l'Odéon, is the original site of Sylvia Beach's bookstore, Shakespeare and Co., where James Joyce's *Ulysses* was first published. Nearby, off rue de Vaugirard at 5, rue de Tournon, resided Marie Lenormand, the *voyante* (fortune-teller) to Napoleon.

Two blocks west of the theater, the 17th-century **Église St-Sulpice** (M. St-Sulpice) is an under-admired marvel. Construction of the elegant façade, designed by Servadoni, began in 1733. Its Greco-Roman simplicity of line was found unbecoming in a Jesuit church, and the current building's obvious asymmetry is a consequence of failed attempts to please the priests: in 1749, the architect Maclaurin was asked to redesign the towers. In 1777, a third architect, Chalgrin, was asked to revamp them; he replaced the north tower but never completed its southern counterpart. It remains unfinished. The church contains Delacroix frescoes in the first chapel on the right, a stunning *Virgin and Child* by Jean-Baptiste Pigalle in one of the rear chapels, and an enormous Chalgrin organ, among the world's largest and most famous, with 6588 pipes. In the transept of the church, an inlaid copper band runs along the floor from north to south, crossing from a plaque in the south arm to an obelisk in the north arm. A ray of sunshine passes through a hole in the upper window of the south transept during the winter solstice, striking marked points on the obelisk at exactly mid-day. A beam of sunlight falls on the copper plaque during the summer solstice and behind the communion table during the spring and autumn equinox. In this way, the church tells its priest exactly when to celebrate Easter mass (open daily 7:30am-7:30pm). From St-Sulpice, move north to the boulevard St-Germain. This area, jam-packed with cafés, restaurants, cinemas, and expensive boutiques, is always crowded, noisy, and exciting.

Begin exploring with a stroll through the **Cour du Commerce St-André,** a historic pedestrian passageway one street west of rue de l'Ancienne Comédie off bd. St-Germain (look for the name of the *cour* arching over the entryway). As you pass under the arch, to your immediate right is a turn-of-the-century bistro, the **Relais Odéon.** Its stylishly painted exterior, decked with floral mosaics and an old-fashioned hanging sign, is a well-maintained period piece from the Belle Époque. The proprietor of the Odéon swears that during the Revolution, Jacobins placed a guillotine on the spot now occupied by his restaurant's terrace and killed some sheep there to test the sharpness of its blade. Others claim that the first guillotine was designed at nearby atelier no. 9 by Doctor Guillotin, intended as a more humane way of killing sheep. Dismayed at the subsequent misuse of his contraption, Dr. Guillotin is said to have ask the Assemblée to change its name. The Assemblée refused in deference to the popular songs of the day; "guillotine" rhymed too well with "machine" to merit the change. In fact, the guillotine was developed as a less painful alternative to death-by-hanging. Already present in other countries, it became associated with Dr. Guillotin only because he advocated its use in the interests of a more humane form of capital punishment.

Farther down this passageway, on the top floor of the building on your left, was the site of the Revolutionary-era clandestine press that published Marat's *L'Ami du Peuple.* Marat himself was assassinated by Charlotte Corday in the bathtub of his home, which once stood where the courtyard meets the rue de l'Ancienne Comédie. The poet Baudelaire was born on another of the small streets off the place St-André-des-Arts, at 15, rue Hautefeuille.

Like bd. Montparnasse, bd. St-Germain has long been a gathering place for literary and artistic notables. **Les Deux Magots,** 6, pl. St-Germain-des-Prés, is named after two porcelain figures that adorned a store that sold Chinese silk and imports at this spot in the 1800s. It was converted into a café in 1875 and by 1885 had become a favorite hangout of Verlaine, Rimbaud, and Mallarmé. Forty years later, it attracted Surrealists Breton, Desnos, and Artaud. Picasso and St-Exupéry (who wrote *The Little Prince*) were also regular patrons. The **Café de Flore,** 172, bd. St-Germain, is two buildings down and just as celebrated. Established in 1890, this café was made famous in the 1940s and 50s by Sartre, Camus, and Jacques Prévert (see "Classic Cafés," p. 134). Across from these two sits the **Brasserie Lipp,** a former haunt of the famous and well-dressed in search of a beer and *choucroute garnie.*

SIGHTS

The nearby **Eglise St-Germain-des-Prés** (M. St-Germain-des-Prés) presides benevolently over all this name-dropping. King Childebert I commissioned the first church on this site to hold relics he had looted from the Holy Land. Completed in 558, it was consecrated by St-Germain, Bishop of Paris, on the very day of King Childebert's death, and not a moment too soon: the king had to be buried inside the church's walls. Sacked by the Normans and rebuilt three times, St-Germain-des-Prés remained for years a heavily fortified abbey outside of Paris. Parts of the modern-day church date from 1163, making it officially the oldest standing church in what is now Paris. The current building is a portmanteau of architectural styles, owing to renovations that spanned centuries. The resulting structure combines Romanesque, Gothic, and Baroque features.

St-Germain-des-Prés got a jump on the Revolutionary desanctification trend. Made a state prison as early as 1674, it was seized by the people on June 30, 1789, providing them with a dress rehearsal for the storming of the Bastille. The church then did a brief stint as a saltpeter mill, which helped to further erode the already deteriorating structure. In 1794, 15 tons of gunpowder that had been stored in the abbey exploded; the ensuing fire devastated the church's collection of artwork and treasures, including much of its renowned monastic library. Baron Haussmann destroyed the last remains of the deteriorating abbey walls and gates when he extended the rue de Rennes to the front of the church and created the **place St-Germain-des-Prés.** Yet the church has maintained an air of sanctity throughout and wears its battle scars well. The magnificent interior, painted in shades of terra cotta and deep green with gold, was restored in the 19th century. Astute wanderers can pick out a millennium's worth of clashing architectural detail: the Romanesque capitals atop some of the pillars, the hidden stonework in the side chapels, the medieval shrines, the 17th-century vaulting. In the second chapel on the right inside the church you'll find a stone marking the interred heart of Descartes and an altar dedicated to the victims of the September 1793 massacre, in which *sans-culottes* slaughtered 186 Parisians in the courtyard. Pick up one of the free maps of the church with information in English on St-Germain's history and its artifacts. (Information office open Mon. 2:30-6:45pm, Tues.-Sat. 10:30am-noon and 2:30-6:45pm.) Come here for one of their frequent concerts. As in most medieval churches, built to accommodate an age without microphones, the acoustics are wonderful. (See "Classical Music, Opera, and Dance," p. 256, for more information. Church open daily 9am-7:30pm.)

Moving north from bd. St-Germain towards the Seine, you'll come upon some of the most tangled streets in central Paris. Haussmann retired before he could figure out a way to extend the rue de Rennes across the Seine to meet up with the rue de Louvre. Subsequent urban designers puzzled over this impassable quarter, seeking a plan to improve local traffic circulation. Before they could destroy the old streets, a preservationist aesthetic kicked in and, as a result, the neighborhood has been left as a largely unreconstructed maze. Don't even try to figure it out; instead, lose yourself in this *quartier* and amble down the rue de Seine, rue Mazarine, rue Bonaparte, and rue Dauphine, past art galleries of every stripe, displaying everything from modern multimedia works to classic oil paintings. Specialty stores carry eclectic decorative arts, elegant home furnishings, and collections of books of every ilk, from parchment manuscripts to sexploitation comic books.

To see what local art students are up to, walk around the **Ecole Nationale Supérieure des Beaux Arts (ENSBA),** 14, rue Bonaparte (tel. 01 47 03 50 00; M. St-Germain-des-Prés), at quai Malaquais. France's most acclaimed art school, the *école* was founded by Napoleon in 1811 and soon became *the* stronghold of French academic painting and sculpture. The current building for ENSBA was finished in 1838 in a gracious style much like that of the nearby **Institut de France.**

Just one block to the east on the *quais,* the **Palais de l' Institut de France,** pl. de l'Institut (M. Pont-Neuf), broods over the Seine beneath its famous *coupole,* the black- and gold-topped dome. This one-time school (1688-1793) and prison (1793-1805) was designed by Le Vau to lodge the college established in Cardinal Mazarin's will. The glorious building has housed the Institut de France since 1806. Founded in 1795, the *institut* was intended to be a storehouse for the nation's knowledge and a meeting place for France's greatest scholars. During the Restoration, appointment to the *institut* was more dependent on one's political position than one's talent, but since 1830 the process has been slightly more meritocratic.

One of the *institut*'s branches is the prestigious **Académie Française,** which, since its founding by Richelieu in 1635, has assumed the tasks of compiling the official French dictionary and serving as guardian of the French language. Having already registered its disapproval of *le weekend, le parking,* and other "Franglais" nonsense, the Academy recently triumphed with the passing of a constitutional amendment affirming French as the country's official language. It is so difficult to become elected to this arcane society, limited to 40 members, that Molière, Balzac, and Proust never made it. In 1981 the first woman, novelist Marguerite Yourcenar, gained membership.

Next door, the **Hôtel des Monnaies,** once the mint for all French coins, still proudly displays its austere 17th-century façade to the heart of the Left Bank. Today it mints only honorary medals. You can still tour its foundry and its significant coin collection by entering the **Musée de la Monnaie de Paris**. The **Pont des Arts,** the footbridge across from the *institut,* is celebrated by poets and artists for its delicate ironwork, its beautiful views of the Seine, and its spiritual locus at the heart of France's most prestigious Academy of Arts and Letters. Built as a toll bridge in 1803, the *pont* was unique on two counts: it was the first bridge to be made of iron, and it was for pedestrians only. On the day it opened, 65,000 Parisians paid to walk across it; today, it is less crowded, absolutely free, and still lovely. Come here at dusk to watch the sun go down against the silhouette of Paris's most famous monuments.

Seventh Arrondissement: The Faubourg St-Germain

Since the eighteenth century, the 7ème has stood its ground as the city's most elegant residential district. Home to the National Assembly, countless foreign embassies, the Invalides, the Musée d'Orsay, and the Eiffel Tower, this section of the Left Bank is a medley of France's diplomatic, architectural, and military achievements.

You might be the only one without a uniform, a gun, or a cellular phone on some streets in the 7ème, where policemen and soldiers guard the area's consulates and ministries. Once owned by Talleyrand, the **Hôtel Matignon,** at 57, rue de Varenne, is the official residence of the French Prime Minister. The nearby **Hôtel Biron,** at no. 77, was built by Gabriel in 1728. Under the state's aegis, it became an artists' *pension* in 1904. The sculptor Auguste Rodin rented a studio on its ground floor in 1908. When the Ministry of Education and Fine Arts evicted all tenants in 1910, Rodin offered to donate all of his works to make the *hôtel* an art museum—on the condition that he be permitted to spend his last years there. The Hôtel Biron now houses the **Musée Rodin** (see "Musée Rodin," p. 233).

A stroll up rue de Bellechasse toward the Seine leads to the elegant **Hôtel de Salm,** built in 1786 by the architect Rousseau for the Prince de Salm-Kyrbourg. The prince, who actually didn't have enough money to pay for the *hôtel,* later returned it to the architect; he continued to live there as a tenant until he was decapitated in 1794, six days after the fall of Robespierre. The state raffled the *hôtel* the following year to a wealthy wig maker named Lieuthraud who called himself Count Beauregard and lived the life of Riley until 1797, when he was jailed as a forger. The mansion was then purchased by the Swedish ambassador and his wife, *salonnière* Mme. de Staël. Benjamin Constant, political theorist and novelist, frequented her world-famous salon. Purchased by Napoleon in 1804, the *hôtel's* current name bears the mark of its most recent owner. Now called the **Palais de la Légion d'Honneur,** it houses the **Musée National de la Légion d'Honneur.** Though the museum's display of medals and other military honoraria may not spark the interest of many tourists, the 25F admission fee (15F for students and seniors) allows a look at the 18th- and 19th-century interiors. The *hôtel* was renovated in 1878 to repair damage done by arsonists during the Commune. Two rooms and the façades facing rue de Lille and the Seine are original (see "Museums," p. 245). Across the street stands the **Musée d'Orsay,** a former train station now known for its glass-and-steel elegance and immense collection of Impressionist works (see "Musée d'Orsay," p. 228).

At 75, rue de Lille, Montesquieu, Marivaux and others frequented the literary salon of Mme. de Tencin. Famous for her adventurous parties during the Regency, she once hosted a *"soirée d'Adam"* for which guests arrived dressed only in fig leaves. Continue down rue de Lille and turn right on rue du Bac. In the 18th century, this street marked the boundary between town and country. Now it is lined with specialty stores. Ponder dessert at **Christian Constant** (no. 26) or at the nearby **Le Nôtre** (no. 44), a ubiquitous but terrific *pâtisserie* chain.

The 17th-century **Eglise St-Thomas-d'Aquin** (tel. 01 42 22 59 74), off rue du Bac on rue de Gribeauval, was originally dedicated to St. Dominique, only to be reconsecrated by Revolutionaries as a Temple of Peace. Built in the form of a Greek cross, the former Jesuit church's dome and 18th-century paintings are worth a glance.

Just off to the left from rue du Bac at 55-57, rue de Grenelle, the **Fontaine des Quatres Saisons** (Fountain of Four Seasons) features a personified, seated version of the city of Paris near reclining figures of the Seine and the Marne. Bouchardon built the fountain in 1739-45 to provide water to this part of Paris year-round. Nearby at 202, bd. St-Germain, the poet Guillaume Apollinaire lived and died.

Following bd. Raspail away from the Seine, turn right on rue de Babylone, and continue to its intersection with rue de Monsieur. There stands **la Pagode,** a Japanese pagoda built in 1895 for M. Morin of the Bon Marché fortune. A gift to his wife, it endures as a testament to the 19th-century Orientalist craze in France and to conjugal love—at least until Mme. Morin left her husband for his colleague's son, prior to World War I. The building then became the scene of Sino-Japanese soirées, although these years saw a period of tension between the two countries (only to deepen with Japan's conquest of Manchuria). The Chinese Embassy, located nearby, thought of renting the elegant building but never did. In 1931, la Pagode opened its doors to the public, becoming a cinema and fashionable address where the likes of silent screen star Gloria Swanson were known to raise a glass. During the period of German occupation and accompanying film censorship, the theater closed. It reopened in 1945 in new resplendence. Today, preserved as a historic monument, it livens up the architectural tedium of ministries and *conseils,* and offers a range of excellent movies, old and new (see "Cinema," p. 250). Walk down rue Monsieur, turn left on rue Oudinot, and take rue Rousselet down to **rue de Sèvres,** a busy market street.

The **Palais Bourbon,** right across the Seine from the pl. de la Concorde, would probably not be recognized by its original occupants. Built in 1722 for the Duchess of Bourbon, daughter of Louis XIV and Mme. de Montespan, the palace was remodeled after 1750 to align with the pl. de la Concorde. Sold to the Prince of Condé in 1764, the building grew in size and ornateness under its new ownership. Napoleon erected the present Greek revival façade in 1807 to harmonize with that of the Madeleine (see "Sights—8ème," p. 180). From 1940 to 1944, the Germans occupied the palace. During the Liberation, parts of it were damaged and many of the library's books were destroyed. Any tourist hoping for a closer look at the allegorical sculpture on the building's façade would need to scale the tall iron gates and sneak past the guards, as the **Assemblée Nationale** currently occupies the palace. Machine-gun-toting police stationed every few yards are ostensibly there to prevent a replay of a 1934 attempted coup, during which rioters stormed the building. French-speakers and policy wonks might want to observe the Assembly in public session (Oct.-June, weekday afternoons and some mornings). Foreigners should expect a one-hour security check before entering the chamber and will be required to present their passports. Appropriate dress is required. Foreign nationals interested in attending a session of the National Assembly must write for permission in advance to 33, quai d'Orsay 75007 Paris.

The security check does not apply to those who take guided tours of the assembly's chambers. Show up at 33, quai d'Orsay (tel. 01 40 63 63 08) on Saturday afternoon at 10am, 2, or 3pm for a free tour (in French, with pamphlet in English available). The tour includes a visit to the **Salon Delacroix** and to the library, both spectacularly painted by Eugène Delacroix. The library's holdings include the original transcripts of Jeanne d'Arc's trial. The tour continues to the assembly's chamber itself, called the **Salle de Séances.** The *Président du conseil* presides over the chamber from a throne-like chair decorated by Lemot and Michallon. Behind him, a framed tapestry of Raphael's *School of Athens* depicts the republic of philosopher-kings. Members of the political right and left sit to the right and left of the president's seat. The Kiosque de l'Assemblée Nationale, 4, rue Aristide-Briand (tel. 01 40 63 61 21) has information about the Assemblée Nationale, as well as the standard collection of souvenirs. (Open Mon.-Fri. 9:30am-7pm, Sat. 9:30am-1pm. In Aug., open Mon.-Fri. only for information and sale of parliamentary documents, 10am-noon and 2-5pm. MC, V.)

The green, tree-lined **Esplanade des Invalides** runs from Pont Alexandre III, lined with gilded lampposts, to the gold-leaf dome of the **Hôtel des Invalides,** 2, av. de Tourville (M. Invalides). In 1670, Louis XIV decided to "construct a royal home, grand and spacious enough to receive all old or wounded officers and soldiers." Architect Libéral Bruand's building accepted its first wounded in 1674, and veterans still live in the Invalides today. Jules Hardouin-Mansart provided the final design for the **Eglise St-Louis,** the chapel within the Invalides complex. This church received Napoleon's body for funeral services in 1840, 19 years after the former emperor died in exile. His body was said to be perfectly preserved when exhumed from its original coffin before the service. Napoleon's ornate sarcophagus, now on display in the *hôtel,* wasn't completed for 20 more years. **Napoleon's tomb,** as well as the **Musée de l'Armée, Musée d'Histoire Contemporaine,** and **Musée de l'Ordre de Libération,**

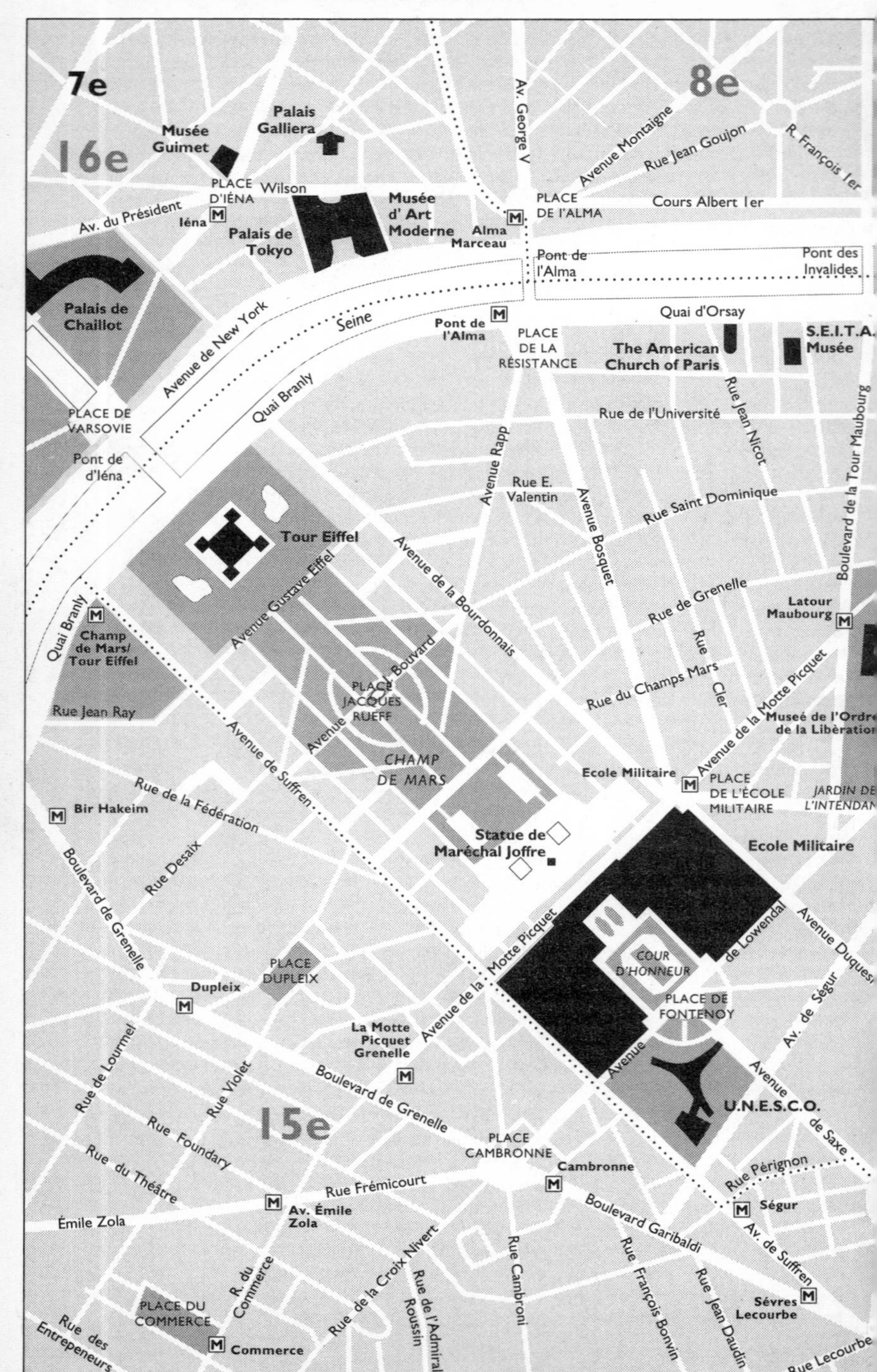
7e
8e
16e
15e
Palais Galliera
Musée Guimet
PLACE D'IÉNA
Wilson
Av. du Président
Iéna
Musée d' Art Moderne
Palais de Tokyo
Alma Marceau
Av. George V
Avenue Montaigne
Rue Jean Goujon
R. François 1er
PLACE DE l'ALMA
Cours Albert 1er
Pont de l'Alma
Pont des Invalides
Palais de Chaillot
Avenue de New York
Seine
Pont de l'Alma
Quai d'Orsay
PLACE DE LA RÉSISTANCE
The American Church of Paris
S.E.I.T.A. Musée
Quai Branly
PLACE DE VARSOVIE
Pont de d'Iéna
Rue de l'Université
Rue Jean Nicot
Boulevard de la Tour Maubourg
Avenue Rapp
Rue E. Valentin
Avenue Bosquet
Rue Saint Dominique
Tour Eiffel
Avenue de la Bourdonnais
Avenue Gustave Eiffel
Rue de Grenelle
Latour Maubourg
Quai Branly
Champ de Mars/ Tour Eiffel
Avenue Bouvard
PLACE JACQUES RUEFF
Rue du Champs Mars
Rue Cler
Avenue de la Motte Picquet
Musée de l'Ordre de la Libération
Rue Jean Ray
Avenue
CHAMP DE MARS
Avenue de Suffren
Ecole Militaire
PLACE DE L'ÉCOLE MILITAIRE
JARDIN DE L'INTENDAN
Rue de la Fédération
Bir Hakeim
Statue de Maréchal Joffre
Ecole Militaire
Boulevard de Grenelle
Rue Desaix
Avenue de la Motte Picquet
COUR D'HONNEUR
de Lowendal
Avenue Duquesne
PLACE DUPLEIX
Dupleix
PLACE DE FONTENOY
Av. de Ségur
La Motte Picquet Grenelle
Avenue
Avenue de Saxe
U.N.E.S.C.O.
Rue de Lourmel
Rue Violet
Boulevard de Grenelle
Rue Foundary
PLACE CAMBRONNE
Rue du Théâtre
Cambronne
Rue Pérignon
Rue Frémicourt
Av. Émile Zola
Émile Zola
Boulevard Garibaldi
Ségur
Av. de Suffren
Rue Cambroni
Rue François Bonvin
Rue Jean Daudin
R. du Commerce
Rue de la Croix Nivert
Rue de l'Admiral Roussin
PLACE DU COMMERCE
Sévres Lecourbe
Rue des Entrepeneurs
Commerce
Rue Lecourbe

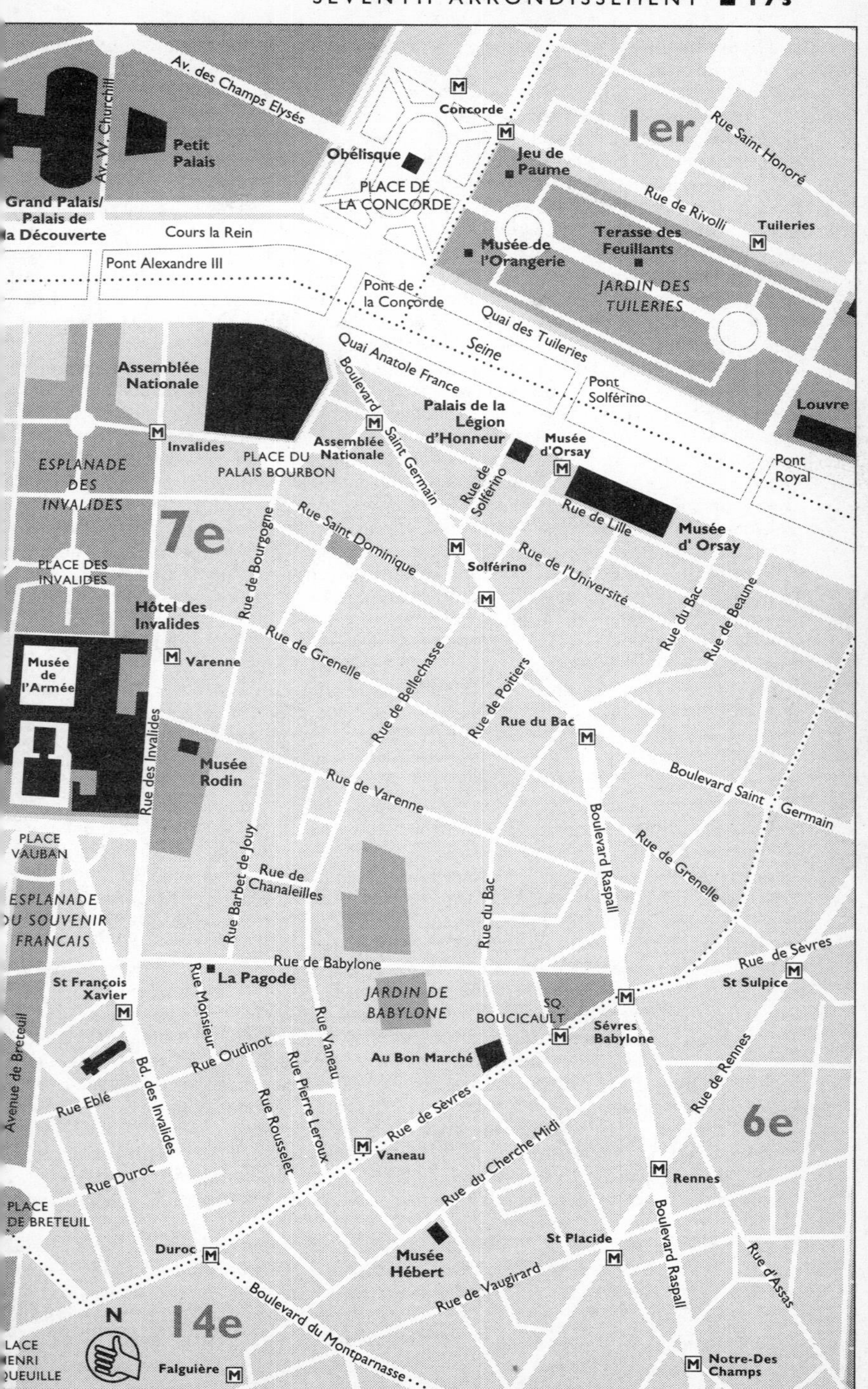
Av. des Champs Elysés
Av. W. Churchill
Petit Palais
Grand Palais/ Palais de la Découverte
Concorde
Obélisque
PLACE DE LA CONCORDE
Jeu de Paume
1er
Rue Saint Honoré
Rue de Rivolli
Tuileries
Cours la Rein
Pont Alexandre III
Musée de l'Orangerie
Terasse des Feuillants
JARDIN DES TUILERIES
Pont de la Concorde
Quai des Tuileries
Seine
Quai Anatole France
Assemblée Nationale
Boulevard Saint Germain
Palais de la Légion d'Honneur
Pont Solférino
Louvre
Invalides
Assemblée Nationale
PLACE DU PALAIS BOURBON
Musée d'Orsay
Pont Royal
ESPLANADE DES INVALIDES
Rue de Solférino
Rue de Lille
Musée d' Orsay
7e
Rue de Bourgogne
Rue Saint Dominique
Rue de l'Université
Solférino
PLACE DES INVALIDES
Hôtel des Invalides
Rue de Grenelle
Rue du Bac
Rue de Beaune
Musée de l'Armée
Varenne
Rue de Bellechasse
Rue de Poitiers
Rue du Bac
Rue des Invalides
Musée Rodin
Rue de Varenne
Boulevard Saint Germain
Boulevard Raspail
PLACE VAUBAN
Rue Barbet de Jouy
Rue de Chanaleilles
Rue de Grenelle
ESPLANADE DU SOUVENIR FRANCAIS
Rue du Bac
Rue de Babylone
Rue de Sèvres
St François Xavier
La Pagode
Rue Monsieur
St Sulpice
JARDIN DE BABYLONE
SQ BOUCICAULT
Rue Vaneau
Sèvres Babylone
Avenue de Breteuil
Rue Oudinot
Au Bon Marché
Bd. des Invalides
Rue Pierre Leroux
Rue Rousselet
Rue Eblé
Rue de Sèvres
Rue de Rennes
6e
Vaneau
Rue du Cherche Midi
Rue Duroc
Rennes
PLACE DE BRETEUIL
Boulevard Raspail
Duroc
St Placide
Musée Hébert
Rue d'Assas
Rue de Vaugirard
Boulevard du Montparnasse
N
14e
LACE ENRI QUEUILLE
Falguière
Notre-Des Champs

are housed within the Invalides museum complex (see "The Invalides Museums," p. 234). Enter from either pl. des Invalides to the north or pl. Vauban and av. de Tourville to the south. Around the "back," to the left of the Tourville entrance, the **Jardin de l'Intendant** provides a shady, almost elegant place to rest on a bench. The ditch, lined with foreign cannons captured in various wars, used to be a moat, and still makes it impossible to leave by any but the official entrance.

The **American Church in Paris,** 65, quai d'Orsay (tel. 01 47 05 07 99), helps out English speakers in search of accommodations, jobs, counseling, cultural programs, sports, support groups, etc. (reception open Mon.-Sat. 9am-1pm and 2-10:30pm, Sun. 2-7:30pm). The rue St-Dominique (off of av. Bosquet) is filled with restaurants, *pâtisseries,* and food stores, with the Eiffel tower looming in the background. The market at rue Cler can satisfy any and all culinary needs. Visit the **Musée des Egouts de Paris** (Sewer Museum), near pl. de la Résistance, to retrace the steps of the French Resistance, or of the Phantom of the Opera (see "Museums," p. 243).

Of the **Tour Eiffel** (Eiffel Tower), Gustave Eiffel wrote in 1889: "France is the only country in the world with a 300m flagpole" (tel. 01 44 11 23 45; M. Bir Hakeim). The tower's design, actually conceived by engineers Emile Nouguier and Maurice Koechlin (who worked for Eiffel's bridge company), was the winning entry in an 1885 contest. Judges chose the "Eiffel" design to be the centerpiece of the 1889 World's Fair, held to coincide with the French Revolution's centennial jubilee. Yet before construction had even begun, shockwaves of dismay reverberated through the city. In February of 1887, one month after builders broke ground on the Champ de Mars, French writers and artists published a scathing letter of protest in *Le Temps.* Writers Guy de Maupassant, Dumas *fils,* Charles Garnier (architect of the Opéra), and the composer Gounod joined countless others in condemning the construction "in the heart of our capital, of the useless and monstrous Eiffel Tower." After the building's completion, Maupassant ate lunch every day in the Eiffel Tower's ground-floor restaurant—the only place in Paris, he claimed, from which he couldn't see the Eiffel Tower. Other Parisians dismissed the tower as "American." Designed as the tallest structure in the world, Eiffel's tower was conceived as a monument to engineering and industry, to rival and surpass the Egyptian pyramids in size and notoriety.

Inaugurated March 31, 1889, it opened for visitors on May 15, 1889 to popular, if not critical, acclaim; nearly two million people ascended the tower during the fair. Numbers dwindled by comparison during the following decades. As time wore on and the twenty-year property lease approached expiration, Eiffel faced the imminent destruction of his masterpiece. The so-called Tower of Babel survived because of its importance as a communications tower, a function Eiffel had helped cultivate in the 1890s. The radio-telegraphic center on the top of the tower worked during World War I to intercept enemy messages, a handful of which, decoded by the French, resulted in the arrest and execution of Mata Hari.

With the 1937 World Exposition, the Eiffel Tower again became a showpiece, now the uncontested symbol of Paris. Eiffel himself walked humbly before it, remarking: "I ought to be jealous of that tower. She is more famous than I am." Renovations for the French Bicentennial gave it new sparkle. Since then, Parisians and tourists alike have reclaimed the monument. The tower, now on everything from postcards to neckties and umbrellas, and is sometimes shunned by tourists as either too "touristy" or too tacky. Don't miss out on one of the most satisfying experiences in Paris. All those kitschy replicas don't even get the Tower's color right. It is a soft brown, not the metallic steel gray that most visitors anticipate. And despite the 18,000 pieces of iron, 2,500,000 rivets, and 9,100,000 kilograms of sheer weight that compose it, the girders appear light and spidery. This is especially true at night, when artfully placed spotlights make the tower a lacy hologram.

While at the Eiffel Tower, you can buy exorbitantly priced souvenirs in the stores, eat good food in the pricey restaurants, or send mail with the "only-available-here" Eiffel Tower postmark. The cheapest way to ascend the tower is by walking up the first two floors (12F). The Cinemax, a relaxing stop midway through the climb on the first floor, shows films about the tower. Also take some time to read one of the posters chronicling its history. If nothing else, they're an excuse to catch your breath and rest your legs. Visitors should, and must, take the elevator to the third story. Tickets can be bought from the *caisse* or from the coin-operated dispenser (16F). Enjoy the unparalleled view of the city from the top floor and consult captioned aerial photographs to locate landmarks. Accompanying blurbs, in English, fill in the history. (Tower open daily July-Aug. 9am-midnight, including holidays. Sept.-June 9:30am-11pm. Elevator tariff to 1st floor 20F, 2nd floor 40F, 3rd floor 56F. Under 12 and over 60: 1st floor 10F, 2nd floor 21F, 3rd floor 28F. Under 4 free.)

Across the river (and the Pont d'Iéna) from the Eiffel Tower are the **Trocadéro** and the **Palais de Chaillot.** Built for the 1937 World's Fair, the Palais de Chaillot's elegant, expansive terrace and gardens provide the city's best views of the tower. Save your pictures for here (see "Sights—16ème," p. 204).

Though close to the 7ème's military monuments and museums, the **Champ de Mars** (the Field of Mars) celebrates the god of war in name alone. This flower-embroidered carpet stretching from the École Militaire to the Eiffel Tower is a great place to hang out at night. You'll find many groups of backpackers sprawled on the grass with bottles of wine in their hands. Travelers don't get a full night's sleep here, regardless of what you've heard—*gardiens* kick them off the grass at 3am. A small playground is nestled in the southwestern corner of this public space. The park's name comes from its previous function as a drill ground for the adjacent École Militaire. In 1780 Charles Montgolfier launched the first hydrogen balloon (with no basket attached) from here. During the Revolution the park witnessed an infamous civilian massacre and numerous political demonstrations. Here, at the 1793 Festival of the Supreme Being, Robespierre proclaimed the new Revolutionary religion. During the 19th and 20th centuries it served as fairgrounds for international expositions in 1889, 1900, and 1937. After the 1900 Exhibition, the municipal council considered parceling off the Champ de Mars for development. They ultimately concluded, as you will, that Paris needed all the open space it could get.

Louis XV created the **École Militaire** at the urging of his mistress, Mme. de Pompadour, who hoped to make educated officers of "poor gentlemen." Jacques-Ange Gabriel's building first accepted students in 1773, when lottery profits and a tax on playing cards financed the school's completion. In 1784, the 15-year-old Napoleon Bonaparte arrived from Corsica to enroll. A few weeks later he presented administrators with a comprehensive plan for the school's reorganization.

As the École Militaire's architectural if not spiritual antithesis, **UNESCO (United Nations Educational, Scientific, and Cultural Organization;** tel. 01 45 68 03 59; M. Ségur) occupies the Y-shaped building across the way at 7, pl. de Fontenoy. Established to foster science and culture throughout the world, the agency developed a reputation for waste, cronyism, and Marxist propaganda, prompting the U.S., the U.K., and Singapore to withdraw in 1984. In so doing, they withdrew 30% of the agency's budget, cramping UNESCO's propensity for spending inordinate sums on its image. Decorating the building and its garden are ceramics by Miró and Artigas, an unnamed painting by Picasso, a Japanese garden, and an angel from the façade of a Nagasaki church destroyed by the Atom bomb. UNESCO often mounts temporary exhibitions of photography as well as exhibits on art, science, and culture—anything from Japanese wood-carving to Ugandan irrigation projects. (Bookstore open Mon.-Fri. 9am-1pm and 2-6pm. Exhibit hours vary. Free.)

Eighth Arrondissement: The Champs-Elysées

To the Arc de Triomphe de l'Etoile:
raise yourself all the way to the heavens, portal of victory
That the giant of our glory
Might pass without bending down.

—Victor Hugo

SIGHTS

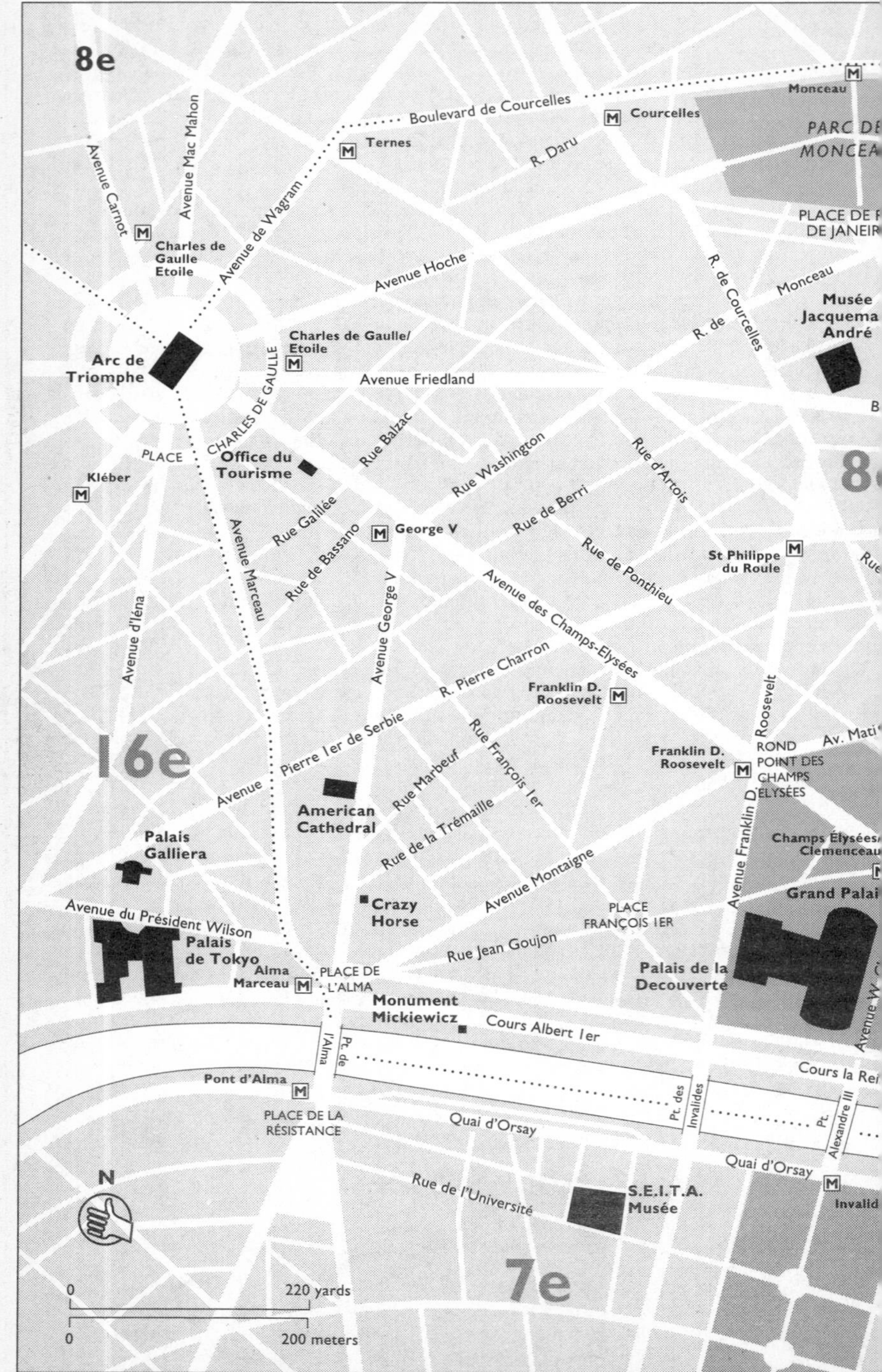
8e
16e
7e
Boulevard de Courcelles
Monceau
Courcelles
Ternes
PARC DE
MONCEAU
R. Daru
Avenue Carnot
Avenue Mac Mahon
Avenue de Wagram
Charles de Gaulle Etoile
PLACE DE R
DE JANEIR
Avenue Hoche
R. de Courcelles
R. de Monceau
Musée Jacquemart André
Charles de Gaulle/ Etoile
Arc de Triomphe
Avenue Friedland
PLACE CHARLES DE GAULLE
Office du Tourisme
Rue Balzac
Rue Washington
Rue d'Artois
Kléber
Rue Galilée
Rue de Berri
George V
Rue de Bassano
Avenue Marceau
Rue de Ponthieu
St Philippe du Roule
Avenue d'Iéna
Avenue George V
Avenue des Champs-Elysées
R. Pierre Charron
Franklin D. Roosevelt
Avenue Pierre 1er de Serbie
Rue François 1er
Rue Marbeuf
Avenue Franklin D. Roosevelt
ROND POINT DES CHAMPS ELYSÉES
American Cathedral
Rue de la Trémaille
Palais Galliera
Champs Elysées/ Clemenceau
Avenue Montaigne
Crazy Horse
Grand Palai
Avenue du Président Wilson
PLACE FRANÇOIS 1ER
Palais de Tokyo
Rue Jean Goujon
Palais de la Decouverte
Alma Marceau
PLACE DE L'ALMA
Monument Mickiewicz
Cours Albert 1er
Pt. de l'Alma
Cours la Rei
Pont d'Alma
Pt. des Invalides
Pt. Alexandre III
PLACE DE LA RÉSISTANCE
Quai d'Orsay
Rue de l'Université
S.E.I.T.A. Musée
Invalid
N
0
220 yards
0
200 meters

Bd. de Batignolles
Place de Clichy
Rome
Villiers
Musée Cernuschi
Bd. Malesherbes
R. de Leningrad
R. de Constantinople
R. de Rome
R. de Moscou
R. d'Amsterdam
R. de Clichy
Musée Nissim de Camondo
R. du Général Foy
PLACE DE L'EUROPE
Europe
Liége
R. de Lisbonne
R. du Rocher
R. de Londres
Av. de Messine
R. du Miromesnil
Haussmann
Gare St Lazare
PLACE ST-AUGUSTIN
St Lazare
St Lazare
St Augustin
R. St Lazare
La Boétie
Miromesnil
Rue Cambacérès
Boulevard Malesherbes
9e
Rue de Penthièvre
Faubourg St Honoré
Rue Pasquier
Havre-Caumartin
Bd. Haussmann
R. Auber
Rue de la Ville l'Evêque
Rue de Surène
Rue Tronchet
Auber
Avenue de Marigny
Rue d'Aguesseau
Madeleine
Opéra
Palais de l'Elysée
R. Boissy d'Anglas
American Embassy
PLACE CLEMENCEAU
Av. Gabriel
Bd. de la Madeleine
Bd. des Capucines
Opéra
Madeleine
R. des Capucines
Avenue de l'Opéra
Statue de Clemenceau
ESPACE PIERRE CARDIN
R. Hôtel Crillon
R. Royale
R. de la Paix
Musée Bouihlet Christofle
Petit Palais
PLACE VENDOME
2e
Chevaux de Marly
Concorde
Hôtel de la Marine
R. du Faubourg St Honoré
La Colonne
Obélisque
Concorde
R. de Castiglione
PLACE DE LA CONCORDE
Jeu de Paume
Pyramides
1er
Bassin Octogonal
Pt. de la Concorde
Musée de l'Orangerie
Tuileries
JARDIN DES TUILERIES
Rue de Rivoli
R. des Pyramides
Seine
Quai des Tuileries
PLACE A.-MALRAUX
Assemblée Nationale
Assemblée Nationale

Almost as elegant as its neighbor to the southwest, the 16ème, the eighth is home to Haussmann's wide sidewalks and tree-lined *grands boulevards,* including the famous **avenue des Champs-Elysées.** Well-known salons and boutiques of *haute couture* pepper fashionable streets like rue du Faubourg St-Honoré. Embassies crowd around the Palais de l'Elysée, the state residence of the French president. Already attractive to the bourgeoisie of the early 19th century, the neighborhood took off with the construction of boulevards Haussmann, Malesherbes, Victor Hugo, Foch, Kléber, and the others that shoot out from the Arc de Triomphe in a radiating formation known as l'Étoile (the star). The whole area bustles, and it should; within a very few blocks, the 8ème provides the resources necessary to dine exquisitely, dress impeccably, and accessorize magnificently. Moreover, you can indulge your esoteric musical tastes, appease your sweet tooth, and buy the ticket for your winter flight to Rio with the greatest amount of ease (and money). Most importantly, the wide open spaces of the 8ème provide you with the chance to show it all off. But be forewarned; in the 8ème you may feel underdressed and overwhelmed. This is the Paris you've seen in *Vogue* and in *Cosmo,* where the scarf is always Hermès and the watch is pure Cartier.

The **Arc de Triomphe** (tel. 01 43 80 31 31; M. Charles-de-Gaulle-Etoile), looming gloriously above the Champs-Elysées at pl. Charles de Gaulle, commemorates France's military victories as well as its long obsession with military history. The world's largest triumphal arch and an internationally recognized symbol of France, this behemoth was commissioned by Napoleon in 1806. When construction began, the Étoile marked the western entrance to the city through the *fermiers généraux* wall. Napoleon was exiled before the monument was completed, but Louis XVIII ordered resumption of work in 1823 and dedicated the arch to the war in Spain and to its commander, the Duc d'Angoulême. The Arc, designed by Chalgrin, was finally consecrated in 1836, 21 years after the defeat of the great army of *"Le Petit Corporal."* There was no consensus on what symbolic figures could cap the monument, and it has retained its simple unfinished form. The names of Napoleon's generals and battles are engraved inside; those generals underlined died in battle. The most famous of the Arc's allegorical sculpture groups depicting the military history of France is François Rude's *Departure of the Volunteers of 1792,* commonly known as *La Marseillaise,* to the right facing the arch from the Champs-Elysées.

The Arc is primarily a military symbol. As such, the horseshoe-shaped colossus has proved a magnet to various triumphal armies. The victorious Prussians marched through in 1871, inspiring the mortified Parisians to purify the ground with fire. On July 14, 1919, however, the Arc provided the backdrop for an Allied celebration parade headed by Maréchal Foch; his memory is now honored by the boulevard that bears his name and stretches out from the west side of the Arc into the 16ème. In 1940, Parisians were brought to tears as the Nazis goose-stepped through the Arc and down the Champs-Elysées. After four years of Nazi occupation, France was liberated by British, American, and French troops who marched through the Arc on August 26, 1944, to the roaring cheers of thousands of grateful Parisians. The Tomb of the Unknown Soldier has rested under the Arc since November 11, 1920; the eternal flame is rekindled every evening at 6:30pm, when veterans and small children lay wreaths decorated with blue, white, and red. De Gaulle's famous cry for *Résistance* is inscribed on a brass plaque in the pavement below the Arc.

The Arc sits in the center of the **Étoile,** which in 1907 became the world's first traffic circle. Rather than risk an early death by crossing the traffic to reach the Arc, use the underpasses on the even-numbered sides of both the Champs-Elysées and av. de la Grande-Armée. Inside the Arc, climb 205 steps up a winding staircase to the *entresol* and then dig deep for the 29 more that take you to the *musée,* or tackle the lines at the elevator for a muscle-pull-free ride. The museum recounts in French the Arc's architectural and ceremonial history, complete with drawings and appropriately tacky souvenirs. The real spectacle lies just 46 steps higher—the *terrasse* at the top of the Arc provides a terrific view of the gorgeous avenue Foch (see "Sights—16ème," p. 204) and the sprawling city. (Observation deck open April-Sept. Sun.-Mon. 9:30am-11pm, Tues.-Sat. 10am-10:30pm, Oct.-March Sun.-Mon. 10am-6pm, Tues.-Sat.

10am-10:30pm. Last entry 30min. earlier. Admission 35F, students 18-25 and seniors 23F, ages 12-17 15F, under 12 free. Expect lines even on weekdays and buy your ticket before going up to the ground level.)

The **avenue des Champs-Elysées** is the most famous of the twelve symmetrical avenues radiating from the huge rotary of place Charles de Gaulle; it may even be the most famous avenue in the world. No one can deny that this 10-lane wonder, flanked by cafés and luxury shops and crowned by the world's most famous arch, deserves its reputation. Le Nôtre planted trees here in 1667 to extend the Tuileries vista, completing the work begun under Marie de Médicis in 1616. In 1709, the area was renamed the "Elysian Fields" because of the shade provided by the trees. During the 19th century, the Champs (as many Parisians call it) developed into a fashionable residential district. Mansions sprang up along its sides, then apartments and smart boutiques, making this strip of pavement the place to see and be seen in Paris. Balls, café-concerts, restaurants, and even circuses drew enormous crowds; the *bal Mabille* opened in 1840 at no. 51, and, at no. 25, in a somewhat more subdued setting, the charming hostess and spy Marquise de Païva entertained her famous guests.

Today, you can escape the crowds and watch the modern-day circus of tourists walk by while relaxing at **Fouquet's,** an outrageously expensive and famous café/restaurant where French film stars hang out. Paris' answer to Hollywood's Sunset Strip, this stretch of the Champs-Elysées bears golden plaques with the names of favorite French recipients of the coveted César award (the French equivalent to the Oscar). Among those with names emblazoned here are Isabelle Adjani, Catherine Deneuve, and the late Louis Malle, director of *My Dinner with André* and *Au Revoir Les Enfants,* and husband of Candice Bergen. Street performers move in at night all along the Champs-Elysées, jamming to an industrial beat. During the day, anyone can enjoy the potpourri of restaurants and overpriced stores, planted next to airlines' and commercial offices.

Six big avenues radiate from the Rond Point des Champs-Elysées. Av. Montaigne runs southwest from the point and shelters the houses of *haute couture* of Christian Dior (no. 30), Chanel (no. 42), and Valentino (no. 17 and 19). St-Laurent (77, av. George V), Nina Ricci (17, rue François 1er), and Pierre Cardin (pl. François 1er) hold sway nearby. You may not be able to afford even the smallest bottle of Chanel (445F per 7mL), but it's fun to look. Nearby, 15, av. Montaigne is home to the **Théâtre des Champs-Elysées,** built by the Perret brothers in 1912 with bas-reliefs by Bourdelle. The three large *salles* still host performances, but the theater is best known for staging the first performance of Stravinsky's *Le Sacre du Printemps* (see "Classical Music, Opera, and Dance," p. 256). Around the corner from the *théâtre*, a long-time cabaret, the **Crazy Horse Saloon,** still entertains a mostly Parisian clientele.

Next to Cartier (no. 51), at 49, rue Pierre Charron, stands Pershing Hall, a 113-year-old, five-story piece of America. Given to the U.S. government, the building has allegedly been used as a brothel, a brawling bar, a casino, a black-market money exchange, and a Council Travel office. Now closed, it awaits its next incarnation.

At the foot of the Champs-Elysées, the **Grand Palais** and the **Petit Palais** face one another on av. Winston Churchill. Built for the 1900 World's Fair, both *palais* are examples of Art Nouveau architecture; the glass over steel and stone composition of the Grand Palais makes its top look like a giant greenhouse. The Petit and Grand Palais host exhibitions on architecture, painting, sculpture, and French history; the Grand Palais also houses the Palais de la Découverte (see "Museums," p. 247). Built at the same time as the palaces, the first stone of **Pont Alexandre III** was placed by the czar's son, Nicholas II. It made a stir as the first bridge to cross the Seine in a single span. Today this is considered the most beautiful bridge across the Seine, providing a noble axis with the Invalides (see "Sights—7ème," p. 171). The statues on pilasters facing the Right Bank represent Medieval France and Modern France; facing the Left Bank, they show Renaissance France and France of the Belle Époque.

The guards pacing around the house at the corner of avenue de Marigny and rue du Faubourg St-Honoré are protecting the **Palais de l'Elysée.** The palace was built in 1718 but was spiffed up to its present glory as the residence of the Marquis de Marigny, brother of Madame de Pompadour. During the Restoration, July Monarchy, and Second Empire, the Elysée was used to house royal guests. Since 1870, it has served as state residence of the French president, now Jacques Chirac. Although entrance requires a personal invitation, the persistent visitor can catch a glimpse of the luscious gardens (M. Champs-Elysées-Clemenceau). The Union Jack flying overhead at no. 35, rue du Faubourg-St-Honoré marks the British embassy. At 2, av. Gabriel, an equally large building flies the Stars and Stripes.

The **place de la Concorde** (M. Concorde), Paris' largest and most infamous public square, forms the eastern terminus of the Champs-Elysées. Like many sights in Paris, this immense *place* was born from pride—constructed between 1757 and 1777 to provide a home for a monument to Louis XV. A fitting punishment for this royal hubris, the vast area soon became the place de la Révolution, the site of the guillotine which severed 1,343 necks. On Sunday, January 21, 1793, Louis XVI was beheaded by guillotine on a site near where the Brest statue now stands. In 1993, hundreds of French (and the American ambassador) honored this event with flowers placed on the very spot. The celebrated heads of Louis XVI, Marie-Antoinette, Charlotte Corday (Marat's assassin), Lavoisier, Robespierre, and others rolled into baskets here and were held up to the cheering crowds who packed the pavement. After the Reign of Terror, the square was optimistically renamed place de la Concorde (*place* of Harmony).

At the center of the pl. de la Concorde, the **Obélisque de Louxor** was one of those king-pleasing gifts offered by Mehemet Ali, Viceroy of Egypt, to Charles X in 1829. Getting the obelisk from Egypt to the center of Paris was no simple task; a canal to the Nile had to be dug, the monolith had to be transported by sea, and a special boat built to transport it up the Seine. Finally erected in 1836, Paris' oldest monument dates back to the 13th century BC and recalls the deeds of Ramses II. On July 14th, a marvelous fireworks display lights up the sky over the place de la Concorde. Every other night, the obelisk, fountains, and turn-of-the-century cast-iron lamps are illuminated, creating a romantic glow from the *place's* otherwise dark and dismal past. Don't be surprised if you see a commercial being shot on location here.

Flanking the Champs-Elysées at the pl. de la Concorde stand the **Chevaux de Marly** (also called *Africans Mastering the Numidian Horses*), 18th-century creations of Guillaume Coustou, who originally designed them for Marly, Louis XIV's château near Versailles. Although the originals are now in the Louvre to protect them from the devastating effects of city pollution, perfect replicas boldly hold their places. Eight large statues representing the major French cities also grace the *place;* Juliette Drouet (Victor Hugo's mistress) allegedly posed for the town of Strasbourg.

Directly north of the *place,* like two sentries guarding the gate to the Madeleine, stand the **Hôtel de Crillon** (on your left) and the **Hôtel de la Marine** (on your right). Architect Jacques-Ange Gabriel built the impressive colonnaded façades between 1757 and 1770. On February 16, 1778, the Franco-American treaties were signed here, making France the first European nation to recognize the independence of the U.S. Chateaubriand lived in the Hôtel de Crillon between 1805 and 1807. Today it is one of the most expensive, elegant hotels in Paris; Michael Jackson stayed here when he gave his concert in Paris. If you're dressed for the occasion, step inside and have an espresso in the plush salon to the accompaniment of soft chamber music (decor by Sonia Rykiel). Coffee runs 30F, but you'll be able to experience Parisian life in a different form. The businesses along rue Royale boast their own proud history. At no. 9, Christofle has been producing works in gold and crystal since 1830. Next door, at 11 rue Royale, stands the famed crystal shop Lalique, named after the Art Nouveau artist who foreshadowed it. World-renowned Maxim's restaurant, 3, rue Royale, won't even allow you a peek into what was once Richelieu's home.

The **Madeleine,** formally called Église Ste-Marie-Madeleine (Mary Magdalene), is the commanding building ahead at the end of rue Royale. It was begun in 1764 at the command of Louis XV and modeled after a Greek temple. Construction was halted during the Revolution, when the Cult of Reason proposed making the generically monumental building into a bank, a theater, or a courthouse. Completed in 1842, the

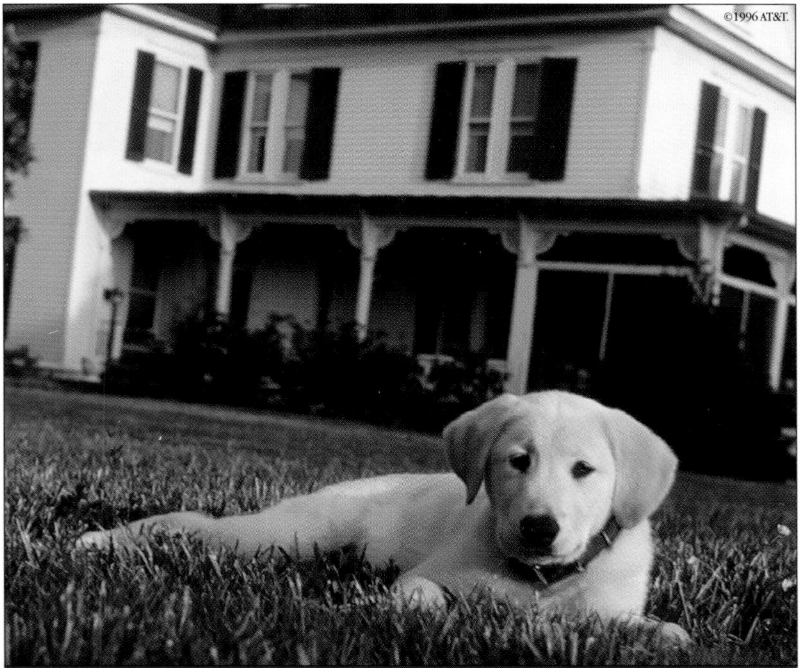

Photo: R. Olken

Greetings from LET'S GO

With pen and notebook in hand, a change of clothes in our backpack, and the tightest of budgets, we've spent our summer roaming the globe in search of travel bargains.

We've put the best of our research into the book that you're now holding. Our intrepid researcher-writers went on the road for months of exploration, from Anchorage to Angkor, Estonia to Ecuador, Iceland to India. Editors worked from spring to fall, massaging copy into witty and informative prose. A brand-new edition of each guide hits the shelves every fall, just months after it is researched, so you know you're getting the most reliable, up-to-date, and comprehensive information available.

We try to make this book an indispensable companion, but sometimes the best discoveries are the ones you make on your own. If you've got something to share, please drop us a line. We're Let's Go Publications, 67 Mount Auburn Street, Cambridge, MA 02138 USA (e-mail: fanmail@letsgo.com). Good luck and happy travels!

structure stands alone in the medley of Parisian churches, distinguished by its four ceiling domes that light the interior in lieu of windows, 52 exterior Corinthian columns, and the lack of even one cross. An immense sculpture of the ascension of Mary Magdalene into Heaven adorns the altar (open Mon.-Sat. 7:30am-7pm, Sun. 7:30am-1:30pm and 3:30-7pm; occasional organ and chamber concerts, look for posters). Marcel Proust spent most of his childhood at 9, bd. Malesherbes, which runs northwest from the pl. de la Madeleine.

At the end of the Madeleine's rue Royale, the high-fashion, high-priced **rue du Faubourg St-Honoré** stretches out like a Cartier necklace. You could spend hours window-shopping at the lavish, outrageous, and oh-so-French *vitrines* of Karl Lagerfeld (no. 19), Cartier (no. 23), Hermès (no. 24), Guy Laroche (no. 30), Yves St-Laurent (no. 38), and others. You'll find no number 13, rue du Faubourg St-Honoré; the superstitious Empress Josephine banned the number during the reign of Napoleon.

Square Louis XVI, on rue Pasquier below bd. Haussmann, includes the improbably large **Chapelle Expiatoire** and a park whose many benches make it a popular spot for lunch. The intriguing Chapelle holds monuments of Marie-Antoinette and Louis XVI. A cemetery, affiliated with the Madeleine, was opened on the site in 1722; during the Revolution victims of the guillotine, Louis and Marie among them, were dumped here. Although Louis XVIII had his brother and sister-in-law's remains removed to St-Denis in 1815, Charlotte Corday and Philippe-Egalité (Louis XVI's cousin, who voted for the king's death, only to be beheaded himself) are buried on either side of the staircase. Statues of the expiatory ex-king and queen, displaced crowns at their feet, stand inside the Chapelle. Their last letters are engraved in French on the statue bases. (Open April-Sept. 10am-6pm; Nov.-Jan. 10am-4pm; Oct. and Feb.-March 10am-5pm.)

A few blocks north squats the **Gare St-Lazare,** whose platforms and iron-vaulted canopy are not to be missed by train riders and fans of Monet and Emile Zola. To the north of the train station is the pl. de Dublin, the setting for Caillebotte's famous painting, *A Rainy Day in Paris,* which hangs in the Art Institute of Chicago.

The **Parc Monceau,** a bizarre preserve guarded by gold-tipped, wrought-iron gates, borders the elegant bd. de Courcelles. While the Jardin du Luxembourg emphasizes show over relaxation, the Parc Monceau serves as a pastoral setting for kids to play and parents to unwind in the shade—all in a series of false ruins and strange grottoes built in the best of the Romantic tradition. The painter Carmontelle designed the park for the Duc d'Orléans; it was brought to its present form in 1862 by Haussmann. The Rotonde de Monceau is a remnant of the *fermiers généraux* wall of the 1780s. Designed to enforce customs duties rather than to keep out invaders, the wall and its fortifications reflected their creator's penchant for ornament. An array of architectural follies—a pyramid, covered bridge, pagoda, Dutch windmills, and Roman ruins—make this one of Paris' most whimsical spots for a *déjeuner sur le* bench. As in other Parisian parks, frolicking on the grass is forbidden. Unlike in most Parisian parks, this rule is not always strictly enforced. (Open April-Oct. 7am-10pm; Nov.-March 7am-8pm. Gates close 15min. earlier; M. Monceau.)

In the days of pre-revolutionary Russia, many Russian aristocrats owned vacation houses in France. Paris still retains a sizable Russian community. The onion-domed **Eglise Russe,** also known as **Cathédrale Alexandre-Nevski,** 12, rue Daru (tel. 01 42 27 37 34; M. Ternes), built in 1860, is an Eastern Orthodox church. The gold domes, spectacular from the outside, are equally beautiful on the inside; they were intricately painted by artists from St. Petersburg. The church is undergoing restorations which will last until spring 1997. Services held Sun. at 10am.

Ninth Arrondissement: Opéra

The ninth arrondissement goes by the name *"Opéra"*—the Opéra Garnier and the boulevards nearby form this area's core. The Opéra lies on the southernmost border of the 9ème, and this part of the arrondissement is definitely the most prosperous and the most visited by tourists. Along the boulevards des Capucines, des Italiens, and

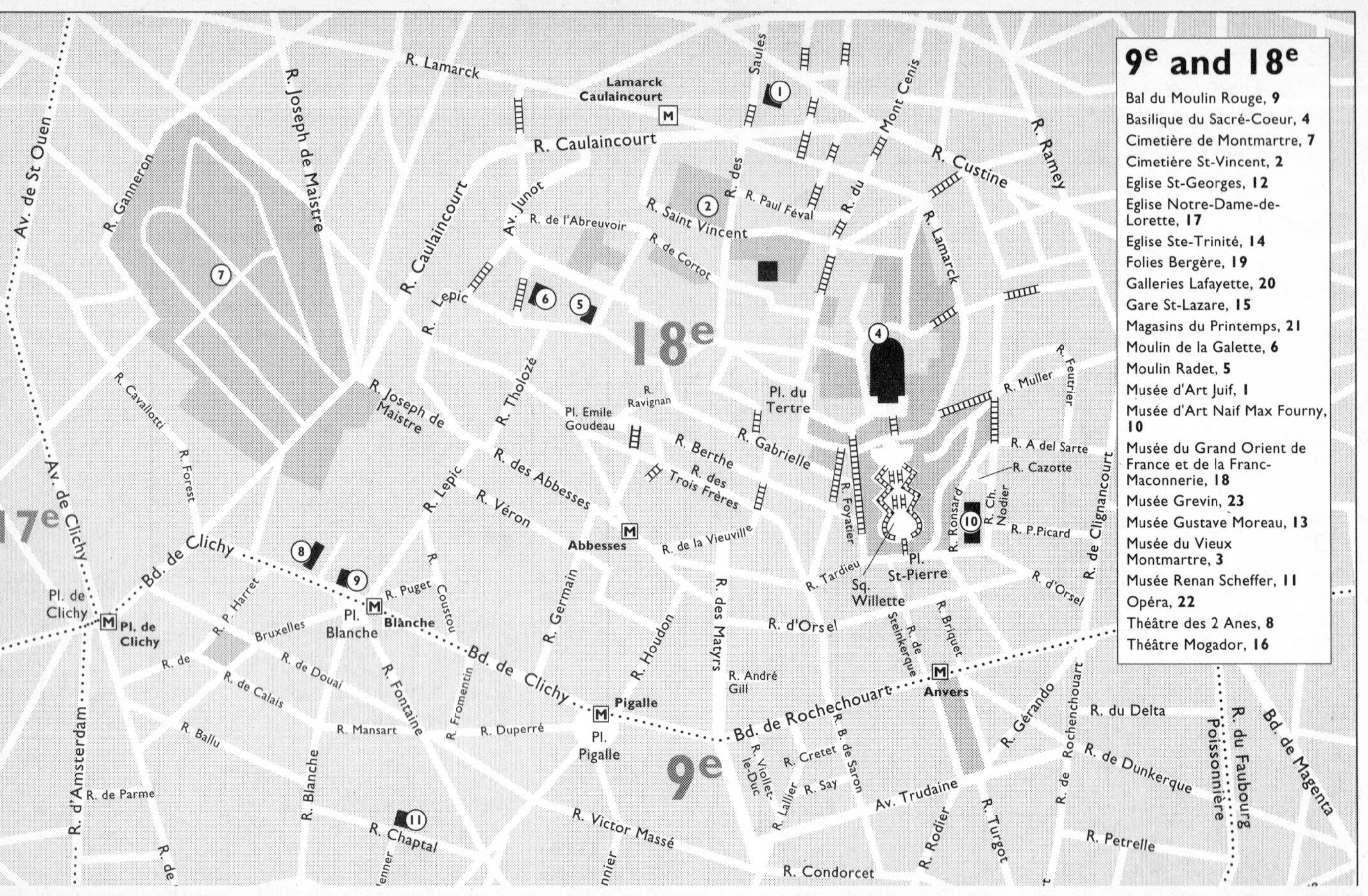
9e and 18e
Bal du Moulin Rouge, 9
Basilique du Sacré-Coeur, 4
Cimetière de Montmartre, 7
Cimetière St-Vincent, 2
Eglise St-Georges, 12
Eglise Notre-Dame-de-Lorette, 17
Eglise Ste-Trinité, 14
Folies Bergère, 19
Galleries Lafayette, 20
Gare St-Lazare, 15
Magasins du Printemps, 21
Moulin de la Galette, 6
Moulin Radet, 5
Musée d'Art Juif, 1
Musée d'Art Naif Max Fourny, 10
Musée du Grand Orient de France et de la Franc-Maconnerie, 18
Musée Grevin, 23
Musée Gustave Moreau, 13
Musée du Vieux Montmartre, 3
Musée Renan Scheffer, 11
Opéra, 22
Théâtre des 2 Anes, 8
Théâtre Mogador, 16

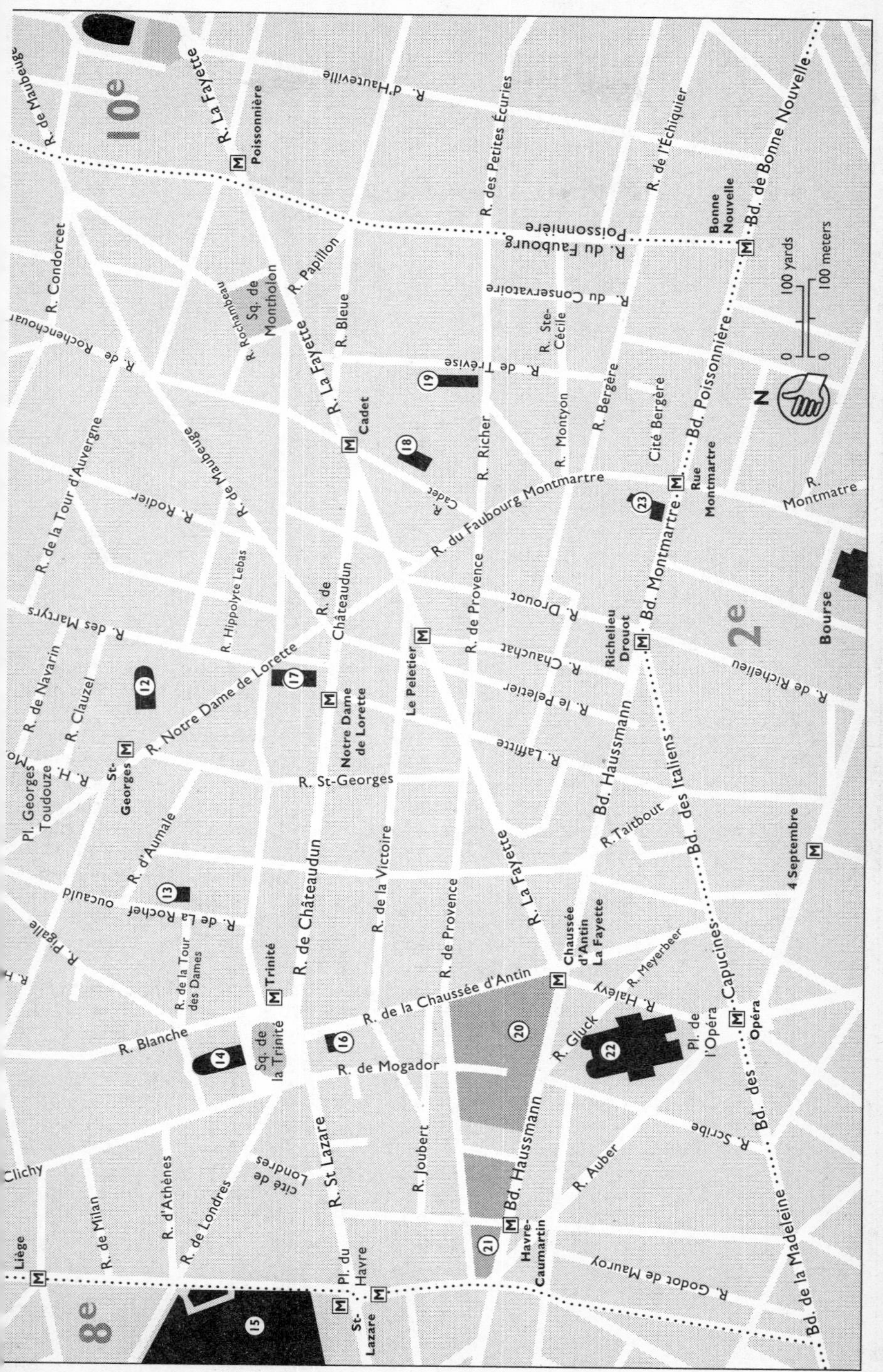

10e
8e
2e
R. de Maubeuge
R. La Fayette
Poissonnière
R. d'Hauteville
R. des Petites Écuries
R. de l'Échiquier
Bonne Nouvelle
Bd. de Bonne Nouvelle
R. du Faubourg Poissonnière
R. Condorcet
R. Rochambeau
Sq. de Montholon
R. Papillon
R. Bleue
R. du Conservatoire
R. Ste-Cécile
R. de Rochechouart
R. de Trévise
Cadet
R. Montyon
R. Bergère
Cité Bergère
Bd. Poissonnière
R. de la Tour d'Auvergne
R. Rodier
R. Cadet
R. Richer
R. du Faubourg Montmartre
Rue Montmartre
R. Montmartre
R. Hippolyte Lebas
R. de Châteaudun
R. de Provence
R. Drouot
Bd. Montmartre
R. des Martyrs
Le Peletier
R. Chauchat
Richelieu Drouot
Bourse
R. de Richelieu
R. de Navarin
R. Clauzel
R. Notre Dame de Lorette
Notre Dame de Lorette
R. le Peletier
R. Laffitte
Bd. Haussmann
Bd. des Italiens
Pl. Georges Toudouze
St-Georges
R. St-Georges
R. d'Aumale
R. de la Victoire
R. Taitbout
4 Septembre
R. de La Rochefoucauld
R. Pigalle
R. de la Tour des Dames
Trinité
R. La Fayette
Chaussée d'Antin La Fayette
R. Meyerbeer
R. Halévy
Capucines
R. Blanche
Sq. de la Trinité
R. de la Chaussée d'Antin
R. Gluck
Pl. de l'Opéra
Opéra
R. de Mogador
Bd. des
R. Scribe
Clichy
R. d'Athènes
cité de Londres
R. St Lazare
R. Joubert
Bd. Haussmann
R. Auber
R. de Milan
R. de Londres
Liège
Pl. du Havre
Havre-Caumartin
R. Godot de Mauroy
Bd. de la Madeleine
St-Lazare
N
100 yards
100 meters
12
13
14
15
16
17
18
19
20
21
22
23

Montmartre, many pleasant restaurants serve mouth-watering delicacies and cater to the post-theater and post-cinema crowd. This area also contains quite a few major movie houses showing big American and European box office hits. Near the Opéra, many large banks and chic boutiques greet their affluent clientele. Perhaps the busiest site of the 9ème, however, is the American Express office, where hordes of tourists go each day to change their Traveler's Cheques commission-free.

Most tourists, willy-nilly, begin their tour with the Opéra Garnier. Emerging from the underground den of the Opéra *métro* station, feast your eyes on Charles Garnier's grandiose **Opéra** (tel. 01 44 73 13 99; 01 44 73 13 98 for recorded program and schedule information; 01 44 73 13 00 for reservations), built under Napoleon III in the showy eclecticism of the Second Empire. This is Haussmann's most extravagant creation: an outpouring of opulence and allegory, not actually opened until 1875, five years after the Empire's collapse. Towering high above the *grands boulevards* of the southern 9ème, the Opéra epitomizes both the Second Empire's obsession with canonized ostentation and its rootlessness; a mix of styles and odd details ties it to no formal tradition. Queried by the Empress Eugénie as to whether his building was in the style of Louis XIV, Louis XV, or Louis XVI, Garnier responded that his creation belonged to Napoleon III. The interior of the Opéra demonstrates the fabric of 19th-century bourgeois social life, with its grand staircase, enormous golden foyer, vestibule, and five-tiered auditorium—all designed so that the audience members could watch each other as much as the action on stage.

Garnier's elaborate design beat out hundreds of competing plans in an 1861 competition, outshining even the entry of the "Pope of Architects," Viollet-le-Duc. At that time, Garnier was a virtual unknown; the Opéra made him famous. The magnificent and eclectic interior is adorned by Gobelin tapestries, gilded mosaics, a 1964 Chagall ceiling (with a whimsical, Chagallian view of Paris), and the six-ton chandelier, which fell on the audience in 1896. Since 1989, when the new Opéra de la Bastille was inaugurated, most operas have been performed at the newer hall and Garnier's opera has been used mainly for ballets. Ballet these days tends to perform its own elegy, staging retrospectives on the work of 20th-century greats. In 1992, Rudolf Nureyev made his last public appearance here shortly before his death.

SIGHTS

The Opéra's library and museum hold documents about costumes and objects tracing the history of opera and dance. They focus particularly on the *ballet russe*, Diaghilev's innovative troupe that liberated classical dance from fluffy Romanticism, and launched 20th-century experimentation with such works as Stravinsky's *Firebird.* (The Opéra is open for visits daily 10am-6pm, last entry 5:30pm. Visits cost a hefty 30F, ages 10-16 20F, and include all public parts of the theater, except for the auditorium on performance days. 1½-hr. guided tours in English and French 60F, ages 10-16 45F, under 10 25F; meet at the Rameau statue in the main hall at 10:15am or 2:15pm. Library open daily 10am-noon and 2–5pm. Gift shop open daily 10am-1pm and 2:15-6pm. For concert schedules and information, see "Classical Music, Opera, and Dance," p. 256. To arrange for private tours, call 01 40 01 25 14.)

To the right of the Opéra is the **Café de la Paix,** 12, bd. des Capucines, *the* quintessential 19th-century-café. Today, it caters to the after-theater crowd and anyone else who doesn't mind paying 30F for coffee (see "Frozen in Time," p. 134). Cartier is at no. 11, and banking institutions swarm the area like actors at Cannes. Of more historic interest, a bit farther down the bd. des Capucines, are the giant red glowing letters of the **Olympia** music hall, where Edith Piaf achieved her fame, along with Jacques Brel, Yves Montand, and many others. Popular artists still perform here, in a strongly nostalgic vein; check posters for concerts. Returning up bd. des Capucines, you will arrive at bd. des Italiens and bd. Montmartre. These three *grands boulevards* represent one of the busiest areas in the *quartier,* overflowing with popular restaurant/cafés (pricey, but perfect for watching the crowds), cinemas, and shops. Thomas Jefferson, in Paris in the 1780s as the American ambassador, lived near what is now the intersection of bd. Haussmann and rue du Helder. At no. 10, bd. Montmartre stands the carnivalesque **Musée Grévin** (see "Museums," p. 244).

West from this area along bd. Haussmann, toward M. Chaussée d'Antin and Trinité, you'll find the largest clothes shopping area in Paris. Two of Paris' most important department stores, **Au Printemps** and **Galeries Lafayette,** are located on the bd. Haussmann, and the streets around here are littered with stores selling clothes and shoes (see "Window Shopping," p. 271, and "Department Stores," p. 272). At the northern end of the rue de la Chaussée (M. Trinité), is the **Église de la Sainte-Trinité.** This church, built at the end of the 19th century in Italian Renaissance style, has beautiful, painted vaults and is surrounded by a restful park with a fountain and tree-shaded benches. The quixotic **Musée Gustave Moreau** is also located in this area, up the rue de La Rochefoucauld (see "Museums," p. 247) in the painter's house and studio on a quiet residential street.

A short walk west from here, on the pl. Kossuth, at M. Notre-Dame-de-Lorette, is the church **Notre-Dame-de-Lorette,** built in 1836 to "the glory of the Virgin Mary." This Neoclassical church is filled with statues of the saints and frescoes of scenes from the life of Mary. The street of the same name, constructed in 1840, quickly gained low-rent apartments of ill repute, stomping ground for Emile Zola's Nana (whose name has made its way into French *argot*—slang for girl, on par with "chick"). The term *lorette* came to refer to the quarter's crop of young *demoiselles* of easy virtue—post-adolescent adventuresses who came to the city from the provinces, their reputations forever tarnished. The mere mention of Notre-Dame-de-Lorette made men look away and good girls blush. Rue des Martyrs, once home to bars and restaurants for the kind of crowd that rents hotel rooms by the hour, revelled in an equally bad reputation. Now filled with fruit stands, cheese shops, and multi-ethnic *épiceries,* the street has mended its sordid ways. Continuing up rue Notre-Dame-de-Lorette near the place St-Georges, you will reach the **square Alex Biscarre,** a small park with young children, stroller-pushing parents, and a sandbox.

North of the rue de Châteaudun is a quiet, mostly residential area with a large student population and many small, well-priced, ethnic restaurants. The streets are narrow and quiet, full of small shops, *tabacs,* little hotels, and modest private residences. The **Musée Renan-Scheffer,** or Musée de la Vie Romantique, is up one of these charming narrow streets, rue Chaptal, off rue Fontaine (see "Museums," p. 248). The interior courtyard and garden of the house are representative of the layout of most of the buildings on these streets.

Farther north, at the border of the 18ème, is the area called **Pigalle,** the so-called un-chastity belt of Paris. Stretching along the bd. de Clichy from pl. Pigalle to pl. Blanche and two or so blocks on either side of it is a salacious, voracious neighborhood. Sex-shops, brothels, porn stores, lace, leather, and latex boutiques line the streets. In Pigalle, people look one another in the eye; usually with money, sex, or both in mind. One salient characteristic of the region is that it swarms with policemen. Tourists, (especially women) should never walk alone here, though Pigalle is not as dangerous as it once was. The areas to the north of bd. Clichy and south of pl. Blanche are particularly calm. This neighborhood has experienced something of a revival as retro and kitsch have become trendy. The surrounding neighborhood is fairly mainstream with classy restaurants and bars on side-streets, a few fashionable night-clubs, and numerous artists studios. Keep your eyes peeled for out-moded French crooners who have taken refuge in the bars of Pigalle; they can provide a hilarious throwback to the by-gone days of Paris.

Tenth Arrondissement

I live between two train stations, at the edge of a canal, in one of the arrondissements of Paris most rich in prisons, hideouts, pleasures, and hospitals. It is a rather vague arrondissement...much like one of those animal-molecules that can both expand and be cut in half. Half-worm, half-butterfly, one never knows which is the head and which the tail, and it is permanently caught at the mid-point of creation, straddling flight on the one side, abjectly crawling on the other.

SIGHTS

These words, written by a resident of the tenth arrondissement in the 1920s, are still accurate today. Far from the normal tourist route, and not the safest or most well-kept of areas, the 10ème offers a few gems of its own to the adventurous soul. In the southern portion, along the Faubourg St-Denis, a curious and bustling market area offers ethnic foods and spices. The rue de Paradis in the western section is home to some of the world's finest china and crystal. Travelers looking to stretch their legs on a layover at the Gare de l'Est or Nord should head for the tree-lined Canal St-Martin and relax in the shade, away from the noise of downtown Paris.

The **Gare du Nord** (M. Gare du Nord) is generally encountered out of necessity rather than curiosity, but it merits a look. Jacques-Ignace Hittorf created the enormous station in 1863, in the midst of the great re-building of Paris. The grandiose Neoclassical exterior is topped by statues representing the great cities of France. Inside, the platforms are covered by a vast *parapluie* (umbrella), as Napoleon III called the glass and steel heaven which creates the giant vault of the train station. Across from the station, a fringe of *brasseries* and cafés caters to the thousands of travelers who go through here every day.

Facing away from the Gare du Nord and walking one block down the rue de Compiègne takes you to the rue de Belzunce and the **Église St-Vincent de Paul,** a Neoclassical structure built in the early 19th century by architects Hittorf and Jean-Baptiste Lepère. The entrance, in the shape of a temple, is topped with a dramatic sculpted frieze of the Glorification of St. Vincent de Paul by Leboeuf-Nanteuil. (Church open to the public Mon.-Sat. 7:30am-noon and 2-7pm, Sun. 7:30am-12:30pm and 3:30-7:30pm. Mass with Gregorian chant Sun. at 9:30am.)

The **Marché St-Quentin,** 85, bd. de Magenta, is a massive, elegant construction of iron and glass, built in 1866. Inside is an enormous variety of goods, from flowers to fresh produce and skinned rabbits for your delectable *lapin à la moutarde* (see "Food Markets and Noteworthy Streets," p. 108). From the Marché St-Quentin, cross bd. de Magenta and follow rue du 8 Mai 1945 until it arrives at the **Gare de l'Est.** Directly across from the train station, the place du 11 Nov. 1918 opens into the bd. de Strasbourg, a thoroughfare teeming with cafés, shops, and fruit stands.

Close by, tiny **rue de Paradis** teeters with shops displaying fine china and crystal. The beautiful (and expensive) objects mark the road to the **Baccarat Co.** headquarters and the **Cristalleries Baccarat,** housed in an 18th-century building at 30-32, rue de Paradis (see "Museums," p. 240). Farther up the street, at 18, rue de Paradis, the art gallery **Le Monde de l'Art** displays remarkable tile murals and contemporary exhibits; it is housed in what was once the headquarters of the Boulanger china company (see "Museums," p. 247).

Going south on the **rue du Faubourg St-Denis,** you pass through crowds of Parisians buying dinner ingredients in a very active market area. Individual stores, many owned by African, Arab, and Indian vendors, specialize in seafood, cheese, bread, or produce, rebuking supermarkets everywhere with their quality and selection. **Passage Brady,** which intersects with bd. de Strasbourg and rue du Faubourg St-Martin, is lined with Indian and Pakistani stores that are stocked with exotic foodstuffs and prepared delicacies that the budget traveler can afford. At night it becomes a challenge to thread your way through the sea of tables, as Parisians and tourists enjoy a spicy meal outside. With intimate, fancy restaurants next to more rudimentary, honest establishments, the animated alley is a bold departure from the deserted commercial area of the lower bd. de Strasbourg.

At the end of rue Faubourg St-Denis, the majestic **Porte St-Denis** (M. Strasbourg/St-Denis) welcomes the visitor into the inner city. Built in 1672 to celebrate the victories of Louis XIV in the Rhineland and Flanders, it imitates the Arch of Titus in Rome. In the Middle Ages, this was the site of a gate in the city walls, but the present arch, which André Breton called *très belle et très inutile* (very beautiful and very useless), served only as a ceremonial marker and a royal entrance on the old road to St-Denis. On July 28, 1830, it was the scene of intense fighting; revolutionaries scrambled to the top of the old Bourbon icon and rained cobblestones on the monarchist troops below. At its side, two blocks down the bd. St-Denis, the **Porte St-Martin** is a smaller

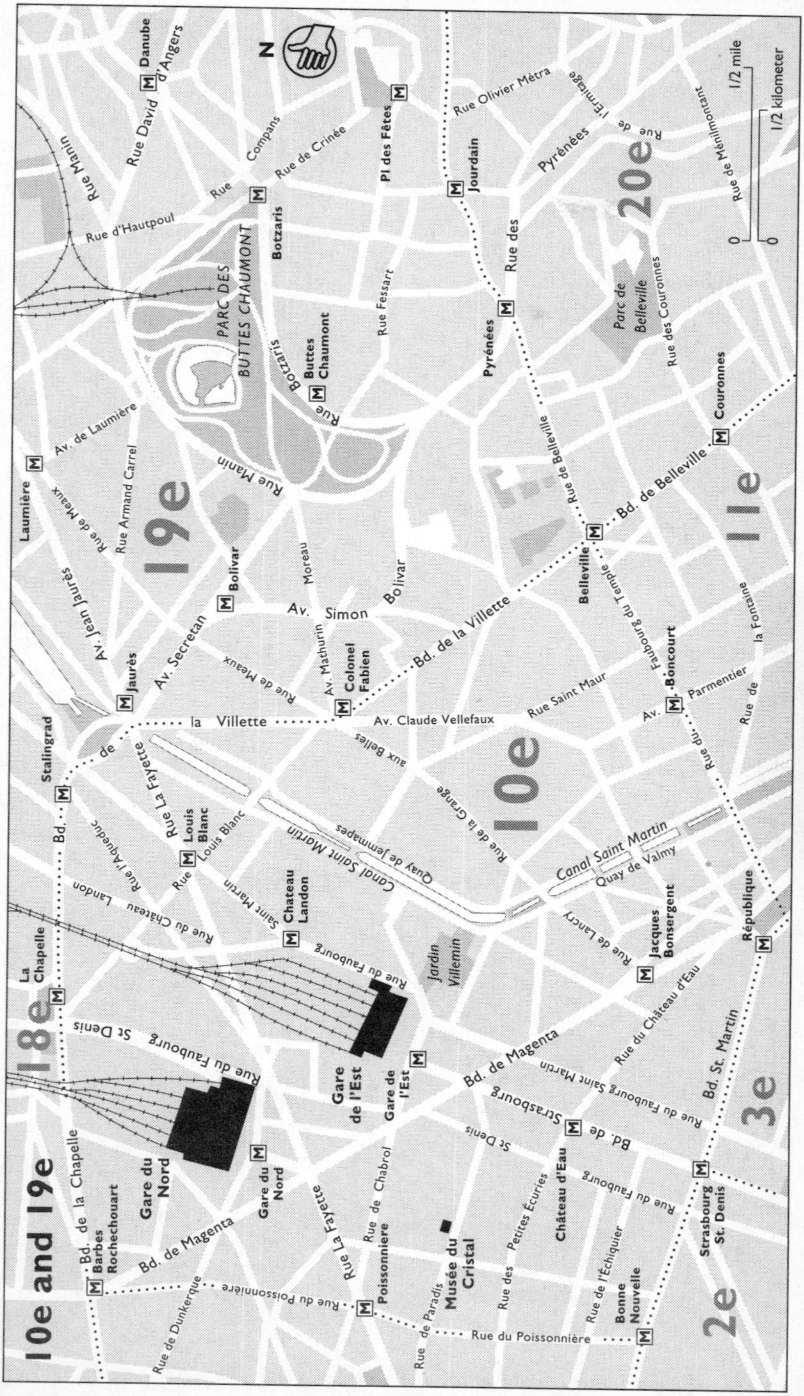
10e and 19e
N
18e
19e
10e
11e
20e
2e
3e
PARC DES BUTTES CHAUMONT
Parc de Belleville
Jardin Villemin
Canal Saint Martin
Gare du Nord
Gare de l'Est
Musée du Cristal
Barbes Rochechouart
La Chapelle
Stalingrad
Jaurès
Laumière
Danube
Louis Blanc
Chateau Landon
Gare du Nord
Gare de l'Est
Poissonniere
Château d'Eau
Jacques Bonsergent
Bonne Nouvelle
Strasbourg St. Denis
République
Colonel Fabien
Bolivar
Buttes Chaumont
Botzaris
Pl des Fêtes
Jourdain
Pyrénées
Belleville
Couronnes
Goncourt
Bd. de la Chapelle
Bd. de Magenta
Rue du Faubourg St Denis
Rue La Fayette
Rue de Chabrol
Rue de Dunkerque
Rue du Poissonnière
Rue de Paradis
Rue des Petites Écuries
Rue de l'Échiquier
Rue du Faubourg St Denis
Bd. de Strasbourg
Rue du Faubourg Saint Martin
Rue du Château d'Eau
Bd. St. Martin
Rue du Faubourg Saint Martin
Rue du Château Landon
Rue de l'Aqueduc
Rue Louis Blanc
Rue de Lancry
Quay de Valmy
Quay de Jemmapes
Rue de la Grange aux Belles
Bd. de la Villette
Av. Claude Vellefaux
Rue Saint Maur
Av. Parmentier
Rue du Faubourg du Temple
Rue de la Fontaine
Rue de Belleville
Bd. de Belleville
Rue des Couronnes
Rue des Pyrénées
Rue de Ménilmontant
Rue de l'Ermitage
Rue Olivier Métra
Rue Fessart
Rue Botzaris
Rue Manin
Av. Simon Bolivar
Rue Moreau
Av. Mathurin Moreau
Rue de Meaux
Av. Secretan
Av. Jean Jaurès
Rue Armand Carrel
Av. de Laumière
Rue d'Hautpoul
Rue Compans
Rue de Crinée
Rue David d'Angers
Rue Manin
0
1/2 mile
1/2 kilometer

SIGHTS

copy, built in 1674 to celebrate yet another victory. On the façade, look for Louis XIV represented as Hercules (nude, except for the wig).

The stretch from Porte St-Martin to pl. de la République, along rue René Boulanger and bd. St-Martin, served as a lively theater district in the 19th century and has recently begun to retrieve some of its former sparkle. Newly refurbished, the **Théâtre de la Renaissance,** with a sculpted façade of griffins and arabesques, has breathed new life into neighboring streets. Not quite a new Bohemian enclave yet, it may arrive in the future.

Going east from here along the bd. St-Martin, you will arrive at the **place de la République** (M. République), the meeting point of the 10*ème*, 3*ème*, and 11*ème* arrondissements. Buzzing with crowds during the day, the area can be dangerous at night. (See "Sights—3*ème*," p. 151, for more about this *place*.)

A bit farther east lies the **Canal St-Martin,** 4.5km long and connecting the Canal de l'Ourcq to the Seine. The canal has several locks, which can be traveled by boat on one of the **canauxrama** trips (see "Sights," p. 139). You can also walk along the tree-lined banks—though again, be careful in this area after dark. East of the canal, follow rue Bichat to the entrance of **Hôpital St-Louis,** one of the oldest hospitals in Paris. Built by Henri IV as a sanctuary/prison for victims of the plague, it was located across a marsh from the city, and downwind of both the smelly mess at Buttes-Chaumont (see "Sights—19*ème*," p. 211) and a gallows. Its distance from any source of fresh water suggests that it was intended more to protect the city from contamination than to help the unfortunates inside. Today, Hôpital St-Louis specializes in dermatology, and offers a peaceful Renaissance courtyard to those willing to brave any plague bacilli that might have survived the centuries.

Just north of hôpital St-Louis, in the area between the canal, rue des Ecluses St-Martin, rue Louis Blanc, and rue de la Grange aux Belles, once stood the **Montfaucon gallows**—famous for its hanging capacity of 60, an efficiency unrivaled until the invention of the guillotine several centuries later. In the early 14th century, the initial wooden structure was replaced by a two-story stone framework, designed by Pierre Rémy, treasurer to Charles IV. (Rémy had a chance to test his creation in 1328, when he was hanged with great pomp and circumstance.) By the 17th century, the Montfaucon gallows had fallen into disuse, and today only memories linger. But in 1954, workers building the garage at 53, rue de la Grange aux Belles uncovered an eerie reminder of this area's former use: two of the original pillars, along with several human bones.

Eleventh Arrondissement

Near the dressed-down, plexiglass opera house at **pl. de la Bastille** (M. Bastille) disgruntled shopkeepers stormed the Bastille prison on July 14, 1789. Long since demolished, the prison was originally commissioned by Charles V to safeguard the eastern entrance to Paris. A treasury vault under Henri IV, the fortress became a state prison under his successor Louis XIII; internment there, generally reserved for religious heretics and political undesirables, followed specific orders from the king. The man in the iron mask sojourned here for a time at Louis XIV's request. The prison was always more of a deluxe hotel than a draconian nightmare, though. Its titled inmates furnished their suites, brought their servants, and received guests. The Cardinal de Rohan held a dinner party for 20 in his cell. The prison itself provided fresh linen. Notable prisoners included Mirabeau, Voltaire, and the Marquis de Sade, one of the last seven prisoners to be held there. Seldom one to miss a party, he left July 7, 1789, just a week before the prison's liberation.

When Revolutionary militants stormed the Bastille, they came for its supply of gunpowder. After sacking the Invalides for weapons, they needed munitions. Surrounded by an armed rabble, too short on food to entertain a siege, and unsure of the loyalty of the Swiss mercenaries who defended the prison, the Bastille's governor surrendered. Soon after, while he was under armed escort to the Hôtel de Ville, the mob hacked off his head with a pocketknife and paraded it around on a pike.

In spite of the incident's gruesome details, the storming of the Bastille has come to symbolize the triumph of liberty over despotism. Its first annual anniversary was the cause for great celebration. Since the late 19th century, July 14th has been the official state holiday of the French Republic.

Demolition of the prison began the morrow of its capture and concluded in October 1792. Some of its stones were incorporated into the Pont de la Concorde. A commemorative pile can also be found in square Henri Galli, a few blocks down bd. Henri IV from pl. de la Bastille. A certain Citizen Palloy, the main demolition contractor, used the stones to construct 83 models of the prison which he sent to the provinces as reminders of "the horror of despotism." Louis XVI got a copy, too, before becoming an ex-despot. Original stones also outline the prison's former location.

The **Opéra Bastille,** a space-age conversation piece and almost the only sight left standing in the 11*ème*, is regularly the butt of jokes by passersby. Designed by Canadian architect Carlos Ott, the building is second only to Disneyland Paris in the minds of Parisians as an example of North American barbarism. It has further been described as a huge *toilette,* a version no doubt of the coin-operated facilities in the streets of Paris. Many complain that the acoustics of the hall leave much to be desired. Worse yet, the "people," for whom the opera was supposedly designed, can't afford to go there. Tours are the only way to see the interior unless you attend a performance (50F, students, under 16, and over 60 30F; 1-2 per day at 1 or 5pm). Call 01 40 01 19 70 for more information about tours. (See "Classical Music, Opera, and Dance," p. 256, for concert information.)

In 1831, King Louis-Philippe laid the cornerstone for the **July Column** at the center of the *place.* It commemorates the Republicans who died in the Revolutions of 1789 and 1830, the latter of which brought Louis-Philippe to *bien sûr* power. The column's vault contains the bodies of 504 martyrs of 1830, along with two mummified Egyptian pharaohs that were moved from the Louvre when they began to decompose.

The neighborhood near the Opéra Bastille has eclipsed the Latin Quarter as the youthful, artistic center of Paris. This portion of the 11*ème* has become, like Montmartre, Montparnasse, and the *quartier latin* before it, the city's latest Bohemia. Don't count on the BCBG glamor of the Left Bank; styles here change as quickly as new galleries open and close. Today's Beautiful People sport tiny t-shirts, teeny backpacks, and sparkly jelly shoes.

Along the streets radiating from the *place* lived many of the Revolution's profiteers and victims. Nos. 157-161, rue de Charonne housed the infamous Dr. Belhomme, whose Maison de Retraite et de Santé sheltered condemned aristocrats and other notables with ready cash during the Terror (1792-1795). For 1000 *livres* a month, Dr. Belhomme would let a room in his sham sanatorium and certify his clients as too ill to brave the scaffold. Arrested himself after word got out, the savvy Dr. Belhomme holed up in a like establishment on the rue de Picpus (12*ème*). Thrown in jail for uncivicism under the Directory, he died peacefully at home at the age of 87.

Off rue de Charonne at 36, rue St-Bernard, **Eglise Ste-Marguerite** was built in 1627 to save parishioners in the village of Charonne the commute to St-Paul in the Marais (see "Sights—4*ème*," p. 156). The Chapelle des Ames du Purgatoire, added to the church in 1764 by architect Louis, is decorated with *trompe l'oeil* paintings by Brunetti. The pietà behind the altar is by Girardon. During the Revolution, Ste-Marguerite continued as a place of worship, though not for traditional Catholicism: its vicar was among the first priests to get married (open daily 9am-noon, 5-7pm).

Next to the church, the **Cimetière Ste-Marguerite** is another stop on the Revolution's trail of blood. At least 73 victims of the guillotine from June 1794 fertilized these grounds, the most enigmatic of whom remains "the child dead in the dungeon of the Temple"—rumored to be Louis XVII. Located near the outside wall of the Chapelle des Ames du Purgatoire, the headstone reads, "L...XVII 1785-1795." Though 19th-century forensic tests confirmed that the body is that of a boy aged 18-20, his identity has never been conclusively proven.

SIGHTS

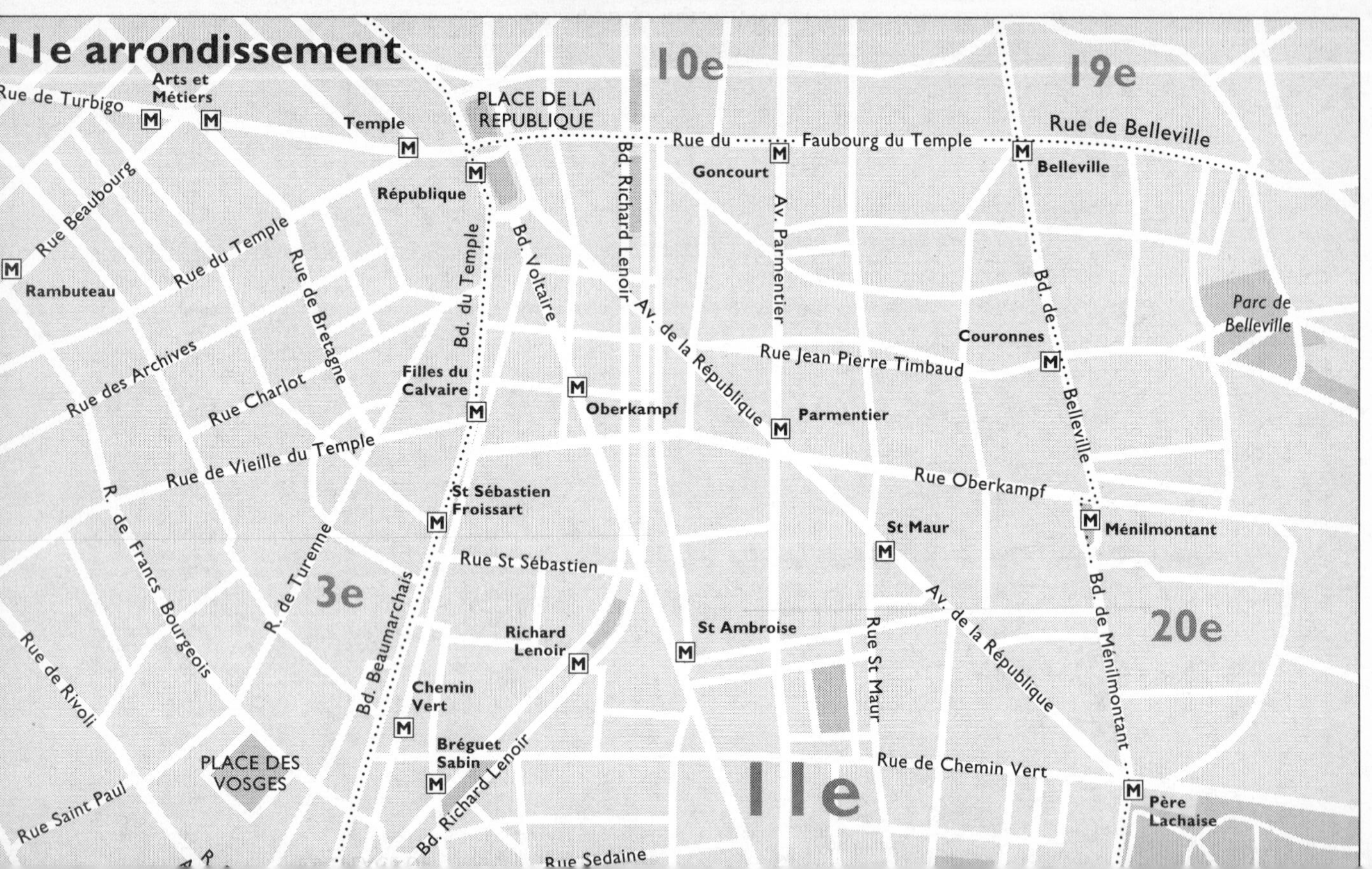
11e arrondissement
Arts et Métiers
Rue de Turbigo
PLACE DE LA REPUBLIQUE
10e
19e
Temple
Rue du Faubourg du Temple
Rue de Belleville
Goncourt
Belleville
République
Rue Beaubourg
Rue du Temple
Bd. du Temple
Bd. Voltaire
Bd. Richard Lenoir
Av. Parmentier
Rambuteau
Rue de Bretagne
Av. de la République
Bd. de Belleville
Parc de Belleville
Couronnes
Rue Jean Pierre Timbaud
Rue des Archives
Rue Charlot
Filles du Calvaire
Oberkampf
Parmentier
Rue de Vieille du Temple
Rue Oberkampf
St Sébastien Froissart
St Maur
Ménilmontant
Rue St Sébastien
3e
R. de Francs Bourgeois
R. de Turenne
Bd. Beaumarchais
Richard Lenoir
St Ambroise
Rue St Maur
Bd. de Ménilmontant
20e
Rue de Rivoli
Chemin Vert
Bréguet Sabin
PLACE DES VOSGES
Rue de Chemin Vert
11e
Père Lachaise
Rue Saint Paul
Rue Sedaine

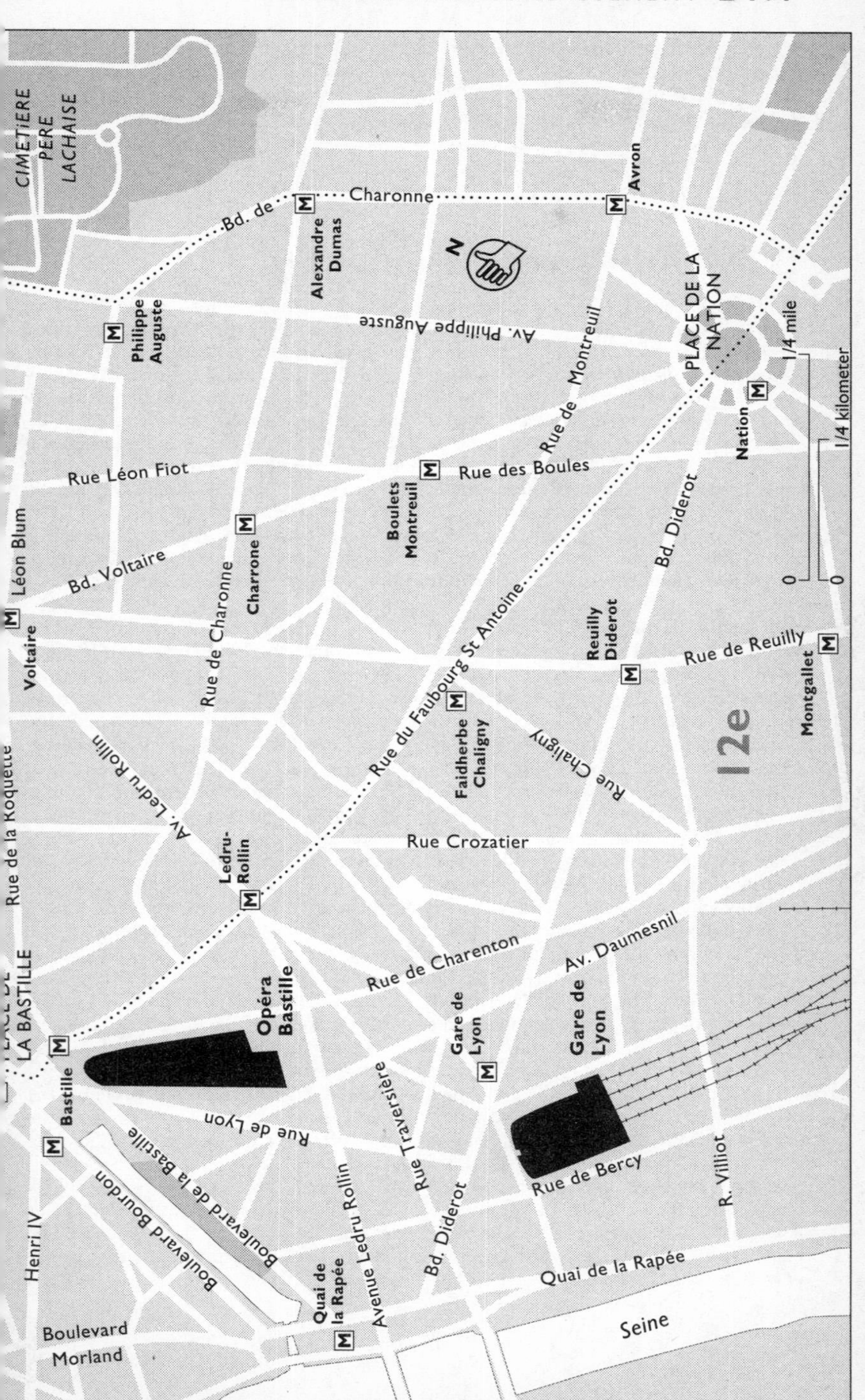

CIMETIERE PERE LACHAISE
Bd. de Charonne
Alexandre Dumas
Avron
Philippe Auguste
Av. Philippe Auguste
PLACE DE LA NATION
Nation
1/4 mile
1/4 kilometer
0
0
Rue Léon Fiot
Rue des Boules
Rue de Montreuil
Boulets Montreuil
Léon Blum
Bd. Voltaire
Charrone
Bd. Diderot
Voltaire
Rue de Charonne
Reuilly Diderot
Rue de Reuilly
Montgallet
Rue du Faubourg St Antoine
Faidherbe Chaligny
Rue Chaligny
12e
Av. Ledru Rollin
Rue de la Roquette
Ledru-Rollin
Rue Crozatier
PLACE DE LA BASTILLE
Opéra Bastille
Rue de Charenton
Av. Daumesnil
Gare de Lyon
Gare de Lyon
Bastille
Rue de Lyon
Rue Traversière
Rue de Bercy
R. Villiot
Boulevard de la Bastille
Boulevard Bourdon
Henri IV
Quai de la Rapée
Avenue Ledru Rollin
Bd. Diderot
Quai de la Rapée
Seine
Boulevard Morland

Head back on the rue de Charonne toward the Bastille and turn left on **rue de Lappe** for a showcase of 17th- and 18th-century everyday life and architecture. In this heart of Bastille chic, the streets are lined with cafés, galleries, old passageways, and gardens. This is the 11*ème* at its most accessible and most charming. Michelet, the great 19th-century historian of the Revolution, lived at no. 49. His statue may be seen on the **Hôtel de Ville** (see "Sights—4*ème*," p. 159). Turn right from rue de Lappe onto **rue de la Roquette** for a glimpse of another 17th-century byway. The poet Verlaine lived at no. 17.

Twelfth Arrondissement

Until joining Paris proper, the area east of pl. de la Bastille comprised the Faubourg (suburb) St-Antoine. Royal decree exempted this artisanal district from duties levied against residents of the wealthier, center city. Hard hit by food shortages in the late 18th century, *faubourg* residents spiritedly joined the Revolution's more radical contingents. Participating in both the 1830 and ill-fated 1848 Revolutions, the *faubourg* became known as the "red belt" around Paris. In the 20th century, the region has proved a bastion of both left- and right-leaning unrest. Residents numbered importantly among the pre-1944 resistance movement; plaques to this effect, conspicuously absent in central Paris, are sprinkled along the city's eastern fringe. On May 28, 1958, over 150,000 people marched to combat an attempted *coup d'état* by the armed forces, whose right-wing elements had waxed rebellious over De Gaulle's policy in Algeria. In their pro-government march, *faubourg* residents followed what historian Jean Lacouture has called "the traditional left-wing route from the pl. de la Nation to the pl. de la République."

Besides its history, the 12*ème*, made up mostly of businesses and tree-lined boulevards, offers little to the sight-seer. One exception is the **Ministère des Finances (Ministry of Finances),** 238, quai de Bercy. Until recently, the Finance Ministry shared space with the Louvre art museum, but something had to give when construction began on the Louvre's new pyramid. Former president Mitterrand commissioned the current finance building. Looking like nothing so much as an obsidian wafer cookie, Chemetov and Huidobro's shiny, spiky design yawns across the Seine—the only of Mitterrand's *grands projets* accessible by both dinghy and parachute. (Its flat top serves as a helicopter landing pad and its dock enables employees to drive speedboats from here to the Assemblée Nationale in three minutes.)

In the arrondissement's southeastern corner, the radial **pl. de la Nation** (M. Nation) marks the boundary between the 12*ème* and the 11*ème*. Dalou's statue *Triomphe de la République* (1899) surveys the *place,* formerly known as the **pl. du Trône** because of a throne placed here in 1660, when Louis XIV married Marie-Thérèse. During the Revolution, the throne was replaced by a guillotine; 1300 nobles were executed on this spot, and the square was renamed the **place du Trône-Renversé** (Square of the Toppled Throne). It became the **place de la Nation** on July 14, 1880. East of the *place,* twin tollhouses—part of Claude-Nicolas Ledoux's 18th-century city walls—flank the cours de Vincennes, a broad avenue leading to the Château de Vincennes and to the wooded park that surrounds it.

Don't miss the new "green spot," the *promenade plantée,* which is probably the only park in the world accessible only by train, elevator, or stairs, and possibly the longest and skinniest as well. Trees, roses, and shrubs were planted on an old railroad track that ran alone the *avenue Daumesnil.* Take a stroll above the traffic and stores underfoot (M. Gare de Lyon, Ledru-Rollin, or Daumesnil. From M. Gare de Lyon, walk up rue Michel Chasles to av. Daumesnil). Under the *promenade* is the **Viaduc des Arts,** 15-121, av. Daumesnil, M. Bastille, Ledru-Rollin, or Gare de Lyon, another fine place for a stroll if heights aren't your thing. Artists, designers, and craftspeople display their work in renovated spaces with huge glass windows.

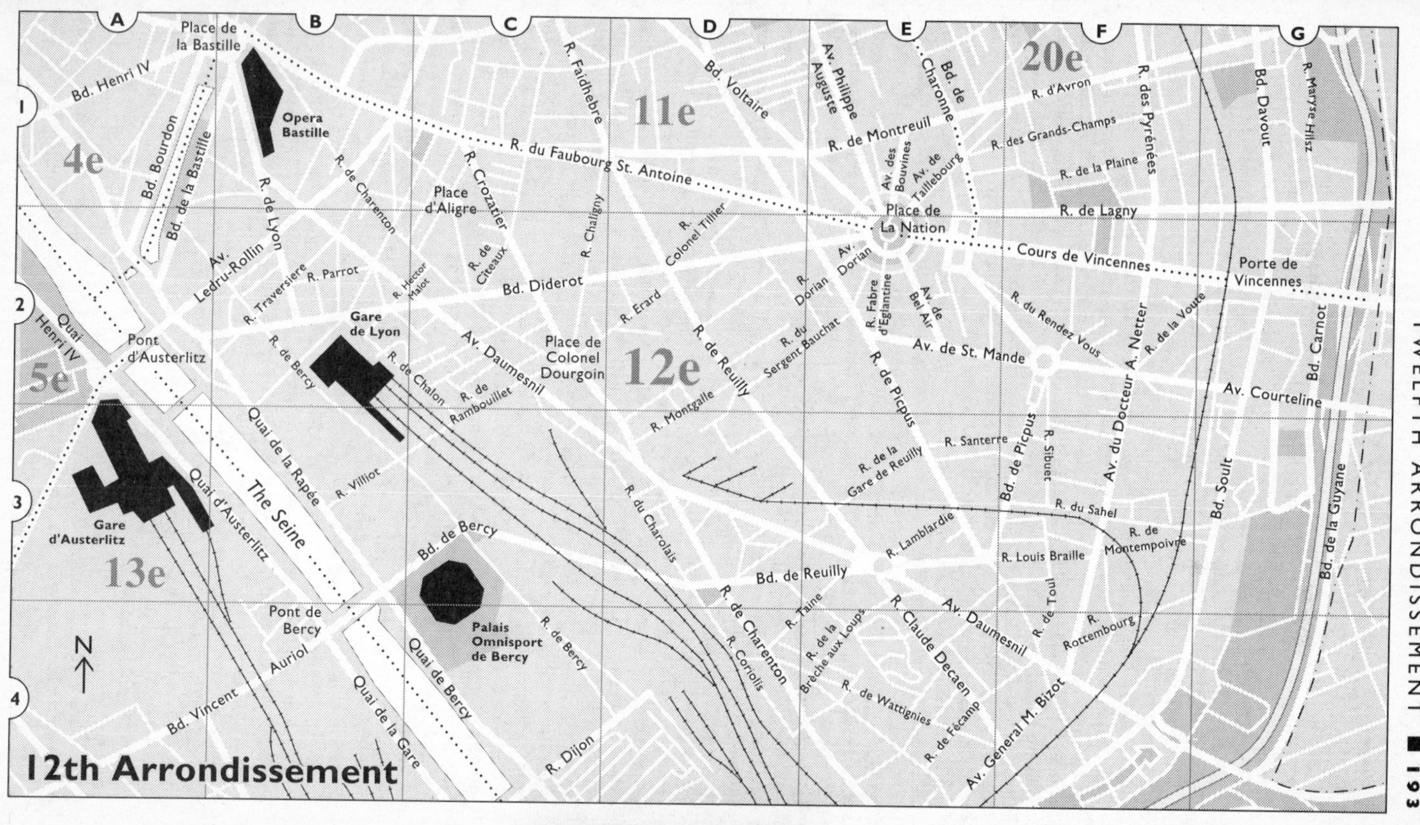
12th Arrondissement
A
B
C
D
E
F
G
1
2
3
4
4e
5e
11e
12e
13e
20e
N
Place de la Bastille
Opera Bastille
Bd. Henri IV
Bd. Bourdon
Bd. de la Bastille
R. de Lyon
Av. Ledru-Rollin
R. Traversiere
R. Parrot
R. Hector Malot
R. de Charenton
R. du Faubourg St. Antoine
Place d'Aligre
R. Crozatier
R. de Citeaux
Bd. Diderot
Gare de Lyon
R. de Chalon
R. de Rambouillet
R. de Bercy
R. Villiot
Quai de la Rapée
The Seine
Quai d'Austerlitz
Pont d'Austerlitz
Quai Henri IV
Gare d'Austerlitz
Pont de Bercy
Auriol
Bd. Vincent
Quai de la Gare
Quai de Bercy
Bd. de Bercy
Palais Omnisport de Bercy
R. de Bercy
R. Dijon
Av. Daumesnil
Place de Colonel Dourgoin
R. Chaligny
R. Faidhebre
R. Erard
R. Montgalle
R. du Charolais
R. de Reuilly
R. Colonel Tillier
Bd. Voltaire
R. du Sergent Bauchat
R. Dorian
R. de Charenton
R. Coriolis
Bd. de Reuilly
R. Taine
R. de la Brèche aux Loups
R. de Wattignies
R. Claude Decaen
R. de Fécamp
Av. General M. Bizot
Av. Daumesnil
R. de Toul
R. Rottembourg
R. Louis Braille
R. Lamblardie
R. de Montempoivre
R. du Sahel
R. Santerre
R. de la Gare de Reuilly
R. de Picpus
R. Fabre d'Eglantine
Av. Dorian
Av. de Bel Air
Av. de St. Mande
Bd. de Picpus
R. Sibuet
R. du Rendez Vous
Av. du Docteur A. Netter
R. de la Voute
Av. Courteline
Bd. Soult
Bd. Carnot
Bd. de la Guyane
Porte de Vincennes
Cours de Vincennes
R. de Lagny
R. de la Plaine
R. des Grands-Champs
R. d'Avron
R. des Pyrénées
Bd. Davout
R. Maryse Hilsz
Place de La Nation
Av. de Taillebourg
Av. des Bouvines
Bd. de Charonne
R. de Montreuil
Av. Philippe Auguste

SIGHTS

Thirteenth Arrondissement

Although its battery of office towers offers little to the sight-seer, the 13ème is a gem for gourmands. Come to explore Paris' **Chinatown,** located along av. de Choisy, or to wander the tangled, ancient streets of the **Butte aux Cailles,** a teensy pocket of artsy restaurants and bars. In the near future, the 13ème is likely to surface as an important axis of French intellectual and cultural life; it is the site of the new Bibliothèque de France (Library of France).

Until the 20th century, the 13ème was one of Paris' poorest, most squalid neighborhoods; Victor Hugo used parts of the 13ème as a setting for *Les Misérables.* Traversed by the **Bièvre,** a stagnant stream clogged with industrial refuse, it was notoriously the city's worst-smelling district. Environmentalists eventually won their campaign to close its tanneries and paper factories. In 1910, the Bièvre was filled in. While no longer a health risk, the 13ème throws few bones to even the Most Dedicated Tourist. Among its highlights, however, is the **Manufacture des Gobelins,** 42, av. des Gobelins (tel. 01 44 08 52 00; M. Gobelins), a tapestry workshop over 300 years old. Masters and journeymen still employ 17th-century weaving techniques, and can spend a full year on one square meter of tapestry. In the mid-17th century, the Gobelins was a prison-like establishment, where whole families lived in poverty to produce what have become priceless tapestry artworks, displayed in the Cluny museum and châteaux near Paris. Still an adjunct of the state, the factory receives commissions from French ministries and foreign embassies. Guided tours, the only way to get inside the factory, explain the intricacies of the weaving process. (Tours in French with free English-language handout, 90 min.; Tues.-Thurs. 2 and 2:45pm; 35F, ages 7-24 25F.)

Farther southwest, narrow streets wag through the **Butte aux Cailles** (quail knoll) district, one of the few old Parisian neighborhoods to escape the notice of both Picasso and Hemingway. (It did not, however, escape the notice of Pilâtre de Rosier or of the Marquis d'Arlandes, who landed the world's first hot-air balloon here on Nov. 21, 1783.) It might not enjoy secluded status much longer, though; trendy, painterly Parisians have begun to frequent its bars. On weekends, the junction of Butte aux Cailles with rue des Cinq Diamants becomes downright frisky.

Due south on rue Tolbiac stands the Romano-Byzantine **Eglise Sainte-Anne de la Maison Blanche,** built 1894-1912. Construction halted in 1898 due to lack of funds, but resumed with a grant from the Lombarts, a local family who owned a chocolate store on av. de Choisy. The front of the church is nicknamed *"la façade chocolat"* in their honor. Although Ste-Anne's pointed twin towers and rose-shaped clock make it impressive from the outside, the dark, plain interior is entirely forgettable.

Chinatown, located east of Ste-Anne's on av. de Choisy and av. d'Ivry, is populated not only by myriad Chinese, Vietnamese, and Cambodians, but also by hundreds of Asian restaurants and grocery stores. Like Chinatowns the world over, it offers delicious Asian cuisine for half the price of dinners elsewhere in the city.

Believe it or not, the panchromatic, Lego-like building in the southeast corner of the 13ème is a Salvation Army shelter, designed by Le Corbusier in 1931. The Princesse de Polignac, patron of the avant garde and friend to the architect, financed the project, named the **Cité de Refuge** (tel. 01 45 83 24 23; 12, rue Cantagrel).

The 13ème is also the site of the new **Bibliothèque de France (Library of France),** scheduled to open its doors in the fall of 1997. The new complex has replaced, in function if not in spirit, the old **Bibliothèque Nationale** (see "Sights—2ème," p. 149). One major difference, however, is that parts of the new library will be open to the public, whereas the old library was reserved for scholars. Designed by architect Dominique Perrault, the new library is a 7-billion-franc endeavor encompassing 7.5 hectares along the Seine, across from the Ministry of Finance. The Bibliothèque de France is just one piece of the 13ème's urban renewal puzzle; a new project called **ZAC (Zone d'Aménagement Concerte) Seine-Rive Gauche** provides for the construction of a university, five schools, a sports complex, a public garden, and a new metro line (Méteor). Librarians' associations and ad-hoc committees of intellectuals (including Claude Lévi-Strauss) wrote open letters to then-President François Mitter-

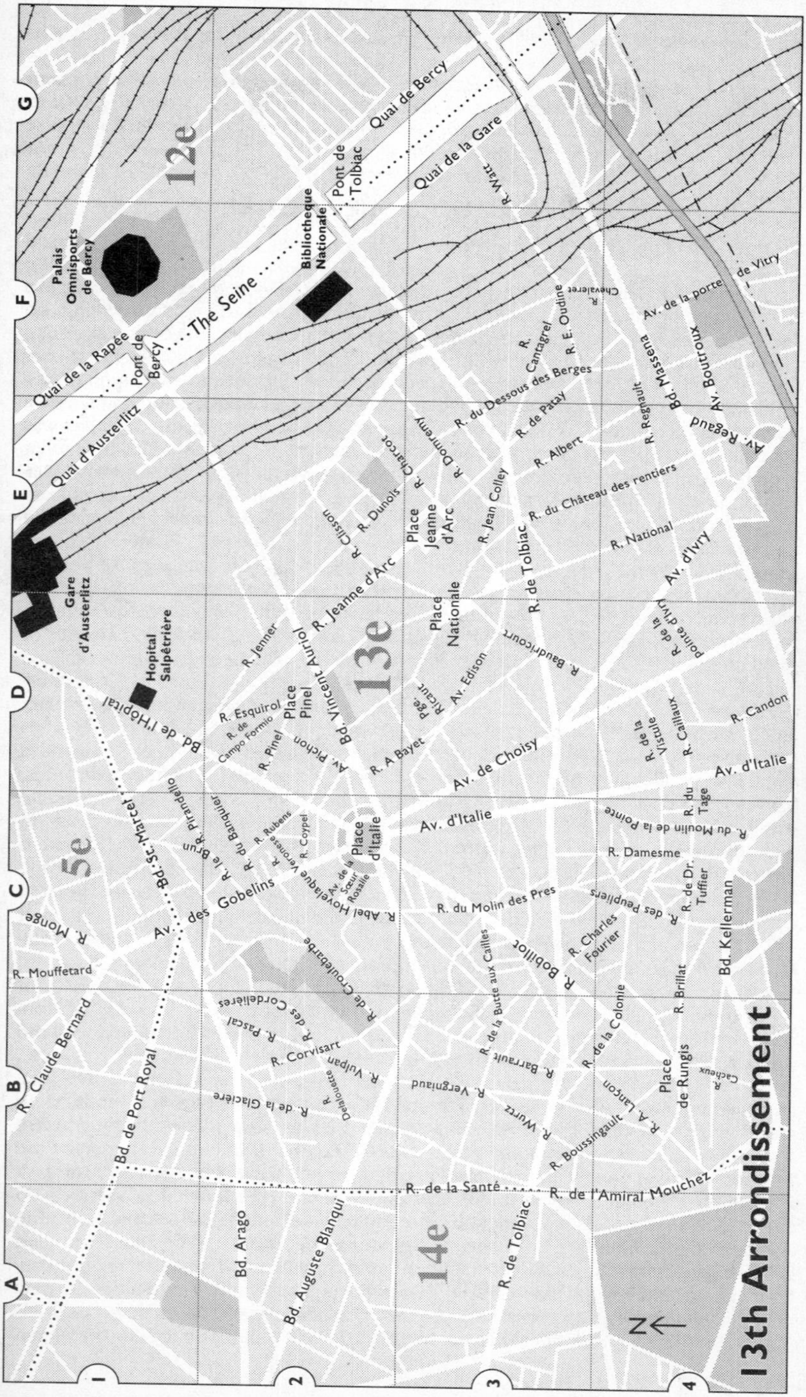

13th Arrondissement

Palais Omnisports de Bercy
Bibliotheque Nationale
Gare d'Austerlitz
Hopital Salpêtrière
The Seine
Quai de la Rapée
Quai d'Austerlitz
Quai de Bercy
Quai de la Gare
Pont de Bercy
Pont de Tolbiac
12e
13e
5e
14e
R. Watt
R. Chevaleret
R. E. Oudine
R. Cantagrel
R. du Dessous des Berges
R. de Patay
R. Albert
R. du Château des rentiers
R. National
R. de Tolbiac
R. Jean Colley
R. Domremy
R. Charcot
R. Dunois
R. Clisson
Place Jeanne d'Arc
R. Jeanne d'Arc
Place Nationale
R. Baudricourt
Av. d'Ivry
R. de la Pointe d'Ivry
Av. de la porte de Vitry
Bd. Massena
R. Regnault
Av. Boutroux
Av. Regaud
R. Jenner
Bd. Vincent Auriol
R. Esquirol
R. de Campo Formio
Place Pinel
R. Pinel
Av. Pichon
R. A Bayet
Pge. Ricaut
Av. Edison
Av. de Choisy
R. de la Vistule
R. Caillaux
R. Candon
Av. d'Italie
Place d'Italie
R. du Tage
R. du Moulin de la Pointe
R. Damesme
R. des Peupliers
R. de Dr. Tuffier
Bd. Kellerman
R. du Molin des Pres
R. Charles Fourier
R. Bobillot
R. de la Colonie
R. Brillat
R. de la Butte aux Cailles
R. Barrault
R. Verginaud
R. Wurz
R. Boussingault
R. A. Lançon
Place de Rungis
R. Cacheux
R. de l'Amiral Mouchez
R. de la Santé
Bd. de l'Hôpital
Bd. St. Marcel
R. Pirandello
R. le Brun
R. du Banquier
R. Rubens
R. Véronese
R. Coypel
Av. de la Sœur Rosalie
R. Abel Hovelaque
Av. des Gobelins
R. Monge
R. Mouffetard
R. de Croulebarbe
R. des Cordelières
R. Pascal
R. Corvisart
R. Vulpian
R. Desbouette
R. de la Glacière
R. Claude Bernard
Bd. de Port Royal
Bd. Arago
Bd. Auguste Blanqui
R. de Tolbiac
N

SIGHTS

rand arguing the inadequacy of Perrault's design. Critics warn that the four L-shaped towers, designed to serve as the library's depositories (and to look like open books from above), would be difficult for researchers who needed one book from the 15th story of tower A and another from the 16th story of tower B across the way. Others worry that light streaming through the clear, glass walls will damage rare volumes. The books on the shelves await their fate in silence.

Fourteenth Arrondissement: Montparnasse

Montparnasse has served as a magnet for an impressive array of residents since the turn of the century. The first to arrive were Bretons, who had lost their livelihoods after failed harvests. Arriving *en masse* at the Gare de Montparnasse, they settled around the station so that they could cut a quick path home if the agricultural tide turned. Vestiges of Breton culture—*crêperies,* stores selling traditional Breton crafts and books, and even Breton cultural associations—remain strong in this area. Montparnasse next became a center for the artistic and political avant garde, marking the beginning of a veritable golden age of Bohemia. Artists including Modigliani, Utrillo, Soutine, Chagall, and Léger migrated from the lamentably less hip Montmartre, forming the base of the artistic movement called the Paris School. Political exiles, notably Lenin and Trotsky, spent evenings planning strategies over cognac in the much acclaimed cafés along the bd. Montparnasse.

After WWI, Montparnasse attracted other artists, especially Americans who wanted to escape Prohibition and profit from a favorable exchange rate. Man Ray transformed an apartment into a photo lab; Calder worked on his first sculptures; Hemingway did some of his most serious writing (and drinking); and Henry Miller created the shocking, steamy *Tropic of Cancer* at Seurat's villa with the encouragement of Anaïs Nin and Lawrence Durrell. It was all fun and games until the outbreak of the Spanish Civil War, followed by WWII, which put the final kibosh on the Bohemian community in Montparnasse. Although pockets of struggling artists persist, the *quartier* has become predominantly residential, especially in the working class neighborhoods north and west of Parc Montsouris. Bordered on the southeast by the sprawling Cité Universitaire, an international Animal House for the university set, the 14ème is dominated at its opposite corner by a mammoth ode to modern design in the form of the **Tour Montparnasse.** Yes, it is as tall and unattractive as you've heard—all 209m of it. Rising from the intersection of the 6ème, 14ème, and 15ème arrondissements like a rook in a monumental game of urban renewal, the *tour* casts a black pall on the area around it which teems with commercialism and caters to tourists (see "Sights—15ème," p. 200). The nighttime excitement around nearby rue de la Gaité may sometimes reach XXX proportions, but the plentiful clothes shops along rue d'Alésia and international eateries lining rue Daguerre are tailored for a wider audience.

Visitors to the 14ème will come most often either to drink where famous dead folk once drank or to see where famous dead folk now lie. The **Cimetière Montparnasse,** 3, bd. Edgar Quinet (tel. 01 44 10 86 50; M. Edgar Quinet) is less than romantic. Shrouded in the shadow of the Tour Montparnasse, crisscrossed by avenues, too crowded with tombs for grass, and occupied by cats and other city wildlife, the cemetery is less than restful, too. Armed with a free *Index des Célébrités* (the detailed map available at the Conservation building just left of the main entrance), determined sightseers thread their way through unknowns to pay their respects to writers like Guy de Maupassant, Samuel Beckett, Jean-Paul Sartre and Simone de Beauvoir (who share a grave), François Truffaut, and Marguerite Duvas, car manufacturer André Citroën, composer Camille Saint-Saens, sculptor Ossip Zadkine, editor Pierre Larousse (of dictionary fame), artist Man Ray, newly arrived composer Serge Gainsbourg, and loyal Frenchman Alfred Dreyfus. Don't miss the memorial to Charles Baudelaire who greeted Death willingly in his *Fleurs du Mal,* published six years before he died: "O Death, old captain, it is time! Lift the anchor! We wish...to plunge into the abyss,

Heaven or Hell, what matters? To the very edge of knowledge in order to find something *new!*" (Open Mon.-Fri. 7:30am-6pm, Sat. 8:30am-6pm, Sun. 9am-6pm; Nov. 6-March 15 closes 5:30pm. Free.)

Place Denfert-Rochereau is presided over by a lion sculpted by Bartholdi, the creator of the Statue of Liberty. Most visitors, however, observe Bartholdi's beast from their place in the line to visit **Les Catacombs,** 1, pl. Denfert-Rochereau (tel. 01 43 22 47 63; M. Denfert-Rochereau), a series of subterranean tunnels 20m below ground level that were originally excavated to provide stone for building the city. By the 1770s, much of the Left Bank was in danger of caving in, and digging promptly stopped. The former quarry was then converted to a mass grave in order to relieve the unbearable stench emanating from cemeteries around Paris. Near the entrance to the ossuary reads the ominous caution, "Stop! Beyond Here Is the Empire of Death." Many have ignored the sign. In 1793, a Parisian got lost and was not found for nine years, at which point he'd become, so to speak, one with the pile of bones. During World War II, the Empire of Death was actually full of life when the resistance set up headquarters among these old and loyal Parisian bones.

The depths of the ossuary compose an underground city (note the "street" names on the walls) with bones for bricks and marrow for mortar. Navigate your way through femur-lined tunnels, complete with fibulas, and anchored by craniums. The ghoulish arrangement is tidy, practical, and often quite artistic. Some rooms even sport cheery sayings to make the journey more interesting—*"Pensez le matin que vous n'irez peut être pas jusques au soir et au soir que vous n'irez pas jusques au matin."* (Think each morning that you may not be alive in the evening, and each evening that you may not be alive in the morning.) Beware the low ceilings and unidentifiable liquid seeping from the walls, and bring a sweater, a flashlight, and a friend for support. Not recommended for the faint of heart or leg; the 85 steep steps you climb on the way in and out provide a day's worth of exercise. Not wheelchair accessible. (Open Tues.-Fri. 2-4pm, Sat.-Sun. 9-11am and 2-4pm. Admission 27F, ages 7-25 19F, particularly brave under 7 free.)

Parc Montsouris offers a sunny return to the land of the living. Begun in 1867 by the Baron Haussmann, this park doubles as an arboretum, offering sanctuary to hundreds of rare and unusual trees, all well-labeled and cared for. An amazing variety of birds, ducks, and geese splashes contentedly in the artificial lake at one end of the park. (The designer of this lake killed himself after the water mysteriously drained during the park's opening ceremony.) Sunbathers, children, and *clochards* are even allowed to stretch out on a 50m x 50m strip of grass along the street side of the lake. Don't give in to the temptation to pet a lesser snow goose, Australian rajah shelduck, or fulvous whistling duck—they'll all hiss a warning, then deliver a nasty bite (open Mon-Fri. 7:30am-10pm, Sat.-Sun. 9am-10pm).

Across the bd. Jourdan, thousands of students study, argue, and/or drink themselves silly in the **Cité Universitaire,** a 40-hectare display case for students who have come from no less than 122 countries to no less than 30 dorms, two of them designed by Le Corbusier. The "vertical slab" called the **Pavilion Suisse** (1932) is adored by architects as a monument of his early career. With its *pilotis* (stilts) underneath and its garden on the roof, the building reflects the architect's dream of a vertical city, with life lived on several levels. During the German occupation, the roof garden housed a battery of anti-aircraft guns. Le Corbusier returned in 1959, with the **Maison du Brasil.** South and west of the dorms, the expansive greenery flaunts Parisian park customs, while hundreds of joggers, frisbee throwers, bikers, and boombox players flout the "keep off" signs that ring the lawns.

North of the Parc Montsouris is the **Hôpital Ste-Anne,** 15, rue Cabanis, a psychiatric hospital with an interesting history. It first opened its doors to the nervous citizens of Paris in 1221 but did not begin to thrive until Louis XIV took the throne, when state funds, mostly earmarked for the imprisonment of "wanton girls and women," poured in. After a series of fires, the hospital went through several incarnations—including one as a dairy farm in the 18th century with a full complement of 140 cows and 700 pigs—before finally being restored to its original life as a clinic by Napoleon

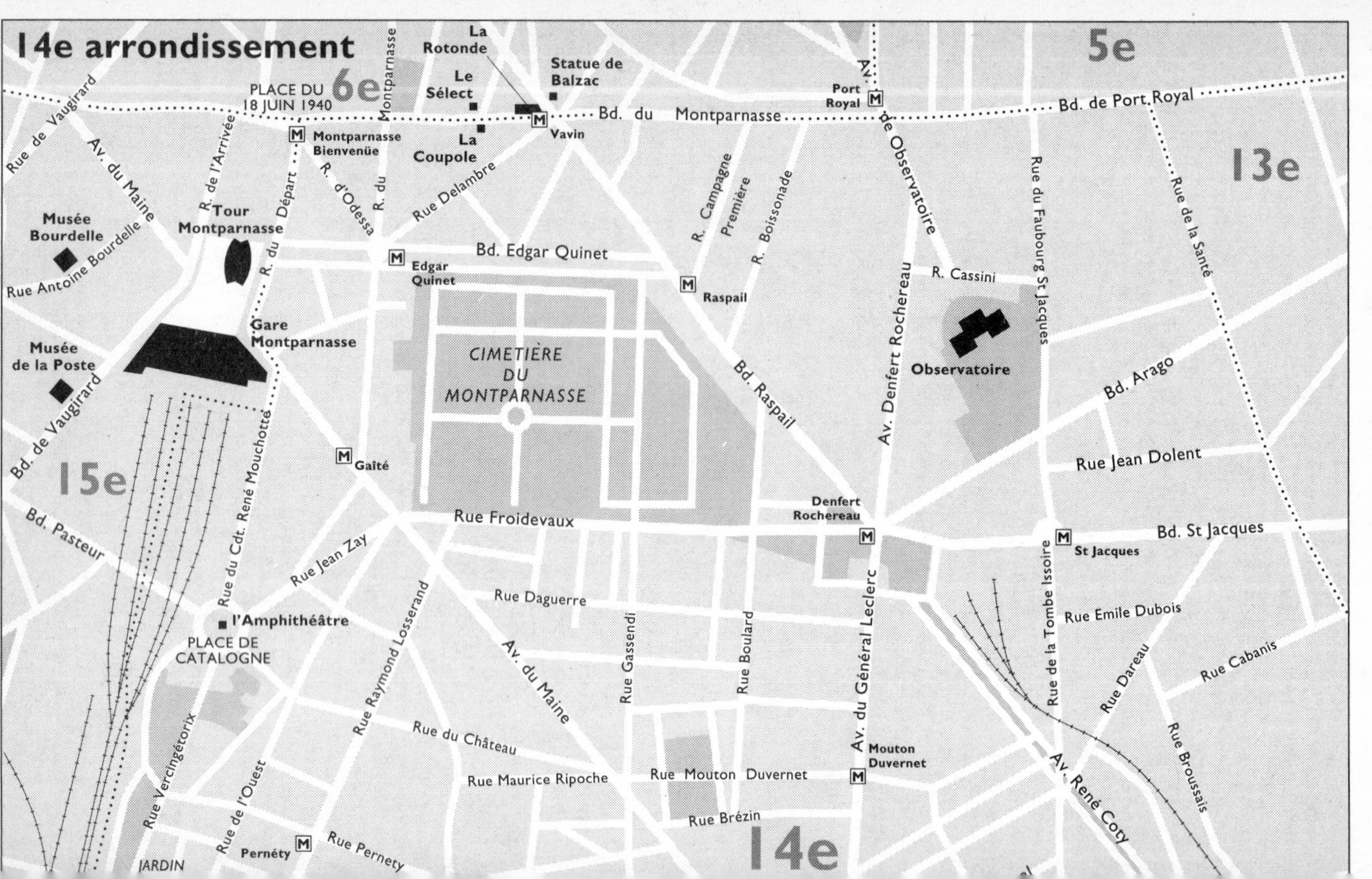
14e arrondissement
La Rotonde
Statue de Balzac
5e
Le Sélect
PLACE DU 18 JUIN 1940
6e
Montparnasse
Port Royal
Av. de Observatoire
Bd. du Montparnasse
Bd. de Port Royal
Vavin
Rue de Vaugirard
Montparnasse Bienvenüe
La Coupole
13e
Av. du Maine
R. de l'Arrivée
R. d'Odessa
R. du Montparnasse
Rue Delambre
R. Campagne Première
R. Boissonade
Rue du Faubourg St Jacques
Rue de la Santé
Musée Bourdelle
Tour Montparnasse
Rue Antoine Bourdelle
R. du Départ
Bd. Edgar Quinet
Edgar Quinet
Raspail
R. Cassini
Av. Denfert Rochereau
Gare Montparnasse
Musée de la Poste
CIMETIÈRE DU MONTPARNASSE
Bd. Raspail
Observatoire
Bd. Arago
Bd. de Vaugirard
Rue du Cdt. René Mouchotte
Gaîté
Rue Jean Dolent
15e
Rue Froidevaux
Denfert Rochereau
Bd. St Jacques
St Jacques
Bd. Pasteur
Rue Jean Zay
Rue Daguerre
Rue Emile Dubois
l'Amphithéâtre
PLACE DE CATALOGNE
Rue Raymond Losserand
Av. du Maine
Rue Gassendi
Rue Boulard
Av. du Général Leclerc
Rue de la Tombe Issoire
Rue Dareau
Rue Cabanis
Rue Vercingétorix
Rue du Château
Rue de l'Ouest
Rue Maurice Ripoche
Rue Mouton Duvernet
Mouton Duvernet
Av. René Coty
Rue Broussais
Rue Brézin
Pernéty
Rue Pernety
JARDIN
14e

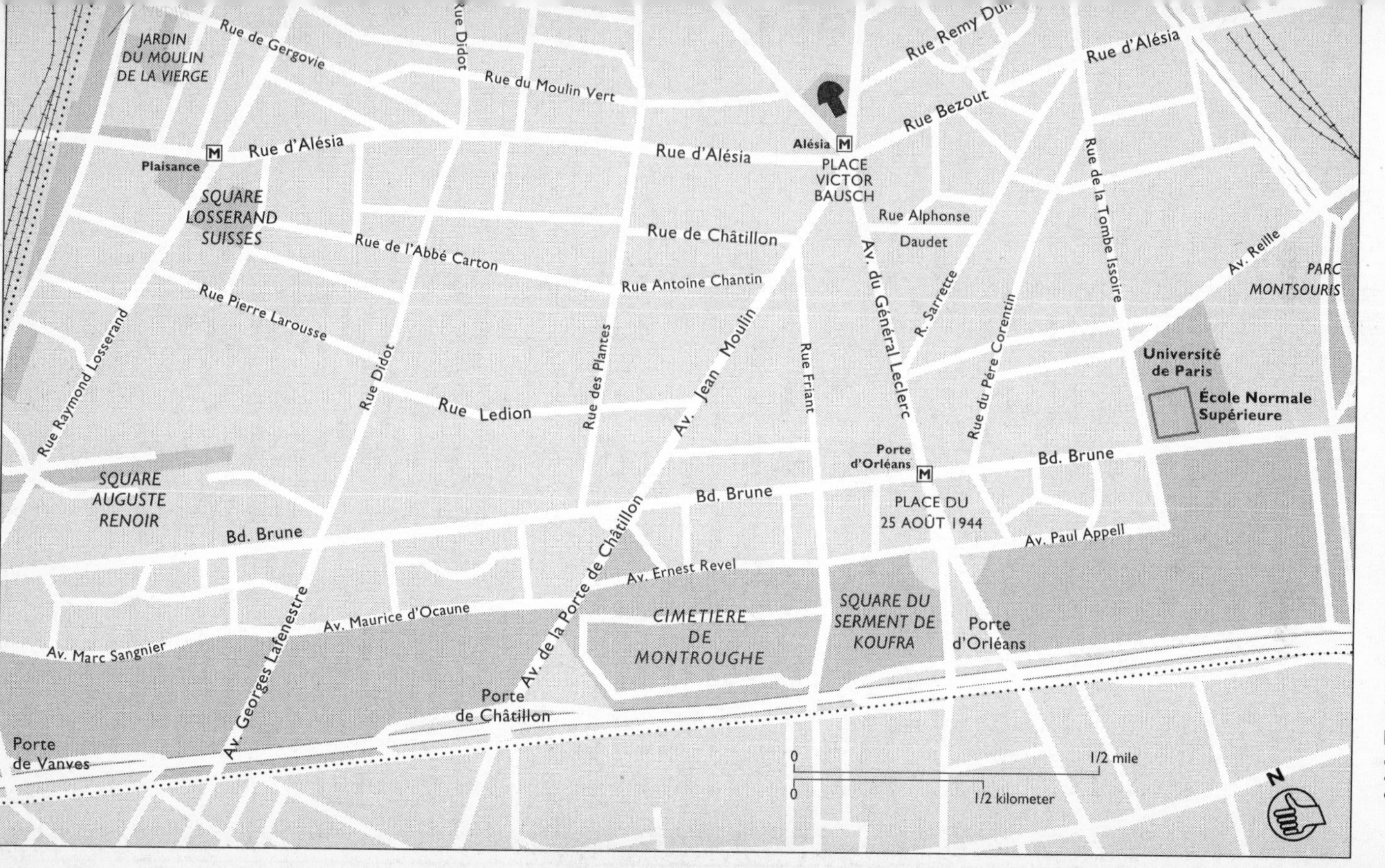
JARDIN DU MOULIN DE LA VIERGE
Rue de Gergovie
Rue Didot
Rue du Moulin Vert
Rue Remy Du
Rue d'Alésia
Rue Bezout
Plaisance
Rue d'Alésia
Rue d'Alésia
Alésia
PLACE VICTOR BAUSCH
SQUARE LOSSERAND SUISSES
Rue Alphonse Daudet
Rue de Châtillon
Rue de l'Abbé Carton
Rue de la Tombe Issoire
Av. Reille
PARC MONTSOURIS
Rue Antoine Chantin
Av. du Général Leclerc
R. Sarrette
Rue Pierre Larousse
Rue du Père Corentin
Av. Jean Moulin
Rue Friant
Université de Paris
École Normale Supérieure
Rue Raymond Losserand
Rue Didot
Rue des Plantes
Rue Ledion
Porte d'Orléans
Bd. Brune
SQUARE AUGUSTE RENOIR
Bd. Brune
PLACE DU 25 AOÛT 1944
Bd. Brune
Av. Paul Appell
Av. Ernest Revel
Av. de la Porte de Châtillon
Av. Maurice d'Ocaune
CIMETIERE DE MONTROUGHE
SQUARE DU SERMENT DE KOUFRA
Porte d'Orléans
Av. Marc Sangnier
Av. Georges Lafenestre
Porte de Châtillon
Porte de Vanves
0
1/2 mile
0
1/2 kilometer
N

III in 1863. Although access to most of the buildings is restricted to the medical staff and patients (neither of whom you probably want to visit), a tour of the grounds affords a quick respite from the bustle of the streets (open 24 hrs.). Curiously enough, all of the streets within the hospital complex are named after artists like Camille Claudel and Vincent Van Gogh, who themselves had breakdowns.

The opposite edge of the 14ème, just south of l'Amphithéâtre, harbors its own schizophrenic tendencies, though these are of an architectural nature. **Notre-Dame du Travail,** 59, rue Vercingétorix (tel. 01 44 10 72 92), was built to tend to the spiritual needs of the hordes of workers who settled in this quarter during the turn-of-the-century Universal Exposition on the Champs de Mars. Facing onto a street named for a Gaullic chief, the church's sand-colored, Roman-style exterior demurely hides a surprising interior infested with iron girders and metal supports. Long before the Musée d'Orsay evolved as a fusion of function with art forms, architect Jules Astrac designed Notre-Dame du Travail to symbolized the devotion of the workers—through the products of their labor—to the church. The alcoves between the grey, metal beams are painted with fanciful flowers to relieve the monotony and remind the faithful that they've indeed left the factory. (Open Mon.-Fri. 8:30am-noon and 2-7pm, Sat. 2-7pm, Sun. 8:30am-noon). Next to the church rears up another tribute to architectural time travel in the form of the **Pl. de Séoul** in the Centre Catalogue, 16-18, rue Guilleminot. This mild-mannered medical office building appears from the outside to be a cream-colored coliseum, sedate and unremarkable. Step into the inner courtyard, however, and there's no more Clark Kent; the circular interior and even the Roman-esque columns are coated from floor to rooftop in mirrored glass.

Fifteenth Arrondissement: Tour Montparnasse

Perhaps the best introduction to the 15ème is the metro ride that takes you there. Metro line 6 runs on an elevated track; board at Trocadéro and ride to the 15ème's central stop, **La Motte-Picquet-Grenelle.** From the car window there's a lovely view of the Seine, the Eiffel Tower, and the rooftops. Called "the new 16ème" by some, this area is nearly as elegant and much more affordable. A mostly residential quarter, the neighborhood has little in the way of sights, but does present a charming picture of daily Parisian life. Most of the brighter cafés, stores, and specialty shops in the 15ème are strung along bd. de Grenelle, while the festive rue du Commerce overflows with flower shops, fashionable clothing stores, and markets. For more people-watching, hop out at the Convention metro stop, where cafés with abundant tables occupy each corner at the intersection of rue de la Convention and rue de Vaugirard. If you're still interested in seeing the city's sights from afar, take the elevator to the top of the towering Tour Montparnasse.

The **Tour Montparnasse** (tel. 01 45 38 52 56; M. Montparnasse-Bienvenue) dominates the *quartier's* northeast corner. Standing 59 stories tall, the controversial building looks somewhat out of place amidst the older architecture of Montparnasse. But the group of French architects who designed the tower believed that it would revolutionize the Paris skyline. It has, but not without the disapproval of many Parisians. Some argue that the *tour,* completed in 1973, is a slice of Manhattan inserted awkwardly in the middle of Paris. Shortly after it was completed, the city of Paris passed an ordinance forbidding any further structures to be built within Paris proper, designating La Défense as the only possible home of looming monsters like the Tour Montparnasse. The *tour,* which houses a huge underground shopping mall and train station, once held the European record for the tallest office building. Take advantage of this by riding an elevator to the 56th floor, then climbing the few remaining flights to the rooftop terrace, where a fabulous view of the unobstructed Paris skyline awaits (open May-Sept. daily 9:30am-11:30pm; Oct.-April Mon.-Fri. 9:30am-10:30pm; admission 42F, seniors 36F, students 33F, under age 14 26F).

I'll Trade You My '52 Mantle for Your '88 Gerard Longuet

If you're going to be in France for any length of time and need to make a phone call, you'll eventually give up the constant (and futile) search for coin-operated telephones, and invest in a *télécarte*. While making your call, look down at your feet. You'll probably see numerous cigarette butts mixed in with many pieces of plastic wrap similar to the one you just shucked off your own card. But where are the spent cards? Where is the *télécarte* graveyard? The answer is simple and classically French: collectors' albums. That's right: the ads and artwork on the cards turn some designs into valuable commodities. So valuable, in fact, that an entire *télécarte* collection business has developed around the credit-card sized *chef d'oeuvres*. Trading and collecting the cards is as intense and lucrative a hobby as that of collecting baseball cards in the U.S. Stores and markets may have boxes of common and uncommon cards (for 5-10F each), while the rarities preen under protective covering in binders and acrylic cases. The condition of a card, of course, drastically affects its value, while the number of call-enabling *unités* is irrelevant. A 1987-88 carte by Gerard Longuet is one of the gems in the *télécarte* collector's crown. Only 40 exist, and an unblemished one will net you 34,000F. But for the real prize, seek out the November 1988 card "Les Boxeurs," with artwork by Gilles Chagny. There are 100 out there, but only one is signed by the artist. Maybe it's down at your feet right now as you make your call—it's worth checking, because if it *is* there, you've just stumbled across a cool 60,000F. Now that's a lot of phone calls.

In front of the Tour Montparnasse, the **pl. du 18 juin** commemorates two important events from World War II. The name recalls the June 18, 1940, BBC radio broadcast from London by General de Gaulle in which he called on his fellow citizens to resist the occupying Nazi forces and the Vichy collaborationist régime of Maréchal Pétain. It was also on this *place* that General Leclerc, the leader of the French forces, accepted the surrender of General von Choltitz, the Nazi commander of the Paris occupation, on August 25, 1944. It is due to von Choltitz's love of the city that the Tour Montparnasse is not Paris' only monument. Despite continual orders from Hitler to destroy Paris ("Is Paris burning?") and retreat, von Choltitz disobeyed, thus saving countless Parisian historical and architectural landmarks.

A roundabout walk southwest will take you past the **Musée Bourdelle,** a well-stocked collection of the works of the French sculptor Emile-Antoine Bourdelle, and past the surprisingly interesting **Musée de la Poste** (see "Museums," p. 248).

Only a metro stop from the *tour* or four blocks south of the Musée de la Poste is **L'Institut Pasteur,** 25, rue du Dr. Roux (tel. 01 45 68 82 82 or 01 45 68 82 83 for museum information; M. Pasteur). Founded by the French scientist Louis Pasteur in 1887, the *institut* is now an international center for biochemical research, development, and treatment facilities. It was here that Pasteur, a champion of germ theory in the 19th century, developed his famous technique for purifying milk products. Today, some of the most advanced research on HIV is conducted here. In 1983, the *institut* gained notoriety for Dr. Luc Montaigner's isolation of HIV, the virus that causes AIDS. For years, Montaigner was embroiled in an international legal and scientific dispute with Dr. Robert Gallo of the American Centers for Disease Control over who had first isolated the HIV virus, but he continues his work here on HIV.

The Institute houses an extensive museum on Pasteur and his work. The museum offers an exhaustive run-down of Pasteur's medical and artistic projects, a lively tour of his lab equipment and preserved living quarters, and a visit to the crypt which houses the scientist's corpse. Pasteur's son designed the symbolic fantasyland on the ceiling, a mosaic recalling Pasteur *père's* work with wine casks, rabid dogs, sheep, and of course, lots of happy cows. Tours are in French with photocopied English translations so you won't let any of it slip *past your eyes* (open Sept.-July Mon.-Fri. 2-5:30pm; admission 15F, students 8F. Closed in August.). Should Pasteur's life spur you to perform some selfless act, a blood donation center is across the street.

Off rue de la Convention, **La Ruche,** 52, rue Dantzig (M. Convention), is a group of round brick buildings designed as a wine pavilion by Gustave Eiffel for the exposition of 1900, a decade after the more famous exposition. During the early 1900s the building, whose name means "the beehive," was bought by the private charitable foundation La Ruche Seydoux, and used to house struggling artists (among them Chagall and Soutine). Today the foundation still gives artists grants, studios, and housing. The garden surrounding the building is studded with sculpture, the work of the house's residents. As La Ruche is a private foundation, visitors can only gain access to the garden when an entering or exiting resident is willing to let you in.

Architecture buffs may wish to hop on the metro and go to the Félix Faure stop. Right outside, the 1905 spaghetti-façade of the building at 24, pl. Étienne Pernet, gives a visceral sense of what people mean when they call Art Nouveau "noodle style." A few steps away on av. Félix Faure, no. 31 is a little less daring, though a little newer; constructed in 1912, its façade is festooned with stone flowers. Down the street, a sculpted representation of Aesop's fable, *The Crow and the Fox,* built in 1907, adorns the front of 40, av. Félix Faure.

Sixteenth Arrondissement

On January 1, 1860, the wealthy villages of Auteuil, Passy, and Chaillot banded together and joined Paris, forming what is now the 16ème arrondissement. More than a century later, the area's original aristocratic families continue to hold their ground, making the 16ème a stronghold of conservative politics, fashion, and culture. It is rumored that some members of the local nobility forbid their children to sing *La*

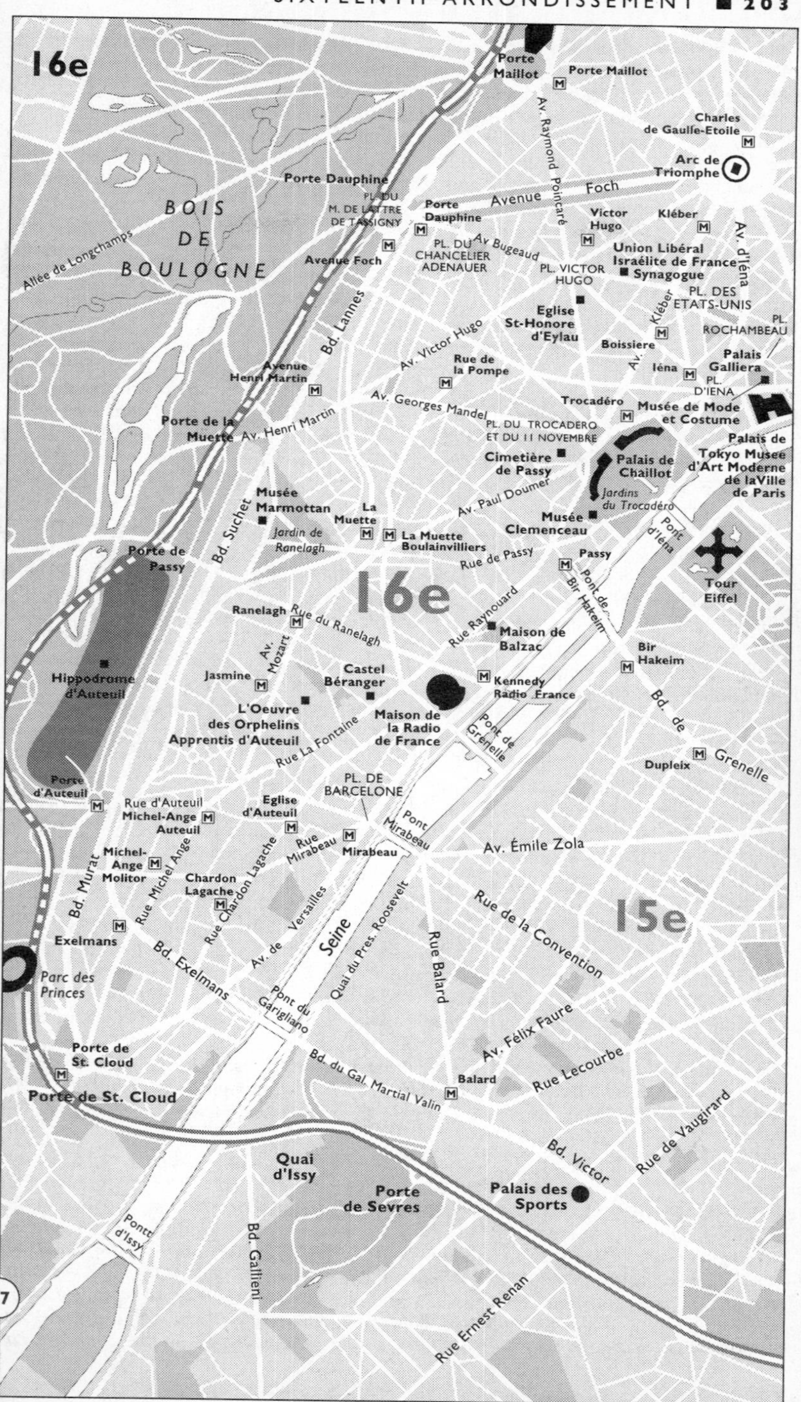
16e
Porte Maillot
Porte Maillot
Av. Raymond Poincaré
Charles de Gaulle-Etoile
Arc de Triomphe
BOIS DE BOULOGNE
Allée de Longchamps
Porte Dauphine
PL. DU M. DE LATTRE DE TASSIGNY
Porte Dauphine
Avenue Foch
Victor Hugo
Kléber
Av. d'Iéna
Av Bugeaud
PL. DU CHANCELIER ADENAUER
Avenue Foch
Union Libéral Israélite de France Synagogue
PL. VICTOR HUGO
PL. DES ETATS-UNIS
Av. Kléber
Bd. Lannes
Eglise St-Honore d'Eylau
PL. ROCHAMBEAU
Boissiere
Av. Victor Hugo
Rue de la Pompe
Iéna
Palais Galliera
PL. D'IENA
Avenue Henri Martin
Av. Georges Mandel
Trocadéro
Musée de Mode et Costume
Porte de la Muette
Av. Henri Martin
PL. DU TROCADERO ET DU 11 NOVEMBRE
Palais de Tokyo Musee d'Art Moderne de laVille de Paris
Cimetière de Passy
Palais de Chaillot
Jardins du Trocadéro
Musée Marmottan
La Muette
Av. Paul Doumer
Musée Clemenceau
Pont d'Iéna
Bd. Suchet
Jardin de Ranelagh
La Muette Boulainvilliers
Porte de Passy
Rue de Passy
Passy
Tour Eiffel
16e
Pont de Bir Hakeim
Ranelagh
Rue du Ranelagh
Rue Raynouard
Maison de Balzac
Av. Mozart
Bir Hakeim
Hippodrome d'Auteuil
Jasmine
Castel Béranger
Kennedy Radio France
L'Oeuvre des Orphelins Apprentis d'Auteuil
Maison de la Radio de France
Bd. de Grenelle
Rue La Fontaine
Pont de Grenelle
Dupleix
Porte d'Auteuil
Rue d'Auteuil
PL. DE BARCELONE
Michel-Ange Auteuil
Eglise d'Auteuil
Pont Mirabeau
Rue Mirabeau
Mirabeau
Av. Émile Zola
Michel-Ange Molitor
Rue Michel Ange
Chardon Lagache
Rue Chardon Lagache
Bd. Murat
Quai du Pres. Roosevelt
Rue de la Convention
Seine
Av. de Versailles
Rue Balard
15e
Exelmans
Bd. Exelmans
Parc des Princes
Pont du Garigliano
Av. Félix Faure
Porte de St. Cloud
Bd. du Gal. Martial Valin
Balard
Rue Lecourbe
Porte de St. Cloud
Bd. Victor
Rue de Vaugirard
Quai d'Issy
Porte de Sevres
Palais des Sports
Pontt d'Issy
Bd. Gallieni
Rue Ernest Renan
7

SIGHTS

Marseillaise, the anthem of the Revolutionaries who beheaded their ancestors. In this lavish residential neighborhood, *hôtels particuliers* (small mansions or townhouses, often with little gardens) retire graciously from wide, quiet roads; businesses, storefronts, and tackiness are at a minimum. Instead, this quarter has embassies (there are 64), museums (the 16ème boasts about half of Paris' museums), and *la crème de la crème* of Parisian high society (the only people who can afford the real estate). To do the 16ème justice, you'll want to flip back and forth repeatedly between these pages and the Museums chapter.

Enter by M. Porte Dauphine, one of the few surviving examples of Hector Guimard's Art Nouveau Paris metro stops. If you don't know it from photographs and vodka ads, it's recognizable by its green, spidery, winged metal frame. To the west lies the Bois de Boulogne; the av. de Foch stretches east to the Arc de Triomphe. One of Haussmann's finest creations, this avenue's expansive width (about 120m) features stretches of lawn running up each of its sides and through its center. Fashionable Parisians of yesteryear drove carriages down av. de Foch on their way to the Bois de Boulogne. The stately *hôtels particuliers* lining both sides of the street are some of the city's most expensive addresses; those on the sun-bathed south side are even more desirable. Stop at the **Musée d'Ennery** and the **Musée Arménien** at no. 59 as you walk down the avenue towards the Arc de Triomphe. While enjoyable for a stroll during the day, don't walk here alone at night; this area has become a cruising strip for prostitutes.

Many of the 16ème's busiest avenues radiate from the pl. de l'Etoile (also called pl. Charles de Gaulle), home to the Arc de Triomphe. Following the commercial av. Marceau down to the Seine takes you past the **Eglise St-Pierre de Chaillot,** between rue de Chaillot and av. Pierre-1er de Serbie. This church, located at the former heart of the village of Auteuil, is a neo-Romanesque structure with brilliantly lit stained glass and a striking sculpture by Henri Bouchard over its front three arches. Stop in for detailed information about foreign-language religious services around Paris or the schedule of free organ concerts. (Office open Mon.-Sat. 9:30am-12:30pm and 3-7pm; Sun 9:30am-12:30pm.) At the end of av. Marceau is the place de l'Alma and a life-size replica of the Statue of Liberty's golden torch, one of several tributes in the neighborhood to France's most famous gift to the United States.

The **Palais de Tokyo,** to your left as you turn up av. du Président Wilson, houses the **Musée d'Art Moderne de la Ville de Paris** and numerous other exhibition halls. Built for the 1937 World Expo, the palace took its name from the adjacent quai de Tokyo. (After WWII, in which Japan fought as an Axis power, it was renamed the quai de New York.) The gardens of the **Palais Galliera,** across from the Palais de Tokyo, draw both young children and sculpture enthusiasts who come to contemplate the three allegorical figures (representing painting, architecture, and sculpture) framed by arches high above the greenery. If you pack a lunch, the gardens make a perfect place for a peaceful meal and a great way to avoid the area's expensive restaurants. The Palais Galliera was built for the Duchess of Galliera by Louis Ginain as a repository for her collection of Italian Baroque art, but never served that function. Instead, the collection went to Genoa; the Italianate structure, completed in 1892, now houses the more contemporary and international **Musée de Mode et Costume.** To enter the museum, follow either of the streets next to the garden to av. Pierre-1er de Serbie. Farther down the avenue at pl. d'Iéna, the **Musée Guimet** contains a spectacular collection of Asian art.

Following av. du Président Wilson from pl. d'Iéna to pl. du Trocadéro et 11 Novembre (generally referred to as "Trocadéro") leads to the radical modernist structure located in the *place* called the **Palais de Chaillot.** A museum and entertainment complex, the Palais houses the **Musée du Cinéma Henri-Langlois,** the **Musée de l'Homme,** the **Musée de la Marine,** and the **Musée National des Monuments Français** as well as the **Théâtre National de Chaillot** and the **Cinémathèque Française** (see "Entertainment," p. 251 and p. 253). Built for the 1937 World Expo, Jacques Carlu's design features two curved wings cradling a paved courtyard. Surveyed by the 7.5m-tall bronze Apollo—another Bouchard sculpture—the building's

SIGHTS

open-air centerpiece attracts tourists, vendors, roller-skating dancers, and political demonstrators. It also offers the best view in all of Paris of the nearby Eiffel Tower and Champ de Mars.

The Palais de Chaillot is actually the last of a series of buildings built on this site. Catherine de Médicis had a château here, later transformed into a convent by Queen Henrietta of England. Napoleon razed the old château and planned to build a more lavish one on the same site for his son until his rotten luck at Waterloo brought construction to a screeching halt. In the 1820s, the Duc d'Angoulême built a fortress-like memorial to his Spanish victory at Trocadéro—hence the present name. That in turn was replaced in 1878 by a supposed exemplar of "Islamic" architecture built for the World Expo, also since demolished. Below the palace, the **Jardins du Trocadéro** extend to the Seine. The fountains lining the central avenues (av. Gustave V de Suède and Albert 1er de Monaco) are particularly striking when lit at night. After a day of sight-seeing, children might enjoy the carrousel in pl. de Varsovie (10F a ride), while adults munch happily on a crêpe from one of the many outdoor stands.

Passy, the area immediately south and southwest of Trocadéro, was known in the past for its restorative waters, although more recent distinction derives from the local filming of *Last Tango in Paris.* The **Cimetière de Passy** runs along its northern walls. The small cemetery, shaded by a chestnut bower, contains the tombs of Claude Debussy, Gabriel Fauré, and Edouard Manet. Ask the concierge at the cemetery entrance, 2, rue de Commandant Schloesing, for directions to these or other grave sites. (Open Mon.-Fri. 8am-6pm, Sun. 9am-6pm. Nov. 6-March 15 closes at 5:30pm.)

Rue Benjamin Franklin commemorates the elder statesmen's one-time residence in Passy and runs south from Trocadéro past the **Musée Clemenceau** (no. 8), located in Clemenceau's own home. The museum chronicles the life and times of the former Prime Minister who, despite a lifetime of accomplishments, is most remembered as France's hard-line negotiator of the Versailles Treaty. Walk all the way down rue Benjamin Franklin and continue on rue Raynouard to the **Maison de Balzac,** located at no. 47. Balzac lived here while completing the last volumes of *La comédie humaine* and keeping one step ahead of his clamoring creditors. Farther down rue Raynouard, between what is now av. du Colonel-Bonnet and rue Singer, Benjamin Franklin built France's first lightning rod. He lived at no. 66 from 1777-1785 while negotiating a treaty between the new U.S. and the old Louis XVI; the present building was built long after his stay.

As you pass the **Maison de Radio-France,** the unmistakable, large, white, round building at the end of rue Raynouard, take rue de Boulainvilliers down to the miniature **Statue of Liberty** near the pont de Grenelle. Donated by a group of American expatriates in 1885, it was moved to this spot for the 1889 World Expo.

The end of rue Raynouard marks the boundary of Passy with **Auteuil.** A 17th-century meeting ground for men of letters such as Racine, Molière, and Boileau, Auteuil currently assembles a startling array of old and new architectural styles, combining *hôtels particuliers* with Art Nouveau and Modernist residential buildings.

Follow rue La Fontaine (an extension of rue Raynouard) to admire a collection of Hector Guimard's work. The award-winning **Castel Béranger** (1898), located at no. 14, flaunts its distinctively Art Nouveau flourishes: swooping arabesques of the *castel's* balconies, staircases, and rooftops that made one skeptical *hôtelier* call it "noodle style." Guimard himself lived there briefly before decamping to another of his creations at 122, av. Mozart. Farther down rue La Fontaine, there is an entire cluster of Guimard works, including no. 17, which dates from 1911. At no. 19, take a left on rue Agar, an odd, T-shaped street which is Art Nouveau down to its street sign. Guimard also designed no. 8 and no. 10 on rue Agar, as you can tell from the decorated, sculpted drainpipes. Back on rue La Fontaine, stop by at no. 40 to visit one of the churches or enjoy the beautiful gardens of **l'Oeuvre des Orphelins Apprentis d'Auteuil** (Society of Apprenticed Orphans). The society was founded in 1866 to provide a home and future for local orphans, who now perform apprenticeships in 30 occupations throughout France (the Auteuil "campus" does printing). Apprentice gardeners tend the grounds. Proust fans might want to walk the extra blocks to no. 96, where the writer was born on July 10, 1871.

Seventeenth-century *hôtels particuliers* cluster along rue d'Auteuil. No. 11bis is one splendid example, and John Adams and his son John Quincy Adams lived at nos. 43-47. For a dramatically different cityscape, return to rue La Fontaine: walk up rue Pierre Guérin, down rue de la Source, then left on rue Raffet; pink stucco, black marble, and mosaic-covered townhouses adjoin more familiar-looking gray façades and iron grillwork along this street. Around the corner and set back behind 55, rue du Docteur-Blanche stand two Le Corbusier villas, completed in 1925. The **Villa La Roche** and **Villa Jeanneret** are stark, white structures maintained by the **Fondation Le Corbusier.** The Villa La Roche contains a small collection of 20th-century paintings, sculpture, and furniture, although the masterpiece of the collection is the building itself.

Bd. de Beauséjour is the continuation of bd. Montmorency as it approaches M. La Muette. Northwest of the metro once stood the Château de la Muette, where Louis XV entertained his mistresses. In 1783 Pilâtre de Rozier and the Marquis d'Arlandes became the first two humans to escape gravity, lifting off from the castle's lawn in a Montgolfier balloon and landing 20 minutes later in what is now the 13ème. Past the playgrounds, old-style carousel, and *guignol* (puppet show) of the **Jardin de Ranelagh,** located just west of M. La Muette, the **Musée Marmottan** displays exquisite Impressionist paintings and medieval illuminations.

Seventeenth Arrondissement

SIGHTS

The seventeenth is a hodgepodge, an entity that wouldn't exist were it not for the willful mix-and-match played by Haussmann when creating Paris' arrondissements. On its southern and southwestern edges, the 17ème borders the 8ème and the 16ème and, like them, smells like old money. Part and parcel of the conservative wealth of the old towns of Neuilly and Passy, this corner of the arrondissement is just off the Champs Elysées, and basks its the glamorous aura. While the region around the Arc de Triomphe epitomizes bourgeois respectability, the eastern portion of the 17ème—only a short distance away—is lively and at times lurid, especially around pl. de Clichy. Inhabited by much the same cast of disreputable characters as pl. Pigalle (see p. 211), pl. de Clichy has started to draw on animated, young crowd at night. With caution and company it can make for an interesting neon-lit coffee break.

The network of small streets spreading between these two polar personalities of the 17ème is primarily residential, and there isn't much to see. While barricades were erected, nobles beheaded, and novels written in the heart of the city, *les Batignolles* was little more than farmers' fields until the mid-19th century. If you happen to be staying in the area, though, the **Musée Jean-Jacques Henner,** 43, av. de Villiers, might be worth a gander (see "Museums," p. 244). Nearby, at 1, pl. Général Catroux, a building belonging to the **Banque de France** (tel. 01 42 27 78 14) dominates a small garden with its huge mosaic brickwork. Built in 1884 as the residence of the bank's regent, the house features gargoyle capitals leering from the façade and serpentine iron drainpipes which slither down the building's sides, spiralled by gold paint and ending with spitting fish as spouts. Inside, the public lobby's vaulted ceilings rise to impossible heights (open Mon.-Fri. 8:45am-noon and 1:45-3:30pm).

The far-ranging flavor of the 17ème is perhaps best explored through the vast repertoire of foods available in its marketplaces and specialty stores. Rue des Batignolles is considered the center of the **Village Batignolles,** now a chic and quiet village of shops and residences starting at av. des Batignolles and extending to place du Dr. Felix Lobligeois. To the west, the restaurant-laden rue des Dames links the Village Batignolles with the street musicians and bustle of the shops and stands along rue des Lévis (M. Villiers). On the other side of rue des Batignolles, rue Lemercier (M. Brochant) has a daily covered market filled with meat, cheese, flowers, produce, and old bourgeois women who have shopped on this street since before World War II. Farther down, at no. 45, is yet another of Verlaine's Parisian addresses. Several blocks

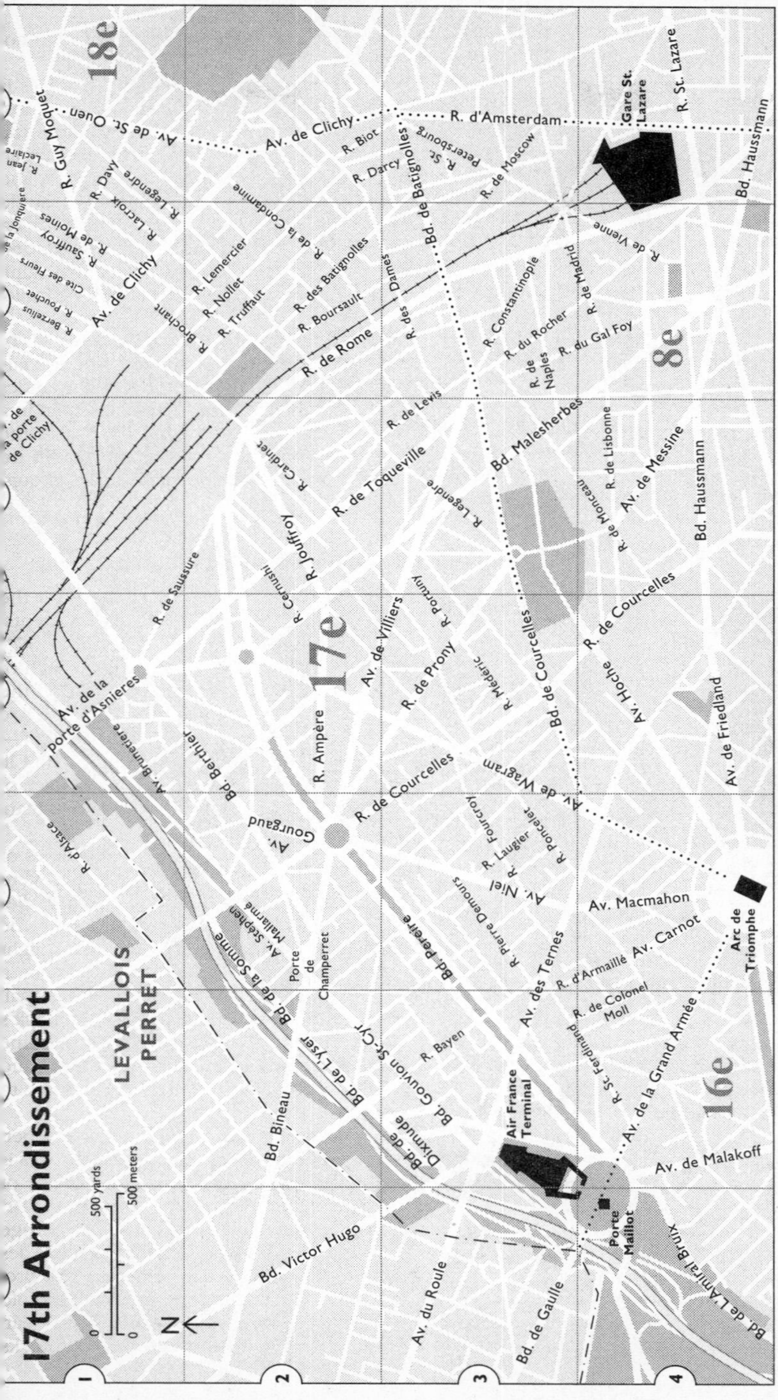
17th Arrondissement
N
0
500 yards
0
500 meters
1
2
3
4
17e
18e
8e
16e
LEVALLOIS PERRET
Av. de St. Ouen
R. Guy Moquet
R. Jean Leclaire
Av. de Clichy
R. Davy
R. Legendre
R. Lacroix
R. de Moines
R. Sauffroy
Cite des Fleurs
R. Pouchet
R. Berzelius
Av. de la porte de Clichy
R. Biot
R. d'Amsterdam
Gare St. Lazare
R. St. Lazare
Bd. Haussmann
R. Darcy
R. St. Petersbourg
R. de Moscow
Bd. des Batignolles
R. de la Condamine
R. des Batignolles
R. Lemercier
R. Nollet
R. Truffaut
R. Brochant
R. Boursault
R. de Rome
R. des Dames
R. Constantinople
R. de Madrid
R. de Vienne
R. du Rocher
R. du Gal Foy
R. de Naples
R. de Levis
Bd. Malesherbes
R. de Lisbonne
Av. de Messine
R. Cardinet
R. de Toqueville
R. Legendre
R. de Monceau
R. Jouffroy
R. Cernuschi
R. de Saussure
R. Portuny
R. de Courcelles
Av. Hoche
Av. de Villiers
R. de Prony
R. Médéric
Bd. de Courcelles
Av. de la Porte d'Asnieres
Av. Brunetiere
Bd. Berthier
R. Ampère
Av. de Friedland
R. d'Alsace
Av. Gourgaud
R. de Courcelles
Av. de Wagram
R. Fourcroy
R. Laugier
R. Poncelet
Av. Niel
R. Pierre Demours
Av. Macmahon
Arc de Triomphe
Av. Carnot
Av. Stephen Mallarmé
Bd. de la Somme
Porte de Champerret
Bd. Pereire
Av. des Ternes
R. d'Armaillé
R. de Colonel Moll
R. St. Ferdinand
Av. de la Grand Armée
Bd. de L'Yser
Bd. Gouvion St.-Cyr
R. Bayen
Bd. Bineau
Bd. de Dixmude
Air France Terminal
Av. de Malakoff
Porte Maillot
Bd. Victor Hugo
Av. du Roule
Bd. de Gaulle
Bd. de L'Amiral Bruix

SIGHTS

north, rue de la Jonquière (M. Guy Môquet) is lined with shops and restaurants and forms the focus of an active North African community. La Cité des Fleurs, between no. 59 and no. 61 on rue de la Jonquière, boasts a row of exquisite private homes and gardens that wouldn't seem out of place in a novel by Balzac himself. Created in 1847, this prototypical condominium required each owner to plant at least three trees in the gardens. Don't miss the houses at no. 29 and no. 33, both of which have elegantly sculpted façades.

The **Cimetière des Batignolles,** 8, rue St-Just (tel. 01 46 27 03 18; M. Porte de Clichy), sandwiched anything-but-restfully between a high school and the bd. Périphérique in the northwest corner of the 17ème, contains the graves of André Breton, Paul Verlaine, and Benjamin Peret. The friendly guards at the front give out maps and can refer you to other sources of information on the resident stars. To get to the cemetery from the metro, follow av. de Porte de Clichy toward the highway, then turn right onto av. du Cimetière des Batignolles. (Open Mon.-Fri. 8am-6pm, Sat. 8:30am-6pm, Sun. 9am-6pm. Nov.6-March 15 closes at 5:30pm.) Not too far away on the other side of the Seine, the less famous and somewhat comic, though touching **Cimetière des Chiens,** 4, Pont de Clichy, Asnières (M. Gabriel Péri Asnières-Gennevilliers; tel. 01 40 86 21 11) is the final resting spot for countless Parisians' beloved pets. Names like Fifi, Jean-Pierre, Jack, and Chérie mark small stones and tiny graves for all these beloved pups. From the metro station, double back along rue Gabriel Péri, then continue through pl. Voltaire on bd. Voltaire to the *cimetière.* (Open Wed.-Mon. 10am-noon and 3-7pm; Oct. 15-March 15 Wed.-Mon. 10am-noon and 2-5pm; admission 15F, kids under 10 5F).

Back within the city limits, the enormous and ultra-modern **Palais des Congrès** stands at the very farthest western end of the 17ème (M. Porte Maillot). The high-rising glass tower's upper-crust restaurants, shopping galleries, and conference halls house a year-round convention center, keeping guests entertained with the Palais' in-house disco and cinema. When not welcoming a variety of business groups, the conference hall hosts music, theater, and dance performances with the likes of Ray Charles and (unfortunately not together) the choir of the former Red Army. It is considered one of the most modern and acoustically effective performance spaces in Europe. (For more info on performances call 01 40 68 00 05.) The open-air terrace on the seventh floor offers a free view of the sprawling Bois de Boulogne to the south and of La Défense to the west.

Nearby, the lovely **pl. des Ternes** (M. Ternes), on the border of the 8ème, has a number of cafés and a daily flower market that brings color to the drab quarter. From the pl. des Ternes, it's a quick walk down bd. des Courcelles to the **Parc Monceau** (M. Monceau). Technically in the 8ème, the park provides an open space for joggers and strollers and a number of architectural follies (see "Sights—8ème," p. 181). In the summertime, the flower beds can be exquisite but you have to admire them from afar since, as in many of the well-groomed parks near the city's center, the grass is off-limits. (Open 7am-10pm; Nov.-March 7am-8pm. Gates begin closing 15min. earlier.)

Eighteenth Arrondissement: Montmartre

Built high above the rest of Paris on a steep *butte* (knoll), Montmartre gets its name from its ancient history of Roman occupation and Christian martyrdom, and a series of etymological coincidences. A site of worship since before the arrival of the druids, the hilltop was once home to an altar dedicated to Mercury and a shrine in honor of Mars. Referred to as *Mons Mercurii* in 840 and *Mons Martis* in 885, the mini-mountain suffered from confused identity until a bishop named Dionysus, now known as St. Denis, came to this hill to introduce Christianity to the Gauls. The unimpressed Romans hadn't heard about constructive criticism; they cut off his head in AD272. Legend has it that he and two other martyred bishops then picked up their heads and carried them north to their final resting point, 7km away, now the site of the Basilique de St-Denis (see "Saint-Denis," p. 299). Aside from a brief re-baptism during the Revolution when the hill was renamed Mont-Marat as a tribute to that "friend of the people," it has borne the name **Montmartre** (hill of martyrs) ever since.

Along with the Montagne Ste-Geneviève (see "Sights—5ème," p. 162), Montmartre is one of the two Parisian hills and few Parisian neighborhoods Baron Haussmann left intact when he overhauled the city and its environs. A rural area outside the city limits until the 20th century, the *butte* used to be covered with vineyards, wheat fields, windmills, and gypsum mines. Its picturesque beauty and low rents attracted notable bohemians like Gustave Charpentier, Toulouse-Lautrec, and Eric Satie, as well as performers and impresarios like "la Goulue" and Aristide Bruant. Henri de Toulouse-Lautrec, in particular, immortalized Montmartre through his paintings of life in disreputable nightspots like the **Bal du Moulin Rouge,** 82, bd. de Clichy (tel. 01 46 06 00 19, fax 01 42 23 02 00; M. Blanche). A generation later, just before WWI smashed its spotlights and destroyed its crops, the *butte* welcomed Picasso, Modigliani, Utrillo, and Apollinaire into its artistic circle. As years passed, Montmartre grew in reputation and diminished in rural charm. Where wheat fields once grew, there rose city blocks. The last quaint traces of rural Montmartre are those profitably maintained by area residents and businesses. The neighborhood's reputation for countrified bohemia is now, for the most part, little more than a pose. With that said, parts of the *butte* are charming, if touristed, preserves of what Montmartre once was. You'll see windmills on top of restaurants, a few vineyards, another generation of painted ladies, women in high-kicking chorus lines, and so on. The *butte* also provides a dramatic panorama of Parisian rooftops, a host of musicians, mimes, and peddlers who gather in front of Sacré-Coeur throughout the day and night, and a plethora of portrait artists in the adjacent pl. du Tertre. At dusk, gas lamps trace the stairways up the hillside to the basilica.

One does not merely visit Montmartre; one climbs it. Entering this *quartier* at M. Barbès-Rochechouart, M. Anvers, M. Pigalle, M. Blanche, or M. Clichy, all along its southern boundary, you can wander slowly upward through any of the small streets draped lazily around the butte like lopsided strands of pearls. The walk up rue Steinkerque from M. Anvers will carry you through a bustling fabric and clothing district, while approaching the hill from M. Château-Rouge along its eastern border gives you the chance to explore the African cloth, food, and gift shops which gather around rue Doudeauville and rue des Poissonniers. At night, use M. Abbesses even if it makes for a more roundabout route. The deepest metro station in Paris, Abbesses has a large elevator and a long spiral staircase which provides a warm-up for the climb ahead, and a delightful series of murals to keep you company. To ascend from M. Abbesses to Sacré Coeur, follow rue la Vieuville until it intersects with rue des Trois Frères, then continue straight up the stairs along rue Drevet, turning right on rue Gabrielle then left up the stairs to rue du Cardinal Dubois, directly below Sacré-Coeur. For a more scenic, if circuitous, route, walk up rue des Abbesses, turn right on rue Tholozé, and take rue Lepic through pl. Marcel Aymé to rue Norvins.

For the classic approach to Sacré-Coeur, climb up the switchbacked stairs leading away from sq. Willette (up the disreputable rue Steinkerque from M. Anvers). Though steep, the walk is not difficult. Day and night, students and tourists mingle in the square to play guitars, drink wine, and smoke whatever's handy. To the east of the square, **Musée d'Art Naïf Max Fourny** houses its neoprimitivist art collection in a 19th-century iron and glass market-pavilion. For a less wearying ascent to the basilica, take the glass-covered *funiculaire* from the base of the rue Tardieu (from M. Anvers, walk up rue Steinkerque and take a left on rue Tardieu). Reminiscent of a ski lift or a San Francisco cable car, the *funiculaire* is operated by the metro service and can be used with a normal metro ticket (8F). In 45 seconds, you are miraculously whisked up an impressive 45-degree gradient while the city below comes almost immediately and spectacularly into sight (open 6am-12:45am).

However you choose to get there, the **Basilique du Sacré-Coeur (Basilica of the Sacred Heart),** 35, rue du Chevalier de la Barre (tel. 01 42 51 17 02; M. Anvers,

SIGHTS

Abbesses, or Château-Rouge), is inviting and odd, an exotic headdress or a white meringue floating serenely above Paris. In 1873, the Assemblée Nationale selected the birthplace of the Commune as the location for Sacré-Coeur, "in witness of repentance and as a symbol of hope," although politician Eugène Spuller called it "a monument to civil war." The basilica was not completed until 1914, after a massive fund-raising effort, and not consecrated until 1919. Both its style—pseudo-Romanesque-cum-Byzantine, a hybrid of onion domes and arches—and its white color sets it apart from the sedate, smoky grunge of most Parisian buildings. The church's bleached look is a quirk of its stone, which secretes white lime when wet. As a result, the parts of the building sheltered from rain are noticeably darker than more exposed ones. While outside, accordion players compete with mimes and illegal street vendors, inside the church the hushed, steady tread of visitors' feet reigns. The mosaics inside the basilica are striking, especially the ceiling depiction of Christ and the mural of the Passion found at the back of the altar. The narrow climb up the 112-m bell tower offers the highest vantage point in Paris and a view that stretches as far as 50km on clear days. A bit farther down, the crypt contains a relic of what many believe to be a piece of the sacred heart of Christ. (Basilica open daily 7am-11pm; free. Dome and crypt open daily 9am-7pm; in winter 9am-6pm. Admission to dome 15F, students 8F; to crypt 15F, students 8F.)

As you exit the basilica, turn right on the winding rue du Mont to arrive at **place du Tertre.** Impossibly crowded with cafés, restaurants, and portrait and silhouette artists, the *place* can be a lovely spot for coffee or a photograph. At 21, pl. du Tertre, the **tourist office** (tel. 01 42 62 21 21) changes money and gives out annotated maps (5F) and information about the area (open daily 10am-10pm; Oct.-March 10am-7pm). Around the corner, the **Musée Salvador Dalí** displays a funky collection of the mustachio'd artist's lithographs and sculptures (see "Museums," p. 243).

Moving away from the overpopulated pl. du Tertre you'll find narrow, winding streets, hidden, walled gardens, and other whimsical remnants of the old bohemian-pastoral Montmartre. The **Clos Montmartre** stretches and twines its vines along rue des Saules. The only remaining vineyard on the butte, the Clos was actually planted in 1933 to emulate the vineyards and pastures which once covered the hill; it hosts an annual harvest festival in October. Below the vineyard at 22, rue des Saules is the **Lapin Agile,** a popular cabaret which has welcomed Verlaine, Renoir, Modigliani, and Max Jacob. When a former dancer came into possession of the cabaret in the 1860s, it gained renown as the "Cabaret des Assassins" until André Gill decorated its façade with a *lapin* (rabbit) striking a pose as it leaps out of a pot, all the while balancing a hat on its head and a bottle on its paw. The cabaret immediately became know as the "Lapin à Gill," and by the time Picasso began to frequent the establishment, walking over from his first studio at 49, rue Gabrielle, the name had contracted to "Lapin Agile." In a zany satire of Picasso's work, other regulars at the Lapin Agile borrowed the owner's donkey, tied a canvas to its back and a paintbrush to its tail, and produced their own painting. (Later exhibited as the work of an unknown Italian artist, the painting received favorable reviews and fetched a respectable sum when sold.) Overlooking the vineyard at no. 12, rue Cortot, the **Musée du Vieux Montmartre** presents a scintillating history of the neighborhood, with in-depth information about Montmartre's bloody history during the Prussian siege of Paris (1870) and the short-lived Paris Commune (1871). Walking down rue de l'Abreuvoir and left on rue Girardon to rue Lepic, will carry you past the **Moulin Radet,** one of the last remaining windmills on Montmartre. Farther down are the **Moulin de la Galette,** depicted by Renoir during one of the frequent dances held there, and one of Van Gogh's former homes at no. 54, rue Lepic. These days, restaurants, antique stores, and *boulangeries* crowd this corner of Montmartre along the rue des Abbesses, rue des Trois Frères, and rue Lepic. Tall iron gates hide the beautiful gardens of 18th-century townhouses. Rue Caulaincourt, below and parallel to rue Lepic, leads downhill to the landscaped, secluded **Cimetière Montmartre,** 20, av. Rachel (tel. 01 43 87 64 24; M. Pl. de Clichy or Blanche). Writers such as Alexandre Dumas, Théophile Gautier, Emile and Delphine Gay de Girardin, and Stendhal, painters including Edgar Degas, Benjamin Constant, and Gustave Moreau, physicist André Ampère, composer Hector Berlioz, dancer Yaslav Nijinski, and film director François Truffaut are all buried here; Emile Zola used to be until his corpse joined the Panthéon in 1908. In 1871, this cemetery became the site of huge mass graves after the Siege and the Commune. (Open Mon.-Fri. 8am-6pm, Sat. 8:30am-6pm, Sun. 8am-7pm; Nov. 6-March 15 open until 5:30pm.)

Along the bd. de Clichy and bd. de Rochechouart, you'll find many of the cabarets and nightclubs that were the definitive hangouts of the Belle Époque, including the infamous **Bal du Moulin Rouge,** immortalized by the paintings of Toulouse-Lautrec and the music of Offenbach. After World War I, Parisian bohemians relocated to the Left Bank and the area around pl. Pigalle became a world-renowned seedy, red-light district (see "Sights—9ème," p. 185). At the turn of the century, Paris' (otherwise respectable) upper bourgeoisie came to the Moulin Rouge to play at being bohemian; today, the crowd consists of (otherwise respectable) tourists out for an evening of sequins, tassels, and glitz (see "Guignols," p. 255). The revues are still risqué, but the admission is ridiculously and prohibitively expensive. Place Pigalle hosts several discos and trendy nightspots for Parisian and foreign youth (see "Discos and Rock Clubs," p. 259). Other than that, it offers a somewhat uniform diet of peep-shows, prostitutes, and XXX movie theaters. During World War II, American servicemen aptly called Pigalle "Pig-alley," and the area is still unsafe for anyone walking alone at night. Farther down bd. de Clichy, at the edge of the 17ème, the **pl. de Clichy** is resplendent in the glowing neon of popular restaurants and cinemas; busy during the day, it can be dangerous at night.

Nineteenth Arrondissement

The nineteenth is predominantly a working-class residential quarter. A host of recent emigrés from Africa, India, and East Asia have settled here, making this a culturally diverse neighborhood frowned upon by many established Parisians. The notable exception to this rule is the rue de Mouzaïa, where wealthy Parisians pay handsomely for houses with small gardens, and others go to stroll and fantasize about living there.

Parc de la Villette (see "La Villette," p. 236, for information on Villette's museums and theaters), is the only major sight in the 19ème. The park has a big grassy area for frisbee and soccer playing, paths for jogging and biking, and hidden corners where people congregate to play African drums and dance. There are wacky sculptures such as an enormous bike which appears to be partly buried, with a wheel, seat, and peddle sticking out of the grass. Villette is a kid's paradise with a "moon-walk", and windmills that only turn if you peddle hard.

To the south, the **Parc des Buttes-Chaumont** (M. Buttes-Chaumont) is an engaging mix of man-made topography and transplanted vegetation. Before its construction in the 19th century, however, the Buttes-Chaumont area of Paris was an eyesore. From the 13th century until the Revolution it contained a gibbet, an iron cage filled with the rotting corpses of criminals and intended for public display. After the Revolution it was a garbage dump, then a dumping-ground for dead horses. After a stint as a commercial breeding-ground for worms (sold as bait), it became a gypsum quarry, the source of "plaster of Paris."

As a young man, Louis Napoleon was exiled to England and for the rest of his life waxed nostalgic for Hyde Park. Once emperor, he added four public parks to the Paris area: the Bois de Boulogne, the Bois de Vincennes, the Parc Montsouris, and the Parc des Buttes-Chaumont, all English gardens—i.e., filled with artificial lakes and tangled trees instead of the immaculately trimmed, rigidly geometrical forms of French formal gardens like the Jardin du Luxembourg or the Tuileries.

Making a park out of this mess took four years and 1000 workers. In order for trees to grow, all of the soil had to be replaced. Furthermore, designer Adolphe Alphand ordered that the heavily quarried remains of a hill be built up with new rock to create fake cliffs surrounding a lake. Workers made a fake waterfall and a fake cave with fake stalactites. A pioneering suspension bridge leads to a fake Roman temple on top of the fake mountain. From this "temple", you have a view of the whole park and of the *real* surrounding city. The park is well-policed at night, and is one of the rare spots in Paris where you can sit on the grass. This is also one of the only Paris parks where people can go for serious exercise (open May-Aug. 7am-11pm; Oct.-April 7am-9pm).

Twentieth Arrondissement: Belleville and Ménilmontant

As Haussmann's 19th-century rebuilding expelled many of Paris' workers from the central city, thousands migrated east to Belleville (the northern part of the arrondissement) and Ménilmontant (the southern). By the late Second Empire, the 20*ème* was known as a "red" arrondissement, solidly proletarian and radical. In January 1871, just before the lifting of the Prussian siege, members of Belleville's National Guard stormed a prison to demand the release of some leftist political leaders—an omen of the civil war to come. Some of the heaviest fighting during the suppression of the Commune took place in these streets, as the *communards* made desperate last stands on their home turf. Caught between the *Versaillais* troops to the west and the Prussian lines outside the city walls, the Commune fortified the Parc des Buttes-Chaumont and Père-Lachaise cemetery, but soon ran out of ammunition. On May 28, 1871, the *communards* abandoned their last barricade and surrendered.

After the Commune, the 20*ème* continued on as the fairly isolated home of those workers who survived the massacres. As historian Eugene Weber observed, "Many a workman's child grew to adolescence before World War I without getting out of Ménilmontant or Belleville." Today, locals freely admit that the only tourist site in the area is Père Lachaise, but they nonetheless consider it the best neighborhood in town. If you're seeking a panoramic view of Paris and have already been to the top floor of the Centre Pompidou and to Sacre Coeur, the 20ème holds a secret that most Parisians don't even know about. From Metro Pyrénées, walk down the rue de Belleville and make a left on rue Piat. At the top of the Parc de Belleville is an overlook which should not be overlooked, if you're in the neighborhood. (Be careful at night, however, when this area is a bit too deserted to feel particularly safe.) Another secret of the 20*ème* is a tiny "provincial" neighborhood with winding streets, small houses and gardens. (Exit M. Porte de Bagnolet at pl. Edith Piaf and walk north up rue du Cap Ferber.)

The **Cimetière Père Lachaise,** bd. de Ménilmontant (tel. 01 43 70 70 33; M. Père-Lachaise), encloses the decaying remains of Balzac, Colette, Seurat, Danton, David, Delacroix, La Fontaine, Haussmann, Molière, and Proust within its winding paths and elaborate sarcophagi. This most illustrious of Parisian cemeteries, named after Louis XIV's confessor, is not restricted to the French; foreigners inhumed here include Chopin, Jim Morrison, Gertrude Stein, and Oscar Wilde.

The land for Père Lachaise was bought in 1803 by Napoleon's government to create a "modern and hygienic necropolis" that would relieve the overcrowding of city cemeteries. At first, Parisians were reluctant to bury their dead so far from the city. To increase the cemetery's popularity, Napoleon ordered that the remains of a few famous figures be dug up and reburied in Père Lachaise. Thus abruptly arrived the remains of Molière, La Fontaine, and several other pre-19th century luminaries. (Héloïse and Abélard have a memorial here, though their bodies lie elsewhere.)

Over one million people have been buried in this cemetery; however, there are only 100,000 tombs. The discrepancy is due to the practice of burying the poor in unmarked mass graves. Corpses are removed from the unmarked plots of the cemetery at regular intervals to make room for new generations of the dead. This grisly process is necessary in a densely populated city like Paris. The 44 hectares of Père Lachaise are filled to bursting, so the government makes room by digging up any grave which has not been visited in a certain number of years. (In other words, if this likely event seems unattractive to the soon-to-be-dead, it's best to hire an official

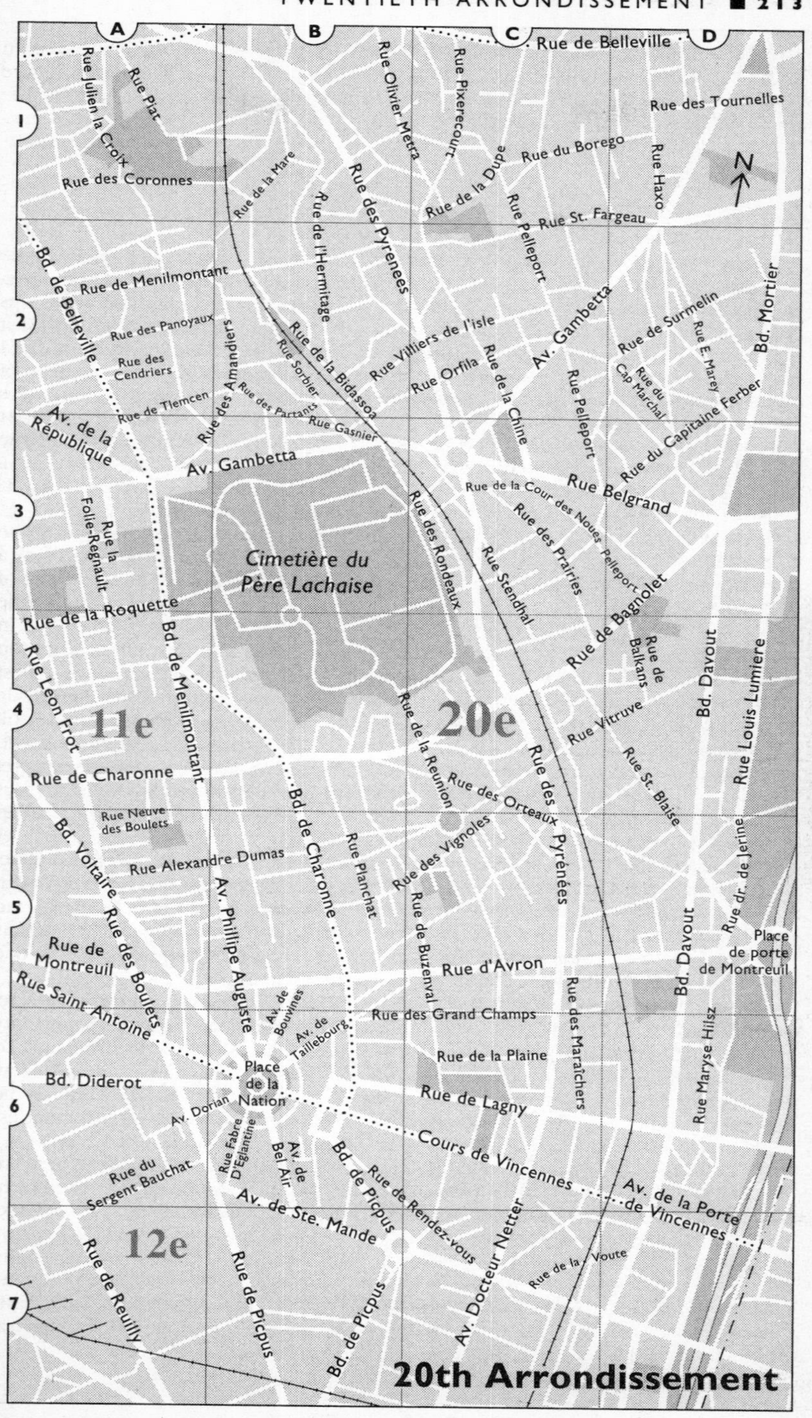
A
B
C
D
1
2
3
4
5
6
7
Rue de Belleville
Rue Julien la Croix
Rue Piat
Rue des Coronnes
Rue Olivier Metra
Rue Pixerecourt
Rue des Tournelles
Rue du Borego
Rue Haxo
Rue de la Dupe
Rue de la Mare
Rue des Pyrenees
Rue de l'Hermitage
Rue St. Fargeau
Rue Pelleport
Bd. de Belleville
Rue de Menilmontant
Rue des Panoyaux
Rue des Cendriers
Rue des Amandiers
Rue de la Bidassoa
Rue Sorbier
Rue Villiers de l'isle
Rue Orfila
Rue de la Chine
Av. Gambetta
Rue de Surmelin
Rue E. Marey
Rue du Cap Marchal
Bd. Mortier
Rue du Capitaine Ferber
Rue de Tlemcen
Rue des Partants
Rue Gasnier
Av. de la République
Av. Gambetta
Rue Belgrand
Rue de la Cour des Noues
Rue des Prairies
Pelleport
Rue la Folie-Regnault
Cimetière du Père Lachaise
Rue des Rondeaux
Rue Stendhal
Rue de Bagnolet
Rue de Balkans
Rue de la Roquette
Bd. de Menilmontant
Rue Leon Frot
11e
20e
Rue de la Reunion
Rue Vitruve
Bd. Davout
Rue Louis Lumiere
Rue de Charonne
Rue des Orteaux
Rue des Pyrénées
Rue St. Blaise
Rue Neuve des Boulets
Bd. Voltaire
Rue Alexandre Dumas
Bd. de Charonne
Rue Planchat
Rue des Vignoles
Rue de Buzenval
Rue dr. de Jerine
Av. Philippe Auguste
Rue des Boulets
Rue de Montreuil
Rue d'Avron
Bd. Davout
Place de porte de Montreuil
Rue Saint Antoine
Av. de Bouvines
Av. de Taillebourg
Rue des Grand Champs
Rue des Maraîchers
Rue Maryse Hilsz
Place de la Nation
Rue de la Plaine
Bd. Diderot
Av. Dorian
Rue de Lagny
Rue Fabre D'Eglantine
Av. de Bel Air
Bd. de Picpus
Cours de Vincennes
Rue du Sergent Bauchat
Rue de Rendez-vous
Av. de la Porte de Vincennes
Av. de Ste. Mande
12e
Av. Docteur Netter
Rue de la Voute
Rue de Reuilly
Rue de Picpus
Bd. de Picpus
20th Arrondissement

SIGHTS

"mourner," much as wealthy patrons used to hire church choirs to sing their masses every year after their death.)

Père Lachaise is the antithesis of the church cemetery; a tribute to this world and not to the next, it's a 19th-century garden party for the dead. Many of the tombs in this landscaped grove strive to remind visitors of the dead's many worldly accomplishments. The tomb of Géricault wears a bronzed reproduction of *The Raft of the Medusa;* on Chopin's tomb sits his muse Calliope with a lyre in her hand. Recognize Oscar Wilde's by the life-sized, streaking Egyptian figure atop it. The most-visited grave is that of **Jim Morrison** (lead singer of The Doors). The graffiti-covered bust of Morrison was removed from his tomb, leaving his fans to fill the rest of the cemetery with their messages. From the main gate, you should be able to follow arrows scribbled on the cobblestones and the other headstones all the way to his plot. In summer, dozens of young people bring flowers, joints, beer, poetry, or general Doors paraphernalia to leave on his tomb; the sandbox in front of the stone is now the sanctioned site for the creative expression of those pensive mourners. Some take hits, others photographs, but there's a rule against filming Morrison's grave. At least one guard polices the spot at all times.

How did Jim Morrison and Oscar Wilde end up here? Simply by dying in Paris. Anybody who was born in or who died in Paris has the right to burial in a Parisian cemetery. Because of overcrowding, however, city policy now requires a family to pay a hefty fee for a departed member to be inhumed in a popular cemetery like Père Lachaise. Still, if you're looking for a unique gift for that special someone, a gravesite near a path is only 38,395F, one away from a path only 23,595F. If these prices are beyond your reach, but you still want your remains to be near those of Jim Morrison, your family can rent shelf space for your cremated ashes in the columbarium. (50 years 9000F, 30 years 6000F, 10 years 2000F).

Remembered by inauspicious plaques in the columbarium are Isadora Duncan and Richard Wright, whose monument, hidden behind a stairwell, is hard to find. The columbarium, a landscape of memorials to the cremated, is located beyond the entrance from Gambetta. The plaques of Maria Callas and Max Ernst may also be found there. You won't be able to help noticing that many visitors to Père Lachaise have had love, rather than death, on their minds; it's a popular rendezvous spot, and many happy congresses here are remembered by plenty of incongruous graffiti.

Père Lachaise's other big pilgrimage site is the **Mur des Fédérés (Wall of the Federals).** Nobody actually hangs out at this small wall, but most French people have heard of it and will at least have had a look. In May 1871 a group of *communards* murdered the Archbishop of Paris, who had been taken hostage at the beginning of the Commune. They dragged his mutilated corpse to their stronghold in Père Lachaise, where they tossed it in a ditch. Four days later the victorious *Versaillais* found the body. In retaliation, they lined up 147 *Fédérés* against the eastern wall of the cemetery, shot them, and buried them on the spot. Since 1871, the Mur des Fédérés has been a rallying point for the French Left, which recalls the massacre's anniversary every Pentecost. Ironically, Republican Adolphe Thiers shares the cemetery with them; he died of natural causes in 1877. Near the wall, a number of monuments containing human remains from concentration camps commemorate the victims of the Nazis. Père Lachaise is open March 16-Nov. 5, Mon.-Fri. 8am-6pm, Sat. 8:30am-6pm, Sun. and holidays 9am-6pm; Nov. 6-March 15 Mon.-Fri. 8am-5:30pm, Sat. 8:30am-5:30pm, Sun., and holidays 9am-5:30pm. Last entrance 15min. before closing. 2-hr. guided general visits of the cemetery (in French) Tues. and Sat. 2:30-4:30. Wed. and Fri. tours 2:30-4:30 have a theme. Tours 35F, students 25F; meet at the main entrance. Call 01 40 71 75 23 for more info about guided visits.

Bois de Boulogne

An 846-hectare green canopy at the western edge of Paris, the Bois de Boulogne (M. Porte Maillot, Sablons, Pont de Neuilly, Porte Dauphine, or Porte d'Auteuil) is a popular place for walks, jogs, and picnics. Formerly a royal hunting ground, the Bois was

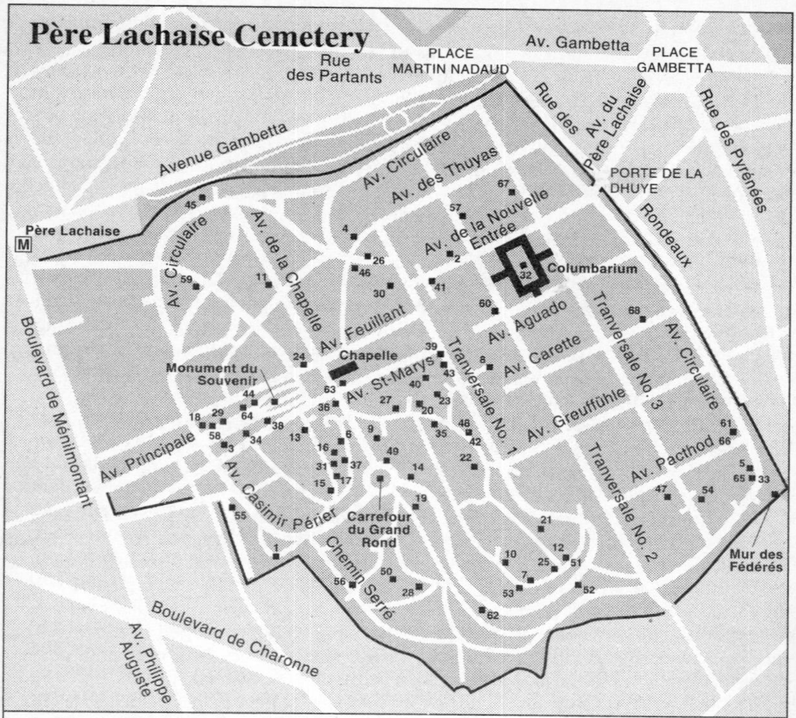

Père Lachaise Cemetery

1 Abélard and Héloïse
2 Guillaume Apollinaire
3 Arago
4 Honoré de Balzac
5 Henri Barbusse
6 Vincenzo Bellini
7 Beaumarchais
8 Sarah Bernhardt
9 C. Bernard
10 Anna Bibesco
11 Georges Bizet
12 Caroline Bonaparte
13 Eduoard Branly
14 Jean Champollion
15 Gustave Charpentier
16 Luigi Cherubini
17 Frédéric Chopin
18 Colette
19 Auguste Comte
20 Camille Corot
21 David d'Angers
22 Alphonse Daudet
23 Honoré Daumier
24 Jacques-Louis David
25 Maréchal Davout
26 Eugène Delacroix
27 Gustave Doré
28 Ferdinand de Lesseps
29 Alfred de Musset
30 Gérard de Nerval
31 Bernardin de St-Pierre
32 Isadora Duncan
33 Paul Éluard
34 Félix Faure
35 Joseph Gay-Lussac
36 Thédore Gericault
37 André Grétry
38 Baron Haussmann
39 Jean Auguste Ingres
40 General Junot
41 Allan Kardec
42 Jean La Fontaine
43 René Lalique
44 General Lecomte
25 Maréchal Lefebvre
25 Maréchal Masséna
45 Georges Méliès
46 Michelet
47 Modigliani
48 Molière
49 Monge
50 Jim Morrison
51 Prince Murat
52 Nadar
53 Maréchal Ney
54 Edith Piaf
55 Camille Pissarro
56 Francis Poulenc
57 Marcel Proust
58 Rossini
59 Georges Seurat
60 Simone Signoret
61 Gertrude Stein
62 Talleyrand
63 Adolphe Thiers
64 Général Thomas
65 Maurice Thorez
66 Alice B. Toklas
67 Général Trujillo
68 Oscar Wilde

given to the city of Paris by Napoleon III in 1852. The Emperor had become a dilettante landscape-architect during his exile in England and wanted Paris to have something comparable to Hyde Park. Acting on these instructions, Baron Haussmann filled in sand-pits, dug artificial lakes, and cut winding paths through thickly wooded areas. This attempt to copy nature marked a break with the tradition of French formal gardens, rectilinear hedges, and flower beds established by Le Nôtre.

When Paris annexed Auteuil in 1860, the park, though outside the city walls, became part of the 16ème. In 1871, it was the site of a massacre of *communards.* General Gallifet shot the most politically and socially undesirable he could discern among the prisoners bound for Versailles—men with gray hair, with watches, with "intelligent faces." At the turn of the century, the park became a fashionable spot for carriage rides. Families of aristocrats rode weekly to the park to spend their "Sunday afternoon in the country" eyeing the finery of their friends from back home.

The Bois de Boulogne contains several stadiums, the most famous of which are the **hippodromes de Longchamp** and **d'Auteuil.** During the Belle Époque, the Grand Prix at Longchamp in June was one of the premier events of the social calendar. Also within the Bois, the **Parc des Princes** hosts soccer matches; the **Stade Roland Garros** is home of the French Open tennis tournament (see "Spectator Sports," p. 269). The Bois further consists of several separate parks, and boathouses that rent rowboats (see below). You may also rent faster, more stylish, remote-control boats, from the classic tug to a swanky cigarette boat.

There are some amusements, however, that the government has tried to discourage. Until a couple of years ago, the Bois by night was a bazaar of sex and drugs, where transvestite prostitutes would stand along the roads and violent crime was quite common. Moreover, in 1991, a flood of newly liberated Eastern Europeans visiting Paris camped out in the park, in an odd imitation of the Cossacks who bivouacked here after Waterloo. The lawn-crashers have been nudged out, but police are now especially attentive to the Bois, closing the roads at night and stepping up patrols. Nonetheless, it's a bad idea to come here for a moonlight stroll.

The **Jardin d'Acclimatation** (tel. 01 40 67 90 82), at the northern end of the Bois (M. Sablons), offers a small zoo, a mini-golf course, carousels, and kiddie motorcycle racetrack. Except for the bumper cars, you must be child-size to ride. This eclectic, old-fashioned spot for a family outing also offers pony rides and holds outdoor jazz concerts. (Park open daily 10am-6:30pm. Ticket office closes 5:45pm. Admission 10F, under 3 free. No dogs allowed; no bikes for kids over 6 years old.)

Within the park, the **Musée en Herbe** (tel. 01 40 67 97 66) is a modern art museum designed for children. The wee ones learn about artists through puzzles and games. Previous shows have featured Chagall and Picasso. The museum also offers a studio workshop. (Museum open Sun.-Fri. 10am-6pm, Sat 2-6pm; 16F. Studio sessions during school term Wed. and Sun., during holidays daily. Participation 35F, 45-60min.) Also within the garden is a participatory theater company for children (shows Oct.-July Wed. and Sat.-Sun.) and a puppet show (Wed., Sat.-Sun., holidays, and daily during school vacations 3:15pm and 4:15pm; free). To get to the park from M. Porte Maillot, go to the big house marked l'Orée du Bois and follow the brown signs that point to the right of the building. Or you can go to the left of the building and take a wee little train. (Trains run Wed., Sat.-Sun., and public holidays, daily during school vacations, every 10min., 1:30-6:30pm, 5F, under 3 free.)

Hear pins drop at the **Bowling de Paris** (tel. 01 40 67 94 00), near the route Mahatma Gandhi entrance of the Jardin d'Acclimatation (18-34F per game; see "Sports—Bowling," p. 269). On the edge of the garden, the **Musée National des Arts et Traditions Populaires** (tel. 01 44 17 60 00; M. Sablons) displays exhibits of tools and everyday artifacts illustrating French rural life before the Industrial Revolution. Enter from the Jardin or from route Mahatma Gandhi. (Museum open Wed.-Mon. 10am-5pm. 22F, under 25, over 60, and Sun. 13F.)

Pré Catelan (tel. 01 46 47 73 20) is a neatly manicured park supposedly named for a troubadour who died in these woods. Arnault Catelan, who rode from Provence to Paris in order to deliver gifts to Philippe le Bel, hired a group of men to protect him

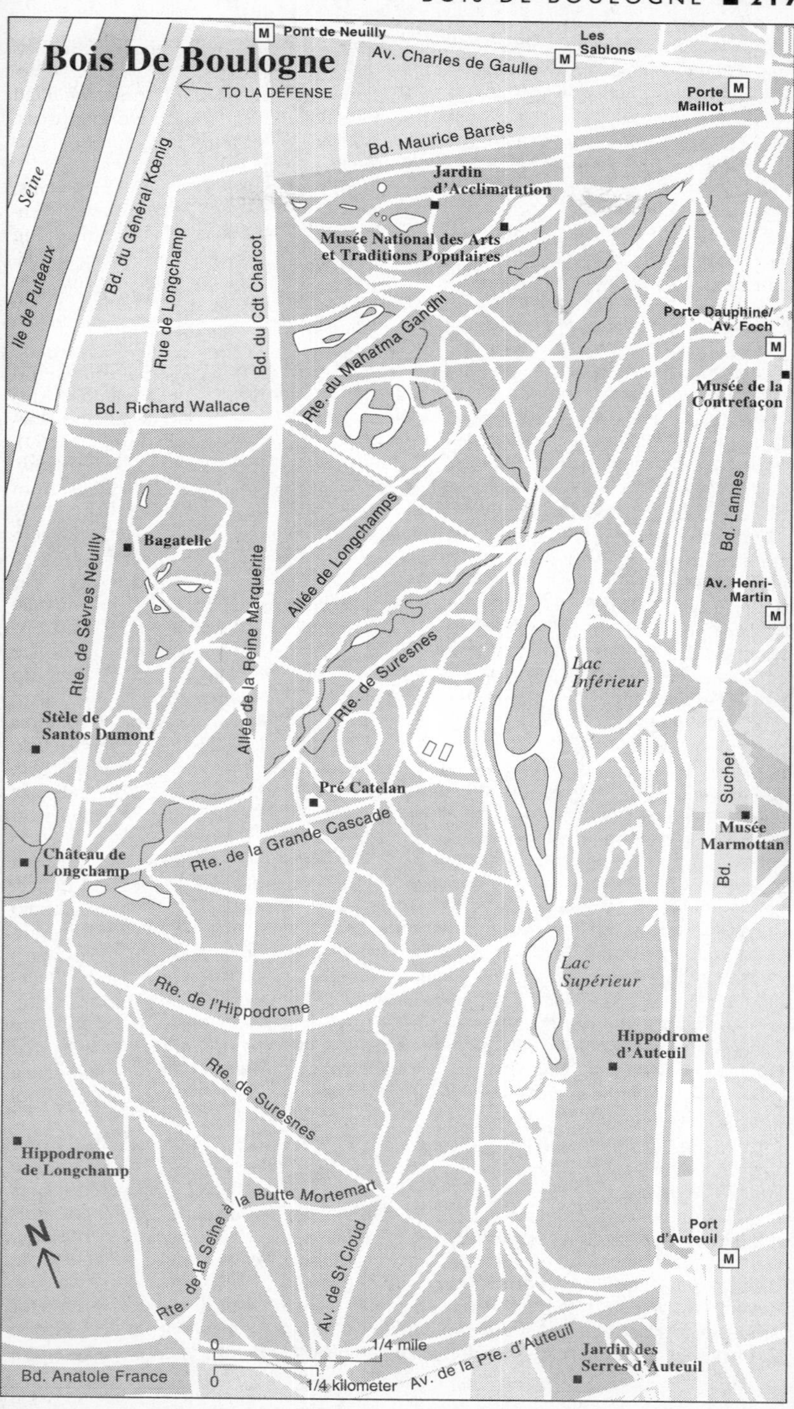

Bois De Boulogne
Pont de Neuilly
Les Sablons
Av. Charles de Gaulle
TO LA DÉFENSE
Porte Maillot
Bd. Maurice Barrès
Seine
Ile de Puteaux
Bd. du Général Kœnig
Rue de Longchamp
Bd. du Cdt Charcot
Jardin d'Acclimatation
Musée National des Arts et Traditions Populaires
Rte. du Mahatma Gandhi
Porte Dauphine/ Av. Foch
Musée de la Contrefaçon
Bd. Richard Wallace
Allée de Longchamps
Bd. Lannes
Bagatelle
Rte. de Sèvres Neuilly
Allée de la Reine Marguerite
Av. Henri-Martin
Rte. de Suresnes
Lac Inférieur
Stèle de Santos Dumont
Pré Catelan
Suchet
Musée Marmottan
Bd.
Rte. de la Grande Cascade
Château de Longchamp
Lac Supérieur
Rte. de l'Hippodrome
Hippodrome d'Auteuil
Rte. de Suresnes
Hippodrome de Longchamp
Rte. de la Seine à la Butte Mortemart
Av. de St Cloud
Port d'Auteuil
N
0
1/4 mile
0
1/4 kilometer
Av. de la Pte. d'Auteuil
Jardin des Serres d'Auteuil
Bd. Anatole France
SIGHTS

on his journey. The men robbed and murdered him in the dead of night, believing that Arnault carried valuable parcels. In fact, Arnault carried only rare perfumes and essences. Authorities later captured the marauders, who, doused in scent, were easily identified. The huge purple beech tree on the park's central lawn is almost 200 years old. You can sit on the grass, except where there are *pelouse interdite* signs.

Inside the Pré Catelan, the **Jardin de Shakespeare** (created 1952-53) features plants mentioned by the bard, grouped by play—there is a collection of Scottish highland vegetation in the *Macbeth* area, a Mediterranean section for *The Tempest,* etc. In the center, a lovely open-air theater, the **Théâtre de Verdure du Jardin Shakespeare** (tel. 01 40 19 95 33), gives popular performances of Shakespeare's and others' plays (in French) in the summer, usually Saturdays and Sundays at 4pm (see "Private Theaters," p. 254). Take the metro to Porte Maillot, then take bus #244 to Bagatelle-Pré-Catelan. (Pré Catelan open 8:30am-7:30pm. Jardin de Shakespeare open daily 3-3:30pm and 4:30-5pm; admission 5F, students 3F, under 10 2F.)

The **Parc de la Bagatelle** (tel. 01 40 67 97 00; same bus stop as Pré Catelan) was once a private estate within the Bois; Bagatelle did not become a public park until 1905. The Count of Artois, the future Charles X, built the little Château de la Bagatelle in 64 days in 1777 on a wager with Marie-Antoinette, his sister-in-law. The garden is famous for its June rose exhibition (35F, seniors 25F, plus park admission; call for specific dates) and for its water lilies, which the gardener added in tribute to Monet. It frequently plays host to art exhibits. Do *not* walk on the grass. They really care about this—enough to put up signs in English along with the normal *"pelouse interdite"* (stay off the grass) signs. Guided French tours of the castle at 3 and 4:30pm (25F plus park admission) and of the park at 3pm (35F, seniors 25F) run from April 1 through October on weekends and public holidays. Meet at the castle. Call 01 40 71 75 23 to check these times. (Admission to park 10F, ages 6-10 5F. Open Jan. 1-15 9am-4:30pm; Jan. 16-Feb. 15 and Oct. 16-Nov. 30 9am-5:30pm; Feb. 16-28 and Oct. 1-15 9am-6pm; March 1-15 8:30am-6:30pm; March 16-April 30 and Sept. 8:30am-7pm; June-July 8:30am-8pm. Ticket office closes 30min. earlier. No, we don't know why they made it this complicated.)

The two **artificial lakes** stretching down the eastern edge of the Bois make for a delightful stroll. Come on a weekday to avoid the crowds; come on a weekend to watch them. The manicured islands of the **Lac Inférieur** (M. Porte Dauphine) can be reached by rented rowboat only. (Boathouses open late Feb. to early Nov. daily 10am-7pm. Daily and annual schedules depend on the weather. Rentals 45F per hr., 400F deposit; with insurance against damage to boat 52F per hr., 200F deposit.)

Dedicated horticulturists may want to stroll through the **Jardin des Serres d'Auteuil** (Greenhouse Garden), full of hothouse flowers and trees (open daily spring-summer 10am-6pm; autumn-winter 10am-5pm; admission 3F). Enter at 1, av. Gordon-Bennett, off bd. d'Auteuil (M. Porte d'Auteuil or Michel Ange Molitor). Free and prettier, if something of a make-out spot, is the neighboring **Jardin des Poètes.** Poems are attached to each flower bed: scan Ronsard, Corneille, Racine, Baudelaire, and Apollinaire. Rodin's sculpture of Victor Hugo is partially obscured by a thicket. Those bored by preciosity and poems may attend **soccer** or **rugby** matches at the **Parc des Princes,** one of several stadiums in the Porte d'Auteuil area.

Bicycles, a delightful way to get around the park, can be rented at two locations: across the street from the boathouse at the northern end of the Lac Inférieur and in front of the entrance to the Jardin d'Acclimatation. (Open April 16-Oct. 15 daily 10am-7pm; Oct. 16-Apr. 15 Wed., Sat., and Sun. 10am-7pm. 30F per hr., 80F per day, passport or driver's license deposit.)

Bois de Vincennes

Like the Bois de Boulogne, the Bois de Vincennes (M. Château de Vincennes or Porte Dorée) was once a royal hunting forest, walled in to keep the exotic game from escaping. Since it lay outside the city limits—and thus outside the reach of Parisian authorities—it was also a favorite ground for dueling. Alexandre Dumas, *père,* was

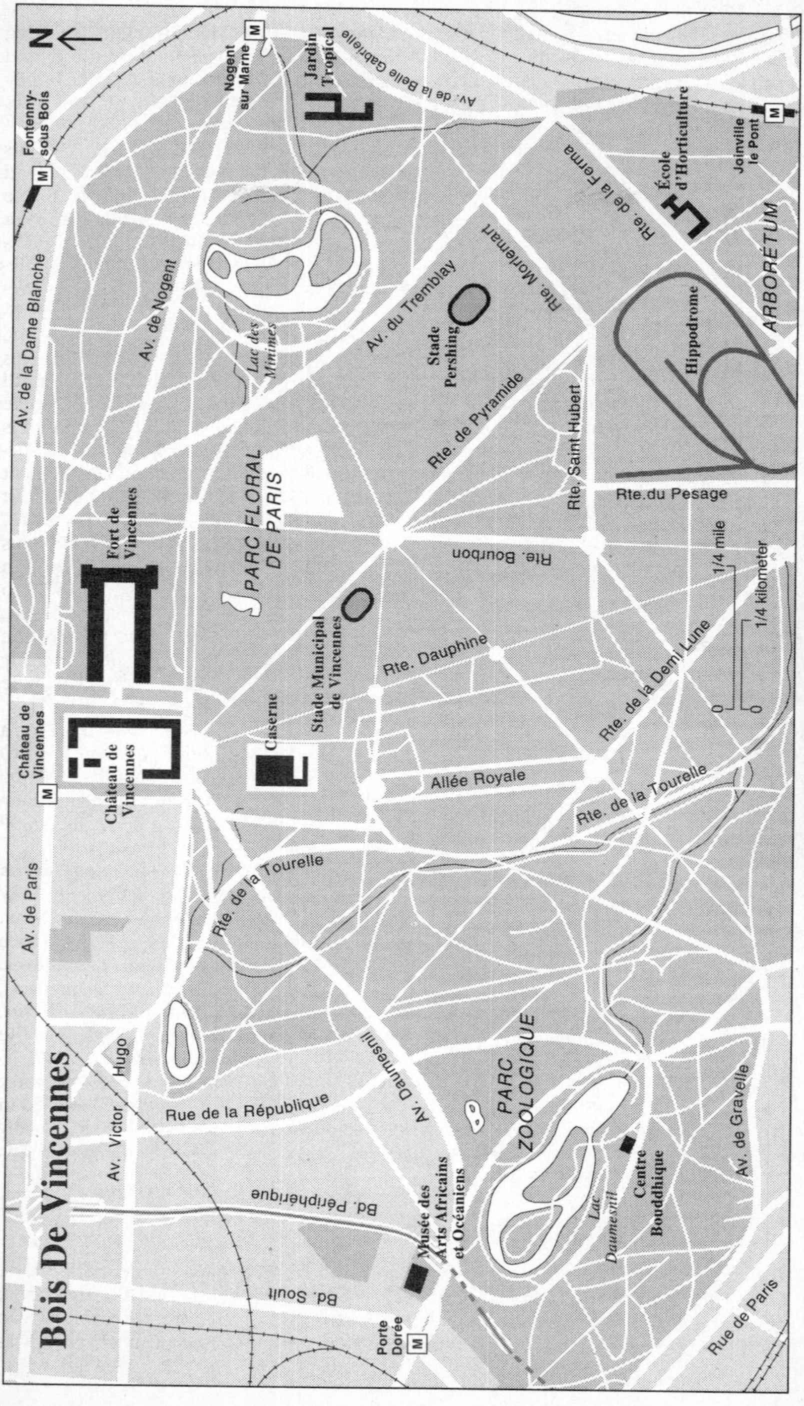

Bois De Vincennes

N

Fontenny-sous Bois
Nogent sur Marne
Jardin Tropical
Av. de la Belle Gabrielle
Av. de la Dame Blanche
Av. de Nogent
Lac des Minimes
Av. du Tremblay
Stade Pershing
Rte. Mortemart
Rte. de la Ferme
École d'Horticulture
Joinville le Pont
ARBORÉTUM
Hippodrome
Rte. de Pyramide
Rte. Saint Hubert
Rte. du Pesage
Fort de Vincennes
PARC FLORAL DE PARIS
Rte. Bourbon
1/4 mile
1/4 kilometer
0
0
Stade Municipal de Vincennes
Rte. Dauphine
Rte. de la Demi Lune
Château de Vincennes
Château de Vincennes
Caserne
Allée Royale
Rte. de la Tourelle
Av. de Paris
Rte. de la Tourelle
Av. Victor Hugo
Rue de la République
Av. Daumesnil
PARC ZOOLOGIQUE
Bd. Périphérique
Musée des Arts Africains et Océaniens
Lac Daumesnil
Centre Bouddhique
Av. de Gravelle
Bd. Soult
Porte Dorée
Rue de Paris

SIGHTS

frustrated here in his duel with a literary collaborator who claimed to have written the *Tour de Nesle.* Dumas's pistol misfired, and the author had to content himself with using the experience as the basis for a scene in *The Corsican Brothers.* Along with its fellow *bois,* the Vincennes forest was given to Paris by Napoleon III, to be transformed into an English-style garden. Not surprisingly, Haussmann oversaw the planning of lakes and pathways. Annexed to a much poorer section of Paris than the Bois de Boulogne, Vincennes was never quite as fashionable or as formal. As one *fin-de-siècle* observer wrote, "At Vincennes, excursionists do not stand on ceremony, and if the weather is sultry, men may be seen lounging in their shirt sleeves, and taking, in other respects, an ease which the inhabitants of the boulevards, who resort to the Bois de Boulogne, would contemplate with horror." Today's *bois,* officially part of the 12*ème*, is still neither as swish nor as well-known as the Bois de Boulogne.

The **Parc Zoologique de Paris,** 53, av. de St-Maurice (tel. 01 44 75 20 10; M. Porte Dorée), on the other hand, is considered the best zoo in France. Unlike their brethren in the Jardin des Plantes, the animals promenade in relatively natural surroundings. While it's disturbing to see waterbucks prance on hard, dry ground when the sign says their natural habitat is swampy, the zoo has been working hard to improve the animals' environment. The *phoques* (pronounced just like you think it is)—seals—are fed with great spectacle daily at 4:30pm. (Open May-Sept. Mon.-Sat. 9am-6pm, Sun. 9am-6:30pm; Oct.-April Mon.-Sat. 9am-5pm, Sun. 9am-5:30pm. Ticket office closes ½hr. before zoo. Admission 40F; ages 4-16, students 16-25, and over 60 20F; under 4 and disabled free. Train tour leaves from restaurant: 10F, under 10 8F.)

Joggers, cyclists, and park bench-sitters happily share the turf around **Lac Daumesnil.** There, people dare to sit on the grass. Discover the lake in a rented rowboat. (Boat rental May-Nov. 15 daily 10:30am-5:30pm. 1-2 people 45F per hr., 3-4 people 51F per hr., 50F deposit, plus tip.) Penetrate farther into the park for running and cycling paths. The **Vélodrome Jacques Anquetil,** the **Hippodrome de Vincennes,** and other sports facilities lie within the sizable *bois* (see "Sports," p. 267).

The **Château de Vincennes,** on the northern edge of the park, is called "the Versailles of the Middle Ages" (M. Château de Vincennes). French kings held court here as early as the 13th century. Although the Louvre was royalty's principal home, every French monarch from Charles V to Henri IV spent at least part of his time at Vincennes. Charles V built up a true medieval fortress on the site his ancestor Philippe-Auguste chose for a royal hunting residence. Henri III found it a useful refuge during the Wars of Religion, and Mazarin and the court found its defenses useful in the wake of the Fronde. Château-lovers will recognize the hand of Louis Le Vau in the buildings farthest from the entry: the Queen's palace and the King's palace, built for Louis XIV, face each other across the courtyard, bounded by an arch-filled wall. In the 18th century, Vincennes became a country-club prison for well-known enemies of the state. Mirabeau spent 3½ years here, killing time by writing lecherous letters to his (married) mistress. When Diderot was imprisoned in the château, Rousseau walked through the forest to visit him.

In the 19th century, the complex resumed its military functions, serving as fortress, arsenal, and artillery park. In 1917, the infamous Mata Hari, convicted of spying for the Germans, faced a firing squad within its walls. In 1940, the château served as headquarters for General Maurice Gamelin, Supreme Commander of French Land Forces. De Gaulle later criticized Gamelin for holing himself up in the *Thébaïde*—ivory tower—of Vincennes, without even a radio tower to connect him with the front. Today, the Services Historiques des Armées and other military-history institutes are headquartered at the château.

The 52m-high **donjon** (keep) was built between 1360 and 1370; it's a striking piece of medieval architecture and an impressive hideout for any king. It has been closed for restoration for the past five years, however, and unfortunately will probably not be open until early in the next millennium. The **Sainte-Chapelle** was founded as a church in 1379, but the building was not inaugurated until 1552. Dainty in its decor and especially beautiful in late afternoon, the Sainte-Chapelle is looking even better these days after restoration of the exterior. (Open daily May-Sept. 10am-6pm; Oct.-

April 10am-5pm.) Guided tours of the Ste-Chapelle and *donjon* daily, every half hour 10:15am-5:15pm, are the only way to get inside, but this church, stripped down to its bare bones over the centuries, is more impressive from the outside than from the inside. Tours are in French, with info sheets in English (32F; students, ages 18-25, and seniors 14F; under 12 free). Survey the archeological digs in the main courtyard, or wander the ramparts for a pleasant, if unexciting, view of the area. If you go on the appropriate day, check out the **Musée des Chasseurs,** dedicated to the art of hunting (open Wed. 10am-5pm and the last Sat. of each month 9am-3pm).

One of the gems of the Bois de Vincennes is the **Parc Floral de Paris,** esplanade du Château (tel. 01 43 43 92 95; M. Château de Vincennes), reached by walking down rue de la Pyramide from the castle. The park has miniature golf and all kinds of games (10 that cost, 60 that don't) for kids. Picnic areas, restaurants, and open-air concerts make it a center of summer entertainment (open daily 9:30am-8pm; shorter winter hours; admission 10F, children 5F).

La Défense

Located just outside the city limits, La Défense is a comic-book city come to life; a techno theme park that exposes all that is ridiculous about the French yen for modernity. It is a mass of concrete, steel, and glass buildings and sculptures, few of them memorable. A glorified office complex, the area boasts the sleeker-than-thou headquarters of 14 of France's top 20 corporations, whose public relations departments are responsible for most of the positive press you'll hear about the place. Clustered around the Grande Arche (a 35-story office block in the shape of a hollowed cube), shops, galleries, trees, and a sprinkling of sculptures make the pedestrian esplanade nice for a stroll, but no great shakes, even for architecture students. The artwork to be found here—by such European notables as Miró, Calder, and César—consists for the most part of open-air sculptures; your whole visit probably won't take longer than a few hours, including lunch.

The proliferation of office towers in the area began in 1956 as part of a scheme to provide office space for Paris without drastically altering the city center. Originally the planners intended to limit buildings to certain heights and styles to create a unified complex; however, by the late 60s and early 70s, companies were allowed to build distinctive *gratte-ciels* (skyscrapers), "Manhattan-style." This haphazard building rapidly threatened the grandeur of the *axe historique,* the line that stretches from the Louvre down the Champs-Elysées to the Arc de Triomphe. In 1969, I. M. Pei suggested the first plan for a monument to anchor the end of the axis. (Ultimately, Pei's plan was not used for this side of the *voie triomphale;* instead, he was asked to redesign the eastern terminus—the courtyard of the Louvre.) French Presidents Pompidou, Giscard d'Estaing, and Mitterrand all sponsored international contests for such a monument, though only Mitterrand acted on the results. Of 424 projects entered, four were presented anonymously to the president, who chose the plan of previously unknown Danish architect Otto von Spreckelsen for its "purity and strength." Spreckelsen backed out of the project before its completion, disheartened by red tape and by his own design, which he deemed a "monument without a soul." Others celebrated the arch as a "window to the world" whose slight asymmetry gives the empty cube a dash of humanity. Spreckelsen, who died of cancer in 1987, never saw the completion of his work.

The **Grande Arche de la Défense** was inaugurated on the French Republic's bicentennial, July 14, 1989. The roof of this unconventional office building covers 2.5 acres—Notre-Dame cathedral could nestle in its hollow core. Its walls are covered with white marble that shines blindingly in sunlight. Most of all, the Arche blends into the centuries-old architectural context of the *axe historique,* though, unlike the smaller arches, this one is aligned six degrees off the axis. Ride the outdoor glass elevators for an unparalleled view at the top. Tickets for the roof are sold at a booth near the elevator shaft. (Ticket office open daily 10am-6pm; roof closes 1 hr. after ticket office; admission 40F, under 18, students and seniors 30F.)

The rest of the plaza deserves only brief mention. Near to and left of the Grande Arche as you face Paris, the funny-looking building which looks as if it's had a piece cut out of it is the **Bull Tower.** Also on the left is the **CNIT building.** At only 37 years of age, it's the oldest building in the complex, the second-most-famous form in the *place,* and primarily a center for congresses, exhibitions, and conferences (open daily 7am-11pm). To the right sits the **Musée de l'Automobile**, 1, place du Dome, of interest to anyone who needs a breather from the Minis and Fiats which clog the streets of central Paris. Car-related accessories and 110 vintage *voitures* tell of the developments of the automobile in its historical/social contexts. (Open Mon., Wed., Fri. noon-7pm, Tues., Thurs., Sun. noon-8pm, Sat. noon-10pm; admission 30F, students, seniors, and under 16 20F). The globe-shaped hi-tech cinema **Dôme IMAX** offers programs in-the-round (see "Cinema," p. 250). The brightly colored sculpture at pl. de la Défense that looks remarkably like one of **Joan Miró's** anthropomorphic paintings come to life is, in fact, his work. Across the *place,* **Alexander Calder's** linear, spidery red steel sculpture provides a fitting counterpart. Calder seems to have thought Miró's work resembled a popsicle: when he first saw a model of it, he asked, "Is that good to lick?" Just past the little lawn in front of you is a white tube where you can find the **Info Défense** booth (tel. 01 47 74 84 24). They sell maps and guides to the works of art (15F), and provide information about La Défense. Downstairs is a free permanent exhibit about the architectural history and future of the area, (open Mon.-Fri. 9am-6pm, Sat.-Sun. 10am-6pm). For French tours of La Défense, call Défense-venement (tel. 01 46 92 17 50; admission 35F, students 25F). By 1997, construction should have started on the latest project of La Défense: **l'Eglise Nôtre Dame de la Pentecôte,** a church planned for a site on the Paris side of the CNIT building. On the other hand, the economic recession has caused several other much-touted additions to La Défense to be abandoned, including the *Tour sans fin* (endless tower), which was to have been the tallest building in Europe. Don't hold your breath.

To the right of the information booth, on a high pedestal, is the bronze statue after which La Défense was named. Louis-Ernest Barrias's design beat 100 other proposals, including one by Auguste Rodin, in an 1871 contest to commemorate the defense of Paris against the Prussians. Moved briefly while the modern complex was built, the statue has been here since. The name, though, has caused quite a fuss: an urban-planning official whose title was "Managing Director of La Défense" was not allowed off a plane in Egypt once because that country did not welcome military personnel during wartime. Also to the right of the booth is the **Galerie de l'esplanade,** an area art gallery (open for temporary exhibits daily noon-7pm). A tree-lined path, flanked on both sides by low blocks of apartment buildings, takes you the rest of the way to the Esplanade de la Défense metro stop. At the end of the path, the stark steel lamps rising out of water are the work of the Greek artist Takis.

If you want to eat or shop in La Défense, there is the huge **4 Temps shopping center**—one of the largest shopping malls in Europe. Enter from the Grande Arche metro stop, from doors behind the Miró sculpture, or from next to the Musée de l'Automobile to marvel at its 30 restaurants. The multilingual information desk on the first floor near the escalator to the metro distributes maps of the complex. (Shops open Mon.-Sat. 10am-8pm. Supermarkets—*hypermarchés*—open Mon.-Sat. 9am-10pm.) The CNIT building is a bit more manageable, however, with six restaurants, (including a café and a sandwich shop with outdoor seats where you can gaze at the Grande Arche).

To get to La Défense from Paris you can take the metro or RER. Older maps might not show the Grande Arche de la Défense metro stop at the end of line 1 (it opened in 1992). The RER is faster, but the metro is cheaper. If you do take the RER, buy the RER ticket before going through the turnstile. A normal metro ticket may get you into the RER station in Paris, but won't get you out without a fine at La Défense.

Museums

Since Charles de Gaulle appointed France's first Minister of Culture in 1956, thousands of hours and millions of francs have been spent shaking the dust off the reputation of the Parisian museum. Paris' national museums are multi-purpose, user-friendly machines shaped by public interest and state funds. Serving as forums for lectures, art films, concerts, and the occasional play, the museums here—most prominently the Louvre, Orsay, and Pompidou—broadcast Paris, past and present.

Paris' *grands musées* cater to an international public and are mobbed, particularly in summer. Take advantage of evening hours and be forewarned: the *Mona Lisa* will be obscured by raised cameras and clamoring schoolchildren. If you tire of dangling from chandeliers for a better view, look for Paris's smaller museums, which display specialized collections often comparable in content to wings of their larger cousins. For listings of temporary exhibits, consult the bimonthly *Le Bulletin des Musées et Monuments Historiques,* available at the tourist office at 127, av. des Champs-Elysées. *Paris Museums and Monuments* not only provides phone numbers, addresses, and hours, but also describes the museums (including wheelchair access). *Pariscope* and *l'Officiel des Spectacles* contain weekly updates of hours and temporary exhibits (see "Publications About Paris," p. 71).

Frequent museum-goers may want to invest in a **Carte Musées et Monuments,** which offers admission to 65 museums in the Paris area so you don't have to wait in line—an important consideration in summer, when lines can be more than half an hour long. The card is available at major museums and metro stations (1 day 70F, 3 consecutive days 140F, 5 consecutive days 200F). For more information, call **Association InterMusées,** 25, rue du Renard, 4ème (tel. 01 44 78 45 81; fax 44 78 12 23), or the central tourist office. It saves money only for speed-walkers and die-hard museum fans who do not qualify for student, teacher, or senior discounts.

Larger museums often offer group tours in various languages. Prices are typically around 500F for a group of adults, 250F for students and seniors. (Seniors means 60 and over unless otherwise stated.) In the past few years, many of Paris' museums have turned their attention towards a national audience, foregoing regularly scheduled English-language tours for more extensive programs in French. This is particularly the case in smaller museums with major collections. Relatively inexpensive English pamphlets can usually be found at bookstores within these museums.

Galleries are an art lover's quick fix when *en route* to the cinema or a bar. Pick up the indispensable *l'Officiel des Galleries* (35F), a reader-friendly monthly publication available at newsstands and *librairies* (bookstores) in chic areas of town, and at the Pompidou bookstore. Inside, you'll find comprehensive listings of temporary exhibitions at both museums and galleries throughout town.

Most of the city's 200 galleries specialize in one type of art, such as neoprimitive painting, modern sculpture, prints, or sketches of Parisian scenes. The eighth arrondissement is loaded with galleries of a more canonical sort; those near M. Franklin Roosevelt on the Champs-Elysées (av. Matignon, rue du Faubourg St-Honoré, and rue de Miromesnil) focus on Impressionism and post-Impressionism. Thanks to the new opera house, the Bastille area has become a haven for artists and galleries with an *épater-les-bourgeois* (shock-the-bourgeoisie) spin. The highest concentration of galleries is in the Marais; a casual stroll through the third and fourth arrondissements (especially on rue Quincampoix and rue des Blancs-Manteaux) will take you past several. The St-Germain-des-Prés (rue Mazarine, rue de Seine, rue des Beaux-Arts, and rue Bonaparte) area also contains an assembly of small, enticing galleries focusing on 20th-century art. Walk right in and don't feel intimidated; you're not usually expected to buy. Most galleries are closed Sunday and Monday and are open until 7pm on other days, often with a break at lunch. The galleries that require appointments are not appropriate for casual browsing.

■ Musée du Louvre

Built on the site of a medieval castle, constructed by a team of French architects to house the king's court, restructured by a 20th-century Socialist politician and a Chinese-American architect, and filled with priceless objects from the tombs of ancient Egyptian pharaohs, the halls of Roman emperors, the studios of French painters, and the walls of Italian churches, the Louvre is an enormous intersection of time, space, and national boundaries. And you thought museums were boring. Just think of how many eons (5000 years, to be specific), how many millions of lives, and how many traditions are represented in the Louvre's building and collection. Even the hordes of visitors add a final impressive touch; just imagine, you may be the 53-millionth visitor to smile back at the *Mona Lisa*.

PRACTICAL INFORMATION

Entrance to the Louvre (tel. 01 40 20 51 51) from the surface is through the center pyramid, where an escalator descends into the **Hall Napoléon;** from the metro stop M. Palais-Royal/Musée du Louvre, you can reduce your wait in lines and enter directly by following signs through the mall. Tickets are sold in the Hall. If you are buying full-priced tickets, save time by using coins or a credit card in one of the automatic ticket machines. Pick up an updated map at the circular information desk in the center of the Hall Napoléon.

Visiting the Louvre's Brobdingnagian collection warrants one rule of thumb: don't be too ambitious. Taking in the whole thing in one day is quite impossible. If you can't afford to spend more than one day here, at least take a couple of breaks; your ticket, valid all day, entitles you to leave the museum and come back. To avoid heat and crowds, visit on weekday afternoons or on Monday and Wednesday evenings, when the museum stays open until 9:45pm. Holders of a **Carte Musée et Monuments** can skip the line by entering the Louvre from the Richelieu entrance (in the passage connecting the Cour Napoléon to the rue de Rivoli).

There are three **places to eat** in the Hall Napoléon. Two cafés (sandwiches 25-35F) are located on the upper and main floors. A pricier restaurant is on the main floor. It's best to pack a lunch and to picnic in the Louvre courtyard or the Tuileries.

The Louvre is fully **wheelchair-accessible.** You may borrow a wheelchair for free at the central information desk (passport deposit). The Louvre has begun a series of **workshops for children** in English (see the information desk in the Hall Napoléon for info). The **auditorium** in the Hall Napoléon hosts concerts (65-130F), films, lectures, and colloquia (all 25F). For information on lectures and colloquia, call (01) 40 20 51 12. (For films and concerts, see "Cinema," p. 250.) There is also a small theater in the hall with free one-hour films relating to the museum (every 90 min., from 11am). The **bookstore** sells a range of postcards and posters, as well as various guides (open Wed.-Mon. 9:30am-10pm).

Audioguides, available at the top of both the Denon and Sully escalators, describe museum highlights; recorded commentaries on selected works last from 30 seconds to three minutes (audioguide rental 30F; deposit of driver's license, passport, or 500F). To operate these gadgets, enter the three-digit code listed on the sheet you've been handed and presto—the voice of a friendly British gentleman appears. English-language **guided tours** leave Monday and Wednesday-Saturday at 10, 11:30am, 2, and 3:30pm (33F, ages 13-18 22F, under 13 free with museum ticket). Call 01 40 20 52 09 for more info. You can only reserve spots for morning tours in the morning, for afternoon tours after 1:15pm. Tours fill up quickly. Temporary exhibitions are housed in the **Hall Napoléon** (open at 10am; additional admission 30F, under 18 free; ticket to both regular and temporary expositions 60F before 3pm, 40F after 3pm and on Sun.; under 18 free first Sun. of each month).

(Museum open Mon. and Wed. 9am-9:45pm and Thurs.-Sun. 9am-6pm. Last entry 45min. before closing, but they start asking people to leave 30min. before closing. The Hall Napoléon is open until 10pm Wed.-Sun. Admission to the museum 40F before 3pm, 20F after 3pm and on Sun., under 18 free.)

THE BUILDING

Construction of the Louvre began in 1190 and isn't finished yet. King Philippe-Auguste built the original structure to protect Paris while he was away on a crusade. In the 14th century, Charles V extended the city walls beyond what is now the Jardin des Tuileries, thus stripping the Louvre of its defensive utility. Not one to let a good castle go to waste, Charles converted the austere fortress into a residential château. Later monarchs avoided the narrow, dank, and rat-infested Louvre, preferring more modern and more grandiose homes in Paris or on the banks of the Loire. In 1527, however, François I returned to the Louvre in an attempt to flatter the Parisian bourgeoisie, whom he hoped to distract from their raised taxes. François razed Charles' palace and commissioned Pierre Lescot to build a new royal palace in the open style of the Renaissance. All that remains of the old Louvre are its foundations, unearthed in the early stages of Mitterrand's renovations and displayed in an underground exhibit called "Le Louvre Mediéval" (admission included in museum ticket).

François I started work on the **Cour Carrée** (Square Courtyard) in 1546. Except for its west wall, finished by Louis XIII, the Cour owes its ponderous classicism to Louis XIV, who hired a domestic trio—Le Vau, Le Brun, and Perrault—to transform the Louvre into the grandest palace in Europe. Louis eventually abandoned the Louvre in favor of Versailles, and construction did not get past the Cour Carrée. Through the passage in the Renaissance wing is the **Cour Napoléon,** a larger courtyard conceptualized by Catherine de Médicis 200 years before it was completed by Napoleon III. The two wings stretching into the distance were once connected by the Palais des Tuileries, a royal residence begun in 1563 to grant Catherine privacy. Henri IV completed the Tuileries and embarked on what he called the Grand Design—a project to link the Louvre and the Tuileries with two large wings like the ones you see today. He only built a fraction of the project before his death in 1610.

With the departure of the court to Versailles, the buildings around the Cour Carrée (the **Sully** wing) fell into disrepair, while indigent artists, prostitutes, and soldiers settled in much of the palace. In 1725, the Academy of Painting inaugurated annual *salons* in the halls to show the work of its members. For over a century, French painting would revolve around the *salons,* and, in 1793, the Revolution made the exhibit permanent, thus creating the first Musée du Louvre.

The museum's fortunes took a turn for the better when Napoleon filled the Louvre with plundered art from continental Europe and Egypt. With his defeat at Waterloo, however, most of this art had to be returned to the countries from which it had been "borrowed." More durably, Napoleon I built the **Arc de Triomphe du Carrousel,** a copy of Rome's Arch of Septimus Severus, to commemorate his victories.

In 1857, Napoleon III finally instituted Henri IV's Grand Design, extending the Louvre's two wings to the Tuileries palace. In order to give architectural unity to the newly dubbed Cour Napoléon, Napoleon III ordered his architects to redo the façades of all the older buildings. As a result, the François I wing gained a new façade on its west side but retained its original design on the Cour Carrée side. Only 14 years after the completion of the Grand Design, the Tuileries palace was burned to the ground by the Paris Commune. Ever since, the Louvre's two large wings (**Denon** and **Richelieu**) reach out to grasp only empty space.

The glass **pyramid** in the courtyard made its dazzling appearance in 1989. It was the crucial step in Mitterrand's campaign to turn the Louvre into a museum that welcomes visitors instead of sending them away cursing the French. Internationally renowned architect I.M. Pei came up with the idea of moving the museum's entrance to the center of the Cour Napoléon, on an underground level surmounted by a glass pyramid. At first, Pei's proposal met with intense disapproval, and many still lament its stark contrast with the courtyard's Baroque façades. Others consider Pei's pyramid a stroke of genius. An enlarged reception area facilitates welcoming services, and escalators provide ready access to each of the palace's wings. Equipped with a bookstore, a cafeteria, and an auditorium, this **Halle Napoléon** glows in the sunbeams streaming through the glass pyramid, cleaned (at great expense) by robots of its grime and pigeon droppings. Legend has it there are exactly 666 panes of glass on the Pyramid; we haven't counted.

Another pyramid, this one inverted, coifs the newly opened underground shopping center attached to the Hall Napoléon, called the Galerie Le Carrousel du Louvre. There is little for the average traveler in this pricey collection of shops and boutiques (except maybe the Virgin Megastore). A Mastercard- and Visa-compatible ATM is located on the main floor. The mall is linked to an underground parking lot, and to M. Palais-Royal/Musée du Louvre (link open 8:15am-11pm). It is possible to reach the museum's entrance directly through this underground network; this approach may have a shorter wait in line than the Pyramides entrance.

THE MUSEUM

Because of the ongoing Grand Louvre project, scheduled to be finished by 1998, curators are relocating 80% of the museum's collection. Until then, some galleries will be closed for renovations. All of this juggling means that no guidebook can give you an adequate walking tour of the museum. Be sure to pick up an updated map in the entrance hall or take a guided tour. Whatever your visiting pace, consider purchasing *The Guide for the Visitor in a Hurry* (20F), an English-language brochure available in the bookstore of the Hall Napoléon and at booths at the tops of escalators in each museum wing. Otherwise, make frequent use of the free info sheets found in gallery corners. Often overlooked by visitors, they provide intelligent commentary on nearby paintings.

Though best known for its European paintings, the Louvre contains seven departments and also exhibits the building's original medieval foundations on the underground level of the Sully wing. **Oriental Antiquities** houses an impressive collection of some of the oldest pre-Christian antiques and sculpture from the Mesopotamian region. This collection includes the world's oldest legal document, a basalt slab from the 18th century BC on which is inscribed the code of King Hammurabi—the first written set of laws. The **Egyptian Antiquities** section is stocked with statues of jeweled cats and interesting tools, and keeps several mummies under wraps. The **Greek, Etruscan, and Roman Antiquities** department displays two of the museum's most famous pieces: the *Venus de Milo* and the *Winged Victory (Nike) of Samothrace.* A 2nd-century BC piece copied from a 4th-century BC statue, the *Venus de Milo's* harmonious proportions and voluptuous form present an image of the goddess of love that would become the 19th century ideal of classical female beauty. Placed atop a flight of stairs, *Winged Victory,* sculpted around 190 BC, portrays the Greek goddess of victory resplendent in all her glory. Her sensuous figure is defined by the folds of her dress, pulled tight against her body by the wind against which her outstretched wings struggle.

The **Sculpture** department includes everything after the Roman period until the 19th century. The undisputed stars of the collection are two of **Michelangelo's** *Slaves,* originally planned to decorate the outside of the tomb of Pope Julius II. The physical vitality and torsion of the *Slaves* is characteristic of the sculptural style which made Michelangelo great. Michelangelo said that he attempted to free each of his sculptures from the marble block in which it was imprisoned; his *Slaves* seem to embody this idea as much as their personal, physical struggles.

Napoleon III's lavishly furnished apartments form part of the **Objets d'Art,** a collection of furniture, jewelry, and porcelain located in the Richelieu wing. The 140,000 works comprising the **Prints and Drawings Collection** rotate through temporary exhibits held in the Pavillon de Flore.

Paintings

The Louvre's painting collection begins with the Middle Ages and includes works dating up to the mid-19th century. The collection extends through the second floors of the Richelieu and Sully wings, and along the length of the first floor of the Denon wing.

The Flemish Gallery houses such masterworks as **Hieronymous Bosch's** small *Ship of Fools,* a surreal allegory of greed and folly, and **Jan Van Eyck's** *Madonna of Chancellor Rolin,* remarkable for the minute detail of the countryside that can be seen beyond the window of the foreground. This is thought to be one of the earliest oil paintings, if not the first. **Peter Paul Rubens's** many-paneled *Médicis Cycle* (1621-25), occupies its very own room. Returning from an exile imposed by her son, Louis XIII, Marie de Médicis hired Rubens to retell her personal history to the world (or at least to the treacherous French court). These wall-size Baroque canvases depict a glorious Marie de Médicis as well as oodles of Rubens's famous buxom maidens: nymphs, muses, and goddesses all aid and cheer Marie on in her path to glorious distinction.

French works stretch from the Richelieu wing through the entire Sully wing and part of the Denon wing. These works include paintings from the Neoclassical, Rococo, and romantic schools of 16th- and 17th-century painting. The Rococo works of Antoine Watteau, Jean-Honoré Fragonard, and François Boucher showcase aristocratic styles of architecture and dress, as well as the upper class sensibilities of the age that culminated in the reign of Louis XIV, the Sun King. Watteau's *Gilles* (also called *Pierrot*) is one of the stranger paintings in the collection: the foreground has an awkward boy in a clown suit staring uncomfortably out at the observer; in the background, other characters mock the boy and an ass, which itself looks balefully at you. In all, the painting is both unsettling and mysterious. The allegorical, pastoral, classical motifs of Nicholas Poussin's *Four Seasons* inspired one of the greatest and most influential of French painters, **Jacques-Louis David,** whose greatest masterpieces also reside in these galleries. David's pivotal, 1785 work, *The Oath of the Horatii,* is as stimulating visually as it was politically. It focuses on three Roman brothers swearing allegiance to their father and country before going off to battle, an ominous theme for Paris on the eve of the Revolution. David accents strength and power in the hard, angular bodies of the men, in contrast to the soft, fluid lines of the weeping women. This combination of rigid, Classical motifs with a deliberate, awkward flatness that flew in the face of convention created quite a stir in the salon, and not to mention electrified audience members who were tired of the aristocratic delicacy of Rococo (and of the aristocracy itself).

Jean Auguste Dominique Ingres, one of David's students, abandoned his mentor's hard, sculptural physiques in favor of the fleshy roundness of that Italian renaissance master, Raphael. His *Grand Odalisque* incorporates exotic oriental themes; and his trademark nudes, with their flawless skin, hearken back not just to Raphael but also to the Mannerists' distortion of the human form. **Théodore Géricault's** *Raft of the Medusa* (1819) was the painting that put Romanticism in the public eye. The gigantic canvas tells the true story of the survivors of the sunken ship *Medusa,* who lashed together a raft to avoid drowning, but were forced to resort to cannibalism to make it through two weeks on the open sea. Salon-goers were horrified by the portrayal of half-eaten corpses tumbling into the sea as the survivors struggle to catch the attention of a ship on the horizon. **Eugène Delacroix** also used large scale canvases, notably in two works from the Louvre's collection: *Liberty Leading the People* and *The Death of Sardanapalus.* The former personifies Liberty as a beautiful, half-naked woman on the barricades of the French Revolution; Louis-Philippe thought it so dangerously inspiring that he immediately bought the painting and hid it from the public. The latter depicts the climactic final scene of a play by Lord Byron. As his enemy closes in around his palace, King Sardanapalus slaughters his horses and concubines before incinerating his palace, his treasure, and himself. The drama, the movement, and the color are characteristic of the Romantic movement spearheaded by Delacroix. Like Gericault's *Raft,* the painting was a bit more than the salon public could handle when first exhibited—it was a flop.

The **Italian Renaissance** collection, on the first floor of the Denon wing, is rivaled only by that of the Uffizi in Florence. For the best in Renaissance portraiture, look to **Raphael's** *Portrait of Balthazar Castiglione* and **Titian's** *Man with a Glove,* a great influence upon Baroque portraitists. Titian's *Fête Champêtre* presents a quietly atmospheric feast of the Gods, later reinterpreted scandalously by Manet in his *Déjeuner*

Ms. Mona's Wild Ride

Actually, Mona's fortunate to be here at all. Louvre curators discovered her missing one morning in 1911. Guillaume Apollinaire warned his friend Pablo Picasso, who owned two statues stolen from the Louvre, that a search for the *Mona Lisa* might uncover the contraband sculptures. The pair panicked, and at midnight struck out into the darkness with the statues packed into a suitcase, intending to dump them in the Seine. Near the *quais* they suspected they were being followed and decided instead to leave the statues anonymously with a local newspaper. But the police soon tracked down and jailed Apollinaire as a suspect in the *Mona Lisa* heist. After two days of intense questioning, Apollinaire's resolve broke—the loyal friend accused Picasso of stealing the painting. In spite of this treachery, Picasso cleared his name with a convincing plea. Only through the efforts of local artists, who attested to the fine quality of Apollinaire's character, was the poet released. The *Mona Lisa* turned up two years later in the possession of a former Louvre employee who had snuck it out of the museum under his overcoat, leaving only the frame and a fine impression of his left thumb. Unfortunately, the museum recorded only its employees' right thumbprints. The joyful, albeit embarrassed, museum directors returned the smiling lady to her proper place, where she now resides securely within a glass enclosure.

sur l'Herbe (in the Musée d'Orsay). **Veronese's** gigantic *Wedding Feast at Cana* occupies an entire wall. Recently it was accidentally dropped while being restored; the fall caused a meter-long tear in the canvas, since then repaired. The biblical theme notwithstanding, the characters in the painting are the high society of 16th-century Venice, with Veronese himself playing the cello.

The most famous painting among the Italian Renaissance works is also the most famous in the world. **Leonardo da Vinci's Mona Lisa** (or *La Joconde,* The Smiling One; 1503), bought by François I, smiles mysteriously at millions of guests each year. Look at the *Mona Lisa,* but don't forget to look at her remarkable neighbors as well. Leonardo's *Virgin of the Rocks* is unquestionably one of his most beautiful paintings, illustrating the rocky landscapes and *sfumato* (smoky) technique for which he is famous.

MUSEUMS

■ Musée d'Orsay

While works by Monet, Degas, Pissarro, and others have established the **Musée d'Orsay,** 1, rue de Bellechasse, 7*ème* (tel. 01 40 49 48 14, recorded information tel. 01 45 49 11 11; RER Musée d'Orsay; M. Solférino), as the "Impressionist museum," *par excellence,* this former railway station is dedicated to presenting all of the various artistic movements spanning the period from 1848 until the first World War. Incorporating painting, sculpture, decorative arts, architecture, and photography, the museum's substantial collection showcases both the icons and the iconoclasts of the 19th-century art world in the hope that situating artists like the Impressionists alongside their more conservative contemporaries will demonstrate why they were considered so revolutionary. This effort to articulate how one form or genre developed from another is a predominant theme in the museum. Sketches and rough studies occupy places of honor near their more perfected descendants, and the train station's steel beams and huge ornate clocks are preserved in the building's reincarnated state as a museum.

Built in time for the 1900 Universal Exposition, the Gare d'Orsay's industrial purpose was carefully masked by architect Victor Laloux behind glass, stucco, and a 370-room luxury hotel, so as to remain faithful to the station's elegant surroundings in the prestigious 7*ème* arrondissement. For several decades, it was the main departure point for southwest-bound trains, but newer trains were too long for its platforms, and it closed in 1939. Since then, the station has served as the main French repatriation center (receiving thousands of concentration camp survivors following World

War II) and as the set for Orson Welles' film "the Trial" before finally metamorphizing into its current classy state as the Museé d'Orsay.

Since its opening in 1986, the museum has recaptured more than the ceiling of its former self. It features the traffic frenzy of any large *gare.* For all its size and bustle, however, Orsay may be the friendliest museum you'll ever encounter: it's crowded, it's noisy, but it's designed to help you. A specially marked escalator at the far end of the building ascends directly to the Impressionist level. A slew of maps and English-language pamphlets cover the information desks, located both in the entrance hall and just past the ticket booths. One of the most recent addition to the Parisian art museum scene, the Museé d'Orsay pays as much attention to how works are displayed as to the works themselves. The result is fabulous: in contrast to the imposing halls of the Louvre, statues here are on modest pedestals in the lower-level courtyard so that they meet their visitors at eye-level. The museum wants guests to learn a little history, and many a guide book has been compiled for this purpose. The best one is the *Guide to the Musée d'Orsay* by Caroline Mathieu, the museum's curator—more than worth the 110F price. For 20F, you can buy the practical condensed *Guide for the Visitor in a Hurry.* Underneath the main staircase, the display *Ouverture sur l'Histoire* offers a retrospective on the building through newspaper articles, photos, and posters. **Audioguides,** available in English, French, German, Japanese, Spanish, and Italian, provide anecdotal histories and analyses of 60 masterpieces throughout the museum. These hand-held devices permit you to dial up descriptions of any or all of the featured works at your leisure. The recording lasts two hours, but you need at least three to visit all the rooms along the path. (30F; driver's license, passport, credit card, or 500F deposit required).

In addition to the permanent collection, seven temporary exhibitions, called *dossiers,* are dispersed throughout the building. Although most are included in the regular cost of admission, some temporary installations have separate fees. A *billet jumelé* (55F, 38F for ages 18-35 and over 60) gives you access to both the museum and the special exhibit.

PRACTICAL INFORMATION

The museum is least crowded on Thursday evenings when it is open late (until 9:45pm) or early on Sunday mornings. Avoid visiting on a Tuesday if at all possible, since this is the day the Louvre closes and all the tour buses lumber over to the left side of the Seine. For a break while you're inside, unwind in the **Café des Hauteurs,** situated on the upper-level behind one of the train station's huge iron clocks. The adjoining outdoor terrace offers a beautiful view of the Seine and Right Bank and a concession stand with snacks. (Open Tues.-Wed. and Fri.-Sun. 10am-5pm, Thurs. 10am-9pm.). Downstairs, browse in the **bookstore,** which offers reproductions, postcards, and every 19th-century art book imaginable as well as historical and architectural guides to Paris (open Tues.-Wed. and Fri.-Sun. 9:30am-6:30pm, Thurs. 9:30am-9:30pm). The museum's boutique has the same hours as the bookstore and offers jewelry, scarves, and sculptures inspired by the museums collection, some at close to collector's prices.

The **Restaurant du Palais d'Orsay** on the middle floor is worth a peek, even if you don't plan on lunching. A stylish artifact of the Belle Epoque designed by Gabriel Ferrier, the restaurant offers a view of the Seine, a gilt ceiling, and plenty of chandeliers. Despite appearances, mere mortals can afford to eat here—all-you-can-eat buffet and dessert (80F). (Open Tues.-Wed. and Fri.-Sun. 11:30am-2:30pm, Thurs. 11:30am-2:30pm and 7-9:30pm; open Tues.-Wed. and Fri.-Sun. as a *salon de thé* 3:30-5:30pm.)

Guided tours leave regularly from the group reception (Tues.-Sat. 11:30am in French, Tues.-Wed. and Fri.-Sun. 11am and Thurs. 11am and 7pm in English; 90min., 35F). Inquire at the information desk for details. Tours are available in other languages when arranged in advance. The booklet *Nouvelles du Musée d'Orsay,* free at the information desk, gives details about current tours, conferences, concerts, and exhibits. You can also call 01 40 49 49 66 for concert information.

(Museum open June 20-Sept. 20 Tues.-Wed. and Fri.-Sun. 9am-6pm, Thurs. 9am-9:45pm. Sept 21-June 19 museum opens at 10:00am. Last ticket sales at 9:15pm Thurs., 5:15pm all other days. Admission 36F; ages 18-25, seniors, and all on Sun. 24F; under 18 free.)

GROUND FLOOR: FROM CLASSICISM TO PROTO-IMPRESSIONISM

Populated by statues of triumphant Napoleans and other toga-clad figures, the central aisle's collection of sculpture from 1850 to 1870 is dominated by the works of Jean-Baptiste Carpeaux. Carpeaux's *La Danse* (1869), depicting five female figures dancing in delight around a leaping male spirit, was deemed a moral outrage by an unsettled public, and made Carpeaux (in)famous. Academic paintings and portraiture from the Second Empire fill the galleries along the right-hand side of the ground floor. *La Source* (1820-56) by Jean-Auguste-Dominique Ingres highlights the soft, rounded curves and crisp lines that defined Classical style for Ingres and his followers. Representing the rival Romantic school, Eugène Delacroix focused on brilliant colors, swift movement, and dramatic landscapes shown here in his 1854 oil sketch for *La Chasse aux Lions.* The paintings by Jean-François Millet, Jean-Baptiste-Camille Corot, and Théodore Rousseau in the rooms to the left of the central aisle illustrate the spirit of the Barbizon school of painting, named for the village on the edge of the Fontainebleau forest to which the artists retreated in 1849. Nostalgic for the simplicity of rural life and natural surroundings during an era of increasing industrialization, the Barbizon painters made the landscape and the provincial people their primary subjects. Millet's *Des Gleaneuses* (1857) is familiar to anyone who has seen the cartoon in which Pépé le Pew visits the Louvre: the women it shows working in the fields represent an idyllic image of the noble peasantry.

While they shared a common subject matter, Realists like **Gustave Courbet** did not depict as idealized a version of humanity as did the Barbizon painters. "How can it be possible to paint such hideous people?" one critic demanded upon viewing Courbet's *Un Enterrement à Ornans* at the salon of 1850.

For one of the most controversial paintings—and the artist whom many consider to be the first modern painter—look to **Edouard Manet.** His *Olympia* (1863) caused an uproarious scandal at the 1865 salon. Manet took the format of Titian's *Venus of Urbino* (1538), the standard for female nudes in Western art, and gave it a Realist twist. As his model, he used a high-salaried prostitute whose compact body, olive skin, and tied-back hair put her as far as possible from the classical standard of female beauty. Viewers objected to Olympia's fuzzy slippers and the ridiculously awake black cat (taking the place of a sleeping dog in Titian's painting). Caricatures of the painting covered the pages of Paris's newspapers and art journals, while Manet himself was met with insults as he walked down the street. This was pornography, cried the critics, not art. Manet was bewildered by the scandal. The ever-optimistic Baudelaire told him by way of support, "You are only the first in the decrepitude of your art."

Although sidelined by the uproarious trends of Classicism, Romanticism, and Realism in the painting and sculpture on the ground floor, the decorative arts display and the multicultural exhibit dedicated to architecture from 1850 to 1900 track the development of industrial design. Don't miss the chance to stand on top of the Paris Opera or look into its depths—thanks to the two scale models—before moving onwards to the "decrepitude" of the late 19th and 20th centuries.

UPPER LEVEL: IMPRESSIONISM AND POST-IMPRESSIONISM

Upstairs, the Impressionist celebration begins in earnest; the location is ideal. Soft light, filtered through the glass ceiling, illuminates the paintings to highlight the colors and the spontaneity of brushstrokes without producing a glare off the canvases.

Manet's *Déjeuner sur l'Herbe* (*Luncheon on the Grass,* 1863) caused yet another brouhaha. As with *Olympia,* Manet took an icon of Western art, Titian's *Fête Champêtre* (in the Louvre), and brought it scandalously into the everyday, contemporary world. *Why,* critics asked, were two perfectly respectable bourgeois gentlemen (the artist's brother and future brother-in-law) picnicking with a naked lady? *Déjeuner* was refused by the official Salon and subsequently shown in the famous *"Salon des Refusés"* (Salon of the Rejected), where Manet and contemporary "rejected" artists showed their work independent of the Academy.

Paintings like **Claude Monet's** *La Gare St-Lazare* (1877) and **Renoir's** *Le bal du Moulin de la Galette* (1876) capture the Paris of their day—the iron train stations, the huge, crowded boulevards, and the society balls. Paintings by Alfred Sisley, Camille Pissarro, and Berthe Morisot provide a more tranquil expression of daily life, especially in the countryside around Paris. Monet also indulged in an almost scientific endeavor to capture the changing effects of light, as in his stunning series on the Rouen cathedral (1892-93).

Edgar Degas represents an alternative side of Impressionism, focusing on lines, patterns, and simple human expressions. His sculptures and paintings of ballet dancers are set, not on stage, but in rehearsal or backstage. The dancers in *La classe de danse* (1874) irreverently scratch their backs, massage their tense necks, and cross their arms while vaguely listening to the ballet master. Paintings like *l'Absinthe* highlight the loneliness and isolation of life in the city, especially among the female working class.

Pushing on through the museum and through history, you arrive at the Post-Impressionists. Everyone inevitably crowds around **Vincent Van Gogh's** tormented *Portrait de l'artiste* (1889), although the artist's anguish is also suggested by the twisted lines and shifting perspective of *L'eglise d'Auvers-sur-Oise* (1890), and *La Chambre de Van Gogh à Arles* (1889). Meanwhile, **Paul Cézanne** painted his famous still-lifes, portraits, and landscapes, experimenting with the soft colors and broken-down geometric planes that would open the door to cubism.

As you're leaving this area, don't miss the pastels displayed in several dimly-lit rooms. Inside, the strange creations of **Odilon Redon** represent a unique strain of mysticism among his more conventional contemporaries. His *Bouquet of Wildflowers* (1912) glows against the brown paper on which it is drawn.

Moving into the north wing, you arrive at the chaos of the late 19th-century avant-garde. Pointillists like **Paul Signac** and **Georges Seurat** strayed from their Impressionist beginnings to a theory of painting based on tiny dots—a proto-version of the TV-screen. **Henri de Toulouse-Lautrec** left his aristocratic family background behind to paint the dancers and prostitutes who accepted his physical deformity. **Paul Gauguin's** masterpiece, *La belle Angèle* (1889), sets the title figure—a Breton peasant woman—in a circular form reminiscent of Japanese art.

MIDDLE LEVEL: BELLE EPOQUE & ART NOUVEAU

After taking you through the neo-Rococo Salle des Fêtes, once the elegant ballroom of the Hôtel d'Orsay, the middle level displays late-19th-century sculpture, painting, and decorative arts. A display on Salon painting from 1880 to 1900 shows what was going on in the sanctioned art world, while Impressionists were gaining their separate victories away from the Academy. Naturalism that carried an almost photographic realism was one of the favorite art forms under the Third Republic.

Nearly one-third of the middle level's terrace is devoted to Auguste Rodin, who made a stylistic point of posing his figures, often quite awkwardly, as if they were still in the process of emerging from the material of which they were made. *Porte de l'Enfer,* which Rodin never completed, consists of the tangled, confused, recast forms of many of his previous works.

Even if you're exhausted, don't miss a stroll through the furniture, lamps, and general extravaganza of the whimsical Art Nouveau displays—an elegant exhibit of desks, vases, and sofas with wavy lines and arabesques which sought to give "function" new prominence in design. You can walk forward into the 20th century with brilliantly colored works by the Nabis artists, as well as paintings by **Henri Matisse** and **Gustav Klimt.** End your tour with the fascinating *Birth of Cinema* display.

■ Centre Pompidou

Often called the Beaubourg, the Centre National d'Art et de Culture Georges Pompidou, 4ème (tel. 01 44 78 12 33 for recorded information in French, tel. 01 44 78 14 63 for general info; M. Rambuteau) has inspired architectural controversy ever since its inauguration in 1977. Named after French president Georges Pompidou, it fulfills his desire for Paris to have a cultural center embracing music, cinema, books, and the graphic arts. Chosen from 681 competing designs, Richard Rogers and Renzo Piano's building-turned-inside-out bares its circulatory system to all. Piping and ventilation ducts in various colors run up, down, and sideways along the outside (blue for air, green for water, yellow for electricity, red for heating). Framing the building like a cage, huge steel bars support its weight. The Centre Pompidou attracts more visitors per year than any other museum or monument in France—eight million annually compared to the Louvre's three million. It also uses as much electricity daily as a town of 20,000 people.

The **Musée National d'Art Moderne,** the center's main attraction, houses a rich selection of 20th-century art, from the Fauves and Cubists to Pop and Conceptual Art. Most of the works were contributed by the artists themselves or by their estates; Joan Miró and Kandinsky's wife number among the museum's founding members.

The entrance to the museum portion of the Beaubourg is on the fourth floor, which features the work of modernists such as Matisse, Dérain, Picasso, Magritte, Braque, Kandinsky, Léger, Mondrian, Chagall, and Pollock. Three terraces display sculptures by Miró, Laurens, Ernst, and Calder. The lower level of the museum (which can only be reached by a small escalator from the floor above) houses works from 1960 to the present. In addition to the permanent collections of the Musée National d'Art Moderne, the Centre Pompidou has temporary display areas on the ground floor *(Forum),* mezzanine *(Galerie Nord and Galerie Sud),* and fifth floor *(Grande Galerie).* Inquire at the information desk about tours. The museum's gift shops sell posters and postcards (4-6F), as well as an impressive selection of contemporary art journals and books in both French and English. Museum open (with the exception of the *atelier des enfants*) Mon. and Wed.-Fri. noon-10pm; Sat.-Sun. 10am-10pm. Ticket office closes at 9pm. Admission 35F, under 25 and all on Sun. 24F, under 16 free. Temporary exhibits cost extra: *Grande Galerie* 45F, under 25 30F, under 16 free; *Galeries Nord* or *Sud* and the *Forum* 27F, under 25 20F, under 16 free. One-day pass gives access to all exhibitions and the museum: 70F, under 25 45F, under 16 free. Buy your tickets on the main floor, since they are not available at the museum entrance; note that *tickets do not permit reentry.* Wheelchair access through the back on rue Beaubourg.

Displaying art is only one of the functions of the Centre Pompidou. The **Salle Garance,** the Pompidou's cinema (located on the main floor), hosts adventurous film series featuring little-known works from all corners of the globe (see "Cinema," p. 250). The **Bibliothèque Publique d'Information,** a free, non-circulating library, is open to anyone who walks in (entrance on the second floor). It is one of the largest libraries in Paris and occupies parts of three floors of the Centre (see "Other Services," p. 71). The **Institut de la Recherche et de la Coordination Acoustique/Musique (IRCAM),** until recently directed by composer/conductor Pierre Boulez, is an institute of musical research housed next to the Stravinsky fountain. Concert repertories fall somewhere between out and far-out, including multimedia events combining film, theater, ballet, and contemporary music (admission 90F). Finally, the **atelier des enfants,** on the main floor (tel. 01 44 78 49 17), caters to the very young, with multimedia programs aimed at expanding minds six to 12 years old. (Open Mon. and Wed.-Sat. 1:30-5:30pm. Special activities related to museum exhibits Wed., Sat., and daily during school vacations, 2-3:15pm and 3:30-4:45pm; 30F.)

While you're there check out the *salle d'actualité,* a non-circulating reading room, or move up to the fifth floor for coffee or a meal, or simply for the great (free!) view. From left to right, you will see Notre-Dame, the Tour Montparnasse, the golden dome of the Invalides, the Eiffel Tower, the Arc de Triomphe, La Défense and its Arch, and Sacré-Coeur on Montmartre. The Pompidou's restaurant and terraced *salon de thé* offer a lunch menu for 61F.

Some 1997 exhibits: *Face à l'Histoire:* the modern artist's look at history, up until April 1997; *Fernand Léger,* May 29-Sept 29, 1997. Parts of the Pompidou may close at the end of 1997 for renovations. Call for dates.

■ Musée Rodin

The Musée Rodin, 77, rue de Varenne, 7ème (tel. 01 44 18 61 10; M. Varenne), located both inside and outside the elegant 18th-century Hôtel Biron (see "Sights—7ème," p. 170), highlights the work of France's greatest sculptor. During his lifetime, Auguste Rodin (1840-1917) was among the country's most controversial artists, classified by many as sculpture's Impressionist (Monet was a close friend and admirer). Today, almost all acknowledge him as the father of modern sculpture. Born in a working-class district of Paris, Rodin began study at the Petite École, a trade school of sorts, for technical drawing. He tried three times to get into the famous École des Beaux-Arts, and failed each time. Frequenting the Louvre to study Classical sculpture, he later worked as an ornamental carver, eventually setting up a small studio of his own. His travels away from Paris allowed him to articulate a definitive, powerful style, completely unlike the flowery academic style then in vogue. One of his first major pieces, *The Age of Bronze* (1875), was so anatomically perfect that he was accused of molding it directly from the body.

The museum houses many of Rodin's better known sculptures in plaster, bronze, and marble, such as *The Hand of God* (1902), which depicts a rough-hewn hand holding an embracing man and woman, and *The Kiss* (1888-98) which portrays a woman kissing her seated lover. *The Cathedral* shows two hands twisted around each other, palms facing and fingertips touching; look twice and you'll notice that both of the hands are right hands, one a man's and one a woman's.

Rodin's training in drawing is evident everywhere; as he said, "my sculpture is but drawing in three dimensions." One room on the first floor is dedicated to a rotating display of drawings and studies. In addition, the museum has several arresting works by Camille Claudel, Rodin's muse, collaborator, and lover. Her *The Ripe Age* shows an elderly man being led away by Death, while a younger woman tries to hold him back; some say that it describes Claudel's ambivalence about her relationship with Rodin, who was much older than she.

The *hôtel's* expansive garden is a museum unto itself. Flowers, trees, and fountains frame outdoor sculptures. If you're short on time or money, consider paying the smaller admission fee for the grounds only. You won't miss the collection's stars: just inside the gates sits Rodin's most famous work, *The Thinker* (1880-1904).

Balzac (1891-1897), behind *The Thinker,* was commissioned in 1891 by the Société des Gens de Lettres, but a battle over Rodin's design and his inability to meet their deadlines raged for years. Unlike the portrait the Société expected, the finished product shows a dramatic, haunted artist with hollow eyes. The plasticity of the body and the distortion of the author's well-known face enraged countless artists and non-artists. Rodin cancelled the commission and kept the statue for himself, claiming proudly, "I have the formal wish to remain the sole owner of my work." Later in his life, he noted, "Nothing which I made satisfied me as much, because nothing had cost me as much; nothing else sums up so profoundly that which I believe to be the secret law of my art." On the other side of the garden, a cast of the stunning *Burghers of Calais* (1884-95) somberly recreates a moment in the Hundred Years War. Beyond stands one version of Rodin's largest and most intricate sculpture, *The Gates of Hell* (1880-90; another towers inside the Musée d'Orsay).

A small, upscale **caféteria** is tucked away in a leafy and shaded part of the garden to the right, behind the Hôtel Biron. The caféteria, a superb place for lunch, offers an extensive salad bar (35F), desserts (8-26F), packaged sandwiches for 18-22F, and plenty of tables along the shaded west walkway—though you will have to fend off brazen birds with designs on your lunch.

Temporary exhibits are housed in the chapel (to your right as you enter). Entrance is included in the price of museum admission. Museum open April-Sept. Tues.-Sun. 9:30am-5:45pm; Oct.-March Tues.-Sun. 9:30am-4:45pm. Last admission 30min. before closing. Admission 28F; students, seniors, under 18, and all on Sun. 18F; admission to park alone 5F. Cafeteria open April-Sept. 10am-6pm; March 10am-4:30pm. Persons who are blind or visually-impaired may get permission to touch the sculptures, but they must obtain an okay before they begin their visit. For more on Rodin and his sculpture, you can visit the smaller **Musée Rodin,** Villa des Brillants 19, av. Auguste Rodin (tel. 01 45 34 13 09), in Meudon. The "country" house where Rodin spent the final years of his life now contains most of his minor works and the plaster models for *The Thinker, The Gates of Hell,* and his other major bronze casts. In the garden, *The Thinker* sits contemplatively above the tombs of Rodin and his wife, Rose Beurat, whom he married the year of her death—after living with her for 53 years. (Open Fri.-Sun. 1:30-6pm. Last ticket sold at 5:30pm. Admission 10F, students 5F.) Take RER line C to Meudon-val-Fleury. Be sure to take a train that stops at all stations; some express trains zoom right by. When you exit the train station, take your first right, then your next right onto av. A. Rodin. The museum is on the left-hand side (15-min. walk). Or take bus #169 from the station and get off at the Paul Bert stop. Alternately, you can take metro line 12 (direction: Mairie d'Issy) to the end of the line, board bus #190 and get off at the Hôpital Percy stop.

■ The Invalides Museums

The Invalides complex guards a series of museums that revolve around French history and, above all, France's martial glory (M. Invalides; see "Sights—7ème," p. 171).

Lying under the massive gilded dome constructed by Jules Hardouin-Mansart is **Napoleon's Tomb.** Finished in 1861, the tomb actually consists of six concentric coffins, made of materials ranging from mahogany to lead, perhaps to make sure the emperor didn't escape again, like he did from Elba. The tomb is placed on the lower level and viewed first from a round balcony above, forcing everyone who visits to bow down to the emperor even in his death. (This delighted Adolf Hitler on his visit to Paris in 1940.) Names of significant battles are engraved in the marble surrounding the coffins—oddly enough, Waterloo isn't there. Ten bas-reliefs recall the institutional reforms of law, education, and the like under Napoleon, who is depicted wearing that most typical of French attire: a toga and laurels. The tiny Roi de Rome, Napoleon's only son, is buried at his feet. Six chapels dedicated to different saints lie off the main room, sheltering the tombs of famous French Marshals. Bring a 10F coin to the Tomb for a five-minute recorded explanation in English. (Tomb open daily June-Aug. 10am-7pm; Oct.-March 10am-5pm; April-May and Sept. 10am-6pm. Admission 35F; students under 30, seniors, and under 18 25F; under 7 free. Ticket, valid for 2 consecutive days, also permits entry to the Musée de l'Armée, Musée des Plans-Relief, and the Musée de l'Ordre de la Libération. For 30F, you can rent an *audioguide* in English at the information desk in the west wing.)

More war trophies are housed in the **Musée de l'Armée** (tel. 01 44 42 37 72 or 44 42 37 64), which celebrates centuries of French military history. The museum is housed in two wings on opposite sides of the Invalides's cobblestone main courtyard, the Cour d'Honneur. The East Wing *(Aile Orient)* houses war paraphernalia from the 17th, 18th, and 19th centuries and culminates in the First Empire exhibit on the second floor, with a special focus on Napoleon. The West Wing *(Aile Occident)* holds 20th-century exhibits revolving around Charles de Gaulle. Electronic maps trace troop movements during the First and Second World Wars. The General's *képi* and letters join an elaborate model of one of the D-Day beaches. Be prepared for peppy music piped into exhibits of numerous swastikas and pictures of work camps; the effect can be nauseating. (Museum open April-Sept. daily 10am-6pm; Oct.-March 10am-5pm. Admission included in ticket for Napoleon's tomb.)

Escape by climbing the stairs to the **Musée des Plans-Reliefs** (tel. 01 45 51 95 05) on the fourth floor, a collection of a hundred models of fortified cities. Spanning the period from 1668 to 1870, the exhibit is one-of-a-kind, of interest to architects, urban planners, and historians. The collection was established by Louis XIV in 1668, when France acquired cities that it needed to fortify. Most of the descriptions in the museum are in French. Pick up the English brochure (free) at the museum's entrance. (Museum open daily April-Sept. 10am-noon and 1:30-6pm; Oct.-March 10am-noon and 1:30-5pm. Admission included in price for Napoleon's Tomb. No wheelchair access.) One of the least celebrated but most worthwhile parts of the Invalides is the **Musée de l'Ordre de la Libération,** 51bis, bd. de Latour-Maubourg (tel. 01 47 05 04 10), in the *Aile Occident* and accessible from the Cour d'Honneur. The quiet, uncrowded museum tells the story of those who fought for the liberation of France. A diverse collection of Charles de Gaulle-related paraphernalia is complemented by tributes to the fighters of Free France. The staircase and upstairs gallery, dealing with deportation, present by far the most devastating message. *"N'oubliez jamais!"* (Never forget!) cries a newspaper article next to a picture of a five-year-old girl in concentration camp uniform. The exhibit juxtaposes forbidden journals and prisoners' drawings with camp uniforms and instruments of torture in an attempt to document the mental and physical horror endured by so many. (Hours the same as the Musée de l'Armée. Admission included in ticket to Napoleon's Tomb.)

Independent from its warring neighbors, but housed in a gallery off the Invalides's Cour d'Honneur, is the **Musée d'Histoire Contemporaine** (tel. 01 44 42 54 91 or 01 44 42 38 39). M. and Mme. Henri Leblanc decided in 1914 to create a library and museum to hold documents about the history of the unfolding World War. The three-room museum mounts two temporary exhibits per year (April-June and Oct.-Dec.), using posters, magazines, pictures, and other documents from the library to probe recent history. Most of the posters and all of the labels are in French, but the visual nature of the exhibits helps transcend the language barrier, as do the enthusiasm of the staff and the helpful English brochure (free). (Open April-June and Oct.-Dec. Tues.-Sat. 10am-1pm and 2-5:30pm, Sun. 2-5:30pm. Admission 30F, 20F if you have a ticket to the other Invalides museums.)

■ Musée de Cluny

The **Hôtel de Cluny,** 6, pl. Paul Painlevé, 5ème (tel. 01 43 25 62 00; M. Cluny-Sorbonne), not only houses one of the world's finest collections of medieval art, jewelry, and tapestries, but also is itself a perfectly preserved medieval manor, built on top of Roman ruins. One of the three Roman baths in the Paris area, the *thermae* and their surroundings were purchased by the Abbot of Cluny, who then built his own residence upon them. Excavations begun after World War II unearthed the remains of the baths, which have since been re-incorporated into the layout of the building. Visitors may now pass through the flamboyant Gothic museum entry, replete with pointed arches and a cobblestone courtyard, into a time when Paris was not Paris but Lutèce, the Gallo-Roman city that emerged here in the first century AD. Most of the building actually dates from the late 15th century, when it was built for the Order of Cluny, a religious order then led by the powerful Amboise family, whose fondness for Italian forms is evident in their home. In 1843 the state converted the *hôtel* into the National Museum of the Middle Ages.

The best-preserved room of the baths is the *frigidarium,* where third-century Gauls gathered to take cold showers. First they worked out in the *palestre,* then took a hot bath in the *caldarium* and finally a cold one in the *frigidarium.* The shock of this transition was eased by a dip in the *tepidarium,* or lukewarm bath. Only the *frigidarium* and swimming pool remain intact and open to visitors (see Room XII on the ground floor). Call the museum for details about guided tours of the hallways and rooms that comprise the rest of the *thermae.*

The people depicted in the museum's impressive collection of tapestries from the 15th and 16th centuries seem to have rejected the frolicking habits of their ancestors in favor of more gentle and clothed pursuits. The depiction of manorial life hanging in Room IV shows elegant men and women passing their time surrounded by servants and an incredible variety of plants and flowers. The masterpiece of the collection, a series of six panels entitled **La Dame et la Licorne** (The Lady and the Unicorn—all tapestries center upon a lady, a unicorn, and a lion), is generally considered to be the best surviving medieval tapestry series (Room XIII). Each of the first five panels represents one of the five senses, but the purpose of the last one, *A mon seul désir,* has been a source of controversy throughout the 150 years of this series' public display. It pictures a lady holding a necklace near a box carried by her servant. The question on everyone's mind: is she about to put the necklace on or to put it away? George Sand first proposed the popular 19th-century notion that the tapestries had been woven as a gift of love. She believed them to be a present by some captured Muslim prince for his beloved—in other words, that the tapestries were all dedicated "to my only desire." Somewhat less romantic scholars have traced them instead to Jean le Viste, a merchant whose coat of arms (three crescents) appears throughout the series. Today, the debate over the series' meaning continues. Some hold that the tapestry shows the lady removing her necklace and locking it away, symbolically rejecting the material, sensual world of the previous five tapestries. In this interpretation, *"A mon seul désir"* would mean "by my own volition," indicating her wish to abandon the world of the senses and to retreat into spiritual hermeticism. Yet another school argues that *"A mon seul désir"* is in fact the first in the series, and that it shows the lady taking the necklace out of the box and accepting with pleasure the world of the senses, which the weaver goes on to depict in the next five tapestries.

On the ground floor, Room VI glows with light from its colorful display of medieval stained glass which includes some of the original windows that once adorned Ste-Chapelle as well as a selection of those from the cathedrals at Rouen and St-Denis. Down the hall in Room VIII, the **Galerie des Rois** displays a set of 21 stone heads of Judean and Israelite kings, dating from 1210 to 1230. These heads (once attached to bodies) sat atop Notre-Dame's portals until 1793 when Revolutionaries, itching to decapitate royalty, mistook them for statues of French kings and severed them from their bodies. Uncovered in 1977, the heads still bear faint traces of their original paint. Upstairs an entire room (Room XVI) is devoted to medieval royal jewelry and crowns. The gold rush continues down the corridor with an enormously rare and valuable gold altarpiece from Basel, Switzerland (Room XIX).

Museum open Wed.-Mon. 9:15am-5:45pm. Admission 28F; students, under 25, over 60, and Sun. 18F; under 18 free. The museum also sponsors chamber music concerts performed on Renaissance and Baroque instruments. Concerts are held Fri. at 12:30pm and Sat. at 5pm—call ahead to confirm times (52F, students and seniors 33F, under 18 15F with admission to the museum). Evening concerts are also held from May to mid-July; call 01 53 73 78 00 for information and reservations or FNAC (see "Theater," p. 252, for ticket agency information), or stop by the museum for a schedule.

■ La Villette

La Villette, 19ème (M. Porte de la Villette or Porte de Pantin), is a highly successful urban renewal project in the northeastern corner of Paris. Its 55 hectares enclose a landscaped park, a huge science museum, an Omnimax cinema, a conservatory, an exhibition hall, a jazz club, and a concert arena. The area was previously home to a nationalized meat market-*cum*-slaughterhouse compound that provided Paris with most of its beef. With the advent of refrigerated transport in 1969, it became more economical to kill cattle in the countryside and deliver the meat directly to butchers.

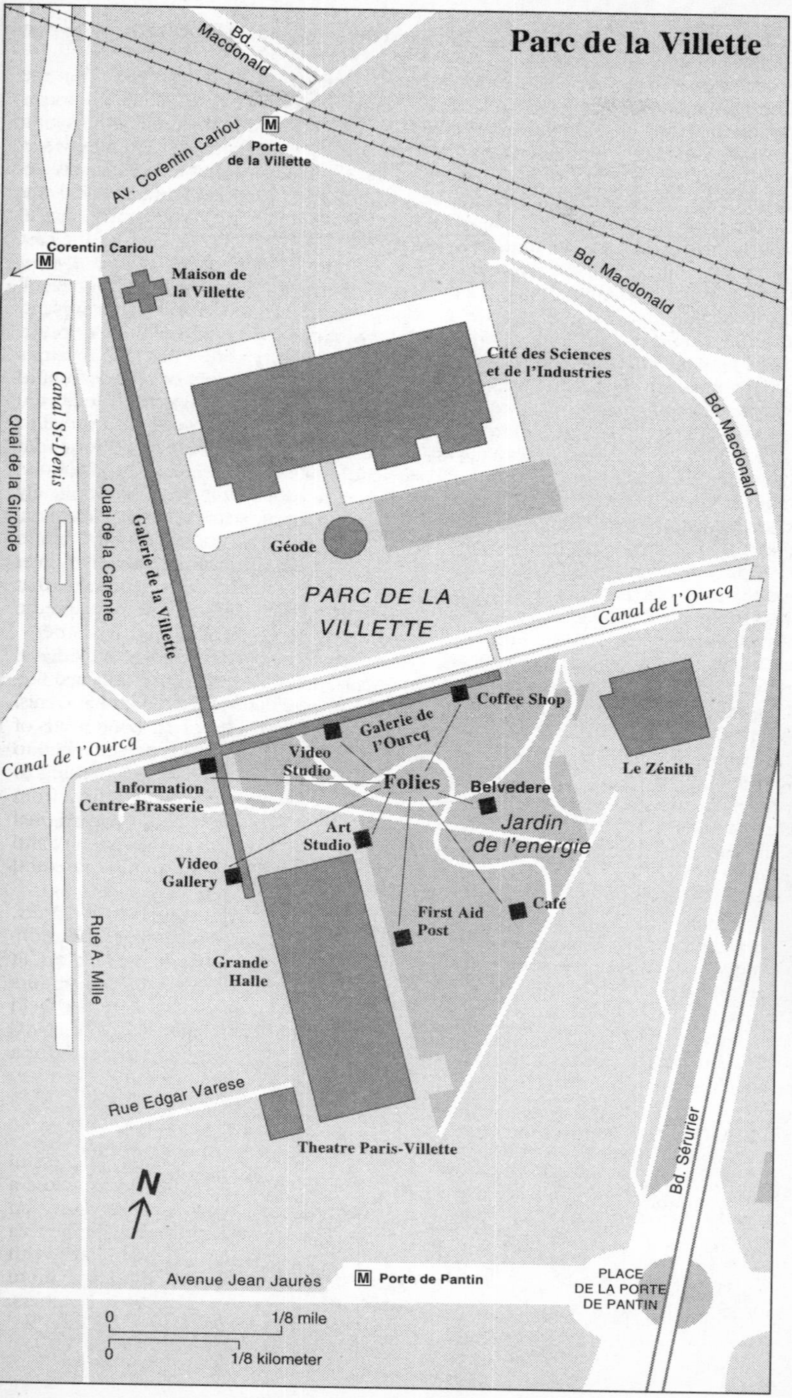

Parc de la Villette

Bd. Macdonald
Av. Corentin Cariou
M Porte de la Villette
M Corentin Cariou
Maison de la Villette
Bd. Macdonald
Cité des Sciences et de l'Industries
Bd. Macdonald
Canal St-Denis
Quai de la Gironde
Quai de la Carente
Galerie de la Villette
Géode
PARC DE LA VILLETTE
Canal de l'Ourcq
Canal de l'Ourcq
Coffee Shop
Galerie de l'Ourcq
Video Studio
Folies
Information Centre-Brasserie
Belvedere
Le Zénith
Jardin de l'energie
Art Studio
Video Gallery
Café
First Aid Post
Grande Halle
Rue A. Mille
Rue Edgar Varese
Theatre Paris-Villette
Bd. Sérurier
N
Avenue Jean Jaurès
M Porte de Pantin
PLACE DE LA PORTE DE PANTIN
0 1/8 mile
0 1/8 kilometer

The government closed down La Villette's meat center in 1974. In 1979, plans began for the new, modern La Villette.

The **Cité des Sciences et de l'Industrie** (tel. 01 36 68 29 30, 2F23 per min.) perches on the northern end of La Villette, next to the Porte de la Villette metro stop. Inaugurated in 1985, this establishment is dedicated to bringing science to the little people. The star attraction, located on the top two stories, is the **Explora** science museum: even when you know the scientific principles behind a particular display, you'll be dazzled by the ingenious way it is presented. There are quite a few English translations throughout the museum. The Cité-Pass ticket allows you to enter the **planetarium** (Floor 2) as well as temporary exhibitions, the 3-D movies in the Cinéma Louis-Lumière (Floor 0), and the modest aquarium (Floor S2). Floor S1 houses the *médiathèque*—a multimedia, open-stack library with more than 300,000 scientific and technical works. As of April 1997, a big greenhouse designed by Dominique Perrot (the architect of the new national library), will explain the latest in agricultural techniques.

If you're traveling with children, this is the place to come. There are two different discovery programs at the **Cité des Enfants** (for ages 3-5 and 5-12; 20F for a 90-min. session). Both programs require adult accompaniment, but no more than two adults per family are admitted. All programs are in French, but because the exhibits explore science using all of the senses, children who don't speak French can have just as much fun as those who do. For example, there are visual exhibits on subjects such as electricity (for ages 5-12). The *vestiare* (Floor 0) rents strollers and wheelchairs; the entire Cité is wheelchair-accessible.

The enormous **La Géode** (tel. 01 40 05 12 12) is a huge mirrored sphere mounted on a water basin in front of the Cité des Sciences that looks like an enormous extraterrestrial golf ball caught in a tiny water trap. The exterior is coated with 6433 polished stainless-steel triangles that reflect every detail of their surroundings. Inside, Omnimax movies are shown on a 1000-square-meter hemispheric screen, "the largest in the world" (or so they say). Come here for the standard Omnimax fare: 3-D documentaries on things like Yellowstone Park and volcanoes. (Showings Tues.-Sun. every hr. on the hour 10am-9pm. Also Mon. during French school holidays 10am-6pm. Reserve tickets early; they can sell out as much as 2 months ahead of time, depending on the show. Buy tickets at the Géode entrance: 57F, reduced 44F. No reduced rates on weekends or holidays 1-6pm.)

To guide you around the Cité and La Géode, headsets with English commentaries on major attractions (including the architecture) can be rented in the Cité on Floor (for 15F. A one-day "Cité-Pass" covers entrance to all exhibits of the museum, includ ing the planetarium and the *Argonaute,* a submarine mock-up with an exhibit inside on submarines (admission 45F, reduced 35F, after 4pm 25F, under 7 free; tickets tc *Argonaute* 25F). A combined ticket for the Géode and Cité 92F, reduced 79F Reduced tickets for seniors, teachers, large families and those under 25. Museun open Tues.-Sat. 10am-6pm, Sun. 10am-7pm; *médiathèque* open Tues.-Sun. noon 8pm, free.

Between the Canal St-Denis and the west side of the Cité is a little marvel called the **Cinaxe** (tel. 01 42 09 34 00). Watch one of several 10-minute movies representing what you would see if you were in a Formula 1 car, in a rocket, or in an airplane flying low over mountains, while sophisticated hydraulic pumps jerk and spin the movie theater, so that you feel the curves and bumps as you see them. (Open Tues.-Sun 11am-6pm; shows every 20min. Forbidden to those under 6; not recommended fo pregnant women or people with heart disorders. Cinaxe tickets 32F, reduced 29F 29F if purchased on the same day as a Géode or Cité ticket.)

At the opposite end of La Villette from the Cité des Sciences is the **Cité de la Musique** (tel. 01 44 84 44 84; reservations open Tues.-Sat. noon-8pm, Sun.-Mon noon-6pm; M. Porte de Pantin). Features a concert hall, information centers, and museum (opening Jan. 1997) where 850 instruments from the 16th century to the present are displayed, along with a history of musicology. (Cité de la Musique ope Tues.-Wed. and Fri.-Sat. noon-6pm, Thurs. noon-9:30pm, Sun. 10am-6pm. The cor cert hall opens 30min. before the performance; buy tickets at the box office Tues.-Sat. noon-6pm, Sun. 10am-6pm.)

The **Parc de la Villette** is a vast open area separating the two Cités, cut in the middle by the Canal de l'Ourcq and bordering the Canal St-Denis. Bernard Tschumi, the Parc de la Villette's designer, rejected the 19th-century notion of a park as an oasis of nature, attempting instead to achieve a 20th-century urban park, "based on cultural invention, education, and entertainment." Unifying this space is a set of roughly cubical red metal structures which form a grid of squares 120m x 120m. Known as *folies,* they serve a variety of purposes. One houses a fast-food restaurant, three are day-care centers, and one, at the park's entrance near M. Pte. de Pantin, is an **information office** (open daily 10am-7pm). Also in the park, the steel-and-glass **Grande Halle** (tel. 01 40 03 75 75), constructed in 1867 as the La Villette beef building, has become a cultural Jack-of-All-Trades, with frequent plays, concerts, temporary exhibitions, and films. Next to the Canal de l'Ourcq is the **Zénith** (tel. 01 42 40 60 00 or 01 42 08 60 00), a concert hall whose high-tech acoustics and 6400-person capacity make it a favorite among such artists as Tina Turner, Ziggy Marley, and Sting. It was also one of the last places Nirvana played, in February of 1994. Directly behind the Zenith is the jazz club **Hot Brass** (tel. 01 42 00 14 14), where acts like George Clinton and the P-funk All Stars come to funk and jazz the nights away.

Finally, the park encompasses a number of thematic **gardens,** which you are likely to miss unless you follow the winding path known as the *promenade cinématique* (the map in the information office helps). Of particular interest, the Mirror Garden uses an array of mirrors to create optical illusions, while the Garden of Childhood Fears takes you through a little wooded grove resonant with spooky sounds. At night the *promenade cinématique* is lit up, and makes for an interesting walk (reasonably safe, too, because the park has plenty of security guards).

■ Other Major Art Collections

Musée Marmottan, 2, rue Louis-Boilly, 16ème (tel. 01 42 24 07 02). M. La Muette. Follow Chausée de la Muette which becomes av. Ranelagh through the Jardin du Ranelagh park. Having inherited from his father both a hunting lodge near the Bois de Boulogne and a propensity to purchase art work, Paul Marmottan indulged his passion for the Napoleonic era by transforming the hunting lodge into a stately mansion and furnishing it with Empire furniture and art. At his death in 1932, he bequeathed the building, his own collection, and his father's group of primitive German, Flemish, and Italian paintings to the Académie des Beaux-Arts. Later, Michel Monet added 80 of *his* father's paintings, many from the later years at Giverny, to the museum's existing Impressionist collection. The numerous Impressionist canvases by Monet, Renoir, and others include stunning works, not the least of which is Monet's *Impression: soleil levant (Impression: Sunrise).* Displayed in 1874 with eight other paintings, it led one critic to refer derisively to "those *impressionistes,"* an epithet Monet and his colleagues enthusiastically embraced. Stolen in 1985, the painting was recently recovered in Corsica. The Wildenstein room, with 228 great medieval illuminations, should not be missed. Open Tues.-Sun. 10am-5:30pm. 35F, students and seniors 15F, under 8 free.

Musée National des Arts Asiatiques (Musée Guimet), 6, pl. d'Iéna, 16ème (tel. 01 47 23 61 65). M. Iéna. Closed until early 1999 for renovations, this large collection of Asian art represents 17 different countries and in the past has been one of the best organized and most peaceful museums in the 16ème. Although much of the museum's collection has been placed in storage, some pieces have been moved to the Musée Guimet's annex, the **Musée du Panthéon Bouddhique,** 19, av. d'Iéna (tel. 01 47 23 61 65), located just a few steps away in the Hôtel Heidelbach. Housed in the turn-of-the-century Neo-Baroque *hôtel,* the Panthéon traces the religious history of Japan and China through a collection of statues, paintings, and sacred figures dating from the 4th through the 19th centuries. The Japanese garden behind the *hôtel,* while not entirely authentic, is entirely restful and refreshing. Open Wed.-Mon. 9:45am-6pm. 15F, under 18 free.

Musée d'Art Moderne de la Ville de Paris, 11, av. du Président Wilson, 16ème (tel. 01 53 67 40 80). M. Iéna. Often overshadowed by its more publicized peer, the Centre Pompidou, this museum contains one of the world's foremost collections of 20th-century art. Works by Matisse *(The Dance)* and Picasso *(The Jester)* are on permanent display while temporary exhibits vary dramatically in topic and scope. The museum offers little more than a brief map and a list of artists to guide you through the labyrinth-like exhibition space. What the collection lacks in overall coherence is more than made up for by its sheer size. A visit will undoubtedly lead to rewarding discoveries, whether your tastes run to 7-ft. pictures of Diana Ross and life-size sculptures of horses made from plastic toys or toward Matisse and Modigliani. Open Wed.-Mon. 10am-5:30pm. Admission to permanent collection 27F, students and seniors 15F; to collection and temporary exhibits 40F, students and seniors 30F.

Musée de l'Orangerie, 1er (tel. 01 42 97 48 16). M. Concorde. A small collection of Impressionist paintings nestled in the southwest corner of the Tuileries. Smaller and less of a knockout than Orsay, this museum is also less crowded, so you can admire the Cézannes, Renoirs, Matisses, Picassos, and other greats in comfort. Claude Monet's *Les Nymphéas (Water Lilies)* occupy 2 rooms of the underground level, each of which is paneled with 4 large curved murals that were created for these chambers. On the day of the Armistice, in lieu of a bouquet of flowers, Monet decided to give France these paintings of the lilies in his garden at Giverny. He spent the rest of his life working on them, finishing just before his death in 1926. The museum also hosts temporary exhibitions. Open Wed.-Mon. 9:45am-5:15pm. 28F; ages 18-25, over 60, and Sun. 18F.

■ From Art Africain to Zadkine

Musée des Arts Africains et Océaniens, 293, av. Daumesnil, 12ème (tel. 01 43 46 51 61), on the western edge of the Bois de Vincennes. M. Porte Dorée. A stunning collection of several millennia of African and Pacific art. Highlights include the immense, breathtaking display of African statues and masks, and jewelry and wedding dresses from the Maghreb (Morocco, Tunisia, and Algeria). Built for the 1931 Colonial Exposition, the museum building still contains its original Eurocentric murals and friezes. There aren't many explanations in the museum, and when there are, they contain no analysis of France's colonialist past or the museum's history in relation to colonialism. Families and young school children crowd downstairs to the tropical fish aquarium; the crocodile room is a perennial favorite. Open Mon. and Wed.-Fri. 10am-noon and 1:30-5:20pm, Sat.-Sun. 12:30-5:50pm. Last entry 30min. before closing. Admission to aquarium, permanent collection, and exhibits 27F, students and seniors 18F, under 18 free.

Musée d'Art Juif, 42, rue des Saules, 18ème (tel. 01 42 57 84 15, fax 01 42 57 26 30). M. Lamarck-Caulaincourt. Housed on the 3rd floor of the Jewish Center, the museum celebrates Judaism through exhibits of objects used during Jewish rituals, pictures, and models of synagogues, as well as an enormous model of Jerusalem during the time of King Solomon. The library displays a variety of beautifully illustrated texts and a collection of works by popular artists from North Africa and Eastern Europe, including several by Marc Chagall. Scholars can call to inquire about access to documents in the museum's library. Closed on Jewish holidays. 30F, students and groups 20F, children 10F. Open Sept.-July Sun.-Thurs. 3-6pm.

Cristalleries Baccarat, 30-32, rue de Paradis, 10ème (tel. 01 47 70 64 30). M. Gare de l'Est. Walk against traffic on bd. Strasbourg and turn right on rue de la Fidelité, which becomes rue de Paradis. The impressive building, built under the Directory between 1798 and 1799, houses both the Baccarat crystal company headquarters and the Baccarat museum. Since its founding in 1764, Baccarat has become one of the most prestigious and expensive of crystal makers, patronized by kings, czars, and shahs. The museum houses an array of every imaginable crystal object, including a life-sized chandelier-woman at the entrance. With exquisite vases, goblets, and sculptures reflected in mirrored tables, the delicate display looks like an ice palace and makes you feel like a bull in a crystal shop. Open Mon.-Fri. 9am-6:30pm, Sat. 10am-6pm. 15F entry to museum.

Maison de Balzac, 47, rue Raynouard, 16ème (tel. 01 42 24 56 38). M. Passy. Honoré de Balzac (1799-1850), one of France's greatest novelists, lived in this house (1840-47) while finishing *La comédie humaine* and evading bill collectors. To ensure the possibility of the former and to leave the latter to the next resident, Balzac required anyone who knocked on his green front door to recite a password such as "la saison des prunes est arrivée" (plum season has arrived) before he or she gained admittance. Access to the house and the museum's collection, which includes portraits, a plaster cast of the author's hand, and Victor Hugo's description of Balzac's death and funeral, is much easier these days. An *audioguide* (15F, in French) or textual guide (25F, French or English) are helpful introductions, especially for those who don't know the genealogy of every character in *La comédie humaine* (copies available 40F). Open Tues.-Sun. 10am-5:40pm. 18F, students 9F, seniors free. Temporary exhibits raise admission fee, usually by 10F.

Musée Henri Bouchard, 25, rue de l'Yvette, 16ème (tel. 01 46 47 63 46). M. Jasmin. The cluttered workshop of Henri Bouchard (1875-1960), sculptor of the Palais de Chaillot's bronze Apollo, illustrates not only his range of media (bronze, tin, plaster, clay, stone, wood) and subjects (monuments, religious decoration, portraits, animals), but also his expertise. Temporary 3-month exhibits in the front hall. Bouchard's son (who speaks English) and daughter-in-law are friendly and knowledgable curators. On the first Sat. of each month at 3pm, Mme. Bouchard guides a tour (free with admission). Ask for a free biography in English. Open July-Sept. 15; Oct.-Dec. 15; Jan. 2-March 15; and April-June 15 Wed.-Sat. 2-7pm. 25F, students 15F. Call about lectures on sculpting technique.

Musée Bourdelle, 18, rue Antoine Bourdelle, 15ème (tel. 01 49 54 73 73). M. Montparnasse. From av. du Maine, turn left onto rue Antoine Bourdelle. People who don't appreciate the raw aggressive style of Antoine Bourdelle (1861-1929) often become fans after spending the afternoon wandering his studio-turned-museum. Room after room packed with statues overwhelm the casual visitor with the sheer productivity and genius of the sculptor, a longtime friend and artistic contemporary of Rodin. Note the impressive series of roughly 40 busts and statues of Beethoven; three small but packed sculpture gardens are also open to the public. Scant captioning does not lessen the museum's impact. Open Tues.-Sun. 10am-5:40pm. Last entry 5:15pm. 18F, students 9F.

Musée Nissim de Camondo, 63, rue Monceau, 8ème (tel. 01 53 89 06 40). M. Villiers or Monceau. This building tells the story not only of 18th-century decorative arts but also of a family that met tragedy. Comte Moïse de Camondo built this *hôtel particulier* from 1911 to 1914, on the model of the Petit Trianon at Versailles, to house his exquisite collection of 18th-century furniture, paintings, tapestries, and porcelain. Camondo's will left the house to the Union des Arts Décoratifs, dedicated to the memory of his son, Nissim, who died in aerial combat in 1917. The rest of the family died at Auschwitz. On a visit in 1990, Barbara Bush—overcome by the combination of Savonnerie carpets, Sèvres porcelain, and a ravishing 1780 mahogany roll-top desk—in a rare burst of strong language exclaimed, "Isn't this the darnedest place you ever saw?" Take one of the 45-min. *audioguides* (25F, 35F for 2, available in English) or buy a 20F brochure (more detailed guides 60F-195F; in French) to supplement otherwise meager explanations. Open Wed.-Sun. 10am-5pm. 27F, students under 25 and seniors 18F.

Musée Carnavalet, 23, rue de Sévigné, 3ème (tel. 01 42 72 21 13, fax 01 42 72 01 61). M. Chemin-Vert. Housed in a 16th-century *hôtel,* this museum traces Paris's history from its origins to the present. There are rooms which reconstitute Parisian homes from the 16th to the 19th centuries; Gallo-Roman and medieval archeological collections, paintings, and all kinds of objects from the revolutionary period. The reconstructed Bijouterie Fouquet may be the star of the show for Art Nouveau junkies. (For information on the courtyard see "Sights—3ème," p. 155.) The museum gets a lot of French schoolchildren on field trips, but don't let that scare you off. Pick up the schedule which includes all tours and workshops offered by the city's public museums at the front desk. Call ahead for partial wheelchair access. Open Tues.-Sun. 10am-5:40pm. Only parts of the museum are open at a time because of renovations and lack of government funding. 27F, students 15F,

MUSEUMS

seniors and under 18 free. French guided tour 25F (Tues. and Sat. at 2:30pm). Optional temporary exhibits sometimes cost extra.

Fondation Cartier pour l'art contemporain, 261, bd. Raspail, 14ème (tel. 01 42 18 56 50, fax 01 42 18 56 52). M. Raspail or Denfert-Rochereau. Housed in a large metal structure dominated by enormous sheets of glass and surrounded by wildflowers and a small outdoor performance space, the Fondation hosts 2-3 temporary exhibitions a year on subjects ranging from Andy Warhol to the history of birds. Soirées Nomades, held every Thurs. Sept.-June at 8pm, are a series of films, lectures, and music, dance, and performance art concerts linked thematically with the current exhibition (prices vary; call for information and reservations, 01 42 18 56 72). 30F, students and seniors 20F, under 10 free. Open Tues.-Wed. and Fri.-Sun. noon-8pm, Thurs. noon-10pm.

Musée Cernuschi, 7, av. Velasquez, 8ème (tel. 01 45 63 50 75), outside the gates of Parc Monceau. M. Villiers or Monceau. A magnificent, charmingly personable collection of Asian art housed in a villa that belonged to Henri Cernuschi (1820-96), a financier of Milanese descent who took off on a trans-world tour after being "affected" by the Commune. Second to the Guimet as an Asian art museum, the Cernuschi contains some very impressive pieces, such as an 18th-century, 3-ton, 3.5m-high, bronze, Japanese Buddha. Open Tues.-Sun. 10am-5:40pm. 18F, art students (age 18-25) 9F, seniors and under 18 free.

Musée de la Chasse (Hunting Museum), 60, rue des Archives, 3ème (tel. 01 42 72 86 43). M. Rambuteau. Housed in the spacious, 17th-century Hôtel Guénégaud, the museum's professionally stuffed animals (whole and in pieces) hold some appeal even for those who dislike *la chasse*. Highlights include the head of a 3-ton white rhino and a rearing polar bear. Portraits of Diana, goddess of the hunt, by Brueghel, Rubens, Velcours, and Monet help make light of the huge collection of animal trophies and weapons (including a crank-operated crossbow). Did we mention the Gabonese bush pig? Open Wed.-Mon. 10am-12:30pm and 1:30-5:30pm. 25F, students and seniors 13F, children ages 5-16 5F. Permission to take photos of the bush pig and friends or to use a video camera 10F.

Musée du Cinéma Henri Langlois, pl. du Trocadéro, in the Palais de Chaillot, 16ème (tel. 01 45 53 74 39). M. Trocadéro. With over 3000 primitive versions of projectors and cameras, as well as demonstrations of how they work, this museum traces the history of film from its beginnings in magic lanterns and shadow theaters to the 1950s. The chronological arrangement of sets, costumes, scripts, and posters may only be visited by guided tour (1hr.) in French. Open Wed.-Sun. for tours at 10, 11am, and 2, 3, 4, and 5pm. 30F.

Musée Clemenceau, 8, rue Benjamin Franklin, 16ème (tel. 01 45 20 53 41), through a small courtyard. M. Passy. Journalist and statesman Georges Clemenceau (1841-1929) has been both revered and vilified for nearly a century. The museum thoroughly documents his life as a journalist, when he published (and titled) Emile Zola's article *"J'accuse,"* thus pronouncing his anti-governmental stance during the Dreyfus affair; as mayor of Montmartre; as Prime Minister of France; as Président du Conseil; as Minister of War (1917-20); and as the much-criticized negotiator of the Versailles Treaty. The documents and clippings (among them scores of political cartoons, both positive and disparaging) present a nuanced portrait of the man, not the hero. On the ground floor, Clemenceau's apartment has been left as it was when he died; even the calendars are all torn off at November 24, 1929. Pamphlet (in French and English) explains some museum contents, though not the painting done for Clemenceau by his close friend Monet or the withered bouquet of flowers given to him by a soldier at the front. Open Tues., Thurs., Sat.-Sun., and holidays 2-5pm. 20F, students and seniors 15F.

Musée Cognacq-Jay, 8, rue Elzévir, 3ème (tel. 01 40 27 07 21). M. St-Paul. Walk up rue Pavée, make a left on rue des Francs Bourgeois and a right on rue Elzévir. Peaceful museum housed in the 16th-century Hôtel Donon. This collection of Enlightenment art, formerly owned by turn-of-the-century orphan-turned-department-store-mogul Ernest Cognacq and his wife, Marie-Louise Jay, has passed into the hands of the city. Works by Watteau, Canaletto, Rembrandt, Greuze, Fragonard, Ingres, and Rubens. A showcase of the Old Regime as it would like to be remembered—lute-strumming nobles at *fêtes galantes* and wind-blown coquettes.

The museum occasionally hosts plays and concerts. Gardens open mid-May to mid-Sept. 10am-12:15pm and 4-5:35pm. Museum open Tues.-Sun. 10am-5:40pm. 18F, students and under 25 9F, seniors and under 18 free.

Musée de Contrefaçon (the Counterfeiting Museum), 16, rue de la Faisanderie, 16ème (tel. 01 45 01 51 11). M. Porte Dauphine. "I can't see the difference. Can you see the difference? Is there a difference?" Direct these questions toward the display of cigars, crackers, handbags, and their illegal counterfeits for about two minutes. Then ask: "Who cares?" A simplistic brochure in English and French details the different forms of counterfeiting and highlights the collection's prize possessions, such as a vase dating from the Gallo-Roman period bearing the oldest known trademark. Open Mon.-Thurs. 2-5pm, Fri. 9:30am-noon. 10F.

Fondation Le Corbusier, 10, sq. du Docteur-Blanche, 16ème (tel. 01 42 88 41 53). M. Jasmin. Walk up rue de l'Yvette, take a left on rue du Docteur-Blanche and another left at no. 55 into sq. du Docteur-Blanche. The foundation is located in the Villas La Roche and Jeanneret, designed—down to the smallest piece of furniture—by Le Corbusier. The Villa La Roche, commissioned by the young banker La Roche to house his collection of Cubist art, contains the museum, or rather, is the museum. It offers an exceptional glimpse of some of Le Corbusier's architectural trademarks: his use of light, his attempt to harmonize with the natural world, his preference for curved forms and for ramps over stairs, and his tendency to build on *pilotis* (piling). The building itself is without question the museum's most impressive artwork. The Villa Jeanneret next door holds the library and the foundation's offices. Pick up the excellent pamphlet guide, only available in French. Open Sept.-July Mon.-Thurs. 10am-12:30pm and 1:30-6pm, Fri. 10am-12:30pm and 1:30-5pm. 15F, students 10F.

Musée Salvador Dalí (Espace Montmartre), 11, rue Poulbot, 18ème (tel. 01 42 64 40 10). M. Anvers or Abbesses. From pl. du Tertre follow rue du Calvaire toward the view, then turn right onto rue Poulbot. This museum dedicated to the "Phantasmic World of Salvador Dalí" is full of lithographs and sculptures by the Spanish surrealist, with scads of incarnations of his famous droopy clocks. The museum is laid out in "Surrealist surroundings," which amount to wonderful spacing, interesting lighting, and slightly ridiculous space-music in the background. Open daily 10am-6pm; last ticket at 5:30pm. 35F, students 25F.

Musée Delacroix, 6, pl. Furstenberg, 6ème (tel. 01 44 41 86 50). M. St-Germain-des-Prés. Behind the Église St-Germain off rue de l'Abbaye. At the round courtyard, follow the sign to the *atelier Delacroix;* you'll pass through another small courtyard to get into the museum. Located in the artist's 3-room apartment and attached studio, this museum contains works spanning the duration of his career. Delacroix (1799-1863) was one of the leaders of French Romanticism, most famous for his painting *Liberty Leading the People.* A surprising number of sketches, watercolors, and engravings found here belie a gentler Delacroix than a visitor to the Louvre might expect. Also displays a few works by other artists (including two Manet watercolors). Open Wed.-Mon. 10am-5pm, last entry 4:30. 15F, ages 18-25 and over 60 10F, under 18 free.

Musée des Egouts de Paris (Museum of the Sewers of Paris), actually inside the sewers, at the corner of the quai d'Orsay and pl. de la Résistance, 7ème (tel. 01 47 05 10 29). M. Pont de l'Alma. In *Les Misérables,* Victor Hugo wrote, "Paris has beneath it another Paris, a Paris of sewers, which has its own streets, squares, lanes, arteries, and circulation." Enjoy a guided tour of the history of this city beneath the city, held on demand whenever enough people are present. Or pick up a brochure in English. The smell can be overwhelming; hold your nose as you approach the two sewage basins that are part of the tour. Close to the exit, you'll find a map of the main arteries of the sewer system. Don't press your guide for a more detailed map of the underground network; the location of smaller subterranean *rues* has been a government secret ever since the Nazis tried to plant bombs in the sewers during World War II. Open May-Sept. Sat.-Wed. 11am-6pm; Oct.-Dec. and Feb.-April Sat.-Wed. 11am-5pm. Last ticket sold 1hr. before closing. 25F, students and under 10 20F. Under 5 free. Closed for 3 weeks in Jan.

Musée d'Ennery, 59, av. Foch, 16ème (tel. 01 45 53 57 96). M. Porte Dauphine. Despite its name and the bust in its front hall, this museum is not the collection of

Adolphe d'Ennery (1811-99), a prolific but not very good French writer of the Second Empire. The ivories, laquerware, and woodcuts here belong to his wife Clémence d'Ennery who scavenged the city's flea markets and antique shops for Orientalia during the 19th-century's Far East craze. Particularly amazing are the *netsuke* (Japanese miniatures originally used to tie pouches to kimonos), of which the museum has over 300 spectacular examples. Open Sept.-July Thurs., Sun., and holidays 2-6pm. Free. On the ground floor of the same building is the **Musée Arménien** (tel. 01 45 56 15 88), which displays Armenian jewelry, paintings, and religious decoration past and present. Open Sept.-July Thurs., Sun., and holidays 2-6pm. Free.

Galerie d'Entomologie (Insect Museum), 45, rue Buffon, 5ème (tel. 01 40 79 34 00). M. Censier-Daubenton or Gare d'Austerlitz. Across the street from the Galerie de Minéralogie in the Jardin des Plantes. Bliss for the bug freak, with beetles as big as your hand and a Peruvian butterfly eerily like the *tricolore*. Most of the 1-room gallery is dedicated to various specimens of beetles and butterflies in different colors and sizes. Open Mon. and Wed.-Fri. 1-4:30pm, Sat. and Sun. 15F, students 10F.

Musée du Grand Orient de France et de la Franc-Maçonnerie, 16, rue Cadet, 9ème (tel. 01 45 23 20 92). M. Cadet. This one-room museum tells the story of the Masons from early Scottish brotherhood to their peak in the 18th and 19th centuries. Folksy captioning, hand-written in French, accompanies one-of-a-kind pamphlets, medals, portraits, and busts of renowned freemasons, including Voltaire and Talleyrand. The museum is housed in the Hôtel Cadet, built in 1852 and designed as the headquarters for French freemasonry. During World War II, Vichy officials used its resources to identify and persecute members of this brotherhood. Open Mon.-Sat. 2-6pm. Free.

Grand Palais, 3, av. du Général Eisenhower, 8ème (tel. 01 44 13 17 30 or recorded info at 01 44 13 17 17). M. Champs-Elysées-Clemenceau. Most of the building houses the Palais de la Découverte (see below), but the other 2 entrances lead the way to temporary exhibits. Call to see what's going on. 1996 saw an impressive exhibition of Romantic painting at the Grand Palais, featuring Delacroix, Ingres, Gericault, and Corot. Open, when an exhibit is there, Thurs.-Mon. 10am-8pm, Wed. 10am-10pm. Last entry 45min. before closing. Admission varies with the exhibit, but anticipate something like 45F, students and Mon. 31F, under 13 free. If two exhibits are showing simultaneously, admission to both 70F, students and Mon. 50F, under 13 free.

Musée Grévin, 10, bd. Montmartre, 9ème (tel. 01 42 46 13 26). M. Rue Montmartre. This wax museum can be fun if you don't mind over-enthusiastic French kids on field trips. The super-ornate halls are filled with illustrious personages, present and past. Marie-Antoinette awaits her execution in the Conciergerie; the cannibals from Géricault's painting *The Raft of the Medusa* reach for the rescue ship on the horizon. The King of Pop stands in the center of the main gallery; a *Sleeper*-era Woody Allen flies overhead. Open daily 1-7pm (during school holidays 10am-7pm), last entry 6pm. 50F, ages 6-14 35F. V, AmEx (130F minimum). The smaller branch at level "-1" of the **Forum des Halles,** near the Porte Berger, 1er (tel. 01 40 26 28 50; M. Châtelet-Les Halles), presents a fascinating spectacle of Paris during the "Belle Epoque" (1885-1900). A terrific *son et lumière,* in French, recreates the turn of the century. The show is easily presented in English; ask at the door and wait for more English-speaking tourists. Open daily 10:30am-7pm, Sun. and holidays 1-7:15pm. Ticket office closes 45min. before museum. 42F, ages 6-14 32F, under 6 free.

Musée Jean-Jacques Henner, 43, av. Villiers, 17ème (tel. 01 47 63 42 73). M. Malsherbes. This museum displays the *études* and paintings of Jean-Jacques Henner (1829-1905) who tended to paint his soft-focus subjects with luminous, bone-white skin, creating a haunting effect most visible in his treatment of St. Sebastian. On the ground floor are a number of portraits of his family and friends, as well as studies of several works. Open Tues.-Sun. 10am-noon and 2-5pm. 20F, students and seniors 15F, under 18 free.

Musée de l'Histoire de France, 60, rue des Francs Bourgeois, 3ème (tel. 01 40 27 60 96). M. Rambuteau. Walk up rue Rambuteau which becomes rue de Francs Bourgeois. Housed in the Hôtel de Soubise, this museum exhibits French documents important and insignificant—falling in the former category are an edict drafted by

Richard the Lionhearted, an extract from Louis XVI's diary on the day he was arrested by Revolutionaries at Varennes, and a letter from Napoleon to Josephine. Temporary exhibits change the selection on display every few months. Labels are in French only. (For more about the Hôtel Soubise, see "Sights—3ème," p. 154.) Open Wed.-Mon. 1:45-5:45pm. 15F; students, seniors, and Sun. 10F; under 18 free.

Musée d'Histoire Naturelle, in the Jardin des Plantes, 5ème (tel. 01 40 79 39 39). M. Gare d'Austerlitz. A 3-building museum which covers 3 fields within the natural sciences. The **Gallery of Comparative Anatomy and Paleontology** houses a dinosaur exhibit, whose triumph is the 7-m skeleton of an iguanodon. The rest of the gallery is devoted to more familiar, though equally large skeletons (like those of elephants and whales) as well as a small collection of fossils. (Open weekdays 10am-5pm, weekends 10am-6pm, closed Tues. 30F, students 20F.) In the Grande Galerie next door, the The **Musée de Minéralogie,** surrounded by luscious rose trellises, contains diamonds, rubies, and sapphires along with assorted *objets d'art* fashioned with them, including two Renaissance Florentine marble tables inlaid with lapis lazuli, amethyst, and other semi-precious stones. Downstairs are a collection of giant crystals and an exhibit addressing the practical uses of minerals. (Both museums share hours and prices.)

Musée de l'Homme (Museum of Man), pl. du Trocadéro, in the Palais de Chaillot, 16ème (tel. 01 44 05 72 00 or 01 44 05 72 72). M. Trocadéro. A painted cart from Sicily, a Turkish store, and a 10m British Columbian totem pole are all elements of the museum's multimedia presentations, covering civilizations and cultures worldwide from prehistory to today. Perpetual renovations don't spoil the show. Labels in French accompany self-explanatory displays. Open Wed.-Mon. 9:45am-5:15pm. 30F, under 27 and seniors 20F, children under 4 and disabled persons free. Films Wed. and Sat. at 3 and 4pm (tel. 01 44 05 72 59 for info).

Maison de Victor Hugo, 6, pl. des Vosges, 4ème (tel. 01 42 72 10 16). M. Chemin Vert. A museum dedicated to the "father of the French Romantics," housed in the building where he lived from 1832 to 1848. The museum offers an assortment of Hugo memorabilia, including his own expressionistic graphic art. One room is devoted to *Les Misérables,* another to *Notre-Dame de Paris;* each displays paintings depicting scenes and characters from the books. Another room showcases furniture from Hauteville House on the island of Guernsey, where Hugo lived in exile from 1852 to 1870. There are also many photographs from this period. Finally (appropriately enough), you can see a reconstruction of the room where the great man died. Clippings of Hugo's hair from 4 different periods of his life are an extra bonus. Open Tues.-Sun. 10am-5:40pm (last admission 5:15pm). 18F, students 9F, under 18 free.

Musée Jacquemart-André, 158, bd. Haussmann, 8ème (tel. 01 42 89 04 91). M. Miromesnil. Newly reopened after lengthy renovations, the museum is home to a relatively small but surprisingly rich collection of mostly French and Italian art of the Renaissance and Baroque periods. The collection includes works of Rembrandt, Van Dyck, Mantegna, Bellini, Boticelli and many others. A peculiar allure also lies in the building itself, the opulent 19th-century mansion of Nélie Jacquemart and her husband Edouard André. Open daily 10am-6pm. Admission 45F, audio tour provided free with admission. Children 7-17, students and groups of 15 or more 30F. Under 7 free. Last visitors admitted at 5:30pm.

Galérie Nationale de Jeu de Paume, 1er (tel. 01 47 03 12 50 or recorded info at 01 42 60 69 69). M. Concorde. Huge windows bathe this spectacular exhibition space in afternoon sunlight, accentuating its graceful curves and sharp angles. Languid connoisseurs and clueless tourists alike come to appreciate the world-class contemporary art exhibitions here. There is also a café with sandwiches (27F) and tarts. Open, when exhibits are on, Tues. noon-9:30pm, Wed.-Fri. noon-7pm, Sat.-Sun. 10am-7pm. 35F, students 25F, under 13 free.

Musée National de la Légion d'Honneur et des Ordres de Chevalerie, 2, rue de Bellechasse, 7ème (tel. 01 40 62 84 25). M. Solférino. Housed in an 18th-century mansion built for Prince Frederick of Salm-Kyrbourg, this museum displays innumerable medals, ribbons, and dress costumes of the French Legion of Honor, created by Napoleon in 1802 to reward civilian and military virtue. Unless the prospect of viewing Jerome Bonaparte's wedding reception glass thrills you, consider admiring the architecture from across the street at the Musée d'Orsay. Open Tues.-Sun. 2-5pm. 25F, students and seniors 15F.

Mémorial du Maréchal Leclerc de Hauteclocque et de la Libération de Paris, 23, allée de la 2*ème* D-B, Dalle-Jardin Atlantique above the tracks of the Gare Montparnasse (tel. 01 40 64 39 44). M. Montparnasse-Bienvenüe. Follow signs to the Jardin Atlantique from the train station, pl. du Pont des Cinq Martyrs du Lycée Buffon, or rue Commandant René Mouchotte. From Africa to the beaches of Normandy and from a liberated Paris to the capture of Berchtesgaden, this museum traces the military maneuvers of Leclerc and the liberation of Paris with a wealth of rare film footage, posters, propaganda, and photographs. A chilling chorus of recorded speeches and explanations rises from the video monitors scattered throughout the exhibition. All written information is in French and English. Included with admission is the more personal exhibition of photographs and interviews presented in the **Musée Jean Moulin,** a space dedicated to the man who unified the French Resistance and whom André Malraux commemorated as "the face of France." Open Tues.-Sun. 10am-5:40pm, last ticket 5:15pm; 18F, students and seniors 9F.

Musée de la Marine (Museum of the Navy), pl. du Trocadéro, in the Palais de Chaillot, 16*ème* (tel. 01 45 53 31 70). M. Trocadéro. An entire fleet of model and real boats from the 17th to 19th centuries have dropped anchor here, including the actual golden dinghy built for Napoleon I in 1810 during a span of 21 days. You might sail past the sea of paintings of naval battles and ancient admirals, but don't miss the enormous nautical rope, the lighthouse windows, or the antique divers' suits. English brochure available at the ticket counter. Open Wed.-Mon. and holidays 10am-6pm. Last entry at 5:30pm. 38F, under 25 and seniors 25F.

Centre de la Mer et des Eaux, 195, rue St-Jacques, 5*ème* (tel. 01 44 32 10 90). M. Luxembourg. More than just the requisite tanks of coral and tropical fish, this is a multimedia marine experience. A "hands-on" learning area lets you push buttons and pull handles to learn about fish disguises and algae life cycles. An entire room is devoted to "The Mysterious Voyage of Eels." Films and exhibitions change, but most come from the adventures of that sea czar, Jacques Cousteau. All labels in French; all chairs for small-sized French students. Open Tues.-Fri. 10am-12:30pm and 1:15-5:30pm, Sat.-Sun. 10am-5:30pm. 30F, students 18F.

Musée Adam Mickiewicz, 6, quai d'Orléans, 4*ème* (tel. 01 43 54 35 61), on the Ile-St-Louis. M. Pont Marie. Ring the doorbell and enter to your left in the courtyard. Located in the former home of famed Polish poet Adam Mickiewicz (1798-1835), the museum exhibits his belongings—including letters he received from Goethe and Victor Hugo, and a sketch by Delacroix on George Sand's letter-head. One room focuses on the life of Chopin, compatriot and friend of Mickiewicz. See first edition manuscripts by the composer, a few letters, and one of the three surviving copies of his death mask. The building also houses a Polish library. Library open Tues.-Fri. 2-6pm and Sat. 10am-1pm. Museum open Thurs. 2-6pm. Visit only by guided tour, conducted by friendly, knowledgeable staff volunteers. Tours begin at 2, 3, 4, and 5pm. 30F, students 15F, children free.

Musée de la Mode et du Costume (Museum of Fashion and Clothing), in the Palais Galleria, 10, av. Pierre 1*er*-de-Serbie, 16*ème* (tel. 01 47 20 85 23). M. Iéna. With 30,000 outfits and 70,000 accessories and only a few display rooms, the museum has no choice but to rotate in temporary exhibitions showcasing fashions of the past 3 centuries. Open Tues.-Sun. 10am-5:40pm. Last entry at 5:15pm. 35F, students and seniors 25F.

Institut du Monde Arabe (Institute of the Arab World), 23, quai St-Bernard, 5*ème* (tel. 01 40 51 38 38). M. Jussieu. Arguably the most architecturally innovative of Parisian museums, it opened in 1987 as a cooperative project between several Arab nations and the French government to promote education about Arab history, art, culture, and language. The riverside façade is shaped like a boat, representing the migration of Arabs to France. The opposite side has ingenious windows with pupil-like "blinds" that open and close in response to the sunlight. Notable for its displays of Arabic rugs and ceramics, the museum assembles art from 3 Arab regions (Maghrib/Spain, the Near East, and the Middle East) from the 3rd through the 18th centuries. Level 4 is devoted entirely to contemporary Arab artists. An extensive library contains works of literature in Arabic, French, and English, as well as periodicals, all of which are open to the public. At night, the auditorium hosts Arab movies (subtitled in English and French; 30F, students 20F) and theater (free). Call for a schedule of events. On Level 9, a delightful cafeteria cooks up 3-course lunches (79F), including many Arabic specialties. The rooftop terrace has a fabulous (free) view of Paris. Museum and library open Tues.-Sun 10am-6pm. Museum admission 25F, ages 12-18 20F, under 12 free. 90min. guided tour of museum Tues.-Fri. at 3pm and Sat.-Sun. at 2 and 4pm, 40F. Admission to temporary exhibits and permanent collection, 50F. Institute open Tues.-Sun. 10am-6pm. Cafeteria open Tues.-Sun. 11:30am-6pm.

Galerie Le Monde de l'Art, 18, rue de Paradis, 10ème (tel. 01 42 46 43 44). M. Gare de l'Est. Go against traffic on bd. Strasbourg and turn right onto rue de la Fidelité, which becomes rue de Paradis. The airy and light-filled interior of this gallery is decorated with tiled Art Nouveau landscapes and Portuguese frescoes, installed when the building served as headquarters for the Boulanger China Company. Upstairs is a private gallery with an exquisitely tiled floor and art that is contemporary, cool, lively, multimedia, hip, happenin', and, unless you're planning to buy some, free. Open Mon. 2-7pm, Tues.-Sat. 1-7:30pm. Closed Aug.

Musée National des Monuments Français, pl. du Trocadéro, in the Palais de Chaillot, 16ème (tel. 01 44 05 39 05). M. Trocadéro. Primarily a scholarly museum of appeal to artists, architects, and medievalists, the museum features life-sized models of façades and tombs from medieval churches all over France. This may be your only chance to see their detailed sculptural decoration at close range. The scant captioning is in French. Interested specialists should ask about the museum's documentation center. Call for info about lectures and temporary exhibits. Open Wed.-Mon. 10am-6pm. Last ticket at 5:30pm. 22F, students ages 18-25 and seniors 14F, under 13 free. Prices are higher during temporary exhibits.

Musée Gustave Moreau, 14, rue de La Rochefoucauld, 9ème (tel. 01 48 74 38 50). M. Trinité. This museum is a gem. Located in the house of the 19th-century symbolist painter Gustave Moreau, it contains thousands of his drawings and paintings. The house itself is charming, and the rooms are lined with works in all stages of completion, from sketches and half-painted canvases to complete works, including the celebrated painting of Salomé dancing before the severed head of John the Baptist. Open Mon. and Wed. 11am-5:15pm, Thurs.-Sun. 10am-12:45pm and 2-5:15pm. 17F, students, children, and Sun. 9F.

Musée d'art Naïf Max Fourny, Halle St-Pierre, 2, rue Ronsard, 18ème (tel. 01 42 58 72 89). M. Anvers. From the metro, walk up rue de Steinkerque and turn right at pl. St-Pierre, then left onto rue Ronsard. Installed within an impressive iron and glass ex-marketplace, the museum is dedicated to presenting neoprimitivist art ranging from childish scrawls to raw, moving tableaus. Most of the artists are developmentally disabled, psychologically impaired, or led by spirits, and none of them appears more than once. Participatory games for visitors ages 3-12. Temporary exhibits sometimes usurp the permanent collection. Open daily 10am-6pm. 40F, students 30F. The Halle St-Pierre also contains a quiet *salon de thé* open the same hours as the museum, with tables for readers. Tea 15-16F. Pastries 18-22F.

Palais de la Découverte (Palace of Discovery), in the Grand Palais, entrance on av. Franklin D. Roosevelt, 8ème (tel. 01 40 74 81 82 or 01 40 74 80 00). M. Franklin Roosevelt. More central and less flashy than the Cité des Sciences. Interactive exhibits run the gamut of scientific subjects remarkably well. Kids tear around at a manic pace to turn wheels that teach about complementary colors, press buttons that start comets on celestial trajectories, spin on seats to investigate angular motion, and glare at all kinds of cleverly camouflaged creepy-crawlies. Open Tues.-Sat. 9:30am-6pm, Sun. 10am-7pm. 25F, students, seniors, and under 18 15F; with planetarium 40F, reduced 25F. Planetarium shows at least 4 times daily.

Petit Palais (also called the **Palais des Beaux-Arts de la Ville de Paris**), av. Winston Churchill, 8ème (tel. 01 42 65 12 73). M. Champs-Elysées-Clemenceau. Built for the 1900 World Expo, this "palace" displays gems from ancient art through 19th- and 20th-century painting and sculpture. Each room in the permanent collection has a theme: 17th-century Flemish and Dutch paintings or canvases depicting the French Revolution, for example. Houses Jean-Baptiste Carpeaux's *Young Fisher with the Shell;* Camille Claudel's bust of Rodin, Monet's *Sunset at Lavacourt,* as well as the occasional Rubens, Rembrandt, Cézanne, Pissarro, and Renoir. Call ahead for wheelchair access. Open Tues.-Sun. 10am-5:40pm, last entry 5pm. Admission to permanent collection 27F, students 15F, seniors and under 18 free. Admission to temporary exhibits roughly 40F, under 25 and seniors 30F. Conference visits (1-1½hr., Thurs. and Sat. at 2:30pm in French and English) on special themes are held in the afternoon; call or visit for schedule.

Musée Picasso, 5, rue de Thorigny, 3*ème* (tel. 01 42 71 25 21). M. Chemin Vert. When the cubist Pablo Picasso died in 1973, his family opted to pay the French inheritance tax in artwork, which is how the French government came to own this collection. (The 17th-century Hôtel Salé, which houses the museum, never belonged to Picasso. See "Sights—3*ème*," p. 151 and p. 155.) Many works are of minor significance, but the collection as a whole is great, thanks to the museum's well-paced and informative layout (with explanations translated into English). Light fixtures by Diego Giacometti (brother of sculptor Alberto) illuminate the first rooms of a circuit that traces the artist's development. Alongside Picasso's pieces are works by artists who influenced him, including Braque, Cézanne, Miró, and anonymous African and Oceanian sculptors. In addition, photos of Picasso's friends—Marie Laurencin, Braque, and Cocteau among others—provide a who's who of the early 20th-century avant-garde. Don't skip the sculpture and pottery on the lower level. A restriction on school groups after 1pm ensures more peaceful viewing. Well-stocked gift shop. Museum open April-Sept. Wed.-Mon. 9:30am-6pm, last entrance 5:15pm; Oct.-March 9:30am-5:30pm, last entrance 4:45pm. 27F, ages 18-25 and over 60, and Sun. 18F. Special exhibition Feb.-May 1997: The photographic sources of Picasso's work, 1899-1930.

Musée de La Poste, 34, bd. de Vaugirard, 15*ème* (tel. 01 42 79 23 45). M. Montparnasse-Bienvenüe. Currently under renovation, the museum is scheduled to reopen in Jan. 1997 with a variety of multimedia presentations. The collection includes several thousand stamps that adorn the walls of an entire floor. Also of note are various mailbox designs, including a high-concept hollow cannonball, which was stuffed with letters and floated downstream to Parisians during the Prussian siege of 1870. Nascent bureaucrats thrill to a scale replica of a post office window; everyone else suffers mysterious waves of impatient anxiety. Funky boutique with quirky momentos and collectors' stamps. Proposed hours: Mon.-Sat. 10am-6pm. 25F, students and seniors 15F.

Musée de la Poupée, Impasse Berthaud 3*ème* (tel./fax 01 42 72 55 90). M. Rambuteau. Off of rue Beaubourg near the Centre Pompidou. 200 dolls from 1860-1960 are shown in 42 glass cases exhibiting scenes such as "the music lesson" and "snack time." Each room is from a different era in doll making. Open Wed. and Fri.-Sun. 10am-6pm, Thurs. 2-10pm. 30F; students, under 26, large families, and over 60, 25F; children 3-10 and disabled 20F. Wheelchair accessible.

Musée de Radio France, 116, av. du Président Kennedy, 16*ème* (tel. 01 42 30 21 80 or 01 42 30 33 83). M. Passy; RER (C) Av. du Pt. Kennedy/Maison de Radio France. Head for the Seine and enter through Door A of the big, white, round building. The museum, visited only by guided tour (in French; call for details about occasional English tours), traces the advent of radio, TV, and the *maison* itself in a whirlwind trip through the evolution of communications. Well-mannered hostesses usher guests past classic radio specimens, such as the *boîte à jambon* (ham box) radio, and into TV studios and concert halls. Inquire about attending free tapings of TV programs. Season tickets to concert with the resident Orchestre National de France are also available. Classic radio specimens on display. Ask for the free English-language brochure at the information desk. Open Mon.-Sat. Tours at 10:30 and 11:30am, 2:30, 3:30, and 4:30pm. 15F, students and seniors 10F.

Musée Renan-Scheffer (also called **Musée de la Vie Romantique**), 16, rue Chaptal, 9*ème* (tel. 01 48 74 95 38). M. St-Georges. Housed in the former residence of 19th-century painter and *salonnier* Ary Scheffer, a friend of George Sand, the small museum displays busts, portraits, letters, and personal belongings (rings, locks of hair, a model of Franz Lizst's right hand) that recall Scheffer, Sand, and other *salonniers.* The house is lovely—with a garden and down a tree-lined lane—and never crowded. Open Tues.-Sun. 10am-5:30pm. 18F, students 9F.

Musée-Galerie de la SEITA (Société d'Exploitation Industrielle des Tabacs et Allumettes), 12, rue Surcouf, 7ème (tel. 01 45 56 60 17). M. Invalides or Latour-Maubourg, on the corner of rue de l'Université and rue Surcouf. Owned and operated by a tobacco company, the museum tells the story of tobacco. Beleaguered smokers can peer fondly at glass cases filled with tobacco-related documents and pipe and cigarette holders depicting everything from nudes to nuns. The attached gallery hosts temporary exhibits throughout the year unrelated to tobacco, previous shows have included Frank Lloyd Wright and Soviet rock posters. Open Mon.-Sat. 11am-7pm. Museum is always free; some gallery exhibitions may require a fee of 25F, 15F reduced tariff.

Musée de la Serrure (Lock Museum), 1, rue de la Perle, 3ème (tel. 01 42 77 79 62). M. Chemin-Vert. From M. Chemin-Vert walk down the rue St. Gilles, which becomes the rue de Parc Royal, and then the rue de la Perle. Housed in the Hôtel Libéral-Bruant, the *cave* of this museum holds a not very interesting collection of locks—padlocks, slide-bolts, hammers, clasps, and latches from the 15th through the 19th century. Intriguing lion's head lock, circa 1780, clamps its jaws around the hands of those who insinuate false keys; a variation on this theme is the pistol lock, which shoots you if you use a wrong key. Open Tues.-Fri. 10am-noon and 2-5pm. 30F, students and seniors 15F, under 18 free.

Musée du Vieux Montmartre, 12, rue Cortot, 18ème (tel. 01 46 06 61 11). M. Lamarck-Caulaincourt. From the metro turn right on rue Larmarck, right again up steep rue des Saules, then left onto rue Cortot. Dedicated to the political, artistic, cultural, and religious past of the *butte,* the museum occupies a beautiful 17th-century house, overlooking a pleasant garden and Montmartre's only vineyard. Once home to diverse artists, including one of Molière's actors, Renoir, and Utrillo, the museum now shelters old maps, paintings, photographs, and a wooden model of the *quartier,* as well as a recreated turn-of-the-century café, complete with one of the few zinc bar counters left after the metal rationing during the Nazi Occupation. The documentation is in French and English. Upcoming special exhibits include *Utrillo, Valadon, Uter* (Oct. '96-March '97), *From Montmartre to Pont-Aven: Emile Bernard, Gauguin, Maurice Denis* (April-Sept. '97), and *La Chanson Française (French Song,* Oct. '97-March '98). Open Tues.-Sun. 11am-6pm; last ticket at 5:30pm. 25F, seniors and students 15F.

Musée du Vin, rue des Eaux or 5-7, sq. Charles Dickens, 16ème (tel. 01 45 25 63 26). M. Passy. From the métro, go down the stairs, turn right on sq. Alboni, and then turn right on rue des Eaux. Set up in a former limestone quarry, this mildly entertaining museum is now filled with wax models making, storing, and tasting wine. Real connoisseurs will learn little; others might appreciate the wine presses, utensils, and bottles exhibited, as well as the wax model of Honoré de Balzac fleeing his creditors. Remind the often forgetful receptionists to offer you a free tasting of red, rosé, or white. Info sheet available in English. Open daily 10am-6pm. 32F, seniors 27F, students 25F.

Musée Zadkine, 100bis, rue d'Assas, 6ème (tel. 01 43 26 91 90). M. Port-Royal. Just south of the Jardin du Luxembourg. This reasonably-sized museum is the perfect antidote to Parisian aesthetic overload. Installed in 1982 in the house and studio where he worked from 1928 until his death, the museum highlights the work of master sculptor Ossip Zadkine (1890-1967). Zadkine's work spans the major developments in modern sculpture, moving from the extremes of Cubism to a renewed Classicism, and using a wide variety of mediums. Even if you don't want to pay the admission to the museum, a visit to the garden is both free and worthwhile; a good selection of the artist's most important works, including his two-faced *Woman with the Bird,* resides there. Relax on the benches in peace while you contemplate his work. Open Tues.-Sun. 10am-5:30pm. 27F, students 19F.

Entertainment

Paris teems with cabarets, discos, and smoky jazz clubs; with U.S. and European cinema; with avant-garde and traditional theater; with rock and classical concerts. When looking for something to do, consult the two bibles of Paris entertainment: the magazine **Pariscope** (3F) and the **Officiel des Spectacles** (2F), both on sale weekly at any newsstand. Even if you don't understand French, you should be able to decipher the listings of times and locations. Or, contact **Info-Loisirs,** a recording that keeps tabs on what's on in Paris (English tel. 01 49 52 53 56; French tel. 01 49 52 53 55).

Paris is one of the world's premier jazz capitals, and big-name American artists make frequent stops here. The city also offers a mixed diet of West African music, Caribbean calypso and reggae, Latin American salsa, North African raï, and rap. Classical concerts are staged both in expensive concert halls and more affordable churches, particularly during the summer. To get more information and to buy tickets for rock, jazz, or classical concerts, head for **FNAC Musique,** 24, bd. des Italiens, 9*ème* (tel. 01 48 01 02 03), or 1, rue de Charenton, 12*ème* (tel. 01 43 42 04 04).

Parisians are inveterate film-goers and are particularly keen on American classics; frequent English-language film series and annual festivals make Parisian cinema a popular, accessible, and affordable entertainment option for visitors and locals alike. The comedy-oriented *café-théâtres* and the music-oriented *chansonniers* perpetuate the ambiance of 30s Parisian cabarets, which helped launch the careers of Edith Piaf and Jacques Brel.

Keep in mind that the neighborhoods around popular night-spots are not always safe. The areas around Pigalle, Gare St-Lazare, and Beaubourg fill nightly with prostitutes and drug dealers. Also remember to keep an eye on the time in order to avoid expensive, late-night taxis; though the metro doesn't stop running until 1am, hop on a train by about 12:30am if you have to make a connection.

Cinema

The true cinophile would never have existed if it wasn't for Paris and the Parisians. After all, cinema was invented here by the Lumière brothers, Auguste and Louis, and the first movie premiered at the Grand Café (14, bd. des Capucines) in 1895. At the time, Louis belittled his discovery as "an invention without a future." Needless to say, he was wrong. What, practically speaking, is a cinophile? Someone who buys *Pariscope* when it comes out on Wednesday and spends hours deciding which films she must see during the week. Paris is probably the city in the world with the greatest number of different films playing every week. There are even Anglophone films that never make it to British or American screens. Despite the quota in the European treaty limiting the importation of Hollywood films, many small alternative theaters are losing the battle against the chains which show mostly contemporary Hollywood movies.

Throughout the city, and particularly on the Left Bank, you'll find more old Hollywood movies—from Hitchcock to Lubïtch—than you ever knew existed. Many theaters in Paris specialize in programs featuring the great European *auteurs,* current independent film, and U.S. classics. **Art-et-essai** is the umbrella term for this particular mix of old and new, but always edifying, cinema.

Catering to the city's enormous student population, Paris's cinemas offer a range of ticket discounts. On Mondays and Wednesdays prices usually drop about 10F for everyone. Check *Pariscope* for details—days and reductions vary with the theater. The confederation of independent cinemas, a bulwark of little-guys competing with Gaumont and UGC, offers reduced tickets for all on both days. In addition to students and seniors, *chômeurs* (the unemployed) get reduced rates, but you must be French to qualify for the last discount.The two big theater chains—**Gaumont** and **UGC**—offer **cartes privilèges** for frequent customers. At 165F for five entries, the *carte*

Gaumont allows bearers to skip past lines and reserve seats in advance. UGC offers a like deal: 120F for 4 entries, 180F for 6. Cards are active for two months, at all shows and franchise locations.

The entertainment weeklies list show times and theaters. Most theaters don't start selling tickets until a few minutes before showtime. Film festivals are listed separately. The notation **v.o. (version originale)** after a non-French movie listing means that the film is being shown in its original language with French subtitles; watching an English-language film with French subtitles is a great way to pick up new (and sometimes very interesting) vocabulary. **v.f. (version française)** means that it has been dubbed—an increasingly rare and entirely avoidable phenomenon. If you're braving Paris's intermittent summertime heat spells, make sure the movie theater is **climatisé (air-conditioned).**

Many theaters show a series of commercials and previews that roll for as long as half an hour. You can skip this part (called the *séance*) as most theaters list the starting time and duration of the *séance* and have a short pause between the *séance* and the actual film so that people may come in freely. However, the *séance* is often as entertaining as the film itself, and French ads can be creative and witty. You should consider tipping the person who points you to your seat (about 3F); an old French law assuring service workers 12-15% accidentally bypassed ushers.

The options below are some of the most interesting, most unusual, or most popular theaters in Paris.

Action Christine, 4, rue Christine, 6ème (tel. 08 36 68 05 98). M. Odéon. Off rue Dauphine. Plays an eclectic, international selection of art and cult films. Always *v.o.* Admission 40F; reduced (for students on weekdays and for all on Mon.) 30F. Weekdays at 6 or 7pm showing only 25F. For 150F (plus a 30F fee at the first purchase), buy a pass good for 1 year that admits you to 6 movies. One of the 2 rooms is wheelchair-accessible; descend a steep staircase to reach the other.

L'Arlequin, 76, rue de Rennes, 6ème (tel. 01 42 56 49 03). M. St-Sulpice. A revival *art-et-essai* cinema with occasional visits from European *auteurs* and first-run preview showings. Some films in *version originale,* others are dubbed; check *Pariscope* for your movie. Buy tickets in advance. Admission 45F, students 35F (Mon.-Fri. only), Wed. all tickets 35F. Sun. matinée 30F. MC, V.

Centre Georges Pompidou, Salle Garance, rue St-Merri, 4ème (tel. 01 42 78 37 29 for schedule info). M. Rambuteau. Multi-cultural programming fills a gap in the U.S.-laden Parisian film scene. Past series have featured Greek and Neapolitan cinema, all in *v.o.* Films Wed.-Mon. 2:30, 7:30, and 8:30pm. Admission 27F, ages 18-25 20F, under 14 12F.

Cinémathèque, Française, pl. du Trocadéro, at the Musée du Cinéma in the Palais de Chaillot, 16ème (tel. 01 45 53 21 86). M. Trocadéro. Enter through the Jardins du Trocadéro. Also 18, rue du Faubourg-du-Temple, 11ème. M. République. Answering machine (tel. 01 47 04 24 24) lists all shows. A must for serious film buffs. 2-3 films per day, many of them classics, near-classics, or soon-to-be classics. Foreign films almost always in *v.o.* Buy tickets 15-20 min. early. Open Wed.-Sun. Shows from 5-9:45pm. Admission 28F.

Dôme IMAX, pl. de la Défense (tel. 01 46 92 45 45). M. Grande Arche de la Défense. The big dome to the right when you have your back to the Grand Arche. Programs in-the-round compensate for lack of plot, substance, or taste with immediacy; past features include *The Fires of Kuwait* and *Antarctica.* Documentaries are in French, but since what you see is of primary importance, non-French speakers can attend without a problem. Admission 55F, students, seniors, and under 16 40F. For 2 shows 75F, students, seniors, and under 16 65F.

L'Entrepôt, 7-9, rue Francis de Pressensé, 14ème (tel. 01 45 43 41 63). M. Pernety. Turn right off rue Raymond Losserand. An international venue for independent films, this cinema organizes a wide variety of week-long festivals, sometimes with director forums. Three screens show films in *v.o.* Admission 39F, students and seniors 29F. The delightful restaurant/bar (tel. 01 45 40 60 70) at the same address will serve your meal amidst live vegetation on the secluded garden terrace or at one of the metal tables near the bar. 55F *menu* at lunchtime includes a main dish and coffee. Salads 38-48F. Beer 18-29F. Restaurant open Mon.-Sat. noon-3pm and 7:30-11:30pm, Sun. noon-3pm. Bar open daily noon-1am. Two branches project high-quality independent, classic, and foreign films. **Les Trois Luxembourg,** 67, rue Monsieur-le-Prince, 6ème (tel. 01 46 33 97 77). M. Odéon. All films in *v.o.* Admission 40F, students 30F. **Le St-Germain-des-Prés,** 22, rue Guillaume Apollinaire, 6ème (tel. 01 42 22 87 23). M. St-Germain-des-Prés. A big, beautiful theater. Admission 40F, students, seniors, Mon., Wed., and noon show 30F.

La Géode, 26, av. Corentin-Cariou, 19ème (tel. 01 40 05 12 12). M. Porte de la Villette, in La Villette. Mostly scientific documentaries, on a huge hemispherical screen, which from the outside looks like the world's biggest disco ball. Shows Tues.-Sun. on the hour 10am-9pm, also Mon. during school holidays. Admission 57F, student rate Mon.-Fri. 44F (no reduced rate on holidays). Reserve in advance.

Le Grand Rex, 1, bd. Poissonnière, 2ème (tel. 01 36 68 70 23). M. Bonne-Nouvelle. This 2800-seat behemoth is the largest theater in Paris; experience "privatized" viewing with thousands of French friends. Amazing sound and a *grand écran* (big screen) which really is. Mostly first-runs. Last show starts around 9:30pm. Admission 46F, students and Mon. 36F. Shows at 11am 25F. A UGC affiliate.

14 Juillet Beaubourg, 50, rue Rambuteau, 3ème (tel. 01 36 68 69 23 for schedules and film descriptions). Six theaters screen talked-about, first-run films. Cannes submissions and prize-winners run May-June. Films competing in Deauville festival screened in September. Matinée repertory of cult favorites like *Blade Runner*, *Eraserhead*, and *Blue Velvet* changes weekly. All foreign films in *v.o.* Admission 47 and 45F. Students, seniors, under 18, and everyone else on Mon. (holidays excluded) and Tues.-Fri. before 6:30pm, 37 and 35F, before 1pm 25F.

Musée du Louvre, 1er (tel. 01 40 20 51 86, reservations 01 40 20 52 29). M. Musée du Louvre. Art flicks and flicks on art. Also silent movies with live musical accompaniment. Movies 25-60F. Call 01 40 20 54 55 for schedule. Open Sept.-June.

La Pagode, 57bis, rue de Babylone, 7ème (tel. 01 36 68 75 07). M. St-François-Xavier. Turn right on rue de Babylone from bd. des Invalides. The intimate *salle japonaise*, with velvet seats and painted screens, helps make this Paris's most charming cinema. Specializing in contemporary films of the artsy ilk, the Pagode is a well-disguised outpost of Gaumont; the *carte Gaumont* works here. Admission 44F, students and seniors Mon.-Fri. before 6pm, and everyone on Wed. 37F. 3-5 shows per day. Shows in the *salle japonaise* are a few francs more. Also visit the *salon de thé,* whose terrace spills into the Japanese garden. Tea or pastries 22F. *Salon de thé* open Mon.-Sat. 4-9:45pm, Sun. and holidays 2-8pm.

Passage du Nord-Ouest, 13, rue du Faubourg Montmartre, 9ème (tel. 08 36 68 03 32 2F per min. recorded info). M. Rue Montmartre. A descent into cutting-edge multi-media productions. The chameleon-like *café-ciné-concert* adapts its interior to the mood of the festival. Also a concert space for jazz fusion, reggae, world music, and whatever else comes into town. Prices vary with the event. Film events 45F, students and seniors 35F.

Studio Galande, 42, rue Galande, 5ème (tel. 01 43 26 94 08). M. St-Michel. A one-screen movie theater with quirky films, mostly prior releases. Put on your best fishnets for the *Rocky Horror Picture Show* Fri.-Sat. night, in English with subtitles. Admission 43F, students, seniors and kids 33F for weekday matinees.

Theater

Generally, Parisian theater-goers are either ushered into large, plush playhouses or crowded onto creaking benches in small, black rooms. Intimate performance spaces like *café-théâtres* and *chansonniers* book anything from Vaudevillian comics to accordionists. National theaters, especially the Comédie Française, are stately venues with generally classical repertoires. The famed *grands guignols* (puppet shows) are intended for children but are likely to attract adults as well. Most theaters close for the month of August. *Pariscope* and *l'Officiel des Spectacles* provide complete listings of current shows; partial 1997 schedules for main theaters are listed in the "National Theaters" section below. The following are a selection of ticket services:

Kiosque Info Jeune, 25, bd. Bourdon, 4ème (tel. 01 42 76 22 60). M. Bastille. Also at 4, rue Louis Armand (in Aquaboulevard), 15ème (tel. 01 40 60 64 06). M. Balard. A youth information service provided by the Paris *Mairie.* Sells theater tickets at half price (in advance, too) and distributes free passes to concerts, plays, and exhibits. You must be under 26 years old to be eligible for discounts. Bastille branch open Mon.-Fri. noon-7pm; Aquaboulevard branch open Tues. and Thurs. 2-7pm, Wed. noon-8pm, Fri.-Sat. 2-8pm.

Kiosque-Théâtre, 15, pl. de la Madeleine, 8ème. M. Madeleine. Far and away the best discount box office. Sells half-price tickets the day of the show, plus 16F per seat commission. No student discounts. Open Tues.-Sat. 12:30-8pm, Sun. 12:30-4pm. Also in metro stop Châtelet-les-Halles. Open Tues.-Sat. noon-5pm.

Alpha FNAC: Spectacles, 136, rue de Rennes, 6ème (tel. 01 49 54 30 00). M. Montparnasse-Bienvenue. Also at Forum des Halles, 1-7, rue Pierre Lescot, 1er (tel. 01 40 41 40 00). M. Châtelet-Les Halles); 26-30, av. des Ternes, 17ème (tel. 01 44 09 18 00). M. Ternes); and 71, bd. St-Germain, 5ème (tel. 01 44 41 31 50). Tickets for theater, concerts, and festivals. Open Mon.-Sat. 10am-7:30pm. MC, V.

Virgin Megastore, 52, av. des Champs-Elysées, 8ème (tel. 01 49 53 50 50; box office tel. 01 44 68 44 08). M. Franklin D. Roosevelt. Like FNAC, easy ticket pick-up but no discounts. Look for the ticket office below the first floor. See "Music," p. 276 for more details. MC, V.

NATIONAL THEATERS

Four of France's five national theaters (add one in Strasbourg) are located in Paris. With the advantages of giant auditoriums, great acoustics, veteran acting troupes, and, in certain cases, centuries of prestige, they stage polished, extremely popular productions. Though modern works are occasionally scheduled, expect Molière, Racine, Goethe, and Shakespeare (all in French). Unless you're banking on last-minute rush tickets, make reservations 14 days in advance.

La Comédie Française: Salle Richelieu, 2, rue de Richelieu, 1er (tel. 01 44 58 15 15). M. Palais Royal. Founded by Molière, now the granddaddy of all French theaters. Much pomp and prestige, with red velvet and chandeliers. Expect wildly gesticulated slapstick farce in the much parodied *"style Comédie Française."* You don't need to speak French to understand the jokes. 892 seats. 1997 will feature works by Racine, Turgenev, and others. Open Sept. 15-July; usually no shows on Mon. Box office open daily 11am-6pm. Admission 60-185F, under 25 60-70F. Rush tickets (25F) available 45min. before show; line up an hour in advance. The *comédiens français,* as actors here are known, also mount plays in the 330-seat **Théâtre du Vieux Colombier,** 21, rue du Vieux-Colombier, 6ème (tel. 01 44 39 87 00 or 01 44 39 87 01; recorded info tel. 08 36 68 01 50). M. St-Sulpice. 1997 will feature works by Hugo and Gênet. Tickets 130F; rush tickets 60F sold 45min. before performances, available to students under 27 and anyone under 25.

Odéon Théâtre de l'Europe, 1, pl. Odéon, 6ème (tel. 01 44 41 36 36). M. Odéon. Eclectic programs run the gamut from classics to avant-garde. 1042 seats. Also **Petit Odéon,** an affiliate with 82 seats. Open Sept.-July. Box office open Mon.-Sat. 11am-6:30pm. 50-165F for most shows; student rush tickets 60F, available 45min. before performance. Petit Odéon 70F, students 50F. MC, V.

Théâtre National de Chaillot, pl. du Trocadéro, in the Palais de Chaillot, 16ème (tel. 01 47 27 81 15; fax 01 47 27 39 23). M. Trocadéro. Plays and occasional music and dance concerts take place in 2 rooms, one with 1000 and the other with 400 seats. Call to make arrangements for wheelchair access. 1997 season includes: *Béjart Ballet Lausanne* (contemporary works choreographed by Maurice Béjart), Jan. 17-Feb. 9; *Macbeth* (William Shakespeare), some performances with English translation, Jan. 23-March 8; Guy Bedos, Feb. 18-23; *Dommage qu'elle soit une putain (Too Bad She's a Whore,* John Ford), some performances with English translation, March 20-June 1; *Adam et Eve* (Jean-Claude Grumberg), April 24-June 28. Box office open Mon.-Sat. 11am-7pm, Sun. 11am-5pm. Admission 160F, under 25 and seniors 120F. Same-day student rush 80F. MC, V.

Théâtre Nationale de la Colline, 15, rue Malte-Brun, 20ème (tel. 01 44 62 52 00, for reservations tel. 01 44 62 52 52, fax 01 44 62 52 90). M. Gambetta. Grand Théâtre, 760 seats, and Petit Théâtre, 200 seats. Founded in 1988, this fledgling national theater features contemporary plays, both French and foreign. Call ahead for wheelchair access. 1997 season includes: *Kinkali* (by Arnaud Bédouet, directed by Phillipe Adrien), Jan. 9-March 2; *Le Radeau de la Meduse ou Gustave et Theo* (Roger Planchon), March 8-April 20; *La Tragedie du Roi Christophe* (directed by Jacques Nichet). Open Sept.-July. Theater box office open Mon.-Sat. 11am-7pm, Sun. 2pm-5pm. Call to reserve tickets Mon.-Sat. 11am-7pm. Admission 160F, under 26 and over 60 110F, under 26 two tickets 160F, and over 60 130F. Petit Théâtre offers a Wed. lunchtime show with a different program (110F).

PRIVATE THEATERS

Paris' private theaters, though less celebrated than their state-run counterparts, often stage outstanding productions. In this realm of the weird and wonderful, risky performances sometimes misfire. Check the reviews in newspapers and entertainment weeklies before investing in a seat. Watch for schedules on the green, cylindrical *spectacles* notice boards posted throughout the city; also, check *Pariscope* or *l'Officiel des Spectacles,* or pick up a schedule from the theater itself.

Athénée-Louis Jouvet, 4, sq. de l'Opéra, 9ème (tel. 01 47 42 67 27). M. Opéra or Auber. 687 seats. Hard-to-find, with a bland exterior, but a magnificent 18th-century interior and outstanding classical productions in two *salles*. Open Oct.-April. Box office open Mon.-Sat. 11:30am-6pm. Admission 95-150F in the large theater (80-100F reduced), 120F in the small theater (90F reduced). 40F for bad seats.

Jardin Shakespeare du Pré Catelan, in the center of the Bois de Boulogne, west of the Lac Inférieur (tel. 01 40 19 95 33). Take bus #244 from Porte Maillot. 450 seats. Summertime Shakespeare (and other classics) in French, set in a garden of plants mentioned by the bard. Tickets at the door or at FNAC. Shows usually Fri.-Sat. night, with Sat.-Sun matinees. Buses stop running before late shows end, and walking in the large deserted Bois de Boulogne is dangerous even if you know your way out. Instead, take a taxi to Porte Maillot. Admission 100F, reduced 60F.

Théâtre de la Huchette, 23, rue de la Huchette, 5ème (tel. 01 43 26 38 99). M. St-Michel. 100 seats. Tiny theater whose productions of Ionesco's *La cantatrice chauve* (The Bald Soprano) and *La leçon* (The Lesson) are still popular after 39 years. A good choice for people with functional high school French. Shows Mon.-Sat. Box office open Mon.-Sat. 5-7pm. *La cantatrice chauve* starts at 7:30pm, *La leçon* at 8:30pm; no one admitted after curtain goes up. Admission 100F, students 70F; for both shows 160F, students 100F. No discounts Sat.

Théâtre Mogador, 25, rue de Mogador, 9ème (tel. 01 53 32 32 00). M. Trinité. With 1792 seats, one of the largest theaters in Paris. Grandiose comedies and musicals on a colossal stage. Frequent matinees Sat. 4pm. Open Sept.-May Tues.-Sat. Box office open Mon.-Fri., 11am-7pm. Admission 160-260F, matinees 140-230F.

Théâtre du Rond Point, Salle Renaud-Barrault, 2bis, av. Franklin D. Roosevelt, 8ème (tel. 01 44 95 98 00; fax 01 40 75 04 48). M. Franklin D. Roosevelt. 920 seats. Also **Salle Jean Vautier** with 150 seats. Large stage hosts a wide range of theatrical spectacles from musical comedy to Beckett. The smaller stage is more experimental. Open Sept.-July. Box office open Tues.-Sat. 11am-6pm. Admission 110-140F, students and seniors 100F. *Petite salle* 120F, reduced 60-90F.

Théâtre de la Ville, 2, pl. du Châtelet, 4ème (tel. 01 42 74 22 77). M. Châtelet. 1000 seats. Excellent productions of all ilks, including classical music concerts and ballets. Open Oct.-June. Box office open Mon.-Fri. 11am-7pm; also open for telephone sales Mon. 9am-6pm, Tues.-Sat. 9am-8pm. Admission 90-190F, student rush tickets half-price. MC, V.

CAFÉ-THÉÂTRES

Visit one of Paris's *café-théâtres* for an evening of word play and social satire in mostly black-box theater settings. Expect low-budget, high-energy skits filled with political puns and double-entendres; in general, knowledge of French slang and politics is a must for audience members. One-person shows are a mainstay.

Au Bec Fin, 6, rue Thérèse, 1er (tel. 01 42 96 29 35). M. Palais Royal. A tiny, 60-seat theater, usually with 2 different shows per night. Dinner and 1 show from 178F, Sat. 210F. Dinner and 2 shows from 300F. Shows at 7, 8:30, and 10:15pm. Seats for auditions occasionally open to the public, 50F. Admission 80F, students 65F; Mon.-Tues. admission 50F.

Café de la Gare, 41, rue du Temple, 4ème (tel. 01 42 78 52 51). M. Hôtel-de-Ville. Couched in the cobbled courtyard of the Centre de Danse du Marais, where it attracts an engaging, youthful crowd to bold performances ranging in comic flavor and cast size. Recent acts include solo comics and a look-alike Addams Family. Reservations daily 3-7pm. Otherwise, the box office opens 45min. before the show. Most shows start at around 8 or 10pm. Admission 50-100F. MC, V.

Petit Casino, 17, rue Chapon, 3ème (tel. 01 42 78 36 50). M. Arts-et-Métiers. Left off rue Beaubourg. Once a plumbing store, now a basement dinner-theater with a stage that's 4 paces wide. Self-serve smorgasbord of salads, charcuteries, desserts, and wine (as much as you want). Performances tend towards low comedy. Dinner starts at 7:30pm, 1st show at 9pm, 2nd show at 10:30pm. Call for reservations daily 9am-8pm. Dinner and 2 shows 130F. Shows without dinner 80F. V.

Le Point Virgule, 7, rue Ste-Croix-de-la-Bretonnerie, 4ème (tel. 01 42 78 67 03). M. Hôtel-de-Ville. As intimate and interactive as theater can be short of sitting on the stage. Capacity crowds of 140 sit shoulder-to-elbow on small benches. Shows generally feature one or two actors. Frequent slapstick acts ideal for non-French speakers. You may leave feeling the actor spent as much time watching you as you did her. Reservations suggested, accepted 24hrs. 3 shows daily at 8, 9:15, and 10:15pm. Tickets to 1 show 80F, students 65F; 2 shows 130F; 3 shows 150F. Open 5pm-midnight.

CHANSONNIERS

The *chansonnier* is the musical cousin of the *café-théâtre.* In the spirit of old Paris, audience members sing along to French folk songs. The better your French, the better the time you'll have. Come to belt out French classics you don't even know. Admission usually includes one drink.

Au Lapin Agile, 22, rue des Saules, 18ème (tel. 01 46 06 85 87). M. Lamarck-Coulaincourt. From the metro turn right on rue Lamark, then right again up rue des Saules. Picasso, Verlaine, Clemenceau, Renoir, Apollinaire, and Max Jacob hung out here during the heyday of Montmartre; now a mainly tourist audience crowds in for comical poems and songs. Arrive early for a good seat. Shows at 9:15pm. Admission and first drink 110F, students 80F. Subsequent drinks 25-30F. Open Tues.-Sun. 9pm-2am.

Caveau de la République, 1, bd. St-Martin, 3ème (tel. 01 42 78 44 45). M. République. A mostly Parisian crowd fills the 482 seats of this 90-year old venue for political satire. Shows string together 6 or 7 separate acts; the sequence is known as the *tour de champs* (tour of the field). Tickets sold up to 6 days in advance, 11am-6pm. Shows Sept.-June Tues.-Sat. 9pm, Sun. 3:30pm. Admission 170F; students and over 60 Tues.-Fri. 105F. MC, V.

Deux Anes, 100, bd. de Clichy, 18ème (tel. 01 46 06 10 26). M. Blanche. 300 seats. Shows Mon.-Sat. 9pm. Reservations by phone or in person 11am-7pm, 2 weeks in advance. Admission 120F, students 95F. Open Sept.-June.

GUIGNOLS

Grand guignol is a traditional Parisian marionette theater featuring the *guignol,* its classic stock character. These antic performances have long thrilled adults as well as children. Though the puppets speak French, you'll have no trouble understanding the slapstick, child-geared humor. Nearly all parks have *guignols;* check *Pariscope* for others that change location weekly.

Marionettes des Champs-Elysées, Rond-Point des Champs-Elysées, 8ème (tel. 01 42 57 43 34), at the intersection of av. Matignon and Gabriel. M. Champs-Elysées-Clemenceau. The classic adventures of the *guignol* character. Shows Sept. to mid-July Wed. and Sat.-Sun. 3, 4, and 5pm. Admission 13F.

Marionettes du Luxembourg, Jardin du Luxembourg, 6ème (tel. 01 43 26 46 47). M. Luxembourg or Notre-Dame-des-Champs. The best *guignol* in Paris. This roofed-in theater plays the same children's classics it has since it opened in 1933: *Little Red Riding Hood, The Three Little Pigs,* and so on. Running time is about 45min. Arrive 30min. early for good seats. 1-2 shows daily at around 3 and 4. Call ahead for precise time. Admission 21F.

Theatre Guignol du Parc des Buttes Chaumont, 19ème. M. Laumière. "If you aren't with your parents, stay in your seat until the end! There are lots of people in the park," warns the sage puppet. Young children love starting a discussion and puppets gladly respond. Seven different rotating shows. Wed. 3 and 4pm. Sat., Sun., and holidays 3, 4, 5pm. Shows last 40min. Admission 12F.

Music

CLASSICAL MUSIC, OPERA, AND DANCE

Paris toasts the classics under lamppost, spire, and chandelier. The city's squares, churches, and concert halls feature world-class performers from home and abroad. Visitors may find France's cultural capital to be a giant with a limp, favoring classical music and opera in lieu of dance. Acclaimed foreign and provincial dance companies swing into town from time to time to take up the slack; watch for posters and read *Pariscope.* Connoisseurs will find the thick and indexed *Programme des Festivals* (free at *mairies* and at the tourist office) an indispensable guide to seasonal music and, to a lesser extent, dance series and celebrations in and around Paris. The monthly publication *Paris Selection,* free at tourist offices throughout the city, also keeps track of the concert in churches and museums, many of which are free or reasonably priced. In general, Paris offers cheap tickets to high culture in great quantities, thanks to a decade of socialism that peddled gentler arts to the masses. Beware, however, of rock-bottom prices. The Opéra Bastille suffers from poor acoustics. And while Balanchine may have said "see the music, hear the dance," you may not be able to do either from the upper eaves of the Opéra Garnier, Paris's ballet-only theater. Try to check a theater floor plan and ask about the obstructed views whenever possible before purchasing a ticket. **Alpha FNAC** is the popular booking agent (see "Theater," p. 252, for this and others). For more information about seasonal events, consult "Festivals and Other Seasonal Events," p. 265.

IRCAM, Institut de Recherche et Coordination Acoustique/Musique, Centre Pompidou, 1, pl. Igor-Stravinsky, 4ème (tel. 01 44 78 48 16). M. Rambuteau. This institute, which invites scholars, composers, and interpreters to come together in the study of music, often holds concerts that are open to the public. Contemporary compositions sometimes accompanied by "film" or "theater." Stop by the office near the Stravinsky fountain or at the information desk in the Centre Pompidou for schedules. (See "Centre Pompidou," p. 232.) There are also two computers in the lobby that allow you to "visit" IRCAM and play musical games. The institute also houses a music library for scholars.

Musée du Louvre, 1er (tel. 01 40 20 52 99 for information; 01 40 20 52 29 for reservations). M. Palais-Royal/Musée du Louvre. Classical music in a classy auditorium. Tickets for individual concerts 65-130F. Music-film combos 25F. Open Sept.-June.

Opéra de la Bastille, pl. de la Bastille, 11ème (tel. 01 43 43 96 96). M. Bastille. The Opéra de la Bastille staged its first performance on July 14, 1989, during the bicentennial jubilee. Hailed by some as the hall to bring opera to the masses, decried by others as offensive to every aesthetic sensibility, this huge theater features elaborate opera and ballet, often with a modern spin. The Bastille Opera has acoustical problems spread democratically throughout the theater, making this a bad place to go all-out for front row seats. Subtitles in English and French during impossible-to-understand lyrical performances. Tickets range 30-610F. Call, write, or stop by for a free brochure of the season's events. Tickets can be purchased: by writing and sending a traveler's check (foreigners can pay on arrival in Paris by presenting their letter of confirmation); by phone (tel. 01 44 73 13 00; open Mon.-Sat. 11am-6pm; by Minitel (3615 code THEA then Opéra Bastille); or in person Mon.-Sat. 11am-6:30pm. Tickets go on sale 14 days in advance of each performance. Reduced rush tickets for under 25, students, and over 65, often available 15min. before show; 110F for operas, 60F for ballets, and 50F for concerts. For events which are sold out, there aren't any reduced rate tickets. Wheelchair access: call (tel. 01 44 73 13 73) at least 15 days in advance. MC, V.

Opéra Comique, 5, rue Favart, 2ème (tel. 01 42 44 45 46; fax 01 49 26 05 93). M. Richelieu-Drouot. Operas on a lighter scale—from Rossini to Offenbach. 1997 season includes: *Les Contes d'Hoffman* (Offenbach), Dec. 3-11; *Le Comte Ory* (Rossini), Jan. 20-Feb 3; *Owen Wingrave* (Britten), Feb. 21-25; *La Dame blanche* (Boieldieu), April 19-29; *La Cantatrice Chauve* (Chailly after Ionesco), March 5-8; *Le Mariage Secret* (Cimarosa), May 5-16.Buy tickets at the box office Mon.-Fri. 11am-6pm or reserve by phone. Tickets 35-490F.

Opéra Garnier, pl. de l'Opéra, 9ème (tel. 01 44 73 13 99 for information, 44 73 13 00 for reservations). M. Opéra. Although the renovations of this historic Opéra will not be finished until 2002, it will be open for the 1996-97 season. The Garnier also hosts the ballet de l'Opéra de Paris. Tickets available at the box office 2 weeks before each performance Mon.-Sat. 11am-6pm. Ballet tickets 30-370F; Opera tickets up to 600F. Lowest-end tickets often have obstructed views. MC, V.

Orchestre de Paris, in the Salle Pleyel, 252, rue du Faubourg St-Honoré, 8ème (tel. 01 45 61 65 65). M. Ternes. The internationally renowned orchestra delivers first-class performances under the baton of music director Semyon Bychkov. 1997 season includes works by Stravinsky, Brahms, Strauss, Mozart, and Mahler. Season runs Sept.-June; call or stop by for concert calendar. Box office open Mon.-Sat. 11am-6pm. Tickets 54-288F. MC, V.

Théâtre des Champs-Elysées, 15, av. Montaigne, 8ème (tel. 01 49 52 50 50). M. Alma Marceau. Top international dance companies and orchestras. To play here is to "arrive" on the highbrow music scene. Season runs Sept.-June. Buy tickets 3 weeks in advance. Reserve by telephone Mon.-Fri. 10am-noon and 2-6pm; box office open Mon.-Sat. 11am-7pm. Tickets 40-500F.

Théâtre Musical de Paris, pl. du Châtelet, 1er (tel. 01 42 33 00 00). M. Châtelet. A superb 2300-seat theater normally reserved for guest orchestras and ballet companies. Magnificent acoustics. Call for a schedule. Tickets run 70-300F. MC, V.

Free concerts are often held in churches and parks, especially during summer festivals. These are extremely popular; get there early if you want to breathe. Check the entertainment weeklies and the Alpha FNAC offices for concert notices. **AlloConcerts'** 24hr. hotline provides info in French on free open-air concerts in the parks (tel. 01 42 76 50 00). The **American Church in Paris,** 65, quai d'Orsay, 7ème (tel. 01 47 05 07 99; M. Invalides or Alma Marceau), sponsors free concerts (Oct.-June Sun. at 6pm). **Eglise St-Merri,** 78, rue St-Martin 4ème (M. Hôtel de Ville) is also known for its free concerts (Sat. at 9pm and Sun. at 4pm, except in Aug.); contact Accueil Musical St-Merri, 76, rue de la Verrerie, 4ème (tel. 01 42 71 40 75 or 01 42 71 93 93; M. Châtelet). The concert series at **Eglise de la Trinité,** pl. Estienne d'Orves, 9ème (tel. 01 48 74 12 77; M. Trinité), is also free and runs from Sept.-June. Sunday concerts take place in the **Jardin du Luxembourg** band shell, 6ème (tel. 01 42 37 20 00); show up early for a seat or prepare to stand. Infrequent concerts in the **Musée d'Orsay** 1, rue Bellechasse, 7ème (tel. 01 40 49 49 66; M. Solferino), are free with a museum ticket. The **Maison de la Radio-France,** 116, av. du President Kennedy, 16ème (tel. 01 42 30 15 16; M. Ranelagh), hosts concerts, both free and not.

Eglise St-Germain-des-Prés, 3, pl. St-Germain-des-Prés, 6ème (M. St-Germain-des-Prés), **Eglise St-Eustache,** 2 rue du Jour, 1er (M. Les Halles), and **Eglise St-Louis-en-l'Ile,** 19bis, rue St-Louis-en-l'Ile, 4ème (M. Pont Marie), also stage frequent concerts that are somewhat expensive, but feature fantastic acoustics and atmosphere (info tel. 01 42 50 70 72; or fax 01 42 50 69 80). Arrive 30-45 minutes ahead to find a front-row seat. **Ste-Chapelle** hosts fabulous concerts a few times per week in the summer. Contact the box office at 4, bd. du

Palais, 1er (tel. 01 46 61 55 41; M. Cité; open daily 1:30-5:30pm; admission 120-150F, students 90-120F).

JAZZ

Aided by a sudden influx of American recordings into post-war France, Paris' status as a jazz hot-spot emerged in the late 1940s. Since then, French jazz musicians, including pianist and native Parisian Michel Petrucciani, have themselves become fixtures of international scale. On the Paris scene, pianist Laurent de Wilde won France's Django Prize in 1993. Funk leader and guitarist Hervé Krief is well-loved by French crowds, as is the old-guard blues organist Eddy Louis. Acid jazz and hip-hop are popular, while 70s fusion has nearly disappeared.

Frequent summer festivals sponsor free or nearly free jazz concerts. The Fête du Marais often features free big-band jazz, while the Parc de la Villette hosts jazz orchestras with a Latin beat during the festival "Halle that Jazze". In fall, the Jazz Festival of Paris comes to town as venues high and low open their doors to celebrity and up-and-coming artists (see "Festivals and Other Seasonal Events," p. 265).

Jazz Hot (45F) and *Jazz Magazine* (35F)—France's answers to *Downbeat* and *Metronome*—are both great sources of information, as is the hard-to-find, bimonthly *LYLO* (*Les Yeux, Les Oreilles;* free). If it isn't in bars or FNACS, try the main office, 55, rue des Vinaigriers, 10ème (tel. 01 42 09 62 05). Also, read *Pariscope.*

Au Duc des Lombards, 42, rue des Lombards, 1er (tel. 01 42 33 22 88). M. Châtelet. Murals of Duke Ellington and Coltrane swathe the exterior of this premier jazz joint. The best French jazz, with occasional American soloists. Dark, smoky, and packed with regulars. English spoken. 70-80F admission, 50F for music students. Beer 28F, cocktails 60F. Featured musicians play from around 8:30-10pm. Thereafter a jazz trio plays until all hours of the night. Open daily 7:30pm-4am. MC, V.

Le Baiser Salé, 58, rue des Lombards, 1er (tel. 01 42 33 37 71). M. Châtelet. This upper-floor club remains one of the few strongholds of 70s-style fusion. Intimate space feels like a student's garret, with murals of troglodytes playing fifes and guitars. African and Antillean music also featured here; watch for the 2-week African music festival in Jan. Concerts at 8:30pm and 10:30pm. Jam sessions Sun. and Mon., free, but with one drink minimum. Usually 35-80F to get in, depending on performers. Beer 28F, Cocktails 49F.

Blue Note, 38, rue Mouffetard, 5ème (tel. 01 45 87 36 09). M. Monge. Excellent samba guitarists and new groups. Try the house drink *aitirissima* (lime juice and vodka). No cover. Drinks 30-40F. Open daily from 9:30pm.

Caveau de la Huchette, 5, rue de la Huchette, 5ème (tel. 01 43 26 65 05; call to find out who's playing). M. St-Michel. You probably haven't seen such enthusiastic jive dancing since junior high. Bebop dance lessons offered weekday evenings before club opens; call 01 42 71 09 09. Swing, blues, and boogie bands are suitable for dancing or listening. The *caves* are thrilling, though, with a gruesome history. They served as tribunal, prison, and execution rooms, used by Danton, Marat, St-Just, and Robespierre during the Revolution. When the club moved into this space in the late 40s, they found 2 skeletons chained together. Great atmosphere. Crowded on weekends. Min. age 18. Cover Sun.-Thurs. 60F, Fri.-Sat. 70F. Students always 55F. Drinks 22-30F. Open daily from 9:30pm.

New Morning, 7-9, rue des Petites-Ecuries, 10ème (tel. 01 45 23 51 41). M. Château d'Eau. 400-seat, former printing plant with the biggest American headliners in the city. Halfway between club and concert hall, it only feels cozy when it's packed; come for music, not ambiance. Sit in the lower front section or in the near wings for best acoustics. Good sound system, a grand piano, and a large stage. Attracts big names like Wynton Marsalis, Bobby McFerrin, and Betty Carter. All the greats have played here—from Chet Baker to Stan Getz and Miles Davis; Archie Shepp is a regular. Open Sept.-July from 9:30pm; times vary. Admission 110-130F. Tickets available at box office or at the FNAC, or the Virgin Megastore. MC, V.

Le Passage du Nord-Ouest, 13, rue du Faubourg Montmartre, 9ème (tel. 08 36 68 03 22 for the 2F per min. info line). M. Rue Montmartre. This *art-et-essai* space books jazz and world beats from Brazil to the Mississippi, Egypt to Cameroon.

Times vary with the event; call or stop by for a program. Beer 30F. Admission around 120F.

Le Petit Journal Montparnasse, 13, rue du Commandant-Mouchotte, 14ème (tel. 01 43 21 56 70). M. Gaîté. Look for the large, animated neon sign featuring a horn player. An elegant club, popular with a well-to-do, older clientele. Very good piano and sound system at the service of the best contemporary mainstream French jazz; 1996 saw Michel Legrand, Eddy Louis, and Joshua Redman. Obligatory first drink 120F. Open Mon.-Sat. 9pm-2am; music begins at 10pm.

Le Petit Journal St-Michel, 71, bd. St-Michel, 5ème (tel. 01 43 26 28 59). M. Luxembourg. A crowded but intimate establishment, where students mix with forty-somethings reminiscing about the riots of 1968. New Orleans bands and first-class performers play in this Parisian center of the "Old Style." Open Mon.-Sat. 9:30pm-1:30am. Obligatory 1st drink 100F.

Le Petit Opportun, 15, rue des Lavandières-Ste-Opportune, 1er (tel. 01 42 36 01 36). M. Châtelet. A relaxed and unpolished pub with some of the best modern jazz trios and quartets around, including a lot of American bands and soloists. The club is tiny (60 seats), but so popular it ought to seat 500. Come early. Open Sept.-July Tues.-Sat. from 11pm; bar open until 3am. Cover charge 50-80F depending on the performer. Drinks from 25F.

Slow Club, 130, rue de Rivoli, 1er (tel. 01 42 33 84 30). M. Châtelet. Miles Davis's favorite jazz club in Paris. Big bands, traditional jazz, and Dixieland in a wonderful old-time setting. Expect dancing and a crowd in their 30s. Weekday cover 60F, women and students 55F. Weekend cover from 75F. Drinks from 19F. Open Tues.-Thurs. 10pm-3am, Fri.-Sat. 10pm-4am.

Le Sunset, 60, rue des Lombards, 1er (tel. 01 40 26 46 60). M. Châtelet. This easy-going club books lesser-known French musicians. The underground room resembles a metro, in its arched ceiling and walls, and in its acoustics; sit close. For Mon. jam sessions, 50-100F cover. Open daily 10pm-dawn.

La Villa, in Hôtel La Villa, 29, rue Jacob, 6ème. (tel. 01 43 26 60 00). M. St-Germain-des-Prés. Downstairs in a 4-star hotel, this exclusive and expensive new club can afford to fly American soloists here for week-long engagements with French rhythm sections. Short list of stars that have appeared here includes Shirley Horn, Joe Lovano, Joshua Redman, and Clifford Jordan. The kind of place where the bar serves cocktails with names like "Night and Day" and "Blue in Paris." 1st drink weekdays 120F, weekend 150F. Special musician price 60F. Open Mon.-Sat. 10pm-2am. MC, V, AmEx.

DISCOS AND ROCK CLUBS

Paris, like New York, is a city which never sleeps. The streets are teeming with clubs, many of them inconspicuous. Some Parisian clubs are small, and nearly impossible to find out about, unless you're a native. Others are larger-than-life and outrageously flashy. The discos that are "in" (or even in business) change drastically from year to year; only a few have been popular since the 1960s. Many Parisian clubs are officially private, which means they have the right to pick and choose their clientele. The management evaluates prospective customers through peepholes in the front doors; be aware that often, people of Arab or African descent find it difficult to win club owners' approval. Parisians tend to dress up more than North Americans for a night on the town; weary backpackers may want to try a bar instead.

In general, word of mouth is the best guide to the current scene. Some of the smaller places in the *quartier latin* admit almost anyone who is sufficiently decked out. To access one of the more exclusive places, you may need to accompany a regular. Women often get a discount or get in free, but don't go alone unless you're looking for lots of amorous attention. Men will generally have an easier time accessing clubs with gay flair, such as Le Queen. Weekdays are cheaper and less crowded so you'll have a better chance of moving, but most action happens on weekends.

L'Arapaho, 30, av. d'Italie, Centre Commercial Italie 2, 13ème (tel. 01 53 79 00 11). M. Place d'Italie. It's the gray door on the right, just past Au Printemps. Since 1983, this place has built up a reputation for hosting some of the best hard-core, rap, pop, and metal bands to come through Paris. Got a hankering for some R.O.C.K.? You'll find that this is a pitstop on most indie rock bands' tour itineraries. Past acts have included Pavement, Sebadoh, Shellac, Bim Skala Bim, and Soul Asylum. Tickets usually around 70-90F. Beer 20F.

Les Bains, 7, rue du Bourg l'Abbé, 3ème (tel. 01 48 87 01 80). M. Réaumur-Sébastopol. Ultra-selective and usually ultra-expensive, ultra-popular club. The man formerly-called-Prince established the club's reputation with a surprise free concert here a few years back. It used to be a public bath, visited at least once by Marcel Proust. More recently, Mike Tyson, Madonna, Roman Polanski, and Jack Nicholson have stopped in. Lots of models and super-attractive people. They sometimes have "fashion shows" that may be considered offensive to women. Cover and 1st drink Sun.-Thurs. 100F, Fri.-Sat. 140F. Subsequent drinks 100F. Open daily, midnight-6am.

Le Balajo, 9, rue de Lappe, 11ème (tel. 01 47 00 07 87). M. Bastille. A youthful, energetic crowd assembles at this seasoned Parisian hang-out, once Edith Piaf's favorite spot. Founded in 1936 by Jo France—thus the name *Bal à Jo.* Wed. 9pm-2am, cover and 1st drink 80F; Thurs.-Sat. 11:30pm-5am, 100F; Sun. 3pm-7pm, 50F.

Le Bataclan, 50, bd Voltaire, 11ème (tel. 01 47 00 39 12). M. Oberkampf. A durn cool place to hang out, drink, and dance the night away. Occasionally hosts indie rock bands like Guided By Voices and Beck. Fri. (80F) is gay night, Sat. (80F) is house, and Thurs. (free) is 80s and disco. Open Thurs.-Sat. 11pm-dawn.

La Casbah, 18-20, rue de la Forge Royale, 11ème (tel. 01 43 71 71 89). M. Faidherbe-Chaligny. This chic, whimsical dance lair mixes pop and Arabic music. Elegant, with a seriously, honestly, we-mean-it, strict door policy. Dress to impress. Cover Wed. and Thurs. 80F, Fri. and Sat. 120F. Open Wed.-Sat. 9pm-6am.

Flash Back, 18, rue des Quatre-Vents, 6ème (tel. 01 43 25 56 10). M. Odéon. Two levels of secluded lounges and a small mirrored dance floor with disco ball. On Tues. retro-nights, DJ spins hits from the 70s and early 80s. Thurs. night floor show features anything from Lola the Showgirl to fly dancers. Comfortable, easy atmosphere among Paris' beautiful youth. Cover 70F, Tues.-Thurs. women free. Drinks 70F. Open Tues.-Sat. 11pm-dawn.

Le Palace, 8, rue du Faubourg Montmartre, 9ème (tel. 01 42 46 10 87). M. Rue Montmartre. A funky disco, although its days as the hottest club in Paris have gone by. If you hit a private party and still get in, the music and crowd can be killer. Otherwise, the music is all-too-top-40. A mix of happy high school students and some older people reliving their youth. Still, the place is huge (up to 2000 people per night), with multi-level dance floors, each with separate bars and different music. American cocktails and occasional rock concerts. Sun. features the Gay Tea Dance, a 15-year institution of the Parisian gay scene. Cover and 1 drink Wed.-Thurs. 50F, Fri. and Sat. 100F, Sun. before 4pm 40F, Sun. after 4pm 60F. Subsequent drinks 60F. Open Tues.-Sat. 11:30pm-6am, Sun. 2-11:30pm.

Le Queen, 102, av. des Champs-Elysées, 8ème (tel. 01 42 89 31 32). Come taste the fiercest funk in town where drag queens, superstars, models, moguls, and Herculean go-go demigods get down to the rhythms of a 10,000 giggawatt sound system. Her majesty is open 7 days a week, midnight to dawn. Mon. is disco with 50F cover plus 50F obligatory drink. Tues. is house music, mostly gay men, and gallons of soap suds (50F cover, 50F drink). Wed. is Latin house, free entry. Thurs. is house, free entry. Fri. and Sat. are house (80F entry, plus 50F obligatory drink), and Sun., hits from the 80s, is free. All drinks 50F. Le Queen is at once the cheapest and most fashionable club in town, and thus the toughest to get in to. Dress your most (insert adjective) and pray to Madonna that you get in.

Le Saint, 7, rue Saint-Séverin, 5ème (tel. 01 43 25 50 04). M. Saint-Michel. Plays a wide range of music, rap, soul, R&B, retro, reggae, and zouk. A small comfortable club set in 13th-century *caves* and filled with regulars who come to dance. Tues.-Thurs. cover 60F, Fri. 80F, Sat. 90F. Drinks 15-50F. Open 11pm-6am.

Scala de Paris, 188bis, rue de Rivoli, 1er (tel. 01 42 61 64 00 or 01 42 60 45 64). M. Palais-Royal. Halfway between a disco and a rollercade; strings of lights and 2 disco balls hang above the central, two-story dance floor. Mixes house and techno for an 18-24 crowd—if even that old. Some claim that it's growing in popularity as others fade. There's a smaller, third-floor dance floor, too. Cover Sun.-Thurs. 80F, women enter free, but must buy one drink. Fri. and Sat. 100F both men and women, one drink included. Additional drinks 45-50F. Open daily 10:30pm-dawn.

Also popular in Paris are clubs specializing in **Brazilian samba** and **African music:**

Le Tango, 13, rue au Maire, 3*ème* (tel. 01 42 72 17 78). M. Arts et Métiers. Crowd dances Thurs.-Sat. to Antillean, African, salsa, and zouk music. Regulars (ages 20-35) all know each other. Kind of square, red decor compensated for by nifty Art Deco lamps and good sound. One Sun. per month is Argentinian tango. Cover for special evenings 50F, regular evenings 60F, Sat. afternoon 25F, Sun. afternoon 35F. Open Thurs.-Fri. 11pm-5am, Sat. 2-7pm and 11pm-5am, Sun. 2-8pm.

Aux Trois Mailletz, 56, rue Galande, 5*ème* (tel. 01 43 54 00 79). M. St-Michel. The basement houses an exceptional jazz café featuring world music. Leans towards the Latin and Afro-Cuban scenes, but also has jazz, blues, and gospel musicians from Europe and the states. 70F admission to club, admission to bar is free. Beer 22-40F, cocktails 65F. Bar open 5pm-dawn every day, *cave* 8:30pm to dawn.

WINE BARS

Although wine bistros have existed since the early 19th century, the modern wine bar emerged only a few years ago with the invention of a machine that pumps nitrogen into the open bottle, protecting wine from oxidation. Rare, expensive wines, exorbitant by the bottle, have become somewhat affordable by the glass. Still, this is not the place for pinching pennies. Expect to pay at least 15F for a glass of high-quality wine; you'll find it quite easy to spend five times as much to develop a distinguishing palate for the stuff. The owners personally and carefully select the wines which constitute their *caves* (cellars) and are usually available to help out less knowledgeable patrons. Over 100-strong, the wine shops in the **Nicolas** chain are reputed for having the world's most inexpensive cellars, though Nicolas himself owns the fashionable and expensive wine bar **Jeroboam,** 8, rue Monsigny, 2*ème* (tel. 01 42 61 21 71; M. Opéra).

Au Sauvignon, 80, rue des Sts-Pères, 7*ème* (tel. 01 45 48 49 02). M. Sèvres-Babylone. At the corner of rue de Sèvres and rue des Sts-Pères. Come here the third Thurs. in Nov. to sample the newest Beaujolais. Also specializes in wines from the Loire valley. Articles and caricatures paper the walls to show the national recognition received by the owner for wines sold here. Lively crowd of well-groomed patrons of the designers' stores which line rue des Sts-Pères. Wine from 19F a glass. Open Mon.-Sat. 8:30am-10pm.

Le Bar du Caveau, 17, pl. Dauphine, 1*er* (tel. 01 43 26 81 84), facing the front steps of the Palais de Justice. M. Cité. Luscious cheeses and delectable wines attract fashionable Parisians to this traditional brass and wood saloon. The Caveau's cuisine is simple, rustic, and delicious. Wines by the glass (12-23F) and by the bottle (70-155F). Plate of cheese 47F. Open Mon.-Fri. 8:30am-8pm.

Le Franc Pinot, 1, quai de Bourbon, 4*ème* (tel. 01 43 29 46 98). M. Pont Marie. A fixture on Ile St-Louis since the island became habitable; notorious in the 17th and 18th centuries as a meeting place for enemies of the state. The exterior's metal grillwork was installed as a security measure in 1642, to prevent prisoners from escaping once trapped inside. The labyrinthine *caves* have been wonderfully preserved as the dining room of this restaurant/wine bar. The wine bar occupies only the main floor. Burgundy wines are a specialty, by the glass 15-36F and up. Check chalkboards for daily specials. Downstairs restaurant has a *menu* and music later in the evening. Open Tues.-Sat. 8am-2am, Sun. 2pm-2am. MC, V, AmEx.

Jacques Mélac, 42, rue Léon Frot, 11*ème* (tel. 01 43 70 59 27). M. Charonne. *The* Parisian family-owned wine bar and bistro. In Sept., Mélac and friends harvest, tread upon, and extract wine from grapes grown in his own vineyard. Wine at 16F a glass or 85F a bottle (38F to go). Daily special, as well as omelettes (33F), plates of cold-cuts (such as ham, 29F). Laid back, no pretension here. Open Sept.-July Mon. 9am-7pm, Tues.-Fri. 9am-10:30pm. MC, V.

Le Relais du Vin, 85, rue St-Denis, 1er (tel. 01 45 08 41 08). M. Châtelet-les-Halles or Etienne-Marcel. Sit terrace-side for a glass of Bordeaux (12-26F), and watch male pedestrians saunter down sometimes-seedy St-Denis. 3-course *menus* of copious French food at 65F and 83F, available all day. À la carte, beef bourgignon (65F) and *bavette aux échalottes* (83F). Extensive dessert selection includes *crème brulée* and yummy *profiteroles* (20-39F). Wines by the glass 12-32F. English spoken. Open Mon.-Sat. 10am-1am; food served until midnight. Closed two weeks in Aug. MC, V.

Le Rouge Gorge, 8, rue St-Paul, 4ème (tel. 01 48 04 75 89). M. St-Paul or Pont-Marie. From M. St-Paul, take rue St-Antoine and turn right on rue St-Paul. Once the home of the Marquise De Brin Villiers (beheaded in 1676 for poisoning her husband, lover, and father), this wine bar is dedicated to reminding you of the vibrant diversity of French regional cuisine. Every two weeks to a month, a selection of approximately 20 wines from a different area are featured, accompanied by appropriate local dishes. Feel free to ask the owner any questions you may have. Wine 19-26F per glass. Entrees 68F. Cheese 28F. Open daily 11am-2am. Food served noon-11:30pm. MC, V.

Willie's Wine Bar, 13, rue des Petits Champs, 1er (tel. 01 42 61 05 09; fax 01 47 03 36 93). M. Palais-Royale. Behind the Palais Royale. The English-run Willy's has become very well known since its founding in 1980. Exposed wooden beams, chic décor and huge windows looking out onto the Palais and Colette's apartment. International clientèle. Glasses from the huge selection of French wines 36-60F. Open Mon.-Sat. 11am-11pm for food, until midnight for wine.

OTHER BARS AND PUBS

To find the bar for you, let arrondissement reputations be your guide. Bars in the 5ème and 6ème often cater to Anglophone students and usually avoid excessive pretension, while the Marais and Bastille are always jumping with crowds of Paris' young and hip, no matter the day or hour. In the 4ème, the rue Vieille du Temple is always hopping. At Bastille, the rue de la Roquette and the rue de Lappe are overflowing with young bar-goers. If you are really adventurous, the 11ème and 20ème, largely working class neighborhoods, hold many hidden hot-spots that have opened in the past few years. Draft beer is *bière pression,* of which the most common incarnation is *un demi* (a half-pint); *kir* is a mixture of white wine and *cassis.* The bartender is the *bar-man.* As with cafés, expect two lists of prices for drinks; stand at the bar and pay less or sit and pay a few francs more for *ambiance.* Law dictates a price increase after 10pm.

Au Caveau Montpensier, 15, rue Montpensier, 1er (tel. 01 47 03 33 78). M. Palais-Royale. Walk around the Comédie Française to the left of the Palais, make a sharp left off of Richelieu and a left up Montpensier. The *caveau* is on the left. Deceptively named, this is not a refined wine tippling establishment but rather a vivacious Irish bar, whose specialties are Guinness, Murphy's and Kilkenney. If you pine for relief from haute couture of the 1er, throw back a few with the boys in this laid-back expatriate watering hole. Open Mon.-Sat. 4pm-1am.

Le Bar sans Nom, 49, rue de Lappe, 11ème (tel. 01 48 05 59 36). M. Bastille. There's nothing more fresh than this bar—cavernous, deep crimson, and packed with the hippest of the hip. Cloths drape the walls of the table-filled front room; head down a few steps towards the womb-like back room, where happening folks sit on carpet-covered wooden benches around the bar. Expensive beer at 30-40F. Cocktails 50F. Open daily 10:30pm-2am.

Café Charbon, 109, rue Oberkampf, 11ème (tel. 01 43 57 55 13). M. Parmentier or Ménilmentant. This old dance hall has become one of the hidden hotspots of young Parisians. High ceilings, hanging lights, and a mural of the days of top hats. Beer 12-16F at the bar, 14-19F at a table. Food served noon-5pm. Salads (35-40F), *entrecôte grillée* (59F). Surprisingly inexpensive. Newspapers for customers with your coffee (6F at the bar, 8F at a table). Open daily 9am-2am.

Café Oz, 184, rue St-Jacques, 5ème (tel. 01 43 54 30 48). M. Luxembourg. Down-to-earth Aussie atmosphere attracts Anglophones and Parisians eager to escape the stress of the city. Happy hour 6:30-8:30pm (beer 15-25F, cocktails 20-25F). Australian wines available. Lunch served until 3pm. Open daily 11am-1:30am.

Caveau des Oubliettes, 11, rue St-Julien-le-Pauvre, 5ème (tel. 01 43 54 94 97). M. St-Michel. Located in what were once the bowels of the Petit-Châtelet Prison. Irish pub with French style and management. Happy hour 5pm-9pm, beer 18-35F. Open Mon.-Sat. 5pm-2am. MC, V.

La Chope des Artistes, 48, rue du Faubourg St-Martin, 10ème (tel. 01 42 02 86 76). M. Strasbourg-St-Denis. The tone is mellow, intimate elegance. You could almost be in a Belle Époque Parisian café, with Apollinaire sinking into one of the spacious chairs next to you and leaning over the slightly-too-small table to whisper sweetly in your ear. The theater crowd shows up before the shows start. Coffee 10F. Beer 25F. Cocktails 28-50F. Open Mon.-Sat. 8:30am-2am.

Finnegan's Wake, 9, rue des Boulangers, 5ème (tel. 01 46 34 23 65). M. Cardinal Lemoine. From the metro walk up rue des Boulangers to this yuppie Irish pub set in a renovated 14th-century wine cellar. Caters to a thirty-something crowd, pours the best pints of Guinness in the city (20-32F), and hosts a variety of Irish cultural events during the school year. Call about poetry readings, jig, and Gaelic and Breton lessons. A Bloomsday extravaganza: come early for the reading, or later for the drinking (June 16). Open Mon.-Fri. 11am-12:30am, Sat.-Sun. 4pm-12:30am.

Le Merle Moqueur, 11, rue de la Butte-aux-Cailles, 13ème (tel. 01 45 65 12 43). M. pl. d'Italie. Take rue Bobillot south until rue de la Butte-aux-Cailles branches right. Psychedelic Beatles posters pepper the walls of this tiny, super-cheap bar (beer 12-30F; nothing over 50F). No table service. Most customers head for the terrace; if you can't find a seat, join the crowds hanging out around the cars. Public music "rehearsals" start during happy hour (5-6pm) most days. Open Sept.-July daily 5pm-2am; Aug. Tues.-Sun. 5pm-2am. 50F minimum for credit cards. MC, V.

Le Petit Fer à Cheval, 30, rue Vieille-du-Temple, 4ème (tel. 01 42 72 47 47). M. Hôtel-de-Ville. Between the horseshoe-shaped, zinc bar and the modern, stainless steel bathroom, one could argue that this favorite Marais institution combines the old and the new as creatively as do the Louvre and its pyramid. The bar, sidewalk terrace, and small, intimate restaurant in the back are lively night and day. Coffee 6F at bar, 10F at tables. Beer 13F at bar, 17F at tables. Cocktails 48F and up. Last call 1:30am. Menu includes a salmon pasta dish (67F), a warm *chèvre* salad (60F), a *plat du jour* (60F, on the weekend 70F), and tarte tatin (37F). Prices go up 4F after 10pm. Open Mon.-Fri. 9am-2am, Sat.-Sun. 11am-2am.

Le Piano Vache, 8, rue Laplace, 5ème (tel. 01 46 33 75 03). M. Cardinal Lemoine or Maubert-Mutualité. A young indie-rock crowd patronizes this poster-plastered alterna-grotto, hidden in the winding streets near the Panthéon. Popular with both French college students and tourists who stumble upon it. Beer on tap 20-34F. Open July-Aug. noon-2pm and 4pm-2am. Sept.-June; Mon.-Sat. noon-2am.

Bisexual, Gay, and Lesbian Entertainment

While the bisexual, gay, and lesbian communities of Paris may not be as politically active as those in New York or San Francisco, the scene is far from closeted. This is Gay Paree, where Eartha Kitt is Queen Camp, where Jean-Paul Gaultier fits Madonna's bullet bras, and where everybody's had a rough day at the gym.

The scene is much more happening for men than women; lesbians are not very visible in Paris, and what lesbian entertainment exists is scattered across the city. That said, the indisputable center of lesbian and gay life is still the Marais, known throughout Paris as the *chic*-est part of the city. There, in the 3ème and the 4ème arrondissements, you will find gay and lesbian café/bars, bookstores, and restaurants, as well as window displays of Gay-Pride-wear. As usual, it's helpful to dress well. Anyone seeking the hippest club scene in Paris might want to drop in at Le Queen, which is an unofficially gay club. Le Bataclan also hosts gay nights (see "Discos and Rock Clubs," p. 259). Quieter gay spots line the rue Vieille-du-Temple.

For the most comprehensive listing of gay and lesbian restaurants, clubs, hotels, organizations, and services, consult Gai Pied's *Guide Gai 1996* (English and French, 69F at any kiosk or *papeterie*). *Lesbia's* ads are a good gauge of what's hot, or at least what's open (25F). *Pariscope* has an English-language section called *A Week of Gay Outings.* The magazines *3 Keller* and *Exit,* available at the Centre Gai et Lesbian (see "Bisexual, Gay, and Lesbian Travelers," p. 44) and at many bars and clubs, can also help point you to the hot spots.

Amnésia Café, 42, rue Vieille-du-Temple, 4ème (tel. 01 42 72 19 64). M. Hôtel-de-Ville. A classy, relaxed, poly-sexual hangout which provides a laid-back atmosphere for people of all races, genders, sexes, and proclivities to meet. Beer 17-30F. Open daily 10am-2am. Brunch daily noon-4pm. MC, V.

Le Bar, 5, rue de la Ferronerie, 1er. M. Châtelet. A throbbing hot-spot of gay nightlife around the corner from its brother organization **Le Club.** Apparently *the* place to drink before going dancing in the St-Denis region. Little space, lots of music and men. Women are welcome upstairs, but not to the mysterious inferno beneath. Happy hour 6-9pm. Open weekends 6pm-6am, weekdays 6pm-3:30am.

Le Bar Central, 33, rue Vieille-du-Temple, 4ème (tel. 01 48 87 99 33). M. Hôtel-de-Ville. At the nerve center of the Marais nightlife. Crowded at night with techno and disco pulsing from a high-powered sound system. The pick-up scene, fueled by free-flowing beer and a steamy atmosphere is of similarly high-voltage. A thirty-something, mostly French crowd with short hair and bulging biceps. Beer 15-18F. Open Sun.-Thurs. 2pm-1am, Fri.-Sat. 2pm-2am. MC, V.

Le Bar du Palmier, 16, rue des Lombards, 4ème (tel. 01 42 78 53 53). M. Châtelet. From bd. Sébastopol turn right on rue des Lombards. Palm trees, pina coladas, and margaritas (50F) mean "exotic" in French. Fantastically mixed clientele, straight and queer, come to this hot-spot and what may be the only terrace in a Marais bar. Music from soul and jazz to techno. Beer 20-33F. Drinks 45-50F. Happy hour (half price on draft beer) daily 6-8pm. Open daily 5pm-5am. MC, V.

Le Champmeslé, 4, rue Chabanais, 2ème (tel. 01 42 96 85 20). M. Pyramides or Bourse. This intimate lesbian bar has comfortable couches, dim lighting, and a young, yuppie clientele. Cabaret show on Thurs. Starting at 10pm, come on the 15th of every month for the *soirée zodiaque;* if it's your birthday month, you get a free drink. No cover. Drinks 25-40F. Open Mon.-Sat. 5pm-dawn. MC, V, AmEx.

Le Club, 14, rue St-Denis, 1er. (tel. 01 45 08 96 25). M. Châtelet-Les Halles. Found in a less chic, but *très* gay area of Beaubourg, next to the Marais. A dark, subterranean, intimate spot to dance. Women and straight men welcome. Wednesday is garage-techno night. Le Club is known for its Thurs. theme parties. Cover (48F including 1st drink) Fri.-Sat. only. Drinks 32-50F. Daily 11:30pm-dawn. MC, V.

Majestic Café, 34, rue Vieille-du-Temple, 4ème (tel. 01 42 74 61 61). M. Hôtel-de-Ville. Loud techno, red lights, and a mostly male crowd by night. Background techno, sunlight, and mostly tourists by day. 68F lunch menu includes espresso, a drink, and a main course. Beer 20-58F (25cL), cocktails 65F. Add 5F after 10pm. Open daily 10am-1:45am. MC, V, AmEx.

Open Bar, 17, rue des Archives, 4ème (tel. 01 42 74 62 60). M. Hôtel-de-Ville. As its name suggests, Open Bar is open to the street and to any and every sex, gender, and preference. A stylish young crowd relaxes to the sounds of disco and house. One of the most fashionable gay establishments in town. Beer 30F, Cocktails 45F. Open daily noon-2am. Monthly ladies night. MC, V, AmEx.

Le Palace Gay Tea Dance, 8, rue Faubourg-Montmartre, 9ème (tel. 01 42 46 10 87). M. Rue Montmartre. A fabulous place to meet on Sunday afternoons. Here, the queer elite sip drinks and gossip about less swanky gay and lesbian establishments. Mostly techno music. Occasional male strip shows. Cover and one drink 40F before 4pm, after 4pm 60F. Both sexes welcome. Open Sun. 2-11:30pm.

Le Piano Zinc, 49, rue des Blancs Manteaux, 4ème (tel. 01 42 74 32 42). M. Rambuteau. According to some, *the* seasoned gay hangout in the Marais. The piano downstairs sparks campy homage performances to Judy, Liza, Eartha, Madonna, Bette, Grace Jones, and Edith Piaf. Xeroxed lyric sheets allow all to join in bar theme song: *"Moi je suis dingue dingue dingue du Piano Zinc."* Happy hour 6-8pm, beer 10F, cocktails 37F. After 8pm, beer 14F, cocktails 44F. Open Tues.-Sun. 6pm-2am; piano bar open Tues.-Sun. 10pm-2am. MC, V, AmEx.

Le Quetzal, 10, rue de la Verrerie, 4ème (tel. 01 48 87 99 07). M. Hôtel-de-Ville. Nicknamed *l'Incontournable* (a Must), this high-tech, neon bar is packed with an under-40s crowd that plays pinball and kisses hello on the lips. All men, all techno. Beer 15-18F. Drinks 30-45F. Open Mon.-Fri. 2pm-3am, Sat.-Sun. 2pm-4am.

Festivals and Other Seasonal Events

At the slightest provocation, Parisians rush to the streets, drink, dance, and generally lose themselves in the spirit of the *fête* (festival) or *foire* (fair). While the city-wide Fête de la Musique (see below) and the pomp and splendor of Bastille Day are difficult to miss—even if you want to—some of the smaller festivities must be ferreted out. The **Office de Tourisme,** 127, av. des Champs-Elysées, 8ème (tel. 01 49 52 53 54; M. Charles de Gaulle-Etoile, see page 63), distributes the multilingual *Saisons de Paris 96/97,* a booklet listing all the celebrations. The English information number (tel. 01 47 20 88 98 or 01 49 52 53 56) gives a weekly summary of current festivals, as does *Pariscope.* You can also get a listing of festivals from the **French Government Tourist Office** (see page 22) before you leave home.

Bastille Day, *Vive la République* and pass the champagne. The day starts with the army parading down the Champs-Elysées and ends with fireworks. The fireworks can be seen from any bridge on the Seine or from the Champs de Mars. Groups also gather in the 19ème where the hilly topography allows a view to the Trocadéro. Traditional street dances are held on the eve at the tip of Ile St-Louis (the Communist Party always throws its gala there), the Hôtel de Ville, pl. de la Contrescarpe, and of course, pl. de la Bastille, where it all began. The so-called *Bals de Pompiers* (yes, firemen's balls) take place in front of every fire station in the city and are free of charge and crowded with jubilant French people. Unfortunately, the entire city also becomes a nightmarish combat zone of leering men cunningly tossing firecrackers under the feet of unsuspecting bystanders; avoid the metro and deserted areas if possible. July 14.

Christmas Eve. At midnight Notre-Dame becomes what it only claims to be the rest of the year: the cathedral of the city of Paris.

Concours International de Danse de Paris (tel. 01 45 22 28 74 for information and auditions). Classical and contemporary dance competition at the Opéra Comique, pl. Boïeldieu, 2ème. Late Nov. to early Dec.

Course des Serveuses et Garçons de Café, starts and finishes at Hôtel de Ville, 4ème (tel. 01 42 96 60 75). If you thought service was slow by necessity, let this race change your mind. Tuxedoed waiters sprint through the streets carrying a full bottle and glass on a tray. One day in mid-June; look for posters.

End of the Tour de France, expect a huge crowd along the banks of the Seine on the Right Bank, as well as along the av. des Champs-Elysées. Join the riotous crowd in the cheering; you may never see calves this strong again in your life. Fourth Sun. in July.

Festival d'Art Sacré (tel. 01 45 61 54 99). Festival of sacred music in churches and cultural centers throughout Paris. Easter and Dec.

Festival d'Automne (tel. 01 42 96 96 94). Drama, ballet, and music arranged around a different theme each year. Many events held at the Théâtre du Chatelet, 1er, the Théâtre de la Ville, 4ème, the Odéon-Théâtre de l'Europe, 6ème, and the Opéra National de Paris Bastille, 12ème. Mid-Sept. to Dec.

Festival Chopin (tel. 01 45 00 22 19 or 01 45 00 69 75). From M. Porte Maillot, take bus #244 to Pré Catelan stop. A dozen concerts and recitals held at the Orangerie du parc de Bagatelle in the Bois de Boulogne. Not all Chopin, but all piano music, arranged each year around a different aspect of the Polish Francophile's *oeuvre.* Times and prices vary annually. Mid-June to mid-July.

Festival du Cinéma en Plein Air, parc de la Villette, 19ème (tel. 01 40 03 76 92). M. Porte de la Villette or Porte de Pantin. A temporary screen is set up, seats are arranged in the Prairie du Triangle, and Paris sits down for its version of a drive-in theater. Movies usually focus on one theme, although exceptions are made for certain cult classics defying notions of theme and category. Theme for 1996 was *les liaisons dangereuses.* Rent a chair for 40F or bring a blanket. All films shown in original version. Mid-July to mid-Aug., Tues.-Sun. 10:30pm.

Festival Foire St-Germain, 6ème (tel. 01 40 46 75 12). Antique and book fair in pl St-Sulpice, concerts in the Auditorium St-Germain (4, rue Félibien; tel. 01 46 33 87 03). Both free. Early June to July.

Festival Internationale de la Guitare (tel. 01 45 23 18 25). Concerts in many Parisian churches. Mid-Nov. to mid-Dec.

Festival du Marais, 68, rue François Miron, 4ème (tel. 01 48 87 60 08). M. St-Paul. Open-air classical music, theater, and exhibits animate the splendid courtyards and backyards of many of the beautiful *hôtels* of the district. Concerts held in the pl des Vosges, at the Musée Cognacq-Jay, and elsewhere. Mid-June to mid July.

Festival de Musique de St-Denis (tel. 01 48 13 12 10; fax 01 48 13 02 81). A four week concert series featuring baroque as well as more classical and contemporary works, both instrumental and choral. Early June to early July.

Festival Musiqueen l'Ile (tel. 01 44 62 70 90; fax 01 44 62 70 89). Chamber and classical music in some of the most exquisite-sounding churches in Paris: Ste Chapelle, Eglise St-Louis, and Eglise St-Germain-des-Près. Mid-July to mid-Sept.

Festival de l'Orangerie de Sceaux, (tel. 01 46 60 07 79) is a weekend series of chamber music concerts from mid-July to mid-Sept. Call for information.

Festival d'Orgue à St-Eustache, 2, rue du Jour, 1er (tel. 01 42 94 82 57). M. Châtelet-Les Halles. Organ concerts in the beautiful St-Eustache church. Tickets 70-120F on sale at ARGOS, 34, rue de Laborde, 8ème (M. St-Augustin). Mid-June to early July.

Fête du Cinéma, purchase one ticket at full price and receive a passport that admits you to an unlimited number of movies for the duration of the 3-day festival at a cost of 10F each. Most cinemas in Paris participate, so choose your first film carefully the maximum ticket price varies considerably from theater to theater. Expect long lines and get there at least 30min. early for popular movies. Look for posters or ask at cinemas for the specific dates (around June 28).

Fête de l'Humanité, parc de la Courneuve. Take the metro to Porte de la Villette and then one of the special buses. The annual fair of the French Communist Party—like nothing you've ever seen. Entertainers in recent years have included Charles Mingus, Marcel Marceau, the Bolshoi Ballet, and radical theater troupes. A cross between the Illinois State Fair and Woodstock; you don't have to be a Communist to enjoy it. 2nd or 3rd week of Sept.

Fête de la Musique (tel. 01 40 03 94 70). Also called *"faîtes de la musique"* (make music!), this summer solstice celebration gives everyone in the city the chance to make as much of a racket as possible; noise laws don't apply on this day. Closet musicians fill the streets, strumming everything from banjos, to ukuleles, to Russian balalaikas. Major concerts at La Villette, pl. de la Bastille, and pl. de la République. Partying in all open spaces: before you join that samba parade, put your wallet in a safe place. Avoid the metro to avoid asphyxiation. Free. June 21.

Fêtes du Pont Neuf (tel. 01 42 77 92 26). M. Pont Neuf. The bridge is opened for dancing, music, street artists, and minstrels. A weekend in late June.

Fête à Neu-Neu, Bois de Boulogne, Chemin du Lac Supérieur, 16ème (tel. 01 46 27 52 29). A big amusement park. Late Aug. to early Oct.

Fête des Vendanges à Montmartre, rue Saules, 18ème (tel. 01 42 62 21 21). M. Lamarck-Caulaincourt. A celebration of the wine-grape harvest from Montmartre's own vineyards. Features costumed picking and tromping of the last vineyard's grapes. First Sat. in Oct.

Feux de la St-Jean (tel. 01 45 08 55 61). Magnificent fireworks at 11pm on the quai St-Bernard, 5ème, in honor of the Feast of St. John the Baptist. For a spectacular, though bird's-eye, view of the spectacle, stand in front of Sacré-Coeur. Call for verification of the location. June 24.

Foire du Trône, Reuilly Lawn, Bois de Vincennes, 12ème (tel. 01 46 27 52 29). M. Porte Dorée. A gigantic amusement park. Open Sun.-Thurs. 2pm-midnight, Fri., Sat., and holidays 2pm-1am. End of March to early June.

Grandes Eaux Musicales de Versailles, Parc du Château de Versailles (tel. 01 39 50 36 22). Weekly outdoor concerts and fountain displays throughout the park. Every Sunday early May to mid-Oct. and Aug. 15.

La Grande Parade de Montmartre, 18ème (tel. 01 42 62 21 21). This newly inaugurated event is just what it sounds like—a big parade. Marching bands from across the world join with Montmartre locals and various costumed brigades (like green Santa Clauses) to parade across the *butte.* New Year's Day.

18h-18F is a newly inaugurated film festival sponsored by the Mairie of Paris. A seat for the 18h (six o'clock) showing of a film at any of the participating theaters throughout Paris will cost 18F. Look for posters or inquire at cinemas for information. Feb. 14-20.

Journées du Patrimoine (tel. 01 44 61 21 50) are the few days each year when national palaces, ministries, monuments, and some townhouses are opened to the public. Free. Sept.

Musique en Sorbonne, 47, rue des Ecoles, 5ème (tel. 01 42 62 71 71 for information and to audition). M. Maubert-Mutualité. Classical music. Admission 60-140F. Late June to early July.

New Year's Eve. Bd. St-Michel and the Champs-Elysées are transformed into pedestrian malls, much to the dismay of the cops, who still attempt to direct traffic. More of the brouhaha that you tried to avoid on the 14th of July.

Piscinéma, in the Piscine des Halles. Before the Fête du Cinéma, the **Vidéothèque de Paris** (2, Grande Galerie, at Porte St-Eustache in the Forum des Halles, 1er; tel. 01 44 76 62 00) hosts this 3-night event which turns movie-watching into a spectator sport. Literally. Don your bathing suit, tread water, and watch a specially selected classic projected on a big screen above the pool. Video clips and documentaries with water themes play in the changing rooms and at the entrance to the pool. Call for tickets and film info. In late June.

Rallye Paris-Deauville (tel. 01 46 24 37 38). More than 100 vintage Parisian cars assemble at the Trocadéro fountains to leave for Deauville (in Normandy). At 7am on a Fri. in early Oct.

La Saison Musicale de L'Abbaye de Royaumont consists of weekend concerts in the great hall of a 13th-century monastery. The *abbaye* arranges for free bus transportation from the train station in nearby Viarmes. Tickets 115F, students and seniors 90F. call 01 34 68 05 50 for information and reservations. From mid-June to late Sept.

Le Temps des Livres (tel. 01 49 54 68 64). Debates, open-houses, lectures, and celebrations with books throughout France. Mid- to late Oct.

Les Trois Heures de Paris (tel. 01 49 77 06 40). A day-long regatta on the Seine. Races between pont d'Austerlitz and Ile St-Louis. On a Sun. in May.

La Villette Jazz Festival, parc de la Villette (tel. 01 40 03 75 75 or 01 44 84 44 84). M. Porte de Pantin. A week-long celebration of jazz from big bands to new international talents, as well as seminars, films, and sculptural exhibits. 1996 saw Max Roach, Cecil Taylor, and B.B. King. Marching bands parade every day and an enormous picnic closes the festival. Some concerts are free; call for info and ticket prices. A *forfait-soirée* gives access to a number of events for one night of the festival for 170F, students and seniors, 135F. Late June to early July.

Sports

PARTICIPATORY SPORTS

You might find it hard to believe while pounding the city's pavement, but Paris and its surroundings teem with indoor and outdoor sports opportunities. For more info. call the Mairie de Paris' sports hotline, **Allô-Sports** (tel. 01 42 76 54 54; open Mon.-Thurs. 10:30am-5pm, Fri. 10:30am-4:30pm). Many of the introductory courses offered by the city are for residents only. The *Pariscope* (see "Publications About Paris," p. 71) "Sports et Loisirs" section lists 10 pages of facilities, hours, and prices for a variety of sports locations. Also see *Paris Pas Cher* for lists of affordable gyms geared toward the long-term visitor. Below are activities for the budget traveler.

Jogging: Joggers are becoming a very common sight in Paris, especially in some of the athletically-oriented parks. Road-running will be difficult in the center city; although the 16ème is often quiet and residential enough to make a jog feasible on smaller roads. Many joggers head instead to one of the following public parks. Keep in mind that running in unknown or deserted areas is dangerous, especially as dark falls or if you're wearing a Walkman.

Central Paris: The **Champs de Mars,** 7ème (M. Bir Hakeim), is a popular in-city jogging spot, with a 2.5km path around the outside, and with gardens that are broken up into 200m lengths. The leafy **Jardin du Luxembourg,** 6ème (M. Cluny-La Sorbonne), offers a 1.6km circuit and a huge crowd. **Parc Monceau,** 8ème (M. Monceau), crawls with kids but remains serenely green; 1km loop.

Periphery: Parc des Buttes-Chaumont, 19ème (M. Buttes Chaumont), offers labyrinthine paths that are great for hill-work. A swooping path (1.6km) rings the park. The **Bois de Boulogne,** 16ème, has 35km of trails. Maps can be found at regular intervals on the periphery of the park. Less renowned, but no less runnable, is the **Bois de Vincennes,** 12ème. Begin at the northwest corner of the park at the medieval **Château de Vincennes** (M. Château de Vincennes). Peripheral path, marked in red and yellow on park maps, is 11km; inside path (marked in blue and white) is 8km. Avoid the southwest corner of the park, especially if you're jogging alone.

Swimming: The Mairie de Paris has created a network of public-access pools. Opening hours vary, but all are open in summer (Mon. 2-7pm, Tues.-Sat. 7am-7:30pm, and Sun. 8am-5pm). Call Allô-Sports to have a copy of *Les Piscines à Paris* sent to you, or pick one up at a *mairie.* It lists hours and services available at each pool. Entry to any **municipal pool** 14F; under 17, over 64, or those accompanying children but not swimming 7F. Ask about 1-yr. passes and youth discounts. Under 8 must be accompanied by an adult. Last entry 30min. before closing; pools are cleared 15min. before closing. Some pools have a *"nocturne,"* 1 or 2 nights a week, when they are open past 8pm.

Tennis: Paris boasts of 170 municipal tennis courts in 45 "tennis centers," each open to the individual player. You must have your own equipment for municipal courts. Free introductory lessons offered to children. To use the municipal courts, apply for a free **Carte Paris Tennis,** which enables you to reserve space through Minitel. Court reservation is crucial, especially in summer. Pick up an application at one of the tennis centers scattered throughout the city. Cards take 5 weeks to process. For municipal courts, rates are low (34F per hour).

Gyms and Fitness: Alésia Club, 143, rue d'Alésia, 14ème (tel. 01 45 42 91 05; M. Alésia), has a gym, sauna, and other facilities and will sell you a membership for the day (200F), or for longer (student rates plus 100F insurance: 300F for 1 month, 1200F for 6 months, 1800F for 1 year; open Mon.-Fri. 11:30am-9pm, Sat. 11:30am-8pm and Sun. 2-8pm). No aerobics. Or try the **Espace Vit'Halles,** 48, rue Rambuteau, 3ème (tel. 01 42 77 21 71), near Les Halles in pl. Beaubourg. With a weight room, a sauna, and aerobics and step classes, Vit'Halles offers both long-term and short-term memberships (students: 80F per day, 600F per month; open Mon.-Fri 8am-10pm, Sat. 10am-7pm, Sun. 11am-4pm). **Gymnase Club**, 149, rue de Rennes 6ème (tel. 01 45 44 24 35). There are at least 20 spread throughout Paris. Call for a free brochure. Each one has different classes and equipment. Most have pools, aerobics, weights, sauna. Some have martial arts, tennis, etc. 140F per day. With 350F membership card good for one year, pay 700F per month, 1500F for three months student membership 2680F per year. If you feel the need for a beach, or perhaps just a jacuzzi, wavepool, and waterslide, satisfy it at **Aquaboulevard,** 4, rue Louis Armand, 15ème (tel. 01 40 60 10 00; M. Balard). Come early in the morning to avoid the crowds (admission 69F for 4hr., 79F on weekends, 50F and 56F for under 12 600F for Sept.-June, 1300F for 1year; open Mon.-Thurs. 9am-11pm, Fri. 9am-midnight, Sat.-Sun. 8am-11pm). Associated fitness club gives access to sauna, gym, tennis and squash courts, aerobic classes, and a golf course, as well as water park (2120F for 1year; open Mon.-Fri. 8am-10pm, Sat.-Sun. 9am-8pm, 160F per day for Aquaboulevard and the club).

Cycling: The city proper is not a good place for a leisurely afternoon pedal, though the highway along the Seine near Châtelet is closed to cars on Sundays. Cyclists happily while away the hours in the **Bois de Vincennes,** 12ème, around Lac Daumesnil (M. Porte Dorée) or deeper into the woods. The **Bois de Boulogne,** 16ème, officially boasts of 8km of bike paths, but any cyclist can make up an original route among the innumerable trees. The **canal de l'Ourcq** passes through the Parc de la Villette, 30, av. Corentin Cariou, 19ème (M. Porte de la Villette), and has a bicycle path alongside. For information about bike rentals, consult "Two Wheelers," p. 77, or see "Bois de Boulogne—Bicycles," p. 218. Long-distance cyclists may want to try the 109km ride out to **Ferté Milon** in the province of Aisne. Also consider the **Forêt de Fontainebleau** (see "Fontainebleau," p. 288).

Roller Skating: Rollerblades are catching on in Paris streets. The Jardins du Trocadéro in front of the Palais de Chaillot fills with motorless Evil Knievals. Rent Rollerblades at **FranScoop**, 47, rue Servan, 11ème (tel. 01 47 00 68 43; M. St- Maur). 45-90F per day, 85-150F per weekend, 170-300F per week (open Mon.-Sat 9:30am-7:30pm). Or check out **La Main Jaune,** pl. de la Porte-de-Champerret, 17ème (tel. 01 47 63 26 47; M. Porte de Champerret). A roller disco with non-skate dancing, it's popular with the high school crowd. Open Wed. and Sat.-Sun. 2:30-7pm, Fri.-Sat. and holidays 10pm-dawn. Admission Wed., Sat., and Sun. 50F (includes a drink), skate rental 10F; Fri. and Sat. night 90F, skate rental 15F.

Fishing: Contact the **Annicale des Pêcheurs de Neuilly, Levallois, et environs,** Base Halientique de la Jatte, 19, bd. de Levallois Prolongé, 92000 Levallois-Perret (tel. 01 43 48 36 34). They'll fill you in on angling in the Bois de Boulogne.

Golf: Golf enthusiasts must reach deep into the suburbs for a real 18-hole game. Nevertheless, Paris contains a number of putting greens. Including club and ball rental, expect to pay about 100F. Try **Golf Club de l'Étoile,** 10, av. de la Grande Armée, 17ème (tel. 01 43 80 30 79) or **Aquagolf École de Golf de Paris,** 26, rue Colonel Pierre Avia, 15ème (tel. 01 45 57 43 06), 9 holes, practice space 70F.

Bowling: Bowling de Paris (tel. 01 40 67 94 00), in the Bois de Boulogne near the route Mahatma Gandhi entrance of the Jardin d'Acclimatation. After the park closes, you have to enter through the park's Mahatma Gandhi entrance, which remains open. Games (Mon.-Fri. 9am-noon 5F, noon-8pm 22F, Fri 8pm-2am, Sat.-Sun. all day 34F). Obligatory bowling shoe rental 10F. Because the Bowling de Paris is inside the garden, you must also pay the garden's admission fee (10F). (Garden open Mon.-Fri. 11am-2am, Sat.-Sun. 10am-2am.) **Bowling International Stadium,** 66, av. d'Ivry, 13ème (tel. 01 45 86 55 52; M. Tolbiac) is a joint bowling alley and billiard hall. American billiards require a 100F deposit, a 5F supplementary fee, and cost 45F per hour before 8:45pm, and 50F per hr. after 8:45pm. Bowling, in any of the 12 lanes, costs 20-33F depending on the time of day, the day of the week, and who you are (reduced prices for senior citizens and students); rent shoes for 7F a pair. Open daily 2pm-2am.

SPECTATOR SPORTS

If you think that Parisians are obsessed with only the very highest of high culture, think again. Parisians follow sports with fierce interest, reading between the lines of their own sports daily, *l'Equipe* (6F), as well as the sports sections of other newspapers. The **Palais Omnisports Paris Bercy,** 8, bd. de Bercy, 12ème (tel. 01 44 68 44 68; M. Bercy), hosts everything from opera and beach volleyball to figure skating, horse jumping, and surfing beneath its radical, sod-covered roof. Ticket prices vary wildly according to the event.

Soccer: Soccer (called *"football"*), France's hands-down national sport, consumes Paris, especially during the big championships like the World Cup *(Le Mondial),* which will take place in France in 1998. Join the Parisian multitudes in waiting to see where *les bleus* will go from here. The **Club de Football Paris St-Germain (PSG;** tel. 01 40 71 91 91) is Paris' own professional *football* team, splitting its time between road games and matches at the enormous **Parc des Princes** (box office tel. 01 49 87 29 29; M. Porte de St-Cloud), the city's premier outdoor stadium venue. The finals of the Coupe de France take place in early May; the Tournoi de Paris is in late July. Tickets to all events can be purchased at the Parc des Princes box office, 24, rue du Commandant-Guibaud, 16ème (M. Porte d'Auteuil), and go on sale anywhere from 2 days to 2 weeks in advance. Games on weekends and some weekday evenings. Prices 50-300F, depending on the seat and the event. Box office open Mon.-Fri., 9am-8pm, Sat. 10am-5pm, when selling tickets for an event; purchase tickets in advance by Mastercard or Visa.

Cycling: The women's **Tour de France** leaves Paris in mid-Aug. near the Eiffel Tower. Call 01 43 57 02 94 for information. Held in July, the **Tour de France** pits 200 of the world's best cyclists against the Alps, the elements, and each other for 21 gruelling stages. Call *l'Equipe* (tel. 01 41 33 15 00), one of the tour's sponsors, for information about the race's itinerary. Spectators turn out in droves along the way, stationed at bends in highways to cheer their favorites to victory. Parisians and tourists alike line the Champs-Elysées for the triumphal last stage, usually between noon and 6pm. Show up early and be prepared for a mob scene. The **Grand Prix Cycliste de Paris** is an annual time trial competition held in June in the Bois de Vincennes, 12ème (tel. 01 43 68 01 27; tickets 50F, available on site).

Tennis: The *terre battue* (red clay) of the **Stade Roland Garros,** 2, av. Gordon Bennett, 16ème (M. Porte d'Auteuil), has ended more than one champion's quest for a Grand Slam. Two weeks each year (May 26-June 8 in 1997), **Les Internationaux de France de Tennis** (The French Open) welcomes the world's top players to Paris. Write to the **Fédération Française de Tennis,** located at the stadium, (tel 01 47 43 48 00) in Feb. for information on tickets for the next spring's tournament. Prices for seats range 45-295F. Also, write or call your national tennis association: they sometimes have an extra supply of tickets.

Horse Racing: The numerous hippodromes in and around town host races of all kinds throughout the year. Far from seedy, an afternoon at the track is a family outing. The level of classiness climbs a notch or two for the season's championship races. **Hippodrome de Vincennes,** 2, route de la Ferme, in the Bois de Vincennes 12ème (tel. 01 05 11 21 14). M. Château de Vincennes. A hike through the woods from the metro stop takes you to the home of Parisian harness racing since 1906 Prix d'Amérique (late Jan.), Prix de France (early Feb.), and Prix du Président de la République (late June). Tickets 15-30F, even for the big races. **Hippodrome d'Auteuil,** in the Bois de Boulogne, 16ème (tel. 01 45 27 12 24). M. Porte d'Auteuil Steeplechases since 1873; the stands date from 1921. For the big races in June and July, shuttles run from the metro and RER stations. Open Sept.-Nov. and Feb.-June Tickets about 25F during the week, 40F on Sun., 50F for major events. No reservations.

Shopping

If you have to ask, you probably can't afford it. When you walk into a boutique, many store owners will take that as a declaration of intent to buy and will approach you immediately. If you want to browse, which they may not like, say: *"Merci. J'aimerais seulement regarder"* (Thank you, I'd just like to look). Do not be coerced into buying something you don't want, but don't be surprised at reactions ranging from disdain to hostility if you leave without making a purchase. Most stores close on Sunday and some of the smaller ones close Monday and during lunch on weekdays.

Window Shopping

The most famous of Paris' clothing boutiques skirt the **rue du Faubourg St-Honoré,** which runs northwest through the 8ème arrondissement. This is the area of *haute couture* (custom-made clothing and accessories). Gawk at the impeccably French scarves and bags at **Hermès** (no. 24), the classically cut velour at **Sonia Rykiel** (no. 70), the untouchables of all types at **Yves Saint Laurent** (no. 38), and the austere design of the Japanese **Ashida** (no. 34). The Pierre Balmain, Karl Lagerfeld, and Versace boutiques mingle nearby. (Pierre Cardin designs for Balmain; Lagerfeld for Chanel.) Nearby, the streets projecting from **pl. des Victoires** (1er and 2ème) harbor more *maisons de couture.* Running southwest from the Rond Point des Champs-Elysées, **av. de Montaigne** shelters the fashion houses of **Christian Dior** (no. 32), **Chanel** (no. 42), **Valentino** (no. 17-19), and **Nina Ricci** (no. 39). The name **Pierre Cardin,** seemingly omnipresent in Paris, appears on a regal house in pl. François 1er. The windows in **pl. Vendôme** and along **rue de la Paix** (north towards the Opéra) glitter with the designs of **Cartier, Van Cleef & Arpels,** and other offerings from the city's jewelry overlords.

Clothing

The sad truth is that Paris, though fashionable to a fault, is not a budget shopper's haven. Regular sales can reduce prices considerably, but clothing is almost always more expensive than in North America. Running smack through the *quartier latin,* bd. St-Michel, 5ème, appeals to the student population with the hippest names in youth fashion. The French equivalents of The Gap and Banana Republic are Chevignon, Creeks, and Naf-Naf; those who miss J. Crew should try Agnès b. Department stores, on the other hand, tend to have more conventional clothing. Stores like Au Printemps and the Galeries Lafayette have high-quality clothes for high prices. Tati, on the other hand, is low on each, giving you the status of a Parisian shirt or skirt for a hard-to-beat price. See "Department Stores," p. 272, for more details.

Magasins de Troc

Essentially snazzy second-hand stores, *magasins de troc* resell clothes bought and returned at more expensive stores. They specialize in adult and business clothing, so shopping for a specific item might be more fruitful than browsing.

Mouton à Cinq Pattes, 8-10-18, rue St-Placide, 6ème (tel. 01 45 48 86 26). M. Sèvres-Babylone. Also at 19, rue Grégoire de Tours, 6ème (tel. 01 43 29 73 56). M. Odéon. A huge selection of lesser-known designer clothing at low prices (for *haute couture*). Little costs less than 200F here. Open Mon.-Fri. 10:30am-7:30pm, Sat. 10:30am-8pm. MC, V, AmEx.

Réciproque, 16ème (tel. 01 47 04 30 28). M. Pompe. Different branches, all on rue de la Pompe, have different specialties: leather, jewelry, and swimwear at no. 92; women's cocktail and evening dresses at no. 93; women's town and sportswear at no. 95; menswear at no. 101; women's coats at no. 123. Greatly discounted, though not inexpensive, big-name designer clothing. Cheapest women's dresse 500F. All branches open Tues.-Sat. 10:30am-7pm. V, MC, AmEx.

Troc'Eve, 25, rue Violet, 15ème (tel. 01 45 79 38 36). M. Dupleix. This tiny shop goe back to the basics with less fashionable and more professional clothes for women including skirts, suits, and jackets. Open Tues.-Sat. 10am-7pm.

Troc Mod, 230, av. du Maine, 14ème (tel. 01 45 40 45 93). M. Alésia. A hit-or-miss selec tion: some things are cheap, some make you say, "No wonder they wanted to get rid o it." Mostly conservative, career-oriented women's clothes from 80F. Open June-Aug Tues.-Sat. 11am-7pm; Sept.-May Tues.-Sat. 10am-7pm.

■ Stock Stores

Stock is French for an outlet store; *magasins stock* feature the big names in French fashion for slightly less than in other stores—often because they have small imperfec tions or are last season's remainders. Rue d'Alésia in the 14ème contains an inordinate number of them, including a Kookaï *stock* store. Keep an eye out for **Cacharel Stock,** 114, rue d'Alésia, 14ème (tel. 01 45 42 53 04; M. Alésia; open Mon.-Sat. 10am 7pm; MC, V, AmEx), which carries men's, women's, and kids' clothes in classi styles, and **Stock Chevignon,** 122, rue d'Alésia, 14ème (tel. 01 45 43 40 25; M. Alésia open Mon. noon-7pm, Tues.-Fri. 10:30am-7:30pm, Sat. 10am-7pm; MC, V), a big name in guy fashion that appeals to any unisex shopper. Others to look out for include **Stock Daniel Hechter,** 16, bd. de l'Hôpital, 5ème (tel. 01 47 07 88 44; M Austerlitz; open Mon.-Sat. 10am-7:30pm; MC, V).

■ Vintage Clothing

Vintage fashion is where Paris shines, though you may have better luck finding a dea on that Catherine Deneuve white peacoat at the flea markets (see page 277).

Antiquités New-Puces, 43, rue Mouffetard, 5ème (tel. 01 43 36 15 75). M. Monge Used clothes from ugly shoes to 70s formal dresses. Clothes upstairs for 100-300F go downstairs to the basement for the real bargains. Some camp and some (almost class, all about 50-150F. Also sells hats, some jewelry and other nick-knacks. Ope Mon.-Fri. 11:30am-11:30pm, Sat 10am-9pm.

La Caverne des Dames, 23, rue des Dames, 17ème (tel. 01 42 93 96 46). M. Pl. d Clichy. Turn left off av. de Clichy onto rue des Dames. Clothing tacky and funky retro and gross. Sequined, tassled dresses mingle with shoes, books, small furniture and bric-a-brac, much of it priced 20-150F. Open Tues.-Fri. 10:30am-7pm.

Guerrisol, 19-29-31 and 33, av. de Clichy, 17ème (tel. 01 42 94 13 21). M. La Fourche Also at 9, 21, and 21bis, bd. Barbès, 18ème (tel. 01 42 52 19 73; M. Barbès Rochech ouart), 45, bd. de la Chapelle, 10ème (tel. 01 45 26 80 85; M. La Chapelle), 116-118 rue Jean-Pierre Timbaud, 11ème (tel. 01 43 38 69 05; M. Courconnes), and 22, bd Poissonière, 9ème (tel. 01 47 70 35 02; M. Bonne Nouvelle). This popular chain ha racks upon racks of second-hand for men and women, and bins of shirts and pant generally starting at 10F. The clothing is more used than vintage and more respect able than retro, but the reasonably priced silk shirts and leather coats can be diff cult to pass up. Jeans 30-60F, most items 10-120F. Most branches open Mon.-Sat 9:30am-6:30pm.

Tandem, 20, rue Houdron, 18ème (tel. 01 44 92 97 60). M. Abbesses. From the metro, go left on rue Abbesses and take a right on rue Houdron. This small stor specializes in *friperie* (fun clothes)—i.e., racks of 60s and 70s polyester and glitte squeezed next to retro-wear from the 40s and 50s. Don't forget to accessorize accessorize with circa 1975 sunglasses (80-90F) and a wide range of baubly jewelr (40-70F). Big selection of men's pants and jackets. Dresses and pants 120F-200F Open Tues.-Sat. 10am-8pm.

■ Department Stores

The first department stores in Paris were also the first in the world, designed as glam orous showplaces for affordable, ready-to-wear goods. When visiting the city's gran old stores like Samaritaine and Bon Marché, keep your eyes peeled for their turn-of-the-century ornamented ceilings and decorative metal work. In recent years, Paris has responded to increased demand for *prêt-à-porter* with newer and bigger *grands magasins* (department stores), offering fabulous one-stop shopping. Shoppers there browse unhassled by the over-aggressive salespeople of Paris' boutiques; sales staff in these stores remain safely behind the counter until you approach them.

At seasonal *soldes* (sales), prepare to elbow through mobs of hell-bent bargain hunters, practice your *"pardon"*s and *"excusez-moi"*s, and fight to the death for that chartreuse slip dress. Also keep in mind that many *grands magasins* are mini-malls; you can often get your hair cut, mail a letter, do your grocery shopping, and have lunch, all without leaving the air conditioned luxury of the store.

Au Printemps, 64, bd. Haussmann, 9ème (tel. 01 42 82 50 00). M. Chaussée d'Antin. Also at 30, pl. d'Italie, 13ème (tel. 01 40 78 17 17; M. pl. d'Italie); 21-25, cours de Vincennes, 20ème (tel. 01 43 71 12 41; M. Porte de Vincennes). Bills itself as "the most Parisian of all the department stores;" the international clientele must be a mirage. Merchandise on par with Galeries Lafayette. Anything you could possibly want (but not necessarily need) at typical (high) department store prices—plus more people than you could possibly want to see in a lifetime. Haussmann store open Mon.-Sat. 9:30am-7pm. Other branches have slightly different hours. MC, V.

BHV, 52, rue de Rivoli, 4ème (tel. 01 42 74 90 00). M. Hôtel-de-Ville. The initials stand for Bazar de l'Hôtel de Ville, logical enough for a department store across the street from the Hôtel de Ville. Heavy on housewares, electronic equipment, and luggage; light on trendy fashions. Less chic than Samaritaine. Open Mon.-Tues. and Thurs.-Sat. 9:30am-7pm, Wed. 9:30am-10pm. MC, V, AmEx.

Bon Marché, 24, rue de Sèvres, 7ème (tel. 01 44 39 80 00). M. Sèvres-Babylone. Paris' oldest department store and perhaps its best. As chic as Galeries Lafayette without the tourists and chaos. Designers of every cant, from Cachet to Laura Ashley. Those with children will enjoy the *Rentrée des Classes* (back to school) section, stocking children's supplies and toys from Tintin backpacks to model airplanes. Across the street is the **Grande Epicerie de Paris,** Bon Marché's gourmet food annex (see "Groceries," p. 106). Open Mon.-Sat. 9:30am-7pm. MC, V.

Galeries Lafayette, 40, bd. Haussmann, 9ème (tel. 01 42 82 34 56). M. Chaussée d'Antin. Also at 22, rue du Départ, 14ème (tel. 01 45 38 52 87; M. Montparnasse). Prices are high, but not outrageous. Keep your eye out for *soldes.* So many American tourists come here that it was considered highly unsafe during the terrorist attacks of the mid-80s. Take the time to admire the ornate Belle Époque dome in the main building. Main store open Mon.-Sat. 9:30am-6:45pm. Rue du Départ branch open Mon.-Sat. 9:45am-7:30pm. MC, V, AmEx.

Samaritaine, 19, rue de la Monnaie, 1er (tel. 01 40 41 20 20). M. Pont-Neuf, Châtelet-Les-Halles, or Louvre. Four large buildings between rue de Rivoli and the Seine, connected by tunnels. Perhaps not as chic as Galeries Lafayettes or Bon Marché, Samaritaine is practically your one-stop shopping center: clothes, furniture, toys, pets… Building 2 has a beautiful ceiling with turquoise and ivory ironwork and a peacock mosaic. Rooftop observation deck provides one of the best views of the city; take the elevator to the top floor and climb the short, spiral staircase (see "Sights—1er," p. 148). Also, **Le Sand's** café (on the 5th floor of Building 2), provides respite and an incredible view of the city. Open Mon.-Wed. 9:30am-7pm, Thurs. 9:30am-10pm, Fri.-Sat. 9:30am-7pm. MC, V, AmEx.

Tati, 11, pl. de la République, 3ème (tel. 01 48 87 72 81). M. République. Also at 106, rue Faubourg du Temple, 11ème (tel. 01 43 57 92 80; M. Belleville); 140, rue de Rennes, 6ème (tel. 01 45 48 68 31; M. Montparnasse); and 4, bd. de Rochechouart, 18ème (tel. 01 42 55 13 09; M. Barbès-Rochechouart). Rub elbows with students, immigrants, and families buying shorts and t-shirts for François and Henri to take to camp. You have never seen a more chaotic, crowded, and cheap department store. Wade through bins of stockings (3 pair for 6F), jeans (60F), bath towels (25F), dishes (6 for 6F). Generally low-quality, but worth rummaging, if only for the experience of this Parisian institution. Get your sales slip made out by one of the clerks (who stand around for just that purpose) before heading to the cashier. République branch open Mon. 10am-7pm, Tues.-Fri. 9:30am-7pm, Sat. 9:15am-7:15pm;

Belleville open Mon.-Sat. 9:45am-6:45pm; Montparnasse open Mon.-Fri. 10am-7:15pm, Sat. 10am-7:30p;. Barbès-Rochechouart open Mon. 10am-7pm, Tues.-Fri. 9:30am-7pm, Sat. 9:15am-7pm. MC, V.

Books and Magazines

Books in Paris, in English or French, are usually much more expensive than in North America. The exception to this rule is French language books, published in paperback "pocket" or "poche" editions. New English-language books sell for about US$20 per novel (paperback). Scope the banks of the Seine, where *bouquinistes* peddle treasures in all languages and at all prices, or try second-hand shops, whose *livres d'occasion* (used books) are often inexpensive. Almost all bookstores will order books for you, but the cost of mailing books from the U.S. can induce apoplexy. Specialty bookshops also provide an excellent resource for information concerning minority groups in the city. The *Sunday New York Times* (75F) may be purchased at W.H. Smith (see below), and at a kiosk on rue Pierre Lescot, 1er, in front of the east entrance to Les Halles.

Alias, 21, rue Boulard, 14ème (tel. 01 43 21 29 82). M. Denfert-Rochereau. Turn right off of av. du Général Leclerc onto rue Daguerre, then turn left onto rue Boulard. Few visitors get past the front door to this bookstore specializing in new and used art books and magazines; the shop is filled from floor to ceiling with sloping stacks of books. Browsers may have better luck elsewhere, but if you know what you're looking for, proprietor Jacques Léobold will usually squeeze through the narrow passage-ways and find it. Open Mon. 2-8pm, Tues.-Sat. 11am-after 8pm, Sun. 11am-2pm. MC, V.

Les Archives de la Presse, 51, rue des Archives, 3ème (tel. 01 42 72 63 93). M. Rambuteau. Huge collection of vintage magazines—especially politics, fashion, photography, music, sports and cinema. Some precious finds from the 50s, including fabulous *Vogue* issues (French and foreign). A magazine from a friend's birthday makes a good present (50F, unless the date happens to mark a more universal interest as well). Open Mon.-Sat. 10:30am-7pm.

Brentano's, 37, av. de l'Opéra, 2ème (tel. 01 42 61 52 50). M. Opéra. An American and French bookstore with an extensive selection of English literature, wide range of guidebooks, and small collection of greeting cards in English. Fiction paperbacks 40-75F. Open Mon.-Wed. and Fri.-Sat. 10am-7pm, Thurs. 10am-8:30pm. MC, V.

Chantelivre, 13, rue de Sèvres, 6ème (tel. 01 45 48 87 90). M. Sèvres-Babylone. A rather pricey children's bookstore with a play area for the wee ones. Classics for the young (Puss-in-Boots) and not so young (Dumas, Jack London). Some adult titles like *Parents en souffrance* (Suffering Parents). Small English-language section. Open Mon. 1-6:50pm, Tues.-Sat. 10am-6:50pm. MC, V (100F minimum).

Les Feux de la Rampe, 2, rue de Luynes, 7ème (tel. 01 45 48 80 97). M. Rue du Bac. Turn left off of bd. Raspail onto rue de Luynes. Books and out-of-print magazines on European and American films for the cinema devotee. If you don't see the giant movie poster you've been looking for, ask to see the thousands in the back room. Also has information on current film showings. Posters start at 20F, postcards at 5F. Open Tues.-Sat. 11am-1pm and 2:30pm-7pm.

Le Funambule, 48, rue Jean-Pierre Timbaud, 11er (tel. 01 48 06 74 94). M. Parmentier. Small bookstore specializing in gay- and lesbian-interest books, from literature to fine arts. Most books are used, out of print, or rare; a few in English. They also carry *Spartacus* and *Gay Pied.* Open Tues.-Sat. 1-7:30pm.

Galignani, 224, rue de Rivoli, 1er (tel. 01 42 60 76 07; fax 42 86 09 31). M. Tuileries The first English bookstore on the continent, Gagliani was founded in 1797 and has inhabited its current location since 1856. Frequented by Thackeray and Garibaldi in the 19th century and occupied by the German general staff during World War II the store is saturated in its own history. Wood paneling, *belles lettres,* coffee table art books, paperbacks, and travel guides. Open Mon.-Sat. 10am-7pm. MC, V.

Gibert Jeune, 5, pl. St-Michel, 5ème (tel. 01 43 25 71 19), near the Seine. M. St Michel. The best bookstore in town. With several branches clustered near each other, Gibert Jeune seems to swallow up the area around the Fontaine St-Michel

SHOPPING

Books in all languages for all tastes, including lots of reduced-price books for the short-on-cash. The store at 27, quai St-Michel (tel. 01 43 54 57 32; M. St-Michel), sells university texts. Main branch open Mon.-Sat. 9:30am-7:30pm.

La Hune, 170, bd. St-Germain, 6*ème* (tel. 45 48 35 85; fax 01 45 44 49 87). M. St-Germain-des-Prés. Next door to one of surrealist André Breton's favorite cafés, this well-stocked bookstore is a hot-spot for literati and art-lovers. Upper level is devoted to the *beaux arts,* organized by artist and period. Open Mon.-Sat. 10am-midnight. MC, V.

La Librairie des Femmes, 74, rue de Seine, 6*ème* (tel. 01 43 29 50 75). M. Odéon. The onetime home of feminist collective MLF. Though it has lost much of its radical edge, the *librarie* is still at the vanguard of the women's liberation movement. Stocks literature in several languages about, by, and generally for women. Open Mon.-Sat. 11am-7pm. MC, V, AmEx.

Librairie Gallimard, 15, bd. Raspail, 7*ème* (tel. 01 45 48 24 84; fax 01 42 84 16 97). M. Rue du Bac. The main store of this famed publisher of French classics features a huge selection of pricey Gallimard books. Basement is filled with Folio paperbacks. Open Mon.-Sat. 10am-7pm. MC, V, AmEx.

Librairie Gourmande, 4, rue Dante, 5*ème* (tel. 01 43 54 37 27; fax 01 43 54 31 16). M. Maubert-Mutualité. Bookstore on the art of living *par excellence;* new and old volumes chronicle food and drink from the Middle Ages to the New Age. Some English-language titles. Books in remainder bins around 30F. Open daily 10am-7pm. MC, V.

Librairie Ulysse, 26, rue St-Louis-en-l'Ile, 4*ème* (tel. 01 43 25 17 35). M. Pont-Marie. Anyone with a passion for travel should head to this magical, one-room bookstore filled floor-to-ceiling with books about every place you've ever dreamed of visiting (and many you haven't). They also have an impressive stock of maps (give Dominique a month and he will find you any map you want). 4000 copies of *National Geographic* from the 1920s on. There is a section in English on Paris and plenty of used books outside. English spoken. Open Tues.-Sat. 2-8pm.

Librairie Un Regard Moderne, 10, rue Git-le-Coeur, 6*ème* (tel. 01 43 29 13 93). M. St-Michel. A wild combination of high and low culture, kitsch and kunst, smut and sublime. Racy comix, glossy art and photo books, high and low-brow porno and gen-x literature stuff a cramped, smoky room. Prices can be high, but you can always just read it in the store. Mon.-Sat. 11am-8pm. MC, V.

Le Monde Libertaire, 145, rue Amelot. M. République. 11*ème* Walk up bd. Voltaire and turn right on rue Amelot. One of the only anarchist, Marxist bookstores in Paris. Books on human rights, revolutions, all kinds of magazines. Lots of sale items (10-50F). Open Mon.-Fri. 2pm-7:30pm, Sat. 10am-7:30pm.

Les Mots à la Bouche, 6, rue Ste-Croix-de-la-Bretonnerie, 4*ème* (tel. 01 42 78 88 30). M. St-Paul or Hôtel-de-Ville. Bookstore with an extensive collection of gay and lesbian literature, including novels, essays, art criticism, and magazines in French and English. Also a small selection of videos. A must-visit for those in search of an inside line on gay and lesbian nightlife and political and cultural events. Open Mon.-Sat. 11am-11pm, Sun. 2-8pm. MC, V.

Office International de Documentation et Librairie (Offilib), 48, rue Gay Lussac, 5*ème* (tel. 01 43 29 21 32). M. Luxembourg. A math and science store with a broad range of technical manuals and textbooks in English and French for 150-200F. Bring your computer queries here. Another branch at 44, rue Gay Lussac (tel. 01 46 33 25 33); offers a similarly wide selection in the social sciences. Open Tues.-Sat. 9am-12:30pm, and 2-6:30pm. Closed Sat. in summer. MC, V, AmEx.

Presence Africaine, 25bis, rue des Ecoles, 5*ème* (tel. 01 43 54 15 88). M. Maubert-Mutualité. French-language texts from Antilles and Africa put out by publishing house of the same name. Children's books, scholarly texts, poetry, and more. Paperbacks 30-70F. Also a helpful resource for travelers seeking businesses which cater to black clientèle. The proprietor keeps a stack of out-of-print guidebooks to Paris behind the desk. Open Mon.-Sat. 10am-7pm. MC, V.

Shakespeare and Co., 37, rue de la Bûcherie, 5*ème*, across the Seine from Notre-Dame. M. St-Michel. Run by George Whitman (alleged great-grandson of Walt), this shop seeks to reproduce the atmosphere of Sylvia Beach's establishment at 8, rue Dupuytren and, later, at 12, rue de l'Odéon, an extraordinary gathering-place for expatriates in the 1920s. Beach published Joyce's *Ulysses* in 1922; avant-garde composer George Antheil wrote *Music for Pianos and Airplane Propellers* as her boarder. Shakespeare and Co.'s current location and proprietor have absolutely no official link to Sylvia Beach, George Antheil, James Joyce, or any other Lost Generation notables. The current store has, however, accumulated a quirky and wide selection of new and used books. Bins outside offer a mixed bag of bargains, including many French classics in English (30F). Profits support impoverished writers who live and work in this literary cooperative—former residents include beatniks Allen Ginsberg and Lawrence Ferlinghetti. Open daily noon-midnight.

Tea and Tattered Pages, 24, rue Mayet, 6ème (tel. 01 40 65 94 35). M. Duroc. The place to go for second-hand English-language fiction, cookbooks, sci-fi, and much more. The crazy-quilt selection is subject to barter and trade; sell books at 3-5F a paperback and get a 10% discount on your next purchase. Books cost 25-45F. If what you want isn't what they've got, sign the wish list and you'll be called if and when it comes in. Adjoining tea room serves root beer floats, brownies, and American coffee with free refills. Holds poetry readings and photography exhibits; call for details. Open Sept.-July daily 11am-7pm.

The Village Voice, 6, rue Princesse, 6ème (tel. 01 46 33 36 47). M. Mabillon. Though it has no connection with its Manhattan-based namesake, this English language bookstore boasts the same dissident intellectual atmosphere and refined risqué taste. Many American newspapers are available. Open Mon. 2-8pm, Tues.-Sat. 11am-8pm. MC, V, AmEx.

W.H. Smith, 248, rue de Rivoli, 1er (tel. 01 44 77 88 99; fax 01 42 96 83 71). M. Concorde. Find the latest publications from Britain and America here, including many scholarly works. Large selection of magazines, from *Lilith* to *Esquire. Sunday New York Times* available by Tues. Open Mon.-Sat. 9:30am-7pm, Sun. 1pm-6pm. MC, V, AmEx.

Music

Highly taxed in France, CDs and cassettes are luxury goods here (CDs 100F or more). *Disques d'occasion* (used LPs) can be found at some music stores and at *marchés aux puces* (flea markets, see page 277). In general, you'll find larger selections of certain musical types (like French, African, and anything by Tom Waits) than you would in North America. Dedicated collectors will jump for joy at finding European labels that never crossed the Atlantic. However, this is no music buyer's mecca; hold off on that CD-shopping spree and stock up on tapes *before* you get to Paris. The following stores are worth a look-see for selection and/or specialization in a genre.

B.P.M. (Bastille Paris Musique), 1, rue Keller, 11ème (tel. 01 40 21 02 88; fax 01 40 21 03 74). M. Bastille. Catering to your rave needs, this address is a clubhouse, information point, and music store for house and techno fans. Rare and expansive collection of records—and record players so you can listen before buying. Check window posters for upcoming raves. Open Mon.-Sat. noon-8pm. MC, V.

FNAC (Fédération Nationale des Achats de Cadres): Several branches. **Montparnasse,** 136, rue des Rennes, 6ème (tel. 01 49 54 30 00; M. Rennes). **Étoile,** 26-30, av. des Ternes, 17ème (tel. 01 44 09 18 00; M. Ternes). **Forum des Halles,** 1-7, rue Porte Lescot, 1er (tel. 01 40 41 40 00; M. Les Halles). **Italiens,** 24, bd. des Italiens, 9ème (tel. 01 48 01 02 03; M. Opéra). Huge selection of tapes, CDs, and stereo equipment. The Les Halles branch contains a well-stocked shelf of books about music. The Italiens branch screens music videos all day in a public viewing room, no charge. Also a box office for concert and theater tickets (see "Theater," p. 252). Montparnasse, Étoile, and Les Halles branches open Mon.-Sat. 10am-7:30pm. Italiens branch open Mon.-Sat. 10am-midnight. MC, V.

Gibert Joseph, 26-30-32-34, bd. St-Michel, 6ème (tel. 01 44 41 88 88; fax 01 40 46 83 62). M. Odéon or Cluny-Sorbonne. A *librairie, papeterie,* and music store all rolled into one with both new and used selections. Gilbert Joseph frequently has sidewalk sales with books, notebooks, and old records starting at 10F. Good selection of used dictionaries and guidebooks. *Papeterie* at 32, bd. St-Michel open Mon.-Sat. 9:30am-7pm; all other departments Mon.-Sat. 9:30am-7:30pm. MC, V.

Rough Trade, 30, rue Charonne, 11ème (tel. 01 40 21 61 62). M. Bastille. Parisian branch of the British record label that brought you the Smiths, Stiff Little Fingers, Wire, Père Ubu, and countless other pop and punk bands. Expensive indie rock outpost in Paris. Techno, hip hop, and house downstairs; rock, pop, noise, and CDs upstairs. They also sell tickets to concerts around town, as well as to all the major European music festivals. Open Mon.-Sat. noon-8pm. MC, V.

Virgin Megastore, 52-60, av. des Champs-Elysées, 8ème (tel. 01 49 53 50 00). M. Franklin Roosevelt. If it's been recorded, it's likely to be at Virgin. This music mecca includes an affordable restaurant and countless headphones that let you listen to the latest hits. Beware of the latter: they invariably have recordings you've never heard of, and find you can't live without. Basement holds a bookstore and a box office (see "Theater," p. 252). Open Mon.-Sat. 10am-midnight, Sun. noon-midnight. MC, V.

Markets

Looking for that special something? From silver serving platters to Stevie Wonder 45s, Balzac to blue jeans, Paris' covered and uncovered markets are an affordable way to discover the charm and occasional chintz of daily life in the neighborhood. If prices aren't marked (and even if they are), feel free to haggle to your heart's content. Wherever you are, watch your wallet; the bustle of market day brings out the pickpockets in hordes. For more information about markets specializing in food, see "Food Markets and Noteworthy Streets," p. 108.

Carreau du Temple, 2-8, rue Perrée, at the corner of rue Dupetit Thouars and rue de Picardie, 3ème. M. Temple. Follow rue du Temple away from the metro and turn left on rue Dupetit Thouars. This structure of blue steel and glass is a neighborhood sports center in the afternoon and a clothes market in the morning. Especially good for leather—coats, bags, and shoes—it also sells other kinds of clothes and fabrics. Don't forget to haggle—you can usually get the already low price down at least 25%. More crowded on weekends. Open Tues.-Fri. 9am-12:30pm, Sat.-Sun. 9am-1pm.

Marché de Clignancourt, at the corner of av. de la Porte de Clignancourt and rue René Binet, 18ème. M. Porte de Clignancourt. Situated at the gateway to the Puces de St-Ouen (see below), this pricey extravaganza of clothes, shoes, leather, and jewelry welcomes unsuspecting tourists who think they've arrived at the famed flea market. You won't find any fleas here, since the merchandise is all new, but you can discover unusual silver and gold jewelers and perfect your bargaining technique. Open Sat.-Mon. 8am-7:30pm.

Marché aux Fleurs, on pl. Louis-Lépine just across from the M. Cité staircase, 4ème. This permanent flower market, filling the plaza near the Palais de Justice with color and fragrance, should be a staple of any walk down the Seine, especially *à deux*. Open Mon.-Sat. 9am-7pm. On Sun., an animal market appears in its stead, featuring goldfish, rabbits, gerbils, bird cages, and petfood stalls. Parakeets 95-800F. Rabbits 100F. Hamsters 20F. Goldfish 10F. Open 9am-6pm.

Marché aux Timbres (stamps), from the Rond-Point des Champs-Elysées to the corner of av. Matignon and av. Gabriel, 8ème. M. Franklin D. Roosevelt. Thurs. and Sat.-Sun. during daylight hours.

Quai de Mégisserie, 1er. M. Pont-Neuf or Châtelet. Creatures caressable and comestible squawk, purr, yelp, and gobble in this 300-year-old animal bazaar. Where the bunnies fit in, we're not quite sure. Cages spill from the stores onto the street, and fauna mingles with luxuriant flora, submerging this average stretch of boulevard into primordial havoc. Open daily until sunset.

PUCES DE ST-OUEN (ST-OUEN FLEA MARKET)

You'll find fleas and just about everything else at the **Puces de St-Ouen,** (M. Porte de Clignancourt), where spangled 1920s dresses rub shoulders with antique armoires, used kitchen sinks, and con artists. The prices and quality of the merchandise vary as widely as the products, beginning with the dirt-cheap, low-quality bargains found among the renegade stalls. At the other end of the spectrum, expensive, high-quality antique dealers use buzzers to ring in their preferred customers while keeping out the riff-raff. The market began during the Middle Ages, when merchants resold the cast-off clothing of aristocrats (crawling with the market's namesake insects) to peasant-folk on the edge of the city; it has gradually developed into a highly structured, regular market alongside a wild, anything-goes street bazaar.

A rule of thumb for first-time visitors: there are no five dollar diamond rings here. If you find the maltese falcon mixed into a pile of schlock jewelry, the vendor planted it there. The one area, however, where peddlers seem not to know what they have is that of rare rock-and-roll recordings. If you know your stuff and have unlimited patience, this is the place—1960s and 70s garage bands, funk, and much more. Best deals are cut on rainy days. The market is least crowded before noon.

If you take the metro, you'll encounter the street bazaar first. The 10-minute walk along av. de la Porte de Clignancourt, under the highway, and left on rue Jean Henri Fabre to the official market is jammed with tiny **unofficial stalls.** Most of these sell flimsy new clothes at exorbitant prices, but the leather jacket stalls have some good buys (suede jackets for 275F), as do some of the music booths. Don't be turned off by the raucous hurriedness of the stalls; once you pass through to the real market you'll be able to browse leisurely. Pickpockets love this crowded area, and Three Card Monte con artists positively proliferate (don't be pulled into the game by seeing someone win lots of money; they're part of the con, planted to attract suckers.

The **official market** is comprised of a number of sales forums, located on rue des Rosiers and rue Jules Vallès in St-Ouen, a town just north of the 18ème arrondissement. You can expect to get lost. From rue Jean Henri Febre, slip into the **Marché Malik,** a warehouse-type space filled with new and used clothing, shoes, music booths, and a tattoo parlor. Exiting onto rue Jules Valles, and walking away from the bongo drums and hard-sell banter of rue Fabre, you'll encounter the indoor **Marché Jules Valles** with its overwhelming collection of old trinkets and antique miscellany. **Marché Paul Bert,** on the street by the same name, has more antique bric-a-brac, as well as a fairly large collection of wooden furniture. Next door at the **Marché Serpette** more specialized furniture stores reign side-by-side with shops dealing in antique firearms. **Marché Biron,** on rue des Rosiers, as well as **Marché Dauphine,** on rue Fabre, will help you plan what to buy when you're rich and famous. The first has an enormous collection of porcelain, gilded furniture, and chandeliers, while the second sports two levels of indoor refinement with everything from velvet couches and Victorian undergarments to 1940s fashion porters and an indoor fountain. **Marché Vernaison,** located between rue des Rosiers and av. Michelet, has more of the same upper-class odds and ends, as well as beads, buttons, and musical instruments.

The **Marché des Rosiers,** rue Paul Bert (lamps, vases, and 20th-century art), and the **Marché Autica,** rue des Rosiers (paintings, furniture), are small, paler shadows of the large markets and deal mainly in new or fairly modern goods. The **Marché Malassie** is as new as any of this gets; more like a mall than a market, this gawky empty space sells "antiques" from the 1960s and similarly uninteresting furniture and artworks. Leaving the markets via av. Michelet will take you past a herd of leather coats, boots, and bags. Wherever you shop, be prepared to bargain; sellers don't expect to get their starting price. (Market open Sat.-Mon. 7am-7:30pm; many of the official stalls close earlier, but the renegade vendors may stay open until 9pm.) If you approach the market from M. Porte de St-Ouen, follow av. de la Porte de St-Ouen under the highway, then turn immediately right onto rue du Docteur Babinski which becomes rue Jean Henri Fabre. Don't be dismayed if the first items you see are batteries and electrical tools—this is only the outskirts of the real thing.

If you want to stop for lunch while at the flea market, try a steaming bowl of *moules marinière* with *frites,* the uncontested specialty of restaurants in the area. Two restaurants in particular stand out: **Chez Louisette,** 130, av. Michelet (tel. 01 40 12 10 14), inside the Marché Vernaison, allée no. 10, all the way at the back, where cigarette-puffin' singers liven up the already boisterous atmosphere. It's an eclectically decorated restaurant with classic French café *chansons*. Unfortunately, the secret is out, and you'll hear as much English and German as French. (*Moules* 58F. Open Sat.-Mon. 12:30-6pm.) A younger, grungier, less-touristy clientèle frequents **Au Baryton,** 50, av. Jules Vallès (tel. 01 40 12 02 74), near the Marché Malik, where people slurp up the *moules-frites* combo as well as an appetizer and dessert for only 59F while taking in the free live blues and rock concerts. (Open Sat.-Mon. 8am-11:30pm. Live music 4:30-8:30pm or 6:30-11:30pm.)

Other *marchés aux puces,* while less impressive, are also less crowded. The **Puces de Vanves,** along rue Marc Sanguier between av. de la Porte de Vanves and av. Georges La Fenestre, 14ème (M. Porte de Vanves), carries a fairly good assortment of antique cameras, jewelry, furniture, lace, and an absurd amount of spoons and dishes, as well as 19th-century texts and 20th-century comic books (open Sat.-Sun. 8am-1pm). The **Puces de Montreuil,** extending from pl. de la Porte de Montreuil along av. du Professeur André Lemierre, then to around 151, av. Galliéni, 20ème, is cheap in every sense. You can pick up an assortment of auto parts, tools, and stereos, but the market's heart is in its piles of used clothes, most priced between 5F and 50F. Bargain freely but be sure to watch your wallet. (Open Sat.-Mon. 7:30am-7:30pm.)

Trips From Paris

Yes, chère maître, I was indeed in Paris during the heat: it was truly "Tro Pical" (to adopt the pronunciation of M. Amat, governor of the palace of Versailles), and I sweated profusely. I was twice at Fontainebleau. And the second time, following your advice, I saw the sands at Arbonne.

—Gustave Flaubert to George Sand, 10 August 1868

DAY TRIPS

Châteaux

A château is literally a "castle," but the magnificent structures that ring Paris are by no means heavy defensive shields. Instead, they were built for 16th- and 17th-century French aristocrats and kings as sometimes whimsical, always elaborate retreats from the city. Surrounding the châteaux are formal French gardens with fountains, trellised rose gardens, and mazes of rectilinear hedges stretching to forest groves. Teams of architects, sculptors, and landscape designers created these compounds with money from the state treasury, while the over-taxed peasantry footed the bill. It is a pleasure to relax and spend a day outside Paris, traipsing through miles of symmetrical, well-kept gardens and reveling in the history of these spectacular residences, hunting lodges, and summer homes.

Versailles

"L'état, c'est moi!" (I am the state) declared Louis XIV, and then proceeded to build a royal residence the size of a small nation. By sheer force of ego, the Sun King converted an already bulky hunting lodge into the world's most famous palace. The sprawling château—its Hall of Mirrors, its oversized royal suites, its endless guest rooms, antechambers, and portrait galleries—stands as a testament to the despotic playboy-king who lived, entertained, and governed on the grandest of scales.

HISTORY

A child during the aristocratic insurgency called the Fronde, Louis XIV is said to have entered his father's bedchamber one night to find (and frighten away) an assassin. Scared of conniving aristocrats for the rest of his life, Louis XIV fled Paris for the 'burbs as soon as he could. Settling in the town of Versailles, the king proceeded to turn his father's hunting lodge into a royal residence, built and decorated mainly by Le Vau, Le Brun, and Le Nôtre (the design team stolen from Vaux-le-Vicomte). The court became the center of noble life, where more than a thousand of France's greatest aristocrats vied for the king's favor. Busily attending to Louis XIV's wake-up *(levée)* and bed-going *(coucher)* rituals, they had little time for subversion. Louis XIV had successfully drawn the high nobility away from their fiefs and under his watchful eye. As a further precaution, he outlawed duels at court.

The château itself is a gilded lily of classical Baroque style. No one knows just how much it cost to build Versailles; Louis XIV himself burned the accounts to keep the price a mystery. At the same time, life there was less luxurious than one might imagine—courtiers wearing rented swords urinated behind statues in the parlors, wine froze in the drafty dining rooms, and dressmakers invented the color *puce* (literally, "flea") to camouflage the insects crawling on the noblewomen. Although Louis XIV and his palace number among the few monarchical successes of 17th-century Europe, the kinds of mass extortions that Versailles represents would spark the French Revolution a century later. On October 5, 1789, 15,000 fishwives and

National Guardsmen marched out to the palace and brought the royal family back with them. Under the July monarchy, King Louis-Philippe established a museum here, dedicated to *toutes les gloires de la France* (all the glories of France). In so doing, he preserved the château, against the wishes of most French people, who wanted Versailles demolished just as the Bastille had been. In 1871, the château took the limelight once again, when Wilhelm of Prussia became Kaiser Wilhelm I of Germany in the Hall of Mirrors. That same year, as headquarters of the Thiers regime, Versailles sent an army against its old rival, Paris, at that time ruled by the Commune. In 1919, a vengeful France forced Germany to sign the ruinous Treaty of Versailles in the very room of that country's birth.

PRACTICAL INFORMATION

Visiting Versailles is a mammoth undertaking; the thorough sightseer may want to take two days to fully appreciate the ostentation. Arrive early in the morning to avoid the worst of the crowds. Versailles is most crowded on Sundays in May-September, when the fountains are turned on, and in late June, when the palace is swamped with French schoolchildren on field trips. (Château open Tues.-Sun. 9am-6:30pm; Oct.-April 9am-5:30pm. Last admission 30min. before closing. Gardens open 7am-sunset. General admission to the palace 42F; ages 18-25, over 60, and Sun. 28F; the *carte musée* includes admission to Versailles. For more information on the *carte,* see "Museums," p. 223.)

For more on Versailles, visit the **Ancienne Comédie Bookshop** in the *cour des Princes* next to the palace. Or call the **Office de Tourisme de Versailles,** Les Manèges, rue du Général de Gaulle (tel. 01 39 53 31 63), across from the train station, which has information about château events, other area sights, lodging, and food. Food is both scarce and expensive at Versailles. There are two pricey restaurants: the **Caféteria** (tel. 01 39 50 58 62; open 9:30am-5pm) and **La Flotille** (tel. 01 39 51 41 58).

For lunch, exit the main gate of the château, turn left, and head for the row of blue parasols on the tree-lined landing just beyond the parked tour buses. There are three cafés there. The middle one has an outdoor sandwich counter with sandwich/drink combo for 35F. You'll also find a few gift shops along this street; prices are as inflated as the Sun King's ego.

The RER has direct and frequent train service between Paris and Versailles. Trains run from M. Invalides on RER Line C5 to the Versailles Rive Gauche station (every 15min., 35-40min., 26F round-trip). From the Invalides metro stop, take trains with labels beginning with "V." Buy your RER ticket *before* going through the turnstile to the platform; though your metro ticket will get you through these turnstiles, it will not get you through the RER turnstiles at Versailles, and could get you in trouble with the dreaded *controlleurs.*

THE MAIN TOUR

When you arrive at the Versailles Rive Gauche RER train stop, exit the station and take a right. The elegant building on the right is the *mairie* of Versailles. Continue walking away from the train station the length of the *mairie's* façade and turn left at the first huge intersection; then walk straight to the gilt-fenced outer courtyard of Versailles. An equestrian statue of a crimped, turned-out Louis XIV stands at the courtyard's center. Overlooking the courtyard is the terrace on which Molière's *Tartuffe* debuted. The clock on the pediment was traditionally set to the time of death of the previous king. The balcony of the **King's Bedroom** is visible at the center of the east-west axis along which the château and gardens are laid out. The location of the room was no mistake; the Sun King's place was at the center of the château and the nation, and he rose each morning, to great ritual, in the east.

Signs in the courtyard point you to Entrance A, B, C, or D. Most of Versailles' visitors enter at **Entrance A,** located on the right-hand side in the north wing. (**Entrance B** is for groups, **Entrance C** leads to the King's Bedchamber, **Entrance D** is where

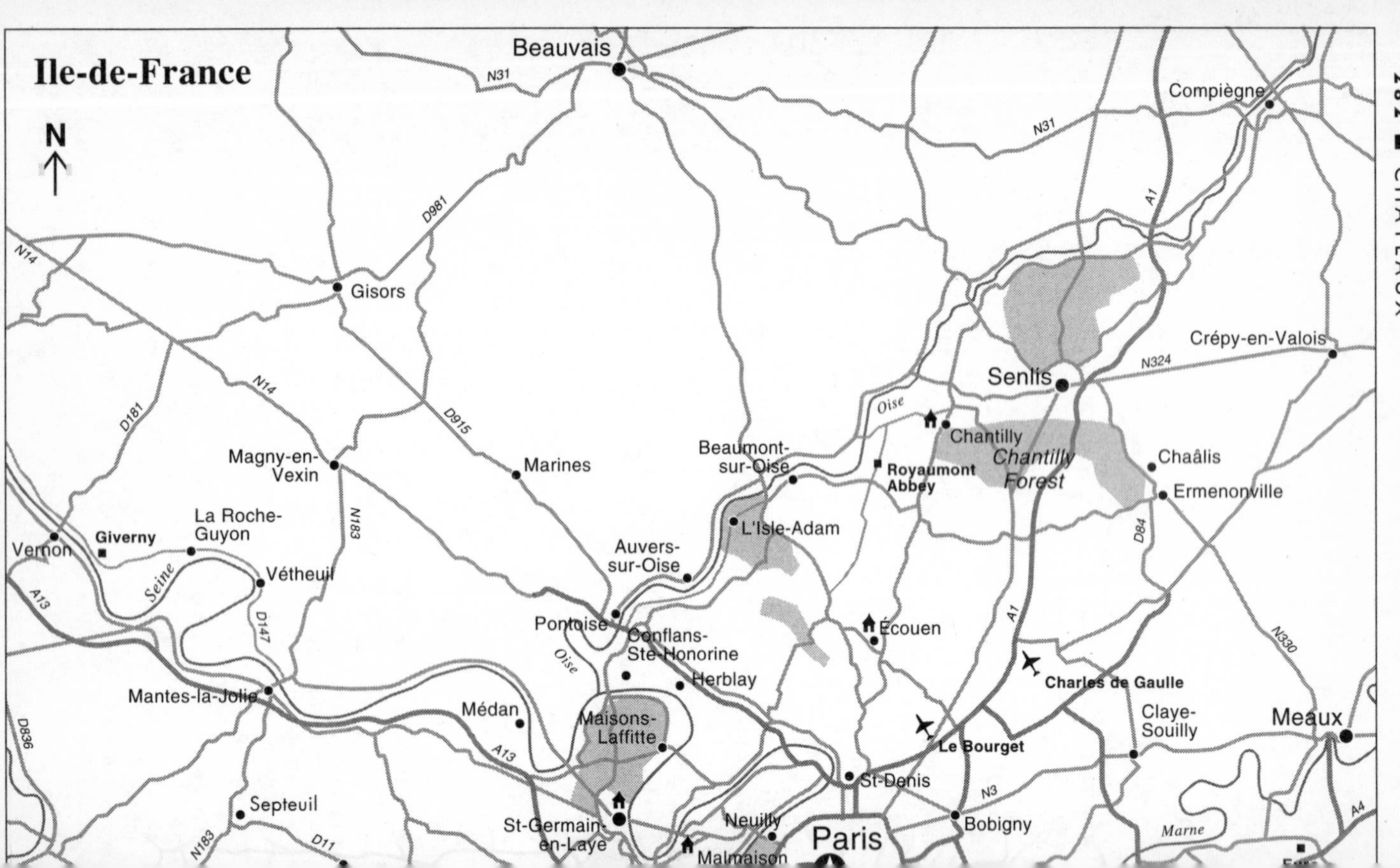
Ile-de-France
N
Beauvais
N31
Compiègne
N31
A1
D981
N14
Gisors
Crépy-en-Valois
N324
Senlis
Oise
N14
D181
D915
Chantilly
Chantilly Forest
Beaumont-sur-Oise
Royaumont Abbey
Chaâlis
Ermenonville
Magny-en-Vexin
Marines
N183
La Roche-Guyon
L'Isle-Adam
D84
Giverny
Vernon
Auvers-sur-Oise
Vétheuil
Seine
A13
D147
Pontoise
Écouen
A1
N330
Conflans-Ste-Honorine
Oise
Charles de Gaulle
Herblay
Mantes-la-Jolie
Médan
Maisons-Laffitte
Claye-Souilly
Meaux
D836
A13
Le Bourget
St-Denis
N3
A4
Septeuil
St-Germain-en-Laye
Neuilly
Paris
Bobigny
Marne
N183
D11
Malmaison

Meudon
Sceaux
N12
D91
Orly
N10
Rambouillet Forest
Dampierre
N306
Chevreuse
Palaiseau
Brie-Comte-Robert
Breteuil
N306
A6
N6
Rambouillet
A10
Evry
Melun-Sénart
Maintenon
Corbeil-Essonnes
N36
Le Marais
A10
Vaux-le-Vicomte
D6
Dourdan Forest
Melun
A11
N154
D906
N7
A6
Seine
A11
N105
Barbizon
Chartres
A10
Etampes
Fontainebleau
D837
Montereau
N6
Fontainebleau Forest
Moret-sur-Loing
Loing
0
10 miles
0
10 kilometers

guided tours start, and **Entrance H** is for visitors in wheelchairs.) Buy general admission tickets at Entrance A (45F; after 3:30pm, Sun., and ages 18-25 35F; under 18 free; the *carte musée et monuments* includes general admission to Versailles). General admission allows entrance to the following rooms: the *grands appartements,* where the king and queen received the public; the War and Peace Drawing Rooms; the *Galerie des Glaces* (the famed Hall of Mirrors); the dauphin and children's apartments. Note that the private suites of the king and queen may only be seen by guided tour. If you intend to take one, proceed directly to Entrance D, purchase the regular admission ticket, and inquire about English-language guided visits. General admission tickets are also for sale at Entrance C, as are tickets for the single tour that leaves from there.

The general admission ticket starts your visit in the **Musée de l'Histoire de France,** created in 1837 by Louis-Philippe to celebrate his country's glory. Along its textured walls hang portraits of men and women who shaped the course of French history. The face of Louis XIV is everywhere; you may wonder if he spent his entire life sitting for portraits. Of particular interest are portraits by Philippe de Champaigne, preeminent court artist under Louis XIII. The 21 rooms (arranged in chronological order) seek to construct a historical context in which to understand the château. In Louis XIV's day, the north wing ground floor was a bustling open-air market where men bought wigs and women ribbons; now thronged with tourists, it has preserved the frenzied, hassled ambiance of its past.

Each of the **drawing rooms** in the **State Apartments** is dedicated to a mythological god—Hercules, Mars, and the ever-present Apollo (the Sun King identified with the sun god), among others. Although less brilliant than you might expect, the gilt wood is still splendid, due to constant, state-funded regilding.

Framed by the **War and Peace Drawing Rooms** is the **Hall of Mirrors.** The hall was a somewhat gloomy passageway until Mansart added a series of mirrored panels, joined together and set in wooden frames, in order to double the light in the room. Each of these mirrors was the largest that 17th-century technology could produce; the ensemble represented an unbelievable extravagance. Although many of the mirrors are aged and clouded, visitors still get a thrill from standing at one end of the Hall and looking past the mirror-filled arches, gold figures, and many chandeliers. Le Brun's ceiling paintings tell the history of Louis XIV's heroism, culminating in the central piece, entitled *The King Governs Alone.*

The **Queen's Bedchamber,** which saw the public births of 20 members of the royal family, is now furnished year-round in its floral summer decor—not the darker plush red and black velvet used during 18th-century winters. A version of the David painting depicting Napoleon's self-coronation (the original is in the Louvre) dominates the **Salle du Sacré** (also known as the Coronation Room). In this room, the king used to wash the feet of a lucky 13 poor children every Holy Thursday.

You can rent a **cassette guide** in English for 28F (with deposit of passport) at the information desk behind the ticket booths. While an *audioguide* may help compensate for the lack of explanatory signs in the château, be aware that the narration is not paced to the sequence of the rooms. An excellent printed guide is Daniel Meyer's 50F color-photo guide to the palace, *Versailles Tour of the Château, Gardens, and Trianon,* on sale at the gift desk. This 96-page book, written by Versailles's curator, has dazzling photos and detailed explanations of the castle's countless paintings, rooms, antiques, gardens, and fountains.

GUIDED TOURS

Start your visit at **Entrance D,** at the left-hand inside corner as you approach the palace (1hr. tours 25F, 1½hr. tours 37F, 2hr. tours 45F; ages 7-17 25F, 26F, and 34F respectively; under 7 free). Choose between seven tours of different parts of the château; only three are offered in English. One good bet is the whirlwind "Best of Versailles" guided visit (1½hr.). Guided tours in sign language are available for the King's State Apartments, the Hall of Mirrors, and the Apartment of the Queen. Reservations must be made in advance with the Bureau d'Action Culturelle (tel. 01 30 84 76 18).

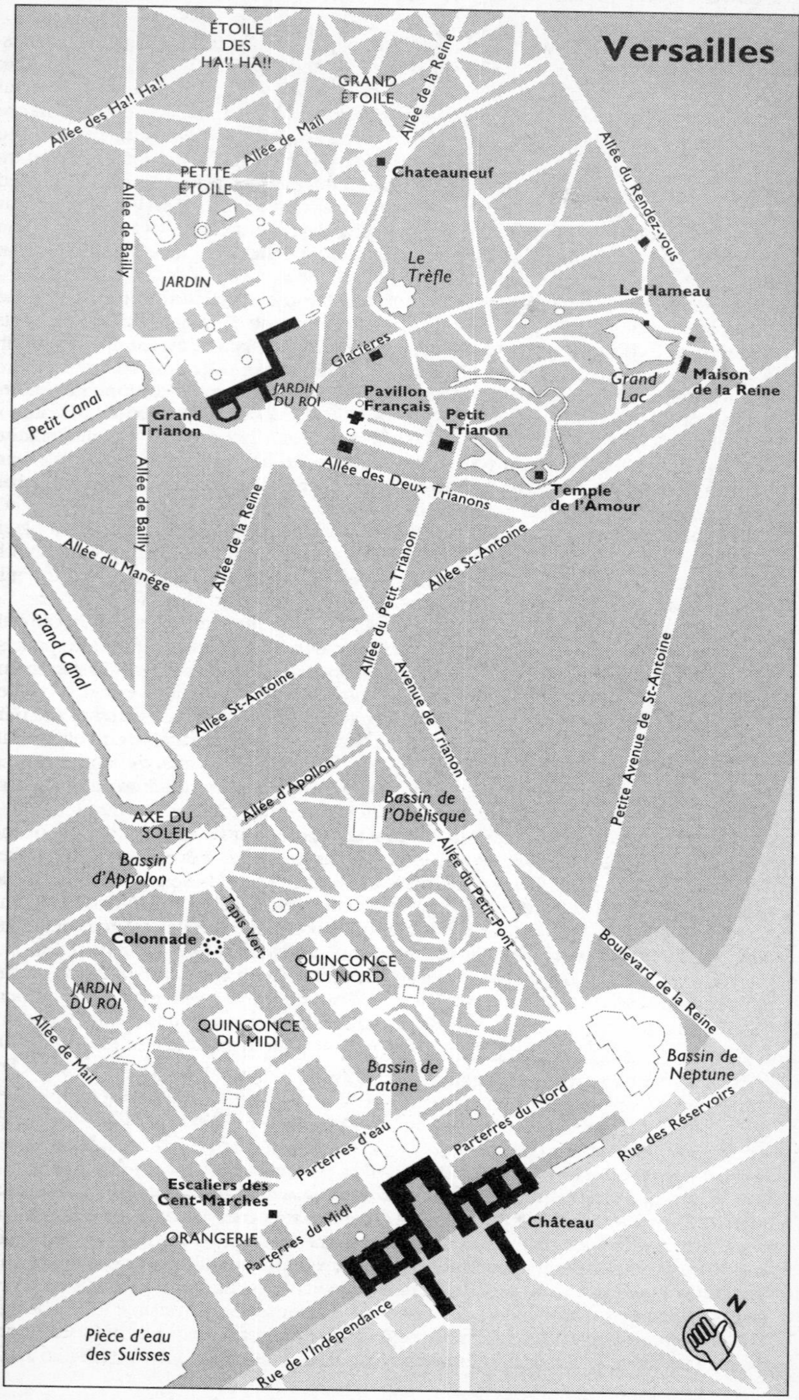
Versailles
ÉTOILE DES HA!! HA!!
Allée des Ha!! Ha!!
GRAND ÉTOILE
Allée de la Reine
Allée de Mail
PETITE ÉTOILE
Chateauneuf
Allée de Bailly
Allée du Rendez-vous
JARDIN
Le Trèfle
Le Hameau
Glacières
JARDIN DU ROI
Pavillon Français
Grand Lac
Maison de la Reine
Petit Canal
Grand Trianon
Petit Trianon
Allée des Deux Trianons
Temple de l'Amour
Allée de Bailly
Allée de la Reine
Allée St-Antoine
Allée du Manége
Allée du Petit Trianon
Grand Canal
Avenue de Trianon
Petite Avenue de St-Antoine
Allée St-Antoine
Allée d'Apollon
Bassin de l'Obélisque
AXE DU SOLEIL
Bassin d'Appolon
Allée du Petit-Pont
Tapis Vert
Colonnade
QUINCONCE DU NORD
Boulevard de la Reine
JARDIN DU ROI
QUINCONCE DU MIDI
Allée de Mail
Bassin de Latone
Bassin de Neptune
Parterres d'eau
Parterres du Nord
Rue des Réservoirs
Escaliers des Cent-Marches
Château
ORANGERIE
Parterres du Midi
Rue de l'Indépendance
Pièce d'eau des Suisses
N

You may wish to take the tour of the opera house, which leaves from Entrances A and C. The *opéra*, which took architect Jacques-Ange Gabriel 20 years to design, was completed at breakneck speed by 20,000 workmen in time for the wedding of Marie-Antoinette and the future Louis XVI. Often considered the world's most beautiful theater, the pink and blue oval room is a marvelous fake. It looks like marble or bronze, but the hall is actually made of wood, because the meticulous Gabriel wanted it to resound like a violin. The mirrored galleries reflect chandeliers and gilt archways, making the theater seem larger than it is. The room's splendor brought Marie-Antoinette to breach royal etiquette on her wedding day; she took her eyes off the stage and ogled the decor. Many of Molière's plays premiered here, accompanied by the music of court composer Jean-Baptiste Lully. Lully's death is one of the saddest, strangest tales in music history. Before the advent of the conducting baton, leaders of musical ensembles used a long, pointed stick to keep time. During a performance celebrating Louis XIV's recovery from illness in 1687, Lully accidentally stabbed himself in the foot with his stick. He died later that year of gangrene.

Most of the other tours take you through practically empty, if historically important, rooms. The tour of **Louis XV's Apartments** showcases a small collection of furnishings, instruments, and tapestries, while providing a history of Versailles under that monarch; Mozart played in one of these rooms on his youthful visits to Versailles (at ages 7 and 22). The visit to **Marie-Antoinette's Apartments** does not trail through as many lavishly decorated rooms as you might hope. Versailles was sacked during the Revolution and only a tiny portion of its original extravagance has been restored. Much of the tour is spent in rooms filled with portraits, learning the who's who of the Hapsburgs, Bourbons, and their ministers. The same is true of apartments belonging to Louis XV's mistresses, Mme. de Pompadour and Mme. du Barry, and to the dauphin, the dauphine, and other royal kids. True French Revolution buffs will not want to miss the door and passageway through which Marie-Antoinette fled to rejoin her king on October 6, 1789, when a crowd of bloodthirsty Parisians stormed her bedroom, demanding the head of the "Austrian whore."

The **King's Bedchamber** yields a blinding look at the Sun King's gold bed and balustrade, and more than a passing glance at Nocret's beautiful family portrait, which depicts Louis XIV as Apollo and his brother, Philippe d'Orléans, as holder of the morning star. Philippe was the first after the morning chaplain to see the Sun King—he was also kept in skirts until he was 18. (Tickets to the Bedchamber tour, in French or in English, on audiocassette or led by a guide, are sold at Entrance C.)

Longer tours go to the **Jardins et Bosquets** (Gardens and Groves) and to the **Petit Trianon.** The two-hour Gardens and Groves tour, with considerable walking, provides the history of Le Nôtre's gardens and their countless fountains (June-Oct. Tues.-Sat. afternoon 3:30pm; 37F, 26F reduced). Guided visits to the **Petit Trianon** illuminate this favored hangout of Marie-Antoinette (same dates, time, and prices as the Gardens and Groves tour; French only). Both tours leave from the entrance to the Petit Trianon.

THE GARDENS

Versailles's gardens are breathtaking and enormous, perfectly scaled to the palace. Numerous artists—Le Brun, Mansart, Coysevox—executed statues and fountains here, but master gardener André Le Nôtre provided the overall plan. Louis XIV, landscape enthusiast, wrote the first guide book to the gardens, entitled the *Manner of Presenting the Gardens at Versailles.* Start, as the Sun King commands, on the terrace, pausing to study the layout of the gardens. During the summer, the grounds at Versailles give an overwhelming impression of green rare to this area of France. Even more rare are the wide paths and tall trees—you can feel totally alone, even with tons of people around. During the summer, the grounds are open until dusk. Some travelers come in the evening to see the immense château without people, like the empty stage of a grand opera.

To the left of the terrace, the **Parterre du Midi** graces the area in front of Mansart's **Orangerie,** once home to 2000 orange trees. The temperature inside the orangerie never drops below 6°C (43°F). In the center of the terrace, the **Parterre d'Eau** boasts statues by the *ancien régime's* greatest sculptors. Below is one of the most extraordinary fountains, the **Bassin de Latone.** Latona, mother of Diana and Apollo, is seen shielding her children from the attack of an oncoming mob, whom Jupiter is turning into frogs. When the fountains are running, part-human, part-frog figures belch water into the air.

Past the *bassin* and to the left is the **Rockwork Grove,** built between 1681 and 1683. Once known as the ballroom because courtiers danced on the long-gone marble floor, the Grove shows off fetid water cascading over shell-encrusted steps. The south gate of the grove leads to the magnificent **Bassin de Bacchus** (or **de l'Automne**), one of four seasonal fountains marking the intersection of pathways on either side of the main alley. The **Bassin du Miroir d'eau** spurts near the peaceful **Jardin du Roi** and the **Bassin de Saturne** (or **de l'Hiver**), sculpted as an old man. The **Colonnade** is a 32-column peristyle decorated by sculptures and 28 white marble basins, in the center of which the king used to take light meals. The north gate to the Colonnade exits onto the **Tapis Vert** (Green Carpet), the central strip of grass linking the château to the much-photographed **Char d'Apollon** (Chariot of Apollo). Pulled by four prancing horses, the Sun King as Sun God rises out of dark water to enlighten the world.

On the north side of the garden is Marsy's incredible **Bassin d'Encelade.** One of the giants who tried to unseat Jupiter from Mount Olympus, Enceladus cries in agony under the weight of rocks that Jupiter hurled to bury him. When the fountains are turned on, a 25-m jet bursts from Enceladus's mouth. Flora reclines more peacefully on a bed of flowers in the **Bassin de Flore** (or **du Printemps**), while Ceres luxuriates in sheaves of wheat in the **Bassin de Cérès** (or **de l'Eté**).

The **Parterre du Nord,** full of flowers, lawns, and trees, overlooks some of the garden's most spectacular fountains. The **Allée d'Eau,** a fountain-lined walkway, provides the best view of the **Bassin des Nymphes de Diane.** The path slopes towards the sculpted **Bassin du Dragon,** where a dying beast spurts water 27m into the air—the highest of any jet in the gardens. The culmination of any visit to the gardens is the **Bassin de Neptune,** the largest of the fountains. Ninety-nine jets of water attached to urns and seahorns surround a menacing Neptune. (Gardens open sunrise-sundown. Free, except May-Sept. Sun. 20F.)

Beyond the **Petit Parc** of Le Nôtre's classical gardens stretch wilder, more natural woods and farmlands. Check out the **Grand Canal,** a rectilinear pond beyond the Bassin d'Apollon. You can rent a bike to the right (north) of the canal, just outside the garden gates, to appreciate Versailles's vast grandeur (35F per hr.). Forgo the unremarkable *bateau-mouche* canal tour (25F, under 16 20F). If you're traveling with friends, rent a *barque* for 4 people at the boathouse to the right of the canal (open 10am-5:30pm, 60F per hr).

THE TRIANONS AND MARIE-ANTOINETTE'S HAMEAU

Also within the grounds of Versailles are the two Trianons—"smaller" châteaux made of lavish pink, white, and black marble—and the **Petit Hameau,** an idyllic peasant village where Marie-Antoinette came to milk cows. Trianon was the name of the village the Sun King bought in 1668 in order to expand his estate. Built by Mansart, the single-story, marble-decorated **Grand Trianon** was intended as a meeker château in which, if need be, the king could reside alone with his family. Stripped of its furniture during the Revolution, the château was restored and inhabited by Napoleon and his second wife. Today, important state meetings (including the one that passed the constitutional amendment for Maastricht) are held at the Grand Trianon, and Versailles again becomes the capital of France.

The **Petit Trianon,** built for Louis XV and Mme. de Pompadour by Gabriel, was presented to Marie-Antoinette by Louis XVI. Restoration has closed off all but four rooms to the public—their cozy feel may not be worth the price of admission. The English Garden, created for Marie-Antoinette, and the Grand Trianon gardens provide calm far from the madding crowds found closer to the château. Quainter still is the **Hameau** (the Queen's Hamlet), a collection of countrified, Norman cottages built for Marie-Antoinette. The young queen liked to play at being a peasant here, to the dismay of people who actually fit that description. The buildings are not open to the public but once contained drawing rooms of rather un-peasant-like elegance.

The Grand and Petit Trianons are open May-Sept., Tues.-Sat. 10am-6:30pm; Oct.-April Tues.-Sun. 10am-12:30pm and 2-5:30pm. Admission to the Grand Trianon is 25F, reduced tariff 15F; to the Petit Trianon 15F, reduced tariff 10F. Combined ticket to the Trianons is 30F, reduced tariff 20F. Shuttle trams from the palace to the Trianons and the Hameau leave from behind the palace (round-trip 31F, 19F for ages 3-12). The train does a 35-minute circuit that allows you to get off, tour the Trianons, and get back on another train, but the commentary it provides on the gardens only repeats what is written in the pamphlet. The walk takes about 25 minutes.

SPECIAL EVENTS

On Sundays from May through September, come to see (and hear) the **Grandes Eaux Musicales,** when the fountains are in full operation. Aglitter with geysers, the park becomes the sensuous feast it was designed to be. A slightly diminished version of this spectacle, called the *grande perspective,* runs 11:15-11:35am. Tour the 24 activated, musically accompanied fountains 3:30-5pm. A free pamphlet lays out a suggested walking path; don't bother with the more expensive 25F guide to the fountain. The same info appears in the Meyer *Guide to the Château and Gardens.* (Admission to park during *Grandes Eaux* 20F.)

The **Grande Fête de Nuit,** a musical and fireworks extravaganza, imitates the huge *fêtes* of Louis XIV. The garden at Versailles had to be finished in 1664 in time for one such party, the Fête of the Enchanted Isle, for which Molière wrote an up-to-the-minute *masque* (theatrical vignette). (*Fêtes* held at the Neptune Fountain 4 Sat. each summer, 10pm rain-or-shine. 90min. 60-185F, reduced rates for children. Call the tourist office at 01 39 59 36 22 for dates and ticket info.) Tickets go on sale at the tourist office and box offices within Paris. Doors open one hour before the show; enter at 2, bd. de la Reine.

The **Centre de Musique Baroque de Versailles,** 16, rue Ste-Victoire, gives concerts, equestrian shows, *masques,* dance performances, and theater presentations in period costume, many focusing on 18th-century French music and drama (June to early Sept. Sat. 5:30pm; tickets 90-200F). Thursday concerts by the Maîtrise Nationale of Versailles are held in the Royal Chapel (Nov.-June 5:30pm; tickets 30F). For info call 01 39 02 30 00 in Versailles; in Paris 01 42 60 58 31 or 01 43 59 24 60.

Versailles offers two ongoing lecture series. The first *(Histoire du Château)* provides an in-depth historical look at various parts of the palace. The second *(Visites approfondies)* provides for a scholarly treatment of themes, with lecture titles like "Court Costumes under the Old Regime," and "Their First Name was Adélaïde." There is much here for both the 18th-century French scholar and the lay Marie-Antoinette aficionado. (1-hr. *"Histoire du Château"* lectures Sat. 10:30am and 2:30pm, admission 23F, under 17 15F. *"Visites approfondies"* Sat.-Sun. 2pm. 46F, under 17 31F. Call 01 30 84 76 18 for more info.)

■ Fontainebleau

When you think "hunting lodge," do you see a log cabin with a stuffed deer head, tucked away in the thick of the woods, maybe with a gun rack and a stone hearth? Not the men who commissioned and designed the Château de Fontainebleau. They thought big, they thought glorious, and their efforts converged in this sprawling structure, deceptively simple when viewed from the main courtyard. Made out of sandstone from the lush tangle of forest surrounding the château, Fontainebleau's warm yellow exterior, accented with red brick, hides the splendiferous extravagance within. Not a bad place for a harried sovereign to get away from it all.

Like its name, believed to spring from a certain Monsieur Bliaut who owned a local fountain, Fontainebleau is a hodge-podge of architectural and decorative styles. It has been a glorified hunting lodge for nearly 500 years and makes a radically different architectural statement from the unity of Vaux-le-Vicomte and Versailles. Kings of France have lived on these grounds since the 12th century, when the exiled Thomas à Beckett consecrated Louis VII's manor chapel. In 1528, François I tore down and rebuilt the castle to bring himself closer to the "red-and-black furred animals" he so loved to hunt. Italian artists designed and decorated the palace, and their paintings, the *Mona Lisa* and the *Virgin in the Rocks* among them, filled François's private collections. Subsequent kings had varying degrees of affection for the château, depending generally on their appreciation for dead and dying furry animals. Most commissioned their favorite designers to add at least one magnificent room, while some attached whole new wings. The château remained an action-packed place throughout. Louis XIII was born here in 1601, Louis XV was married here in 1725, and Louis XIV revoked the Edict of Nantes here in 1685. Fontainebleau was also the perfect place to welcome the Pope, who had come to crown Napoleon in 1804, and to imprison His Holiness between 1812 and 1814. Napoleon popped into Fontainebleau frequently, and it is presented as one of his main residences; but he actually only spent 194 days in the building, whose eclectic architecture led him to dub it *"La Maison des Siècles"* (the House of Centuries). The **Cour des Adieux** was so named after serving as the scene of his dramatic farewell in 1814. Also known as the **White Horse Court,** it is used as the main entry to the château. Note the famous horseshoe-shaped stairway leading to the front door (but don't use it).

The **Grands Appartements,** the standard visitors' circuit, provides a lesson in the history of French architecture and decoration. Guides (available in English) will make the whole visit more meaningful: 20F gets you a pamphlet about the château and some of the gardens or one describing the Grands Appartements alone; 30F buys the glossy booklet with more complete descriptions. Dubreuil's **Gallery of Plates** tells the history of Fontainebleau on a remarkable series of 128 porcelain plates, fashioned in Sèvres between 1838 and 1844. In the **Gallery of François I,** arguably the most famous room at Fontainebleau, muscular figures by Mannerist artist Il Rosso (known in French as Maître Roux) tell mythological tales of heroism and bravado, brilliantly illuminated by light flooding in from windows looking onto the Fountain Courtyard. The **Ball Room's** magnificent octagonal ceiling, with complementary floor, reminds the visitor that much of Fontainebleau should be observed with a craned neck. If you look out the windows, you can see to your left the **Oval Courtyard,** which used to be the castle's main courtyard. The **King's Cabinet** (also known as the **Louis XIII Salon,** because Louis XIII was born there), decorated under Henri IV, was the site of many an important meeting, as well as *le débotter,* the king's post-hunt boot removal. Gobelin tapestries and Savonnerie carpets line walls and floors throughout the palace—three of the four seasons, with floral hoops, are depicted on the wall of the **Empress's Antechamber.** Every Queen of France since the 17th century slept in the gold, green, and leafy **Queen's** (later Empress's) **Bed Chamber;** the gilded wood bed was built for Marie-Antoinette, who never used it. The *N* on the throne of the **Throne Room** is another testament to Napoleon's enduring humility; the red and gold velvet meets in a crown above the throne. **Napoleon's Bed Chamber** boasts predictably fancy decor, but the **Emperor's Small Bed Chamber,** complete with camp bed, is more the style of a military man. In the **Emperor's Private Room,** known today as the **Abdication Chamber,** Napoleon signed off his empire in 1814. As you exit, check out the 16th-century **Trinity Chapel.** (Grands Appartements open Nov.-May, Wed.-Mon. 9:30am-12:30pm and 2-5pm; June and Sept.-Oct. 9:30am-5pm; July-Aug. 9:30am-6pm. Last entry 45min. before closing time. Admission 31F, students, seniors, and Sun. 20F, under 18 free. Call 01 60 71 50 70 for details.)

The same ticket admits you to the **Musée Napoléon,** a collection of paraphernalia including his tiny shoes, his toothbrush, his field tent, and his son's toys. Not to be missed are the gifts (don't you wish you had enemies like this?) from Carlos IV of Spain. (Same tel. and hrs. as Grands Appartements, except closed 11:30am-2:30pm, and closes 5pm weekdays.) Also in the château and included in its admission, the **Musée Chinois de l'Impératrice Eugénie** offers a welcome respite from the sometimes crowded apartments upstairs. Recently restored, these four rooms were remodeled in 1863 by the Empress to house the collection she called her *"Musée chinois"* (Chinese museum), a gathering of Far Eastern decorative art: porcelain, jade, and crystal. These pieces were brought to her after the 1860 Franco-English campaign in China and also by Siamese ambassadors received by Napoleon III in 1861. The rooms are quietly decorated in green and maroon and are among the few in the château that seem to have anything to do with real people living comfortably (open 9:30am-11:30am and 2:30pm-5pm).

The **Petits Appartements,** private rooms of Napoleon and the Empress Josephine, are accessible only by guided tours and only on certain days. Tours on Mondays and holidays, otherwise they are not scheduled until the day they will occur; call for info. (Admission 15F, under 26 and over 60 10F, under 18 free. When available, tours in French are at 10, 11am, 2, and 3pm.)

The gardens in the main courtyard of Fontainebleau are unimpressive but make a pleasant enough stroll. Quieter and more refined are the **Jardin Anglais,** complete with rustic grotto and the famous Fontaine-belle-eau, and the **Jardin de Diane,** guarded by a statue of the huntress. (Courtyard and gardens open daily sunrise-sunset.) You can also tool around the **Etang des Carpes** in a rented boat and admire the fish. (4-person max. per boat. Boat rental June-Aug. daily 10am-12:30pm and 2-7pm; Sept. Sat.-Sun. 2-6pm. 40F per ½hr., 60F per hr.)

The **Forêt de Fontainebleau** is a thickly wooded 20,000-hectare preserve with hiking trails and the famous sandstone rocks used for training alpine climbers. If you'll be in town for a while, you too can learn how to climb (ask at the tourist office). Bikes can be rented in town. Maps of hiking and bike trails are available at the tourist office. Fans of 19th-century art will recognize the thick hardwoods and sandstones made famous by Rousseau and Millet, painters of the Barbizon school.

In the town itself, the **Musée Napoléonien d'Art et d'Histoire Militaire,** 88, rue St-Honoré (tel. 01 64 22 49 80, ext. 424), grew out of Louis Prost's childhood fascination with Napoleon and things military (he grew up to become the creator and conservator of the museum). The place to go if you saw Fontainebleau but, like France, didn't get enough of Napoleon the first time. (Open Tues.-Sat. 2-5pm. Last entrance 4:45pm. Admission 10F, under 12 free.)

Fontainebleau's **tourist office,** 4, rue Royal (tel. 01 60 74 99 99), across from the château, organizes tours of the village surrounding the château, helps find accommodations, and has maps of Fontainebleau and Barbizon. (Open Mon.-Sat. 9:30am-6:30pm; Sun. 10am-12:30pm and 3-5:30pm.) A *petit train* (tel. 01 42 62 24 00) run by the tourist office gives a 30-minute tour of the park and of the town with multilingual commentary (April to mid-Oct. Mon.-Sat. 9:30am-6:30pm, Sun 10am-noon; 30F, children 15F). Hourly **trains** run to the town from the Gare de Lyon, *banlieue* level (45min., 92F round-trip). The château is a 30-minute walk or 10-minute bus ride away. Take **Car Vert A** (tel. 01 64 22 23 88) from the station (8F70). Buses leave after each train arrival from Paris; take direction "Château-Lilas" and get off at the Château stop. You can also rent a **bike** at the train station from **MBK** (tel. 01 64 22 36 14; fax 01 60 72 64 89). (For a basic model, 60F per day; 7-speeds 70F per half-day, 120F per day; mountain bikes 80F per half-day, 120F all day. Helmet rental 10F. Officially open daily 9am-7pm; open just about all day weekends and sometimes only when the train arrives weekdays. MC, V.)

NEAR FONTAINEBLEAU: BARBIZON

On the edge of the Fontainebleau forest blossoms the rustic village of **Barbizon,** a favorite of 19th-century French landscape painters. Théodore Rousseau, Jean-François Millet, and Jean-Baptiste Camille Corot were the key figures in the Barbizon School, living and working in this artistic haven in the mid-1800s. Influenced at once by the writings of Jean-Jacques Rousseau and the paintings of 17th-century Dutch landscapists, they were the spiritual and artistic predecessors of the Impressionists.

The **Musée Municipal de l'Ecole de Barbizon** is housed in **l'Auberge Ganne** at 92, Grande rue (tel. 01 60 66 22 27), where most of these artists lived at one time or another between 1848 and 1870. Just renovated, the museum gives a 30-minute multimedia blitz about the lives of the young artists of Barbizon. The ground floor is a recreation of the inn, whose walls and furniture were used by residents as media for artistic expression (read: were painted on). Upstairs, the museum has more traditional canvases, some by Rousseau and Millet. Pick up the free English-language brochure at the entrance. (Open April-Sept. Mon. and Wed.-Fri. 10am-12:30pm and 2-6pm, Sat.-Sun. 10am-6pm; Oct.-March Mon. and Wed-Fri. 10am-12:30pm and 2-5pm, Sat.-Sun. 10am-5pm. Admission 25F, students 13F, under 12 free.)

The town's other museum, the **Maison et Atelier de Jean-François Millet,** 27, Grande rue (tel. 01 60 66 21 55), shifts focus to Millet, the best-known of the Barbizon masters, famous for his portrayal of the French peasantry as the proud, the victimized, the simple, and the uncorrupted (open Wed.-Mon. 9:30am-12:30pm and 2-5:30pm; free). Galleries dedicated to the Barbizon School, as well as contemporary art, line the main drag, misnamed Grande rue. A little stroll down the road will lead you past most of the places where the Barbizon artists settled after leaving the Auberge Ganne; Rousseau lived at no. 55.

Barbizon is 10km from Fontainebleau. **Buses** (tel. 01 64 23 71 11) linking the two towns are the cheapest and quickest way to go between them, but have limited schedules and don't run during the summer. (Wed. and Sat., the bus leaves the Fontainebleau train station at 2:10pm, the château at 2:20pm, and arrives at Barbizon at 2:30pm; the reverse trip leaves Barbizon at 5:10pm; 13F one-way from the château to Barbizon, 17F80 one-way from Fontainebleau to Barbizon. From the Barbizon bus stop, follow rue René Ménard and turn left on Grande rue.) Biking to Barbizon gives more flexibility; see above for bike rental information, and ask the Fontainebleau tourist office for directions. Otherwise, a taxi from the Fontainebleau train station is about 110F one-way. The tourist office, 55, Grande rue (tel. 01 60 66 41 87), sells a booklet (5F) with descriptions of all the towns to visit in the area.

■ Compiègne

Tranquil Compiègne (pop. 50,000) has tripped through 1200 years of diplomatic notoriety without being much affected by it. The town first gained prominence in the 8th century, welcoming Frankish and Byzantine officials to the banks of the Oise. The English captured Joan of Arc here in 1430 during a siege in yet another round of the Hundred Years War. The armistice ending World War I was signed in a forest clearing about 6km away on November 11, 1918; in 1940 Adolf Hitler forced the French to surrender at the same spot. Beech trees, landscaped grounds, and the 17th-century château make today's Compiègne a picturesque town with a few skeletons hidden in the *armoire*. Under the German occupation, Compiègne served as one of France's largest detention centers for Jews on their way to concentration camps—a journey that ended in death for more than half the voyagers. This dark period in the town's history is carefully neglected by most tour guides, and visitors can enjoy Compiègne's château, three unusual museums, and web of hiking trails in peaceful ignorance.

First stop at the **tourist office** (tel. 03 44 40 01 00; fax 03 44 40 23 28) in the Hôtel de Ville for a free and useful map, one-hour walking tour of the city, and all sorts of useful information. To reach the office from the train station, walk across the parking lot, take a right along the canal, and take the next left across the bridge onto rue Solférino. Continue up this street and the Hôtel de Ville appears soon enough on the left. (Open Easter-Oct. Mon.-Sat. 9am-12:15pm and 1:45-6:15pm, Sun. 9:30am-12:30pm and 2:30-5pm; Nov.-Easter Mon.-Sat. 9am-12:15pm and 1:45-6:15pm.) Compiègne is easily accessible by **train** from Paris (Gare du Nord) and Amiens.

The main attraction of the town is the **Musée National du Château de Compiègne** (tel. 03 44 38 47 00; fax 03 44 38 47 01). Fond of the original château's rustic appeal, Louis XIV quipped, "I am lodged as king at Versailles, as gentleman at Fontainebleau, as peasant at Compiègne." Louis XV found this "quaintness" less beguiling, and in

1751 began building the large palace whose profile you see today. In the 19th century, Compiègne served as second home to Napoleon Bonaparte and later to Napoleon III. The château's interior bears the mark of Bonaparte's ostentatious tastes; it's an opulent ensemble of nude nymphs and tapestried chairs. Compiègne also harbors a *trompe l'oeil* bag of tricks—secret doors, baffling paintings that seem to be carved marble, and other curiosities. Also part of the museum complex is the **Musée de la Voiture,** featuring 18th-, 19th-, and early 20th-century coaches and omnibuses including those used by Napoleons I and II. (Château accessible only by guided tour in French, every 15min. April-Sept. Wed.-Mon. 9:15am-6:15pm, last tour 5:30pm; Oct.-March Wed.-Mon. 9:15am-4:30pm, last tour 3:45pm.)

No visit to the palace is complete without a tour of the **grounds** designed at Napoleon's request in 1811. Meandering walkways, shady trees, natural-looking flower beds, and a 5km long *grande pelouse* (great lawn) make this the perfect place for a stroll or a picnic. Just beyond this vast expanse of manicured grass lies the untamed Forest of Compiègne, a more adventurous setting for a bike ride or hike. Check with the tourist office for details about the hunting season.

Six kilometers into the forest is the **Clairiève de l'Armistice** (Armistice Clearing) (tel. 03 44 85 14 18). It was here in 1918 that the Supreme Commander of the Allies, Maréchal Foch, brought his railway carriage for the signing of the Armistice in November and left it as a monument to the French Victory. On June 20, 1940, that same carriage was taken by Hitler as a trophy of the French capitulation. Destroyed by Allied bombing, it was replaced by a replica and a small **museum** (open May-Sept. Wed.-Mon. 9am-noon and 2-6:15pm; Oct.-April 9am-noon and 2-5pm).

A highlight of the tourist office's walking tour is the **Musée Divenal** (tel. 03 44 20 26 04), with strong collections of Greek vases, regional archaeology, Renaissance *objets d'art,* and an Egyptian collection featuring the mummy of a child. (Open March-Oct. Tues.-Sat. 9am-noon and 2-6pm, Sun. 2-6pm; Nov.-Feb. Tues.-Sat. 9am-noon and 2-5pm, Sun. 2-5pm.) The route also passes the **Tour Jeanne D'Arc (Tour Beauregard),** a striking ruin commemorating Joan's imprisonment in Compiègne, and the **Parc de Sougeons,** from which unfolds an arresting view of the Oise River. The **Eglise St.-Jacques** holds an impressive stained glass of Joan taking communion on May 23, 1430 (the day she was captured). Another church in Compiègne is the **Eglise St-Antoine,** a 16th-century marvel with a gorgeous rose window.

■ Vaux-le-Vicomte

Vaux-le-Vicomte was built by the famous threesome Le Vau, Le Brun, and Le Nôtre before they moved to Versailles. Nicolas Fouquet, Louis XIV's Minister of Finance, assembled the triumvirate of architect, artist, and landscaper to build Vaux for him between 1656 and 1661. In so doing, he financed the creation of a new standard of country château, in a uniquely French, Neoclassical Baroque style. Though smaller and less opulent than Versailles, Vaux impresses with architectural coherence and *trompe l'oeil.* Be attentive to optical tricks in both the château and the gardens. To show off his new pad, Fouquet threw a *fête* to end all *fêtes* on August 17, 1661 with 6,000 guests. Louis XIV and Anne d'Autriche were but two of the witnesses to a sensuous orgy that premiered poetry by La Fontaine and a new ballet by Molière, and concluded in a fireworks extravaganza featuring the King and Queen's coat of arms and pyrotechnic squirrels (Fouquet's symbol).

The celebration of Fouquet's impeccable grace, sophistication, and culture—he was surrounded by a circle of the finest artists and intellectuals—did not last long. Furious at being upstaged by his first minister, young Louis ordered Fouquet arrested. Three weeks later at Nantes, d'Artagnan, the captain of the Musketeers immortalized by Dumas, arrested the hapless man for speculation. Behind Fouquet's downfall were hidden causes. Colbert, another minister, had been turning the monarch against Fouquet for years; Fouquet's ill-advised expression of affection for Mme. de Lavallière, beloved of the king, didn't help matters either. And someone, even the man who had kept the French treasury solvent by raising funds against his own fortune, needed to be the fall guy for the state's abysmal financial condition. In a trial that lasted three years, the judges in Fouquet's case voted narrowly for banishment over death; Louis XIV overturned the judgment in favor of life imprisonment. Pignerol, a dreary citadel, housed the fallen minister until his death in 1680, leading some to speculate that he was the famous man in the iron mask. Louis did appreciate Fouquet's tastes; soon after the minister's arrest, the King confiscated many of Vaux's finest objects (including trees from the garden) and hired the same trio—Le Vau, Le Brun, and Le Nôtre—to work their magic at Versailles.

Everything at Vaux-le-Vicomte is orchestrated to create an impressive whole. The designers integrated painting and sculpture, architecture and decor, building and garden to please the viewer with ideal forms and harmony and impress one with humanity's ability to govern and tame nature through symmetry and invention.

THE CHATEAU

The château itself (tel. 01 64 14 41 90) recalls both the grandeur of a Roman past, with its rusticated columns, and a French fort, complete with squat walls and moat. The first optical trick to be aware of is the appearance of three entries, though there is only one. Another is that the moat is completely invisible from the road. Although the tour begins to your left upon entering, peek up at the dome in the Oval Room ahead and then out to the seemingly infinite space of the gardens.

For a detailed and brilliantly colored souvenir, buy the glossy guide in the gift shop (30F, available in English or French). Notice the ornate scripted *F*s all around the château, and keep an eye out for the ever-present squirrel, Fouquet's industrious symbol, and for the tower with three battlements, his second wife's crest. The **Minister's Bedchamber** may lead you to wonder who the real monarch was in this kingdom. The opulent red and gold bed stands under an allegorical ceiling in which Apollo bears the lights of the world. (One begins to understand why Fouquet was arrested.) **Mme. Fouquet's Closet** once had walls lined with small mirrors, the decorative forerunner of Versailles's Hall of Mirrors. In the **Square Room,** Le Brun's portrait of Fouquet hangs over the fireplace—Fouquet would seem a humble man, except for his penetrating gaze. Divert your own gaze from the beautiful 1877 billiard table long enough to admire the exquisite beams of the Louis XIII-style ceiling. The vivid colors and engaging expressions of the nine muses in the **Room of the Muses** make this one of Le Brun's finest decorative schemes. Le Brun had planned to crown the **Oval Room** (or Grand Salon) with a fresco entitled *The Palace of the Sun,* but Fouquet's arrest halted all activity. The tapestries once bore Fouquet's squirrel, but Colbert seized them and replaced the rodents with his own adders. The ornate **King's Bedchamber** boasts an orgy of cherubs and lions fluttering around the centerpiece of *Time Bearing Truth Heavenward.*

THE GARDENS

Vaux-le-Vicomte presented André Le Nôtre with his first opportunity to create an entire formal garden. Three villages (including Vaux), a small château, and many trees were destroyed to open up the required space, though countless trees were later replanted to draw the contrast between order and wilderness. Even a river was rerouted to provide the desired effect. With Vaux, Le Nôtre gave birth to a truly French style of garden—shrubs were trimmed, lawns shaved, bushes sculpted, and pools strategically placed to create a blend of classical harmony and optical illusion.

The impressive panorama is best viewed from the steps behind the château. From this angle, the garden seems perfectly symmetrical and the grottoes appear to be directly behind the large pool of water. Closer inspection reveals otherwise. The right-hand *parterre* was a flowerbed in its original incarnation, but today is dominated by a statue of Diana. Its matching green area on the left side is actually wider and sunken. The **Pool of the Crown,** named for the gold crown at its center, is the most ornate of the garden pools. The **Round Pool** and its surrounding 17th-century statues mark an important intersection; to the left, down the east walkway, are the

Water Gates, likely backdrop for Molière's performance of *The Annoyances* before Louis XIV. The **Water Mirror,** farther down the central walkway, was designed to reflect the château perfectly, but you may have some trouble positioning yourself to enjoy the effect. The Mirror also hides the sunken canal, known as **La Poêle** (the Frying Pan), fed by the Anqueuil River. The canal is a reminder that Fouquet made his fortune in shipping. Climb to a 19th-century addition to the gardens, the **Farnese Hercules** (the vanishing point when you look out from the castle), and survey the land and imposing château. The old stables today house a fantastic carriage museum, **Les Equipages.** Magnificent carriages of all kinds come complete with piped-in music, dressed-up party-goers, and liveried footmen. Picnicking is prohibited, but the cafeteria-style restaurant **L'Ecureuil** (the squirrel) on the castle grounds provides salads (26-40F) and cooked dishes (54-58F). (Open Mon.-Fri. and Sun. 11:30am-6:30pm, Sat. 11:30am-6pm and 7:30-11:30pm; MC, V, AmEx.)

Vaux is exquisite; getting there is exquisite torture (if you are short on funds), which may explain the absence of crowds. Your best and cheapest option, if traveling in a group, is to rent a car; the castle is 60km out of Paris. Take Autoroute A4 or A6 from Paris and exit at Val-Maubué or Melun, respectively. Head toward Meaux on N36 and follow the signs. Or take the RER to Melun from Châtelet les Halles or Gare du Nord (45min., 80F round-trip). Unfortunately, the station is a smug 6km from the château. You can take a bike on the train free of charge, but riding on the undivided highway without a shoulder next to big trucks is not advisable. It is worth it to splurge and take a taxi. The 6km ride will cost you around 75F each way, Sundays 100F (pick one up at the train station; call 01 64 52 51 50 from Vaux). Fit troopers might not mind the 70- to 90-minute hike for at least one part of the trip, but should be prepared to jump off the highway and into the grass at any minute. The effort may pay off most handsomely on Saturday evenings from May to mid-October (8:30-11pm), when the candle-lit château may remind you of a wedding cake. The fountains in Le Nôtre's gardens are turned on from 3 to 6pm every second and last Saturday of the month from April to October. The **tourist office,** 2, av. Gallieni (tel. 01 64 37 11 31), by the train station in Melun, can help you with accommodations and sight-seeing opportunities, and give you a free map—useful to those planning to walk (open Tues.-Sat. 10am-noon and 2-6pm). If the tourist office is closed, do not fear. While the highway is perilous, the directions are relatively simple: just follow av. de Thiers through its many name-changes to highway 36 (direction: "Meaux") and follow signs to Vaux-Le-Vicomte.

Château open April-Oct. Mon.-Sat. 10am-1pm and 2-6pm, Sun. and holidays 10am-6pm; last entry 5:30pm daily. Visits by appointment the rest of the year; call for more information. Gardens open daily 10am-7pm (last entry 5:30pm); *équipages* open daily 10am-6pm. Admission to château and gardens 56F, students, seniors, and ages 6-16 46F, under 6 free; admission to gardens 30F, students, seniors, and ages 6-16 24F, under 6 free. Estate open May to mid-Oct. Sat. 8:30-11pm for candle-lit evenings. Admission 75F, students, seniors, and under 16 65F.

■ Chantilly

Chantilly says a lot about unreality. The faux-Renaissance castle, built in the late 19th century, looms above a carefully-tended "natural" landscape, while a play village recalls the idealized view of peasant life depicted by a medieval artist. The whole scene testifies to an aristocracy a bit removed from the real world. Fittingly, during World War I, French commander-in-chief Général Joffre established his headquarters here, whence he plotted grand strategy in blithe ignorance of the magnitude of the slaughter taking place on the front.

Set in the magnificent gardens Le Nôtre sculpted from the surrounding forest, the **Château de Chantilly** drapes elegantly over its serene gardens, lakes, and canals. A Roman citizen named Cantilius built his villa here, leaving his name and a tradition of high property values. A succession of medieval lords constructed elaborate fortifications, but the château did not come into its own until the Grand Condé, cousin of

Louis XIV, brought Le Nôtre to create the gardens and eventually commissioned the Grand Château. His château was razed during the Revolution; the present building is a reproduction built in the 1870s by then-owner, the Duc d'Aumale, fifth son of Louis-Philippe. As you approach, the dramatic Renaissance façade, lush greenery, and extravagant entrance hall whet your appetite for something truly remarkable.

Inside, the château houses the **Musée Condé** (tel. 03 44 57 08 00), crowded with the duke's private collection of elegant furniture and dusty paintings. For the castle's most sumptuous experience, head to the wood-paneled library, which displays medieval miniatures, a Gutenberg Bible, and a facsimile of the museum's most famous possession, the **Très Riches Heures du Duc de Berry,** a 15th-century manuscript showing the French peasantry and aristocracy engaged in the labors of the different months. The **Salle de Gardes** displays two Van Dyck paintings, along with a Roman mosaic of *The Rape of Europa* that used to hang over the Duc d'Aumale's mantel. The galleries contain paintings by Raphael, Titian, Poussin, Gros, Corot, Delacroix, and Ingres—an impressive collection, but so crowded that it's hard to appreciate the individual works. For the dedicated connoisseur, the 39F (24F reduced rate) admission fee is well worth it just to see the collection of chairs from **Marie-Antoinette's** dressing room in Versailles.

Even if you skip the museum, consider taking a 17F wander through the **gardens,** the château's main attraction. For another 6F you can buy a map of the gardens with a suggested walking tour; wandering, however, will let you make your own delightfully aimless discoveries. Directly in front of the château, the central expanse is in typical French formal style, with neat rows of carefully pruned trees and calm statues overlooking geometric pools. To the right, hidden within a forest, the rambling English garden attempts to recreate untamed nature, rendered more picturesque by its human element. Here, paths meander around pools where lone swans float; windows carved into the foliage allow you to see fountains in the formal garden as you stroll. The gardens also hide a play village, the inspiration for Marie-Antoinette's infamous hamlet at Versailles. Elsewhere, a statue of Cupid reigns over the "Island of Love." If you want to see the chateau, grounds, and surroundings all at once, you can take a 10-minute hot air balloon ride. Located on the park grounds, the balloon (attached, alas, to the ground by a cable) rises 150m, providing a view as far as the Eiffel Tower in clear weather. (Château open March-Oct. Wed.-Mon. 10am-6pm; Nov.-Feb. Wed.-Mon. 10:30am-12:45pm and 2-5pm. Admission to the château and park 39F, reduced 24F; to park alone 17F, ages 3-11 10F. Balloon rides 45F, children under 12 25F; tel. 01 44 57 35 55 for more info.)

The approach to the castle passes the **Grandes Ecuries,** immense stables that housed 240 horses and hundreds of hunting dogs from 1719 until the Revolution. The stables were originally ordained by Louis-Henri Bourbon, who hoped to live in them when reincarnated as a horse. These stables now house the **Musée Vivant du Cheval** (tel. 01 44 57 13 13 or 01 44 57 40 40), a huge museum dealing with all things equine: on display are saddles, horseshoes, merry-go-rounds, and horse postcards and sculptures. The horses themselves are here only for your viewing pleasure—no touching, no riding. The museum also puts on magnificent horse-training demonstrations (in French), a must-see for all horse lovers. (Museum open April-Oct. Mon. and Wed.-Fri. 10:30am-6:30pm, Sat.-Sun. 10:30am-7pm; May-June also Tues. 10:30am-5:30pm; July-Aug. also Tues. 2-5:30pm; Nov.-March Mon. and Wed.-Fri. 2-4:30pm, Sat.-Sun. 10:30am-5:30pm. Horse shows when museum open May-June 11:30am, 3:30, and 5:15pm; July-Aug. 3:30 and 5:15pm; Nov.-March Mon. and Wed.-Fri. 3:30pm, Sat.-Sun. 11:30am, 3:30, and 5:15pm. Admission to museum and show 50F, students and seniors 40F. Special show Sun. 4pm. Admission 1-4:30pm 80F.) Two of France's premier horse races are held here in June—the **Prix de Diane** and the **Prix du Jockey Club. Polo at the Hippodrome,** in mid-September, is free to the public (matches at 11am, 12:30, 2, 3:15, and 4:30pm).

The **tourist office** is stabled at 23, av. du Mal Joffre (tel. 01 44 57 08 58; open Mon. and Wed.-Sat. 9am-12:30pm and 2:15-5:30pm, Sun. 10am-2pm. April-Sept., also open Tues. 10am-noon). **Trains** run to Chantilly from Paris's Gare du Nord (35min., 80F round-trip). Call ahead for the schedule. To reach the château from the station, either take the arduous walk down rue des Otages, turn left on av. de Marechal Joffre (the tourist office is about a block or two down on the right), then turn right on rue du Connetable, the town's main street (2km) or take a taxi (40F).

NEAR CHANTILLY: SENLIS

Tiny **Senlis,** a 10-minute bus ride from Chantilly, basks in the glory of being officially the quaintest and best-preserved village in the Ile-de-France. Its cobblestone streets, friendly residents, and intimate atmosphere are the closest you'll get to storybook France. The **Cathédrale de Notre-Dame,** begun in 1191, is a prime example of early Gothic architecture. Its Grand Portal influenced the designs of Chartres and Notre-Dame in Paris. Across the *place* from Notre-Dame, the **Eglise St-Frambourg,** founded around 900 by the merciful Queen Adélaïde, also deserves a quick look. Reconstructed in 1177 by Louis VII and ransacked during the Revolution, this beauty found its most recent savior in the great pianist György Cziffra, who restored the church as an international music center, now called the Fondation Cziffra. Enter the park next to the tourist office to reach the **Château Royal,** a hunting lodge for monarchs from Charlemagne to Henri IV, now converted to a hunting museum (open April-Sept. Thurs.-Mon. 10am-noon and 2-6pm, Wed. 2-6pm; admission 20F, reduced 15F). The remains of **Gallo-Roman fortifications,** with 31 towers, surround the town. The old town is a network of medieval alleyways winding up and down cobblestone hills between several of the original gates. Senlis's **tourist office,** pl. du Parvis Notre-Dame (tel. 01 44 53 06 40), has information on concerts and exhibitions (open Tues.-Sun. 10am-noon and 2:15-6:15pm). SNCF buses meet most trains from Paris to Chantilly for the 10-minute ride to Senlis; you can find a schedule and catch them at the Gare Routière, just to the left as you exit the Chantilly train station (14F one-way; railpasses valid).

■ Châteaux de Malmaison and Bois-Preau

Choose a sunny day to visit the **Château de Malmaison,** 1, av. du Château de Malmaison (tel. 01 41 29 05 55), for a trip backstage to the Napoleon and Josephine affair. Bought with borrowed funds in 1799 on the eve of Napoleon's rise to power, the château served as a love nest for the newlyweds, as a conference hall during the Consulate (1801-02), and then as Josephine's own Elba after their marriage was annulled in 1809. It is unknown why the house is called "Mal-maison" or "bad/sick house." The original building was constructed in 1622, upon the order of the Counselor to the Parliament of Paris. It was enlarged in 1690 and again in 1770, when the grounds were landscaped as well. Bonaparte had Fontaine and Percier modernize the château, at which time the veranda (in the shape of a military tent) was added, and the interior renovated.

Malmaison is a mélange of his and hers; the restored Empire interiors mix *trompe l'oeil* marble and sarcophagus-inspired armchairs with a smattering of Romantic landscape paintings, many of the château itself. Private and public apartments feature paintings of the emperor by David, Greuze, Gros, and others. Josephine furnished them in the height of the Empire style: chairs with Egyptian motifs; square tables; short, tentlike beds. The decor may hark back to Napoleon's era, but the house itself is all Josephine. The museum overflows with Empress memorabilia: her jewels, her shoes, her colossal dress bills, her harp, and her perfumes are displayed upstairs. She preferred the modestly sized, sunny bedroom to the lavish one she had for show (and in which she died). At one corner of the house, its two walls of windows look out on her treasured gardens.

Left by Napoleon for the Empress Eugenie after she failed to produce an heir, Josephine lived out her remaining years here, cultivating the grounds of Malmaison in plush seclusion. A devotee of the natural sciences, she consulted botanists worldwide about her gardens and collected exotic animals; camels, zebras, and kangaroos once walked these grounds. Josephine, née Rose—she changed her name to please her husband—devoted much attention to the rose gardens which now surround the château. The **Roseraie Ancienne,** to the left as you enter the château, is a sharp contrast to the Mondrian/Rubic's cube surfaces of the Tuileries. These English gardens are as much worth the trip as Malmaison itself, especially in May and June, when hundreds of varieties of roses bloom on vine and bush. Pierre-Joseph Redouté's roses were painted from the flowers in Josephine's gardens, and some of his drawings are now in the museum's collection. These grounds also hold a memorial to Eugène-Louis-Jean-Joseph Bonaparte, the Prince Imperial, son of Napoleon III.

Those unfamiliar with Napoleon's empire should visit the **Château de Bois-Preau.** Walk across the parking lot and on through the sizeable park up the path from Malmaison. It contains a museum-*cum*-shrine to the emperor. The ground floor summarizes Napoleon's life and then traces the changing images of Napoleon since his death. There are several copies of his death mask here, as well as a funny collection of Russian toys created for the centennial anniversary of Napoleon's failed attempt to take Moscow. The second floor is devoted to Napoleon's final days on St-Helena. Filled with models and sketches of the house, grounds, and his death-chamber, it also displays selected articles of his clothing (boxer shorts, footsy pajamas), and from his toilette. Here is a glimpse into the private life of Napoleon that we never learned about in school, following him off the battlefield and into the boudoir. Curators appear to have emptied the contents of his overnight bag; view his toothbrush, tweezers, and the handkerchief he carried at Toulon, behind glass. The adjoining park of Bois-Preau is one of the few in the Paris area where you can walk on the grass. Take the time to picnic, play frisbee, or walk through the woods. (Château de Malmaison open Mon. and Wed.- Fri. 10am-noon and 1:30-5:45pm; ticket office closes at noon, and at 5pm. Sat.-Sun. 10am-6:30pm; ticket office closes at 5:30pm. Holidays 10am-12:30pm and 1:30-6:30pm. Ticket office closes at 5:30pm. Free guided visit every 20min. on weekends, reserve a spot upon entering the château. Tours are also offered weekdays at 11am and 3pm (occasionally in English). Château de Bois-Preau open Thurs.-Sun. 12:30-6:30pm; ticket office closes ½hr. before château. Both châteaux close 30min. earlier Oct.-March. Admission to both châteaux 28F; students, seniors, and Sun. 18F, under 18 free. Bois-Preau park open May-Sept. Wed.-Mon. 10am-8pm; Oct.-March Wed.-Mon. 9:30am-6pm; April 10am-7pm; free.)

To get there, do not take the bus or metro to Rueil-Malmaison, which is very far from the museum. Instead take the RER or metro to the Grande Arche de la Défense and then take exit A to change to bus #258 (7F). The RER stop is in zone 3 while the metro stop is in zone 2, so you need an extra ticket if you take the RER. The bus stop "Bois-Preau" goes to Bois-Preau; the stop "Château" takes you to Malmaison.

Housed in one of the most popular *guinguettes* (open-air cafés and dance-halls), the **Musée de la Maison Fournaise,** Ile des Impressionnistes, Chatou (tel. 01 34 80 63 22), is dedicated to documenting the era when Parisians and artists alike flocked to dance and dally by the riverside. While the museum's collection includes few originals among its bewildering display of prints, etchings, and paintings, you can still glimpse the porch where Renoir painted *Le déjeuner des canotiers (The Luncheon of the Boating Party)* in 1881 as well as traces of other favorite haunts and subjects of Monet, Degas, Guy de Maupassant, and later Nadar. (Open Wed.-Fri. 11am-5pm, Sat.-Sun. 11am-6pm; 25F, students and seniors 15F, under 13 free.) From M. Grande Arche de la Défense take the RER A1 to Rueile Malmaison (round-trip 16F). From the station follow route N190 in the direction of Chaton and turn right down the off-ramp for the Ile des Impressionnistes. Next door, the **Centre National de la Gravure Contemporaine** (National Center for Contemporary Prints; tel. 01 39 52 45 35) and its small exhibitions drawn from the center's archives inhabit the small space where Maurice de Vlaminck and André Derain prepared their part in the artistic revolution that accompanied the presentation of the Fauves at the Salon of 1905 (same hours and prices as the Maison Fournaise).

■ St-Germain-en-Laye

St-Germain-en-Laye is a wealthy Parisian suburb masquerading as a large provincial town. A day in St-Germain is a relaxing break from the intensity of Paris: people are friendlier, life is slower, and the air is cleaner. The winding streets of the town center are packed with restaurants, cafés, and stores with meticulously crafted displays. Louis VI built the first castle in St-Germain-en-Laye, in the 12th century, near the site on which his ancestor Robert the Pious had constructed a monastery dedicated to St-Germain. Louis' donjon still exists, but the castle was rebuilt by Charles V after its destruction during the Hundred Years War. It took on its present appearance in 1548 under François I. Lover of all things Italian, François I ordered his architects Chabiges and Delormé to construct a Renaissance palace—the current *château vieux*—on the foundations of the old church and castle. (The castle's mix of brick and stone is typical of the Renaissance.) Henri II added the *château neuf,* Louis XIV made it his home (1622-82), and in 1638, his son, the future Louis XV, was born there. An impressive list of names graced these two châteaux—among them Colbert, Mme. de Sévigné, Rousseau, Molière, and Lully (the last two wrote and composed for festivals at the châteaux). James II of England died here in exile in 1701, kicking off a lousy 18th century for the estate. The *château neuf* was torn down; during the Revolution, the Empire, and the July Monarchy, St-Germain was alternately used as a prison, a cavalry school, and a military prison. It was here that the Austro-Hungarian Empire was formally dismantled in 1919, and in 1955, Moroccan independence became fact.

Napoleon III decided to make the castle into a museum of antiquity. Today, the **Musée des Antiquités Nationals** (tel. 01 34 51 53 65) claims to have the richest collection of its kind in the world. At first, the display looks a bit like someone's pet rock collection, but the work gets more sophisticated as you move through the eras (100,000 BC to the 8th century AD), and by the time you plow through to the Iron Age, you can believe these relics were made by the ancestors of the French artists we know and love. The collection's highlight may be its ancient tombs complete with dirt, bones, and burial loot. The explanations, when there are any, are easy to follow only if you read French (the museum has no English explanations or brochures). Call in advance for a schedule of guided tours. (Open Wed.-Mon. 9am-5:15pm. Admission 23F, students, seniors, and Sun. 16F, under 18 free.) If used tools aren't your thing, wander along the **garden terrace** (open daily 8am-10pm), designed by the omnipresent Le Nôtre. His gardens were destroyed along with the *château neuf* at the end of the 18th century, but the terrace survived. While lacking the extraordinary orchestration of Versailles, the gardens and nearby forest make for an energizing stroll or jog, and there is a panoramic view of western Paris and its *banlieue.* Numerous cafés with lounge chairs scattered throughout the park encourage you to sunbathe or read, and lots of shady spots beckon you to lie down and take a nap. A map of forest trails is available from the tourist office.

Across from the château stands the **Eglise St-Germain,** consecrated in 1827 on the site of the 11th-century priory that gave St-Germain its name. Modern white pillars and piped-in religious music give the church a Southern evangelical feel. A 14th-century stone statue of **Notre-Dame-de-Bon-Retour** (Our Lady of the Safe Return) is one of the most venerated images in St-Germain; it was found buried deep underground when they dug the foundations for the church in 1775. James II's tomb is in the back of the church. (Church open daily 8:30am-noon and 2-7pm. Services Sun. 7:30, 9:30, 11:15am, and 6:30pm; weekdays 7:15pm; Sat. 6:30pm.)

Spend some time at the two-room museum of the **Maison Claude Debussy,** 38 rue au Pain (tel. 01 34 51 05 12), the Impressionist composer's birthplace. An autographed copy of *Prélude à l'après-midi d'un faune* and a revealing questionnaire he completed for a young girl—he called Hamlet his hero in fiction—are among the eclectic array of documents and pictures about the man who said, "I want to dare to be myself and to suffer for my truth." To reach the museum, follow rue de la Salle (just left of Eglise St-Germain as you face it) to rue au Pain and turn left. (Open Tues.-Sat. 2-6pm. Free.)

The **Musée Départemental Maurice Denis le Prieuré,** 2bis, rue Maurcie-Denis (tel. 01 39 73 77 87), is dedicated to the works of this painter (1870-1943), the Symbolists, and the Nabis. Built in 1678 for the Marquise de Montespand and used as an almshouse, a hospital, and then a retirement home for Jesuits, *Le Prieuré* (The Priory) was purchased by Denis in 1914. He decorated the chapel with his interpretation of the Beatitudes. Today, one can visit his house and workshop and see works by such artists as Vuillard, Bonnard, and Moret who, like Denis, received Gauguin's challenge to "risk everything." (Open Wed.-Fri. 10am-5:30pm, Sat.-Sun. and holidays 10am-6:30pm. Admission 25F, students 15F, children under 12 free.) Linger in the peaceful garden among winding paths and roses.

A number of spots in town offer fine eating options. **Auberge le Grison,** 28, rue au Pain (tel. 01 39 73 01 00), offers *specialités savoyardes.* This intimate restaurant offers an interesting summer menu: many little portions of different foods in glass bowls served in a basket. *Menu* includes appetizer, main dish, dessert, wine, and cider or coffee (68F). (Open Tues.-Sun. noon-2:30 and 7pm-10:30pm.) Show your *Let's Go* guide for a *kir savoyard* on the house. The **Office Municipal de Tourisme,** Maison Claude Debussy, 38, rue au Pain (tel. 01 34 51 05 12), provides lists of restaurants and hotels, a free detailed map, and information about the town in English (open Tues.-Fri. 9:15am-12:30pm and 2-6:30pm, Sat. 9:15am-6:30pm; March-Oct. also open Sun. 10am-1pm). St-Germain is 20 minutes from metro stop Charles-de-Gaulle-Etoile by RER Line A1 (12F50 there, 16F50 back).

Churches & Cathedrals

The word "cathedral" literally means the "place of the *cathedra,*" which is the archbishop or cardinal's seat (roughly equivalent in symbolic weight to a throne). A cathedral serves as the mother church for an archdiocese, a geographical county within the Roman Catholic Church. Cathedrals, like most churches from the Middle Ages, are most often built in the form of a cross that is rounded at one end, as shown in the composite sketch above. Most are positioned so that you face east—towards Jerusalem—as you enter the main doorway. If the church is still functioning as a place of worship, you probably won't be allowed into the choir area; however, the ambulatory is usually open to the public. Chapels devoted to specific saints and marked as prayer areas are blocked off to tourists. Aside from these basic similarities, cathedrals can be as architecturally diverse as museums and palaces; much of France's history is written in their walls. Some, like Notre-Dame, feature elegant and massive flying buttresses, others boast tall bell-towers or multiple ambulatories wrapping around each other like a rainbow. Still others, like St-Denis, serve as the burial ground for royalty, saints, and other well-known national figures.

Saint-Denis

The home of the famed **Basilique de St-Denis,** the burial place of France's kings and queens, this town is named after the missionary bishop Denis. According to legend, Denis was beheaded by the Romans in Montmartre in AD 250 and walked north carrying his head until he reached the town and was buried here in a plowed field. In 475, a small church was built here to mark St. Denis' grave. This church became a popular destination for religious pilgrimages until King Pepin destroyed it to make way for a larger one, perhaps because he wanted to be buried there—and he was, in 768. Today, St-Denis (M. St-Denis-Basilique) is a working-class town with a large, lively population of West and North African immigrants.

Since 768, the **Basilica,** 2, rue de Strasbourg (tel. 01 48 09 83 54), has been home to the remains of almost all of the kings and queens of France, whose funerary monuments form a progression from medieval simplicity to Renaissance extravagance. Its delicate 12th-century ambulatory is also the first example of Gothic architecture in all of Europe. By the end of the 10th century, the church had become the official necropolis of French royalty.

In 1136, Abbot Suger began rebuilding the basilica in a revolutionary style tha would open its hallowed area to the "light of the divine." Suger was dissatisfied witl dark and heavy Romanesque interiors, with their small windows and forests of thic columns. Instead, he brought together known architectural elements to create a unprecedented openness in the nave. In the final Gothic creation, function melde with aesthetic form—the vaulted arches of the nave, essential to the cathedral's effec of verticality and weightlessness, funnel the weight of the roof into a few points, sup ported with long, narrow columns inside and flying buttresses outside. Freed fror the burden of supporting the roof, the walls gave way to the huge stained-glass wi dows that became the style's trademark, and even disappeared completely in som places. The chapels around the first ambulatory have no walls between them, crea ing a second ambulatory that gracefully encircles the first.

The grandiose stained-glass windows and human-dwarfing nave are breathtakin especially when the afternoon sun casts a rainbow of light over the tombs of France' ancient rulers. However awe-inspiring this height and spaciousness, there is noneth less a heaviness about the pillars that marks the construction as early Gothic. Th flamboyance would come soon, though. Suger's contemporaries were flabbergaste and quickly worked to outdo him with their own cathedrals, building ever more intr cate interiors, larger stained-glass windows, loftier vaults, and higher towers—th Gothic age was ignited.

Suger himself died in 1151, well before most of his basilica had been rebuilt. Hi successors altered his plans, but did not stray from his Gothic pattern. They create an unusually wide transept, complete with magnificent rose windows. The extr space was needed to accommodate the ever-growing number of dead monarchs. I 1593, underneath the newly spacious nave, Henri IV converted to Catholicism wit his famous statement: *"Paris vaut bien une messe"* (Paris is well worth a mass). I 1610, he was buried here with the rest of France's Catholic monarchs.

As both the necropolis of nobility and the keeper of the *Oriflamme* (the royal ba ner which symbolized dominance of the realm), St-Denis became a prime target fo the wrath of the Revolution. Most of the tombs were desecrated or destroyed, an the remains of the Bourbon family were thrown into a ditch. With the restoration c the monarchy in 1815, Louis XVIII ordered that the necropolis be reestablished, an Louis XVI and Marie-Antoinette were buried here with great pomp in 1819. Th remains of the other Bourbons were dug out of their ditch and placed in an ossuar inside the crypt. Tombs that had survived the Revolution were returned from th National Museum of Monuments, where they had been on display. Louis XVIII als added funerary monuments once located within churches that had been complete demolished by Revolutionary marauders.

Not content with defiling the bodies of former rulers, Revolutionaries had wreake further destruction, smashing the church's famous stained glass, which had served a models for many of the windows at Chartres. Virtually all of St-Denis's original wi dows have been replaced, most during the 19th century when the church wa restored, but in the front of the ambulatory you can still find some of the origina 12th-century windows. Look closely and you can discern something other than bib cal tales: the Abbot Suger ensured his immortality by having pictures of himself— small monk piously praying—put into the windows, "signing" each self-portrait t make certain he was recognized. Don't miss the room on the left side of the churc that contains the funerary garments of the royal family. (Church open April-Sept. dai 10am-7pm; Oct.-March 10am-5pm. Admission 25F, seniors and students 20F, unde 18 10F. Ticket booth closes ½hr. before the church. Guided tours in French daily a 3, 3:45, and 4:30pm. Ask about free organ concerts on Sundays.)

For a bite to eat try one of the reasonably priced restaurants that cluster around th park in front of the church or any of the numerous sandwich shops or tea room along rue Gabriel Péri between rue de la République and pl. de la Résistance. There i also a large, enclosed market between rue Auguste-Blanqui and rue Jules-Joffrin teen ing with produce, meats, cheese, and real live locals (open Tues.-Fri. and Sun. 9an

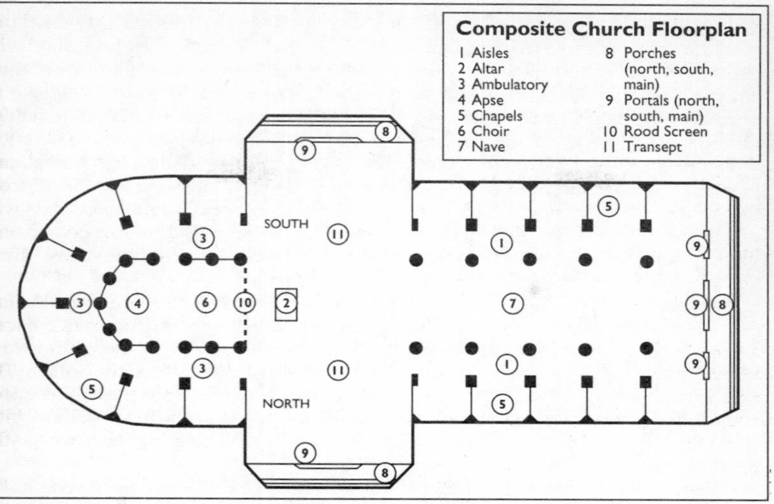

:pm). To reach it, walk straight out the front door of the cathedral, take a right at pl. ean Jaurès, and continue one block up rue Pierre Dupont.

The helpful **tourist office,** at 1, rue de la République (tel. 01 42 43 33 55), has lots of information on the cathedral and the town of St-Denis, including maps, suggested walks, and restaurant guides (open Mon.-Sat. 9:30am-12:30pm and 2-6:30pm, Sun. 0am-12:30pm and 2-6:30pm). The tourist office also provides information on the museums of St-Denis and the **Festival de St-Denis** (tel. 01 48 13 06 07), which brings world-class orchestras and musicians, such as Barbara Hendricks and conductor Charles Dutoit and the Orchestre National de France, to the basilica every June.

From the church, walk down rue de la Légion d'Honneur, turn right on rue Franciade, and then left on rue Gabriel Péri to reach the **Musée d'art et d'histoire,** 22bis, ue Bariel Péri (tel. 01 42 30 05 10). The recipient of the *Prix Européen du Musée* in 983 soon after its opening, the museum is housed in a former Carmelite convent dating back to 1625. In addition to exhibits on the local 18th-century Hôtel-Dieu and daily life in St-Denis during the Middle Ages, the museum chronicles the convent's history and that of its most famous resident, Madame Louise, beloved daughter of Louis XV, who spent most of her life here in quiet devotion. The top floor contains an bsorbing display of satirical cartoons, political declarations, drawings, and paintings. The works of Girardet and Manet trace the history of the Paris Commune of 1791 from Napoleon III's declaration of war with Prussia to the war waged by government troops against the 72-day insurrection, the inspiration for Victor Hugo's *Les Misérables.* The museum also contains works by the second-generation Impressionist painter and friend of Renoir, Albert André, as well as a collection of writings, photographs, and drawings by and about Surrealist poet Paul Éluard, who was born in St-Denis in 1895 with the unlikely name of Eugène Grindel. Call ahead for info regarding the special exhibit on Surrealist artist and writer Max Ernst planned for February-May 997. (Museum open Mon. and Wed.-Sat. 10am-5:30pm, Sun. 2-6:30pm. 20F, students and seniors 10F, under 16 free.)

■ Chartres

THE CATHEDRAL

The **Cathédrale de Chartres** survives today as one of the most sublime creations of the Middle Ages, a patchwork constructed by generations of devoted masons, architects, and artisans. The existing structure is the fifth to occupy this site—three diffe ent churches stood here before the year 1000. In 876, Charlemagne's grandsor Charles the Bald, made a gift to Chartres of the *Sancta Camisia,* the cloth believed t have been worn by Mary when she gave birth to Christ. Pilgrims have been flockin to the cathedral ever since to see the sacred relic and benefit from its supernatur powers. Its magic was confirmed for the citizens of St-Chartres in AD 911, whe under attack from Vikings, they placed the relic on view at the top of the city wal The infidels ran away; their leader Rollin converted to Christianity and became th first duke of Normandy.

The cathedral became one of the continent's foremost centers of learning, led b the brilliant Fulbert who arrived in 990 and supervised the building of the fourt church, a fine Romanesque cathedral. Disaster struck in 1194, when the third fire i 200 years burned all but the crypts, the west tower, and the Royal Portal. When the discovered that Mary's relic (hidden in the crypt by three loyal priests who staye with it, sweating out the fire) had emerged unsinged, the villagers took it as a sign c not only Mary's love but also her desire for a more worthy cathedral. Clerics too advantage of the miracle to solicit funds on a grand scale, and construction pr ceeded at a furious pace: most of the cathedral was completed by 1223 and cons crated in 1260—allowing an unusual unity of style. Chartres's stained-glass window soon gained fame for their clarity and beauty, as did the sculptures adorning each c the main portals. Since then, in a series of miracles as great as the survival of th *Sancta Camisia* in 1194, the Cathédrale de Chartres has emerged intact from Prote tant iconoclasm, the clergy's decision to "modernize" in the 18th century, the Rev lution's attempt to turn it into a Temple of Reason, and two World Wars.

Few cathedrals rival Chartres in size and majesty. A masterpiece of finely crafte detail, the cathedral will appeal to the aesthete in anyone. While the cathedr remains a showcase for the massive, the tall, and the glorious, its minute detail i equally worthy of attention. At the time it was built, Chartres served as a stage for cu ting-edge contemporary artisanry. Sculpture and stained glass here tell the story c Christ, set in medieval castles and lordly dress; remote to the modern visitor, this i roughly like depicting Jesus walking around in the Centre Pompidou. Visitors durin the 13th century might have recognized themselves in the slouching figure of slot or the tunicked and tempted St. Anthony.

An extraordinary fusion of Romanesque and Gothic architectural elements, th Cathedral was built in a record-breaking 29 years (compared to 163 years for Notr Dame de Paris). The famous twin-steepled silhouette is visible from miles around, ri ing above the flat wheat fields that surround it. The flying buttresses, connected t the vaulting inside, fulfill both a functional and aesthetic role: they take the weight c the roof away from the walls and provide an elegant outside expression of the cath dral's interior structure. Towering over the surrounding town, the cathedral is a pow erful embodiment of a time when the Church controlled every aspect of daily lif and the tallest buildings in existence were its cathedrals.

The exterior of the church is marked by three entrances. The famous 12th-centu statues of the Royal Portal present an assembly of Old Testament figures at the heig of late Romanesque sculpture. Those in the central bay, attributed to the "Master c Chartres," are especially beautiful: their elongated, simple figures have an unpara leled elegance. The 13th-century North and South Porches, representing the life c Mary and Christ triumphant, respectively, are highly expressive examples of Goth sculpture. On the North Porch, John the Baptist sadly examines the disc in his hand decorated with a lamb and cross, it symbolically predicts the coming of Christ an the imminence of John's own death. The left bay tells the story of the Visitation an shows Mary and Elizabeth turning to greet each other, like two nuns chatting pr vately in their convent's cloister. Inside the church, the life of Mary is further elab rated in the beautiful Renaissance choir screen, begun by Jehan de Beauce in 151 and finished in the 18th century; it depicts Mary's story from birth, through the life c Christ, to death and ascension.

Most of the stained glass dates from the 13th century and was preserved through both World Wars by heroic town authorities, who dismantled over 2000 square meters and stored the windows piece by piece until the end of hostilities. The origi-ıal merchant sponsors of each window are shown in the lower panels, providing a valuable record of daily life during the 13th century. The famous "Blue Virgin" win-dow, an object of pilgrimage and one of the few pieces of 12th-century glass to sur-vive the fire, is visible at the first window of the choir, on the right. The window has four panels with a large picture of the Virgin Mary dressed in blue (hence its name), cradling Christ on her lap; the other panes of glass were 13th-century additions. The façade holds the rest of the 12th-century glass: on the right is the tree of Jesse and on the left is the Passion and Resurrection of Christ. The center window is the Incarna-tion, which shows the life of Christ from the Annunciation to the ride into Jerusalem. Mary is given the place of honor at the top of the window, flanked by kneeling angels. Bring binoculars if you can (or rent them for 10F per hour plus the deposit of a form of ID or 300F at *La Crypte,* the same place which offers crypt tours; see below); many of the stories told by the stained glass are barely visible with the naked eye.

If it's stories you're seeking, world-renowned tour guide Malcolm Miller, an author-ity on Gothic architecture, has brought the cathedral to life for English-speaking visi-tors for the past 40 years. Miller knows everything about the religion and daily routines that the windows depict, and composes each tour individually to explain the cathedral's history and symbolism. His presentation is intelligent, witty, and enjoy-able for all ages—the only possible gripe is that one can't absorb his rapid-fire vol-umes of information quickly enough. Consider taking notes to help you when you're on your own in the cathedral. He provides countless details about the church; on any given day, he might discuss the labyrinth on the floor, which provided a path for the penitent pilgrim to follow on hands and knees, or the slope of the floor, which per-mitted the cathedral to be washed—particularly necessary because of pilgrims bil-leted on its floor every night. If you can, take both his morning and afternoon tours. They're worth it, and Miller is careful to discuss different aspects of the cathedral depending on how many repeat visitors he has and what days (or years) they last took his tours. Indeed, no two of his visits are alike, and all are fascinating. You may want to invest in a 40F guide as well, available at the shop within the cathedral. (1¼hr. tours April-Jan. Mon.-Sat. noon and 2:45pm. The rest of the year, Miller lectures around the globe. 30F, students 20F. Avoid Sat. and Tues.—busy days in the high sea-son. Private tours on request: tel. 01 37 28 15 58; fax 01 37 28 33 03. Tours also offered in German, Spanish, Italian, and French; check inside the cathedral for more info, or call Accueil Visites Cathédrale at 01 37 21 75 02.)

No present-day visit to Chartres would be complete without a visit to the object that drew millions of people here in the Middle Ages. The sacred cloth is on display at the east end, to the left of the cathedral's **treasury,** where other significant gar-ments and objects from the building's history are preserved. (Open March 16-Oct. 15 Mon.-Sat. 10am-noon and 2-6pm, Sun. and holidays 2-6pm; Oct. 16-March 15 Mon.-Sat. 10am-noon and 2:30-4:30pm, Sun. and holidays 2-5pm. Free.) The adventurous can climb the cathedral towers for a stellar view of the cathedral roof, the flying but-tresses, and the city below. Begin by climbing the south tower and then cross the roof to reach the north tower, **Tour Jehan-de-Beauce,** named after its architect and completed in 1513. The tower is a wonderful example of flamboyant Gothic, a late medieval style named after the flame-like nature of its decoration. Built to replace a wooden steeple which repeatedly burned down, it provides a fascinating counter-part to its more sedate neighbor (and predecessor by three centuries), the octagonal steeple built just before the 1194 fire. (Towers open April-Sept. Mon.-Sat. 9:30am-5:30pm, Sun. 2-5:30pm; Oct. and March Mon.-Sat. 10-11:30am and 2-4:30pm, Sun. 2-4:30pm; Nov.-Feb. Mon.-Sat. 10-11:30am and 2-4pm, Sun. 2-4pm. Admission 14F, ages 12-17 10F, under 12 free.)

Parts of Chartres's **crypt,** one of the largest in Western Christendom, date back to the 9th century. You can only enter the subterranean crypt as part of a tour that leaves from *La Crypte* (18, Cloître Notre Dame, tel. 01 37 21 56 33), the store oppo site the cathedral's south entrance. The tour is in French, but information sheets ar available in English. Even if you can't follow the narration, you'll see the numerou old chapels, the staircase that allowed the relic to be saved from fire, a 4th-centur wall, and the well down which a band of Vikings tossed the bodies of their victim after an 858 raid. The wooden statue of Virgin and Child is a 19th-century copy of th 16th-century original, burnt by Revolutionaries in front of the cathedral (while monk hid the tenacious relic). Look also for some of the statues from the Royal Portal, cop ied and transferred to the crypt after severe weathering had almost erased their fea tures. (30min. tours May-Oct. Mon.-Sat. 11am, 2:15, 3:30, 4:30pm, and, from mid-Jun to mid-Sept., at 5:15pm. Sun. at 2:15, 3:30, 4:30, and 5:15pm. Nov.-April Mon.-Sa 11am and 4:15pm, Sun. 4:15pm. Admission 11F, students 8F.)

The cathedral is open daily in summer from 7:30am to 7:30pm and in winter fro 7:30am to 7pm. No casual visits are allowed Saturdays from 5:45 to 7pm or Sunday from 9:15 to 11am because of religious services. If you want the true Chartres expe ence, however, try attending one of these services. Call the tourist office (see below for information on concerts in the cathedral, as well as the annual student pilgrimag in late May and other festivals throughout the year.

THE TOWN

Rightly called a *ville d'art* (city of art), Chartres celebrates the medieval crafts show cased in its cathedral. In addition to the workshops and galleries, the downtown are is itself a vision to behold. The charming *vieille ville* (old town) has the cobblestor staircases, gabled roofs, half-timbered houses, and iron lamps of a village almost fo gotten by time. Old streets are named for the trades once practiced there; rue de Poissonerie, for example, was home to the fishmonger. Charming stone bridges an iron-trimmed walkways cross the Eure River. Although the town is surrounded by fl wheat fields, Chartres is built on a hill, and some of the best views of the cathedral a found by walking down the well-marked tourist circuit. Free maps are available fro the tourist office (see below).

Le Musée des Beaux-Arts (Museum of Fine Arts), 29, rue du Cloître Notre-Dam (tel. 01 37 36 41 39), next door to the cathedral, resides in the former Episcopal Pa ace. Built mainly in the 17th and 18th centuries on a site occupied by bishops sinc the 11th century, the palace houses a rich, eclectic collection of painting, sculptur and furniture. Zurbarán, Holbein, and Vlaminck all figure prominently, as do loc scenes and medieval wood polychrome statues from the 13th century on. (Ope April-Sept. Wed.-Mon. 10am-6pm; Nov.-March 10am-noon and 2-5pm. Admissic 10F, students and seniors 5F. For temporary exhibits 20F, students and seniors 10F

La Galerie du Vitrail, 17, rue du Cloître Notre-Dame (tel. 01 37 36 10 03), se works of stained glass for anywhere from 400F to 10,000F, but you can admire all yo want without buying. The store also sells books detailing the stained glass at Chartr and other French churches, as well as postcards that might be more in your pri range (postcards 5F, coloring books 22-60F; gallery open April-Sept. Tues.-Sa 9:45am-7pm; Nov.-March Tues.-Sat. 9:45am-1pm and 2-6:30pm). The **Centre Inte national du Vitrail,** 5, rue du Cardinal Pie (tel. 01 37 21 65 72), hosts tempora exhibitions on stained glass, both historical and contemporary, as well as a worki study and a library. The 13th-century barn in which it is housed was once used store wine and grains surrounding farmers gave the clergy. Dedicated to promoti the study of stained glass art, the Centre presents everything from 16th-century fl faced supplicants to late 20th-century machine-dreams, with an emphasis on Art No veau and Art Deco. (Open Mon.-Fri. 9:30am-12:30pm and 1:30-6pm, Sat.-Sun. 10a 12:30pm and 2:30-6pm. Admission 20F, students 12F. Library open Mon.-Tues. a Thurs.-Fri. 2-5pm.) The **Maison de l'Archéologie,** 16, rue Saint-Pierre (tel. 01 37 30 38), is a tiny museum which displays the results of the resident archaeologis research in and around Chartres, and seems to have unearthed mostly pots, cl pieces, and a number of dominoes (open April-Sept. Wed.-Mon. 2-6pm; June-O Wed. and Sun. 2-6pm; admission 5F, students and seniors free).

Chartres is home to houses of worship other than the cathedral. **Eglise St-Aignan,** on rue des Greniers, was rebuilt in the 16th century but boasts feudal origins. The Romanesque **Eglise St-André** sits on a street by the same name overlooking the banks of the Eure River. Fires have ravaged it, but the church has been a part of Chartres since the 12th century. During the 16th and 17th centuries, its gallery was extended to cross the river; one of the arches on which it was supported is still visible. Even if the cathedral sated your urge to see churches, the trip down through the winding, narrow streets of the old city towards Eglise St-André is worth the time. **Eglise St-Pierre,** on the pl. St-Pierre, is a delicate, 13th-century Gothic masterpiece. Once the church of the Benedictine monastery of St-Père-en-Vallée, St-Pierre was renamed during the French Revolution when the monastery was disbanded. (Eglise St-Aignan and Eglise St-Pierre are both open daily 8am-7:30pm; Eglise St-André opens for art exhibitions and concerts—inquire at the tourist office for information on current events.)

Worth the 30- to 40-minute walk across the river (which offers the best view of the cathedral), up rue St-Barthelémy and down rue du Repos past the cemetery, is the **Maison Picassiette,** 22, rue du Repos (tel. 01 37 34 10 78). From 1928 until his death in 1964, Raymond Isidore decorated his house and garden with mosaics made from broken china and colored glass. Beginning with the kitchen, the former graveyard groundskeeper worked with abandon and no preconceived plan, filling courtyards and building shrines, reconstructing Paris and Chartres on wall, planter, and rooftop. Stroll and enjoy the mosaics of plants, animals, people, cathedrals, and panoramas decorating every stationary object on the grounds. Don't miss the Eiffel Tower plant holder in the garden; another room has France's most famous churches on its walls. Mosaic flowers on the walls and near the ceilings are juxtaposed with real flowers, blooming in the garden, and the planters so that Isadore's wish could be fulfilled. "I hope that people will leave here also wanting to live among flowers and within beauty. I'm trying to find a way for men to escape their misery," he said in 1962. The visit isn't long, but it is magical. (Open April-Oct. Wed.-Mon. 10am-noon and 2-6pm. Off-season, call to arrange a visit; admission 10F, students 5F.)

More recent history also looms large in Chartres; filled with streets with names like bd. de la Résistance, the town harbors a monument to **Jean Moulin,** the famous resistance hero who worked closely with de Gaulle. *Préfet* of Chartres before World War II, Moulin attempted suicide rather than be forced by the Nazis to sign a document maintaining that French troops had committed atrocities. Tortured and then killed by the Gestapo in 1943, he was eventually buried in the Panthéon. To get to the monument, walk from the Cathédrale down rue Cheval Blanc until it turns into rue Jean Moulin; the monument will be on your right.

PRACTICAL INFORMATION

The **tourist office** (tel. 01 37 21 50 00), in front of the cathedral's main entrance at pl. de la Cathédrale, helps find accommodations in and near Chartres (10F fee), and supplies visitors with a list of restaurants, brochures, and an excellent map with a walking tour marked. One person for 35F or two people for 40F (plus a deposit) can use an *audioguide* in English, French, or German to see the city. (Tour lasts 1½-2hr. and is great. Available all day, but must be returned while the office is open.) The tourist office staff speaks excellent English, as well as other languages. (Open May-Sept. Mon.-Fri. 9:30am-6:45pm, Sat. 9:30am-6pm, Sun. 10:30am-12:30pm and 2:30-5:30pm; Oct.-April Mon.-Fri. 9:30am-6pm, Sat. 9:30am-5pm, Sun. 10:30am-1pm.)

For **food,** try sandwich or *brasserie* fare in pl. du Cygne or pl. Marceau, open-air pedestrian areas with musicians and great atmosphere. **La Passacaille,** 30, rue Ste-Même (tel. 01 37 21 52 10), offers salads (17-38F) and a large selection of filling pizza (37-57F) in tasteful surroundings; 67F and 82F *menus* (open Mon.-Fri. 11:30am-2pm and 7-10pm, Fri.-Sat. 11:30am-2pm and 7-10:30pm; MC, V, AmEx). **Le Pélagie,** 1, av. Jehan de Beauce (tel. 01 37 36 07 49), serves ample portions of standard meat and potatoes fare as well as Tex-Mex. *Menus* from 59F (open Mon.-Fri. noon-2pm and 7-10:30pm, Sat. 7-10:30pm; MC, V).

Chartres is accessible by frequent **trains** from Gare Montparnasse (1hr., round-trip 138F; in Paris call 08 36 35 35 35 for info; in Chartres call 01 47 20 50 50). Roughly one train per hour during the summer, but many trains run only on certain days or occasions—call ahead. To reach the cathedral from the train station, walk straight to pl. de Châtelet, turn left into the *place,* and then turn right onto rue Ste-Même. When you take another left onto rue Jean Moulin, you will see the cathedral.

NEAR CHARTRES: ILLIERS-COMBRAY

Proust fans should take the time, effort, and half-hour train ride from Chartres to **Illiers-Combray,** the author's childhood vacation home and the setting for much of *A la recherche du temps perdu* (*Remembrance of Things Past*). In Proust's own words, the town remains "a church epitomizing a town, speaking of it and for it to the horizon." Uncut lawns, medieval ruins, half-timbered façades, and sloping roofs mark the town as an unhurried trace of the French past, best seen by tourists armed with *Swann's Way* and a bicycle. In 1971, the Proust centennial birth year, the town came out of hiding, changing its name from Illiers to Combray, its literary pseudonym. Visitors should proceed from the train station down av. Georges-Clémenceau and turn right onto rue de Chartres. Pick-up a map of the town at the *papeterie* across from the Eglise St-Jacques (10F). With Swann's way, the Guermantes way, and other fondly remembered promenades clearly marked, the map is a pilgrim's necessity. Visit **Maison de Tante Léonie,** 4, rue Docteur Léonie (tel. 01 37 24 30 97), the home of Proust's invalid aunt who "had gradually declined to leave, first Combray, then her bedroom, and finally her bed." Proust mementos displayed here may be only seen by guided tour (Tues.-Fri. 2:30 and 4pm, Sat.-Sun. and holidays 11:30am in English, 2:30, and 4pm; mid-June to mid-Sept. Tues.-Fri. 2:30, 3:30, and 4:30pm, Sat.-Sun. and holidays 11:30am in English, 2:30, 3:30, and 4:30pm; call ahead to confirm times and English language tours; admission 25F). **Trains** to Illiers leave from Chartres extremely irregularly; pick up a schedule before you begin your trip, and don't get left behind. First train to Illiers-Combray leaves 12:40pm, last train back at 5:49pm. The ride costs 50F round-trip.

■ Beauvais

Originally known as Caesaromagus—Caesar's market—Beauvais was an important Gallo-Roman settlement until Germanic invasions destroyed it in the 3rd century AD. Heavy bombing during World War II leveled many of the town's medieval buildings. Among the few still in evidence is the Gothic Cathédrale St-Pierre, whose structural flaws have caused its various parts to self-destruct. In the oldest extant portion of Beauvais, located north of the cathedral's ambulatory, fragments of the city's old Roman wall still stand.

During its boom in the 12th century, the town rebuilt its cathedral. The monster **Cathédrale Saint-Pierre** on rue St-Pierre looks like an overgrown Gothic elephant stalking behind the skyline as you approach the city. Its Gothic chancel, the tallest in the world, is the product of architectural ambition pushed beyond reason and engineering principle. This latter-day tower of Babel was smote down in 1284, however, and in spite of efforts to restore it through the 16th century, has toppled every time. The mighty scale of St-Pierre may blind the casual visitor to the fact that construction of the building's nave was never even begun. As Gothic cathedrals go, St-Pierre is certainly not a stupendous artistic masterwork on par with Notre Dame or Chartres. But the sheer scale on which it fails, and the rank luxuriance of the auxiliary buttresses needed to hold the building together confer on it the stumbling charm of a Snuffaluffagus or Boo Radley. Guided tours are in French only, but a pricey 39F English-language guide book is available.

Bordering the cathedral's grassy cloister is the **Basse-Oeuvre,** the ruins of a 10th-century Carolingian church that once stood here. The cathedral also vaunts a one-of-a-kind, 90,000-piece **astronomical clock,** crafted in 1865-68 by Louis-Auguste Vérité. For details on its construction and operation, attend the 25-minute *son et lumière* (sound and light show). Renovations expected to be completed by early 1997, will attempt to prop up what is left of the cathedral; parts may be closed to visitors. (*Son et lumière* about the clock daily at 10:40am, 2:40, 3:40, 4:40pm, except when masses are held. Admission 21F, children 18F. Cathedral open daily 9am-12:15pm and 2-6:15pm; in winter 9am-12:15pm and 2-5:15pm. Call Association "Espaces" at 01 44 48 11 60 for info about the church or the clock.)

Beauvais's three museums display medieval paintings, sculptures, ceramics, and tapestries. The **Musée Departemental de l'Oise,** 1, rue du Musée (tel. 01 44 06 37 37) is located in the former palace of the Bishop de Nesle. Parts of the building date from the 12th, 14th, and 16th centuries. The bishop commissioned the twin **Tours de Nesle,** on either side of the main entrance, after a local peasant uprising; the new fortifications were intended to keep out commoners. The museum assembles local painting, furniture, and sculpture from the 16th century onward, plus a few fossils thrown in for good measure. The precedence it gives to regional artists is not always deserved. Nonetheless, occasional gems do surface, like Nabi painter Maurice Denis's seven-canvas *l'Age d'Or* series (1912). Descend to the museum's basement for a look at Greco-Roman tombs and coins unearthed in nearby excavations. A wan and tragic "Head of Christ," from the old Eglise St-Sauveur, is exhibited on the first floor. (Open Wed.-Mon. 10am-noon and 2-6pm. Admission 16F, students, ages 18-25, and over 65 8F, under 18 and Wed. free.)

On the other side of the cathedral, across from the ruins, the **Galerie Nationale de la Tapisserie** (tel. 01 44 05 14 28), rue St-Pierre, pays homage to the Gobelins tapestry factory built here in 1664. Exhibits change frequently and may feature medieval or modern-day designs. The Gobelins factory itself is depicted in the *"King Visiting the Gobelins Factory"* tapestry (1673-80), which features the Sun King, Colbert, Charles Le Brun—both the designer of the work and the first director of the factory—and countless weavers scrambling to look occupied. Gallo-Roman ramparts and a tower dating from the late 3rd and early 4th centuries AD jut into the gallery's basement. (Open April-Sept. Tues.-Sun. 9:30-11:30am and 2-6pm; Oct.-March Tues.-Sun. 10-11:30am and 2:30-4:30pm. Last entry 1hr. before closing. Admission 22F, students, seniors, and under 18 14F.)

The **Manufacture Nationale de la Tapisserie,** 24, rue Henri Brispot (tel. 01 44 05 14 28), was exiled from Beauvais for 49 years during and following World War II. Visitors may tour the tapestry workshop and watch its staff of weavers in action; craftsmen follow centuries-old techniques that allow the visitor to understand exactly how such masterpieces of tapestries were created in the Middle Ages. (Open Tues.-Thurs. 2-4pm. Admission 19F; students, seniors, and under 18 10F. You must pay separately for the *manufacture* and the *galerie.*)

The **tourist office,** 1, rue Beauregard (tel. 01 44 45 08 18), near the cathedral, offers countless brochures on the surrounding area, a list of hotels and restaurants, and an invaluable map of the town. (English brochures. Open April-Sept. Tues.-Sat. 9:30am-7pm, Sun.-Mon. and holidays 10am-1pm and 2-6pm; Oct.-March Mon.-Sat. 9:30am-6:30pm, Sun. 10am-1:30pm.)

Year-round, the **pl. Jeanne Hachette** brims with cafés, *brasseries,* restaurants, and bakeries. The nearby **pl. des Halles** hosts an all-day market Wednesday and Saturday. Roughly 12 trains leave daily for Beauvais from Paris's Gare du Nord, *grandes lignes* platform (75-90min., 124F round-trip). For more info, call the Beauvais train station (tel. 01 44 21 50 50). To reach the cathedral, follow bd. du Général de Gaulle straight out of the train station and past the garden. Follow the road as it makes a right, and take your second left onto rue des Jacobins. This route leads you to the center of town, passing the tourist office on the left as you approach the cathedral.

■ L'Abbaye de Royaumont

Located in the countryside 35km north of Paris, the Abbaye de Royaumont (tel. 01 30 35 59 00; fax 01 34 68 00 60), Asnières-sur-Oise, is one of the oldest and best-preserved medieval monasteries in Europe. Despite seven centuries of war, political turmoil, and natural disaster, this peaceful cloistered abbey stands as a monument to medieval architecture, monastic life, and years of devotion to literature, music, and learning. Today, the expansive Gothic abbey houses the **Fondation Royaumont,** an international cultural organization which sponsors a center for medieval studies, seminars and conferences for ecclesiastical scholars, a center for poetry and translation, and an annual concert series hosted by the abbey.

Founded by St. Louis (King Louis IX of France) in 1228 and completed in 1235, the abbey was devoted to the order of Cîteaux (Cisterian Order). The king provided the plentiful funds necessary to establish the monastery, and brought learned and devoted men to dedicate their lives to prayer and scholarship within the abbey's walls; the king's brother, three of his sons, and two of his grandsons studied here.

The monks of the Abbaye de Royaumont were divided into two vocations: those who dedicated their lives to a mere 10 hours of daily prayer, called *Réligieux de Coeur,* and those who dedicated their time and energy to scholarship and script-copying. St. Louis invited one of the most celebrated medieval monk-scholars in Europe, Vincent de Beauvais, to lecture on his work, the *Speculum Majus,* an encyclopedia of world leaders, historical figures, and scholars. It was the very first *Who's Who* and, at several thousand pages, was astoundingly comprehensive—a prime example of high quality European medieval monastic scholarship. Since the demolition of the abbey's church by revolutionaries in 1792, the monastery has been used alternately as a prison, a hospital, a mill, and a seat of local government.

While the abbey has passed through multiple identities, the park currently surrounding it is unified by a system of canals and lily-padded pools. The remains of the abbey church, including several stone pillars and a single turret which towers eerily high above the ground, lie just north of the existing buildings. Visitors can also see the *palais abbatial,* the abbot's formal residence, designed by Louis Le Masson.

Inside the abbey you can tour the refectory, where the monks ate in silence while a designated reader recited scripture. In the *anciennes cuisines* (old kitchens), the beautiful 14th-century statue of the Vierge de Royaumont watches tourists pass, where she used to watch monks preparing the daily meals. Colorful fragments of 13th-century floor tiles from the refectory have been re-located to the sacristy, along with other religious and architectural artifacts from the abbey's collection. Next door, the Teilhard de Chardin room houses permanent exhibits on the development of typography since the 15th century and on medieval musical instruments. The Abbaye also has a bar/tea room which serves drinks and snacks in this unusual setting (coffee 9F, ice cream cones 10F; open March-Oct. Sat.-Sun. and holidays noon-6:30pm, Nov.-Feb. Sat.-Sun. and holidays noon-5:30pm; MC, V).

Abbaye open daily 10am-6pm; Nov.-Feb. 10am-5:30pm. Admission 22F, students, scholars, seniors, and ages 7-16 15F, under 7 free. Free tours on weekends only. For more information or a schedule of concerts (held weekends June-Sept.), seminars, or conferences, call 01 34 68 05 50 or write to Fondation Royaumont, 95270 Ansières-Sur-Oise, France.

To get to the Abbaye de Royaumont from Paris, take the Paris-Nord-Montsoult-Muffliers **train,** direction Luzarches, from the Gare du Nord **banlieue** lines and get off at the Gare de Viarmes (1 per hr., 40min., 50F; call 08 36 35 35 35 for schedules). Once you get to Viarmes, avoid the temptation to take a taxi—each way costs 65F. Instead, enjoy an invigorating 7km hike through the town of Viarmes and down rue de Royaumont, following signs to the abbey. From the train station, follow the sign to Centre Ville down the pedestrian walkway and continue straight down rue de la Gare. This street will end at bd. de Paris, the main artery of Viarmes, which becomes rue de Royaumont. Turn right onto bd. de Paris and continue out of town, through two rotaries; you will soon see signs for the abbey. Free shuttle service is offered to and from the train station for concerts. Infrequent bus service is also available on weekdays in the early morning and late afternoon to and from the train station and the abbey (Asnières-Baillon stop, line 14); inquire at the station for schedule information or call Les Courriers de l'Ile de France (CIF; tel. 01 48 62 38 33).

Disneyland Paris

It's a small, small world and Disney seems hell-bent on making it even smaller. When Euro-Disney opened on April 12, 1992, Peter Pan, Mickey Mouse, Cinderella, and Snow White were met by the jeers of French intellectuals and the popular press. Resistance to the park seems to have subsided since Walt & Co. renamed it Disneyland Paris and started serving wine; a touch of class can go a long way. Whether you're there to celebrate or mock, the park is an exciting place to spend a day, even for the budget traveler; every show, attraction, and ride is included in the admission price, as is the chance to see Europeans sway to Michael Jackson's "Captain Eo."

Disneyland Paris' designers (called "Imagineers") and staff (ahem, "Cast Members") have created a resort which celebrates imagination, childhood, fantasy, creativity, technology, and fun. A small army of publicists trumpet Disneyland Paris as a vast entertainment and resort center, the largest on the continent, covering an area one-fifth the size of Paris. Although Disney may eventually develop its 600 hectares, the current theme park doesn't even rank the size of an arrondissement. From the gate it takes only ten minutes to walk to the farthest point inside the park—nothing like the vast reaches of Florida's Disneyworld—a fact which Imagineers have attempted to disguise by designing the park as a veritable maze. On the other hand, this Disney park is the most technologically advanced yet, and the special effects on some rides are enough to knock your socks off.

Despite early financial instability, Disneyland Paris has been a hit, and Disney has had to close the ticket windows repeatedly for hours at a time to keep ride lines down during the summer. Try to get there on a weekday—Tuesdays and Thursdays are the least crowded. Otherwise, expect to spend most of your time fighting to keep your place in line, rather than having fun. Masses of people practice line-cutting, as whole families duck under barriers and worm their way up front. To make things worse, devious architecture hides the true length of the lines; a line just emerging from a building may be only the tail end of a 90-minute wait inside. Discreetly posted signs at the entrances of the more popular rides alert you to how long you can expect to wait for a 5-10-minute rush. The crowds thin out towards 5pm, when parents start crying to go home, reducing waits to as little as 15 minutes. Saving the bigger rides for the evening is probably the best way to go, and considering that the park closes at 11pm during the summer, you'll have plenty of time to catch all of your favorite rides several times over.

ORIENTATION AND PRACTICAL INFORMATION

Everything in Disneyland Paris is in English and French. The staff is extremely helpful, and the detailed guide called the *Disneyland Paris Guest Guidebook,* which you'll receive when you enter the park, has information on everything from restaurants and attractions to bathrooms and first aid.

Tickets: Instead of selling tickets, Disneyland Paris issues *Passeports,* available at the 50 windows located on the ground floor of the Disneyland Hotel. You can also buy *Passeports* at the Paris tourist office on the Champs-Elysées (see "Tourist Offices," p. 63) or at any of the major stations on RER line A, such as Châtelet-Les Halles, Gare de Lyon, or Charles-de-Gaulle-Étoile. Pursue either of these options if you plan on coming out on a weekend, so you won't risk wasting a couple of hours while the windows remain closed due to the crowds. The *passeport* is valid for one day; be sure to have your hand stamped if you plan to leave the park and return later. Admission 195F, ages 3-11 150F. Two- and three-day *passeports* are also available. Open daily 9am-11pm, Sept.-June hours vary. Hours subject to change during the winter when snow and sleet can make your experience less than satisfactory. Reduced prices Oct-Dec. 22 and Jan. 8-March 31.

Restaurants: Pick up the weekly *Programme,* a guide to restaurants, shows, and parades, at the ticket counter or City Hall, or consult your *Disneyland Paris Guest Guidebook.* Restaurants are classified by the type of service: sit-down, cafeteria, or snack bars. For a sit-down, 3-course *menu,* expect to pay 100-200F, on average. Cafeteria meals run 40-50F for simpler *menus* (i.e. hamburger, french fries, and a soft drink). Snack stands located throughout the park offer hot dogs, ice cream, sugared popcorn, and the like for 8-19F. The least expensive options are the very British fish and chips at **Toad Hall Restaurant,** the frontier grub and saloon show at **Lucky Nugget Saloon,** the Italian staples of pasta and pizza at **Pizzeria Bella Notte,** or the burgers at Discoveryland's **Café Hyperion.** The Lucky Nugget Saloon offers what is perhaps the best value in the whole park. 74F at lunch and 150F at dinner buys a 4-course meal with buffalo wings, a bowl of chili, a hot beef sandwich and a brownie. Most restaurants also offer reduced-price *menus* for children. You're not supposed to bring in picnic food, but the French seem to do it anyhow. Most restaurants are open non-stop 11am-10pm during the summer and 11am 'til the park's closing throughout the year. Food lines are generally shorter before noon and after 2:30pm.

Hotels: The resort has six hotels, each designed on a particular theme celebrating a region of the United States. The **Sequoia Lodge** is surrounded by sequoia trees imported from California, the **Hotel Santa Fe** is modeled on the adobes of New Mexico, and the **Hotel Cheyenne** is built to look like a frontier town. A group of four could comfortably and affordably stay for a weekend at the Hotel Cheyenne for 450F per night, or at the Hotel Santa Fe (unpopular with the French because it looks like a French housing project) for 350F per night during off-season. The Resort also had a campground called the **Davy Crockett Ranch,** which has been converted into a resort village with fully equipped bungalows that can house up to six people (350F off-season). Unfortunately, it is also 7km from the center of the park, and buses are no longer available; taxis or cars are the only ways of getting there. High season usually extends from late June until the end of Aug.; call ahead to find the best dates to rent a room. For more info call in France tel. 01 60 30 60 30, in the U.K. tel. 0990 030 303, or in the U.S. tel. (407) W-DISNEY (934-7639). The tourist office (tel. 01 60 43 33 33; fax 01 60 43 74 95) can help you make a hotel reservation outside of Disney (for a 20F commission) and give you information on the area surrounding Disneyland Paris. Open daily Nov.-May 9am-11pm, Oct.-June Sun.-Thurs. 9am-9pm, Fri.-Sat. 9am-11pm.

NIGHTLIFE

Separate from Disneyland Paris and free to enter is **Festival Disney,** a street filled with bars and game rooms where people roam about wearing cowboy hats and clutching beers (average prices 24-40F per bottle or glass). Festival Disney also contains a number of restaurants with classier fare and post-modern architecture, as well as nightclubs, a popular sports bar, and free bands playing cover songs until 1am. With the addition of a Planet Hollywood and an 8-screen Gaumont cinema due to open in March 1997, Festival Disney will become known as Disney Village.

SIGHTS AND ACTIVITIES

For the wildest rides, look for those with the most dire warnings. While "may frighten certain young children" might sound promising, it only means that the ride is dark and things pop out at you. Warnings directed at pregnant women and people with chronic heart problems are the hallmarks of the real thing. The park can be divided into five areas. **Main Street, USA,** a storybook depiction of a turn-of-the-century town, is more American than apple pie and the first area you'll pass through after the gate. Home to the park's welcome center at City Hall, Main Street funnels you through a consumer's paradise of shops and restaurants before depositing you at the center of the park. The arcades on either side of the street are a good way to partially avoid the merchandise megalopolis and reach the rides more quickly. At the heart of the Magical Kingdom, the **Château de la Belle au Bois Dormant** (Sleeping Beauty's Castle) contains one stupendous, high-tech, smoke-breathing dragon in the dungeon, and a shop where you can purchase Cinderella's glass slipper for a paltry 485F. Tall and very, very pink, it makes one heck of a landmark. Exiting out the back of the château, you fall into **Fantasyland.** Although the rides are tame, the spinning **Mad Hat-**

ter's Teacups merit a whirl. **Alice's Curious Labyrinth** is a hedge maze, replete with squirting fountains and a hookah-smoking caterpillar; best visited at night when you just might get lost with a friend, the labyrinth contains a palace which offers a great view of the park. Drift through a world of laughter, a world of tears, a world of hopes, and a world of fears on **It's a Small World,** where tiny automated dolls from around the world sing you into submission.

Off to the left, **Adventureland** awaits both the intrepid explorer and the weary parent with a mix of themes from so-called adventurous regions: the Middle East, West Africa, and the Caribbean. **Pirates of the Caribbean** presents 10 minutes of frighteningly life-like corsairs and a fantastic water-dungeon set. Be warned: the line outside is only a fraction of the total wait. **Indiana Jones et le Temple du Péril** features what was the first 360° loop ever on a Disney ride; unfortunately, the ride lasts only three minutes and the loop is minuscule. The rickety track and sudden dips can bring on the adrenaline, but more demanding thrill-seekers might want to mosey over to rough and ready **Frontierland,** where **Thunder Mesa,** a towering sunset-colored reproduction of a New Mexican desert mesa, hosts the park's most breathtaking ride: **Big Thunder Mountain.** At high noon, the line is almost as deadly as the ride, but the marvelous robot llamas and donkeys that border the track, and the bumpy trip itself, are superb. Set apart on a scraggly hill, the creaky **Phantom Manor** is the park's classic haunted house. While the Haunted Mansion at Disneyland in Florida is a huge scary fortress, the architecture had to be changed in Europe, where fortresses and châteaux are common; this haunted Manor is based instead on the Victorian mansion in the film *Psycho.*

Light-years away on the other side of the park, Discoveryland flaunts the park's latest technological wizardry. **Star Tours** invite you to fly the not-so-friendly skies around the Death Star; after the bumpy ride don't miss a stop in *L'Astroport Services Interstellaires* where a host of high-tech games await. Michael Jackson's **Captain Eo** croons away at nearby *Cinémagique*, and the **Visionarium's** 360° time-travel film is a good break. The newest ride at Disneyland Paris, **Space Mountain** is touted as "the crowning achievement of forty years of innovation by Disney Imagineers." It puts the Florida and California versions of this ride to shame: you'll travel at speeds of 70km per hour through three loops in pitch blackness—a 360° loop, a corkscrew, and a 180° horseshoe—while a synchronized eight-speaker soundtrack immerses you in the illusion that you're on your way to the moon.

In addition to the rides, Disney also puts on a variety of special daily events including a **Disney Character Parade** with myriad elaborate floats; the **Main Street Electrical Parade** (for the best view of the parades stand to the left at the top of Main Street near the pseudo-rotary—that's where the special effects on the floats are timed to go off); and a fantastic *son et lumières* show, set against the background of the château. Musical extravaganzas based on the latest Disney movies and other special events are listed in the *Programmes: Spectacles & Restaurants.*

GETTING THERE

The easiest way to get to Disneyland Paris is by taking **RER** A4 from Paris. Get on at either M. Gare de Lyon or Châtelet-Les Halles and take the train (direction: "Marne-la-Vallée") to the last stop, "Marne-la-Vallée/Chessy." Before boarding the train, check the illuminated electric boards hanging above the platform to make sure there's a light next to the Marne-la-Vallée stop; otherwise the train won't end up there (every 30min., 45min., 74F round-trip). The last train to Paris leaves Disney at 12:22am, but you may have trouble getting the metro at the other end. By **car,** take the A4 highway from Paris and get off at exit 14, marked "Parc Disneyland Paris," about a 30-minute drive from the city. You can park for 40F per day in any one of the 11,000 spaces in the parking lot. **Disneyland Paris Buses** make the rounds between the terminals of both Orly and Roissy/Charles de Gaulle airports and the bus station near the Marne-la-Vallée RER (every 45-60 min., 40min., 85F, 8:30am-7:45pm, 8:30am-10pm at CDG on weekends). TGV service from Roissy/Charles de Gaulle reaches the park in a mere 15 minutes, making Disneyland Paris fantastically accessible for travelers with Eurail passes. Daily train service between Waterloo Station in London and Disneyland Paris via Eurostar is planned to begin in late 1996, creating a mere 3-hr. separation between Mickey Mouse and Big Ben (Eurostar information tel. 08 36 35 35 39).

Gardens

Giverny

Halfway between Rouen and Paris, Giverny is the enchanting embodiment of the old adage "stop and smell the roses." From April well into July, and sometimes longer, the roadsides and gardens of this rural village overflow with roses, hollyhocks, poppies, and the heady scent of honeysuckle. Whether bewitched by the countryside in bloom, the fields filled with hay, or the lilypads floating lazily in the Epte river, arch-Impressionist Claude Monet settled here in 1883 and soon set about painting the grounds around him. By 1887, Giverny had grown into an artists' colony, as John Singer Sargent, Paul Cézanne, and Mary Cassatt set up their easels beside Monet's. Despite his almost obsessive fascination with painting the local countryside, Monet also devoted much horticultural energy and skill to creating the garden surrounding his home, explaining *"Mon jardin est mon plus beau chef d'ouevre"* ("My garden is my most beautiful masterpiece").

Today his property comprises the **Fondation Claude Monet,** 84, rue Claude Monet (tel. 02 32 51 28 21). The gardens have been reconstructed from eyewitness reports and historical documents, now looking (as far as scholars know) as they did to the painter himself. The waterlilies float serenely on the pond, the Japanese bridge and the trailing weeping willows look like—well, like Monets, and the turkeys' gawkiness mars but doesn't negate their harmonious color coordination with the pink, crushed-brick façade of the house. It takes scores of contemporary gardeners to give the grounds' floral palette the color and variety of their master's brushstrokes. Less various—but just as numerous—are the tourists. Though the seven-year-old soccer players and amateur photographers can't rob Giverny of beauty, they can steal its romance and tranquility. Nonetheless, the house is lovely; displayed within are many of Monet's belongings, including his impressive collection of 18th- and 19th-century Japanese prints and his deathbed. The second floor windows offer fabulous views of the garden. (House and garden open April-Oct. Tues.-Sun. 10am-6pm. 35F, students and 12-18 yrs. old 25F, ages 7-12 20F. Gardens only 25F. Bring extra film and arrive early; the line quickly becomes a 1-hr. wait.)

About 100m down rue Claude Monet at no. 99 is the light-filled and spacious **Musée d'Art Américain** (tel. 02 32 51 94 65), a recent addition to Giverny which purports to show American art in comparison and in contrast to the European stuff. Although mostly a collection of paintings by little-known American Impressionists who descended upon Giverny in search of Monet and inspiration between 1887 and the First World War, it has a small room of Whistlers, a few Singer Sargent sketches, and some poignant Mary Cassatts. If you can forget that you've never heard of most of the other artists (John Leslie Breck's 13-canvas tribute to Monet's haystacks, anyone?), their work can be charming. (Open April-Oct. Tues.-Sun. 10am-6pm; 35F, students, seniors, teachers, and ages 12-18 20F, under 12 15F.)

Another 100m farther beyond the territory of the teeming tourists is a rustic treasure. The **Musée Baudy,** at no. 81 (tel. 02 32 21 10 03), is in the old Hôtel Baudy, which lodged most of these Monet hangers-on at some point or other, as well as Monet himself (before he bought his house), and many of his close friends (Renoir, Pissarro, Clémenceau, and so on). The hotel itself contains little more than a contemporary art gallery and the partially restored dining area where Sisley reportedly slurped his soup, much to Cassatt's annoyance, but behind the main building the gardens have wrapped the hillside in wreaths of blossoms. While lacking the familiar vistas of Monet's own property, the tangled greenery and winding paths which lead away from the small studio used by Cézanne and scores of American artists are enchanting and a perfect place to pause for a while. Mainly a rose garden, the grounds are best seen in June. (Museum open daily April 15-July 15 10am-6pm; 25F, seniors 20F, students 15F, ages 8-12 10F; the gallery remains open July 16-Oct. 31 Tues.-Sun. 10am-6pm for free visits.)

To eat in Giverny, click your heels three times and repeat "I want a budget restaurant." For the most part, restaurants and snack bars are priced high for tourists. Most of the staff at the Fondation eats at **La Bonne Étable,** 9, rue de la Falaise (tel. 02 32 51 66 32), rather than any of the closer restaurants. Following rue Claude Monet away from the three museums, turn left at the intersection onto rue de la Falaise. Sandwiches cost 15-22F, salads 38-55F, desserts 12-35F, and 3-course lunch *menu* is 70F. (Open Tues.-Fri. and Sun. noon-3pm, Sat. noon-3pm and 7:30-10pm; MC, V.) A little farther down rue de la Falaise opposite no. 13 is **La Grenouillère** (tel. 02 32 51 23 59), a shaded outdoor luncheon spot beside the Epte river. Salads 38F, grilled meat with fries 38-48F, desserts 12-26F. Bottle of farm cider 38F. (Open daily April-Oct. noon-6pm.) Vernon itself has more options. At bright and floral **Pizza del Teatro,** 34, rue d'Albuféra (tel. 02 32 21 35 49), appetizers are 20-68F and pizzas 40-59F, pasta 39-65F, and a 2-course lunch *menu* 72F (open daily noon-2:30pm and 7-11pm; MC, V). Around the corner at 88, rue Carnot, **L'Exotic** (tel. 02 32 21 58 76) serves salads (40F) and creole specialties (10-40F) behind a facade of two-dimensional palm trees and tropical fruit. Three-course *menus* are 85F, but there's a 50F weekday special. (Open daily April 15-Oct. 15 noon-2pm and 6-10:30pm.)

Over 400,000 tourists a year require Giverny and its lilies to be easily accessible by public transportation. **Trains** run from Paris to Vernon, the nearest station, erratically throughout the day. Checking the timetables posted in the *grandes lignes* reservation rooms at Gare St-Lazare or calling the SNCF (tel. 08 36 35 35 35) will save you from frustration and give you more time with the flowers. (Trains every 1-3hrs., 45-75min., from Gare St-Lazare. 130F round-trip.) To get to Giverny, rent a bike from the station (55F per day cash, 1000F deposit cash or MC, V), or take a bus from the front of the station (tel. 02 35 71 32 99; Mon.-Sat., 6 per day each way, Sun. and holidays 3 per day each way; 10min.; 11F30, round-trip 17F). Taxis abound outside the train station and cost about 55-65F on weekdays and 65-80F on weekends in each direction; if you can become a party of four, the convenience of the ride might outweigh its price. The 6km, hour-long hike from the train station in Vernon across the river to Giverny is calming. And long. The Vernon tourist office supplies free maps to help first-time visitors, or you can retrace the bus or taxi's route on your way back from Giverny; the highway can be unpleasant to follow, but the pedestrian path is tricky to find. Regardless of how you travel back and forth between Giverny and Vernon, you may want to consider a climb up the valley into the **Forêt de Vernon,** alongside Giverny, to see some of the beautiful poppy-covered countryside. The Vernon **tourist office,** 36, rue Carnot (tel. 02 32 51 39 60), distributes free maps of Vernon and hiking trails in the area, as well as historical pamphlets (open April-Oct. Tues.-Sat. 9:30am-noon and 2:30-6:30pm, Sun. 10am-noon; Nov.-March Tues. -Sat. 10am-noon and 2:30-5:30pm). To reach the tourist office from the Vernon station, take rue Emile Loubet, turn left on rue d'Albuféra and right on rue Carnot. If you remain on rue d'Albuféra, pont Clémenceau will carry you across the Seine; to the left on the far side of the river there's a picnic spot beside an old mill, and to the right, frequent signs lead to Giverny.

If you have time to spare, a stroll through some of the cobblestone streets of Vernon past quirky, half-timber houses built up to 500 years ago can be an enjoyable way to end the day and pick up a cheap snack. The **Musée de Vernon,** 12, rue du Pont (tel. 02 32 21 28 09), exhibits an eclectic collection: besides the predictable local colorists (only one is a Monet), it contains archaeological relics found near Vernon and a significant display of *art animalier* (animal art). From rue d'Albuféra as you face the bridge, turn left on rue Carnot and right on rue du Pont. (Open April-Oct. Tues.-Fri. 11am-1pm and 2-6pm, Sat.-Sun. 2-5:30pm; Nov.-March Tues.-Sun. 2-6pm. 15F, students and under 18 free.)

■ Auvers-sur-Oise

I am entirely absorbed by these plains of wheat on a vast expanse of hills like an ocean of tender yellow, pale green, and soft mauve, with a piece of cultivated land dotted with clusters of potato vines in bloom, and all this under a blue sky tinted with shades of white, pink, and violet.

—Vincent Van Gogh, 1890

Despite the turbulent century which followed Van Gogh's arrival in Auvers-sur-Oise, relatively little in this small village, located 30km northwest of Paris, has changed. Today's visitor can walk past the same cottages, medieval church, and beckoning fields of golden grain which once drew a generation of Impressionists (including Pissarro, Cézanne, Daubigny, and Gachet), away from the cities and out into the countryside. Van Gogh, fleeing Provence where he had been so unhappy, arrived at Auvers-sur-Oise in May, 1890, and immediately began to paint and sketch feverishly. In a scant ten weeks he produced over 70 drawings, studies, and canvases. This intense productivity did not bring with it peace of mind; on the afternoon of July 27, the 37-year-old Van Gogh shot himself in the chest while standing in the same wheat fields he had painted only days before. He died two days later in his rented room at the **Auberge Ravaux,** known today as the Maison de Van Gogh, attended by his close friend Dr. Gachet and his beloved younger brother Théo.

While the **Maison de Van Gogh** (8, rue de la Sansonne; tel. 01 34 48 05 47) has little to offer beyond a glimpse of Van Gogh's room and a pretty slideshow in French, English, and Japanese, the cost of admission does include an elegant, illustrated "passport" to Auvers-sur-Oise which details the history of the *auberge* and Van Gogh's sojourn there. The booklet also gives information on the town's other museums, self-guided walking tours, and neighboring villages of interest. (Open April-Sept. Tues.-Sun. 10am-7pm; Oct.-March Tues.-Sun. 10am-6pm; last entrance ½hr. before closing; 30F.) The 15-minute walk from the Maison to the **Cimetière d'Auvers** is well worth the trip, if for nothing other than the view. Following the right-hand path at the end of rue de la Sansonne up to rue Daubigny, turn right on the latter and then bear left up rue Emile Bernard when you reach **Notre-Dame d'Auvers.** Dating back to the 12th century, this church is the subject of Van Gogh's striking *L'eglise d'Auvers* (1890), which hangs in the Musée d'Orsay. Grief-stricken and ill, Vincent's brother Théo died six months after Vincent, and in 1914, his wife had him reburied at his brother's side along the far wall of the cemetery. The bed of ivy which unites the brothers' twin headstones is typically crowned with tributes to the former evangelist and ear-lobeless icon, ranging from the wreaths of wildflowers to phials of *sake.*

The **chemin du cimetière** leads through the fields where Van Gogh painted his *Champ de blé aux corbeaux* (*Wheatfields with Crows,* 1890) and emerges near the **Atelier de Daubigny,** 61, rue Daubigny (tel. 01 34 48 03 03), once the home and studio of pre-Impressionist painter Charles-François Daubigny (1817-78). Daubigny began to make regular trips to Auvers in 1854, found moorings here for his floating studio christened "Le Bottin" in 1857, and built a less water-worthy and more permanent studio in 1861. This *atelier* became a popular meeting place for artists—including Pissarro, Morisot, and Cézanne—and when rain made it impossible to work outdoors, Daubigny, his son Karl, and his friends Daumier and Corot cheerfully set about covering the walls with giant pastoral *tableaux*, bouquets of flowers and fruits, and delicate trim. While most of Daubigny's works hang elsewhere, some smaller works and personal items are still on display in his lovingly maintained studio. (Open Easter-Oct. Tues.-Sun. 2-6:30pm; 20F, under 14 free.)

The **Musée de l'Absinthe,** 44, rue Callé (tel. 01 30 36 83 26), located a few minutes away from the *atelier* on a side street off of rue de Léry, is yet another memorial to the Impressionists. Dedicated to the narcotic, alcoholic beverage that the likes of Manet, Toulouse-Lautrec, and Degas drank and painted, the museum traces the evolution of absinthe from its humble beginnings as a preventative medicine, to the peak of its popularity around 1860 when happy hour was known as *l'heure verte* (green hour) in honor of the drink's cloudy emerald appearance and absinthe was the national drink of France. It was finally banned in 1915 by turn-of-the-century teetotalers who labeled it *le peril vert* (the green peril). Special spoons, fervent poems by Verlaine, Rimbaud, and Baudelaire, satirical cartoons, a re-created period *bistrot,* and lush posters of—well—lushes tell the story of the mythical *fée verte* (green fairy) which seduced and inspired a generation. (Open June-Sept. Wed.-Sun. 11am-6pm; Oct.-May Sat.-Sun. 11am-6pm; 25F, students 20F.)

The **Château d'Auvers** (tel. 01 34 48 48 48), set serenely on a hilltop a little farther down rue de Léry, dates from 1635 but has recently reopened in a new form. Converted into a hi-tech museum, it now offers a "*voyage au temps des impressionists*" (journey into the Impressionists' era), a multimedia exhibit recreating 19th-century Paris and Auvers. Visitors don wild headsets (with audio available in four languages) and take a self-paced, 90-minute tour of the modern museum. Be prepared for a veritable kaleidoscope of films, projections, and slide shows that carry you from Haussmann's Paris to the train station, and from there to the countryside and the seashore. While anyone familiar with either the Impressionists or the Belle Epoque in France will learn relatively little from the visit, the 19th-century photographs and turn-of-the-century film footage may merit a glance. Avoid visiting the Château on weekends, when herds of tourists lumbering from one room to the next prevent you from moving at your own pace. (Open May-Oct. Tues.-Sun. 10am-8pm, Nov.-April 10am-6:30pm. Last entry 1½hr. before closing time. 55F, seniors 45F, under 25 40F, under 6 free.) Once past the Château, the rue de Léry becomes rue du Docteur Gachet and then rue François Coppée. It was in his home along this stretch of road that Dr. Paul Ferdinand Gachet welcomed Renoir, Monet, Pissarro, Van Gogh, and Cézanne, the last of whom stayed in Auvers between 1872 and 1874, painting works such as *La maison du pendu* up and down rue Francois Coppée.

Several package admission deals are offered to the various museums in Auvers: to the Château, Atelier de Daubigny, and Maison de Van Gogh, Tues.-Sat., 75F; to the Château and Musée de l'Absinthe, Sat.-Sun., 65F; to the Château and Atelier Daubigny, Sun. 65F. The **Office de Tourisme d'Auvers-sur-Oise** (tel. 01 30 36 10 06), housed in the Manoir des Colombières, rue de la Sansonne, has more information on the package deals, as well as postcards, books, and a list of the names and telephone numbers of area experts on the Impressionists. The helpful staff hands out free simple maps of Auvers and 3F maps showing walking tours and famous sites, as well as information on the town's museums and annual festival. A free 20-minute video about Van Gogh's sojourn in Auvers runs continuously in French (ask for an English showing) and 90-minute guided tours of the village depart from here (April-Oct. Sun. 3pm; 25F, under 14 10F). Office open daily 9:30am-noon and 2-6pm. The Manoir des Colombières also hosts the small **Musée Daubigny** (tel. 01 30 36 80 20), which contains a few minor works by its namesake, as well as his palette and engraving tools, and an eclectic mix of other works both painted and sculptural, documenting the 150 years of artistic activity in and around Auvers. (Open Wed.-Sun. 2:30-6:30pm; Nov.-March 2-5:30pm; 20F, under 16 free.)

To get to Auvers, take the **train** from Gare St-Lazare to Pontois, then switch to the Persan Creil line and get off at Gare d'Auvers-sur-Oise (both run every hr., 1hr., 56F). Or depart from the Gare du Nord for Valmondois, change there for a train going to Pontoise and get off at Auvers-sur-Oise.

■ St-Cloud

The town of **St-Cloud,** 3km southwest of Paris, harbors a beautiful park, the former site of a château. Framed by orderly hedges and trimmed with rectangular beds of more than 30 varieties of flowers and 30 types of rosebushes, the multi-terraced park marches its way down the hillside, stretching almost all the way to the Seine below. By consulting horticultural guides of the 19th century, modern-day gardeners have painstakingly reconstructed the floral arrangements in the fashion of the court of

Napoleon III during his stays at St-Cloud. The result is a great spot for a bike excursion or a picnic, especially since you can walk and sit on the grass.

The **Château de St-Cloud** was the scene of the assassination of Henri III in 1589 and Napoleon's coup d'état in 1799, when troops loyal to the rising general invaded the chambers of the legislature in session there. In 1870, marauding Prussians bombed and then burned the château; nothing remains but Le Nôtre's magnificent park. To orient yourself, consult the large marble slab at the *bassin de l'oragerie.* A map of the grounds in 1811, the slab shows the parts of the original park that still remain, the parts that were destroyed, and the exact location of the château. To the left of the park's main gates (the *grille d'honneur*), the tiny **Musée Historique** offers drawings and paintings about the park and the ex-château. (Grounds open daily March-April and Sept.-Oct. 7:30am-8:50pm; May-Aug. 7:30am-9:50pm; Nov.-Feb. 7:30am-7:50pm. Museum open Wed., Sat.-Sun., and holidays 2:30-6:30pm. Both free. 25F maps are unnecessary.)

To get to St-Cloud from Paris, take the metro, bus #72 from the Hôtel de Ville, or bus #52 from the Madeleine to "Boulogne-Pt. de St-Cloud." There you can either take a local bus across the Pont de St-Cloud or an unpleasant 15-minute walk across intersecting highways. Take the #160, 467 or 460 bus, look for signs in the metro, or catch them right before the bridge, for Pont de St-Cloud. (If you are arriving by bike, ride on the sidewalk on the left side of the bridge and follow the signs to the park). Get off at pl. Magenta and head down av. du Général Leclerc to the park or get off earlier at the train station and head downhill until you hit the church. To the right of the church is the town hall. There you can find free maps of the town and park as well as a guide to all the restaurants and stores in town. (Open Mon.-Fri. 9am-noon and 2-5:45pm, Sat. 8:45am-noon.)

The most interesting parts of the park are right near the town. If you enter at av. du Général Leclerc, walk down the *Allée de la glacière* until you arrive at the fountains. If you continue to the *Bassin de l'oragerie* you will come upon a panorama of Paris and the surrounding suburbs. The *grille d'honneur* is to your left. You can continue downhill to the *Bassin des cascades* (don't go out of the gates at the *grille d'honneur* or you'll hit the highway). The cascades are a magical fountain with frogs and other creatures spouting water. Go to your left at the bottom of the fountain and exit the park through a tunnel. Cross the street to catch the #75 bus back to Hotel de Ville, or walk across the bridge to the metro.

WEEKEND TRIPS

> *By all which it appears, quoth I, having read it over, a little too rapidly, that if a man sets out in post-chaise from Paris—he must go on travelling in one, all the days of his life—or pay for it.*
>
> —Laurence Stern

Sitting in a Parisian café, it's easy to forget that life exists beyond the Ile de France. The provinces, officially defined as the rest of the country, are where most of French history was played out, where most French landmarks stand, and where most of the French live. Foray into the Pays de la Loire (a mere hour away) or into Normandy (2 hours away) for a glimpse at the France of châteaux, battlefields, and beaches. For more extensive coverage of the provinces, see *Let's Go: France 1997*.

Pays de la Loire

The châteaux along the Loire, France's longest river, range from grim medieval fortresses with defensive walls to elegant Renaissance houses with storybook moats. The buildings themselves buzz with 400 years' worth of stories about royal births and queenly poisonings, arranged marriages and true love. Most of the châteaux were

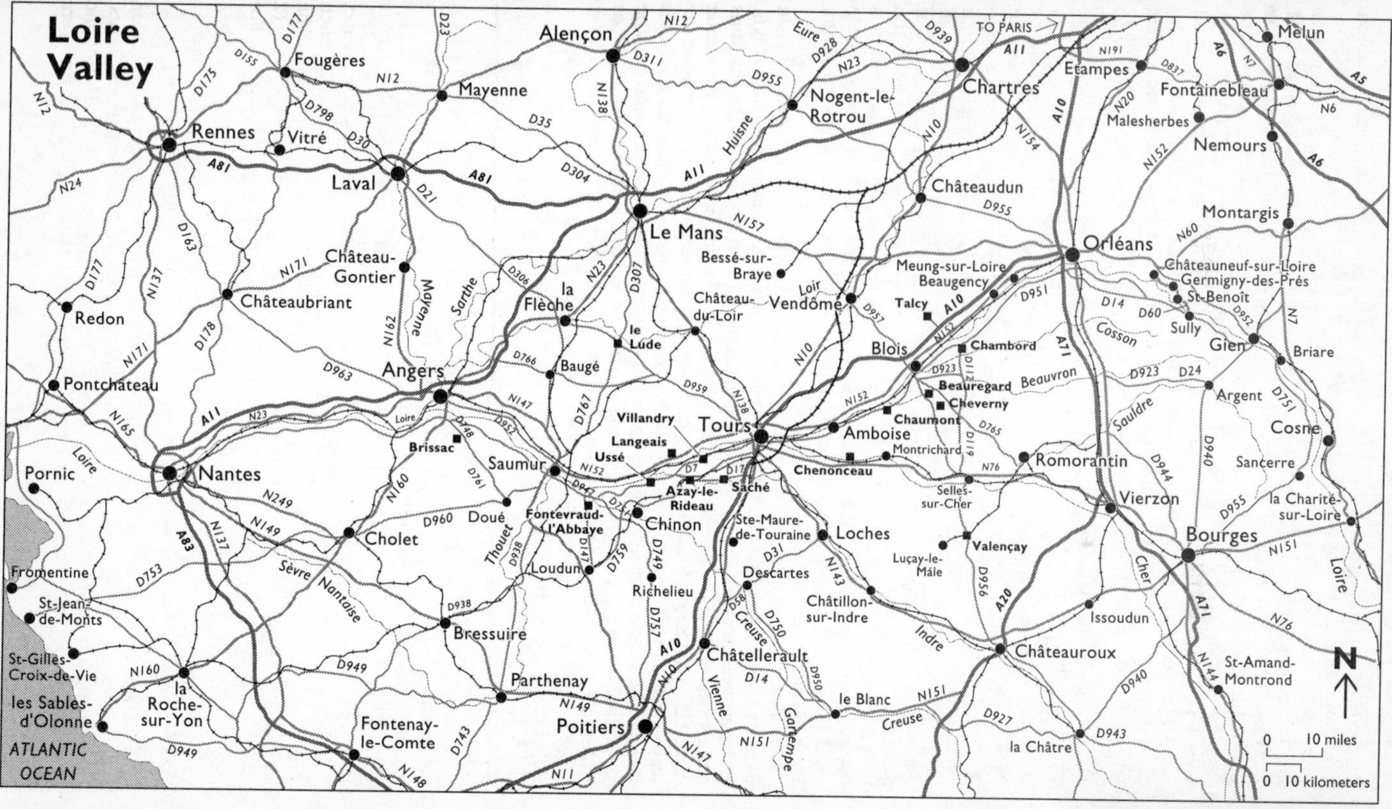
Loire Valley
N
10 miles
10 kilometers
TO PARIS
Melun
Fontainebleau
Nemours
Montargis
Malesherbes
Étampes
Chartres
Châteaudun
Orléans
Châteauneuf-sur-Loire
Germigny-des-Prés
St-Benoît
Sully
Gien
Briare
Cosne
Argent
Sancerre
la Charité-sur-Loire
Bourges
St-Amand-Montrond
Vierzon
Issoudun
Châteauroux
la Châtre
Romorantin
Valençay
Luçay-le-Mâle
Selles-sur-Cher
Meung-sur-Loire
Beaugency
Chambord
Beauregard
Cheverny
Talcy
Blois
Chaumont
Montrichard
Amboise
Chenonceau
Loches
Châtillon-sur-Indre
le Blanc
Nogent-le-Rotrou
Vendôme
Bessé-sur-Braye
Château-du-Loir
Tours
Villandry
Langeais
Azay-le-Rideau
Saché
Ussé
Chinon
Ste-Maure-de-Touraine
Descartes
Richelieu
Châtellerault
Poitiers
Alençon
Le Mans
le Lude
la Flèche
Baugé
Fontevraud-l'Abbaye
Saumur
Loudun
Doué
Brissac
Angers
Mayenne
Laval
Château-Gontier
Fougères
Vitré
Rennes
Châteaubriant
Cholet
Bressuire
Parthenay
Fontenay-le-Comte
Nantes
Redon
Pontchâteau
Pornic
Fromentine
St-Jean-de-Monts
St-Gilles-Croix-de-Vie
les Sables-d'Olonne
la Roche-sur-Yon
ATLANTIC OCEAN
Loire
Cher
Indre
Creuse
Vienne
Gartempe
Thouet
Sèvre Nantaise
Mayenne
Sarthe
Loir
Eure
Huisne
Cosson
Beauvron
Sauldre
A5
A6
A10
A11
A20
A71
A81
A83

built in the 15th and 16th centuries, when French monarchs left Paris and ruled from the countryside around Tours, both to avoid urban grime and to squeeze in hunting excursions between official state decrees. Some structures, however, remain from the days before the region was even French: Henry II and Richard the Lionheart, both English royalty, mobilized two of the oldest communities, Chinon and Beaugency, to defend the region from the Capetian monarchs of the 12th century. The English and the French played hot potato with the Loire until Jeanne d'Arc helped win it for the French in the Hundred Years War (1337-1453). In the 15th century, under the Valois kings, the French monarchy acquired the region in a flux of martial and marital activity; it is at this time that châteaux accumulated the works of the finest Italian masters and an opulence never before imagined.

GETTING AROUND

Blois, Chinon, and Tours are convenient bases for châteaux exploration, especially since the Paris Gare d'Austerlitz serves Blois and Tours directly. Trains then run between Tours and Chinon or Chenonceau, while Chambord is accessible by bus (in summer) or bike from Blois. The Loire Valley is a fantastic spot to rent a car: a group of four can often undercut tour bus prices by doing so, and will be able to see many more of the smaller châteaux. Bikes are available for rent almost everywhere around (50F per day). *Michelin's* road map of the region will steer you away from truck-laden highways and onto delightful country roads.

■ Blois

In their eagerness to visit the out-of-town castles, tourists often overlook the charms of Blois's narrow cobblestone lanes, tempting *pâtisseries*, and historic château. Home to French monarchs Louis XII and François I, Blois' **château** (tel. 02 54 78 06 62) was the center of power of Renaissance France. The ornate octagonal **spiral staircase,** built under François I, juts out into the courtyard; stone salamanders, symbols of his force, wriggle on the staircase (legends held that the salamander is reborn, not harmed, through fire). Start with the **Aile François I** and traipse through a series of swank Renaissance rooms. Don't miss the crafty chamber of Catherine de Médicis. (Open June 15-Aug. daily 9am-8pm; March 15-June 14 and Sept.-Oct. 14 daily 9am-6:30pm; Oct. 15-March 14 daily 9am-12:30pm and 2-7:30pm. Call ahead for English or French tours. Admission 33F, students under 25 17F. The château presents a *son et lumière* every evening May-Sept. at 10:30pm, in French, 60F.) Also in town, the 12th-century Abbaye St-Laumer, now the **St-Nicolas cathedral,** is a towering master-stroke of medieval architecture (open 9am-dusk). At sunset, cross the Loire and turn right on quai Villebois Mareuil for a shimmering view of the château.

Trains (tel. 02 47 20 50 50) run frequently from Paris-Austerlitz (8 per day, 1¾hr., 120F). You can also catch trains to Tours (10 per day, 1hr., 49F). **Banks** and **ATMs** are scattered everywhere in Blois's *centre ville,* especially near the Loire, along rue Denis Papin and around pl. de la Résistance. The **tourist office,** 3, av. Jean Laigret (tel. 02 54 74 06 49) has info about Blois and nearby châteaux. (Open April-Sept. Mon.-Sat. 9am-12:30pm and 2-7pm, Sun. 10am-1pm and 4-7pm; Oct.-March Mon.-Sat. 9:15am-noon and 2-6pm.) The local **hostel (HI),** 18, rue de l'Hôtel Pasquier (tel. 02 54 78 27 21), is a 5km, one hour walk outside Blois; take rue Denis Papin down to the river, then bus 4 "Les Grouets" to "Eglise des Grouets" (10min., 6F). Reception open 7-10am and 6-10:30pm; 41F; open March-Nov. 15. In town, the **Hôtel du Bellay,** 12, rue des Minimes (tel. 02 54 78 23 62; fax 02 54 78 52 04) offers cleanliness and convenience. Singles and doubles 130-185F; reserve ahead; MC, V, AmEx. For **food,** try the restaurants along rue St. Lubin and around pl. Poids du Roi, near the cathedral; don't miss the sweet specialty *le chocolat blésois*.

FROM BLOIS: CHAMBORD

Built by François I for his hunting trips and orgiastic fêtes, Chambord is the largest and most extravagant of the Loire châteaux. Seven hundred of his trademark stone salamanders lurk on Chambord's walls, ceilings, and ingenious staircase, while the 365 fireplaces (one for each day of the year) scattered through the 440 rooms create a forest of decorated chimneys on the rooftop terrace.

At the heart of the symmetrical château rises a spectacular double-helix staircase, attributed to Leonardo da Vinci, and constructed so that one person can ascend and another descend without meeting, while keeping sight of one another through its sculpted openings. The château was a favorite *auberge* of Louis XIV, who planted the magnificent kilometer-long, tree-lined avenue approaching the château. Today, the sprawling grounds cover over 5350 hectares—1200 of which are open to the public—forming a game preserve surrounded by a 2.5-m high and 33-km long wall, the longest wall in France. (Open July-Aug. daily 9:30am-7:15pm; April-June and Sept. daily 9:30am-6:15pm; Feb.-March and Oct.-Dec. daily 9:30am-12:15pm and 2-5:15pm. Closed Jan. Admission 35F, students 22F.)

To get to Chambord from Paris, take a **train** to Blois (info above) then catch a **bus** at the *gare routière,* 2, route Victor Hugo (tel. 02 54 78 15 66). Buses run mid-June to mid-September. Take the **Transports Loir-et-Cher (TLC)** bus, circuit #1 (65F, students 50F.) You could also rent a **bike** in Blois from **Intersport,** 2-4, rue Porte Côté (tel. 02 54 78 06 57), just below pl. Victor Hugo. (Bikes 50F per day; open Mon. 2-7pm, Tues.-Sat. 9am-noon and 2-7pm.) The 40-minute ride is pretty and straightforward; ask for directions at the Blois tourist office (info above) or the one in Chambord (tel. 02 54 20 34 86; open Apr. to mid-Oct.). Blois is your best bet for an overnight stay (info above).

■ Chenonceau

The most romantic château of them all, Chenonceau (tel. 02 47 23 90 07) was designed by three women. Catherine Bohier, the wife of the royal tax-collector, oversaw its practical design, which features four rooms radiating from a central chamber and innovative straight (rather than spiral) staircases. In 1547, Henri II gave the château to his mistress, Diane de Poitiers, who added sublime symmetrical gardens and constructed the arched bridge over the Cher so she could hunt in the nearby forest. When Henri II died in 1559, his wife; Catherine de Médicis, kicked Diane out of her beloved castle, and then designed her own set of gardens and the most spectacular wing of the castle: the two-story gallery spanning the Cher. (Open daily March 16-Sept. 15 9am-7pm; call for off-season hours. 40F, students 25F. Late June-Sept., *son et lumière* at 10:15pm. 40F, students 25F.)

The village of Chenonceaux is 214km from Paris (2hrs.) and 34km from Tours (25min.) by car on the A10. Take a **train** from Paris to Tours (22 per day, 2¼hr., 148F; TGV 16 per day, 1hr., 190-245F with reservation); from the Tours station (tel. 02 47 20 50 50), trains run to the village (3 per day, ¾hr., 34F). The station is 2km from the château. Cross the tracks, immediately turn right, then follow the blue sign to the château. **Tourisme Verney** (tel. 02 47 37 81 81, in Tours) runs buses from Tours via Amboise (3 per day, ½hr., 44F roundtrip) to Chenonceaux (1hr., 62F roundtrip), stopping at the château gates.

For 62F, you can stay at the **hostel (HI)** in Tours, av. d'Arsonval, Parc de Grandmont (tel. 02 47 25 14 45; fax 02 47 48 26 59), 4km from the station in a park by the highway. From the station, take bus #1 (direction: Jotie Blotterie, 7F) or bus #6 (direction: Chambray, 7F) from the stop on the right side of av. de Grammont, 30m down from pl. Jean Jaurès (last bus at 8:15pm). (Reception 5-11pm; off-season 5-10pm; 62F.) Also in Tours, **Mon Hôtel,** 40, rue de la Préfecture (tel. 02 47 05 67 53) has singles with shower 125-180F, doubles with shower 140-200F; MC, V, AmEx. For more information about Tours and Chenonceau, including guided château excursion lists, contact Tours's **tourist office,** rue Bernard Palissy (tel. 02 47 70 37 37).

Chinon

Henry II Plantagenet, Richard the Lionheart, Philippe-Auguste, St. Louis, Charles VII, Jeanne d'Arc, the Templars, and Cesare Borgia, among many others, slept here. The château itself is in ruins, but this diminishes neither its history nor the view of the Vienne river from atop the noble pile of rocks. In the great hall, Jeanne d'Arc passed the court advisors' first major test of her divine mission when she ignored the man dressed in the *dauphin's* robes and addressed herself to the real prince, hidden among 300 nobles. Imagination can go a long way—as ruins go, these are great ones. (Open daily July-Aug. 9am-7pm; April-June and Sept. 9am-6pm; Oct. 9am-5pm; Nov.-March 9am-noon and 2-5pm. Admission 25F, students 17F.)

Other than the château, the town is the birthplace of Rabelais and great wine. The **Musée Animé du Vin et de la Tonnellerie,** 12, rue Voltaire (tel. 02 47 93 25 63), handles the latter: their 15- to 20-minute tour illustrates the wine-making process, glass of Chinon wine included. (Open April-Sept. Fri.-Wed. 10am-12:30pm and 2-7pm; 22F.) From Paris, take a train to Tours (see Chambord, above) and catch a connection to Chinon (3 per day, 1hr., 44F). From the station, walk along quai Jeanne d'Arc; turn right at Café de la Paix to reach pl. du Gén. de Gaulle. The **tourist office,** 12, rue Voltaire (tel. 02 47 93 17 85), off pl. Général de Gaulle, changes money if banks are closed. **Banks** with **ATMs** are scattered around pl. Général de Gaulle. The **HI hostel,** rue Descartes (tel. 02 47 93 10 48), is located along the quai Jeanne d'Arc. (Reception daily 5am-10pm; 44F; reserve in summer.) Otherwise, **Hôtel du Point du Jour,** 102, quai Jeanne d'Arc (tel. 02 47 93 07 20) has singles and doubles (with shower 135-160F).

Normandy

Normandy, whose jagged coastline, gently sloping valleys, and elaborate cathedrals inspired the Impressionists, has had a tumultuous history. The territory was seized by Vikings in the 9th century, and in 911 the French king acknowledged the independence of the Norsemen (Normans). From the 10th to the 13th century, the Normans created a string of mammoth ornate cathedrals. Their most impressive achievement, however, was the conquest in 1066 of a small island to the northwest of France. William the Conqueror's defeat of England was celebrated by a magnificent tapestry that still hangs in the Norman town of Bayeux.

During the Hundred Years War, the English had their revenge; they invaded and overpowered fierce Norman resistors. English troops, led by the Duke of Bedford and aided by French traitors, succeeded in capturing Jeanne d'Arc after a great victory on September 8, 1430. Charged with heresy and sorcery, Jeanne was imprisoned in Rouen's Tour Jeanne d'Arc (still standing) and condemned to be burned at the stake. Although the British were eventually overthrown, they left their mark on the customs of the area. The British did not attempt another invasion until D-Day, June 6, 1944, when they returned with American and Canadian allies to wrest Normandy from German occupation. The beaches near Bayeux, where the Allies landed, still bear scars from the attack.

GETTING AROUND

Trains go between Paris and the major sites of Normandy, including most of the tourist spots listed below and large towns, such as Lille, Le Havre, and Caen. Within Normandy, buses fill in the gaps between smaller towns; a bike or a car helps for extended touring or individual exploring of the Normandy countryside.

Rouen

Best known as the city where Jeanne d'Arc was burned and Emma Bovary was bored, Rouen (pop. 400,000) makes a great weekend trip from Paris. It had its two hundred years of fame from the 10th to the 12th centuries, when it bloomed into a veritable

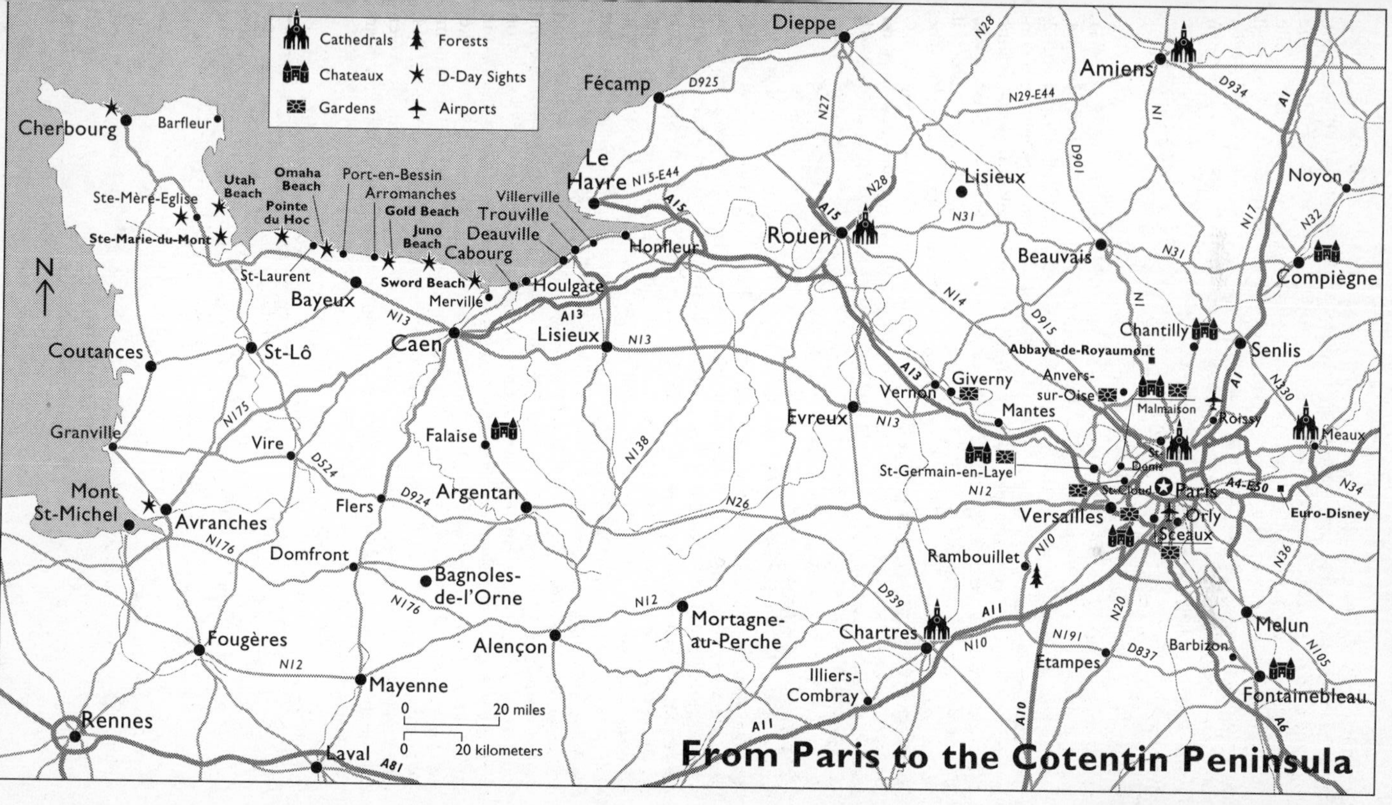
From Paris to the Cotentin Peninsula
Cathedrals
Chateaux
Gardens
Forests
D-Day Sights
Airports
N
0
20 miles
0
20 kilometers
Cherbourg
Barfleur
Ste-Mère-Eglise
Ste-Marie-du-Mont
Utah Beach
Omaha Beach
Pointe du Hoc
St-Laurent
Port-en-Bessin
Arromanches
Gold Beach
Juno Beach
Sword Beach
Merville
Cabourg
Deauville
Trouville
Villerville
Houlgate
Honfleur
Le Havre
Fécamp
Dieppe
Amiens
Noyon
Compiègne
Senlis
Chantilly
Abbaye-de-Royaumont
Beauvais
Lisieux
Rouen
Giverny
Vernon
Mantes
Anvers-sur-Oise
Malmaison
Roissy
St-Denis
St-Cloud
Paris
Orly
Sceaux
Versailles
St-Germain-en-Laye
Meaux
Euro-Disney
Melun
Fontainebleau
Barbizon
Etampes
Rambouillet
Chartres
Illiers-Combray
Evreux
Mortagne-au-Perche
Alençon
Argentan
Falaise
Caen
Bayeux
St-Lô
Coutances
Granville
Vire
Flers
Bagnoles-de-l'Orne
Domfront
Mayenne
Laval
Fougères
Avranches
Mont St-Michel
Rennes
A1
A4-E50
A6
A10
A11
A13
A15
A81
N1
N10
N12
N13
N14
N15-E44
N17
N20
N26
N27
N28
N29-E44
N31
N32
N34
N36
N105
N138
N175
N176
N191
N330
D901
D915
D925
D934
D939
D837
D924
D524

flower garden of Gothic architecture and half-timbered houses, as befitted the capital of the Norman empire. Modern Rouen has been marred by war and pollution. Yet amid the destruction there is reconstruction; in its splendid architecture and its numerous museums, Rouen holds the promise of its rebirth.

To get to the center of town from the station, take rue Jeanne d'Arc for several blocks. A left onto the cobblestone rue du Gros Horloge leads to pl. de la Cathédrale and the tourist office (the shopping district); a right leads to pl. du Vieux Marché (the food district). The **tourist office** is at 25, pl. de la Cathédrale (tel. 02 32 08 32 40). The **HI hostel,** 118, bd. de l'Europe (tel. 02 35 72 06 45), is across the river 5km from the station, at metro stop "Europe." (59F; lockout 10am-5pm.) Call the **train station** (tel. 02 35 98 50 50) for info on trains to Paris (hourly, 1¼hr., 122F).

A walking tour of Rouen easily covers the city's hotspots. The **Tour Jeanne d'Arc,** near the station on rue du Donjon, is the last remaining tower of the château which confined Jeanne d'Arc (open Wed.-Mon. 10am-noon and 2-5:30pm; admission 10F, students 5F). A block up rue Jeanne d'Arc is the **Musée des Beaux-Arts,** sq. Verdrel (tel. 02 35 71 28 40). This excellent museum has works by Rouen's native artists as well as European masters and a collection of Russian icons. (Open Wed.-Sun. 10am-6pm; admission 20F, students 13F.)

Mont-Saint-Michel

Rising abruptly out of a huge expanse of sea and visible for miles in every direction, the abbey and island of Mont-St-Michel are breathtaking. The island first came into existence in the 7th century, when a gigantic wave swamped the forest of Sissy, isolating the Mont from the mainland. In 708, the archangel Michael appeared in the dreams of the Bishop of Avranches, instructing him to build a place of worship on this barren and rocky island north of Pontorson. Today, the Mont is a dazzling labyrinth of immaculately preserved stone arches, spires, and stairways that climb (and keep climbing) to the abbey that shares its name. Just as overwhelming as the Mont's beauty, though, are the crowds that fill its streets (200,000 per day in August). Go off-season or late in the day, if you can.

The only break in the Mont's outer wall is the **Porte de l'Avancée.** Inside, the **tourist office** lies immediately to the left (tel. 02 33 60 14 30); to the right, the **Porte du Boulevard** and **Porte du Roy** open onto the town's major thoroughfare, **Grande Rue.** All hotels, restaurants, and sights are on this spiraling street, but sneak off via several inconspicuous stairwells and archways to explore Mont-St-Michel's less-visited corners. The **abbey** is the departure point for all of the one-hour tours (tel. 02 33 89 80 00; open daily May-Sept. 9:30am-5:30pm; Oct.-April 10am-4pm; tours in English leave roughly every 2hrs; tours in French every 45min., starting at 10am; admission 36F, ages 18-25 22F, under 18 15F). The two-hour *visites conférences* (French only) are a special treat, allowing you to walk atop a flying buttress and creep inside pre-Roman crypts. (Tours daily at 10:15am and 2:30pm. Admission 56F, ages 18-25 and over 60 42F, under 18 35F.) **La Merveille,** an intricate 13th-century cloister housing the monastery, encloses a seemingly endless web of passageways and chambers. Escape down the ramparts and into the abbey garden, where you can reflect upon the soaring stone buttresses that wrap around the entire island, and the coastline of Normandy and Brittany. Or avoid the crowds by descending to the **Porte du Bavole** via the ramparts. Don't wander too far on the sand; the highest tides in Europe rush in to envelop the Mont at speeds of up to 2m per second.

To get to the Mont from Paris, take a **train** (tel. 02 33 60 00 35) to **Pontorson** (1 per day, 4hr., 235F plus 36-90F TGV supplement). The STN **bus** (tel. 02 33 60 00 35; 6 per day, 15min., round-trip 21F) takes you to the Mont from Pontorson. Try Pontorson's **Centre Duguesclin (HI),** rue Gén. Patton (tel. 02 33 60 18 65; 41F; open June to mid-Sept.) or **Hôtel de l'Arrivée,** 14, rue du Docteur Tizon (tel. 02 33 60 01 57; singles/doubles 87-110F, with shower 155F; shower 15F).

Appendices

Time Zones

All of France is one hour ahead of Greenwich Mean Time (Britain and Ireland), six hours ahead of New York and Toronto, and nine hours ahead of California and Vancouver. France is one hour behind most of South Africa, including Johannesburg, seven hours behind Perth, and nine hours behind Sydney. French time falls one hour back in the Fall, and springs one hour forward in the Spring for daylight saving's time; both switches occur about a week before similar changes in U.S. time.

Weather

Average maximum and minimum daily temperatures are given in degrees Celsius followed by degrees Farenheit. Average rainfall is given in centimeters.

MONTH	HIGH	LOW	RAINFALL
June-Aug.	24°/76°	13°/55°	5.25
Sept.-Nov.	15°/59°	7°/44°	5.50
Dec.-Feb.	6°/42°	0°/32°	3.75
March-May	16°/60°	5°/41°	4.25

Weights and Measures

1 millimeter (mm) = 0.04 inch
1 meter (m) = 1.09 yards
1 kilometer (km) = 0.62 mile
1 kilogram (kg) = 2.2 pounds (lb)
1 gram (g) = 0.04 ounce
1 liter = 1.06 quarts

1 inch = 25mm
1 yard = 0.92m
1 mile = 1.61km
1 pound = 0.55kg
1 ounce = 25g
1 quart = 0.94 liter

To convert from °C to °F, multiply by 1.8 and add 32.
To convert from °F to °C, subtract 32 and multiply by 5/9.

°C	35	30	25	20	15	10	5	0	-5	-10
°F	95	86	75	68	59	50	41	32	23	14

Glossary

Here you will find a compilation of some of the French terms *Let's Go* has used, along with their pronounciations. The gender of the noun is indicated in parentheses; "pl." indicates that the word is used only in the plural in French. The glossary is followed by a list of phrases you might find helpful. The masculine definite article in French is "le" ("luh"); feminine is "la" ("lah"); and plural is "les" ("lay"). Eu and eue (pronounced the same) have a pronounciation in between the English "ew" and "uh." In this guide we have used "uh" to indicate this sound.

aller-retour (m.)	round-trip	ah-LAY ruh-TOOR
arc (m.)	arch	AHRK
arrondissement (m.)	district (administrative)	ah-rohn-dees-MEHNT
atelier (m.)	artist's studio	ah-tuh-LYAY
auberge (f.)	inn, tavern	oh-BEHRZH

banlieue (f.)	suburbs	bahn-LYUH
bibliothèque (f.)	library	bihb-lee-oh-TECK
billet (m.)	ticket	bee -YAY
bois (m.)	forest	BWAH
bouquiniste (m.)	second-hand bookseller	boh-keh-NEEST
bureau de change (m.)	money-changing booth	byuh-ROH duh SHANZH
carnet (m.)	notebook; group of tickets	kahr-NAY
cathédrale (f.)	cathedral	kah-tay-DRAHL
cave (f.)	cellar	KAHV
chapelle (f.)	chapel	shah-PEHL
château (m.)	castle	shah-TOH
chômeur (m.)	unemployed person	shoh-MUHR
cimetière (m.)	cemetery	see-meh-TYAYR
cité (f.)	walled city	see-TAY
cloître (m.)	cloister	KLWAH-truh
contrôleur (m.)	ticket collector, inspector	kohn-troh-LEHR
douane (f.)	customs	DWAHN
école (f.)	school	ay-KOHL
écran (m.)	screen	ay-KRAHN
église (f.)	church	ay-GLEEZ
escalier (m.)	stairway	ehs-kahl-YAY
étude (f.)	study; course of study	ay-TOOD
faubourg (m.)	neighborhood, quarter	foh-BOOR
fête (f.)	celebration, festival	FEHT
flâneur (m.)	stroller, wanderer	flah-NEHR
foire (f.)	fair	FWAHR
fontaine (f.)	fountain	fohn-TEHN
forêt (f.)	forest	foh-RAY
foule (f.)	crowd	FOOL
gare (f.)	train station	GAHR
gare routière (f.)	bus station	GAHR root-YAYR
gendarmerie (f.)	(state) police station	zhehn-DAHM-eh-REE
guichet (m.)	window, ticket window	gee-SHAY
halle (f.)	covered market	AHL
horloge (f.)	clock	ohr-LOHZH
hôtel (particulier) (m.)	mansion (townhouse)	oh-TEHL (pahr-tee-cool-YAY)
hôtel de ville (m.)	town hall	oh-TEHL duh VEEL
île (f.)	island	EEL
librairie (f.)	bookstore	lee-breh-REE
magasin (m.)	store	mah-gah-ZEHN
mairie (f.)	mayoralty, town hall	meh-REE
marché (m.)	market	mahr-SHAY
mur (m.)	wall	MYUR
palais (m.)	palace	pah-LAY
papeterie (f.)	stationery store	pah-peh-TREE
parc (m.)	park	PAHR
pilotis (m.)	piling, pillar	pee-loh-TEE
piscine (f.)	pool	peh-SEEN
place (f.)	square	PLAHS
plan (m.)	map	PLAHN
pont (m.)	bridge	POHN
quai (m.)	quay, wharf	KAY
quartier (m.)	section (of town), quarter	kahr-TYAY

rue (f.)	street	RU
salon (m.)	drawing or living room	sah-LOHN
soldes (m. pl.)	(clearance) sale	SOHLD
son et lumière (m.)	sound and light show	SOHN AY loo-MYAYR
tabac (m.)	tobacco store	tuh-BAHK
tour (f.)	tower	TOOR

Helpful Phrases

please	*s'il vous plaît*	see voo PLAY
thank you	*merci*	mehr-SEE
hello	*bonjour*	bohn-ZHOOR
good evening	*bonsoir*	bohn-SWAHR
How are you?	*Comment allez-vous?*	KOH-mehn TAH-lay VOO
I am well.	*Je vais bien.*	ZHUH VAY BYEHN
goodbye	*au revoir*	OH ruh-VWAHR
Excuse me.	*Excusez-moi.*	ehks-KOO-ZAY MWAH
Do you speak English?	*Parlez-vous anglais?*	PAHR-lay VOO zahn-GLAY
I don't understand.	*Je ne comprends pas.*	ZHUH NUH kohm-PRAHN pah
Leave me alone.	*Laissez-moi tranquille.*	LEH-say MWAH trahn-KEEL
How much	*combien*	kohm-BYEHN
I'm sorry.	*Je suis désolé.*	ZHUH SWEE day-soh-LAY
who	*qui*	KEE
what?	*Comment?*	koh-MOH
how	*comment*	koh-MOH
why	*pourquoi*	poor-KWAH
when	*quand*	KAHN
What is it?	*Qu'est-ce que c'est?*	KEHS-kuh SAY
I would like	*Je voudrais*	ZHUH voo-DRAY
I need	*J'ai besoin de*	ZHAY buhz-WAN DUH
I want	*Je veux*	ZHUH VUH
I don't want	*Je ne veux pas*	ZHUH NUH VUH PAH
to rent	*louer*	loo-AY
The bill, please.	*L'addition, s'il vous plaît.*	lah-dees-YOHN, SEE VOO PLAY
Where is/are	*Où est/sont*	OO AY/SOHN
the bathroom?	*les toilettes.*	twa-LET
the police	*la police*	po-LEES
to the right	*à droite*	ah DWAHT
to the left	*à gauche*	ah GOHSH
up	*en haut*	ahn OH
down	*en bas*	ahn BAH
straight ahead	*tout droit*	TOO DWAHT
a room	*une chambre*	oon SHAHM-bruh
—for one	*—simple*	—SAYM-pluh
—for two	*—pour deux*	—POOR DEUH
with	*avec*	ah-VECK
without	*sans*	SAHN
a shower	*une douche*	oon DOOSH
breakfast	*le petit déjeuner*	puh-TEE day-jhuh-NAY
included	*compris*	kohm-PREE

APPENDICES

Numbers

one	*un*
two	*deux*
three	*trois*
four	*quatre*
five	*cinq*
six	*six*
seven	*sept*
eight	*huit*
nine	*neuf*
ten	*dix*
twenty	*vingt*
thirty	*trente*
forty	*quarante*
fifty	*cinquante*
sixty	*soixante*
seventy	*soixante-dix*
eighty	*quatre-vingt*
ninety	*quatre-vingt-dix*
one hundred	*cent*

Menu Reader

à point	medium rare
agneau	lamb
ail	garlic
andouillette	tripe sausage
assiette	plate, platter
bavette	skirt steak
beurre	butter
bien cuit	well done
bière	beer
bifteck	steak
blanc de volaille	breast of chicken
bleu	very rare
boeuf	beef
boissons	drinks
boudin	blood sausage
brioche	buttery bread, almost like pastry
canard	duck
champignon	mushroom
Chantilly	whipped cream with sugar
chaud	hot
chèvre	goat cheese
choix	choice
citron	lemon
confit de canard	duck or goose preserved in its own fat
côte	rib or chop
courgette	zucchini
crème brulée; crème caramel	custard in a caramel sauce
crème fraîche	fresh heavy cream
croque-monsieur	toasted, open-faced ham and cheese sandwich
crudités	raw vegetables, usually with dressing
cuisse	leg or thigh (of poultry)
déjeuner	lunch
dîner	dinner
échalote	shallot
entrecôte	beef rib steak
entrée	appetizer
foie gras	liver of a fattened goose
frais	fresh
fraise	strawberry
framboise	raspberry
frites	french fries
fromage	cheese
fromage blanc	smooth cottage cheese
gâteau	cake
glace	ice cream
grenouille	frog (legs)
haricot vert	green bean
jambon	ham
lait	milk
langue	tongue
lapin	rabbit
lardons	bacon cubes
légume	vegetable
limonade	carbonated lemon/lime drink
magret de canard	breast of duck
mille-feuille	"thousand-layered" pastry
moules	mussels
nature	plain
nouilles	noodles
oeuf	egg
oignon	onion
pain	bread

pâtes	pasta
plat du jour	daily special
poisson	fish
poivre	pepper
pomme	apple
pomme de terre	potato
porc	pork
potage	soup
poulet	chicken
profiteroles	puff pastry filled with ice cream and doused in chocolate sauce
salade verte	green salad
saucisson	big dried sausage
saumon	salmon
sel	salt
tartare	chopped raw meat topped with a raw egg
tarte	pie (salted or sweet)
tarte tatin	caramelized, upside-down apple pie
truite	trout
viande	meat
vin	wine

Index

INDEX

INDEX

INDEX

★Let's Go 1997 Reader Questionnaire

Please fill this out and return it to **Let's Go, St. Martin's Press,**
175 5th Ave. NY, NY 10010

Name: ____________________ **What book did you use?**______________

Address: ____

City: ______________________ **State:** ______ **Zip Code:** __________

How old are you? under 19 19-24 25-34 35-44 45-54 55 or over

Are you (circle one) in high school in college in grad school employed retired between jobs

Have you used Let's Go before? yes no

Would you use Let's Go again? yes no

How did you first hear about Let's Go? friend store clerk CNN bookstore display advertisement/promotion review other

Why did you choose Let's Go (circle up to two)? annual updating reputation budget focus price writing style other: ________________________

Which other guides have you used, if any? Frommer's $-a-day Fodor's Rough Guides Lonely Planet Berkeley Rick Steves other: ________________________

Is Let's Go the best guidebook? yes no

If not, which do you prefer? ________________________

Which part of Let's Go do you feel needs most to be improved, if any (circle up to two)? packaging/cover practical information accommodations food cultural introduction sights practical introduction ("Essentials") directions entertainment gay/lesbian information maps other: ________________________

How would you like to see these things improved?

____

____

How long was your trip? one week two weeks three weeks one month two months or more

Have you traveled extensively before? yes no

Do you buy a separate map when you visit a foreign city? yes no

Have you seen the Let's Go Map Guides? yes no

Have you used a Let's Go Map Guide? yes no

If you have, would you recommend them to others? yes no

Did you use the internet to plan your trip? yes no

Would you buy a Let's Go phrasebook adventure/trekking guide gay/lesbian guide

Which of the following destinations do you hope to visit in the next three to five years (circle one)? Australia China South America Russia other: ________________________

Where did you buy your guidebook? internet chain bookstore independent bookstore college bookstore travel store other: ________________________

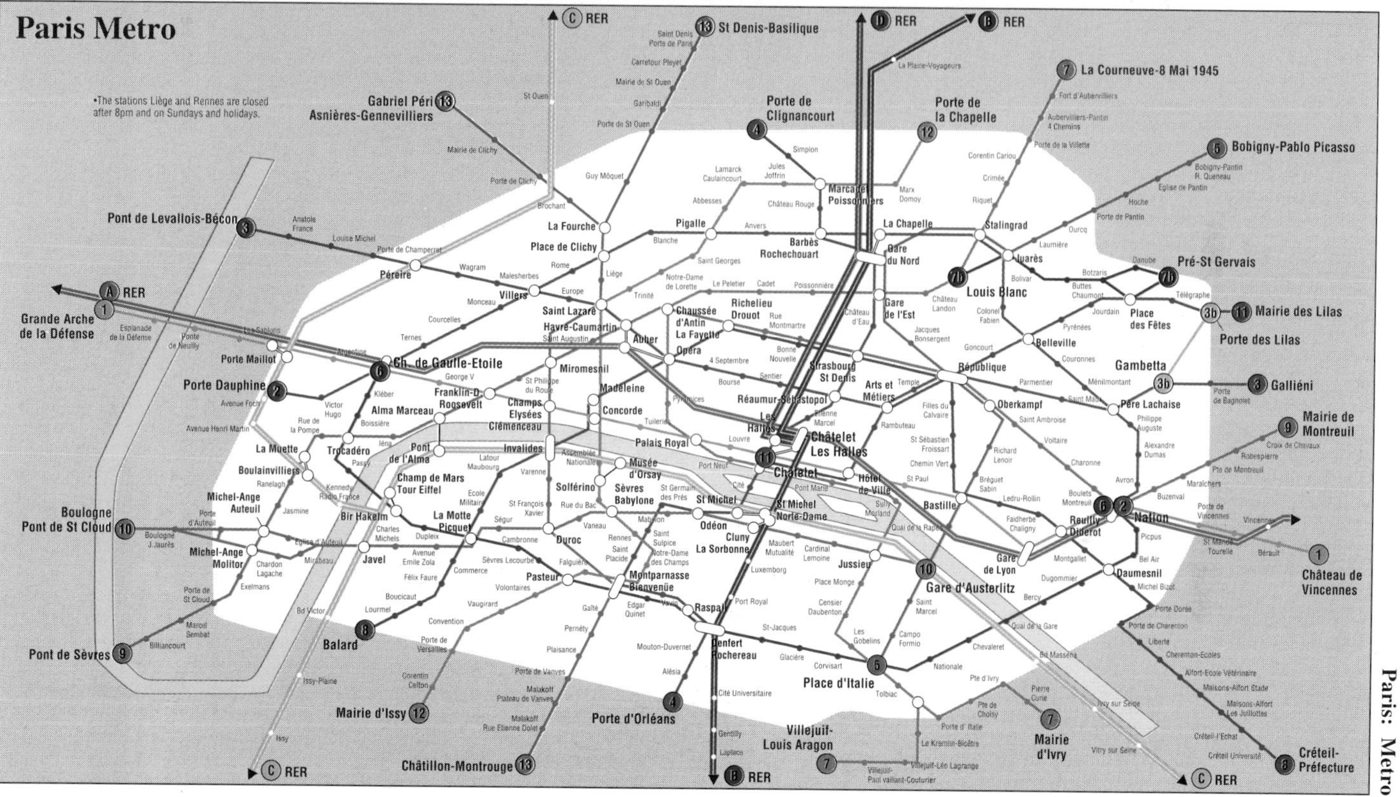
Paris Metro
•The stations Liège and Rennes are closed after 8pm and on Sundays and holidays.
Grande Arche de la Défense
Pont de Levallois-Bécon
Gabriel Péri Asnières-Gennevilliers
St Denis-Basilique
Porte de Clignancourt
Porte de la Chapelle
La Courneuve-8 Mai 1945
Bobigny-Pablo Picasso
Pré-St Gervais
Mairie des Lilas
Porte des Lilas
Galliéni
Mairie de Montreuil
Château de Vincennes
Créteil-Préfecture
Mairie d'Ivry
Villejuif-Louis Aragon
Porte d'Orléans
Châtillon-Montrouge
Mairie d'Issy
Balard
Pont de Sèvres
Boulogne Pont de St Cloud
Porte Dauphine
Porte Maillot
Ch. de Gaulle-Etoile
Pigalle
Stalingrad
Louis Blanc
Gare du Nord
Gare de l'Est
République
Châtelet Les Halles
Bastille
Nation
Gare de Lyon
Gare d'Austerlitz
Place d'Italie
Denfert Rochereau
Montparnasse Bienvenüe
Invalides
Concorde
Opéra
Saint Lazare
RER

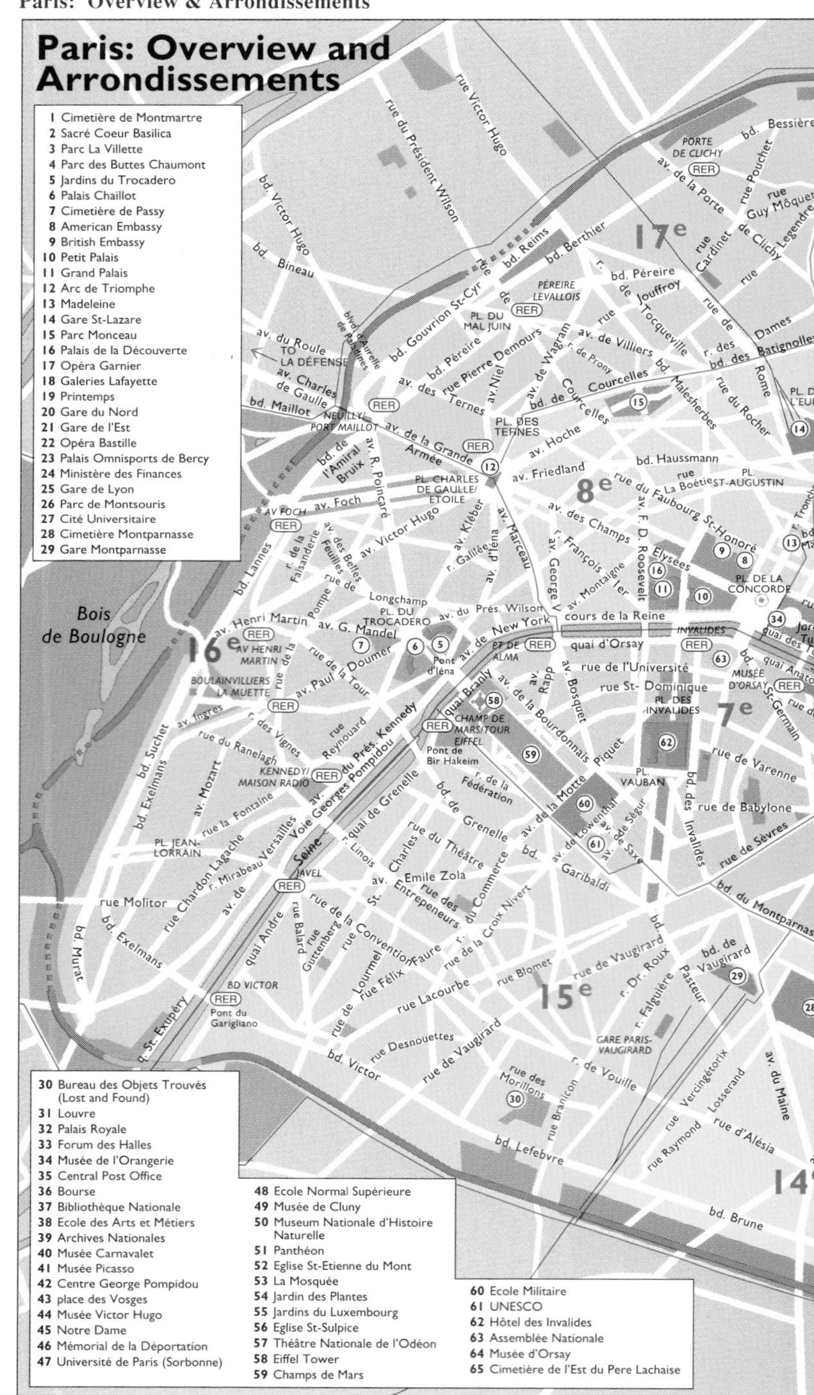
Paris: Overview and Arrondissements
1 Cimetière de Montmartre
2 Sacré Coeur Basilica
3 Parc La Villette
4 Parc des Buttes Chaumont
5 Jardins du Trocadero
6 Palais Chaillot
7 Cimetière de Passy
8 American Embassy
9 British Embassy
10 Petit Palais
11 Grand Palais
12 Arc de Triomphe
13 Madeleine
14 Gare St-Lazare
15 Parc Monceau
16 Palais de la Découverte
17 Opéra Garnier
18 Galeries Lafayette
19 Printemps
20 Gare du Nord
21 Gare de l'Est
22 Opéra Bastille
23 Palais Omnisports de Bercy
24 Ministère des Finances
25 Gare de Lyon
26 Parc de Montsouris
27 Cité Universitaire
28 Cimetière Montparnasse
29 Gare Montparnasse
30 Bureau des Objets Trouvés (Lost and Found)
31 Louvre
32 Palais Royale
33 Forum des Halles
34 Musée de l'Orangerie
35 Central Post Office
36 Bourse
37 Bibliothèque Nationale
38 Ecole des Arts et Métiers
39 Archives Nationales
40 Musée Carnavalet
41 Musée Picasso
42 Centre George Pompidou
43 place des Vosges
44 Musée Victor Hugo
45 Notre Dame
46 Mémorial de la Déportation
47 Université de Paris (Sorbonne)
48 Ecole Normal Supérieure
49 Musée de Cluny
50 Museum Nationale d'Histoire Naturelle
51 Panthéon
52 Eglise St-Etienne du Mont
53 La Mosquée
54 Jardin des Plantes
55 Jardins du Luxembourg
56 Eglise St-Sulpice
57 Théâtre Nationale de l'Odéon
58 Eiffel Tower
59 Champs de Mars
60 Ecole Militaire
61 UNESCO
62 Hôtel des Invalides
63 Assemblée Nationale
64 Musée d'Orsay
65 Cimetière de l'Est du Pere Lachaise
Bois de Boulogne
16e
17e
8e
7e
15e
14e
Seine
TO LA DÉFENSE

18e
19e
10e
2e
3e
11e
20e
4e
5e
12e
13e
N
bd. Ney
bd. Macdonald
Canal de l'Ourcq
bd. Ornano
rue de la Chapelle
rue Poissonniers
rue Riquet
r. l'Evangile
rue d'Aubervilliers
rue Archereau
rue de l'Ourcq
av. Corentin Cariou
bd. Sérurier
av. Jean Lolive
rue de Flandre
rue de Crimée
Bassin de la Villette
av. Jean Jaurès
bd. Indochine
rue Custine
rue de Clignancourt
bd. Barbès
rue des
rue Marx Dormoy
bd. de la Chapelle
PL. DE STALINGRAD
r. Armand Carel
r. David d'Angiers
rue Manin
bd. d'Algérie
RER
av. Secrétan
PL. DU COLONEL FABIEN
Canal St-Martin
rue La Fayette
r. Paradis
rue du Fg. Poissonnière
r. d'Hauteville
r. de Fg. St-Denis
bd. de Strasbourg
bd. de Magenta
r. Château d'Eau
bd. de la Villette
rue du Faubourg du Temple
rue des Pyrénées
PL. GAMBETTA
bd. Mortier
bd. Poissonnière
bd. St-Denis
blvd. St-Martin
Réaumur
PL. DE LA REPUBLIQUE
av. Parmentier
rue St-Maur
bd. de Belleville
av. Gambetta
av. de la République
rue Oberkampf
rue de Turbigo
bd. de Sébastopol
r. St-Denis
r. St-Martin
r. Etienne Marcel
rue Beaubourg
rue du Temple
rue des Archives
rue Vieille du Temple
rue de Rivoli
rue St-Antoine
bd. Beaumarchais
bd. R. Lenoir
rue du Chemin Vert
bd. Voltaire
rue de la Roquette
bd. de Ménilmontant
rue de Charonne
bd. de Charonne
av. Philippe Auguste
bd. Davout
Ile de la Cité
Ile St-Louis
bd. Henri IV
quai de la Tournelle
PL. MAUBERT
r. des Écoles
LUXEMBOURG
rue Monge
PL. DE LA CONTRE-SCARPE
rue d'Ulm
rue Mouffetard
rue Censier
r. G. St-Hilaire
rue Buffon
quai St-Bernard
Seine
Pont de Sully
rue du Faubourg St-Antoine
rue de Lyon
rue Rollin
av. Ledru
rue de Montreuil
NATION
PL. DE LA NATION
Cours de Vincennes
bd. Diderot
bd. Picpus
rue de Picpus
av. du Dr. Arnold Netter
av. Daumesnil
GARE D'AUSTERLITZ
r. C. Bernard
Gay Lussac
bd. de Port Royal
bd. St-Marcel
av. des Gobelins
bd. Arago
bd. de l'Hôpital
Pont de Bercy
bd. de Bercy
rue de Bercy
quai de Bercy
PL. FÉLIX ÉBOUÉ
rue de Charenton
Mi. Bizot
bd. Soult
av. du Gén
bd. Poniatowski
Parc Zoologique
Bois de Vincennes
Pont de Tolbiac
rue de la Gare
rue du Chevaleret
rue Jeanne d'Arc
PL. D'ALESIA
bd. A. Blanqui
av. de Choisy
rue de Tolbiac
rue National
Pont National
BD. MASSÉNA
rue Regnault
bd. de Masséna
av. d'Ivry
av. d'Italie
bd. Kellerman
rue de Paris
0
1 mile
0
1 km

Paris: 1er and 2e

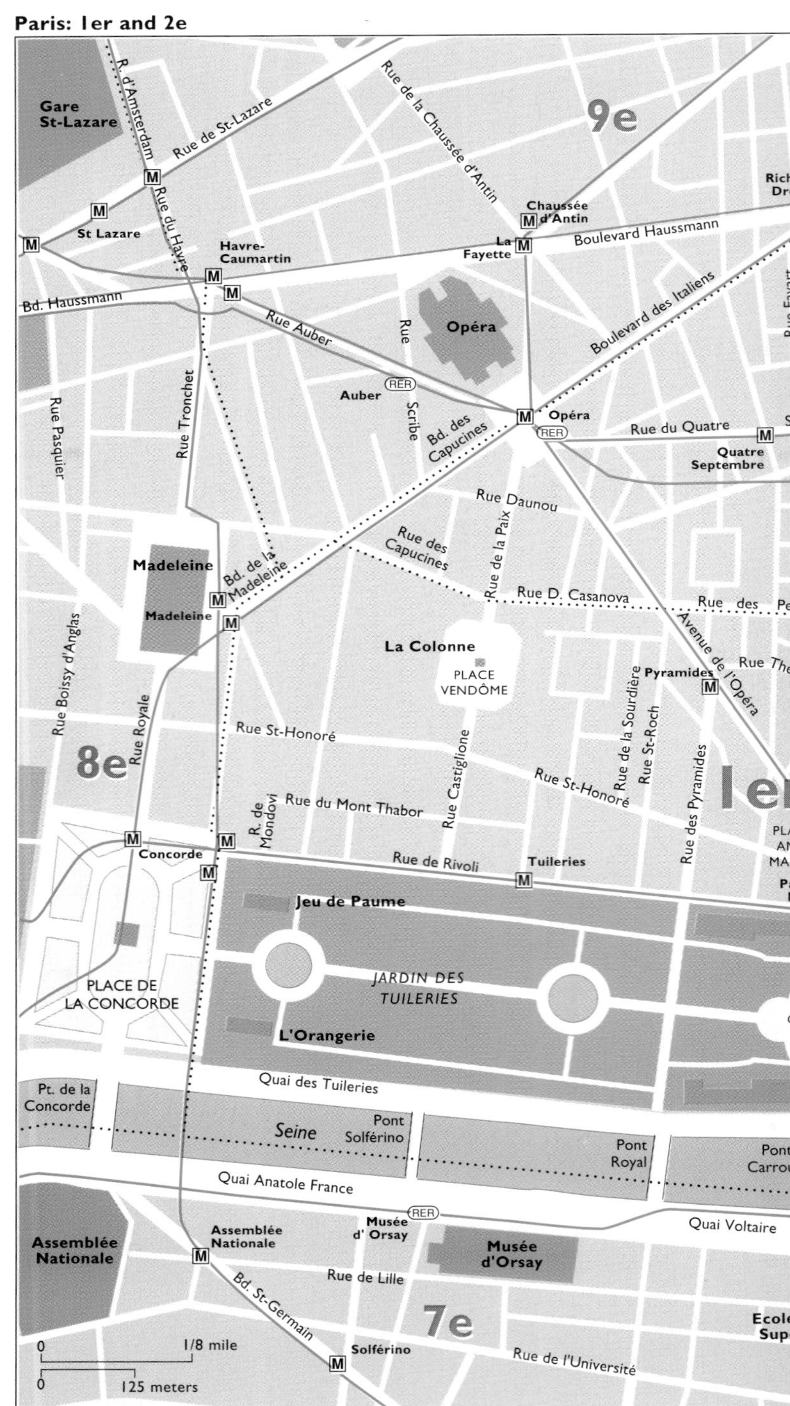

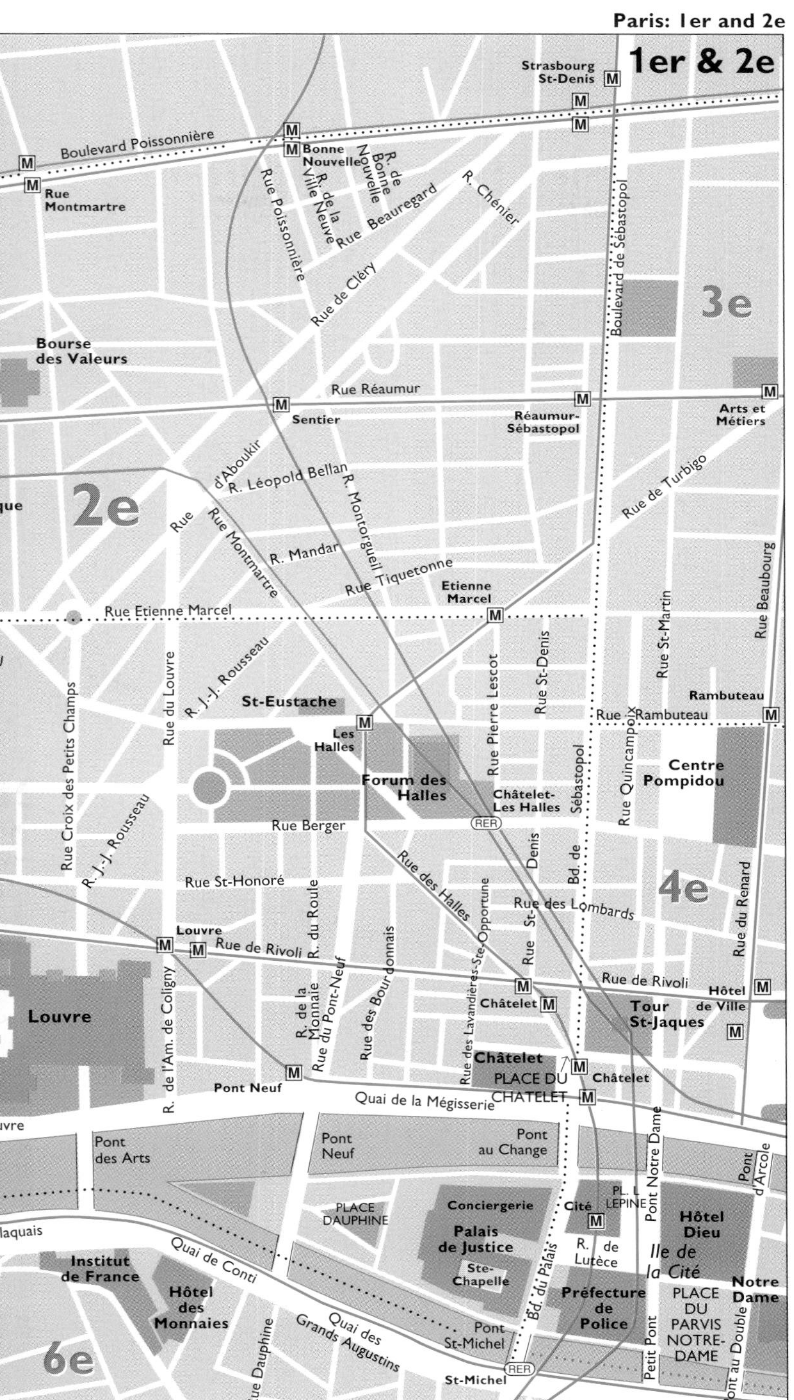

1er & 2e
Strasbourg St-Denis
Boulevard Poissonnière
Bonne Nouvelle
Rue Montmartre
R. de Bonne Nouvelle
R. de la Ville Neuve
Rue Poissonnière
Rue Beauregard
R. Chénier
Boulevard de Sébastopol
Rue de Cléry
3e
Bourse des Valeurs
Rue Réaumur
Sentier
Réaumur-Sébastopol
Arts et Métiers
d'Aboukir
R. Léopold Bellan
R. Montorgueil
Rue de Turbigo
2e
Rue
Rue Montmartre
R. Mandar
Rue Tiquetonne
Etienne Marcel
Rue Beaubourg
Rue Etienne Marcel
R. J.-J. Rousseau
Rue St-Denis
Rue Pierre Lescot
Rue St-Martin
St-Eustache
Rambuteau
Rue du Louvre
Rue Rambuteau
Rue Croix des Petits Champs
Les Halles
Rue Quincampoix
Centre Pompidou
Forum des Halles
Châtelet-Les Halles
Sébastopol
RER
Rue Berger
R. J.-J. Rousseau
Rue des Halles
Denis
Bd. de
4e
Rue St-Honoré
R. du Roule
Rue des Lavandières-Ste-Opportune
Rue St-Denis
Rue des Lombards
Rue du Renard
Louvre
Rue de Rivoli
R. de l'Am. de Coligny
R. de la Monnaie
Rue du Pont-Neuf
Rue des Bourdonnais
Rue de Rivoli
Hôtel de Ville
Châtelet
Tour St-Jaques
Louvre
Châtelet
PLACE DU CHATELET
Châtelet
Pont Neuf
Quai de la Mégisserie
Pont des Arts
Pont Neuf
Pont au Change
Pont Notre Dame
Pont d'Arcole
PL. L LEPINE
PLACE DAUPHINE
Conciergerie
Cité
Hôtel Dieu
Palais de Justice
R. de Lutèce
Ile de la Cité
Institut de France
Quai de Conti
Ste-Chapelle
Bd. du Palais
Préfecture de Police
PLACE DU PARVIS NOTRE-DAME
Notre Dame
Hôtel des Monnaies
Quai des Grands Augustins
Pont St-Michel
Petit Pont
Pont au Double
6e
Rue Dauphine
RER
St-Michel

Paris: 5e and 6e

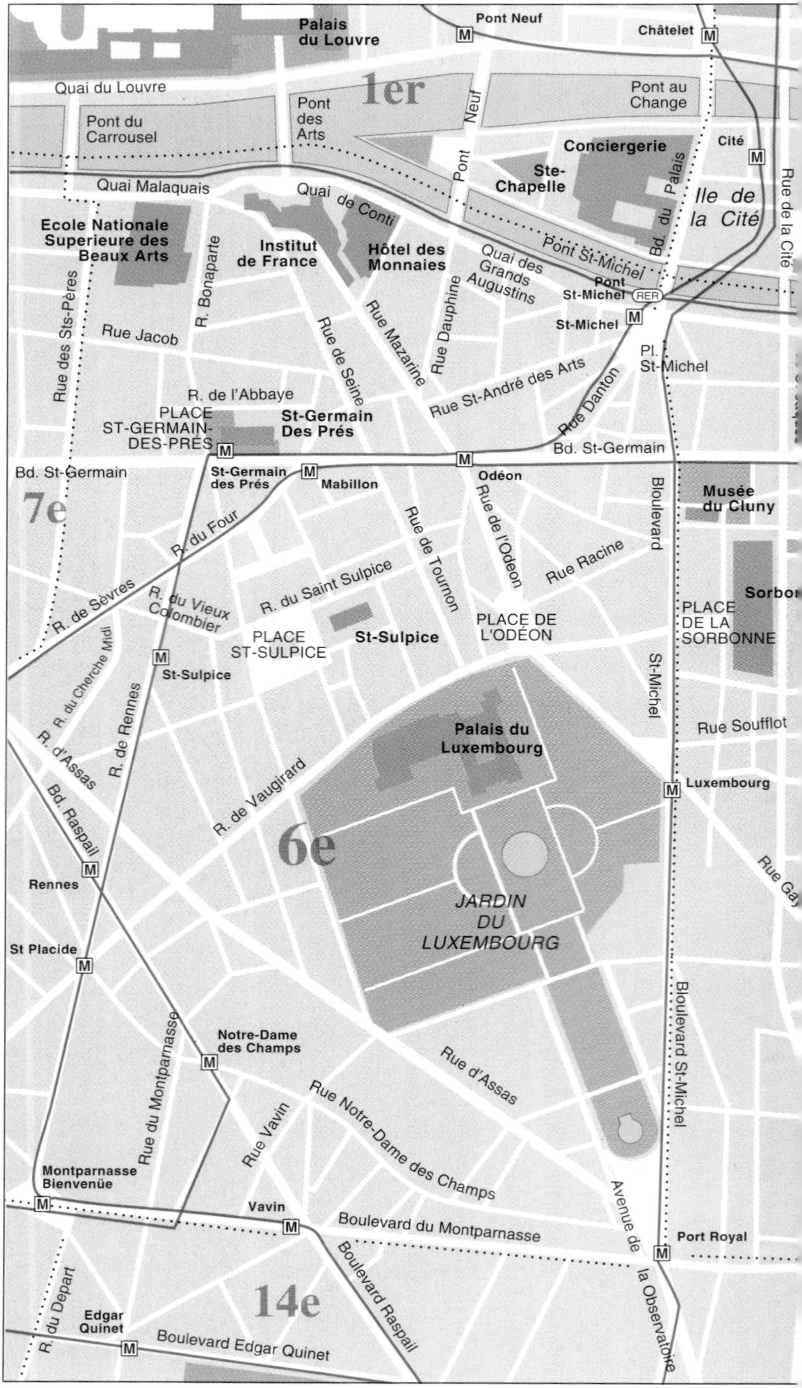

Palais du Louvre
Pont Neuf
Châtelet
1er
Quai du Louvre
Pont du Carrousel
Pont des Arts
Neuf
Pont au Change
Conciergerie
Cité
Ste-Chapelle
Pont
Quai Malaquais
Quai de Conti
Bd. du Palais
Ile de la Cité
Rue de la Cité
Ecole Nationale Superieure des Beaux Arts
R. Bonaparte
Institut de France
Hôtel des Monnaies
Quai des Grands Augustins
Pont St-Michel
Pont St-Michel
RER
Rue des Sts-Pères
Rue Jacob
Rue de Seine
Rue Mazarine
Rue Dauphine
St-Michel
Pl. St-Michel
Rue St-André des Arts
R. de l'Abbaye
PLACE ST-GERMAIN-DES-PRÉS
St-Germain Des Prés
Rue Danton
Bd. St-Germain
Bd. St-Germain
St-Germain des Prés
Mabillon
Odéon
Rue de l'Odeon
Boulevard
Musée du Cluny
7e
R. du Four
Rue de Tournon
Rue Racine
R. de Sevres
R. du Vieux Colombier
R. du Saint Sulpice
Sorbon
PLACE DE LA SORBONNE
PLACE DE L'ODÉON
PLACE ST-SULPICE
St-Sulpice
St-Sulpice
R. du Cherche Midi
St-Michel
Palais du Luxembourg
Rue Soufflot
R. de Rennes
R. d'Assas
R. de Vaugirard
Luxembourg
Bd. Raspail
6e
Rue Ga
Rennes
JARDIN DU LUXEMBOURG
St Placide
Notre-Dame des Champs
Rue du Montparnasse
Rue d'Assas
Boulevard St-Michel
Rue Notre-Dame des Champs
Rue Vavin
Montparnasse Bienvenüe
Avenue de la Observatoire
Vavin
Boulevard du Montparnasse
Port Royal
Boulevard Raspail
R. du Depart
14e
Edgar Quinet
Boulevard Edgar Quinet

Paris: 5e and 6e

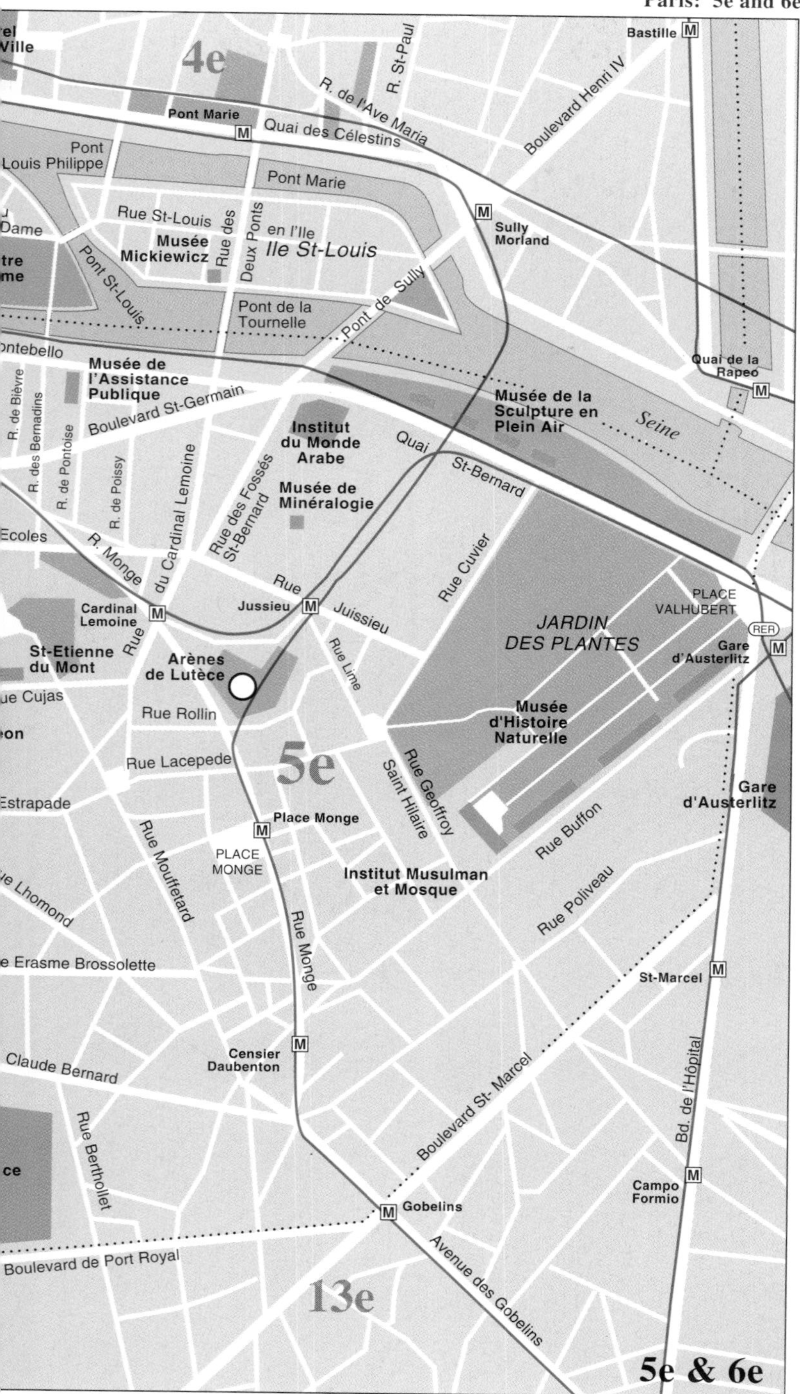

Paris: RER

Paris RER

A1 St-Germain en Laye
Le Vésinet-Le Pecq
La Vésinet-Centre
Chatou-Croissy
Rueil-Malmaison
Nanterre-Ville
Nanterre-Université
Nanterre Préfecture
La Défense Grande Arche de
Charles de Gaulle-Etoile
Auber
Châtelet-Les Halles
Gare de Lyon
Nation
Vincennes
Fontenay sous Bois
Nogent sur Marne
Joinville le Pont
St-Maur-Creteil
Le Parc de St-Maur
Champigny
La Varenne-Chennevierse
Sucy-Bonneuil
A2 Boissy St-Léger
Val de Fontenay
Neuilly-Plaisance
Bry-sur-Marne
Noisy le Grand-Mont d'Est
Noisy-Champs
Noisiel
Lognes
Torcy
A4 Marne-la-Vallée Chessy
A3 Cergy- St-Christophe
Cergy-Préfecture
Conflans Fin d'Oise
Achères-Ville
Maisons-Laffitte
Sartrouville
Houilles Carrières sur Seine
Achères Grand Cormier
A5 Poissy

B3 Roissy-Aeroport Charles de gaulle
Parc des Expositions
Villepinte
Sevran Beaudottes
B5 Mitry-Claye
Villeparisis
Vert Galant
Sevran-Livry
Aulnay sous Bois
Blanc Mesnil
Drancy
Le Bourget
Aubervilliers-La Courneuve
La Plaine-Voyageurs
Gare du Nord
St-Michel Notre-Dame
Luxembourg
Port Royal
Denfert-Rochereau
Cité Universitaire
Gentilly
Laplace
Arcueil-Cachan
Bagneux
Bourg la Reine
Sceaux
Fontenay aux Roses
B2 Robinson
Parc de Sceaux
La Croix de Berny
Antony
Fontaine Michalon
Les Baconnets
Massy-Verrières
Palaiseau
Palaiseau-Villebon
Lozère
Le Guichet
Orsay-Ville
Bures sur Yvette
La Hacquinière
Gif sur Yvette
Courcelle sur Yvette
B4 St-Remy les Chevreuse

D1 Orry-la-Vieille Coy
La Borne-Blanche
Survilliers-Fosses
Louvres
Les Noues
Goussainville
Villiers-le-Bel
Garges-Sarcelles
Pierrefitte Stains
St Denis
D2

C1 Montigny-Beauchamp
Franconville Plessis-Bouchard
Cernay
Ermont Eaubonne
St-Gratien
Epinay sur Seine
Gennevilliers
Les Grésillons
St-Ouen
C3 Argenteuil
Sannois
Pereire
Pte Maillot
Av. Foch
Av. H. Martin
Boulainvilliers
Kennedy Radio France
Pont de l'Alma
Invalides
Musée d'Orsay
Seine
Champ de Mars Tour Eifel
Javel
Bd Victor
Issy-Plaine
Issy
Meudon-Val Fleury
Chaville-Vélizy
Viroflay-RG
Porchefontaine
C5 Versailles-RG
Versailles-Chantiers
St-Cyr
C7 St-Quentin en Yvelines
Gare d'Austerlitz
Bd Masséna
Ivry sur Seine
Vitry sur Seine
Les Ardoines
Choisy le Roi
Villeneuve le Roi
Ablon
Athis-Mons
Juvisy
Les Saules
Orly Ville
Pont de Rungis Aéroport d'Orly
Rungis La Fraternelle
Chemin d'Antony
C2 Palaiseau
Savigny sur Orge
Epinay sur Orge
St-Geneviève des Bois
St-Michel sur Orge
Brétigny sur Orge
La Norville St-Germain les Arpajon
Arpajon
Egly
Breuillet-Bruyères le Châtel
Breuillet Village
St-Chéron
Sermaise
C4 Dourdan
Marolles en Hurepoix
Bouray
Lardy
Chamarande
Etrechy
Etampes
C6 St-Martin d'Etampes